Building iOS 17 Apps with Xcode Storyboards

Building iOS 17 Apps with Xcode Storyboards

ISBN-13: 978-1-951442-84-2

Rev: 1.0

Find more books at *https://www.payloadbooks.com.*

Contents

Table of Contents

1. Start Here

This book aims to teach the skills necessary to create iOS apps using the iOS 17 SDK, UIKit, Xcode 15 Storyboards, and the Swift programming language.

Beginning with the basics, this book outlines the steps necessary to set up an iOS development environment. Next, an introduction to the architecture of iOS 17 and programming in Swift is provided, followed by an in-depth look at the design of iOS apps and user interfaces. More advanced topics such as file handling, database management, graphics drawing, and animation are also covered, as are touch screen handling, gesture recognition, multitasking, location management, local notifications, camera access, and video playback support. Other features include Auto Layout, local map search, user interface animation using UIKit dynamics, iMessage app development, and biometric authentication.

Additional features of iOS development using Xcode are also covered, including Swift playgrounds, universal user interface design using size classes, app extensions, Interface Builder Live Views, embedded frameworks, collection and stack layouts, CloudKit data storage, and the document browser.

Other features of iOS 17 and Xcode 15 are also covered in detail, including iOS machine learning features.

The aim of this book, therefore, is to teach you the skills necessary to build your own apps for iOS 17. Assuming you are ready to download the iOS 17 SDK and Xcode 15, have a Mac, and some ideas for some apps to develop, you are ready to get started.

1.1 Source Code Download

The source code and Xcode project files for the examples contained in this book are available for download at:

https://www.payloadbooks.com/product/ios17xcode/

1.2 Download the Color eBook

Thank you for purchasing the print edition of this book. Your purchase includes a color copy of the book in PDF format. If you would like to download the PDF version of this book, please email proof of purchase (for example, a receipt, delivery notice, or photo of the physical book) to *info@payloadbooks.com*, and we will provide you with a download link.

1.3 Feedback

We want you to be satisfied with your purchase of this book. Therefore, if you find any errors in the book or have any comments, questions, or concerns, please contact us at *info@payloadbooks.com*.

1.4 Errata

While we make every effort to ensure the accuracy of the content of this book, inevitably, a book covering a subject area of this size and complexity may include some errors and oversights. Any known issues with the book will be outlined, together with solutions, at the following URL:

https://www.payloadbooks.com/ios-17-xcode-errata/

If you find an error not listed in the errata, please email our technical support team at *info@payloadbooks.com*.

1.5 Find more books

Visit our website to view our complete book catalog at *https://www.payloadbooks.com.*

2. Joining the Apple Developer Program

The first step in the process of learning to develop iOS 17 based applications involves gaining an understanding of the advantages of enrolling in the Apple Developer Program and deciding the point at which it makes sense to pay to join. With these goals in mind, this chapter will outline the costs and benefits of joining the developer program and, finally, walk through the steps involved in enrolling.

2.1 Downloading Xcode 15 and the iOS 17 SDK

The latest versions of both the iOS SDK and Xcode can be downloaded free of charge from the macOS App Store. Since the tools are free, this raises the question of whether to enroll in the Apple Developer Program, or to wait until it becomes necessary later in your app development learning curve.

2.2 Apple Developer Program

Membership in the Apple Developer Program currently costs $99 per year to enroll as an individual developer. Organization level membership is also available.

Much can be achieved without the need to pay to join the Apple Developer program. There are, however, areas of app development which cannot be fully tested without program membership. Of particular significance is the fact that Siri integration, iCloud access, Apple Pay, Game Center and In-App Purchasing can only be enabled and tested with Apple Developer Program membership.

Of further significance is the fact that Apple Developer Program members have access to technical support from Apple's iOS support engineers (though the annual fee initially covers the submission of only two support incident reports, more can be purchased). Membership also includes access to the Apple Developer forums; an invaluable resource both for obtaining assistance and guidance from other iOS developers, and for finding solutions to problems that others have encountered and subsequently resolved.

Program membership also provides early access to the pre-release Beta versions of Xcode, macOS and iOS.

By far the most important aspect of the Apple Developer Program is that membership is a mandatory requirement in order to publish an application for sale or download in the App Store.

Clearly, program membership is going to be required at some point before your application reaches the App Store. The only question remaining is when exactly to sign up.

2.3 When to Enroll in the Apple Developer Program?

Clearly, there are many benefits to Apple Developer Program membership and, eventually, membership will be necessary to begin selling your apps. As to whether to pay the enrollment fee now or later will depend on individual circumstances. If you are still in the early stages of learning to develop iOS apps or have yet to come up with a compelling idea for an app to develop then much of what you need is provided without program membership. As your skill level increases and your ideas for apps to develop take shape you can, after all, always enroll in the developer program later.

If, on the other hand, you are confident that you will reach the stage of having an application ready to publish, or know that you will need access to more advanced features such as Siri support, iCloud storage, In-App Purchasing and Apple Pay then it is worth joining the developer program sooner rather than later.

2.4 Enrolling in the Apple Developer Program

If your goal is to develop iOS apps for your employer, then it is first worth checking whether the company already has membership. That being the case, contact the program administrator in your company and ask them to send you an invitation from within the Apple Developer Program Member Center to join the team. Once they have done so, Apple will send you an email entitled *You Have Been Invited to Join an Apple Developer Program* containing a link to activate your membership. If you or your company is not already a program member, you can enroll online at:

https://developer.apple.com/programs/enroll/

Apple provides enrollment options for businesses and individuals. To enroll as an individual, you will need to provide credit card information in order to verify your identity. To enroll as a company, you must have legal signature authority (or access to someone who does) and be able to provide documentation such as a Dun & Bradstreet D-U-N-S number and documentation confirming legal entity status.

Acceptance into the developer program as an individual member typically takes less than 24 hours with notification arriving in the form of an activation email from Apple. Enrollment as a company can take considerably longer (sometimes weeks or even months) due to the burden of the additional verification requirements.

While awaiting activation you may log in to the Member Center with restricted access using your Apple ID and password at the following URL:

https://developer.apple.com/membercenter

Once logged in, clicking on the *Your Account* tab at the top of the page will display the prevailing status of your application to join the developer program as *Enrollment Pending*. Once the activation email has arrived, log in to the Member Center again and note that access is now available to a wide range of options and resources, as illustrated in Figure 2-1:

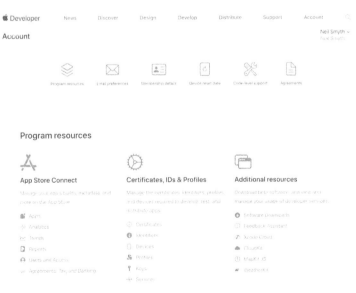

Figure 2-1

2.5 Summary

An important early step in the iOS 17 application development process involves identifying the best time to enroll in the Apple Developer Program. This chapter has outlined the benefits of joining the program, provided some guidance to keep in mind when considering developer program membership and walked briefly through the enrollment process. The next step is to download and install the iOS 17 SDK and Xcode 15 development environment.

3. Installing Xcode 15 and the iOS 17 SDK

iOS apps are developed using the iOS SDK and Apple's Xcode development environment. Xcode is an integrated development environment (IDE) within which you will code, compile, test and debug your iOS applications.

All of the examples in this book are based on Xcode version 15 and use features unavailable in earlier Xcode versions. This chapter will cover the steps involved in installing Xcode 15 and the iOS 17 SDK on macOS.

3.1 Identifying Your macOS Version

When developing with iOS apps, the Xcode 15 environment requires a system running macOS Ventura 13.5 or later. If you are unsure of the version of macOS on your Mac, you can find this information by clicking on the Apple menu in the top left-hand corner of the screen and selecting the *About This Mac* option from the menu. In the resulting dialog, check the *macOS* line:

Figure 3-1

If the "About This Mac" dialog does not indicate that macOS 13.5 or later is running, click on the *Software Update...* button to download and install the appropriate operating system upgrades.

3.2 Installing Xcode 15 and the iOS 17 SDK

The best way to obtain the latest Xcode and iOS SDK versions is to download them from the Apple Mac App Store. Launch the App Store on your macOS system, enter Xcode into the search box and click on the *Get* button to initiate the installation. This will install both Xcode and the iOS SDK.

3.3 Starting Xcode

Having successfully installed the SDK and Xcode, the next step is to launch it so we are ready to start development work. To start up Xcode, open the macOS Finder and search for *Xcode*. Since you will be frequently using this tool, take this opportunity to drag and drop it onto your dock for easier access in the future. Click on the Xcode icon in the dock to launch the tool. The first time Xcode runs you may be prompted to install additional components. Follow these steps, entering your username and password when prompted.

Once Xcode has loaded, and assuming this is the first time you have used Xcode on this system, you will be presented with the *Welcome* screen from which you are ready to proceed:

Figure 3-2

3.4 Adding Your Apple ID to the Xcode Preferences

Whether or not you enroll in the Apple Developer Program, it is worth adding your Apple ID to Xcode now that it is installed and running. Select the *Xcode -> Settings…* menu option followed by the *Accounts* tab. On the Accounts screen, click on the + button highlighted in Figure 3-3, select *Apple ID* from the resulting panel and click on the *Continue* button. When prompted, enter your Apple ID and password before clicking on the *Sign In* button to add the account to the preferences.

Figure 3-3

3.5 Developer and Distribution Signing Identities

Once the Apple ID has been entered the next step is to generate signing identities. To view the current signing identities, select the newly added Apple ID in the Accounts panel and click on the *Manage Certificates…* button to display a list of available signing identity types. To create a signing identity, simply click on the + button highlighted in Figure 3-4 and make the appropriate selection from the menu:

Figure 3-4

If the Apple ID has been used to enroll in the Apple Developer program, the option to create an *Apple Distribution* certificate will appear in the menu which will, when clicked, generate the signing identity required to submit the app to the Apple App Store. You will also need to create a *Developer ID Application* certificate if you plan to integrate features such as iCloud and Siri into your app projects. If you have not yet signed up for the Apple Developer program, select the *Apple Development* option to allow apps to be tested during development.

3.6 Summary

This book was written using Xcode 15 and the iOS 17 SDK running on macOS 14.0 (Sonoma). Before beginning iOS development, the first step is to install Xcode and configure it with your Apple ID via the accounts section of the Preferences screen. Once these steps have been performed, a development certificate must be generated which will be used to sign apps developed within Xcode. This will allow you to build and test your apps on physical iOS-based devices.

When you are ready to upload your finished app to the App Store, you will also need to generate a distribution certificate, a process requiring membership in the Apple Developer Program as outlined in the previous chapter.

Having installed the iOS SDK and successfully launched Xcode 15, we can now look at Xcode in more detail, starting with a guided tour.

4. A Guided Tour of Xcode 15

Just about every activity related to developing and testing iOS apps involves the use of the Xcode environment. This chapter is intended to serve two purposes. Primarily it is intended to provide an overview of many key areas that comprise the Xcode development environment. In the course of providing this overview, the chapter will also work through creating a straightforward iOS app project to display a label that reads "Hello World" on a colored background.

By the end of this chapter, you will have a basic familiarity with Xcode and your first running iOS app.

4.1 Starting Xcode 15

As with all iOS examples in this book, the development of our example will take place within the Xcode 15 development environment. Therefore, if you have not already installed this tool with the latest iOS SDK, refer first to the   chapter of this book. Then, assuming that the installation is complete, launch Xcode either by clicking on the icon on the dock (assuming you created one) or using the macOS Finder to locate Xcode in the Applications folder of your system.

When launched for the first time the screen illustrated in Figure 4-1 will appear by default:

Figure 4-1

If you do not see this window, select the *Window -> Welcome to Xcode* menu option to display it. Within this window, click on the option to *Create a New Project*. This selection will display the main Xcode project window together with the *project template* panel, where we can select a template matching the type of project we want to develop. Within this window, select the iOS tab so that the template panel appears as follows:

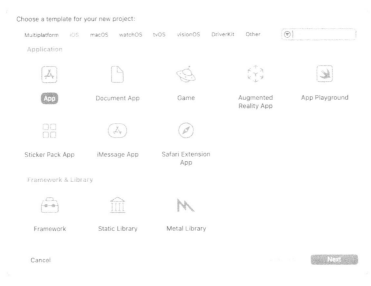

Figure 4-2

The toolbar on the window's top edge allows for selecting the target platform, providing options to develop an app for iOS, watchOS, visionOS, tvOS, or macOS. An option is also available for creating multiplatform apps using SwiftUI.

Begin by making sure that the *App* option located beneath *iOS* is selected. The main panel contains a list of templates available to use as the basis for an app. The options available are as follows:

- **App** – This creates a basic template for an app containing a single view and corresponding view controller.

- **Document App** – Creates a project intended to use the iOS document browser. The document browser provides a visual environment where the user can navigate and manage local and cloud-based files from within an iOS app.

- **Game** – Creates a project configured to take advantage of Sprite Kit, Scene Kit, OpenGL ES, and Metal for developing 2D and 3D games.

- **Augmented Reality App** – Creates a template project pre-configured to use ARKit to integrate augmented reality support into an iOS app.

- **Sticker Pack App** – Allows a sticker pack app to be created and sold within the Message App Store. Sticker pack apps allow additional images to be made available for inclusion in messages sent via the iOS Messages app.

- **iMessage App** – iMessage apps are extensions to the built-in iOS Messages app that allow users to send interactive messages, such as games, to other users. Once created, iMessage apps are available through the Message App Store.

- **Safari Extension App** - This option creates a project to be used as the basis for developing an extension for the Safari web browser.

For our simple example, we are going to use the *App* template, so select this option from the new project window and click *Next* to configure some more project options:

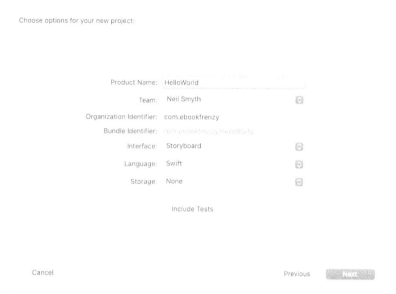

Figure 4-3

On this screen, enter a Product name for the app that will be created, in this case, "HelloWorld". Next, choose your account from the Team menu if you have already signed up for the Apple developer program. Otherwise, leave the option set to None.

The text entered into the Organization Name field will be placed within the copyright comments of all the source files that make up the project.

The company identifier is typically the reverse URL of your website, for example, "com.mycompany". This identifier will be used when creating provisioning profiles and certificates to enable the testing of advanced features of iOS on physical devices. It also uniquely identifies the app within the Apple App Store when it is published.

When developing an app in Xcode, the user interface can be designed using either Storyboards or SwiftUI. For this book, we will be using Storyboards, so make sure that the Interface menu is set to Storyboard. SwiftUI development is covered in our *iOS 17 App Development Essentials* book:

https://www.payloadbooks.com/index.php/product/ios-17-app-development-essentials-ebook/

Apple supports two programming languages for the development of iOS apps in the form of *Objective-C* and *Swift*. While it is still possible to program using the older Objective-C language, Apple considers Swift to be the future of iOS development. Therefore, all the code examples in this book are written in Swift, so make sure that the *Language* menu is set accordingly before clicking on the *Next* button.

On the final screen, choose a location on the file system for the new project to be created. This panel also allows placing the project under Git source code control. Source code control systems such as Git allow different project revisions to be managed and restored, and for changes made over the project's development lifecycle to be tracked. Since this is typically used for larger projects, or those involving more than one developer, this option can be turned off for this and the other projects created in the book.

Once the new project has been created, the main Xcode window will appear as illustrated in Figure 4-4:

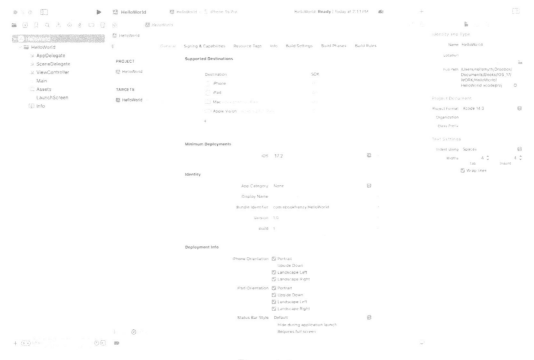

Figure 4-4

Before proceeding, we should take some time to look at what Xcode has done for us. First, it has created a group of files we will need to complete our app. Some of these are Swift source code files, where we will enter the code to make our app work.

In addition, the *Main* storyboard file is the save file used by the Interface Builder tool to hold the user interface design we will create. A second Interface Builder file named *LaunchScreen* will also have been added to the project. This file contains the user interface design for the screen that appears on the device while the app is loading.

Also present will be one or more *Property List* files that contain key/value pair information. For example, the *Info. plist* file contains resource settings relating to items such as the language, executable name, and app identifier and, as will be shown in later chapters, is the location where several properties are stored to configure the capabilities of the project (for example to configure access to the user's current geographical location). The list of files is displayed in the *Project Navigator* located in the left-hand panel of the main Xcode project window. In addition, a toolbar at the top of this panel contains options to display other information, such as build and run history, breakpoints, and compilation errors.

By default, the center panel of the window shows a general summary of the settings for the app project. This summary includes the identifier specified during the project creation process and the target devices. In addition, options are also provided to configure the orientations of the device that are to be supported by the app, together with opportunities to upload icons (the small images the user selects on the device screen to launch the app) and launch screen images (displayed to the user while the app loads) for the app.

The Signing section allows selecting an Apple identity when building the app. This identity ensures that the app is signed with a certificate when it is compiled. If you have registered your Apple ID with Xcode using the Preferences screen outlined in the previous chapter, select that identity now using the Team menu. Testing apps on physical devices will not be possible if no team is selected, though the simulator environment may still be used.

The Supported Destinations and Minimum Deployment sections of the screen also include settings to specify the device types and iOS versions on which the completed app is intended to run, as shown in Figure 4-5:

Figure 4-5

The iOS ecosystem now includes a variety of devices and screen sizes. When developing a project, it is possible to indicate that it is intended to target either the iPhone or iPad family of devices. With the gap between iPad and iPhone screen sizes now reduced by the introduction of the Pro range of devices, it no longer makes sense to create a project that targets just one device family. A much more sensible approach is to create a single project that addresses all device types and screen sizes. As will be shown in later chapters, Xcode 15 and iOS 17 include several features designed specifically to make the goal of *universal* app projects easy to achieve. With this in mind, ensure that the destination list at least includes the iPhone and iPad.

In addition to the General screen, tabs are provided to view and modify additional settings consisting of Signing & Capabilities, Resource Tags, Info, Build Settings, Build Phases, and Build Rules.

As we progress through subsequent chapters of this book, we will explore some of these other configuration options in greater detail. To return to the project settings panel at any future time, ensure the *Project Navigator* is selected in the left-hand panel and select the top item (the app name) in the navigator list.

When a source file is selected from the list in the navigator panel, the contents of that file will appear in the center panel, where it may then be edited.

4.2 Creating the iOS App User Interface

Simply by the very nature of the environment in which they run, iOS apps are typically visually oriented. Therefore, a vital component of any app involves a user interface through which the user will interact with the app and, in turn, receive feedback. While it is possible to develop user interfaces by writing code to create and position items on the screen, this is a complex and error-prone process. In recognition of this, Apple provides a tool called Interface Builder, which allows a user interface to be visually constructed by dragging and dropping components onto a canvas and setting properties to configure the appearance and behavior of those components.

As mentioned in the preceding section, Xcode pre-created several files for our project, one of which has a .storyboard filename extension. This is an Interface Builder storyboard save file, and the file we are interested in for our HelloWorld project is named *Main.storyboard*. To load this file into Interface Builder, select the *Main* item in the list in the left-hand panel. Interface Builder will subsequently appear in the center panel, as shown in Figure 4-6:

Figure 4-6

In the center panel, a visual representation of the app's user interface is displayed. Initially, this consists solely of a *View Controller* (UIViewController) containing a single View (UIView) object. This layout was added to our design by Xcode when we selected the App template option during the project creation phase. We will construct the user interface for our HelloWorld app by dragging and dropping user interface objects onto this UIView object. Designing a user interface consists primarily of dragging and dropping visual components onto the canvas and setting a range of properties. The user interface components are accessed from the Library panel, which is displayed by clicking on the Library button in the Xcode toolbar, as indicated in Figure 4-7:

Figure 4-7

This button will display the UI components used to construct our user interface. The layout of the items in the library may also be switched from a single column of objects with descriptions to multiple columns without descriptions by clicking on the button located in the top right-hand corner of the panel and to the right of the search box.

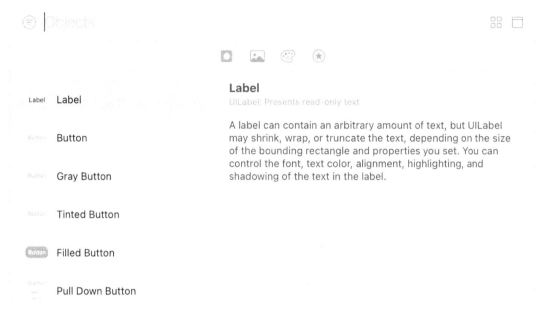

Figure 4-8

By default, the library panel will disappear either after an item has been dragged onto the layout or a click is performed outside of the panel. Hold the Option key while clicking on the required Library item to keep the panel visible in this mode. Alternatively, displaying the Library panel by clicking on the toolbar button highlighted in Figure 4-7 while holding down the Option key will cause the panel to stay visible until it is manually closed.

To edit property settings, we need to display the Xcode right-hand panel (if it is not already shown). This panel is referred to as the *Utilities panel* and can be displayed and hidden by clicking the right-hand button in the Xcode toolbar:

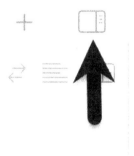

Figure 4-9

The Utilities panel, once displayed, will appear as illustrated in Figure 4-10:

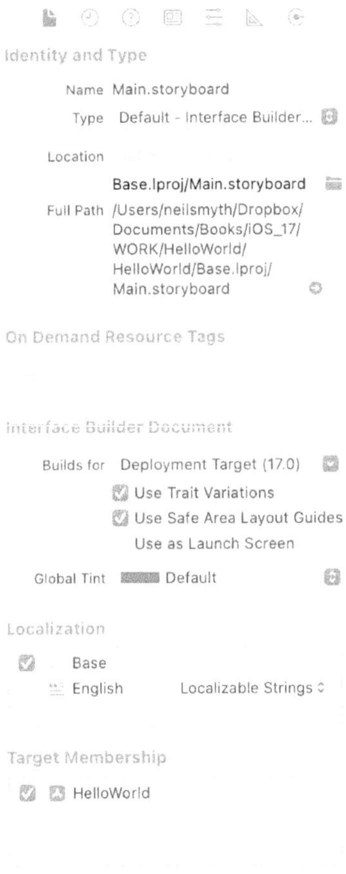

Identity and Type

Name Main.storyboard

Type Default - Interface Builder...

Location

Base.lproj/Main.storyboard

Full Path /Users/neilsmyth/Dropbox/
Documents/Books/iOS_17/
WORK/HelloWorld/
HelloWorld/Base.lproj/
Main.storyboard

On Demand Resource Tags

Interface Builder Document

Builds for Deployment Target (17.0)

Use Trait Variations

Use Safe Area Layout Guides

Use as Launch Screen

Global Tint Default

Localization

Base

English   Localizable Strings

Target Membership

HelloWorld

Figure 4-10

Along the top edge of the panel is a row of buttons that change the settings displayed in the upper half of the panel. By default, the *File Inspector* is typically shown. Options are also provided to display quick help, the *Identity Inspector, History Inspector, Attributes Inspector, Size Inspector*, and *Connections Inspector*. Take some time to review each of these selections to familiarize yourself with the configuration options each provides. Throughout the remainder of this book, extensive use of these inspectors will be made.

4.3 Changing Component Properties

With the property panel for the View selected in the main panel, we will begin our design work by changing the background color of this view. Start by ensuring the View is selected and that the Attributes Inspector (*View -> Inspectors -> Attributes*) is displayed in the Utilities panel. Next, click on the current property setting next to the *Background* setting and select the Custom option from the popup menu to display the *Colors* dialog. Finally, choose a visually pleasing color using the color selection tool and close the dialog. You will now notice that the view window has changed from white to the new color selection.

4.4 Adding Objects to the User Interface

The next step is to add a Label object to our view. To achieve this, display the Library panel as shown in Figure 4-7 above and either scroll down the list of objects in the Library panel to locate the Label object or, as illustrated in Figure 4-11, enter *Label* into the search box beneath the panel:

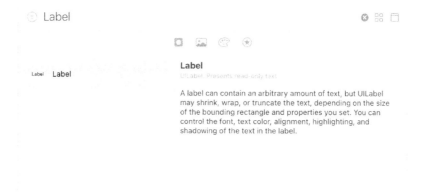

Figure 4-11

After locating the Label object, click on it and drag it to the center of the view so that the vertical and horizontal center guidelines appear. Once it is in position, release the mouse button to drop it at that location. We have now added an instance of the UILabel class to the scene. Cancel the Library search by clicking on the "x" button on the right-hand edge of the search field. Next, select the newly added label and stretch it horizontally so that it is approximately three times the current width. With the Label still selected, click on the centered alignment button in the Attributes Inspector (*View -> Inspectors -> Attributes*) to center the text in the middle of the label view:

Figure 4-12

Double-click on the text in the label that currently reads "Label" and type in "Hello World". Locate the font setting property in the Attributes Inspector panel and click the "T" button to display the font selection menu next to the font name. Change the Font setting from *System – System* to *Custom* and choose a larger font setting, for example, a Georgia bold typeface with a size of 24, as shown in Figure 4-13:

Figure 4-13

The final step is to add some layout constraints to ensure that the label remains centered within the containing view regardless of the size of the screen on which the app ultimately runs. This involves using the Auto Layout capabilities of iOS, a topic that will be covered extensively in later chapters. For this example, select the Label object, display the Align menu as shown in Figure 4-14, and enable both the *Horizontally in Container* and *Vertically in Container* options with offsets of 0 before clicking on the *Add 2 Constraints* button.

Figure 4-14

At this point, your View window will hopefully appear as outlined in Figure 4-15 (allowing, of course, for differences in your color and font choices).

Figure 4-15

Before building and running the project, it is worth taking a short detour to look at the Xcode *Document Outline* panel. This panel appears by default to the left of the Interface Builder panel. It is controlled by the small button in the bottom left-hand corner (indicated by the arrow in Figure 4-16) of the Interface Builder panel.

Figure 4-16

When displayed, the document outline shows a hierarchical overview of the elements that make up a user interface layout, together with any constraints applied to views in the layout.

Figure 4-17

4.5 Building and Running an iOS App in Xcode

Before an app can be run, it must first be compiled. Once successfully compiled, it may be run either within a simulator or on a physical iPhone or iPad device. For this chapter, however, it is sufficient to run the app in the simulator.

Within the main Xcode project window, make sure that the menu located in the top left-hand corner of the window (marked C in Figure 4-18) has the *iPhone 15* simulator option selected:

Figure 4-18

Click on the *Run* toolbar button (A) to compile the code and run the app in the simulator. The small panel in the center of the Xcode toolbar (D) will report the progress of the build process together with any problems or errors that cause the build process to fail. Once the app is built, the simulator will start, and the HelloWorld app will run:

Figure 4-19

Note that the user interface appears as designed in the Interface Builder tool. Click on the stop button (B), change the target menu from iPhone 15 to iPad Air (5th Generation), and rerun the app. Once again, the label will appear centered on the screen even with the larger screen size. Finally, verify that the layout is correct in landscape orientation by using the *Device -> Rotate Left* menu option. This indicates that the Auto Layout constraints are working and that we have designed a *universal* user interface for the project.

4.6 Running the App on a Physical iOS Device

Although the Simulator environment provides a valuable way to test an app on various iOS device models, it is important to also test on a physical iOS device.

If you have entered your Apple ID in the Xcode preferences screen as outlined in the previous chapter and selected a development team for the project, it is possible to run the app on a physical device simply by connecting it to the development Mac system with a USB cable and selecting it as the run target within Xcode.

With a device connected to the development system and an app ready for testing, refer to the device menu in the Xcode toolbar. There is a reasonable chance that this will have defaulted to one of the iOS Simulator configurations. Switch to the physical device by selecting this menu and changing it to the device name, as shown in Figure 4-20:

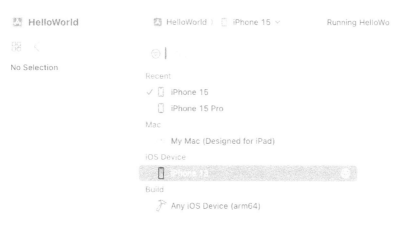

Figure 4-20

If the menu indicates that developer mode is disabled on the device, navigate to the Privacy & Security screen in the device's Settings app, locate the Developer Mode setting, and enable it. You will then need to restart the device. After the device restarts, a dialog will appear in which you will need to turn on developer mode. After entering your security code, the device will be ready for use with Xcode.

With the target device selected, ensure the device is unlocked and click on the run button, at which point Xcode will install and launch the app. As will be discussed later in this chapter, a physical device may also be configured for network testing, whereby apps are installed and tested via a network connection without needing to have the device connected by a USB cable.

4.7 Managing Devices and Simulators

Currently connected iOS devices and the simulators configured for use with Xcode can be viewed and managed using the Xcode Devices window, accessed via the *Window -> Devices and Simulators* menu option. Figure 4-21, for example, shows a typical Device screen on a system where an iPhone has been detected:

Figure 4-21

A wide range of simulator configurations are set up within Xcode by default and can be viewed by selecting the *Simulators* button at the top of the left-hand panel. Other simulator configurations can be added by clicking on the + button in the window's bottom left-hand corner. Once selected, a dialog will appear, allowing the simulator to be configured in terms of the device model, iOS version, and name.

4.8 Enabling Network Testing

In addition to testing an app on a physical device connected to the development system via a USB cable, Xcode also supports testing via a network connection. This option is enabled on a per device basis within the Devices and Simulators dialog introduced in the previous section. With the device connected via the USB cable, display this dialog, select the device from the list and enable the *Connect via network* option as highlighted in Figure 4-22:

Figure 4-22

Once the setting has been enabled, the device may continue to be used as the run target for the app even when the USB cable is disconnected. The only requirement is that the device and development computer be connected to the same WiFi network. Assuming this requirement has been met, clicking the run button with the device selected in the run menu will install and launch the app over the network connection.

4.9 Dealing with Build Errors

If for any reason, a build fails, the status window in the Xcode toolbar will report that an error has been detected by displaying "Build" together with the number of errors detected and any warnings. In addition, the left-hand panel of the Xcode window will update with a list of the errors. Selecting an error from this list will take you to the location in the code where corrective action needs to be taken.

4.10 Monitoring Application Performance

Another useful feature of Xcode is the ability to monitor the performance of an application while it is running, either on a device or simulator or within the Live Preview canvas. This information is accessed by displaying the *Debug Navigator.*

When Xcode is launched, the project navigator is displayed in the left-hand panel by default. Along the top of this panel is a bar with various of other options. The seventh option from the left displays the debug navigator when selected, as illustrated in Figure 4-23. When displayed, this panel shows real-time statistics relating to the performance of the currently running application such as memory, CPU usage, disk access, energy efficiency, network activity, and iCloud storage access.

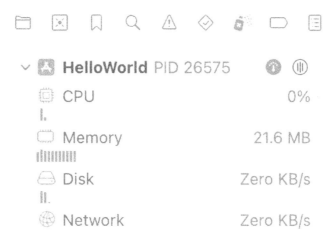

Figure 4-23

When one of these categories is selected, the main panel (Figure 4-24) updates to provide additional information about that particular aspect of the application's performance:

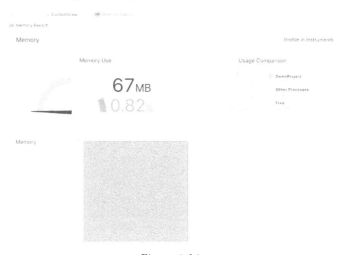

Figure 4-24

Yet more information can be obtained by clicking on the *Profile in Instruments* button in the top right-hand corner of the panel.

4.11 Exploring the User Interface Layout Hierarchy

Xcode also provides an option to break the user interface layout out into a rotatable 3D view that shows how the view hierarchy for a user interface is constructed. This can be particularly useful for identifying situations where one view instance is obscured by another appearing on top of it or a layout is not appearing as intended. This is also useful for learning how iOS works behind the scenes to construct a layout if only to appreciate how much work iOS is saving us from having to do.

To access the view hierarchy in this mode, the app needs to be running on a device or simulator. Once the app is running, click on the *Debug View Hierarchy* button indicated in Figure 4-25:

Figure 4-25

Once activated, a 3D "exploded" view of the layout will appear. Clicking and dragging within the view will rotate the hierarchy allowing the layers of views that make up the user interface to be inspected:

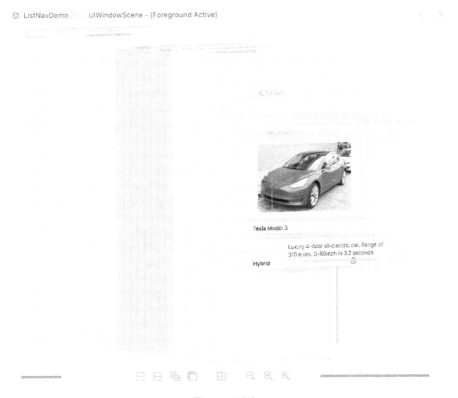

Figure 4-26

Moving the slider in the bottom left-hand corner of the panel will adjust the spacing between the different views in the hierarchy. The two markers in the right-hand slider (Figure 4-27) may also be used to narrow the range of views visible in the rendering. This can be useful, for example, to focus on a subset of views located in the middle of the hierarchy tree:

Figure 4-27

While the hierarchy is being debugged, the left-hand panel will display the entire view hierarchy tree for the layout as shown in Figure 4-28 below:

Figure 4-28

Selecting an object in the hierarchy tree will highlight the corresponding item in the 3D rendering and vice versa. The far right-hand panel will also display the Object Inspector populated with information about the currently selected object. Figure 4-29, for example, shows part of the Object Inspector panel while a Label view is selected within the view hierarchy.

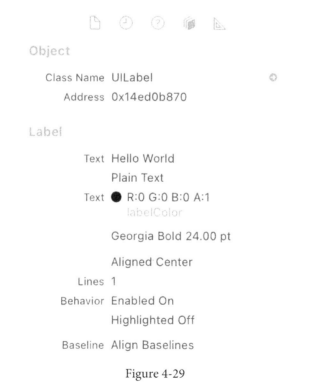

Figure 4-29

4.12 Summary

Apps are primarily created within the Xcode development environment. This chapter has provided a basic overview of the Xcode environment and worked through creating a straightforward example app. Finally, a brief overview was provided of some of the performance monitoring features in Xcode 15. In subsequent chapters of the book, many more features and capabilities of Xcode and Interface Builder will be covered.

5. An Introduction to Xcode 15 Playgrounds

Before introducing the Swift programming language in the following chapters, it is first worth learning about a feature of Xcode known as *Playgrounds*. This is a feature of Xcode designed to make learning Swift and experimenting with the iOS SDK much easier. The concepts covered in this chapter can be put to use when experimenting with many of the introductory Swift code examples contained in the chapters that follow.

5.1 What is a Playground?

A playground is an interactive environment where Swift code can be entered and executed with the results appearing in real-time. This makes an ideal environment in which to learn the syntax of Swift and the visual aspects of iOS app development without the need to work continuously through the edit/compile/run/debug cycle that would ordinarily accompany a standard Xcode iOS project. With support for rich text comments, playgrounds are also a good way to document code for future reference or as a training tool.

5.2 Creating a New Playground

To create a new Playground, start Xcode and select the *File -> New -> Playground...* menu option. Choose the iOS option on the resulting panel and select the Blank template.

The Blank template is useful for trying out Swift coding. The Single View template, on the other hand, provides a view controller environment for trying out code that requires a user interface layout. The game and map templates provide preconfigured playgrounds that allow you to experiment with the iOS MapKit and SpriteKit frameworks respectively.

On the next screen, name the playground *LearnSwift* and choose a suitable file system location into which the playground should be saved before clicking on the *Create* button.

Once the playground has been created, the following screen will appear ready for Swift code to be entered:

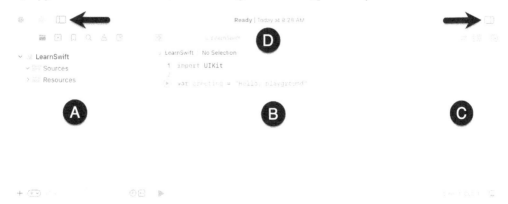

Figure 5-1

The panel on the left-hand side of the window (marked A in Figure 5-1) is the Navigator panel which provides access to the folders and files that make up the playground. To hide and show this panel, click on the button indicated by the left-most arrow. The center panel (B) is the *playground editor* where the lines of Swift code are entered. The right-hand panel (C) is referred to as the *results panel* and is where the results of each Swift expression entered into the playground editor panel are displayed. The tab bar (D) will contain a tab for each file currently open within the playground editor. To switch to a different file, simply select the corresponding tab. To close an open file, hover the mouse pointer over the tab and click on the "X" button when it appears to the left of the file name.

The button marked by the right-most arrow in the above figure is used to hide and show the Inspectors panel (marked A in Figure 5-2 below) where a variety of properties relating to the playground may be configured. Clicking and dragging the bar (B) upward will display the Debug Area (C) where diagnostic output relating to the playground will appear when code is executed:

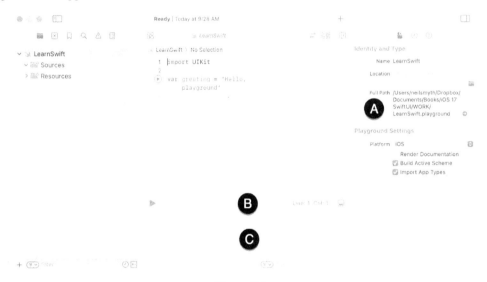

Figure 5-2

By far the quickest way to gain familiarity with the playground environment is to work through some simple examples.

5.3 A Swift Playground Example

Perhaps the simplest of examples in any programming language (that at least does something tangible) is to write some code to output a single line of text. Swift is no exception to this rule so, within the playground window, begin adding another line of Swift code so that it reads as follows:

```
import UIKit

var greeting = "Hello, playground"

print("Welcome to Swift")
```

All that the additional line of code does is make a call to the built-in Swift *print* function which takes as a parameter a string of characters to be displayed on the console. Those familiar with other programming languages will note the absence of a semi-colon at the end of the line of code. In Swift, semi-colons are optional and generally only used as a separator when multiple statements occupy the same line of code.

Note that although some extra code has been entered, nothing yet appears in the results panel. This is because the code has yet to be executed. One option to run the code is to click on the Execute Playground button located in the bottom left-hand corner of the main panel as indicated by the arrow in Figure 5-3:

Figure 5-3

When clicked, this button will execute all the code in the current playground page from the first line of code to the last. Another option is to execute the code in stages using the run button located in the margin of the code editor, as shown in Figure 5-4:

```
LearnSwift
1   import UIKit
2
⊙   var greeting = "Hello, playground"

    print("Welcome to Swift")
6
```

Figure 5-4

This button executes the line numbers with the shaded blue background including the line on which the button is currently positioned. In the above figure, for example, the button will execute lines 1 through 3 and then stop.

The position of the run button can be moved by hovering the mouse pointer over the line numbers in the editor. In Figure 5-5, for example, the run button is now positioned on line 5 and will execute lines 4 and 5 when clicked. Note that lines 1 to 3 are no longer highlighted in blue indicating that these have already been executed and are not eligible to be run this time:

```
LearnSwift
    import UIKit

    var greeting = "Hello, playground"
4
⊙   print("Welcome to Swift")
6
```

Figure 5-5

This technique provides an easy way to execute the code in stages making it easier to understand how the code functions and to identify problems in code execution.

To reset the playground so that execution can be performed from the start of the code, simply click on the stop button as indicated in Figure 5-6:

Figure 5-6

Using this incremental execution technique, execute lines 1 through 3 and note that output now appears in the results panel indicating that the variable has been initialized:

Figure 5-7

Next, execute the remaining lines up to and including line 5 at which point the "Welcome to Swift" output should appear both in the results panel and debug area:

Figure 5-8

5.4 Viewing Results

Playgrounds are particularly useful when working and experimenting with Swift algorithms. This can be useful when combined with the Quick Look feature. Remaining within the playground editor, enter the following lines of code beneath the existing print statement:

```
var x = 10

for index in 1...20 {
    let y = index * x
    x -= 1
}
```

This expression repeats a loop 20 times, performing arithmetic expressions on each iteration of the loop. Once the code has been entered into the editor, click on the run button positioned at line 13 to execute these new lines of code. The playground will execute the loop and display in the results panel the final value for each variable. More interesting information, however, may be obtained by hovering the mouse pointer over the results line so that an additional button appears, as shown in Figure 5-9:

```
5  print("Welcome to Swift")                    "Welcome to Swift\n"

6
7  var x = 10                                    10

8
9  for index in 1...20 {
10     let y = index * x                         -180
11     x -= 1                                    -10
   }
```

Figure 5-9

Hovering over the output will display the *Quick Look* button on the far right which, when selected, will show a popup panel displaying the results, as shown in Figure 5-10:

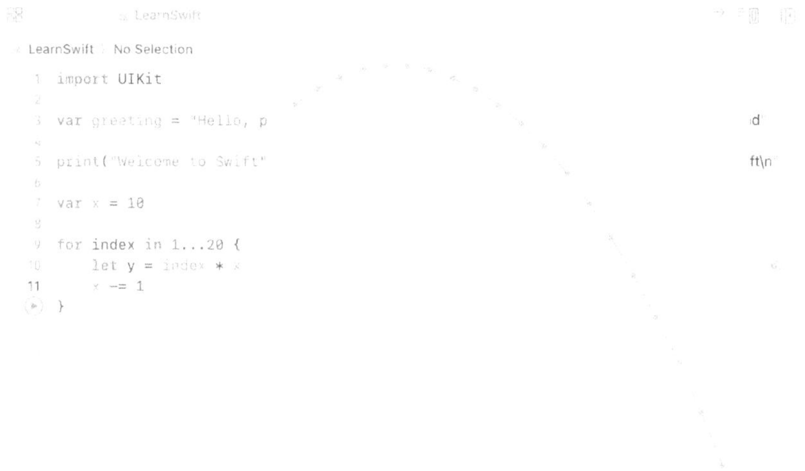

Figure 5-10

The left-most button is the *Show Result* button which, when selected, displays the results in-line with the code:

```
9  for index in 1...20 {
10     let y = index * x                         -180
11     x -= 1                                    -10
```

Figure 5-11

5.5 Adding Rich Text Comments

Rich text comments allow the code within a playground to be documented in a way that is easy to format and read. A single line of text can be marked as being rich text by preceding it with a //: marker. For example:

```
//: This is a single line of documentation text
```

Blocks of text can be added by wrapping the text in /*: and */ comment markers:

```
/*:
This is a block of documentation text that is intended
to span multiple lines
*/
```

The rich text uses the Markup language and allows text to be formatted using a lightweight and easy-to-use syntax. A heading, for example, can be declared by prefixing the line with a '#' character while text is displayed in italics when wrapped in '*' characters. Bold text, on the other hand, involves wrapping the text in '**' character sequences. It is also possible to configure bullet points by prefixing each line with a single '*'. Among the many other features of Markup is the ability to embed images and hyperlinks into the content of a rich text comment.

To see rich text comments in action, enter the following markup content into the playground editor immediately after the *print("Welcome to Swift")* line of code:

```
/*:
# Welcome to Playgrounds
This is your *first* playground which is intended to demonstrate:
* The use of **Quick Look**
* Placing results **in-line** with the code
*/
```

As the comment content is added it is said to be displayed in *raw markup* format. To display in *rendered markup* format, either select the *Editor -> Show Rendered Markup* menu option, or enable the *Render Documentation* option located under *Playground Settings* in the Inspector panel (marked A in Figure 5-2). If the Inspector panel is not currently visible, click on the button indicated by the right-most arrow in Figure 5-1 to display it. Once rendered, the above rich text should appear, as illustrated in Figure 5-12:

```
import UIKit

print("Welcome to Swift")
```

Welcome to Playgrounds

This is your *first* playground which is intented to demonstrate:

* The use of **Quick Look**
* Placing results **in-line** with the code

Figure 5-12

Detailed information about the Markup syntax can be found online at the following URL:

https://developer.apple.com/library/content/documentation/Xcode/Reference/xcode_markup_formatting_ref/index.html

5.6 Working with Playground Pages

A playground can consist of multiple pages, with each page containing its own code, resources and, rich text comments. So far, the playground used in this chapter contains a single page. Add a page to the playground now by selecting the LearnSwift entry at the top of the Navigator panel, right-clicking, and selecting the *New Playground Page* menu option. If the Navigator panel is not currently visible, click the button indicated by the left-most arrow in Figure 5-1 above to display it. Note that two pages are now listed in the Navigator named "Untitled Page" and "Untitled Page 2". Select and then click a second time on the "Untitled Page 2" entry so that the name becomes editable and change the name to *UIKit Examples* as outlined in Figure 5-13:

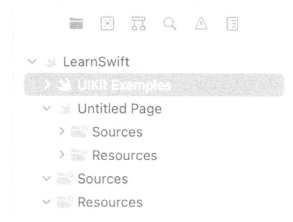

Figure 5-13

Note that the newly added page has Markdown links which, when clicked, navigate to the previous or next page in the playground.

5.7 Working with UIKit in Playgrounds

The playground environment is not restricted to simple Swift code statements. Much of the power of the iOS SDK is also available for experimentation within a playground.

When working with UIKit within a playground page, we first need to import the iOS UIKit Framework. The UIKit Framework contains most of the classes required to implement user interfaces for iOS apps and is an area that will be covered in considerable detail throughout the book. A compelling feature of playgrounds is that it is possible to work with UIKit and many other frameworks that comprise the iOS SDK.

The following code, for example, imports the UIKit Framework, creates a UILabel instance, and sets color, text, and font properties on it:

```
import UIKit


let myLabel = UILabel(frame: CGRect(x: 0, y: 0, width: 200, height: 50))


myLabel.backgroundColor = UIColor.red
myLabel.text = "Hello Swift"
myLabel.textAlignment = .center
myLabel.font = UIFont(name: "Georgia", size: 24)
myLabel
```

Enter this code into the playground editor on the UIKit Examples page (the existing code can be removed) and run the code. This code provides an excellent demonstration of how the Quick Look feature can be helpful.

Each line of the example Swift code configures a different aspect of the appearance of the UILabel instance. For example, clicking the Quick Look button for the first line of code will display an empty view (since the label exists but has yet to be given any visual attributes). Clicking on the Quick Look button in the line of code which sets the background color, on the other hand, will show the red label:

```
let myLabel = UILabel(frame: CGRect(x: 0, y: 0, width: 200,     UILabel
    height: 50))

myLabel.backgroundColor = UIColor.red                           UILabel
myLabel.text = "Hello Swift"                                    UILabel
myLabel.textAlignment = .center                                UILabel
myLabel.font = UIFont(name: "Georgia", size: 24)               UILabel
myLabel                                                        UILabel
```

Figure 5-14

Similarly, the quick look view for the line where the text property is set will show the red label with the "Hello Swift" text left aligned:

```
let myLabel = UILabel(frame: CGRect(x: 0, y: 0, width: 200,     UILabel
    height: 50))

myLabel.backgroundColor = UIColor.red                           UILabel
myLabel.text = "Hello Swift"                                    UILabel       Hello Swift
myLabel.textAlignment = .center                                UILabel
myLabel.font = UIFont(name: "Georgia", size: 24)               UILabel
myLabel                                                        UILabel
```

Figure 5-15

The font setting quick look view, on the other hand, displays the UILabel with centered text and the larger Georgia font:

```
let myLabel = UILabel(frame: CGRect(x: 0, y: 0, width: 200,     UILabel
    height: 50))

myLabel.backgroundColor = UIColor.red                           UILabel
myLabel.text = "Hello Swift"                                    UILabel
myLabel.textAlignment = .center                                UILabel
myLabel.font = UIFont(name: "Georgia", size: 24)               UILabel       Hello Swift
myLabel                                                        UILabel
```

Figure 5-16

5.8 Adding Resources to a Playground

Another helpful feature of playgrounds is the ability to bundle and access resources such as image files in a playground. For example, within the Navigator panel, click on the right-facing arrow (known as a *disclosure arrow*) to the left of the UIKit Examples page entry to unfold the page contents (Figure 5-17) and note the presence of a folder named *Resources*:

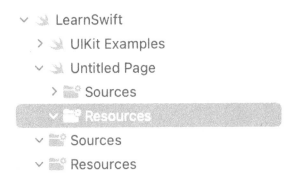

Figure 5-17

If you have not already done so, download and unpack the code samples archive from the following URL:

https://www.payloadbooks.com/product/ios17xcode/

Open a Finder window, navigate to the *playground_images* folder within the code samples folder, and drag and drop the image file named *waterfall.png* onto the *Resources* folder beneath the UIKit Examples page in the Playground Navigator panel:

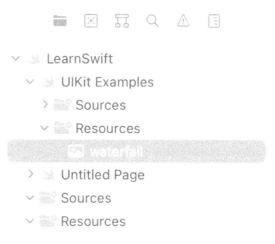

Figure 5-18

With the image added to the resources, add code to the page to create an image object and display the waterfall image on it:

```
let image = UIImage(named: "waterfall")
```

With the code added, run the new statement and use either the Quick Look or inline option to view the results of the code:

Figure 5-19

5.9 Working with Enhanced Live Views

So far in this chapter, all UIKit examples have presented static user interface elements using the Quick Look and inline features. It is, however, also possible to test dynamic user interface behavior within a playground using the Xcode Enhanced Live Views feature. First, create a new page within the playground named Live View Example to demonstrate live views in action. Then, within the newly added page, remove the existing lines of Swift code before adding import statements for the UIKit Framework and an additional playground module named PlaygroundSupport:

```
import UIKit
import PlaygroundSupport
```

The PlaygroundSupport module provides several useful playground features, including a live view within the playground timeline.

Beneath the import statements, add the following code:

```
let container = UIView(frame: CGRect(x: 0,y: 0,width: 200,height: 200))
container.backgroundColor = UIColor.white
let square = UIView(frame: CGRect(x: 50,y: 50,width: 100,height: 100))
square.backgroundColor = UIColor.red

container.addSubview(square)

UIView.animate(withDuration: 5.0, animations: {
    square.backgroundColor = UIColor.blue
    let rotation = CGAffineTransform(rotationAngle: 3.14)
    square.transform = rotation
})
```

The code creates a UIView object as a container view and assigns it a white background color. A smaller view is then drawn and positioned in the center of the container view and colored red. The second view is then added as a child of the container view. Animation is then used to change the smaller view's color to blue and rotate it 360 degrees. If you are new to iOS programming, rest assured that these areas will be covered in detail in later chapters. At this point, the code is provided to highlight the capabilities of live views.

Once the code has been executed, clicking on any of the Quick Look buttons will show a snapshot of the views at each stage in the code sequence. None of the quick-look views, however, show the dynamic animation. Therefore, the live view playground feature will be necessary to see how the animation code works.

The PlaygroundSupport module includes a class named PlaygroundPage that allows playground code to interact with the pages that make up a playground. This is achieved through a range of methods and properties of the class, one of which is the *current* property. This property, in turn, provides access to the current playground page. To execute the live view within the playground timeline, the *liveView* property of the current page needs to be set to our new container. To enable the timeline, enable the Xcode *Editor -> Live View* menu option as shown in Figure 5-20:

Figure 5-20

Once the timeline is enabled, add the code to assign the container to the live view of the current page as follows:

```
import UIKit
import PlaygroundSupport

let container = UIView(frame: CGRect(x: 0,y: 0,width: 200,height: 200))

PlaygroundPage.current.liveView = container

container.backgroundColor = UIColor.white
let square = UIView(frame: CGRect(x: 50,y: 50,width: 100,height: 100))
square.backgroundColor = UIColor.red

container.addSubview(square)

UIView.animate(withDuration: 5.0, animations: {
    square.backgroundColor = UIColor.blue
    let rotation = CGAffineTransform(rotationAngle: 3.14)
    square.transform = rotation
})
```

Once the call has been added, re-execute the code, at which point the views should appear in the timeline (Figure 5-21). During the 5-second animation duration, the red square should rotate through 360 degrees while gradually changing color to blue:

Figure 5-21

To repeat the execution of the code on the playground page, click on the stop button highlighted in Figure 5-6 to reset the playground and change the stop button into the run button (Figure 5-3). Then, click the run button to repeat the execution.

5.10 When to Use Playgrounds

Swift Playgrounds provide an ideal environment for learning to program using the Swift programming language, and the use of playgrounds in the Swift introductory chapters is recommended.

It is also essential to remember that playgrounds will remain useful long after the basics of Swift have been learned and will become increasingly useful when moving on to more advanced areas of iOS development.

The iOS SDK is a vast collection of frameworks and classes. As a result, it is not unusual for even experienced developers to experiment with unfamiliar aspects of iOS development before adding code to a project. Historically this has involved creating a temporary iOS Xcode project and then repeatedly looping through the somewhat cumbersome edit, compile, and run cycle to arrive at a programming solution. Rather than fall into this habit, consider having a playground on standby to conduct experiments during your project development work.

5.11 Summary

This chapter has introduced the concept of playgrounds. Playgrounds provide an environment in which Swift code can be entered, and the results of that code are viewed dynamically. This provides an excellent environment for learning the Swift programming language and experimenting with many of the classes and APIs included in the iOS SDK without creating Xcode projects and repeatedly editing, compiling, and running code.

6. Swift Data Types, Constants and Variables

Prior to the introduction of iOS 8, the stipulated programming language for the development of iOS applications was Objective-C. When Apple announced iOS 8, however, the company also introduced an alternative to Objective-C in the form of the Swift programming language.

Due entirely to the popularity of iOS, Objective-C had become one of the more widely used programming languages. With origins firmly rooted in the 40-year-old C Programming Language, however, and despite recent efforts to modernize some aspects of the language syntax, Objective-C was beginning to show its age.

Swift, on the other hand, is a relatively new programming language designed specifically to make programming easier, faster and less prone to programmer error. Starting with a clean slate and no burden of legacy, Swift is a new and innovative language with which to develop applications for iOS, iPadOS, macOS, watchOS and tvOS with the advantage that much of the syntax will be familiar to those with experience of other programming languages.

The next several chapters will provide an overview and introduction to Swift programming. The intention of these chapters is to provide enough information so that you can begin to confidently program using Swift. For an exhaustive and in-depth guide to all the features, intricacies and capabilities of Swift, some time spent reading Apple's excellent book entitled "The Swift Programming Language" (available free of charge from within the Apple Books app) is strongly recommended.

6.1 Using a Swift Playground

Both this and the following few chapters are intended to introduce the basics of the Swift programming language. As outlined in the previous chapter, entitled *"An Introduction to Xcode 15 Playgrounds"* the best way to learn Swift is to experiment within a Swift playground environment. Before starting this chapter, therefore, create a new playground and use it to try out the code in both this and the other Swift introduction chapters that follow.

6.2 Swift Data Types

When we look at the different types of software that run on computer systems and mobile devices, from financial applications to graphics intensive games, it is easy to forget that computers are really just binary machines. Binary systems work in terms of 0 and 1, true or false, set and unset. All the data sitting in RAM, stored on disk drives and flowing through circuit boards and buses are nothing more than sequences of 1s and 0s. Each 1 or 0 is referred to as a *bit* and bits are grouped together in blocks of 8, each group being referred to as a *byte*. When people talk about 32-bit and 64-bit computer systems they are talking about the number of bits that can be handled simultaneously by the CPU bus. A 64-bit CPU, for example, is able to handle data in 64-bit blocks, resulting in faster performance than a 32-bit based system.

Humans, of course, don't think in binary. We work with decimal numbers, letters and words. In order for a human to easily (easily being a subjective term in this context) program a computer, some middle ground between human and computer thinking is needed. This is where programming languages such as Swift come into play. Programming languages allow humans to express instructions to a computer in terms and structures we understand, and then compile that down to a format that can be executed by a CPU.

One of the fundamentals of any program involves data, and programming languages such as Swift define a set of *data types* that allow us to work with data in a format we understand when programming. For example, if we want to store a number in a Swift program, we could do so with syntax similar to the following:

```
var mynumber = 10
```

In the above example, we have created a variable named *mynumber* and then assigned to it the value of 10. When we compile the source code down to the machine code used by the CPU, the number 10 is seen by the computer in binary as:

```
1010
```

Now that we have a basic understanding of the concept of data types and why they are necessary we can take a closer look at some of the more commonly used data types supported by Swift.

6.2.1 Integer Data Types

Swift integer data types are used to store whole numbers (in other words a number with no decimal places). Integers can be *signed* (capable of storing positive, negative and zero values) or *unsigned* (positive and zero values only).

Swift provides support for 8, 16, 32 and 64-bit integers (represented by the Int8, Int16, Int32 and Int64 types respectively). The same variants are also available for unsigned integers (UInt8, UInt16, UInt32 and UInt64).

In general, Apple recommends using the *Int* data type rather than one of the above specifically sized data types. The Int data type will use the appropriate integer size for the platform on which the code is running.

All integer data types contain bounds properties which can be accessed to identify the minimum and maximum supported values of that particular type. The following code, for example, outputs the minimum and maximum bounds for the 32-bit signed integer data type:

```
print("Int32 Min = \(Int32.min) Int32 Max = \(Int32.max)")
```

When executed, the above code will generate the following output:

```
Int32 Min = -2147483648 Int32 Max = 2147483647
```

6.2.2 Floating Point Data Types

The Swift floating point data types are able to store values containing decimal places. For example, 4353.1223 would be stored in a floating-point data type. Swift provides two floating point data types in the form of *Float* and *Double*. Which type to use depends on the size of value to be stored and the level of precision required. The Double type can be used to store up to 64-bit floating point numbers with a level of precision of 15 decimal places or greater. The Float data type, on the other hand, is limited to 32-bit floating point numbers and offers a level of precision as low as 6 decimal places depending on the native platform on which the code is running. Alternatively, the Float16 type may be used to store 16-bit floating point values. Float16 provides greater performance at the expense of lower precision.

6.2.3 Bool Data Type

Swift, like other languages, includes a data type for the purpose of handling true or false (1 or 0) conditions. Two Boolean constant values (*true* and *false*) are provided by Swift specifically for working with Boolean data types.

6.2.4 Character Data Type

The Swift Character data type is used to store a single character of rendered text such as a letter, numerical digit, punctuation mark or symbol. Internally characters in Swift are stored in the form of *grapheme clusters*. A grapheme cluster is made of two or more Unicode scalars that are combined to represent a single visible character.

The following lines assign a variety of different characters to Character type variables:

```
var myChar1 = "f"
var myChar2 = ":"
var myChar3 = "X"
```

Characters may also be referenced using Unicode code points. The following example assigns the 'X' character to a variable using Unicode:

```
var myChar4 = "\u{0058}"
```

6.2.5 String Data Type

The String data type is a sequence of characters that typically make up a word or sentence. In addition to providing a storage mechanism, the String data type also includes a range of string manipulation features allowing strings to be searched, matched, concatenated and modified. Strings in Swift are represented internally as collections of characters (where a character is, as previously discussed, comprised of one or more Unicode scalar values).

Strings can also be constructed using combinations of strings, variables, constants, expressions, and function calls using a concept referred to as *string interpolation*. For example, the following code creates a new string from a variety of different sources using string interpolation before outputting it to the console:

```
var userName = "John"
var inboxCount = 25
let maxCount = 100

var message = "\(userName) has \(inboxCount) messages. Message capacity remaining
is \(maxCount - inboxCount) messages."
```

```
print(message)
```

When executed, the code will output the following message:

```
John has 25 messages. Message capacity remaining is 75 messages.
```

A multiline string literal may be declared by encapsulating the string within triple quotes as follows:

```
var multiline = """

    The console glowed with flashing warnings.
    Clearly time was running out.

    "I thought you said you knew how to fly this!" yelled Mary.

    "It was much easier on the simulator" replied her brother,
     trying to keep the panic out of his voice.

"""
```

```
print(multiline)
```

The above code will generate the following output when run:

```
    The console glowed with flashing warnings.
    Clearly time was running out.
```

```
"I thought you said you knew how to fly this!" yelled Mary.

"It was much easier on the simulator" replied her brother,
trying to keep the panic out of his voice.
```

The amount by which each line is indented within a multiline literal is calculated as the number of characters by which the line is indented minus the number of characters by which the closing triple quote line is indented. If, for example, the fourth line in the above example had a 10-character indentation and the closing triple quote was indented by 5 characters, the actual indentation of the fourth line within the string would be 5 characters. This allows multiline literals to be formatted tidily within Swift code while still allowing control over indentation of individual lines.

6.2.6 Special Characters/Escape Sequences

In addition to the standard set of characters outlined above, there is also a range of *special characters* (also referred to as *escape sequences*) available for specifying items such as a new line, tab or a specific Unicode value within a string. These special characters are identified by prefixing the character with a backslash (a concept referred to as *escaping*). For example, the following assigns a new line to the variable named newline:

```
var newline = "\n"
```

In essence, any character that is preceded by a backslash is considered to be a special character and is treated accordingly. This raises the question as to what to do if you actually want a backslash character. This is achieved by *escaping* the backslash itself:

```
var backslash = "\\"
```

Commonly used special characters supported by Swift are as follows:

- **\n** - New line

- **\r** - Carriage return

- **\t** - Horizontal tab

- \\ - Backslash

- \" - Double quote (used when placing a double quote into a string declaration)

- \' - Single quote (used when placing a single quote into a string declaration)

- **\u{*nn*}** – Single byte Unicode scalar where *nn* is replaced by two hexadecimal digits representing the Unicode character.

- **\u{*nnnn*}** – Double byte Unicode scalar where *nnnn* is replaced by four hexadecimal digits representing the Unicode character.

- **\u{*nnnnnnnn*}** – Four-byte Unicode scalar where *nnnnnnnn* is replaced by eight hexadecimal digits representing the Unicode character.

6.3 Swift Variables

Variables are essentially locations in computer memory reserved for storing the data used by an application. Each variable is given a name by the programmer and assigned a value. The name assigned to the variable may then be used in the Swift code to access the value assigned to that variable. This access can involve either reading the value of the variable or changing the value. It is, of course, the ability to change the value of variables which gives them the name *variable*.

6.4 Swift Constants

A constant is like a variable in that it provides a named location in memory to store a data value. Constants differ in one significant way in that once a value has been assigned to a constant it cannot subsequently be changed.

Constants are particularly useful if there is a value which is used repeatedly throughout the application code. Rather than use the value each time, it makes the code easier to read if the value is first assigned to a constant which is then referenced in the code. For example, it might not be clear to someone reading your Swift code why you used the value 5 in an expression. If, instead of the value 5, you use a constant named interestRate the purpose of the value becomes much clearer. Constants also have the advantage that if the programmer needs to change a widely used value, it only needs to be changed once in the constant declaration and not each time it is referenced.

As with variables, constants have a type, a name and a value. Unlike variables, however, once a value has been assigned to a constant, that value cannot subsequently be changed.

6.5 Declaring Constants and Variables

Variables are declared using the *var* keyword and may be initialized with a value at creation time. If the variable is declared without an initial value, it must be declared as being *optional* (a topic which will be covered later in this chapter). The following, for example, is a typical variable declaration:

```
var userCount = 10
```

Constants are declared using the *let* keyword.

```
let maxUserCount = 20
```

For greater code efficiency and execution performance, Apple recommends the use of constants rather than variables whenever possible.

6.6 Type Annotations and Type Inference

Swift is categorized as a *type safe* programming language. This essentially means that once the data type of a variable has been identified, that variable cannot subsequently be used to store data of any other type without inducing a compilation error. This contrasts to *loosely typed* programming languages where a variable, once declared, can subsequently be used to store other data types.

There are two ways in which the type of a constant or variable will be identified. One approach is to use a *type annotation* at the point the variable or constant is declared in the code. This is achieved by placing a colon after the constant or variable name followed by the type declaration. The following line of code, for example, declares a variable named userCount as being of type Int:

```
var userCount: Int = 10
```

In the absence of a type annotation in a declaration, the Swift compiler uses a technique referred to as *type inference* to identify the type of the constant or variable. When relying on type inference, the compiler looks to see what type of value is being assigned to the constant or variable at the point that it is initialized and uses that as the type. Consider, for example, the following variable and constant declarations:

```
var signalStrength = 2.231
let companyName = "My Company"
```

During compilation of the above lines of code, Swift will infer that the signalStrength variable is of type Double (type inference in Swift defaults to Double for all floating-point numbers) and that the companyName constant is of type String.

When a constant is declared without a type annotation it must be assigned a value at the point of declaration:

```
let bookTitle = "iOS 17 App Development Essentials"
```

If a type annotation is used when the constant is declared, however, the value can be assigned later in the code. For example:

```
let bookTitle: String
.
.
.
if iosBookType {
    bookTitle = "iOS 17 App Development Essentials"
} else {
    bookTitle = "Android Studio Development Essentials"
}
```

It is important to note that a value may only be assigned to a constant once. A second attempt to assign a value to a constant will result in a syntax error.

6.7 The Swift Tuple

Before proceeding, now is a good time to introduce the Swift tuple. The tuple is perhaps one of the simplest, yet most powerful features of the Swift programming language. A tuple is, quite simply, a way to temporarily group together multiple values into a single entity. The items stored in a tuple can be of any type and there are no restrictions requiring that those values all be of the same type. A tuple could, for example, be constructed to contain an Int value, a Double value and a String as follows:

```
let myTuple = (10, 432.433, "This is a String")
```

The elements of a tuple can be accessed using a number of different techniques. A specific tuple value can be accessed simply by referencing the index position (with the first value being at index position 0). The code below, for example, extracts the string resource (at index position 2 in the tuple) and assigns it to a new string variable:

```
let myTuple = (10, 432.433, "This is a String")
let myString = myTuple.2
print(myString)
```

Alternatively, all the values in a tuple may be extracted and assigned to variables or constants in a single statement:

```
let (myInt, myFloat, myString) = myTuple
```

This same technique can be used to extract selected values from a tuple while ignoring others by replacing the values to be ignored with an underscore character. The following code fragment extracts the integer and string values from the tuple and assigns them to variables, but ignores the floating-point value:

```
var (myInt, _, myString) = myTuple
```

When creating a tuple, it is also possible to assign a name to each value:

```
let myTuple = (count: 10, length: 432.433, message: "This is a String")
```

The names assigned to the values stored in a tuple may then be used to reference those values in code. For example, to output the *message* string value from the *myTuple* instance, the following line of code could be used:

```
print(myTuple.message)
```

Perhaps the most powerful use of tuples is, as will be seen in later chapters, the ability to return multiple values from a function.

6.8 The Swift Optional Type

The Swift optional data type is a new concept that does not exist in most other programming languages. The purpose of the optional type is to provide a safe and consistent approach to handling situations where a variable or constant may not have any value assigned to it.

Variables are declared as being optional by placing a ? character after the type declaration. The following code declares an optional Int variable named index:

```
var index: Int?
```

The variable *index* can now either have an integer value assigned to it or have nothing assigned to it. Behind the scenes, and as far as the compiler and runtime are concerned, an optional with no value assigned to it actually has a value of nil.

An optional can easily be tested (typically using an if statement) to identify whether it has a value assigned to it as follows:

```
var index: Int?

if index != nil {
    // index variable has a value assigned to it
} else {
    // index variable has no value assigned to it
}
```

If an optional has a value assigned to it, that value is said to be "wrapped" within the optional. The value wrapped in an optional may be accessed using a concept referred to as *forced unwrapping*. This simply means that the underlying value is extracted from the optional data type, a procedure that is performed by placing an exclamation mark (!) after the optional name.

To explore this concept of unwrapping optional types in more detail, consider the following code:

```
var index: Int?

index = 3

var treeArray = ["Oak", "Pine", "Yew", "Birch"]

if index != nil {
    print(treeArray[index!])
} else {
    print("index does not contain a value")
}
```

The code simply uses an optional variable to hold the index into an array of strings representing the names of tree species (Swift arrays will be covered in more detail in the chapter entitled *"Working with Array and Dictionary Collections in Swift"*). If the index optional variable has a value assigned to it, the tree name at that location in the array is printed to the console. Since the index is an optional type, the value has been unwrapped by placing an exclamation mark after the variable name:

```
print(treeArray[index!])
```

Had the index not been unwrapped (in other words the exclamation mark omitted from the above line), the compiler would have issued an error similar to the following:

```
Value of optional type 'Int?' must be unwrapped to a value of type 'Int'
```

As an alternative to forced unwrapping, the value assigned to an optional may be allocated to a temporary variable or constant using *optional binding*, the syntax for which is as follows:

```
if let constantname = optionalName {


}

if var variablename = optionalName {


}
```

The above constructs perform two tasks. In the first instance, the statement ascertains whether the designated optional contains a value. Second, in the event that the optional has a value, that value is assigned to the declared constant or variable and the code within the body of the statement is executed. The previous forced unwrapping example could, therefore, be modified as follows to use optional binding instead:

```
var index: Int?

index = 3

var treeArray = ["Oak", "Pine", "Yew", "Birch"]

if let myvalue = index {
    print(treeArray[myvalue])
} else {
    print("index does not contain a value")
}
```

In this case the value assigned to the index variable is unwrapped and assigned to a temporary (also referred to as *shadow*) constant named *myvalue* which is then used as the index reference into the array. Note that the *myvalue* constant is described as temporary since it is only available within the scope of the if statement. Once the if statement completes execution, the constant will no longer exist. For this reason, there is no conflict in using the same temporary name as that assigned to the optional. The following is, for example, valid code:

```
.

.
if let index = index {
    print(treeArray[index])
} else {
.

.
```

When considering the above example, the use of the temporary value begins to seem redundant. Fortunately, the Swift development team arrived at the same conclusion and introduced the following shorthand if-let syntax in Swift 5.7:

```
var index: Int?

index = 3
```

```
var treeArray = ["Oak", "Pine", "Yew", "Birch"]

if let index {
    print(treeArray[index])
} else {
    print("index does not contain a value")
}
```

Using this approach it is no longer necessary to assign the optional to a temporary value.

Optional binding may also be used to unwrap multiple optionals and include a Boolean test condition, the syntax for which is as follows:

```
if let constname1 = optName1, let constname2 = optName2,
    let optName3 = ..., <boolean statement> {


}
```

The shorthand if-let syntax is also available when working with multiple optionals and test conditions avoiding the need to use temporary values:

```
if let constname1, let constname2,
    let optName3, ... <boolean statement> {


}
```

The following code, for example, uses shorthand optional binding to unwrap two optionals within a single statement:

```
var pet1: String?
var pet2: String?

pet1 = "cat"
pet2 = "dog"

if let pet1, let pet2 {
    print(pet1)
    print(pet2)
} else {
    print("insufficient pets")
}
```

The code fragment below, on the other hand, also makes use of the Boolean test clause condition:

```
if let pet1, let pet2, petCount > 1 {
    print(pet1)
    print(pet2)
} else {
    print("insufficient pets")
}
```

In the above example, the optional binding will not be attempted unless the value assigned to *petCount* is greater than 1.

It is also possible to declare an optional as being *implicitly unwrapped*. When an optional is declared in this way, the underlying value can be accessed without having to perform forced unwrapping or optional binding. An optional is declared as being implicitly unwrapped by replacing the question mark (?) with an exclamation mark (!) in the declaration. For example:

```
var index: Int! // Optional is now implicitly unwrapped

index = 3

var treeArray = ["Oak", "Pine", "Yew", "Birch"]

if index != nil {
    print(treeArray[index])
} else {
    print("index does not contain a value")
}
```

With the index optional variable now declared as being implicitly unwrapped, it is no longer necessary to unwrap the value when it is used as an index into the array in the above print call.

One final observation with regard to optionals in Swift is that only optional types are able to have no value or a value of nil assigned to them. In Swift it is not, therefore, possible to assign a nil value to a non-optional variable or constant. The following declarations, for instance, will all result in errors from the compiler since none of the variables are declared as optional:

```
var myInt = nil // Invalid code
var myString: String = nil // Invalid Code
let myConstant = nil // Invalid code
```

6.9 Type Casting and Type Checking

When writing Swift code, situations will occur where the compiler is unable to identify the specific type of a value. This is often the case when a value of ambiguous or unexpected type is returned from a method or function call. In this situation it may be necessary to let the compiler know the type of value that your code is expecting or requires using the *as* keyword (a concept referred to as *type casting*).

The following code, for example, lets the compiler know that the value returned from the *object(forKey:)* method needs to be treated as a String type:

```
let myValue = record.object(forKey: "comment") as! String
```

In fact, there are two types of casting which are referred to as *upcasting* and *downcasting*. Upcasting occurs when an object of a particular class is cast to one of its superclasses. Upcasting is performed using the *as* keyword and is also referred to as *guaranteed conversion* since the compiler can tell from the code that the cast will be successful. The UIButton class, for example, is a subclass of the UIControl class as shown in the fragment of the UIKit class hierarchy shown in Figure 6-1:

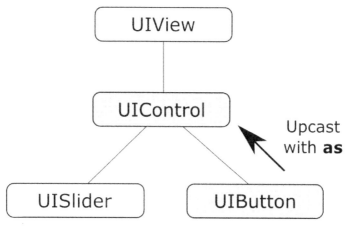

Figure 6-1

Since UIButton is a subclass of UIControl, the object can be safely upcast as follows:

```
let myButton: UIButton = UIButton()
```

```
let myControl = myButton as UIControl
```

Downcasting, on the other hand, occurs when a conversion is made from one class to another where there is no guarantee that the cast can be made safely or that an invalid casting attempt will be caught by the compiler. When an invalid cast is made in downcasting and not identified by the compiler it will most likely lead to an error at runtime.

Downcasting usually involves converting from a class to one of its subclasses. Downcasting is performed using the *as!* keyword syntax and is also referred to as *forced conversion*. Consider, for example, the UIKit UIScrollView class which has as subclasses both the UITableView and UITextView classes as shown in Figure 6-2:

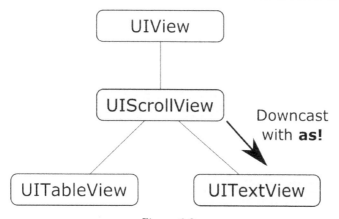

Figure 6-2

In order to convert a UIScrollView object to a UITextView class a downcast operation needs to be performed. The following code attempts to downcast a UIScrollView object to UITextView using the *guaranteed conversion* or *upcast* approach:

```
let myScrollView: UIScrollView = UIScrollView()
```

```
let myTextView = myScrollView as UITextView
```

The above code will result in the following error:

```
'UIScrollView' is not convertible to 'UITextView'
```

The compiler is indicating that a UIScrollView instance cannot be safely converted to a UITextView class instance. This does not necessarily mean that it is incorrect to do so, the compiler is simply stating that it cannot guarantee the safety of the conversion for you. The downcast conversion could instead be forced using the *as!* annotation:

```
let myTextView = myScrollView as! UITextView
```

Now the code will compile without an error. As an example of the dangers of downcasting, however, the above code will crash on execution stating that UIScrollView cannot be cast to UITextView. Forced downcasting should, therefore, be used with caution.

A safer approach to downcasting is to perform an optional binding using *as?*. If the conversion is performed successfully, an optional value of the specified type is returned, otherwise the optional value will be nil:

```
if let myTextView = myScrollView as? UITextView {
    print("Type cast to UITextView succeeded")
} else {
    print("Type cast to UITextView failed")
}
```

It is also possible to *type check* a value using the *is* keyword. The following code, for example, checks that a specific object is an instance of a class named MyClass:

```
if myobject is MyClass {
    // myobject is an instance of MyClass
}
```

6.10 Summary

This chapter has begun the introduction to Swift by exploring data types together with an overview of how to declare constants and variables. The chapter has also introduced concepts such as type safety, type inference and optionals, each of which is an integral part of Swift programming and designed specifically to make code writing less prone to error.

7. Swift Operators and Expressions

So far we have looked at using variables and constants in Swift and also described the different data types. Being able to create variables, however, is only part of the story. The next step is to learn how to use these variables and constants in Swift code. The primary method for working with data is in the form of *expressions*.

7.1 Expression Syntax in Swift

The most basic Swift expression consists of an *operator*, two *operands* and an *assignment*. The following is an example of an expression:

```
var myresult = 1 + 2
```

In the above example, the (+) operator is used to add two operands (1 and 2) together. The *assignment operator* (=) subsequently assigns the result of the addition to a variable named *myresult*. The operands could just have easily been variables (or a mixture of constants and variables) instead of the actual numerical values used in the example.

In the remainder of this chapter we will look at the basic types of operators available in Swift.

7.2 The Basic Assignment Operator

We have already looked at the most basic of assignment operators, the = operator. This assignment operator simply assigns the result of an expression to a variable. In essence, the = assignment operator takes two operands. The left-hand operand is the variable or constant to which a value is to be assigned and the right-hand operand is the value to be assigned. The right-hand operand is, more often than not, an expression which performs some type of arithmetic or logical evaluation, the result of which will be assigned to the variable or constant. The following examples are all valid uses of the assignment operator:

```
var x: Int? // Declare an optional Int variable
var y = 10 // Declare and initialize a second Int variable

x = 10 // Assign a value to x
x = x! + y // Assign the result of x + y to x
x = y // Assign the value of y to x
```

7.3 Swift Arithmetic Operators

Swift provides a range of operators for the purpose of creating mathematical expressions. These operators primarily fall into the category of *binary* operators in that they take two operands. The exception is the *unary negative operator* (-) which serves to indicate that a value is negative rather than positive. This contrasts with the *subtraction operator* (-) which takes two operands (i.e. one value to be subtracted from another). For example:

```
var x = -10 // Unary - operator used to assign -10 to variable x
x = x - 5 // Subtraction operator. Subtracts 5 from x
```

The following table lists the primary Swift arithmetic operators:

Operator	Description
-(unary)	Negates the value of a variable or expression

*	Multiplication
/	Division
+	Addition
-	Subtraction
%	Remainder/Modulo

Table 7-1

Note that multiple operators may be used in a single expression.

For example:

```
x = y * 10 + z - 5 / 4
```

7.4 Compound Assignment Operators

In an earlier section we looked at the basic assignment operator (=). Swift provides a number of operators designed to combine an assignment with a mathematical or logical operation. These are primarily of use when performing an evaluation where the result is to be stored in one of the operands. For example, one might write an expression as follows:

```
x = x + y
```

The above expression adds the value contained in variable x to the value contained in variable y and stores the result in variable x. This can be simplified using the addition compound assignment operator:

```
x += y
```

The above expression performs exactly the same task as $x = x + y$ but saves the programmer some typing.

Numerous compound assignment operators are available in Swift, the most frequently used of which are outlined in the following table:

Operator	Description
x += y	Add x to y and place result in x
x -= y	Subtract y from x and place result in x
x *= y	Multiply x by y and place result in x
x /= y	Divide x by y and place result in x
x %= y	Perform Modulo on x and y and place result in x

Table 7-2

7.5 Comparison Operators

Swift also includes a set of logical operators useful for performing comparisons. These operators all return a Boolean result depending on the result of the comparison. These operators are *binary operators* in that they work with two operands.

Comparison operators are most frequently used in constructing program flow control logic. For example, an *if* statement may be constructed based on whether one value matches another:

```
if x == y {
    // Perform task
}
```

The result of a comparison may also be stored in a *Bool* variable. For example, the following code will result in a *true* value being stored in the variable result:

```
var result: Bool?
var x = 10
var y = 20

result = x < y
```

Clearly 10 is less than 20, resulting in a *true* evaluation of the *x < y* expression. The following table lists the full set of Swift comparison operators:

Operator	Description
x == y	Returns true if x is equal to y
x > y	Returns true if x is greater than y
x >= y	Returns true if x is greater than or equal to y
x < y	Returns true if x is less than y
x <= y	Returns true if x is less than or equal to y
x != y	Returns true if x is not equal to y

Table 7-3

7.6 Boolean Logical Operators

Swift also provides a set of so-called logical operators designed to return Boolean *true* or *false* values. These operators both return Boolean results and take Boolean values as operands. The key operators are NOT (!), AND (&&) and OR (||).

The NOT (!) operator simply inverts the current value of a Boolean variable, or the result of an expression. For example, if a variable named *flag* is currently true, prefixing the variable with a '!' character will invert the value to false:

```
var flag = true // variable is true
var secondFlag = !flag // secondFlag set to false
```

The OR (||) operator returns true if one of its two operands evaluates to true, otherwise it returns false. For example, the following code evaluates to true because at least one of the expressions either side of the OR operator is true:

```
if (10 < 20) || (20 < 10) {
        print("Expression is true")
}
```

The AND (&&) operator returns true only if both operands evaluate to be true. The following example will return false because only one of the two operand expressions evaluates to true:

```
if (10 < 20) && (20 < 10) {
    print("Expression is true")
}
```

7.7 Range Operators

Swift includes several useful operators that allow ranges of values to be declared. As will be seen in later chapters, these operators are invaluable when working with looping in program logic.

The syntax for the *closed range operator* is as follows:

x…y

This operator represents the range of numbers starting at x and ending at y where both x and y are included within the range. The range operator 5…8, for example, specifies the numbers 5, 6, 7 and 8.

The *half-open range operator*, on the other hand uses the following syntax:

x..<y

In this instance, the operator encompasses all the numbers from x up to, but not including, y. A half-closed range operator 5..<8, therefore, specifies the numbers 5, 6 and 7.

Finally, the *one-sided range* operator specifies a range that can extend as far as possible in a specified range direction until the natural beginning or end of the range is reached (or until some other condition is met). A one-sided range is declared by omitting the number from one side of the range declaration, for example:

x…

or

…y

The previous chapter, for example, explained that a String in Swift is actually a collection of individual characters. A range to specify the characters in a string starting with the character at position 2 through to the last character in the string (regardless of string length) would be declared as follows:

2…

Similarly, to specify a range that begins with the first character and ends with the character at position 6, the range would be specified as follows:

…6

7.8 The Ternary Operator

Swift supports the *ternary operator* to provide a shortcut way of making decisions within code. The syntax of the ternary operator (also known as the conditional operator) is as follows:

```
condition ? true expression : false expression
```

The way the ternary operator works is that *condition* is replaced with an expression that will return either *true* or *false*. If the result is true then the expression that replaces the *true expression* is evaluated. Conversely, if the result was *false* then the *false expression* is evaluated. Let's see this in action:

```
let x = 10
let y = 20


print("Largest number is \(x > y ? x : y)")
```

The above code example will evaluate whether x is greater than y. Clearly this will evaluate to false resulting in y being returned to the print call for display to the user:

```
Largest number is 20
```

7.9 Nil Coalescing Operator

The *nil coalescing operator* (??) allows a default value to be used in the event that an optional has a nil value. The following example will output text which reads "Welcome back, customer" because the *customerName* optional is set to nil:

```
let customerName: String? = nil
print("Welcome back, \(customerName ?? "customer")")
```

If, on the other hand, *customerName* is not nil, the optional will be unwrapped and the assigned value displayed:

```
let customerName: String? = "John"
print("Welcome back, \(customerName ?? "customer")")
```

On execution, the print statement output will now read "Welcome back, John".

7.10 Bitwise Operators

As previously discussed, computer processors work in binary. These are essentially streams of ones and zeros, each one referred to as a bit. Bits are formed into groups of 8 to form bytes. As such, it is not surprising that we, as programmers, will occasionally end up working at this level in our code. To facilitate this requirement, Swift provides a range of *bit operators*.

Those familiar with bitwise operators in other languages such as C, C++, C#, Objective-C and Java will find nothing new in this area of the Swift language syntax. For those unfamiliar with binary numbers, now may be a good time to seek out reference materials on the subject in order to understand how ones and zeros are formed into bytes to form numbers. Other authors have done a much better job of describing the subject than we can do within the scope of this book.

For the purposes of this exercise we will be working with the binary representation of two numbers (for the sake of brevity we will be using 8-bit values in the following examples). First, the decimal number 171 is represented in binary as:

```
10101011
```

Second, the number 3 is represented by the following binary sequence:

```
00000011
```

Now that we have two binary numbers with which to work, we can begin to look at the Swift bitwise operators:

7.10.1 Bitwise NOT

The Bitwise NOT is represented by the tilde (~) character and has the effect of inverting all of the bits in a number. In other words, all the zeros become ones and all the ones become zeros. Taking our example 3 number, a Bitwise NOT operation has the following result:

```
00000011 NOT
========
11111100
```

The following Swift code, therefore, results in a value of -4:

```
let y = 3
let z = ~y


print("Result is \(z)")
```

7.10.2 Bitwise AND

The Bitwise AND is represented by a single ampersand (&). It makes a bit by bit comparison of two numbers. Any corresponding position in the binary sequence of each number where both bits are 1 results in a 1 appearing in the same position of the resulting number. If either bit position contains a 0 then a zero appears in the result. Taking our two example numbers, this would appear as follows:

```
10101011 AND
```

```
00000011
========
00000011
```

As we can see, the only locations where both numbers have 1s are the last two positions. If we perform this in Swift code, therefore, we should find that the result is 3 (00000011):

```
let x = 171
let y = 3
let z = x & y

print("Result is \(z)")
```

7.10.3 Bitwise OR

The bitwise OR also performs a bit by bit comparison of two binary sequences. Unlike the AND operation, the OR places a 1 in the result if there is a 1 in the first or second operand. The operator is represented by a single vertical bar character (|). Using our example numbers, the result will be as follows:

```
10101011 OR
00000011
========
10101011
```

If we perform this operation in a Swift example the result will be 171:

```
let x = 171
let y = 3
let z = x | y

print("Result is \(z)")
```

7.10.4 Bitwise XOR

The bitwise XOR (commonly referred to as *exclusive OR* and represented by the caret '^' character) performs a similar task to the OR operation except that a 1 is placed in the result if one or other corresponding bit positions in the two numbers is 1. If both positions are a 1 or a 0 then the corresponding bit in the result is set to a 0. For example:

```
10101011 XOR
00000011
========
10101000
```

The result in this case is 10101000 which converts to 168 in decimal. To verify this we can, once again, try some Swift code:

```
let x = 171
let y = 3
let z = x ^ y

print("Result is \(z)")
```

7.10.5 Bitwise Left Shift

The bitwise left shift moves each bit in a binary number a specified number of positions to the left. Shifting an integer one position to the left has the effect of doubling the value.

As the bits are shifted to the left, zeros are placed in the vacated right most (low order) positions. Note also that once the left most (high order) bits are shifted beyond the size of the variable containing the value, those high order bits are discarded:

```
10101011 Left Shift one bit
========
101010110
```

In Swift the bitwise left shift operator is represented by the '<<' sequence, followed by the number of bit positions to be shifted. For example, to shift left by 1 bit:

```
let x = 171
let z = x << 1

print("Result is \(z)")
```

When compiled and executed, the above code will display a message stating that the result is 342 which, when converted to binary, equates to 101010110.

7.10.6 Bitwise Right Shift

A bitwise right shift is, as you might expect, the same as a left except that the shift takes place in the opposite direction. Shifting an integer one position to the right has the effect of halving the value.

Note that since we are shifting to the right there is no opportunity to retain the lower most bits regardless of the data type used to contain the result. As a result, the low order bits are discarded. Whether or not the vacated high order bit positions are replaced with zeros or ones depends on whether the *sign bit* used to indicate positive and negative numbers is set or not.

```
10101011 Right Shift one bit
========
01010101
```

The bitwise right shift is represented by the '>>' character sequence followed by the shift count:

```
let x = 171
let z = x >> 1

print("Result is \(z)")
```

When executed, the above code will report the result of the shift as being 85, which equates to binary 01010101.

7.11 Compound Bitwise Operators

As with the arithmetic operators, each bitwise operator has a corresponding compound operator that allows the operation and assignment to be performed using a single operator:

Operator	Description
x &= y	Perform a bitwise AND of x and y and assign result to x
x |= y	Perform a bitwise OR of x and y and assign result to x
x ^= y	Perform a bitwise XOR of x and y and assign result to x
x <<= n	Shift x left by n places and assign result to x
x >>= n	Shift x right by n places and assign result to x

Table 7-4

7.12 Summary

Operators and expressions provide the underlying mechanism by which variables and constants are manipulated and evaluated within Swift code. This can take the simplest of forms whereby two numbers are added using the addition operator in an expression and the result stored in a variable using the assignment operator. Operators fall into a range of categories, details of which have been covered in this chapter.

8. Swift Control Flow

Regardless of the programming language used, application development is largely an exercise in applying logic, and much of the art of programming involves writing code that makes decisions based on one or more criteria. Such decisions define which code gets executed, how many times it is executed and, conversely, which code gets by-passed when the program is executing. This is often referred to as *control flow* since it controls the *flow* of program execution. Control flow typically falls into the categories of *looping control* (how often code is executed) and *conditional control flow* (whether code is executed). This chapter is intended to provide an introductory overview of both types of control flow in Swift.

8.1 Looping Control Flow

This chapter will begin by looking at control flow in the form of loops. Loops are essentially sequences of Swift statements which are to be executed repeatedly until a specified condition is met. The first looping statement we will explore is the *for-in* loop.

8.2 The Swift for-in Statement

The *for-in* loop is used to iterate over a sequence of items contained in a collection or number range and provides a simple to use looping option.

The syntax of the for-in loop is as follows:

```
for constant name in collection or range {
    // code to be executed
}
```

In this syntax, *constant name* is the name to be used for a constant that will contain the current item from the collection or range through which the loop is iterating. The code in the body of the loop will typically use this constant name as a reference to the current item in the loop cycle. The *collection* or *range* references the item through which the loop is iterating. This could, for example, be an array of string values, a range operator or even a string of characters (the topic of collections will be covered in greater detail within the chapter entitled *"Working with Array and Dictionary Collections in Swift"*).

Consider, for example, the following for-in loop construct:

```
for index in 1...5 {
    print("Value of index is \(index)")
}
```

The loop begins by stating that the current item is to be assigned to a constant named *index*. The statement then declares a closed range operator to indicate that the for loop is to iterate through a range of numbers, starting at 1 and ending at 5. The body of the loop simply prints out a message to the console panel indicating the current value assigned to the *index* constant, resulting in the following output:

```
Value of index is 1
Value of index is 2
Value of index is 3
Value of index is 4
Value of index is 5
```

As will be demonstrated in the *"Working with Array and Dictionary Collections in Swift"* chapter of this book, the *for-in* loop is of particular benefit when working with collections such as arrays and dictionaries.

The declaration of a constant name in which to store a reference to the current item is not mandatory. In the event that a reference to the current item is not required in the body of the *for* loop, the constant name in the *for* loop declaration can be replaced by an underscore character. For example:

```
var count = 0

for _ in 1...5 {
    // No reference to the current value is required.
    count += 1
}
```

8.2.1 The while Loop

The Swift *for* loop described previously works well when it is known in advance how many times a particular task needs to be repeated in a program. There will, however, be instances where code needs to be repeated until a certain condition is met, with no way of knowing in advance how many repetitions are going to be needed to meet that criteria. To address this need, Swift provides the *while* loop.

Essentially, the *while* loop repeats a set of tasks while a specified condition is met. The *while* loop syntax is defined as follows:

```
while condition {
    // Swift statements go here
}
```

In the above syntax, *condition* is an expression that will return either *true* or *false* and the // *Swift statements go here* comment represents the code to be executed while the *condition* expression is *true*. For example:

```
var myCount = 0

while myCount < 100 {
    myCount += 1
}
```

In the above example, the *while* expression will evaluate whether the *myCount* variable is less than 100. If it is already greater than 100, the code in the braces is skipped and the loop exits without performing any tasks.

If, on the other hand, *myCount* is not greater than 100 the code in the braces is executed and the loop returns to the *while* statement and repeats the evaluation of *myCount*. This process repeats until the value of *myCount* is greater than 100, at which point the loop exits.

8.3 The repeat ... while loop

The *repeat ... while* loop replaces the Swift 1.x *do .. while* loop. It is often helpful to think of the *repeat ... while* loop as an inverted *while* loop. The *while* loop evaluates an expression before executing the code contained in the body of the loop. If the expression evaluates to *false* on the first check then the code is not executed. The *repeat ... while* loop, on the other hand, is provided for situations where you know that the code contained in the body of the loop will *always* need to be executed at least once. For example, you may want to keep stepping through the items in an array until a specific item is found. You know that you have to at least check the first item in the array to have any hope of finding the entry you need. The syntax for the *repeat ... while* loop is as follows:

```
repeat {
    // Swift statements here
}
```

```
} while conditional expression
```

In the *repeat ... while* example below the loop will continue until the value of a variable named *i* equals 0:

```
var i = 10

repeat {
        i -= 1
} while (i > 0)
```

8.4 Breaking from Loops

Having created a loop, it is possible that under certain conditions you might want to break out of the loop before the completion criteria have been met (particularly if you have created an infinite loop). One such example might involve continually checking for activity on a network socket. Once activity has been detected it will most likely be necessary to break out of the monitoring loop and perform some other task.

For the purpose of breaking out of a loop, Swift provides the *break* statement which breaks out of the current loop and resumes execution at the code directly after the loop. For example:

```
var j = 10

for _ in 0 ..< 100
{
    j += j

    if j > 100 {
        break
    }

    print("j = \(j)")
}
```

In the above example the loop will continue to execute until the value of j exceeds 100 at which point the loop will exit and execution will continue with the next line of code after the loop.

8.5 The continue Statement

The *continue* statement causes all remaining code statements in a loop to be skipped, and execution to be returned to the top of the loop. In the following example, the print function is only called when the value of variable *i* is an even number:

```
var i = 1

while i < 20
{
        i += 1

        if (i % 2) != 0 {
            continue
        }

        print("i = \(i)")
```

```
}
```

The *continue* statement in the above example will cause the print call to be skipped unless the value of *i* can be divided by 2 with no remainder. If the *continue* statement is triggered, execution will skip to the top of the while loop and the statements in the body of the loop will be repeated (until the value of *i* exceeds 19).

8.6 Conditional Control Flow

In the previous chapter we looked at how to use logical expressions in Swift to determine whether something is *true* or *false*. Since programming is largely an exercise in applying logic, much of the art of programming involves writing code that makes decisions based on one or more criteria. Such decisions define which code gets executed and, conversely, which code gets by-passed when the program is executing.

8.7 Using the if Statement

The *if* statement is perhaps the most basic of control flow options available to the Swift programmer. Programmers who are familiar with C, Objective-C, C++ or Java will immediately be comfortable using Swift *if* statements.

The basic syntax of the Swift *if* statement is as follows:

```
if boolean expression {
    // Swift code to be performed when expression evaluates to true
}
```

Unlike some other programming languages, it is important to note that the braces ({}) are mandatory in Swift, even if only one line of code is executed after the *if* expression.

Essentially if the *Boolean expression* evaluates to *true* then the code in the body of the statement is executed. The body of the statement is enclosed in braces ({}). If, on the other hand, the expression evaluates to *false* the code in the body of the statement is skipped.

For example, if a decision needs to be made depending on whether one value is greater than another, we would write code similar to the following:

```
let x = 10

if x > 9 {
    print("x is greater than 9!")
}
```

Clearly, x is indeed greater than 9 causing the message to appear in the console panel.

8.8 Using if ... else ... Statements

The next variation of the *if* statement allows us to also specify some code to perform if the expression in the *if* statement evaluates to *false*. The syntax for this construct is as follows:

```
if boolean expression {
    // Code to be executed if expression is true
} else {
    // Code to be executed if expression is false
}
```

Using the above syntax, we can now extend our previous example to display a different message if the comparison expression evaluates to be *false*:

```
let x = 10
```

```
if x > 9 {
        print("x is greater than 9!")
} else {
        print("x is less than 10!")
}
```

In this case, the second print statement would execute if the value of x was less than or equal to 9.

8.9 Using if ... else if ... Statements

So far we have looked at *if* statements which make decisions based on the result of a single logical expression. Sometimes it becomes necessary to make decisions based on a number of different criteria. For this purpose, we can use the *if ... else if ...* construct, an example of which is as follows:

```
let x = 9

if x == 10 {
        print("x is 10")
} else if x == 9 {
        print("x is 9")
} else if x == 8 {
        print("x is 8")
}
```

This approach works well for a moderate number of comparisons but can become cumbersome for a larger volume of expression evaluations. For such situations, the Swift *switch* statement provides a more flexible and efficient solution. For more details on using the *switch* statement refer to the next chapter entitled "*The Swift Switch Statement*".

8.10 The guard Statement

The *guard* statement is a Swift language feature introduced as part of Swift 2. A guard statement contains a Boolean expression which must evaluate to true in order for the code located *after* the guard statement to be executed. The guard statement must include an *else* clause to be executed in the event that the expression evaluates to false. The code in the else clause must contain a statement to exit the current code flow (i.e. a *return*, *break*, *continue* or *throw* statement). Alternatively, the *else* block may call any other function or method that does not itself return.

The syntax for the guard statement is as follows:

```
guard <boolean expressions> else {
   // code to be executed if expression is false
   <exit statement here>
}

// code here is executed if expression is true
```

The guard statement essentially provides an "early exit" strategy from the current function or loop in the event that a specified requirement is not met.

The following code example implements a guard statement within a function:

```
func multiplyByTen(value: Int?) {
```

```
    guard let number = value, number < 10 else {
        print("Number is too high")
        return
    }

    let result = number * 10
    print(result)
}

multiplyByTen(value: 5)
multiplyByTen(value: 10)
```

The function takes as a parameter an integer value in the form of an optional. The guard statement uses optional binding to unwrap the value and verify that it is less than 10. In the event that the variable could not be unwrapped, or that its value is greater than 9, the else clause is triggered, the error message printed, and the return statement executed to exit the function.

If the optional contains a value less than 10, the code after the guard statement executes to multiply the value by 10 and print the result. A particularly important point to note about the above example is that the unwrapped *number* variable is available to the code outside of the guard statement. This would not have been the case had the variable been unwrapped using an *if* statement.

8.11 Summary

The term *control flow* is used to describe the logic that dictates the execution path that is taken through the source code of an application as it runs. This chapter has looked at the two types of control flow provided by Swift (looping and conditional) and explored the various Swift constructs that are available to implement both forms of control flow logic.

9. The Swift Switch Statement

In *"Swift Control Flow"* we looked at how to control program execution flow using the *if* and *else* statements. While these statement constructs work well for testing a limited number of conditions, they quickly become unwieldy when dealing with larger numbers of possible conditions. To simplify such situations, Swift has inherited the *switch* statement from the C programming language. Those familiar with the switch statement from other programming languages should be aware, however, that the Swift switch statement has some key differences from other implementations. In this chapter we will explore the Swift implementation of the *switch* statement in detail.

9.1 Why Use a switch Statement?

For a small number of logical evaluations of a value the *if… else if…* construct is perfectly adequate. Unfortunately, any more than two or three possible scenarios can quickly make such a construct both time consuming to write and difficult to read. For such situations, the *switch* statement provides an excellent alternative.

9.2 Using the switch Statement Syntax

The syntax for a basic Swift *switch* statement implementation can be outlined as follows:

```
switch expression
{
    case match1:
        statements

    case match2:
        statements

    case match3, match4:
        statements

    default:
        statements
}
```

In the above syntax outline, *expression* represents either a value, or an expression which returns a value. This is the value against which the *switch* operates.

For each possible match a *case* statement is provided, followed by a *match* value. Each potential match must be of the same type as the governing expression. Following on from the *case* line are the Swift statements that are to be executed in the event of the value matching the case condition.

Finally, the *default* section of the construct defines what should happen if none of the case statements present a match to the *expression*.

9.3 A Swift switch Statement Example

With the above information in mind we may now construct a simple *switch* statement:

```
let value = 4

switch (value)
{
      case 0:
        print("zero")

      case 1:
        print("one")

      case 2:
        print("two")

      case 3:
        print("three")

      case 4:
        print("four")

      case 5:
        print("five")

      default:
        print("Integer out of range")
}
```

9.4 Combining case Statements

In the above example, each case had its own set of statements to execute. Sometimes a number of different matches may require the same code to be executed. In this case, it is possible to group case matches together with a common set of statements to be executed when a match for any of the cases is found. For example, we can modify the switch construct in our example so that the same code is executed regardless of whether the value is 0, 1 or 2:

```
let value = 1

switch (value)
{
      case 0, 1, 2:
        print("zero, one or two")

      case 3:
        print("three")

      case 4:
        print("four")

      case 5:
```

```
    print("five")

  default:
    print("Integer out of range")
}
```

9.5 Range Matching in a switch Statement

The case statements within a switch construct may also be used to implement range matching. The following switch statement, for example, checks a temperature value for matches within three number ranges:

```
let temperature = 83

switch (temperature)
{
    case 0...49:
      print("Cold")

    case 50...79:
      print("Warm")

    case 80...110:
      print("Hot")

    default:
      print("Temperature out of range")
}
```

9.6 Using the where statement

The *where* statement may be used within a switch case match to add additional criteria required for a positive match. The following switch statement, for example, checks not only for the range in which a value falls, but also whether the number is odd or even:

```
let temperature = 54

switch (temperature)
{
    case 0...49 where temperature % 2 == 0:
      print("Cold and even")

    case 50...79 where temperature % 2 == 0:
      print("Warm and even")

    case 80...110 where temperature % 2 == 0:
      print("Hot and even")

    default:
      print("Temperature out of range or odd")
}
```

9.7 Fallthrough

Those familiar with switch statements in other languages such as C and Objective-C will notice that it is no longer necessary to include a *break* statement after each case declaration. Unlike other languages, Swift automatically breaks out of the statement when a matching case condition is met. The fallthrough effect of other switch implementations (whereby the execution path continues through the remaining case statements) can be emulated using the *fallthrough* statement:

```
let temperature = 10

switch (temperature)
{
    case 0...49 where temperature % 2 == 0:
      print("Cold and even")
      fallthrough

    case 50...79 where temperature % 2 == 0:
      print("Warm and even")
      fallthrough

    case 80...110 where temperature % 2 == 0:
      print("Hot and even")
      fallthrough

    default:
      print("Temperature out of range or odd")
}
```

Although *break* is less commonly used in Swift switch statements, it is useful when no action needs to be taken for the default case. For example:

```
    .
    .
    .
default:
     break
}
```

9.8 Summary

While the *if.. else..* construct serves as a good decision-making option for small numbers of possible outcomes, this approach can become unwieldy in more complex situations. As an alternative method for implementing flow control logic in Swift when many possible outcomes exist as the result of an evaluation, the *switch* statement invariably makes a more suitable option. As outlined in this chapter, however, developers familiar with switch implementations from other programming languages should be aware of some subtle differences in the way that the Swift switch statement works.

10. Swift Functions, Methods and Closures

Swift functions, methods and closures are a vital part of writing well-structured and efficient code and provide a way to organize programs while avoiding code repetition. In this chapter we will look at how functions, methods and closures are declared and used within Swift.

10.1 What is a Function?

A function is a named block of code that can be called upon to perform a specific task. It can be provided data on which to perform the task and is capable of returning results to the code that called it. For example, if a particular arithmetic calculation needs to be performed in a Swift program, the code to perform the arithmetic can be placed in a function. The function can be programmed to accept the values on which the arithmetic is to be performed (referred to as *parameters*) and to return the result of the calculation. At any point in the program code where the calculation is required the function is simply called, parameter values passed through as *arguments* and the result returned.

The terms *parameter* and *argument* are often used interchangeably when discussing functions. There is, however, a subtle difference. The values that a function is able to accept when it is called are referred to as *parameters*. At the point that the function is actually called and passed those values, however, they are referred to as *arguments*.

10.2 What is a Method?

A method is essentially a function that is associated with a particular class, structure or enumeration. If, for example, you declare a function within a Swift class (a topic covered in detail in the chapter entitled *"The Basics of Swift Object-Oriented Programming"*), it is considered to be a method. Although the remainder of this chapter refers to functions, the same rules and behavior apply equally to methods unless otherwise stated.

10.3 How to Declare a Swift Function

A Swift function is declared using the following syntax:

```
func <function name> (<para name>: <para type>,
                      <para name>: <para type>, ... ) -> <return type> {
    // Function code
}
```

This combination of function name, parameters and return type are referred to as the *function signature*. Explanations of the various fields of the function declaration are as follows:

- **func** – The prefix keyword used to notify the Swift compiler that this is a function.

- **<function name>** - The name assigned to the function. This is the name by which the function will be referenced when it is called from within the application code.

- **<para name>** - The name by which the parameter is to be referenced in the function code.

- **<para type>** - The type of the corresponding parameter.

- **<return type>** - The data type of the result returned by the function. If the function does not return a result then no return type is specified.

- **Function code** - The code of the function that does the work.

As an example, the following function takes no parameters, returns no result and simply displays a message:

```
func sayHello() {
    print("Hello")
}
```

The following sample function, on the other hand, takes an integer and a string as parameters and returns a string result:

```
func buildMessageFor(name: String, count: Int) -> String {
    return("\(name), you are customer number \(count)")
}
```

10.4 Implicit Returns from Single Expressions

In the previous example, the *return* statement was used to return the string value from within the *buildMessageFor()* function. It is worth noting that if a function contains a single expression (as was the case in this example), the return statement may be omitted. The *buildMessageFor()* method could, therefore, be rewritten as follows:

```
func buildMessageFor(name: String, count: Int) -> String {
    "\(name), you are customer number \(count)"
}
```

The return statement can only be omitted if the function contains a single expression. The following code, for example, will fail to compile since the function contains two expressions requiring the use of the return statement:

```
func buildMessageFor(name: String, count: Int) -> String {
    let uppername = name.uppercased()
    "\(uppername), you are customer number \(count)" // Invalid expression
}
```

10.5 Calling a Swift Function

Once declared, functions are called using the following syntax:

```
<function name> (<arg1>, <arg2>, ... )
```

Each argument passed through to a function must match the parameters the function is configured to accept. For example, to call a function named *sayHello* that takes no parameters and returns no value, we would write the following code:

```
sayHello()
```

10.6 Handling Return Values

To call a function named *buildMessageFor* that takes two parameters and returns a result, on the other hand, we might write the following code:

```
let message = buildMessageFor(name: "John", count: 100)
```

In the above example, we have created a new variable called *message* and then used the assignment operator (=) to store the result returned by the function.

When developing in Swift, situations may arise where the result returned by a method or function call is not used. When this is the case, the return value may be discarded by assigning it to '_'. For example:

```
_ = buildMessageFor(name: "John", count: 100)
```

10.7 Local and External Parameter Names

When the preceding example functions were declared, they were configured with parameters that were assigned names which, in turn, could be referenced within the body of the function code. When declared in this way, these names are referred to as *local parameter names*.

In addition to local names, function parameters may also have *external parameter names*. These are the names by which the parameter is referenced when the function is called. By default, function parameters are assigned the same local and external parameter names. Consider, for example, the previous call to the *buildMessageFor* method:

```
let message = buildMessageFor(name: "John", count: 100)
```

As declared, the function uses "name" and "count" as both the local and external parameter names.

The default external parameter names assigned to parameters may be removed by preceding the local parameter names with an underscore (_) character as follows:

```
func buildMessageFor(_ name: String, _ count: Int) -> String {
       return("\(name), you are customer number \(count)")
}
```

With this change implemented, the function may now be called as follows:

```
let message = buildMessageFor("John", 100)
```

Alternatively, external parameter names can be added simply by declaring the external parameter name before the local parameter name within the function declaration. In the following code, for example, the external names of the first and second parameters have been set to "username" and "usercount" respectively:

```
func buildMessageFor(username name: String, usercount count: Int)
                                                   -> String {
       return("\(name), you are customer number \(count)")
}
```

When declared in this way, the external parameter name must be referenced when calling the function:

```
let message = buildMessageFor(username: "John", usercount: 100)
```

Regardless of the fact that the external names are used to pass the arguments through when calling the function, the local names are still used to reference the parameters within the body of the function. It is important to also note that when calling a function using external parameter names for the arguments, those arguments must still be placed in the same order as that used when the function was declared.

10.8 Declaring Default Function Parameters

Swift provides the ability to designate a default parameter value to be used in the event that the value is not provided as an argument when the function is called. This simply involves assigning the default value to the parameter when the function is declared. Swift also provides a default external name based on the local parameter name for defaulted parameters (unless one is already provided) which must then be used when calling the function.

To see default parameters in action the *buildMessageFor* function will be modified so that the string "Customer" is used as a default in the event that a customer name is not passed through as an argument:

```
func buildMessageFor(_ name: String = "Customer", count: Int ) -> String
```

```
{
    return ("\(name), you are customer number \(count)")
}
```

The function can now be called without passing through a name argument:

```
let message = buildMessageFor(count: 100)
print(message)
```

When executed, the above function call will generate output to the console panel which reads:

```
Customer, you are customer number 100
```

10.9 Returning Multiple Results from a Function

A function can return multiple result values by wrapping those results in a tuple. The following function takes as a parameter a measurement value in inches. The function converts this value into yards, centimeters and meters, returning all three results within a single tuple instance:

```
func sizeConverter(_ length: Float) -> (yards: Float, centimeters: Float,
                                        meters: Float) {

    let yards = length * 0.0277778
    let centimeters = length * 2.54
    let meters = length * 0.0254

    return (yards, centimeters, meters)
}
```

The return type for the function indicates that the function returns a tuple containing three values named yards, centimeters and meters respectively, all of which are of type Float:

```
-> (yards: Float, centimeters: Float, meters: Float)
```

Having performed the conversion, the function simply constructs the tuple instance and returns it.

Usage of this function might read as follows:

```
let lengthTuple = sizeConverter(20)

print(lengthTuple.yards)
print(lengthTuple.centimeters)
print(lengthTuple.meters)
```

10.10 Variable Numbers of Function Parameters

It is not always possible to know in advance the number of parameters a function will need to accept when it is called within application code. Swift handles this possibility through the use of *variadic parameters*. Variadic parameters are declared using three periods (…) to indicate that the function accepts zero or more parameters of a specified data type. Within the body of the function, the parameters are made available in the form of an array object. The following function, for example, takes as parameters a variable number of String values and then outputs them to the console panel:

```
func displayStrings(_ strings: String...)
{
    for string in strings {
        print(string)
```

```
    }
}

displayStrings("one", "two", "three", "four")
```

10.11 Parameters as Variables

All parameters accepted by a function are treated as constants by default. This prevents changes being made to those parameter values within the function code. If changes to parameters need to be made within the function body, therefore, *shadow copies* of those parameters must be created. The following function, for example, is passed length and width parameters in inches, creates shadow variables of the two values and converts those parameters to centimeters before calculating and returning the area value:

```
func calcuateArea(length: Float, width: Float) -> Float {

    var length = length
    var width = width

    length = length * 2.54
    width = width * 2.54
    return length * width
}

print(calcuateArea(length: 10, width: 20))
```

10.12 Working with In-Out Parameters

When a variable is passed through as a parameter to a function, we now know that the parameter is treated as a constant within the body of that function. We also know that if we want to make changes to a parameter value we have to create a shadow copy as outlined in the above section. Since this is a copy, any changes made to the variable are not, by default, reflected in the original variable. Consider, for example, the following code:

```
var myValue = 10

func doubleValue (_ value: Int) -> Int {
    var value = value
    value += value
    return(value)
}

print("Before function call myValue = \(myValue)")

print("doubleValue call returns \(doubleValue(myValue))")

print("After function call myValue = \(myValue)")
```

The code begins by declaring a variable named *myValue* initialized with a value of 10. A new function is then declared which accepts a single integer parameter. Within the body of the function, a shadow copy of the value is created, doubled and returned.

The remaining lines of code display the value of the *myValue* variable before and after the function call is made. When executed, the following output will appear in the console:

```
Before function call myValue = 10
doubleValue call returns 20
After function call myValue = 10
```

Clearly, the function has made no change to the original myValue variable. This is to be expected since the mathematical operation was performed on a copy of the variable, not the *myValue* variable itself.

In order to make any changes made to a parameter persist after the function has returned, the parameter must be declared as an *in-out parameter* within the function declaration. To see this in action, modify the *doubleValue* function to include the *inout* keyword, and remove the creation of the shadow copy as follows:

```
func doubleValue ( _ value: inout Int) -> Int {
    var value = value
    value += value
    return (value)
}
```

Finally, when calling the function, the inout parameter must now be prefixed with an & modifier:

```
print ("doubleValue call returned \(doubleValue(&myValue))")
```

Having made these changes, a test run of the code should now generate output clearly indicating that the function modified the value assigned to the original *myValue* variable:

```
Before function call myValue = 10
doubleValue call returns 20
After function call myValue = 20
```

10.13 Functions as Parameters

An interesting feature of functions within Swift is that they can be treated as data types. It is perfectly valid, for example, to assign a function to a constant or variable as illustrated in the declaration below:

```
func inchesToFeet ( _ inches: Float) -> Float {
    return inches * 0.0833333
}


let toFeet = inchesToFeet
```

The above code declares a new function named *inchesToFeet* and subsequently assigns that function to a constant named *toFeet*. Having made this assignment, a call to the function may be made using the constant name instead of the original function name:

```
let result = toFeet(10)
```

On the surface this does not seem to be a particularly compelling feature. Since we could already call the function without assigning it to a constant or variable data type it does not seem that much has been gained.

The possibilities that this feature offers become more apparent when we consider that a function assigned to a constant or variable now has the capabilities of many other data types. In particular, a function can now be passed through as an argument to another function, or even returned as a result from a function.

Before we look at what is, essentially, the ability to plug one function into another, it is first necessary to explore the concept of function data types. The data type of a function is dictated by a combination of the parameters it accepts and the type of result it returns. In the above example, since the function accepts a floating-point parameter and returns a floating-point result, the function's data type conforms to the following:

```
(Float) -> Float
```

A function which accepts an Int and a Double as parameters and returns a String result, on the other hand, would have the following data type:

```
(Int, Double) -> String
```

In order to accept a function as a parameter, the receiving function simply declares the data type of the function it is able to accept.

For the purposes of an example, we will begin by declaring two unit conversion functions and assigning them to constants:

```
func inchesToFeet ( _ inches: Float) -> Float {

    return inches * 0.0833333
}

func inchesToYards ( _ inches: Float) -> Float {

    return inches * 0.0277778
}


let toFeet = inchesToFeet
let toYards = inchesToYards
```

The example now needs an additional function, the purpose of which is to perform a unit conversion and print the result in the console panel. This function needs to be as general purpose as possible, capable of performing a variety of different measurement unit conversions. In order to demonstrate functions as parameters, this new function will take as a parameter a function type that matches both the inchesToFeet and inchesToYards function data type together with a value to be converted. Since the data type of these functions is equivalent to (Float) -> Float, our general-purpose function can be written as follows:

```
func outputConversion( _ converterFunc: (Float) -> Float, value: Float) {

    let result = converterFunc(value)

    print("Result of conversion is \(result)")
}
```

When the outputConversion function is called, it will need to be passed a function matching the declared data type. That function will be called to perform the conversion and the result displayed in the console panel. This means that the same function can be called to convert inches to both feet and yards, simply by "plugging in" the appropriate converter function as a parameter. For example:

```
outputConversion(toYards, value: 10) // Convert to Yards
outputConversion(toFeet, value: 10) // Convert to Feet
```

Functions can also be returned as a data type simply by declaring the type of the function as the return type. The following function is configured to return either our toFeet or toYards function type (in other words a function which accepts and returns a Float value) based on the value of a Boolean parameter:

```
func decideFunction( _ feet: Bool) -> (Float) -> Float
{
    if feet {
        return toFeet
```

```
    } else {
        return toYards
    }
}
```

10.14 Closure Expressions

Having covered the basics of functions in Swift it is now time to look at the concept of *closures* and *closure expressions*. Although these terms are often used interchangeably there are some key differences.

Closure expressions are self-contained blocks of code. The following code, for example, declares a closure expression and assigns it to a constant named sayHello and then calls the function via the constant reference:

```
let sayHello = { print("Hello") }
sayHello()
```

Closure expressions may also be configured to accept parameters and return results. The syntax for this is as follows:

```
{(<para name>: <para type>, <para name> <para type>, ... ) ->
                                                <return type> in
        // Closure expression code here
}
```

The following closure expression, for example, accepts two integer parameters and returns an integer result:

```
let multiply = {(_ val1: Int, _ val2: Int) -> Int in
    return val1 * val2
}
let result = multiply(10, 20)
```

Note that the syntax is similar to that used for declaring Swift functions with the exception that the closure expression does not have a name, the parameters and return type are included in the braces and the *in* keyword is used to indicate the start of the closure expression code. Functions are, in fact, just named closure expressions.

Before the introduction of structured concurrency in Swift 5.5 (a topic covered in detail in the chapter entitled "*An Overview of Swift Structured Concurrency*"), closure expressions were often (and still are) used when declaring completion handlers for asynchronous method calls. In other words, when developing iOS applications, it will often be necessary to make calls to the operating system where the requested task is performed in the background allowing the application to continue with other tasks. Typically, in such a scenario, the system will notify the application of the completion of the task and return any results by calling the completion handler that was declared when the method was called. Frequently the code for the completion handler will be implemented in the form of a closure expression. Consider the following code example:

```
eventstore.requestAccess(to: .reminder, completion: {(granted: Bool,
                error: Error?) -> Void in
    if !granted {
            print(error!.localizedDescription)
    }
})
```

When the tasks performed by the *requestAccess(to:)* method call are complete it will execute the closure expression declared as the *completion:* parameter. The completion handler is required by the method to accept a Boolean value and an Error object as parameters and return no results, hence the following declaration:

```
{(granted: Bool, error: Error?) -> Void in
```

In actual fact, the Swift compiler already knows about the parameter and return value requirements for the completion handler for this method call and is able to infer this information without it being declared in the closure expression. This allows a simpler version of the closure expression declaration to be written:

```
eventstore.requestAccess(to: .reminder, completion: {(granted, error) in
    if !granted {
            print(error!.localizedDescription)
    }
})
```

10.15 Shorthand Argument Names

A useful technique for simplifying closures involves using *shorthand argument names*. This allows the parameter names and "in" keyword to be omitted from the declaration and the arguments to be referenced as $0, $1, $2 etc.

Consider, for example, a closure expression designed to concatenate two strings:

```
let join = { (string1: String, string2: String) -> String in
    string1 + string2
}
```

Using shorthand argument names, this declaration can be simplified as follows:

```
let join: (String, String) -> String = {
    $0 + $1
}
```

Note that the type declaration (*(String, String) -> String*) has been moved to the left of the assignment operator since the closure expression no longer defines the argument or return types.

10.16 Closures in Swift

A *closure* in computer science terminology generally refers to the combination of a self-contained block of code (for example a function or closure expression) and one or more variables that exist in the context surrounding that code block. Consider, for example the following Swift function:

```
func functionA() -> () -> Int {

    var counter = 0

    func functionB() -> Int {
        return counter + 10
    }
    return functionB
}

let myClosure = functionA()
let result = myClosure()
```

In the above code, *functionA* returns a function named *functionB*. In actual fact functionA is returning a closure since functionB relies on the *counter* variable which is declared outside the functionB's local scope. In other words, functionB is said to have *captured* or *closed over* (hence the term closure) the counter variable and, as such, is considered a closure in the traditional computer science definition of the word.

To a large extent, and particularly as it relates to Swift, the terms *closure* and *closure expression* have started to be used interchangeably. The key point to remember, however, is that both are supported in Swift.

10.17 Summary

Functions, closures and closure expressions are self-contained blocks of code that can be called upon to perform a specific task and provide a mechanism for structuring code and promoting reuse. This chapter has introduced the concepts of functions and closures in terms of declaration and implementation.

11. The Basics of Swift Object-Oriented Programming

Swift provides extensive support for developing object-oriented applications. The subject area of object-oriented programming is, however, large. It is not an exaggeration to state that entire books have been dedicated to the subject. As such, a detailed overview of object-oriented software development is beyond the scope of this book. Instead, we will introduce the basic concepts involved in object-oriented programming and then move on to explaining the concept as it relates to Swift application development. Once again, while we strive to provide the basic information you need in this chapter, we recommend reading a copy of Apple's *The Swift Programming Language* book for more extensive coverage of this subject area.

11.1 What is an Instance?

Objects (also referred to as class *instances*) are self-contained modules of functionality that can be easily used and re-used as the building blocks for a software application.

Instances consist of data variables (called *properties*) and functions (called *methods*) that can be accessed and called on the instance to perform tasks and are collectively referred to as *class members*.

11.2 What is a Class?

Much as a blueprint or architect's drawing defines what an item or a building will look like once it has been constructed, a class defines what an instance will look like when it is created. It defines, for example, what the methods will do and what the properties will be.

11.3 Declaring a Swift Class

Before an instance can be created, we first need to define the class 'blueprint' for the instance. In this chapter we will create a bank account class to demonstrate the basic concepts of Swift object-oriented programming.

In declaring a new Swift class we specify an optional *parent class* from which the new class is derived and also define the properties and methods that the class will contain. The basic syntax for a new class is as follows:

```
class NewClassName: ParentClass {
    // Properties
    // Instance Methods
    // Type methods
}
```

The *Properties* section of the declaration defines the variables and constants that are to be contained within the class. These are declared in the same way that any other variable or constant would be declared in Swift.

The *Instance methods* and *Type methods* sections define the methods that are available to be called on the class and instances of the class. These are essentially functions specific to the class that perform a particular operation when called upon and will be described in greater detail later in this chapter.

To create an example outline for our BankAccount class, we would use the following:

```
class BankAccount {
```

```
}
```

Now that we have the outline syntax for our class, the next step is to add some instance properties to it.

When naming classes, note that the convention is for the first character of each word to be declared in uppercase (a concept referred to as UpperCamelCase). This contrasts with property and function names where lower case is used for the first character (referred to as lowerCamelCase).

11.4 Adding Instance Properties to a Class

A key goal of object-oriented programming is a concept referred to as *data encapsulation*. The idea behind data encapsulation is that data should be stored within classes and accessed only through methods defined in that class. Data encapsulated in a class are referred to as *properties* or *instance variables*.

Instances of our BankAccount class will be required to store some data, specifically a bank account number and the balance currently held within the account. Properties are declared in the same way any other variables and constants are declared in Swift. We can, therefore, add these variables as follows:

```
class BankAccount {
    var accountBalance: Float = 0
    var accountNumber: Int = 0
}
```

Having defined our properties, we can now move on to defining the methods of the class that will allow us to work with our properties while staying true to the data encapsulation model.

11.5 Defining Methods

The methods of a class are essentially code routines that can be called upon to perform specific tasks within the context of that class.

Methods come in two different forms, *type methods* and *instance methods*. Type methods operate at the level of the class, such as creating a new instance of a class. Instance methods, on the other hand, operate only on the instances of a class (for example performing an arithmetic operation on two property variables and returning the result).

Instance methods are declared within the opening and closing braces of the class to which they belong and are declared using the standard Swift function declaration syntax.

Type methods are declared in the same way as instance methods with the exception that the declaration is preceded by the *class* keyword.

For example, the declaration of a method to display the account balance in our example might read as follows:

```
class BankAccount {

    var accountBalance: Float = 0
    var accountNumber: Int = 0

    func displayBalance()
    {
        print("Number \(accountNumber)")
        print("Current balance is \(accountBalance)")
    }
```

```
}
```

The method is an *instance method* so it is not preceded by the *class* keyword.

When designing the BankAccount class it might be useful to be able to call a type method on the class itself to identify the maximum allowable balance that can be stored by the class. This would enable an application to identify whether the BankAccount class is suitable for storing details of a new customer without having to go through the process of first creating a class instance. This method will be named *getMaxBalance* and is implemented as follows:

```
class BankAccount {

    var accountBalance: Float = 0
    var accountNumber: Int = 0

    func displayBalance()
    {
       print("Number \(accountNumber)")
       print("Current balance is \(accountBalance)")
    }

    class func getMaxBalance() -> Float {
        return 100000.00
    }

}
```

11.6 Declaring and Initializing a Class Instance

So far all we have done is define the blueprint for our class. In order to do anything with this class, we need to create instances of it. The first step in this process is to declare a variable to store a reference to the instance when it is created. We do this as follows:

```
var account1: BankAccount = BankAccount()
```

When executed, an instance of our BankAccount class will have been created and will be accessible via the *account1* variable.

11.7 Initializing and De-initializing a Class Instance

A class will often need to perform some initialization tasks at the point of creation. These tasks can be implemented by placing an *init* method within the class. In the case of the BankAccount class, it would be useful to be able to initialize the account number and balance properties with values when a new class instance is created. To achieve this, the *init* method could be written in the class as follows:

```
class BankAccount {

    var accountBalance: Float = 0
    var accountNumber: Int = 0

    init(number: Int, balance: Float)
    {
        accountNumber = number
        accountBalance = balance
```

```
   }

   func displayBalance()
   {
      print("Number \(accountNumber)")
      print("Current balance is \(accountBalance)")
   }
}
```

When creating an instance of the class, it will now be necessary to provide initialization values for the account number and balance properties as follows:

```
var account1 = BankAccount(number: 12312312, balance: 400.54)
```

Conversely, any cleanup tasks that need to be performed before a class instance is destroyed by the Swift runtime system can be performed by implementing the de-initializer within the class definition:

```
class BankAccount {

   var accountBalance: Float = 0
   var accountNumber: Int = 0

   init(number: Int, balance: Float)
   {
      accountNumber = number
      accountBalance = balance
   }

   deinit {
      // Perform any necessary clean up here
   }

   func displayBalance()
   {
      print("Number \(accountNumber)")
      print("Current balance is \(accountBalance)")
   }
}
```

11.8 Calling Methods and Accessing Properties

Now is probably a good time to recap what we have done so far in this chapter. We have now created a new Swift class named *BankAccount*. Within this new class we declared some properties to contain the bank account number and current balance together with an initializer and a method to display the current balance information. In the preceding section we covered the steps necessary to create and initialize an instance of our new class. The next step is to learn how to call the instance methods and access the properties we built into our class. This is most easily achieved using *dot notation*.

Dot notation involves accessing an instance variable, or calling an instance method by specifying a class instance followed by a dot followed in turn by the name of the property or method:

```
classInstance.propertyName
```

```
classInstance.instanceMethod()
```

For example, to get the current value of our *accountBalance* instance variable:

```
var balance1 = account1.accountBalance
```

Dot notation can also be used to set values of instance properties:

```
account1.accountBalance = 6789.98
```

The same technique is used to call methods on a class instance. For example, to call the *displayBalance* method on an instance of the BankAccount class:

```
account1.displayBalance()
```

Type methods are also called using dot notation, though they must be called on the class type instead of a class instance:

```
ClassName.typeMethod()
```

For example, to call the previously declared *getMaxBalance* type method, the BankAccount class is referenced:

```
var maxAllowed = BankAccount.getMaxBalance()
```

11.9 Stored and Computed Properties

Class properties in Swift fall into two categories referred to as *stored properties* and *computed properties*. Stored properties are those values that are contained within a constant or variable. Both the account name and number properties in the BankAccount example are stored properties.

A computed property, on the other hand, is a value that is derived based on some form of calculation or logic at the point at which the property is set or retrieved. Computed properties are implemented by creating *getter* and optional corresponding *setter* methods containing the code to perform the computation. Consider, for example, that the BankAccount class might need an additional property to contain the current balance less any recent banking fees. Rather than use a stored property, it makes more sense to use a computed property which calculates this value on request. The modified BankAccount class might now read as follows:

```
class BankAccount {

    var accountBalance: Float = 0
    var accountNumber: Int = 0;
    let fees: Float = 25.00

    var balanceLessFees: Float {
        get {
            return accountBalance - fees
        }
    }

    init(number: Int, balance: Float)
    {
        accountNumber = number
        accountBalance = balance
    }
    .
    .
```

```
.
}
```

The above code adds a getter that returns a computed property based on the current balance minus a fee amount. An optional setter could also be declared in much the same way to set the balance value less fees:

```
var balanceLessFees: Float {
    get {
        return accountBalance - fees
    }

    set(newBalance)
    {
        accountBalance = newBalance - fees
    }
}
```

The new setter takes as a parameter a floating-point value from which it deducts the fee value before assigning the result to the current balance property. Although these are computed properties, they are accessed in the same way as stored properties using dot-notation. The following code gets the current balance less the fees value before setting the property to a new value:

```
var balance1 = account1.balanceLessFees
account1.balanceLessFees = 12123.12
```

11.10 Lazy Stored Properties

There are several different ways in which a property can be initialized, the most basic being direct assignment as follows:

```
var myProperty = 10
```

Alternatively, a property may be assigned a value within the initializer:

```
class MyClass {
  let title: String

  init(title: String) {
    self.title = title
  }
}
```

For more complex requirements, a property may be initialized using a closure:

```
class MyClass {

    var myProperty: String = {
        var result = resourceIntensiveTask()
        result = processData(data: result)
        return result
    }()
    .

    .
}
```

Particularly in the case of a complex closure, there is the potential for the initialization to be resource intensive and time consuming. When declared in this way, the initialization will be performed every time an instance of the class is created, regardless of when (or even if) the property is actually used within the code of the app. Also, situations may arise where the value assigned to the property may not be known until a later stage in the execution process, for example after data has been retrieved from a database or user input has been obtained from the user. A far more efficient solution in such situations would be for the initialization to take place only when the property is first accessed. Fortunately, this can be achieved by declaring the property as *lazy* as follows:

```
class MyClass {

    lazy var myProperty: String = {
        var result = resourceIntensiveTask()
        result = processData(data: result)
        return result
    }()
    .
    .
}
```

When a property is declared as being lazy, it is only initialized when it is first accessed, allowing any resource intensive activities to be deferred until the property is needed and any initialization on which the property is dependent to be completed.

Note that lazy properties must be declared as variables (*var*).

11.11 Using self in Swift

Programmers familiar with other object-oriented programming languages may be in the habit of prefixing references to properties and methods with *self* to indicate that the method or property belongs to the current class instance. The Swift programming language also provides the *self* property type for this purpose and it is, therefore, perfectly valid to write code which reads as follows:

```
class MyClass {
    var myNumber = 1

    func addTen() {
        self.myNumber += 10
    }
}
```

In this context, the *self* prefix indicates to the compiler that the code is referring to a property named *myNumber* which belongs to the MyClass class instance. When programming in Swift, however, it is no longer necessary to use self in most situations since this is now assumed to be the default for references to properties and methods. To quote The Swift Programming Language guide published by Apple, "in practice you don't need to write *self* in your code very often". The function from the above example, therefore, can also be written as follows with the *self* reference omitted:

```
func addTen() {
    myNumber += 10
}
```

In most cases, use of self is optional in Swift. That being said, one situation where it is still necessary to use *self* is when referencing a property or method from within a closure expression. The use of self, for example, is mandatory in the following closure expression:

```
document?.openWithCompletionHandler({(success: Bool) -> Void in
    if success {
        self.ubiquityURL = resultURL
    }
})
```

It is also necessary to use self to resolve ambiguity such as when a function parameter has the same name as a class property. In the following code, for example, the first print statement will output the value passed through to the function via the myNumber parameter while the second print statement outputs the number assigned to the myNumber class property (in this case 10):

```
class MyClass {

    var myNumber = 10 // class property

    func addTen(myNumber: Int) {
        print(myNumber) // Output the function parameter value
        print(self.myNumber) // Output the class property value
    }
}
```

Whether or not to use self in most other situations is largely a matter of programmer preference. Those who prefer to use self when referencing properties and methods can continue to do so in Swift. Code that is written without use of the *self* property type (where doing so is not mandatory) is, however, just as valid when programming in Swift.

11.12 Understanding Swift Protocols

By default, there are no specific rules to which a Swift class must conform as long as the class is syntactically correct. In some situations, however, a class will need to meet certain criteria in order to work with other classes. This is particularly common when writing classes that need to work with the various frameworks that comprise the iOS SDK. A set of rules that define the minimum requirements which a class must meet is referred to as a *Protocol*. A protocol is declared using the *protocol* keyword and simply defines the methods and properties that a class must contain in order to be in conformance. When a class *adopts* a protocol, but does not meet all of the protocol requirements, errors will be reported stating that the class fails to conform to the protocol.

Consider the following protocol declaration. Any classes that adopt this protocol must include both a readable String value called *name* and a method named *buildMessage()* which accepts no parameters and returns a String value:

```
protocol MessageBuilder {

    var name: String { get }
    func buildMessage() -> String
}
```

Below, a class has been declared which adopts the MessageBuilder protocol:

```
class MyClass: MessageBuilder {

}
```

Unfortunately, as currently implemented, MyClass will generate a compilation error because it contains neither the *name* variable nor the *buildMessage()* method as required by the protocol it has adopted. To conform to the protocol, the class would need to meet both requirements, for example:

```
class MyClass: MessageBuilder {

    var name: String

    init(name: String) {
      self.name = name
    }

    func buildMessage() -> String {
        "Hello " + name
    }
}
```

11.13 Opaque Return Types

Now that protocols have been explained it is a good time to introduce the concept of opaque return types. As we have seen in previous chapters, if a function returns a result, the type of that result must be included in the function declaration. The following function, for example, is configured to return an Int result:

```
func doubleFunc1 (value: Int) -> Int {
    return value * 2
}
```

Instead of specifying a specific return type (also referred to as a *concrete type*), opaque return types allow a function to return any type as long as it conforms to a specified protocol. Opaque return types are declared by preceding the protocol name with the *some* keyword. The following changes to the *doubleFunc1()* function, for example, declare that a result will be returned of any type that conforms to the Equatable protocol:

```
func doubleFunc1(value: Int) -> some Equatable {
    value * 2
}
```

To conform to the Equatable protocol, which is a standard protocol provided with Swift, a type must allow the underlying values to be compared for equality. Opaque return types can, however, be used for any protocol, including those you create yourself.

Given that both the Int and String concrete types are in conformance with the Equatable protocol, it is possible to also create a function that returns a String result:

```
func doubleFunc2(value: String) -> some Equatable {
    value + value
}
```

Although these two methods return entirely different concrete types, the only thing known about these types is that they conform to the Equatable protocol. We therefore know the capabilities of the type, but not the actual type.

In fact, we only know the concrete type returned in these examples because we have access to the source code of the functions. If these functions resided in a library or API framework for which the source is not available to us, we would not know the exact type being returned. This is intentional and designed to hide the underlying return type used within public APIs. By masking the concrete return type, programmers will not come to rely on a function returning a specific concrete type or risk accessing internal objects which were not intended to be accessed. This also has the benefit that the developer of the API can make changes to the underlying implementation (including returning a different protocol compliant type) without having to worry about breaking dependencies in any code that uses the API.

This raises the question of what happens when an incorrect assumption is made when working with the opaque return type. Consider, for example, that the assumption could be made that the results from the *doubleFunc1()* and *doubleFunc2()* functions can be compared for equality:

```
let intOne = doubleFunc1(value: 10)
let stringOne = doubleFunc2(value: "Hello")



if (intOne == stringOne) {
    print("They match")
}
```

Working on the premise that we do not have access to the source code for these two functions there is no way to know whether the above code is valid. Fortunately, although we, as programmers, have no way of knowing the concrete type returned by the functions, the Swift compiler has access to this hidden information. The above code will, therefore, generate the following syntax error long before we get to the point of trying to execute invalid code:

```
Binary operator '==' cannot be applied to operands of type 'some
 Equatable' (result of 'doubleFunc1(value:)') and 'some Equatable'
(result of 'doubleFunc2(value:)')
```

11.14 Summary

Object-oriented programming languages such as Swift encourage the creation of classes to promote code reuse and the encapsulation of data within class instances. This chapter has covered the basic concepts of classes and instances within Swift together with an overview of stored and computed properties and both instance and type methods. The chapter also introduced the concept of protocols which serve as templates to which classes must conform and explained how they form the basis of opaque return types.

12. An Introduction to Swift Subclassing and Extensions

In *"The Basics of Swift Object-Oriented Programming"* we covered the basic concepts of object-oriented programming and worked through an example of creating and working with a new class using Swift. In that example, our new class was not derived from any base class and, as such, did not inherit any traits from a parent or super class. In this chapter we will introduce the concepts of subclassing, inheritance and extensions in Swift.

12.1 Inheritance, Classes and Subclasses

The concept of inheritance brings something of a real-world view to programming. It allows a class to be defined that has a certain set of characteristics (such as methods and properties) and then other classes to be created which are derived from that class. The derived class inherits all of the features of the parent class and typically then adds some features of its own.

By deriving classes we create what is often referred to as a *class hierarchy*. The class at the top of the hierarchy is known as the *base class* or *root class* and the derived classes as *subclasses* or *child classes*. Any number of subclasses may be derived from a class. The class from which a subclass is derived is called the *parent class* or *super class*.

Classes need not only be derived from a root class. For example, a subclass can also inherit from another subclass with the potential to create large and complex class hierarchies.

In Swift a subclass can only be derived from a single direct parent class. This is a concept referred to as *single inheritance*.

12.2 A Swift Inheritance Example

As with most programming concepts, the subject of inheritance in Swift is perhaps best illustrated with an example. In *"The Basics of Swift Object-Oriented Programming"*, we created a class named *BankAccount* designed to hold a bank account number and corresponding current balance. The BankAccount class contained both properties and instance methods. A simplified declaration for this class is reproduced below:

```
class BankAccount {

    var accountBalance: Float
    var accountNumber: Int

    init(number: Int, balance: Float)
    {
        accountNumber = number
        accountBalance = balance
    }

    func displayBalance()
    {
        print("Number \(accountNumber)")
```

```
        print("Current balance is \(accountBalance)")
    }
}
```

Though this is a somewhat rudimentary class, it does everything necessary if all you need it to do is store an account number and account balance. Suppose, however, that in addition to the BankAccount class you also needed a class to be used for savings accounts. A savings account will still need to hold an account number and a current balance and methods will still be needed to access that data. One option would be to create an entirely new class, one that duplicates all of the functionality of the BankAccount class together with the new features required by a savings account. A more efficient approach, however, would be to create a new class that is a *subclass* of the BankAccount class. The new class will then inherit all the features of the BankAccount class but can then be extended to add the additional functionality required by a savings account.

To create a subclass of BankAccount that we will call SavingsAccount, we simply declare the new class, this time specifying BankAccount as the parent class:

```
class SavingsAccount: BankAccount {


}
```

Note that although we have yet to add any instance variables or methods, the class has actually inherited all the methods and properties of the parent BankAccount class. We could, therefore, create an instance of the SavingsAccount class and set variables and call methods in exactly the same way we did with the BankAccount class in previous examples. That said, we haven't really achieved anything unless we take steps to extend the class.

12.3 Extending the Functionality of a Subclass

So far we have been able to create a subclass that contains all the functionality of the parent class. For this exercise to make sense, however, we now need to extend the subclass so that it has the features we need to make it useful for storing savings account information. To do this, we simply add the properties and methods that provide the new functionality, just as we would for any other class we might wish to create:

```
class SavingsAccount: BankAccount {

    var interestRate: Float = 0.0

    func calculateInterest() -> Float
    {
        return interestRate * accountBalance
    }
}
```

12.4 Overriding Inherited Methods

When using inheritance, it is not unusual to find a method in the parent class that almost does what you need, but requires modification to provide the precise functionality you require. That being said, it is also possible you'll inherit a method with a name that describes exactly what you want to do, but it actually does not come close to doing what you need. One option in this scenario would be to ignore the inherited method and write a new method with an entirely new name. A better option is to *override* the inherited method and write a new version of it in the subclass.

Before proceeding with an example, there are two rules that must be obeyed when overriding a method. First, the overriding method in the subclass must take exactly the same number and type of parameters as the overridden method in the parent class. Second, the new method must have the same return type as the parent method.

In our BankAccount class we have a method named *displayBalance* that displays the bank account number and current balance held by an instance of the class. In our SavingsAccount subclass we might also want to output the current interest rate assigned to the account. To achieve this, we simply declare a new version of the *displayBalance* method in our SavingsAccount subclass, prefixed with the *override* keyword:

```
class SavingsAccount: BankAccount {

    var interestRate: Float

    func calculateInterest() -> Float
    {
        return interestRate * accountBalance
    }

    override func displayBalance()
    {
        print("Number \(accountNumber)")
        print("Current balance is \(accountBalance)")
        print("Prevailing interest rate is \(interestRate)")
    }
}
```

It is also possible to make a call to the overridden method in the super class from within a subclass. The *displayBalance* method of the super class could, for example, be called to display the account number and balance, before the interest rate is displayed, thereby eliminating further code duplication:

```
override func displayBalance()
{
    super.displayBalance()
    print("Prevailing interest rate is \(interestRate)")
}
```

12.5 Initializing the Subclass

As the SavingsAccount class currently stands, it inherits the init initializer method from the parent BankAccount class which was implemented as follows:

```
init(number: Int, balance: Float)
{
    accountNumber = number
    accountBalance = balance
}
```

Clearly this method takes the necessary steps to initialize both the account number and balance properties of the class. The SavingsAccount class, however, contains an additional property in the form of the interest rate variable. The SavingsAccount class, therefore, needs its own initializer to ensure that the interestRate property is initialized when instances of the class are created. This method can perform this task and then make a call to the *init* method of the parent class to complete the initialization of the remaining variables:

```
class SavingsAccount: BankAccount {

    var interestRate: Float
```

```
init(number: Int, balance: Float, rate: Float)
{
    interestRate = rate
    super.init(number: number, balance: balance)
}
    .
    .
    .
}
```

Note that to avoid potential initialization problems, the *init* method of the superclass must always be called *after* the initialization tasks for the subclass have been completed.

12.6 Using the SavingsAccount Class

Now that we have completed work on our SavingsAccount class, the class can be used in some example code in much the same way as the parent BankAccount class:

```
let savings1 = SavingsAccount(number: 12311, balance: 600.00,
                              rate: 0.07)


print(savings1.calculateInterest())
savings1.displayBalance()
```

12.7 Swift Class Extensions

Another way to add new functionality to a Swift class is to use an extension. Extensions can be used to add features such as methods, initializers, computed properties and subscripts to an existing class without the need to create and reference a subclass. This is particularly powerful when using extensions to add functionality to the built-in classes of the Swift language and iOS SDK frameworks.

A class is extended using the following syntax:

```
extension ClassName {
  // new features here
}
```

For the purposes of an example, assume that we need to add some additional properties to the standard Double class that will return the value raised to the power 2 and 3. This functionality can be added using the following extension declaration:

```
extension Double {

    var squared: Double {
        return self * self
    }

    var cubed: Double {
        return self * self * self
    }
}
```

Having extended the Double class with two new computed properties we can now make use of the properties as we would any other properties of the Double class:

```
let myValue: Double = 3.0
print(myValue.squared)
```

When executed, the print statement will output the value of 9.0. Note that when declaring the myValue constant we were able to declare it as being of type Double and access the extension properties without the need to use a subclass. In fact, because these properties were added as an extension, rather than using a subclass, we can now access these properties directly on Double values:

```
print(3.0.squared)
print(6.0.cubed)
```

Extensions provide a quick and convenient way to extend the functionality of a class without the need to use subclasses. Subclasses, however, still have some advantages over extensions. It is not possible, for example, to override the existing functionality of a class using an extension and extensions cannot contain stored properties.

12.8 Summary

Inheritance extends the concept of object re-use in object-oriented programming by allowing new classes to be derived from existing classes, with those new classes subsequently extended to add new functionality. When an existing class provides some, but not all, of the functionality required by the programmer, inheritance allows that class to be used as the basis for a new subclass. The new subclass will inherit all the capabilities of the parent class, but may then be extended to add the missing functionality.

Swift extensions provide a useful alternative option to adding functionality to existing classes without the need to create a subclass.

13. An Introduction to Swift Structures and Enumerations

Having covered Swift classes in the preceding chapters, this chapter will introduce the use of structures in Swift. Although at first glance structures and classes look similar, there are some important differences that need to be understood when deciding which to use. This chapter will outline how to declare and use structures, explore the differences between structures and classes and introduce the concepts of value and reference types.

13.1 An Overview of Swift Structures

As with classes, structures form the basis of object-oriented programming and provide a way to encapsulate data and functionality into re-usable instances. Structure declarations resemble classes with the exception that the *struct* keyword is used in place of the *class* keyword. The following code, for example, declares a simple structure consisting of a String variable, initializer and method:

```
struct SampleStruct {

    var name: String

    init(name: String) {
        self.name = name
    }

    func buildHelloMsg() {
        "Hello " + name
    }
}
```

Consider the above structure declaration in comparison to the equivalent class declaration:

```
class SampleClass {

    var name: String

    init(name: String) {
        self.name = name
    }

    func buildHelloMsg() {
        "Hello " + name
    }
}
```

Other than the use of the *struct* keyword instead of *class*, the two declarations are identical. Instances of each type are also created using the same syntax:

```
let myStruct = SampleStruct(name: "Mark")
let myClass = SampleClass(name: "Mark")
```

In common with classes, structures may be extended and are also able to adopt protocols and contain initializers.

Given the commonality between classes and structures, it is important to gain an understanding of how the two differ. Before exploring the most significant difference it is first necessary to understand the concepts of *value types* and *reference types*.

13.2 Value Types vs. Reference Types

While on the surface structures and classes look alike, major differences in behavior occur when structure and class instances are copied or passed as arguments to methods or functions. This occurs because structure instances are value type while class instances are reference type.

When a structure instance is copied or passed to a method, an actual copy of the instance is created, together with any data contained within the instance. This means that the copy has its own version of the data which is unconnected with the original structure instance. In effect, this means that there can be multiple copies of a structure instance within a running app, each with its own local copy of the associated data. A change to one instance has no impact on any other instances.

In contrast, when a class instance is copied or passed as an argument, the only thing duplicated or passed is a reference to the location in memory where that class instance resides. Any changes made to the instance using those references will be performed on the same instance. In other words, there is only one class instance but multiple references pointing to it. A change to the instance data using any one of those references changes the data for all other references.

To demonstrate reference and value types in action, consider the following code:

```
struct SampleStruct {

    var name: String

    init(name: String) {
        self.name = name
    }

    func buildHelloMsg() {
        "Hello " + name
    }
}


let myStruct1 = SampleStruct(name: "Mark")
print(myStruct1.name)
```

When the code executes, the name "Mark" will be displayed. Now change the code so that a copy of the myStruct1 instance is made, the name property changed and the names from each instance displayed:

```
let myStruct1 = SampleStruct(name: "Mark")
var myStruct2 = myStruct1
myStruct2.name = "David"
```

```
print(myStruct1.name)
print(myStruct2.name)
```

When executed, the output will read as follows:

```
Mark
David
```

Clearly, the change of name only applied to myStruct2 since this is an actual copy of myStruct1 containing its own copy of the data as shown in Figure 13-1:

```
+------------------+        +------------------+
|    myStruct1     |        |    myStruct2     |
|                  |        |                  |
|   name: Mark     |        |   name: David    |
+------------------+        +------------------+
```

Figure 13-1

Contrast this with the following class example:

```
class SampleClass {

    var name: String

    init(name: String) {
        self.name = name
    }

    func buildHelloMsg() {
        "Hello " + name
    }
}

let myClass1 = SampleClass(name: "Mark")
var myClass2 = myClass1
myClass2.name = "David"

print(myClass1.name)
print(myClass2.name)
```

When this code executes, the following output will be generated:

```
David
David
```

In this case, the name property change is reflected for both myClass1 and myClass2 because both are references pointing to the same class instance as illustrated in Figure 13-2 below:

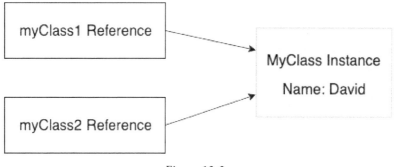

Figure 13-2

In addition to these value and reference type differences, structures do not support inheritance and sub-classing in the way that classes do. In other words, it is not possible for one structure to inherit from another structure. Unlike classes, structures also cannot contain a de-initializer (deinit) method. Finally, while it is possible to identify the type of a class instance at runtime, the same is not true of a struct.

13.3 When to Use Structures or Classes

In general, structures are recommended whenever possible because they are both more efficient than classes and safer to use in multi-threaded code. Classes should be used when inheritance is needed, only one instance of the encapsulated data is required, or extra steps need to be taken to free up resources when an instance is de-initialized.

13.4 An Overview of Enumerations

Enumerations (typically referred to as enums) are used to create custom data types consisting of pre-defined sets of values. Enums are typically used for making decisions within code such as when using switch statements. An enum might, for example be declared as follows:

```
enum Temperature {
    case hot
    case warm
    case cold
}
```

Note that in this example, none of the cases are assigned a value. An enum of this type is essentially used to reference one of a pre-defined set of states (in this case the current temperature being hot, warm or cold). Once declared, the enum may, for example, be used within a switch statement as follows:

```
func displayTempInfo(temp: Temperature) {
    switch temp {
        case .hot:
            print("It is hot.")
        case .warm:
            print("It is warm.")
        case .cold:
            print("It is cold.")
    }
}
```

It is also worth noting that because an enum has a definitive set of valid member values, the switch statement does not need to include a default case. An attempt to pass an invalid enum case through the switch will be caught by the compiler long before it has a chance to cause a runtime error.

To test out the enum, the *displayTempInfo()* function must be passed an instance of the Temperature enum with one of the following three possible states selected:

```
Temperature.hot
Temperature.warm
Temperature.cold
```

For example:

```
displayTempInfo(temp: Temperature.warm)
```

When executed, the above function call will output the following information:

```
It is warm.
```

Individual cases within an enum may also have *associated values*. Assume, for example, that the "cold" enum case needs to have associated with it a temperature value so that the app can differentiate between cold and freezing conditions. This can be defined within the enum declaration as follows:

```
enum Temperature {
    case hot
    case warm
    case cold(centigrade: Int)
}
```

This allows the switch statement to also check for the temperature for the cold case as follows:

```
func displayTempInfo(temp: Temperature) {
    switch temp {
        case .hot:
            print("It is hot")
        case .warm:
            print("It is warm")
        case.cold(let centigrade) where centigrade <= 0:
            print("Ice warning: \(centigrade) degrees.")
        case .cold:
            print("It is cold but not freezing.")
    }
}
```

When the cold enum value is passed to the function, it now does so with a temperature value included:

```
displayTempInfo(temp: Temperature.cold(centigrade: -10))
```

The output from the above function will read as follows:

```
Ice warning: -10 degrees
```

13.5 Summary

Swift structures and classes both provide a mechanism for creating instances that define properties, store values and define methods. Although the two mechanisms appear to be similar, there are significant behavioral differences when structure and class instances are either copied or passed to a method. Classes are categorized as being reference type instances while structures are value type. When a structure instance is copied or passed, an entirely new copy of the instance is created containing its own data. Class instances, on the other hand, are passed and copied by reference, with each reference pointing to the same class instance. Other features unique to classes include support for inheritance and deinitialization and the ability to identify the class type at runtime. Structures should typically be used in place of classes unless specific class features are required.

Enumerations are used to create custom types consisting of a pre-defined set of state values and are of particular use in identifying state within switch statements.

14. Working with Array and Dictionary Collections in Swift

Arrays and dictionaries in Swift are objects that contain collections of other objects. In this chapter, we will cover some of the basics of working with arrays and dictionaries in Swift.

14.1 Mutable and Immutable Collections

Collections in Swift come in mutable and immutable forms. The contents of immutable collection instances cannot be changed after the object has been initialized. To make a collection immutable, assign it to a *constant* when it is created. Collections are mutable, on the other hand, if assigned to a *variable*.

14.2 Swift Array Initialization

An array is a data type designed specifically to hold multiple values in a single ordered collection. An array, for example, could be created to store a list of String values. Strictly speaking, a single Swift based array is only able to store values that are of the same type. An array declared as containing String values, therefore, could not also contain an Int value. As will be demonstrated later in this chapter, however, it is also possible to create mixed type arrays. The type of an array can be specified specifically using type annotation or left to the compiler to identify using type inference.

An array may be initialized with a collection of values (referred to as an *array literal*) at creation time using the following syntax:

var variableName: [type] = [value 1, value2, value3, …….]

The following code creates a new array assigned to a variable (thereby making it mutable) that is initialized with three string values:

```
var treeArray = ["Pine", "Oak", "Yew"]
```

Alternatively, the same array could have been created immutably by assigning it to a constant:

```
let treeArray = ["Pine", "Oak", "Yew"]
```

In the above instance, the Swift compiler will use type inference to decide that the array contains values of String type and prevent values of other types being inserted into the array elsewhere within the application code.

Alternatively, the same array could have been declared using type annotation:

```
var treeArray: [String] = ["Pine", "Oak", "Yew"]
```

Arrays do not have to have values assigned at creation time. The following syntax can be used to create an empty array:

```
var variableName = [type]()
```

Consider, for example, the following code which creates an empty array designated to store floating point values and assigns it to a variable named priceArray:

```
var priceArray = [Float]()
```

Another useful initialization technique allows an array to be initialized to a certain size with each array element pre-set with a specified default value:

```
var nameArray = [String](repeating: "My String", count: 10)
```

When compiled and executed, the above code will create a new 10 element array with each element initialized with a string that reads "My String".

Finally, a new array may be created by adding together two existing arrays (assuming both arrays contain values of the same type). For example:

```
let firstArray = ["Red", "Green", "Blue"]
let secondArray = ["Indigo", "Violet"]

let thirdArray = firstArray + secondArray
```

14.3 Working with Arrays in Swift

Once an array exists, a wide range of methods and properties are provided for working with and manipulating the array content from within Swift code, a subset of which is as follows:

14.3.1 Array Item Count

A count of the items in an array can be obtained by accessing the array's count property:

```
var treeArray = ["Pine", "Oak", "Yew"]
var itemCount = treeArray.count

print(itemCount)
```

Whether or not an array is empty can be identified using the array's Boolean *isEmpty* property as follows:

```
var treeArray = ["Pine", "Oak", "Yew"]

if treeArray.isEmpty {
    // Array is empty
}
```

14.3.2 Accessing Array Items

A specific item in an array may be accessed or modified by referencing the item's position in the array index (where the first item in the array has index position 0) using a technique referred to as *index subscripting*. In the following code fragment, the string value contained at index position 2 in the array (in this case the string value "Yew") is output by the print call:

```
var treeArray = ["Pine", "Oak", "Yew"]

print(treeArray[2])
```

This approach can also be used to replace the value at an index location:

```
treeArray[1] = "Redwood"
```

The above code replaces the current value at index position 1 with a new String value that reads "Redwood".

14.3.3 Random Items and Shuffling

A call to the *shuffled()* method of an array object will return a new version of the array with the item ordering randomly shuffled, for example:

```
let shuffledTrees = treeArray.shuffled()
```

To access an array item at random, simply make a call to the *randomElement()* method:

```
let randomTree = treeArray.randomElement()
```

14.3.4 Appending Items to an Array

Items may be added to an array using either the *append* method or + and += operators. The following, for example, are all valid techniques for appending items to an array:

```
treeArray.append("Redwood")
treeArray += ["Redwood"]
treeArray += ["Redwood", "Maple", "Birch"]
```

14.3.5 Inserting and Deleting Array Items

New items may be inserted into an array by specifying the index location of the new item in a call to the array's *insert(at:)* method. An insertion preserves all existing elements in the array, essentially moving them to the right to accommodate the newly inserted item:

```
treeArray.insert("Maple", at: 0)
```

Similarly, an item at a specific array index position may be removed using the *remove(at:)* method call:

```
treeArray.remove(at: 2)
```

To remove the last item in an array, simply make a call to the array's *removeLast* method as follows:

```
treeArray.removeLast()
```

14.3.6 Array Iteration

The easiest way to iterate through the items in an array is to make use of the for-in looping syntax. The following code, for example, iterates through all of the items in a String array and outputs each item to the console panel:

```
let treeArray = ["Pine", "Oak", "Yew", "Maple", "Birch", "Myrtle"]

for tree in treeArray {
    print(tree)
}
```

Upon execution, the following output would appear in the console:

```
Pine
Oak
Yew
Maple
Birch
Myrtle
```

The same result can be achieved by calling the *forEach()* array method. When this method is called on an array, it will iterate through each element and execute specified code. For example:

```
treeArray.forEach { tree in
    print(tree)
}
```

Note that since the task to be performed for each array element is declared in a closure expression, the above example may be modified as follows to take advantage of shorthand argument names:

```
treeArray.forEach {
    print($0)
```

```
}
```

14.4 Creating Mixed Type Arrays

A mixed type array is an array that can contain elements of different class types. Clearly an array that is either declared or inferred as being of type String cannot subsequently be used to contain non-String class object instances. Interesting possibilities arise, however, when taking into consideration that Swift includes the *Any* type. Any is a special type in Swift that can be used to reference an object of a non-specific class type. It follows, therefore, that an array declared as containing Any object types can be used to store elements of mixed types. The following code, for example, declares and initializes an array containing a mixture of String, Int and Double elements:

```
let mixedArray: [Any] = ["A String", 432, 34.989]
```

The use of the Any type should be used with care since the use of Any masks from Swift the true type of the elements in such an array thereby leaving code prone to potential programmer error. It will often be necessary, for example, to manually cast the elements in an Any array to the correct type before working with them in code. Performing the incorrect cast for a specific element in the array will most likely cause the code to compile without error but crash at runtime. Consider, for the sake of an example, the following mixed type array:

```
let mixedArray: [Any] = [1, 2, 45, "Hello"]
```

Assume that, having initialized the array, we now need to iterate through the integer elements in the array and multiply them by 10. The code to achieve this might read as follows:

```
for object in mixedArray {
    print(object * 10)
}
```

When entered into Xcode, however, the above code will trigger a syntax error indicating that it is not possible to multiply operands of type Any and Int. In order to remove this error it will be necessary to downcast the array element to be of type Int:

```
for object in mixedArray {
    print(object as! Int * 10)
}
```

The above code will compile without error and work as expected until the final String element in the array is reached at which point the code will crash with the following error:

```
Could not cast value of type 'Swift.String' to 'Swift.Int'
```

The code will, therefore, need to be modified to be aware of the specific type of each element in the array. Clearly, there are both benefits and risks to using Any arrays in Swift.

14.5 Swift Dictionary Collections

String dictionaries allow data to be stored and managed in the form of key-value pairs. Dictionaries fulfill a similar purpose to arrays, except each item stored in the dictionary has associated with it a unique key (to be precise, the key is unique to the particular dictionary object) which can be used to reference and access the corresponding value. Currently only String, Int, Double and Bool data types are suitable for use as keys within a Swift dictionary.

14.6 Swift Dictionary Initialization

A dictionary is a data type designed specifically to hold multiple values in a single unordered collection. Each item in a dictionary consists of a key and an associated value. The data types of the key and value elements type may be specified specifically using type annotation, or left to the compiler to identify using type inference.

A new dictionary may be initialized with a collection of values (referred to as a *dictionary literal*) at creation time using the following syntax:

var *variableName*: [*key type*: *value type*] = [*key 1: value 1, key 2: value2 .... *]

The following code creates a new dictionary assigned to a variable (thereby making it mutable) that is initialized with four key-value pairs in the form of ISBN numbers acting as keys for corresponding book titles:

```
var bookDict = ["100-432112" : "Wind in the Willows",
                "200-532874" : "Tale of Two Cities",
                "202-546549" : "Sense and Sensibility",
                "104-109834" : "Shutter Island"]
```

In the above instance, the Swift compiler will use type inference to decide that both the key and value elements of the dictionary are of String type and prevent values or keys of other types being inserted into the dictionary.

Alternatively, the same dictionary could have been declared using type annotation:

```
var bookDict: [String: String] =
                ["100-432112" : "Wind in the Willows",
                "200-532874" : "Tale of Two Cities",
                "202-546549" : "Sense and Sensibility",
                "104-109834" : "Shutter Island"]
```

As with arrays, it is also possible to create an empty dictionary, the syntax for which reads as follows:

var *variableName* = [*key type*: *value type*]()

The following code creates an empty dictionary designated to store integer keys and string values:

```
var myDictionary = [Int: String]()
```

14.7 Sequence-based Dictionary Initialization

Dictionaries may also be initialized using sequences to represent the keys and values. This is achieved using the Swift *zip()* function, passing through the keys and corresponding values. In the following example, a dictionary is created using two arrays:

```
let keys = ["100-432112", "200-532874", "202-546549", "104-109834"]
let values = ["Wind in the Willows", "Tale of Two Cities",
                "Sense and Sensibility", "Shutter Island"]

let bookDict = Dictionary(uniqueKeysWithValues: zip(keys, values))
```

This approach allows keys and values to be generated programmatically. In the following example, a number range starting at 1 is being specified for the keys instead of using an array of predefined keys:

```
let values = ["Wind in the Willows", "Tale of Two Cities",
                "Sense and Sensibility", "Shutter Island"]

var bookDict = Dictionary(uniqueKeysWithValues: zip(1..., values))
```

The above code is a much cleaner equivalent to the following dictionary declaration:

```
var bookDict = [1 : "Wind in the Willows",
                2 : "Tale of Two Cities",
                3 : "Sense and Sensibility",
```

```
          4 : "Shutter Island"]
```

14.8 Dictionary Item Count

A count of the items in a dictionary can be obtained by accessing the dictionary's count property:

```
print(bookDict.count)
```

14.9 Accessing and Updating Dictionary Items

A specific value may be accessed or modified using key subscript syntax to reference the corresponding value. The following code references a key known to be in the bookDict dictionary and outputs the associated value (in this case the book entitled "A Tale of Two Cities"):

```
print(bookDict["200-532874"])
```

When accessing dictionary entries in this way, it is also possible to declare a default value to be used in the event that the specified key does not return a value:

```
print(bookDict["999-546547", default: "Book not found"])
```

Since the dictionary does not contain an entry for the specified key, the above code will output text which reads "Book not found".

Indexing by key may also be used when updating the value associated with a specified key, for example, to change the title of the same book from "A Tale of Two Cities" to "Sense and Sensibility"):

```
bookDict["200-532874"] = "Sense and Sensibility"
```

The same result is also possible by making a call to the *updateValue(forKey:)* method, passing through the key corresponding to the value to be changed:

```
bookDict.updateValue("The Ruins", forKey: "200-532874")
```

14.10 Adding and Removing Dictionary Entries

Items may be added to a dictionary using the following key subscripting syntax:

dictionaryVariable[key] = value

For example, to add a new key-value pair entry to the books dictionary:

```
bookDict["300-898871"] = "The Overlook"
```

Removal of a key-value pair from a dictionary may be achieved either by assigning a *nil* value to the entry, or via a call to the *removeValueForKey* method of the dictionary instance. Both code lines below achieve the same result of removing the specified entry from the books dictionary:

```
bookDict["300-898871"] = nil
bookDict.removeValue(forKey: "300-898871")
```

14.11 Dictionary Iteration

As with arrays, it is possible to iterate through dictionary entries by making use of the for-in looping syntax. The following code, for example, iterates through all of the entries in the books dictionary, outputting both the key and value for each entry:

```
for (bookid, title) in bookDict {
  print("Book ID: \(bookid) Title: \(title)")
}
```

Upon execution, the following output would appear in the console:

```
Book ID: 100-432112 Title: Wind in the Willows
```

```
Book ID: 200-532874 Title: The Ruins
Book ID: 104-109834 Title: Shutter Island
Book ID: 202-546549 Title: Sense and Sensibility
```

14.12 Summary

Collections in Swift take the form of either dictionaries or arrays. Both provide a way to collect together multiple items within a single object. Arrays provide a way to store an ordered collection of items where those items are accessed by an index value corresponding to the item position in the array. Dictionaries provide a platform for storing key-value pairs, where the key is used to gain access to the stored value. Iteration through the elements of Swift collections can be achieved using the for-in loop construct.

15. Understanding Error Handling in Swift 5

In a perfect world, a running iOS app would never encounter an error. The reality, however, is that it is impossible to guarantee that an error of some form or another will not occur at some point during the execution of the app. It is essential, therefore, to ensure that the code of an app is implemented such that it gracefully handles any errors that may occur. Since the introduction of Swift 2, the task of handling errors has become much easier for the iOS app developer.

This chapter will cover the handling of errors using Swift and introduce topics such as *error types*, *throwing methods and functions*, the *guard* and *defer* statements and *do-catch* statements.

15.1 Understanding Error Handling

No matter how carefully Swift code is designed and implemented, there will invariably be situations that are beyond the control of the app. An app that relies on an active internet connection cannot, for example, control the loss of signal on an iPhone device, or prevent the user from enabling "airplane mode". What the app can do, however, is to implement robust handling of the error (for example displaying a message indicating to the user that the app requires an active internet connection to proceed).

There are two sides to handling errors within Swift. The first involves triggering (or *throwing*) an error when the desired results are not achieved within the method of an iOS app. The second involves catching and handling the error after it is thrown by a method.

When an error is thrown, the error will be of a particular error type which can be used to identify the specific nature of the error and to decide on the most appropriate course of action to be taken. The error type value can be any value that conforms to the Error protocol.

In addition to implementing methods in an app to throw errors when necessary, it is important to be aware that a number of API methods in the iOS SDK (particularly those relating to file handling) will throw errors which will need to be handled within the code of the app.

15.2 Declaring Error Types

As an example, consider a method that is required to transfer a file to a remote server. Such a method might fail to transfer the file for a variety of reasons such as there being no network connection, the connection being too slow or the failure to find the file to be transferred. All these possible errors could be represented within an enumeration that conforms to the Error protocol as follows:

```
enum FileTransferError: Error {
    case noConnection
    case lowBandwidth
    case fileNotFound
}
```

Once an error type has been declared, it can be used within a method when throwing errors.

15.3 Throwing an Error

A method or function declares that it can throw an error using the *throws* keyword. For example:

```
func transferFile() throws {

}
```

In the event that the function or method returns a result, the *throws* keyword is placed before the return type as follows:

```
func transferFile() throws -> Bool {

}
```

Once a method has been declared as being able to throw errors, code can then be added to throw the errors when they are encountered. This is achieved using the *throw* statement in conjunction with the *guard* statement. The following code declares some constants to serve as status values and then implements the guard and throw behavior for the method:

```
let connectionOK = true
let connectionSpeed = 30.00
let fileFound = false

enum FileTransferError: Error {
    case noConnection
    case lowBandwidth
    case fileNotFound
}

func fileTransfer() throws {

    guard connectionOK else {
        throw FileTransferError.noConnection
    }

    guard connectionSpeed > 30 else {
        throw FileTransferError.lowBandwidth
    }

    guard fileFound else {
        throw FileTransferError.fileNotFound
    }
}
```

Within the body of the method, each guard statement checks a condition for a true or false result. In the event of a false result, the code contained within the *else* body is executed. In the case of a false result, the throw statement is used to throw one of the error values contained in the FileTransferError enumeration.

15.4 Calling Throwing Methods and Functions

Once a method or function is declared as throwing errors, it can no longer be called in the usual manner. Calls to such methods must now be prefixed by the *try* statement as follows:

```
try fileTransfer()
```

In addition to using the try statement, the call must also be made from within a *do-catch* statement to catch and handle any errors that may be thrown. Consider, for example, that the *fileTransfer* method needs to be called from within a method named *sendFile*. The code within this method might be implemented as follows:

```
func sendFile() -> String {

    do {
        try fileTransfer()
    } catch FileTransferError.noConnection {
        return("No Network Connection")
    } catch FileTransferError.lowBandwidth {
        return("File Transfer Speed too Low")
    } catch FileTransferError.fileNotFound {
        return("File not Found")
    } catch {
        return("Unknown error")
    }

    return("Successful transfer")
}
```

The method calls the *fileTransfer* method from within a *do-catch* statement which, in turn, includes catch conditions for each of the three possible error conditions. In each case, the method simply returns a string value containing a description of the error. In the event that no error was thrown, a string value is returned indicating a successful file transfer. Note that a fourth catch condition is included with no pattern matching. This is a "catch all" statement that ensures that any errors not matched by the preceding catch statements are also handled. This is required because do-catch statements must be exhaustive (in other words constructed so as to catch all possible error conditions).

Swift also allows multiple matches to be declared within a single catch statement, with the list of matches separated by commas. For example, a single catch declaration could be used to handle both the noConnection and lowBandwidth errors as follows:

```
func sendFile() -> String {

    do {
        try fileTransfer()
    } catch FileTransferError.noConnection, FileTransferError.lowBandwidth {
        return("Connection problem")
    } catch FileTransferError.fileNotFound {
        return("File not Found")
    } catch {
        return("Unknown error")
    }

    return("Successful transfer")
}
```

15.5 Accessing the Error Object

When a method call fails, it will invariably return an Error object identifying the nature of the failure. A common requirement within the catch statement is to gain access to this object so that appropriate corrective action can be taken within the app code. The following code demonstrates how such an error object is accessed from within a catch statement when attempting to create a new file system directory:

```
do {
    try filemgr.createDirectory(atPath: newDir,
                        withIntermediateDirectories: true,
                        attributes: nil)
    } catch let error {
            print("Error: \(error.localizedDescription)")
}
```

15.6 Disabling Error Catching

A throwing method may be forced to run without the need to enclose the call within a do-catch statement by using the *try!* statement as follows:

```
try! fileTransfer
```

In using this approach we are informing the compiler that we know with absolute certainty that the method call will not result in an error being thrown. In the event that an error is thrown when using this technique, the code will fail with a runtime error. As such, this approach should be used sparingly.

15.7 Using the defer Statement

The previously implemented *sendFile* method demonstrated a common scenario when handling errors. Each of the catch clauses in the do-catch statement contained a return statement that returned control to the calling method. In such a situation, however, it might be useful to be able to perform some other task before control is returned and regardless of the type of error that was encountered. The *sendFile* method might, for example, need to remove temporary files before returning. This behavior can be achieved using the *defer* statement.

The defer statement allows a sequence of code statements to be declared as needing to be run as soon as the method returns. In the following code, the *sendFile* method has been modified to include a defer statement:

```
func sendFile() -> String {

    defer {
        removeTmpFiles()
        closeConnection()
    }

    do {
        try fileTransfer()
    } catch FileTransferError.noConnection {
        return("No Network Connection")
    } catch FileTransferError.lowBandwidth {
        return("File Transfer Speed too Low")
    } catch FileTransferError.fileNotFound {
        return("File not Found")
    } catch {
```

```
        return("Unknown error")
    }

    return("Successful transfer")
}
```

With the defer statement now added, the calls to the *removeTmpFiles* and *closeConnection* methods will always be made before the method returns, regardless of which return call gets triggered.

15.8 Summary

Error handling is an essential part of creating robust and reliable iOS apps. Since the introduction of Swift 2 it is now much easier to both trigger and handle errors. Error types are created using values that conform to the Error protocol and are most commonly implemented as enumerations. Methods and functions that throw errors are declared as such using the *throws* keyword. The *guard* and *throw* statements are used within the body of these methods or functions to throw errors based on the error type.

A throwable method or function is called using the *try* statement which must be encapsulated within a do-catch statement. A do-catch statement consists of an exhaustive list of catch pattern constructs, each of which contains the code to be executed in the event of a particular error being thrown. Cleanup tasks can be defined to be executed when a method returns through the use of the *defer* statement.

16. The iOS 17 App and Development Architecture

So far, we have covered a considerable amount of ground intended to provide a sound foundation of knowledge on which to begin building iOS 17-based apps. Before plunging into more complex apps, however, you must have a basic understanding of some key methodologies associated with the overall architecture of iOS apps.

These methodologies, also called design patterns, clearly define how your apps should be designed and implemented in terms of code structure. The patterns we will explore in this chapter are *Model View Controller (MVC)*, *Subclassing*, *Delegation*, and *Target-Action*.

It is also helpful to understand how iOS is structured in terms of operating system layers.

While these concepts can initially seem a little confusing if you are new to iOS development, much of this will become apparent once we start working on some examples in subsequent chapters.

16.1 An Overview of the iOS 17 Operating System Architecture

iOS consists of several software layers, each providing programming frameworks for developing apps that run on top of the underlying hardware.

These operating system layers can be diagrammatically presented as illustrated in Figure 16-1:

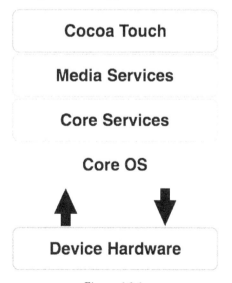

Figure 16-1

Some diagrams designed to graphically depict the iOS software stack show an additional box positioned above the Cocoa Touch layer to indicate the apps running on the device. In the above diagram, we have yet to do so since this would suggest that the only interface available to the app is Cocoa Touch. In practice, an app can directly call down to any of the layers of the stack to perform tasks on the physical device.

However, each operating system layer provides an increasing level of abstraction away from the complexity of working with the hardware. Therefore, as an iOS developer, you should always look for solutions to your programming goals in the frameworks located in the higher-level iOS layers before writing code that reaches down to the lower-level layers. In general, the higher level the layer you program to, the less effort and fewer lines of code you will have to write to achieve your objective. And as any veteran programmer will tell you, the less code you have to write, the less opportunity you have to introduce bugs.

16.2 Model View Controller (MVC)

In the days before object-oriented programming (and even for a time after object-oriented programming became popular), there was a tendency to develop apps where the code for the user interface was tied tightly to the code containing the app logic and data handling. This coupling made app code challenging to maintain and locked the app to a single user interface. If, for example, an app written for Microsoft Windows needed to be migrated to macOS, all the code written specifically for the Windows UI toolkits had to be ripped out from amongst the data and logic code and replaced with the macOS equivalent. If the app then needed to be turned into a web-based solution, the process would have to be repeated. Attempts to achieve this feat were usually prohibitively expensive and ultimately ended up with the apps being completely rewritten each time a new platform needed to be targeted.

The MVC design pattern separates an app's logic and data handling code from the presentation code. In this concept, the Model encapsulates the data for the app, and the View presents and manages the user interface. The Controller provides the basic logic for the app and acts as the go-between, providing instructions to the Model based on user interactions with the View and updating the View to reflect responses from the Model. The value of this approach is that the Model knows absolutely nothing about the app's presentation. It just knows how to store and handle data and perform specific tasks when called upon by the Controller. Similarly, the View knows nothing about the data and logic model of the app.

Within the context of an object-oriented programming environment such as the iOS SDK and Swift, the Model, View, and Controller components are objects. It is also worth pointing out that apps are not restricted to a single model, view, and controller. An app can consist of multiple view objects, controllers, and model objects.

A view controller object interacts with a Model through the methods and properties exposed by that model object. This is no different from how one object interacts with another in any object-oriented programming environment.

However, things get a little more complicated in terms of the view controller's interactions with the view. In practice, this is achieved using the *Target-Action pattern* and *Outlets* and *Actions*.

16.3 The Target-Action pattern, IBOutlets, and IBActions

When you create an iOS app, you will typically design the user interface (the view) using the Interface Builder tool and write the view controller and model code in Swift using the Xcode code editor. The previous section looked briefly at how the view controller interacts with the model. In this section, we will look at how the view created in Interface Builder and our view controller code interact with each other.

When a user interacts with objects in the view, for example, by touching and releasing a button control, an *event* is triggered (in this case, the event is called a *Touch Up Inside* event). The purpose of the *Target-Action* pattern is to allow you to specify what happens when such events are triggered. In other words, this is how you connect the objects in the interface you designed in the Interface Builder tool to the back-end Swift code you have written in the Xcode environment. Specifically, this allows you to define which method of which controller object gets called when a user interacts in a certain way with a view object.

The process of wiring up a view object to call a specific method on a view controller object is achieved using an *Action*. An action is a method defined within a view controller object designed to be called when an event is triggered in a view object. This allows us to connect a view object created within Interface Builder to the code we have written in the view controller class. This is one of the ways that we bridge the separation between the *View* and the *Controller* in our MVC design pattern. As we will see in *"Creating an Interactive iOS 17 App"*, action methods are declared using the *IBAction* keyword.

The opposite of an *Action* is the *Outlet*. As previously described, an Action allows a view object to call a method on a controller object. On the other hand, an Outlet allows a view controller object method to access the properties of a view object directly. A view controller might, for example, need to set the text on a UILabel object. To do so, an Outlet must first have been defined using the *IBOutlet* keyword. In programming terms, an *IBOutlet* is simply an instance variable that references the view object to which access is required.

16.4 Subclassing

Subclassing is an essential feature of any object-oriented programming environment, and the iOS SDK is no exception to this rule. Subclassing allows us to create a new class by deriving from an existing class and extending the functionality. In so doing, we get all the functionality of the parent class combined with the ability to extend the new class with additional methods and properties.

Subclassing is typically used where a pre-existing class does most, but not all, of what you need. By subclassing, we get all that existing functionality without duplicating it, allowing us to simply add on the functionality that was missing.

We will see an example of subclassing in the context of iOS development when we start to work with view controllers. The UIKit Framework contains a class called the UIViewController. This is a generic view controller from which we will create a subclass to add our own methods and properties.

16.5 Delegation

Delegation allows an object to pass the responsibility for performing one or more tasks onto another object. This allows the behavior of an object to be modified without having to go through the process of subclassing it.

A prime example of delegation can be seen in the case of the UIApplication class. The UIApplication class, of which every iOS app must have one (and only one) instance, is responsible for the control and operation of the app within the iOS environment. Much of what the UIApplication object does happens in the background. There are, however, instances where it allows us to include our functionality into the mix. UIApplication allows us to do this by delegating some methods to us. For example, UIApplication delegates the *didFinishLaunchingWithOptions* method to us so that we can write code to perform specific tasks when the app first loads (for example, taking the user back to the point they were at when they last exited). If you still have a copy of the Hello World project created earlier in this book, you will see the template for this method in the *AppDelegate.swift* file.

16.6 Summary

In this chapter, we have provided an overview of several design patterns and discussed the importance of these patterns in structuring iOS apps. While these patterns may seem unclear to some, the relevance and implementation of such concepts will become more apparent as we progress through the examples in subsequent chapters of this book.

17. Creating an Interactive iOS 17 App

The previous chapter looked at the design patterns we need to learn and use regularly while developing iOS-based apps. In this chapter, we will work through a detailed example intended to demonstrate the View-Controller relationship together with the implementation of the Target-Action pattern to create an example interactive iOS app.

17.1 Creating the New Project

The purpose of the app we are going to create is to perform unit conversions from Fahrenheit to Centigrade. The first step is creating a new Xcode project to contain our app. Start Xcode and, on the Welcome screen, select *Create a new Xcode project*. Make sure iOS is selected in the toolbar on the template screen before choosing the *App* template. Click *Next*, set the product name to *UnitConverter*, enter your company identifier, and select your development team if you have one. Before clicking *Next*, change the *Language* to Swift and the *Interface* to Storyboard. On the final screen, choose a location to store the project files and click *Create* to proceed to the main Xcode project window.

17.2 Creating the User Interface

Before we begin developing the logic for our interactive app, we will start by designing the user interface. When we created the new project, Xcode generated a storyboard file for us and named it *Main.storyboard*. Within this file, we will create our user interface, so select the *Main* item from the project navigator in the left-hand panel to load it into Interface Builder.

Figure 17-1

Display the Library panel by clicking on the toolbar button shown in Figure 17-2 while holding down the Option key and dragging a Text Field object from the library onto the View design area:

Figure 17-2

Resize the object and position it so it appears as outlined in Figure 17-3:

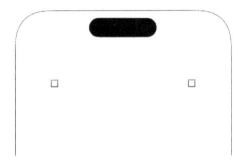

Figure 17-3

Within the Attributes Inspector panel (*View -> Inspectors -> Attributes*), type the words *Enter temperature* into the *Placeholder* text field. This text will then appear in light gray in the text field as a visual cue to the user. Since only numbers and decimal points will be required to be input for the temperature, locate the *Keyboard Type* property in the Attributes Inspector panel and change the setting to *Numbers and Punctuation*.

Now that we have created the text field into which the user will enter a temperature value, the next step is adding a Button object that may be pressed to initiate the conversion. To achieve this, drag and drop a *Button* object from the Library to the View. Next, double-click the button object to change to text edit mode and type the word *Convert* onto the button. Finally, select the button and drag it beneath the text field until the blue dotted line indicates it is centered horizontally within the containing view before releasing the mouse button.

The last user interface object we need to add is the label where the result of the conversion will be displayed. Add this by dragging a Label object from the Library panel to the View and positioning it beneath the button. Stretch the width of the label so that it is approximately two-thirds of the overall width of the view, and reposition it using the blue guidelines to ensure it is centered relative to the containing view. Finally, modify the Alignment attribute for the label object so that the text is centered.

Double-click on the label to highlight the text and press the backspace key to clear it (we will set the text from within a method of our View Controller class when the conversion calculation has been performed). Though the label is no longer visible when it is not selected, it is still present in the view. If you click where it is located, it will be highlighted with the resize dots visible. It is also possible to view the layout outlines of all the scenes' views, including the label, by selecting the *Editor -> Canvas -> Bounds Rectangles* menu option.

For the user interface design layout to adapt to the many different device orientations and iPad and iPhone screen sizes, it will be necessary to add some Auto Layout constraints to the views in the storyboard. Auto Layout will be covered in detail in subsequent chapters, but for this example, we will request that Interface Builder add what it considers to be the appropriate constraints for this layout. In the lower right-hand corner of the Interface Builder panel is a toolbar. Click on the background view of the current scene followed by the

Resolve Auto Layout Issues button as highlighted in Figure 17-4:

Figure 17-4

From the menu, select the *Reset to Suggested Constraints* option listed under *All Views in View Controller*:

Figure 17-5

At this point, our project's user interface design phase is complete, and the view should appear as illustrated in Figure 17-6. We are now ready to try out a test build and run.

Figure 17-6

17.3 Building and Running the Sample App

Before we implement the view controller code for our app and then connect it to the user interface we have designed, we should perform a test build and run of the app. Click on the run button in the toolbar (the triangular "play" button) to compile the app and run it in the simulator or a connected iOS device. If you are unhappy with how your interface looks, feel free to reload it into Interface Builder and make improvements. Assuming the user interface appears to your satisfaction, we are ready to start writing Swift code to add logic to our controller.

17.4 Adding Actions and Outlets

When the user enters a temperature value into the text field and touches the convert button, we need to trigger an action to calculate the temperature. The calculation result will then be presented to the user via the label object. The *Action* will be a method we will declare and implement in our View Controller class. Access to the text field and label objects from the view controller method will be implemented through *Outlets*.

Before we begin, now is a good time to highlight an example of subclassing as previously described in the chapter titled *"The iOS 17 App and Development Architecture"*. The UIKit Framework contains a class called UIViewController which provides the basic foundation for adding view controllers to an app. To create a functional app, however, we inevitably need to add functionality specific to our app to this generic view controller class. This is achieved by subclassing the UIViewController class and extending it with the additional functionality we need.

When we created our new project, Xcode anticipated our needs, automatically created a subclass of UIViewController, and named it ViewController. In so doing, Xcode also created a source code file named *ViewController.swift*.

Selecting the *ViewController.swift* file in the Xcode project navigator panel will display the contents of the file in the editing pane:

```
import UIKit


class ViewController: UIViewController {

    override func viewDidLoad() {
        super.viewDidLoad()
        // Do any additional setup after loading the view.
    }
}
```

As we can see from the above code, a new class called ViewController has been created that is a subclass of the UIViewController class belonging to the UIKit framework.

The next step is to extend the subclass to include the two outlets and our action method. This could be achieved by manually declaring the outlets and actions within the *ViewController.swift* file. However, a much more straightforward approach is to use the Xcode Assistant Editor to do this for us.

With the *Main.storyboard* file selected, display the Assistant Editor by selecting the *Editor -> Assistant* menu option. Alternatively, it may also be displayed by selecting the *Adjust Editor Options* button in the row of Editor toolbar buttons in the top right-hand corner of the main Xcode window and selecting the Assistant menu option, as illustrated in the following figure:

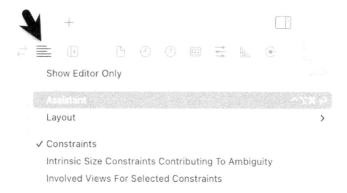

Figure 17-7

The editor panel will, by default, appear to the right of the main editing panel in the Xcode window. For example, in Figure 17-8, the panel (marked A) to the immediate right of the Interface Builder panel is the Assistant Editor:

Figure 17-8

By default, the Assistant Editor will be in *Automatic* mode, whereby it automatically attempts to display the correct source file based on the currently selected item in Interface Builder. If the correct file is not displayed, use the toolbar at the top of the editor panel to select the correct file. The button displaying interlocking circles in this toolbar can be used to switch to *Manual* mode allowing the file to be selected from a pull-right menu containing all the source files in the project.

Make sure that the *ViewController.swift* file is displayed in the Assistant Editor and establish an outlet for the Text Field object by right-clicking on the Text Field object in the view. Drag the resulting line to the area immediately beneath the class declaration line in the Assistant Editor panel, as illustrated in Figure 17-9:

Figure 17-9

Upon releasing the line, the configuration panel illustrated in Figure 17-10 will appear, requesting details about the outlet to be defined.

Figure 17-10

Since this is an outlet, the *Connection* menu should be left as *Outlet*. The type and storage values are also correct for this type of outlet. The only task that remains is to enter a name for the outlet, so in the *Name* field, enter *tempText* before clicking on the *Connect* button.

Once the connection has been established, select the *ViewController.swift* file and note that the outlet property has been declared for us by the assistant:

```
import UIKit

class ViewController: UIViewController {

    @IBOutlet weak var tempText: UITextField!
.
.
.
}
```

Repeat the above steps to establish an outlet for the Label object named *resultLabel*.

Next, we need to establish the action that will be called when the user touches the Convert button in our user interface. The steps to declare an action using the Assistant Editor are the same as those for an outlet. Once again, select the *Main.storyboard* file, but this time right-click on the button object. Drag the resulting line to the area beneath the existing *viewDidLoad* method in the Assistant Editor panel before releasing it. The connection box will once again appear. Since we are creating an action rather than an outlet, change the *Connection* menu to *Action*. Name the action *convertTemp* and make sure the *Event* type is set to *Touch Up Inside*:

Figure 17-11

Click on the *Connect* button to create the action.

Close the Assistant Editor panel, select the *ViewController.swift* file, and note that a stub method for the action has now been declared for us by the assistant:

```
@IBAction func convertTemp(_ sender: Any) {
}
```

All that remains is to write the Swift code in the action method to perform the conversion:

```
@IBAction func convertTemp(_ sender: Any) {
    guard let tempString = tempText.text else { return }

    if let fahrenheit = Double(tempString) {
        let celsius = (fahrenheit - 32)/1.8
        let resultText = "Celsius \(celsius)"
        resultLabel.text = resultText
    }
}
```

Before proceeding, it is probably a good idea to pause and explain what is happening in the above code. However, those already familiar with Swift may skip the following few paragraphs.

In this file, we are implementing the *convertTemp* method, a template for which was created for us by the Assistant Editor. This method takes as a single argument a reference to the *sender*. The sender is the object that triggered the call to the method (in this case, our Button object). The sender is declared as being of type *Any* (different type options are available using the *Type* menu in the connection dialog shown in Figure 17-11 above). This special type can be used to represent any type of class. While we won't be using this object in the current example, this can be used to create a general-purpose method in which the method's behavior changes depending on how (i.e., via which object) it was called. We could, for example, create two buttons labeled *Convert to Fahrenheit* and *Convert to Celsius,* respectively, each of which calls the same *convertTemp* method. The method would then access the *sender* object to identify which button triggered the event and perform the corresponding type of unit conversion.

Within the method's body, we use a guard statement to verify that the tempText view contains some text. If it does not, the method simply returns.

Next, dot notation is used to access the *text* property (which holds the text displayed in the text field) of the UITextField object to access the text in the field. This property is itself an object of type String. This string is converted to be of type Double and assigned to a new constant named *fahrenheit*. Since it is possible that the user has not entered a valid number into the field, optional binding is employed to prevent an attempt to perform the conversion on invalid data.

Having extracted the text entered by the user and converted it to a number, we then perform the conversion to Celsius and store the result in another constant named *celsius*. Next, we create a new string object and initialize it with text comprising the word Celsius and the result of our conversion. In doing so, we declare a constant named *resultText*.

Finally, we use dot notation to assign the new string to the text property of our UILabel object to display it to the user.

17.5 Building and Running the Finished App

From within the Xcode project window, click on the run button in the Xcode toolbar (the triangular "play" style button) to compile the app and run it in the simulator or a connected iOS device. Once the app is running, click inside the text field and enter a Fahrenheit temperature. Next, click the Convert button to display the equivalent temperature in Celsius. Assuming all went to plan, your app should appear as outlined in the following figure:

Figure 17-12

17.6 Hiding the Keyboard

The final step in the app implementation is to add a mechanism for hiding the keyboard. Ideally, the keyboard should withdraw from view when the user touches the background view or taps the return key on the keyboard (note when testing on the simulator that the keyboard may not appear unless the *I/O -> Keyboard -> Toggle Software Keyboard* menu option is selected).

To achieve this, we will begin by implementing the *touchesBegan* event handler method on the view controller in the *ViewController.swift* file as follows:

```
override func touchesBegan(_ touches: Set<UITouch>, with event: UIEvent?) {
    tempText.endEditing(true)
}
```

The keyboard will now be hidden when the user touches the background view.

The next step is to hide the keyboard when the return key is tapped. To do this, display the Assistant Editor and right-click and drag from the Text Field to a position beneath the *viewDidLoad* method within the *ViewController*.

swift file. On releasing the line, change the settings in the connection dialog to establish an Action connection named *textFieldReturn* for the *Did End on Exit* event with the Type menu set to UITextField as shown in Figure 17-13 and click on the *Connect* button to establish the connection.

Connection	Action
Object	View Controller
Name	textFieldReturn
Type	UITextField
Event	Did End On Exit
Arguments	Sender

Cancel   Connect

Figure 17-13

Select the *ViewController.swift* file in the project navigator, locate and edit the *textFieldReturn* stub method so that it now reads as follows:

```
@IBAction func textFieldReturn(_ sender: UITextField) {
    _ = sender.resignFirstResponder()
}
```

In the above method, we call the *resignFirstResponder* method of the object that triggered the event. The *first responder* is the object with which the user is currently interacting (in this instance, the virtual keyboard displayed on the device screen). Note that the result of the method call is assigned to a value represented by the underscore character (_). The *resignFirstResponder()* method returns a Boolean value indicating whether or not the resign request was successful. Assigning the result this way indicates to the Swift compiler that we are intentionally ignoring this value.

Save the code and then build and run the app. When the app starts, select the text field so the keyboard appears. Touching any area of the background or tapping the return key should cause the keyboard to disappear.

17.7 Summary

In this chapter, we have demonstrated some of the theories covered in previous chapters, in particular, separating the view from the controller, subclassing, and implementing the Target-Action pattern through actions and outlets.

This chapter also provided steps to hide the keyboard when the user touches either the keyboard Return key or the background view.

18. Understanding iOS 17 Views, Windows, and the View Hierarchy

In the preceding chapters, we created several user interfaces in building our example iOS apps. In doing so, we have been using views and windows without actually providing much in the way of explanation. Before moving on to other topics, however, it is essential to understand the concepts behind how iOS user interfaces are constructed and managed. This chapter will cover the concepts of views, windows, and view hierarchies.

18.1 An Overview of Views and the UIKit Class Hierarchy

Views are visual objects assembled to create an iOS app's user interface. They essentially define what happens within a specified rectangular area of the screen, visually and in terms of user interaction. All views are subclasses of the UIView class, which is part of the UIKit class hierarchy. Common types of view that subclass from UIView include items such as the label (UILabel) and image view (UIImageView) and controls such as the button (UIButton) and text field (UITextField).

Another type of view that is of considerable importance is the UIWindow class.

18.2 The UIWindow Class

If you have developed (or even used) applications for desktop systems such as Windows or macOS, you will be familiar with the concept of windows. A typical desktop application will have multiple windows, each with a title bar containing controls that allow you to minimize, maximize or close the window. Windows, in this context, essentially provide a surface area on the screen onto which the application can present information and controls to the user.

The UIWindow class provides a similar function for iOS-based apps in that it also provides the surface on which the view components are displayed. There are, however, some differences in that an iOS app typically only has one window, which usually fills the entire screen (the exception being when the app is in multitasking mode, as outlined in the chapter entitled *"A Guide to iPad Multitasking"*) and it lacks the title bar we've come to expect on desktop applications.

As with the views described previously, UIWindow is also a subclass of the UIView class and sits at the root of the view hierarchy, which we will discuss in the next section. The user does not see or interact directly with the UIWindow object. These windows may be created programmatically, but Interface Builder typically creates them automatically when you design your user interface.

18.3 The View Hierarchy

iOS user interfaces are constructed using a hierarchical approach whereby different views are related through a parent/child relationship. At the top of this hierarchy sits the UIWindow object. Other views are then added to the hierarchy. If we take the example from the chapter entitled *"Creating an Interactive iOS 17 App"*, we have a design that consists of a window, a view, a text field, a button, and a label. The view hierarchy for this user interface would be drawn as illustrated in Figure 18-1:

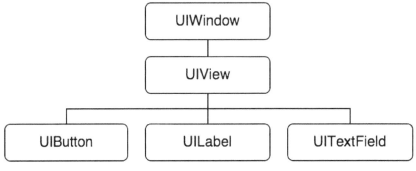

Figure 18-1

In this example, the UIWindow object is the parent or *superview* of the UIView instance, and the UIView is the child or *subview* of the UIWindow. Similarly, the text, label, and button objects are all *subviews* of the UIView. A subview can only have one direct parent. As shown in the above example, a superview may have multiple subviews.

In addition, view hierarchies can be nested to any level of depth. Consider, for example, the following hierarchy diagram:

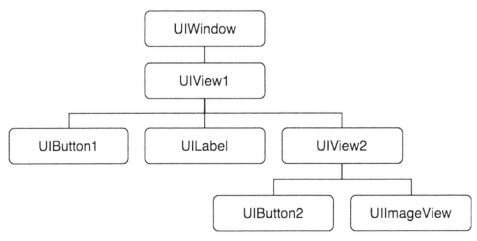

Figure 18-2

The hierarchical structure of a user interface has significant implications for how the views appear and behave. Visually, subviews always appear on top of and within the visual frame of their corresponding parent. The button in the above example, therefore, appears on top of the parent view in the running app. Furthermore, the resizing behavior of subviews (in other words, how the views change size when the device is rotated) is defined relative to the parent view. Superviews also can modify the positioning and size of their subviews.

If we were to design the above-nested view hierarchy in Interface Builder, it might appear as illustrated in Figure 18-3.

In this example, the UIWindow instance is not visible because the UIView1 instance entirely obscures it. Displayed on top of and within the frame of UIView1 are the UIButton1, UILabel, and UIView2 subviews. Displayed on top of, and within the frame of, UIView2 are its respective subviews, namely UIButton2 and UIImageView.

Figure 18-3

The view hierarchy also defines how events are handled when users interact with the interface, essentially defining the *responder chain*. If, for example, a subview receives an event that it cannot handle, that event is passed up to the immediate superview. If that superview can also not handle the event, it is passed up to the next parent until it reaches a level within the responder chain where it can be dealt with.

18.4 Viewing Hierarchy Ancestors in Interface Builder

A helpful technique for displaying the hierarchical ancestors of a view object is to perform a Ctrl-Shift-Click operation (or a mouse pad force touch on newer MacBook devices) over the object in Interface Builder. Figure 18-4, for example, shows the results of this operation on the Convert button from the UnitConverter project storyboard scene:

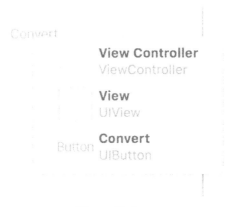

Figure 18-4

18.5 View Types

Apple groups the various views included in the UIKit Framework into several different categories:

18.5.1 The Window

The UIWindow is the root view of the view hierarchy and provides the surface on which all subviews draw their content.

18.5.2 Container Views

Container views enhance the functionality of other view objects. The UIScrollView class, for example, provides scrollbars and scrolling functionality for the UITableView and UITextView classes. Another example is the UIToolbar view, which groups together multiple controls in a single view.

18.5.3 Controls

The controls category encompasses views that present information and respond to user interaction. Control views inherit from the UIControl class (a subclass of UIView) and include items such as buttons, sliders, and text fields.

18.5.4 Display Views

Display views are similar to *controls* in that they provide visual feedback to the user, the difference being that they do not respond to user interaction. Examples of views in this category include the UILabel and UIImageView classes.

18.5.5 Text and WebKit Views

The UITextView and WKWebView classes both fall into this category and are designed to provide a mechanism for displaying formatted text to the user. The WKWebView class, for example, is designed to display HTML content formatted so that it appears as it would if loaded into a web browser.

18.5.6 Navigation Views and Tab Bars

Navigation views and tab bars provide mechanisms for navigating an app user interface. They work with the view controller and are typically created from within Interface Builder.

18.5.7 Alert Views

Views in this category are designed to prompt the user with urgent or important information and optional buttons to call the user to action.

18.6 Summary

In this chapter, we have explored the concepts of using views in constructing an iOS app user interface and how these views relate to each other within the context of a view hierarchy. We have also discussed how the view hierarchy dictates issues such as the positioning and resize behavior of subviews and defines the response chain for the user interface.

19. An Introduction to Auto Layout in iOS 17

Arguably one of the most important parts of designing the user interface for an app involves getting the layout correct. In an ideal world, designing a layout would consist of dragging view objects to the desired location on the screen and fixing them at these positions using absolute X and Y screen coordinates. However, in reality, the world of iOS devices is more complex than that, and a layout must be able to adapt to variables such as the device rotating between portrait and landscape modes, dynamic changes to content, and differences in screen resolution and size.

Before the release of iOS 6, layout handling involved using a concept referred to as *autosizing*. Autosizing involves using a series of "springs" and "struts" to define, on a view-by-view basis, how a subview will be resized and positioned relative to the superview in which it is contained. Limitations of autosizing, however, typically meant that considerable amounts of coding were required to augment the autosizing in response to orientation or other changes.

One of the most significant features in iOS 6 was the introduction of Auto Layout, which has continued to evolve with the release of subsequent iOS versions. Auto Layout is an extensive subject area allowing layouts of just about any level of flexibility and complexity to be created once the necessary skills have been learned.

The goal of this and subsequent chapters will be to introduce the basic concepts of Auto Layout, work through some demonstrative examples and provide a basis to continue learning about Auto Layout as your app design needs evolve. Auto Layout introduces a lot of new concepts and can, initially, seem a little overwhelming. By the end of this sequence of chapters, however, it should be more apparent how the pieces fit together to provide a powerful and flexible layout management system for iOS-based user interfaces.

19.1 An Overview of Auto Layout

The purpose of Auto Layout is to allow the developer to describe the behavior required from the views in a layout independent of the device screen size and orientation. This behavior is implemented by creating *constraints* on the views that comprise a user interface screen. A button view, for example, might have a constraint that tells the system that it is to be positioned in the horizontal center of its superview. A second constraint might also declare that the bottom edge of the button should be positioned a fixed distance from the bottom edge of the superview. Having set these constraints, no matter what happens to the superview, the button will always be centered horizontally and a fixed distance from the bottom edge.

Unlike autosizing, Auto Layout allows constraints to be declared between a subview and superview and between subviews. Auto Layout, for example, would allow a constraint to be configured such that two button views are always positioned a specific distance apart from each other regardless of changes in size and orientation of the superview. Constraints can also be configured to cross superview boundaries to allow, for example, two views with different superviews (though on the same screen) to be aligned. This is a concept referred to as *cross-view hierarchy constraints*.

Constraints can also be explicit or variable (otherwise referred to in Auto Layout terminology as *equal* or *unequal*). Take, for example, a width constraint on a label object. An explicit constraint could be declared to fix the width of the label at 70 points. This might be represented as a constraint equation that reads as follows:

```
myLabel.width = 70
```

However, this explicit width setting might become problematic if the label is required to display dynamic content. For example, an attempt to display text on the label that requires a greater width will result in the content being clipped.

Constraints can, however, be declared using less than, equal to, greater than, *or equal to* controls. For example, the width of a label could be constrained to any width as long as it is less than or equal to 800:

```
myLabel.width <= 800
```

The label is now permitted to grow in width up to the specified limit, allowing longer content to be displayed without clipping.

Auto Layout constraints are by nature interdependent. As such, situations can arise where a constraint on one view competes with a constraint on another view to which it is connected. In such situations, it may be necessary to make one constraint *stronger* and the other *weaker* to provide the system with a way of arriving at a layout solution. This is achieved by assigning *priorities* to constraints.

Priorities are assigned on a scale of 0 to 1000, with 1000 representing a *required constraint* and lower numbers equating to *optional constraints*. When faced with a decision between the needs of a required constraint and an optional constraint, the system will meet the needs of the required constraint exactly while attempting to get as close as possible to those of the optional constraint. In the case of two optional constraints, the needs of the constraint with the higher priority will be addressed before those of the lower.

19.2 Alignment Rects

When working with constraints, it is important to be aware that constraints operate on the content of a view, not the frame in which a view is displayed. This content is referred to as the *alignment rect* of the view. Alignment constraints, such as those that cause the center of one view to align with that of another, will do so based on the alignment rects of the views, disregarding any padding that may have been configured for the frame of the view.

19.3 Intrinsic Content Size

Some views also have what is known as an *intrinsic content size*. This is the preferred size that a view believes it needs to be to display its content to the user. A Button view, for example, will have an intrinsic content size in terms of height and width based primarily on the text or image it is required to display and internal rules on the margins that should be placed around that content. When a view has an intrinsic content size, Auto Layout will automatically assign two constraints for each dimension for which the view has indicated an intrinsic content size preference (i.e., height and/or width). One constraint is intended to prevent the view's size from becoming larger than the size of the content (otherwise known as the *content hugging* constraint). The other constraint is intended to prevent the view from being sized smaller than the content (referred to as the *compression resistance* constraint).

19.4 Content Hugging and Compression Resistance Priorities

The resizing behavior of a view with an intrinsic content size can be controlled by specifying compression resistance and content hugging priorities. For example, a view with high compression resistance and low content hugging priority will be allowed to grow but will resist shrinking in the corresponding dimension. Similarly, a high compression resistance and a high content hugging priority will cause the view to resist any resizing, keeping the view as close as possible to its intrinsic content size.

19.5 Safe Area Layout Guide

In addition to the views that comprise the layout, a screen may also contain navigation and tab bars at the top and bottom of the screen. If the layout is designed to use the full screen height, there is a risk that some views will be obscured by navigation and tab bars. To avoid this problem, UIView provides a *safe area layout guide* for constrained views. Constraining views to the safe area instead of the outer edges of the parent UIView ensures that the views are not obscured by title and tab bars. For example, the screen in Figure 19-1 includes both navigation and tab bars. The dotted line represents the safe area layout guide to which the top edge of the Button and bottom edge of the Label has been constrained:

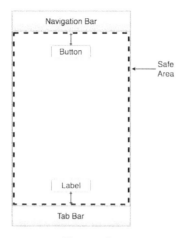

Figure 19-1

19.6 Three Ways to Create Constraints

There are three ways in which constraints in a user interface layout can be created:

- **Interface Builder** – Interface Builder has been modified extensively to support the visual implementation of Auto Layout constraints in user interface designs. Examples of using this approach are covered in the *"Working with iOS 17 Auto Layout Constraints in Interface Builder"* and *"Implementing Cross-Hierarchy Auto Layout Constraints in iOS 17"* chapters of this book.

- **Visual Format Language** – The visual format language defines a syntax that allows constraints to be declared using a sequence of ASCII characters that visually approximate the nature of the constraint being created to make constraints in code both easier to write and understand. Use of the visual format language is documented in the chapter entitled *"Understanding the iOS 17 Auto Layout Visual Format Language"*.

- **Writing API code** – This approach involves directly writing code to create constraints using the standard programming API calls. This topic is covered in *"Implementing iOS 17 Auto Layout Constraints in Code"*.

Wherever possible, Interface Builder is the recommended approach to creating constraints. When creating constraints in code, the visual format language is generally recommended over the API-based approach.

19.7 Constraints in More Detail

A constraint is created as an instance of the NSLayoutConstraint class, which, having been created, is then added to a view. The rules for a constraint can generally be represented as an equation, the most complex form of which can be described as follows:

```
view1.attribute = multiplier * view2.attribute2 + constant
```

The above equation establishes a constraint relationship between view1 and view2, respectively. In each case, an attribute is targeted by the constraint. Attributes are represented by NSLayoutConstraint.Attribute.*<name>* constants where *<name>* is one of several options, including left, right, top, bottom, leading, trailing, width, height, centerX, centerY, and baseline (i.e., NSLayoutConstraint.Attribute.width). The multiplier and constant elements are floating point values that modify the constraint.

A simple constraint that dictates that view1 and view2 should, for example, be the same width would be represented using the following equation:

```
view1.width = view2.width
```

Similarly, the equation for a constraint to align the horizontal center of view1 with the horizontal center of view2 would read as follows:

```
view1.centerX = view2.centerX
```

A slightly more complex constraint to position view1 so that its bottom edge is positioned a distance of 20 points above the bottom edge of view2 would be expressed as follows:

```
view1.bottom = view2.bottom - 20
```

The following constraint equation specifies that view1 is to be twice the width of view2 minus a width of 30 points:

```
view1.width = view2.width * 2 - 30
```

So far, the examples have focused on equality. As previously discussed, constraints also support inequality through <= and >= operators. For example:

```
view1.width >= 100
```

A constraint based on the above equation would limit the width of view1 to any value greater than or equal to 100.

The reason for representing constraints in equations is less apparent when working with constraints within Interface Builder. Still, it will become invaluable when using the API or the visual format language to set constraints in code.

19.8 Summary

Auto Layout uses constraints to descriptively express a user interface's geometric properties, behavior, and view relationships.

Constraints can be created using Interface Builder or in code using either the visual format language or the standard SDK API calls of the NSLayoutConstraint class.

Constraints are typically expressed using a linear equation, an understanding of which will be particularly beneficial when working with constraints in code.

Having covered the basic concepts of Auto Layout, the next chapter will introduce the creation and management of constraints within Interface Builder.

20. Working with iOS 17 Auto Layout Constraints in Interface Builder

By far, the most productive and intuitive way to work with constraints is using the Auto Layout features of Interface Builder. Not only does this avoid the necessity to write time-consuming code (though for complex layout requirements, some code will be inevitable), but it also provides instant visual feedback on constraints as they are configured.

Within this chapter, a simple example will be used to demonstrate the effectiveness of Auto Layout, together with an in-depth look at the Auto Layout features of Interface Builder. The chapter will then demonstrate the concepts of content hugging and constraint priorities.

20.1 An Example of Auto Layout in Action

Before digging deeper into the Auto Layout features of Interface Builder, the first step in this chapter will be to demonstrate the basic concept of Auto Layout quickly. Begin, therefore, by creating a new Xcode project using the iOS *App* template with the Swift and Storyboard options selected, entering *AutoLayoutExample* as the product name.

20.2 Working with Constraints

Although Auto Layout is enabled by default, the Interface Builder tool does not automatically apply any default constraints as views are added to the layout. Views are instead positioned using absolute x and y coordinates. To see this in action, drag a label view from the Library and position it towards the bottom of the view in the horizontal center of the view canvas so the vertical blue guideline appears, indicating that it is centered before dropping the view into place. The location of the view has just been defined using hard-coded absolute x and y coordinates on the screen. As far as the view is concerned, the label is positioned perfectly as long as the device remains in portrait orientation:

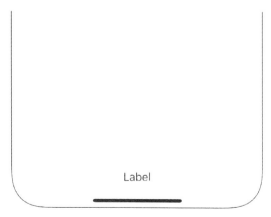

Figure 20-1

A problem arises, however, when the device rotates to landscape orientation. This can be demonstrated by compiling and running the app on a physical iPhone or iPad device or iOS Simulator in the usual way.

Alternatively, the effect of an orientation change can be tested within the Interface Builder environment. To rotate to landscape mode, click on the *Orientation* entry located in the status bar positioned along the bottom edge of the Interface Builder panel as highlighted in Figure 20-2 below:

Figure 20-2

As illustrated in Figure 20-3, the label is no longer visible with the device in landscape orientation. This is because it remains positioned at the same geographical coordinates in relation to the parent view, which, in landscape orientation, is outside the visible bounds of the parent view as shown in Figure 20-3:

Figure 20-3

Similar problems can occur when the app runs on different sizes of iPhone devices which can be tested by clicking on the *Devices* button (Figure 20-4) and selecting different device models:

Figure 20-4

For example, return the orientation to portrait mode and switch between iPhone 15 Pro and iPhone SE (1st Generation). Note that the label is again positioned incorrectly on larger and smaller display form factors. Clearly, layout is essential for handling device orientation and ensuring correct user interface appearance on different device models.

Before the introduction of Auto Layout, options to address this would have either involved using springs and struts or writing code to detect the device's rotation and moving the label to the new location on the screen. Now, however, the problem can be solved using Auto Layout.

Xcode provides several different ways to add constraints to a layout. These options will be covered later in this chapter, but by far, the easiest is to use the Auto Layout toolbar. With the Label selected, click on the *Add New Constraints* menu (Figure 20-5):

Figure 20-5

The goal for this example is to add a constraint to the label such that the bottom edge of the label is always positioned the same distance from the bottom of the containing superview, and so that it remains centered horizontally. To do this, we are first interested in this panel's *Spacing to nearest neighbor* section. This visualizes the view in question (in this case, the label) represented by the square in the middle. Extending from each square side are faded and dotted I-beam icons connecting with fields containing values. The fact that the I-beams are dotted and faded indicates that these constraints have not been set. The values indicate the current distances within the layout of the corresponding side to the nearest neighbor. The "nearest neighbor" will either be the nearest view to that side of the selected view or the corresponding side of the superview.

Select the constraint I-beam icon located beneath the view so that it appears in solid red (as shown in Figure 20-6) to indicate that the constraint is now set before clicking on the *Add 1 Constraint* button to add the constraint to the view.

Figure 20-6

Having added a constraint, Auto Layout now knows that the bottom edge of the label must always be positioned a fixed distance from the bottom edge of the containing superview. However, the layout is still missing a constraint to designate the horizontal position of the label in the superview. One way to add this constraint is to use the *Align* menu. With the label still selected in the view canvas and the Align menu panel displayed, enable the checkbox next to the *Horizontally in Container* property (Figure 20-7). Since no offset from the center is required, leave the offset value at 0.

Figure 20-7

With the constraint appropriately configured, click the *Add 1 Constraint* button to add the constraint to the view.

Having configured some constraints, rotate the orientation once again, noting that the label is visible and positioned sensibly. Testing different display form factors should also demonstrate that the constraints work to keep the label correctly positioned for different devices.

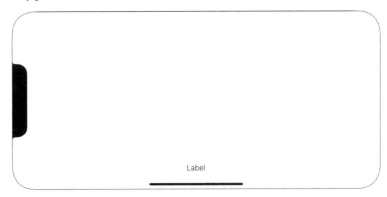

Figure 20-8

In this example, only a small subset of the Auto Layout features provided by Xcode has been used. Xcode provides a wide range of options and visual cues to ease creating Auto Layout constraints.

20.3 The Auto Layout Features of Interface Builder

Several features are provided in Xcode to assist in implementing Auto Layout-based constraints. This section will present a guided tour of many of these features.

20.3.1 Suggested Constraints

When objects are added to a layout canvas, Interface Builder does not implement any default constraints on those views leaving the developer to add constraints as needed. There is, however, the option to have Interface

Builder apply suggested constraints. When this option is used, Interface Builder will apply what it believes to be the correct constraints for the layout based on the positioning of the views. Suggested constraints can be added to the currently selected view objects or an entire scene layout.

In situations where constraints are missing from a layout resulting in warnings, Interface Builder also provides the option to automatically add the constraints it believes are missing.

The options to perform these tasks are accessed via the toolbar's *Resolve Auto Layout Issues menu,* as illustrated in Figure 20-9.

The menu's top section represents tasks that relate to the currently selected views in the canvas, while the options in the lower section apply to all views in the currently selected view controller scene.

Figure 20-9

Most of the time, the suggested constraints will exactly match the required layout behavior, and occasionally, the suggested constraints will be incorrect. Most of the time, however, the suggested constraints provide an excellent starting point for implementing Auto Layout. For example, a typical process for designing a user interface might involve positioning the views by dragging and dropping them into place, applying suggested constraints, and then editing and fine-tuning those constraints to perfect the layout.

To see suggested constraints in action, select the label view in the AutoLayoutExample project and select the *Clear Constraints* option from the *Resolve Auto Layout Issues* menu. There are no constraints in the layout at this point, and the old positioning problem appears when the view is rotated. With the label still selected, choose the *Reset to Suggested Constraints* menu option listed under *Selected Views*. Reviewing the view canvas and orientation change should demonstrate that Interface Builder has suggested and applied the same constraints we previously added manually.

20.3.2 Visual Cues

Interface Builder includes several visual cues in the layout canvas to highlight the constraints currently configured on a view and to draw attention to areas where problems exist. When a view is selected within the layout canvas, the constraints that reference that view will be represented visually. Consider, for example, the label view created in our *AutoLayoutExample* app. When selected in the canvas, several additional lines appear, as shown in Figure 20-10:

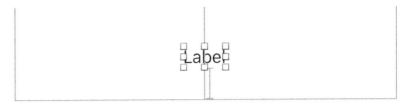

Figure 20-10

The vertical line that runs through the center of the label indicates the presence of a constraint that positions the label in the horizontal center of the parent view (analogous to the NSLayoutConstraint.Attribute.centerX attribute). If expressed as an equation, therefore, this would read as:

```
label.NSLayoutConstraint.Attribute.centerX =
            superview.NSLayoutConstraint.Attribute.centerX
```

The I-beam line running from the bottom edge of the label view to the bottom edge of the parent view indicates that a vertical space constraint is in place between the label and the safe area. The absence of additional visual information on the line indicates that this is an *equality* constraint. Figure 20-11 shows an example of a "greater than or equal to" horizontal constraint between two button views:

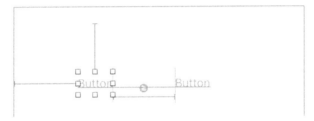

Figure 20-11

The horizontal line running beneath the Button label text indicates that constraints are in place to horizontally align the content baseline (represented by NSLayoutConstraint.Attribute.baseline) of the two buttons.

Width constraints are indicated by an I-beam line running parallel to the edge of the view in the corresponding dimension. The text view object in Figure 20-12, for example, has a "greater than or equal to" width constraint configured:

Figure 20-12

20.3.3 Highlighting Constraint Problems

Interface Builder also uses a range of visual cues and decorations to indicate that constraints are either missing, ambiguous, or in conflict. For example, valid and complete Auto Layout configurations are drawn using blue lines. However, when part of a layout is ambiguous, the constraint lines are orange.

Ambiguity typically occurs when a constraint is missing. Take, for example, the label view used earlier in the chapter. If only the horizontal center constraint is set, that constraint line will appear in orange because Auto Layout does not know where to position the view in the vertical plane. However, once the second constraint is set between the bottom edge of the label and the bottom of the superview, the constraint line will turn blue to indicate that the layout is no longer ambiguous.

Red constraint lines are used to indicate that constraints conflict. Consider, for example, a view object on which two width constraints have been configured, each for a different width value. The Auto Layout system categorizes such a situation as a constraint conflict, and Interface Builder draws the offending constraint lines on the layout canvas in red. Figure 20-13, for example, illustrates a conflict where one constraint is attempting to set the width of a view to 110 points while a second constraint dictates that the width must be greater than or equal to 120 points:

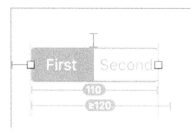

Figure 20-13

The layout canvas will dynamically update the positions and sizes of the views that make up a user interface as constraints are added. Under certain circumstances, however, it is possible to have constraints configured that will result in layout behavior different from that currently displayed within the canvas. When such a situation arises, Interface Builder will draw a dotted orange outline indicating the actual size and location of the frame for the currently selected item. This is, perhaps, best demonstrated with an example. Within the *AutoLayoutExample* project, add a Text Field object to the layout so that it is positioned near the top of the view and to the right of the horizontal center, as shown in Figure 20-14:

Figure 20-14

Select the new Text Field object and, using the *Add New Constraints* menu, establish a *Spacing to nearest neighbor* constraint from the top of the text view to the top of the safe area. Then, using the *Align* menu, add another constraint that aligns the view with the horizontal center in the container. Having established these constraints, review the layout within the view canvas and note that the Text View is positioned in compliance with the newly added constraints.

Click and drag the Text View to no longer be in the correct position. As outlined in Figure 20-15, the horizontal center constraint appears in orange with a number assigned to it. A dotted box also appears on this line, level with the Text View object. Interface Builder is attempting to warn us that the size and position of this view will resemble the dotted orange box at run time and not the size and position currently shown for the view in the canvas. The number on the horizontal center constraint tells us that the object's horizontal position will be a specific number of points to the left of the current position.

Figure 20-15

To reset the view to the size and position dictated by the constraints so that the canvas matches the runtime layout, select the Text View object and click on the *Update Frames* button located in the Interface Builder status bar, as highlighted in Figure 20-16:

Figure 20-16

The canvas will subsequently update to reflect the correct layout appearance (Figure 20-17):

Figure 20-17

If, on the other hand, the text view had been positioned correctly (in other words, the visual position was correct, but the constraints were wrong), the current constraints could have been adjusted to match the actual position of the view using the *Update Constraint Constants* option of the *Resolve Auto Layout Issues* menu.

20.3.4 Viewing, Editing, and Deleting Constraints

All of the constraints currently set on the views of a user interface may be viewed at any time from within the Document Outline panel positioned to the left of the Interface Builder canvas area. Hidden by default, this panel can be displayed by clicking on the button in the bottom left-hand corner of the storyboard canvas (marked by the arrow in Figure 20-18).

Figure 20-18

Within this outline, a category listed as *Constraints* will be present, which, when unfolded, will list all of the constraints currently configured for the layout. Note that when more than one container view is present in the view hierarchy, there will be a separate constraints list for each one. Figure 20-19, for example, lists the constraints for the user interface represented in Figure 20-10 above:

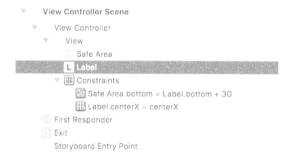

Figure 20-19

Also listed within the outline is the safe area belonging to the UIView component. As indicated, the bottom of the label is constrained to the bottom edge of the safe area.

As each constraint is selected from the outline list, the corresponding visual cue element will highlight within the layout canvas.

The details of a particular constraint may be viewed and edited at any time using various methods. For example, one method is to double-click on the constraint line in the canvas to display a constraint editing panel:

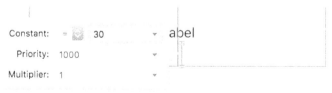

Figure 20-20

Another option is to select the constraint from the layout canvas or the Document Outline panel. Once selected, display the Attributes Inspector in the Utilities panel (*View -> Utilities -> Show Attributes Inspector*) to view and edit the properties of the constraint. For example, Figure 20-20 illustrates the settings for an equality spacing constraint.

Figure 20-21

A listing of the constraints associated with a specific view can be obtained by selecting that view in the layout canvas and displaying the Size Inspector in the Utilities panel. Figure 20-21, for example, lists two constraints that reference the currently selected view. Clicking the edit button on any constraint will provide options to edit the constraint properties. In addition, constraints can be removed by selecting them in the layout canvas and pressing the keyboard Delete key.

Figure 20-22

20.4 Creating New Constraints in Interface Builder

New user constraints can be created in Interface Builder using a variety of approaches, keeping in mind that constraints can relate to more than one view at a time. For example, to configure an alignment constraint, all of the views to be included in the alignment operation must be selected before creating the constraints.

As demonstrated earlier in this chapter, one of the easiest ways is to use the various options in the toolbar in the bottom right-hand corner of the storyboard canvas.

Another helpful option is simply to right-click within a view and then drag the resulting line outside the view's boundary. A context menu will appear on releasing the line, providing constraint options. The menu options will depend on the direction in which the line was dragged. If the line is dragged downwards, the menu will include options to add a constraint to the bottom of the view or to center vertically within the container. On the other hand, Dragging horizontally provides the option to attach to the corresponding edge of the safe area or to center horizontally. Dragging the line to another view in the canvas will provide options (Figure 20-23) to set up spacing, alignment, and size equality constraints between those views.

Figure 20-23

20.5 Adding Aspect Ratio Constraints

The height and width of a view can be constrained to retain the aspect ratio by right-clicking in the view, dragging diagonally, and then releasing. In the resulting menu, selecting *Aspect Ratio* ensures that the current aspect ratio will be preserved regardless of whether the view shrinks or grows.

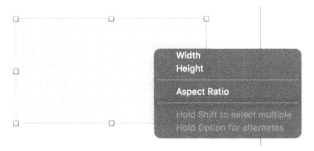

Figure 20-24

20.6 Resolving Auto Layout Problems

Another advantage of implementing Auto Layout constraints in Xcode is that several features are available in Xcode to assist in resolving problems.

In the first instance, descriptions of current issues can be obtained by clicking on the yellow warning triangle in the top right-hand corner of the canvas area:

Figure 20-25

Solutions to some problems may be implemented by using the options in the *Resolve Auto Layout Issues* menu to perform tasks such as automatically adding missing or resetting to suggested constraints.

More detailed resolution options are available from within the document outline panel. When issues need to be resolved, a red circle with a white arrow appears next to the corresponding view controller name in the outline panel, as shown in Figure 20-26:

Figure 20-26

Clicking on the red circle displays all current layout issues listed by category:

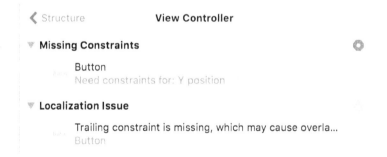

Figure 20-27

Hovering over a category title (for example, Missing Constraints) will display an information symbol that, when clicked, will display a detailed description of the problem type.

Clicking on the error or warning symbol will display a panel providing one or more possible solutions together with a button to apply the selected change:

Figure 20-28

20.7 Summary

This chapter has looked at a very simplistic example of the benefits of using Auto Layout in iOS user interface design. The remainder of the chapter has been dedicated to providing an overview of the Auto Layout features available in Interface Builder.

21. Implementing iOS 17 Auto Layout Constraints in Code

In addition to using Interface Builder, it is also possible to create Auto Layout constraints directly within the code of an app. These approaches, however, are not necessarily mutually exclusive. There are, for example, situations where a layout will be constructed using a combination of Interface Builder and manual coding. Furthermore, some types of constraint cannot yet be implemented in Interface Builder, constraints that cross-view hierarchies being a prime example. Finally, interface Builder is also of limited use when user interfaces are created dynamically at run time.

Given these facts, understanding how to create Auto Layout constraints in code is an important skill. In this chapter, we will explore two ways to create constraints in code. We will begin by exploring constraints using the NSLayoutConstraint class and then look at a more straightforward solution involving the NSLayoutAnchor class.

21.1 Creating Constraints Using NSLayoutConstraint

Implementing constraints using the NSLayoutConstraint class is a two-step process that involves creating the constraint and then adding the constraint to a view.

To create a constraint, an instance of the NSLayoutConstraint class must be created and initialized with the appropriate settings for the Auto Layout behavior it is to implement. This is achieved by initializing an NSLayoutConstraint instance, passing through a set of arguments for the constraint.

When considering this syntax, it is helpful to recall how constraints can be represented using linear equations (as outlined in *"An Introduction to Auto Layout in iOS 17"*) because the equation elements match the arguments used to create an NSLayoutConstraint instance.

Consider, for example, the following constraint expressed as an equation:

```
view1.bottom = view2.bottom - 20
```

The objective of this constraint is to position view1 so that its bottom edge is positioned at a distance of 20 points above the bottom edge of view2. This same equation can be represented in code as follows:

```
var myConstraint =
        NSLayoutConstraint(item: view1,
            attribute: NSLayoutConstraint.Attribute.bottom,
            relatedBy: NSLayoutRelation.equal,
            toItem: view2,
            attribute: NSLayoutConstraint.Attribute.bottom,
            multiplier: 1.0,
            constant: -20)
```

As we can see, the arguments to the method match those of the equation (except for the multiplier, which is absent from the equation and therefore equates to 1 in the method call).

The following equation sets the width of a Button view named *myButton* to be five times the width of a Label

153

view named *myLabel:*

```
var myConstraint =
          NSLayoutConstraint(item: myButton,
               attribute: NSLayoutConstraint.Attribute.width,
               relatedBy: NSLayoutRelation.equal,
               toItem: myLabel,
               attribute: NSLayoutConstraint.Attribute.width,
               multiplier: 5.0,
               constant: 0)
```

So far, the examples shown in this chapter have been *equality*-based constraints, and, as such, the *relatedBy:* argument has been set to NSLayoutRelation.Equal. The following equation uses a greater than or equal to operator:

```
myButton.width >= 200
```

Translated into code, this reads as follows:

```
var myConstraint =
          NSLayoutConstraint(item: myButton,
               attribute: NSLayoutConstraint.Attribute.width,
               relatedBy: NSLayoutRelation.greaterThanOrEqual,
               toItem: nil,
               attribute: NSLayoutConstraint.Attribute.width,
               multiplier: 1.0,
               constant: 200)
```

Note that since this constraint is not related to another view, the *toItem:* argument is set to *nil.*

21.2 Adding a Constraint to a View

Once a constraint has been created, it needs to be assigned to a view to become active. This is achieved by passing it through as an argument to the *addConstraint* method of the view instance to which it is being added. In the case of multiple constraints, each is added by a separate call to the *addConstraint* method. This leads to deciding the view to which the constraint should be added.

In the case of a constraint that references a single view, the constraint must be added to the immediate parent of the view. When a constraint references two views, the constraint must be applied to the closest ancestor of the two views. Consider, for example, the view hierarchy illustrated in Figure 21-1.

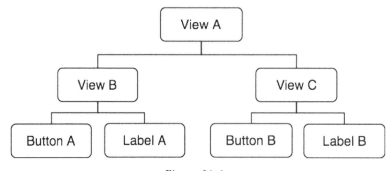

Figure 21-1

A constraint referencing only *Label A* should be added to the immediate parent, *View B.* On the other hand, a constraint referencing Button B and Label B must be added to the nearest common ancestor, which in this case is *View C*. Finally, a constraint referencing *Button A* and *Button B* must, once again, be added to the nearest common ancestor which equates to *View A*.

For example, the following code excerpt creates a new constraint and adds it to a view:

```
var myConstraint =
        NSLayoutConstraint(item: myButton,
            attribute: NSLayoutConstraint.Attribute.width,
            relatedBy: NSLayoutRelation.equal,
            toItem: myLabel,
            multiplier: 5.0,
            constant: 0)


self.view.addConstraint(myConstraint)
```

21.3 Turning off Auto Resizing Translation

When adding views to a layout in code, the toolkit will, by default, attempt to convert the autosizing mask for that view to Auto Layout constraints. Unfortunately, those auto-generated constraints will conflict with any constraints added within the app code. It is essential, therefore, that translation is turned off for views to which constraints are to be added in the code. This is achieved by setting the *setTranslatesAutoresizingMaskIntoConstraints* property of the target view to *false*. For example, the following code creates a new Button view, turns off translation, and then adds it to the parent view:

```
let myButton = UIButton()


myButton.setTitle("My Button", forState: UIControlState.normal)
myButton.translatesAutoresizingMaskIntoConstraints = false


self.view.addSubview(myButton)
```

21.4 Creating Constraints Using NSLayoutAnchor

An alternative to using the NSLayoutConstraint class is configuring constraints using layout anchors. Layout Anchors are created using the NSLayoutAnchor class, which creates NSLayoutConstraint instances for us, resulting in more concise code that is easier to write and understand.

UIView and all of its subclasses (UIButton, UILabel, etc.) contain a set of anchor properties that can be used to create constraints relative to anchor properties on other views in a layout. These anchor properties are instances of the NSLayoutAnchor class. The complete set of anchor properties is as follows:

Horizontal Anchors

- centerXAnchor

- leadingAnchor

- trailingAnchor

- leftAnchor

- rightAnchor

Vertical Anchors

- centerYAnchor

- bottomAnchor

- topAnchor

- firstBaselineAnchor

- lastBaselineAnchor

Size Anchors

- heightAnchor

- widthAnchor

A constraint is created by calling the *constraint()* method on one of the above properties of a view and passing it details of the view and anchor to which it is to be constrained. Suppose, for example, that we want to center a UILabel horizontally and vertically within a parent view. The required code would read as follows:

```
myLabel.centerXAnchor.constraint(equalTo: myView.centerXAnchor).isActive=true
myLabel.centerYAnchor.constraint(equalTo: myView.centerYAnchor).isActive=true
```

Using this approach, we can establish constraints between different anchor property types and include constant values. The following code, for example, constrains the bottom of a view named myLabel to the top of a view named myButton using an offset of 100:

```
myLabel.bottomAnchor.constraint(equalTo: myButton.topAnchor,
                                constant: 100).isActive=true
```

Not only do layout anchors require considerably less code than NSLayoutConstraint, but they also make the code easier to understand.

21.5 An Example App

Create a new Xcode project using the iOS App template, enter *AutoLayoutCode* as the product name, and set the Interface and Language menus to Storyboard and Swift, respectively.

21.6 Creating the Views

For this example, the code to create the views and constraints will be implemented in a new method named *createLayout* which will, in turn, be called from the *viewDidLoad* method of the *AutoLayoutCode* view controller. Select the *ViewController.swift* file and add this code to create a button and a label and add them to the main view:

```
override func viewDidLoad() {
    super.viewDidLoad()
    createLayout()
}

func createLayout() {
    let superview = self.view

    let myLabel = UILabel()
    myLabel.translatesAutoresizingMaskIntoConstraints = false
    myLabel.text = "My Label"
```

```
let myButton = UIButton()

myButton.setTitle("My Button", for: UIControl.State.normal)
myButton.backgroundColor = UIColor.blue
myButton.translatesAutoresizingMaskIntoConstraints = false

superview?.addSubview(myLabel)
superview?.addSubview(myButton)
}
```

21.7 Creating and Adding the Constraints

Constraints will be added to position the label in the horizontal and vertical center of the superview. The button will then be constrained to be positioned to the left of the label with the baselines of both views aligned. To achieve this layout, the *createLayout* method needs to be modified as follows:

```
func createLayout() {

    let superview = self.view

    let myLabel = UILabel()
    myLabel.translatesAutoresizingMaskIntoConstraints = false
    myLabel.text = "My Label"

    let myButton = UIButton()

    myButton.setTitle("My Button", for: UIControlState.normal)
    myButton.backgroundColor = UIColor.blue
    myButton.translatesAutoresizingMaskIntoConstraints = false

    superview?.addSubview(myLabel)
    superview?.addSubview(myButton)

    var myConstraint =
        NSLayoutConstraint(item: myLabel,
                attribute: NSLayoutConstraint.Attribute.centerY,
                relatedBy: NSLayoutConstraint.Relation.equal,
                toItem: superview,
                attribute: NSLayoutConstraint.Attribute.centerY,
                multiplier: 1.0,
                constant: 0)

    superview?.addConstraint(myConstraint)

    myConstraint =
        NSLayoutConstraint(item: myLabel,
                attribute: NSLayoutConstraint.Attribute.centerX,
```

```
            relatedBy: NSLayoutConstraint.Relation.equal,
            toItem: superview,
            attribute: NSLayoutConstraint.Attribute.centerX,
            multiplier: 1.0,
            constant: 0)


    superview?.addConstraint(myConstraint)


    myConstraint =
        NSLayoutConstraint(item: myButton,
                attribute: NSLayoutConstraint.Attribute.trailing,
                relatedBy: NSLayoutConstraint.Relation.equal,
                toItem: myLabel,
                attribute: NSLayoutConstraint.Attribute.leading,
                multiplier: 1.0,
                constant: -10)


    superview?.addConstraint(myConstraint)


    myConstraint =
        NSLayoutConstraint(item: myButton,
                attribute: NSLayoutConstraint.Attribute.lastBaseline,
                relatedBy: NSLayoutConstraint.Relation.equal,
                toItem: myLabel,
                attribute: NSLayoutConstraint.Attribute.lastBaseline,
                multiplier: 1.0,
                constant: 0)


    superview?.addConstraint(myConstraint)
}
```

When the app is compiled and run, the layout of the two views should match that illustrated in Figure 21-2:

Figure 21-2

21.8 Using Layout Anchors

Now that we have implemented constraints using the NSLayoutConstraint class, we can make a comparison by replacing this code with the equivalent layout anchor code. Remaining in the *ViewController.swift* file, remove or comment out the previously added constraint code and replace it with the following:

```
myLabel.centerXAnchor.constraint(equalTo: superview!.centerXAnchor).isActive=true
myLabel.centerYAnchor.constraint(equalTo: superview!.centerYAnchor).isActive=true
myButton.trailingAnchor.constraint(equalTo: myLabel.leadingAnchor, constant: -10)
                                        .isActive=true
myButton.lastBaselineAnchor.constraint(equalTo: myLabel.lastBaselineAnchor)
                                        .isActive=true
```

Rerun app to confirm the layout anchor code creates the same layout as before.

21.9 Removing Constraints

While it has not been necessary in this example, it is important to be aware that removing constraints from a view is possible. This can be achieved simply by calling the *removeConstraint* method of the view to which the constraint was added, passing through as an argument the NSLayoutConstraint object matching the constraint to be removed:

```
self.myview.removeConstraint(myconstraint)
```

It is also worth knowing that constraints initially created in Interface Builder can be connected to outlet properties, thereby allowing them to be referenced in code. The steps involved in creating an outlet for a constraint are covered in more detail in *"Implementing Cross-Hierarchy Auto Layout Constraints in iOS 17"*.

Layout anchor constraints can be enabled and disabled by saving the constraint to a variable and changing the *isActive* property as follows:

```
var constraint = myLabel.centerXAnchor.constraint(
                                equalTo: superview!.centerXAnchor)


constraint.isActive=true    // Enable the constraint
constraint.isActive=false   // Disable the constraint
```

21.10 Summary

While Interface Builder is the recommended method for implementing Auto Layout constraints, there are still situations where it may be necessary to implement constraints in code. This is typically necessary when dynamically creating user interfaces or when specific layout behavior cannot be achieved using Interface Builder (a prime example of these being constraints that cross view hierarchies, as outlined in the next chapter).

Constraints are created in code by instantiating instances of the NSLayoutConstraint class, configuring those instances with the appropriate constraint settings, and then adding the constraints to the appropriate views in the user interface.

22. Implementing Cross-Hierarchy Auto Layout Constraints in iOS 17

One of the few types of Auto Layout constraints that cannot be implemented within the Interface Builder environment references views contained in different view hierarchies. Constraints of this type must, therefore, be implemented in code. Fortunately, however, the steps to achieve this are quite simple. The objective of this chapter is to work through an example that demonstrates the creation of a cross-view hierarchy Auto Layout constraint.

22.1 The Example App

For this example, a straightforward user interface will be created consisting of two Views, a Button, and a Label. In terms of the physical view hierarchy, the user interface will be constructed as outlined in Figure 22-1.

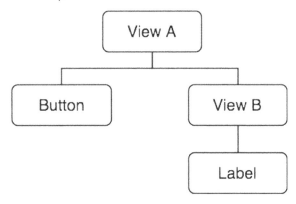

Figure 22-1

The goal will be to implement a constraint that aligns the centers of the Button and Label, which are part of different view hierarchies - the button being part of the hierarchy contained by View A and the label being part of the View B sub-hierarchy.

In terms of visual layout, the user interface should appear as illustrated in Figure 22-2. Key points to note are that the label should have constraints associated with it which horizontally and vertically center it within View B, and the button view should be positioned so that it is off-center in the horizontal axis:

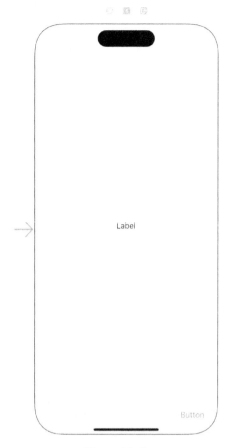

Figure 22-2

Begin by launching Xcode and selecting the options to create a new iOS app based on the App template. Enter *CrossView* as the product name and set the Language to Swift and the Interface to Storyboard.

Select the *Main.storyboard* file from the project navigator panel, select the view and change the background color to a light shade of grey using the Attributes Inspector. Next, display the Library dialog and drag a View, Button, and Label onto the design canvas as illustrated in Figure 22-2. Making sure to center the label object horizontally and vertically within the parent view.

Select the newly added View object, click on the *Resolve Auto Layout Issues* menu from the toolbar in the lower right-hand corner of the canvas, and select the *Reset to Suggested Constraints* option listed under *All Views in View Controller*.

22.2 Establishing Outlets

We will need to implement some outlets to set a cross-hierarchy constraint within the code. Since the constraint will need to reference both the button and the label, outlets need to be configured for these views. Select the label object and display the Assistant Editor using the *Editor -> Assistant* menu option

Make sure that the Assistant Editor is showing the *ViewController.swift* file. Right-click on the Label object in the view and drag the resulting line to the area immediately beneath the class declaration directive in the Assistant Editor panel. Upon releasing the line, the connection panel will appear. Configure the connection as an *Outlet* named *myLabel* and click on the *Connect* button. Repeat the above steps to add an outlet for the button object named *myButton.*

As currently constrained, the label object is centered horizontally within the view we refer to as View B. In place of this constraint, we need the label to be aligned with the center of the button object. This will involve removing and replacing the CenterX constraint with a new constraint referencing the button. This requires outlets for both the View B instance and the CenterX constraint.

Right-click on the View B parent of the label object and drag the resulting line to the area immediately beneath the previously declared outlets in the Assistant Editor. Release the line and configure an outlet named *viewB.*

Next, select the label object so that the associated constraint lines appear. Click on the vertical line passing through the label view so that it highlights. Next, right-click on the constraint line, drag to the Assistant Editor panel (Figure 22-3), and create a new outlet for this object named *centerConstraint.*

Figure 22-3

22.3 Writing the Code to Remove the Old Constraint

With the necessary outlets created, the next step is to write some code to remove the center constraint from the label object. For this example, all code will be added to the *viewDidLoad* method of the view controller. Select the *ViewController.swift* file and locate and modify the method as follows:

```
override func viewDidLoad() {
    super.viewDidLoad()
    viewB.removeConstraint(centerConstraint)
}
```

All the code is doing is calling the removeConstraint method of view B using the previously configured outlet, passing through a reference to the CenterX constraint, and again using the previously configured outlet to that object.

22.4 Adding the Cross Hierarchy Constraint

All that remains is to add the constraint to align the centers of the label and button. With the appropriate outlets already configured, this is simply a matter of adding a layout anchor constraint between the label and button views:

```
override func viewDidLoad() {
    super.viewDidLoad()
```

```
viewB.removeConstraint(centerConstraint)

    myLabel.trailingAnchor.constraint(
                    equalTo: myButton.trailingAnchor).isActive=true
}
```

22.5 Testing the App

Compile and run the app on a physical iOS device or the iOS Simulator. When the app runs, the label view should be aligned with the button, which should be maintained when the device is rotated into landscape orientation.

22.6 Summary

The current version of Interface Builder does not provide a way to select two views that reside in different view hierarchies and configure a constraint between them. However, as outlined in this chapter, the desired result can be achieved in code. Of crucial importance in this process is the fact that constraints, just like any other view object in a user interface, may be connected to an outlet and accessed via code.

23. Understanding the iOS 17 Auto Layout Visual Format Language

The third and final option for creating Auto Layout constraints involves a combination of code and the visual format language. This chapter aims to introduce the visual format language and work through code samples demonstrating the concept in action.

23.1 Introducing the Visual Format Language

The visual format language is not a new programming language in the way that C++, Java, and Swift are all programming languages. Instead, the visual format language defines a syntax through which Auto Layout constraints may be created using sequences of ASCII characters. These visual format character sequences are then turned into constraints by passing them through to the *constraints(withVisualFormat:)* method of the NSLayoutConstraint class.

What makes the language particularly appealing and intuitive is that the syntax used to define a constraint involves characters sequences that, to a large extent, visually represent the constraint being created.

23.2 Visual Format Language Examples

The easiest way to understand the concepts behind the visual format language is to look at some syntax examples. Take, for example, visual format language syntax to describe a view object:

```
[myButton]
```

As we can see, view objects are described in the visual format language by surrounding the view name with square brackets ([]).

Two views may be constrained to be positioned flush with each other by placing the views side by side in the visual format string:

```
[myButton1][myButton2]
```

Similarly, a horizontal spacer between two view objects is represented by a hyphen:

```
[myButton1]-[myButton2]
```

The above example instructs the Auto Layout system to create a constraint using the standard spacing for views. The following construct, on the other hand, specifies a spacing distance of 30 points between the two views:

```
[myButton1]-30-[myButton2]
```

By default, constraints of the type outlined above are assumed to be horizontal constraints. Vertical constraints are declared using a *V:* prefix. For example, the following syntax establishes a vertical spacing constraint between two views:

```
V:[myLabel]-50-[myButton]
```

For consistency and completeness, horizontal constraints may, optionally, be prefixed with *H:*.

The width of a view can be set specifically as follows:

```
[myButton(100)]
```

Alternatively, inequality can be used:

```
[myButton(<=100)]
```

The width of one view can be constrained to match that of a second view using a similar syntax:

```
[myLabel(==myButton2)]
```

When using the visual format language, the superview of the view for which the constraint is being described is represented by the | character. For example, the following visual format language construct declares a constraint for the myButton1 view that attaches the leading and trailing edges of the view to the left and right edges of the containing superview with a spacing of 20 and 30 points, respectively:

```
|-20-[myButton1]-30-|
```

The language also allows priorities to be declared. The following excerpt specifies that the width of myButton1 must be greater than or equal to 70 points with a priority value of 500:

```
[myButton1(>=70@500)]
```

Of particular importance, however, is the fact that the language may be used to construct multiple constraints in a single sequence, for example:

```
V:|-20-[myButton1(>=70@500)]-[myButton2(==myButton1)]-30-[myButton3]-|
```

23.3 Using the constraints(withVisualFormat:) Method

As previously described, visual language format-based constraints are created via a call to the *constraints(withVisualFormat:)* method of the NSLayoutConstraint class. However, there are several other arguments that the method can accept. The syntax for the method is as follows:

```
NSLayoutConstraint.constraints(withVisualFormat: <visual format string>,
        options: <options>,
        metrics: <metrics>,
        views: <views dictionary>)
```

The <visual format string> is, of course, the visual format language string that describes the constraints to be created. The <options> values must be set when the constraint string references more than one view. The purpose of this is to indicate how the views are to be aligned, and the value must be of type NSLayoutFormatOptions, for example, .alignAllLeft, .alignAllRight, .alignAllTop, .alignAllLastBaselines, etc.

The <metrics> argument is an optional Dictionary object containing the corresponding values for any constants referenced in the format string.

Finally, the <views dictionary> is a Dictionary object that contains the view objects that match the view names referenced in the format string.

When using a visual format string that will create multiple constraints, the options should include an alignment directive such as NSLayoutFormatOptions.alignAllLastBaseLines.

Since the method can create multiple constraints based on the visual format string, it returns an array of NSLayoutConstraint objects, one for each constraint, which must then be added to the appropriate view object.

Some sample code to create views and then specify multiple constraints using a visual format language string would, therefore, read as follows:

```
// Get a reference to the superview
let superview = self.view

//Create a label
```

```
let myLabel = UILabel()
myLabel.translatesAutoresizingMaskIntoConstraints = false
myLabel.text = "My Label"

// Create a button
let myButton = UIButton()
myButton.backgroundColor = UIColor.red
myButton.setTitle("My Button", for: UIControlState.normal)
myButton.translatesAutoresizingMaskIntoConstraints = false

// Add the button and label to the superview
superview?.addSubview(myLabel)
superview?.addSubview(myButton)

// Create the views dictionary
let viewsDictionary = ["myLabel": myLabel, "myButton": myButton]

// Create and add the vertical constraints
superview?.addConstraints(NSLayoutConstraint.constraints(
    withVisualFormat: "V:|-[myButton]-|",
        options: NSLayoutConstraint.FormatOptions.alignAllLastBaseline,
        metrics: nil,
        views: viewsDictionary))

// Create and add the horizontal constraints
superview?.addConstraints(NSLayoutConstraint.constraints(
    withVisualFormat: "|-[myButton]-[myLabel(==myButton)]-|",
        options: NSLayoutConstraint.FormatOptions.alignAllLastBaseline,
        metrics: nil,
        views: viewsDictionary))
```

23.4 Summary

The visual format language allows Auto Layout constraints to be created using sequences of characters designed to represent the constraint being described visually. Visual format strings are converted into constraints via a call to the *constraints(withVisualFormat:)* method of the NSLayoutConstraints class, which, in turn, returns an array containing an NSLayoutConstraint object for each new constraint created as a result of parsing the visual format string.

24. Using Trait Variations to Design Adaptive iOS 17 User Interfaces

In 2007 developers only had to design user interfaces for single screen size and resolution (that of the first generation iPhone). However, considering the range of iOS devices, screen sizes, and resolutions available today, designing a single user interface layout to target the full range of device configurations now seems a much more daunting task.

Although eased to some degree by the introduction of Auto Layout, designing a user interface layout that would work on both iPhone and iPad device families (otherwise known as an *adaptive interface*) typically involved creating and maintaining two storyboard files, one for each device type.

iOS 9 and Xcode 7 introduced the concepts of *trait variations* and *size classes*, explicitly intended to allow a user interface layout for multiple screen sizes and orientations to be designed within a single storyboard file. In this chapter, the concept of traits and size classes will be covered together with a sample app demonstrating how to use them to create an adaptive user interface.

24.1 Understanding Traits and Size Classes

Traits define the features of the environment an app is likely to encounter when running on an iOS device. Traits can be defined both by the device's hardware and how the user configures the iOS environment. Examples of hardware-based traits include hardware features such as the range of colors supported by the device display (also referred to as the *display gamut*) and whether or not the device supports features such as 3D Touch. The traits of a device that are dictated by user configuration include the dynamic type size setting and whether the device is configured for left-to-right or right-to-left text direction.

Arguably the most powerful trait category, however, relates specifically to the size and orientation of the device screen. Therefore, these trait values are referred to as *size classes*.

Size classes categorize the screen areas an app user interface will likely encounter during execution. Rather than represent specific screen dimensions and orientations, size classes represent *width* (w) and *height* (h) in terms of being *compact* (C) or *regular* (R).

All iPhone models in portrait orientation are represented by the compact width and regular height size class (wC hR). However, when smaller models such as the iPhone SE are rotated to landscape orientation, they are considered to be of compact height and width (wC hC). On the other hand, larger devices such as iPhone Pro and Pro Max models in landscape orientation are categorized as compact height and regular width (wR hC).

Regarding size class categorization, all iPad devices (including the iPad Pro) are classified as regular height and width (wR hR) in both portrait and landscape orientation. In addition, a range of different size class settings are used when apps are displayed on the iPad using multitasking, a topic covered in detail in this book's *"A Guide to iPad Multitasking"* chapter.

24.2 Size Classes in Interface Builder

Interface Builder in Xcode 15 allows different Auto Layout constraints to be configured for different size class settings within a single storyboard file. In other words, size classes allow a single user interface file to store multiple sets of layout data, with each data set targeting a particular size class. At runtime, the app will use the layout data set for the size class that matches the device and prevailing orientation on which it is executing, ensuring that the user interface appears correctly.

By default, any layout settings configured within the Interface Builder environment will apply to all size classes. Only when *trait variations* are specifically specified will the layout configuration settings differ between size classes.

Customizing a user interface for different size classes goes beyond the ability to configure different Auto Layout constraints for different size classes. Size classes may also be used to designate which views in a layout are visible within each class and which version of a particular image is displayed to the user. A smaller image may be used when an app is running on an iPhone SE, for example, or extra buttons might be made to appear to take advantage of the larger iPad screen.

24.3 Enabling Trait Variations

Xcode enables trait variations by default for new Xcode projects. This setting can be viewed and changed by opening the Main storyboard file, selecting a scene, and displaying the File inspector as illustrated in Figure 24-1:

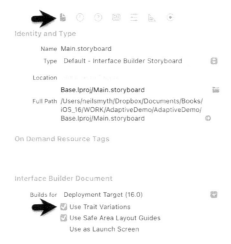

Figure 24-1

24.4 Setting "Any" Defaults

When designing user interfaces using size classes, there will often be situations where particular Auto Layout constraints or view settings will be appropriate for all size classes. Rather than configure these same settings for each size class, these can be configured within the *Any* category. Such settings will be picked up by default by all other size classes unless specifically overridden within those classes.

24.5 Working with Trait Variations in Interface Builder

A key part of working with trait variations involves using the device configuration bar. Located along the bottom edge of the Interface Builder storyboard canvas is an indicator showing the currently selected device, marked A in Figure 24-2:

Figure 24-2

Clicking on the current setting (A) in the status bar will display the device configuration menu shown in Figure 24-3, allowing different iOS device types to be selected:

Figure 24-3

Note that when an iPad model is selected, the button marked B is enabled so that you can test layout behavior for multitasking split-screen and slide-over modes. In addition, the device's orientation can be switched between portrait and landscape using the button (C).

When you make device and orientation selections from the configuration bar, the scenes within the storyboard canvas will resize to match precisely the screen size corresponding to the selected device and orientation. This provides a quick way to test the adaptivity of layouts within the storyboard without compiling and running the app on different devices or emulators.

24.6 Attributes Inspector Trait Variations

Regardless of the current selection in the device configuration panel, any changes made to layouts or views within the current storyboard will, by default, apply to all devices and size classes (essentially the "Any" size class). Trait variations (in other words, configuration settings that apply to specific size classes) are configured in two ways.

The first option relates to setting size-specific properties such as fonts and colors within the Attributes Inspector panel. Consider, for example, a Label view contained within a storyboard scene. This label is required to display text at a 17pt font size for all size classes except for regular width and height, where a 30pt font is needed. Reviewing the Attributes Inspector panel shows that the 17pt font setting is already configured, as shown in Figure 24-4:

Figure 24-4

The absence of any size class information next to the attribute setting tells us that the font setting corresponds to the any width, any height, any gamut size class and will be used on all devices and orientations unless overridden. To the left of the attribute field is a + button, as indicated in Figure 24-5:

Figure 24-5

This is the *Add Variation* button which, when selected, displays a panel of menus allowing size class selections to be made for a trait variation. To configure a different font size for regular height, regular width, and any gamut, for example, the menu selections shown in Figure 24-6 would need to be made:

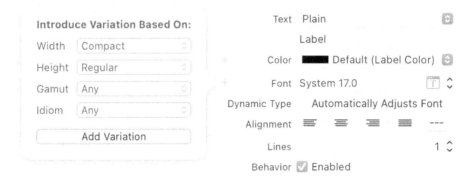

Figure 24-6

Once the trait configuration has been added, it appears within the Attributes Inspector panel labeled as wR hR and may be used to configure a larger font for regular width and height size class devices:

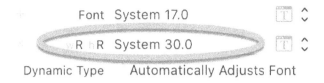

Figure 24-7

24.7 Using Constraint Variations

Layout size and constraint variations are managed using the Size inspector, which is accessed using the button marked A in Figure 24-8:

Figure 24-8

The Size inspector will update to reflect the currently selected object or constraint within the design layout. Constraints are selected either by clicking on the constraint line in the layout canvas or by making selections within the Document outline panel. In Figure 24-9, for example, a centerX constraint applied to a Label is selected within Interface Builder:

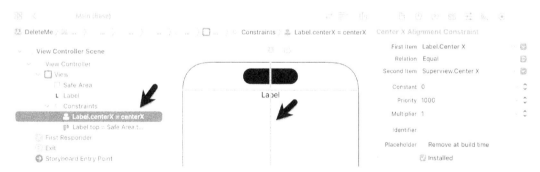

Figure 24-9

The area marked B in Figure 24-8 above contains a list of variations supported by the currently selected constraint (in this example, only the default constraint is installed, which will apply to all size classes). As demonstrated later in this chapter, we can add additional variations by clicking on the + button (C) and selecting the required class settings as outlined above when working with fonts. Once the new variation has been set up, the default variation must be disabled so that only the custom variation is active. In Figure 24-10, for example, a Label width constraint variation has been configured for the wR hR size class:

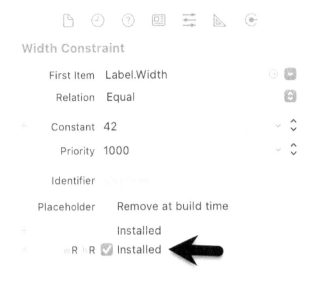

Figure 24-10

If we needed a different width for compact width, regular height devices, we would add a second width constraint to our Label and configure it with a wC hR variation containing the required width value. Then, the system will select the appropriate width constraint variation for the current device when the app runs.

24.8 An Adaptive User Interface Tutorial

The remainder of this chapter will create an adaptive user interface example. This tutorial aims to create a straightforward adaptive layout that demonstrates each of the key features of trait variations, including setting individual attributes, using the vary for traits process, and implementing image asset catalogs in the context of size classes.

Begin by creating a new Xcode iOS app project named *AdaptiveDemo* with the language option set to Swift.

24.9 Designing the Initial Layout

The iPhone 15 Pro in portrait orientation will serve as the base layout configuration for the user interface, so begin by selecting the *Main.storyboard* file and ensuring that the device configuration bar currently has the iPhone 15 Pro device selected.

Drag and drop a Label view so that it is positioned in the horizontal center of the scene and slightly beneath the top edge of the safe area of the view controller scene. With the Label still selected, use the *Align* menu to add a constraint to center the view horizontally within the container. Using the *Add New Constraints* menu, set a *Spacing to nearest neighbor* constraint on the top edge of the Label using the current value and with the *Constrain to Margins* option enabled.

Double-click on the Label and change the text to read "A Sunset Photo". Next, drag an Image View object from the Library panel to be positioned beneath the Label and centered horizontally within the scene. Resize the Image View so that the layout resembles that illustrated in Figure 24-11:

Figure 24-11

With the Image View selected, display the Align menu and enable the option to center the view horizontally within the container, then use the *Add New Constraints* menu to add a nearest neighbor constraint on the top edge of the Image View with the *Constrain to Margins* option disabled and to set a Width constraint of 320:

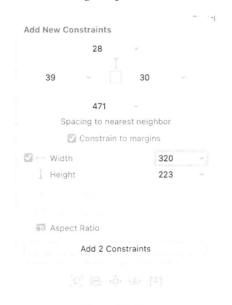

Figure 24-12

Right-click and drag diagonally across the Image View, as shown in Figure 24-13. On releasing the line, select *Aspect Ratio* from the resulting menu.

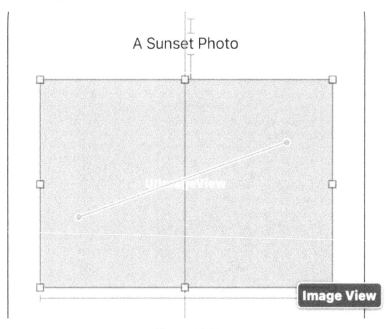

Figure 24-13

If necessary, click the Update Frames button in the status bar to reset the views to match the constraints.

24.10 Adding Universal Image Assets

The tutorial's next step is adding some image assets to the project. The images can be found in the *adaptive_images* directory of the code samples download, which can be obtained from:

https://www.payloadbooks.com/product/ios17xcode/

Within the project navigator panel, locate and click on the Assets entry, click on the + button in the panel's bottom left-hand corner, and select the Image Set option. Next, double-click on the new image set, which will have been named *Image*, and rename it to *Sunset*.

Locate the *sunset_wAny_hAny@2x.jpg* file in a Finder window and drag and drop it onto the 2x image box as illustrated below:

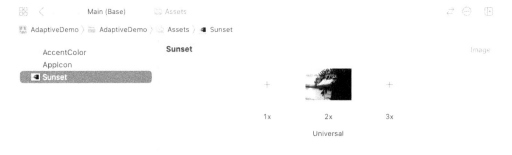

Figure 24-14

Return to the *Main.storyboard* file, select the Image View and display the Attributes Inspector panel. Next, click the down arrow to the right of the Image field and select *Sunset* from the resulting menu. The Image View in the view controller canvas will update to display the sunset image from the asset catalog.

Switch between device types and note that the same image is used for all size classes. The next step is to add a different image to be displayed in regular-width size class configurations.

Once again, select *Assets* from the project navigator panel and, with the *Sunset* image set selected, display the Attributes Inspector and change the *Width Class* attribute to *Any & Compact*. An additional row of image options will appear within the Sunset image set. Once again, locate the images in the sample source code download, this time dragging the *sunset_wCompact_hRegular@2x.jpg* file onto the 2x image well in the compact row, as shown in Figure 24-15:

Figure 24-15

Return to the *Main.storyboard* file and verify that different sunset images appear when switching between compact and regular width size class configurations.

24.11 Increasing Font Size for iPad Devices

The next step in the tutorial is to add some trait variations that will apply when the app runs in regular width and regular height size class device configurations (in other words, when running on an iPad). The first variation is to use a larger font on the Label object.

Begin by selecting the Label object in the scene. Next, display the Attributes Inspector panel and click on the + button next to the font property, as illustrated in Figure 24-6 above. Select the Regular Width | Regular Height menu settings from the resulting menu and click on the *Add Variation* button. Within the new wR hR font attribute field, increase the font size to 35pt.

Using the device configuration bar, test that the new font applies only to iPad device configurations.

24.12 Adding Width Constraint Variations

The next step is to increase the Image View size when the app encounters an iPad device size class. Since the Image View has a constraint that preserves the aspect ratio, only the width constraint needs to be modified to achieve this goal.

Earlier in the tutorial, we added a width constraint to the Image view that is currently being used for all size classes. The next step, therefore, is to adjust this constraint so that it only applies to compact width devices. To do this, select the width constraint for the Image view in the Document outline as shown below:

Figure 24-16

With the constraint selected, display the Size inspector, click on the button marked C in Figure 24-8 above and add a new compact width, regular height variation. Once the variation has been added, disable the default variation so that only the new variation is installed:

Figure 24-17

Now that we have a width constraint for compact width devices, we need to add a second width constraint to the Image view for regular width size classes. Select the Image view in the layout and use the Add New Constraints menu to add a width constraint with a value of 600:

Figure 24-18

Locate this new width constraint in the Document outline and select it as outlined in Figure 24-19:

Figure 24-19

With the constraint selected, display the Size inspector, add a regular width, regular height variation and disable the default variation. If the Relation field is set to *Greater Than or Equal to*, change it to *Equal*:

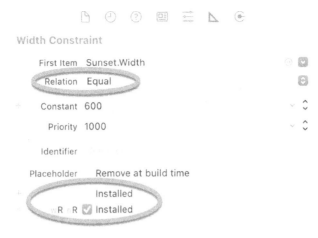

Figure 24-20

24.13 Testing the Adaptivity

Use the device configuration bar to test a range of size class permutations. Assuming that the adaptivity settings are working, a larger font and a larger, different image should appear when previewing iPad configurations. Use the device configuration bar to test a range of size class permutations. Assuming that the adaptivity settings are working, a larger font and a larger, different image should appear when previewing iPad configurations.

Before continuing to the next chapter, take some time to experiment by adding other variations, for example, to adjust the image size for smaller iPhone devices in landscape orientation (wC hC).

24.14 Summary

The range of iOS device screen sizes and resolutions is much more diverse than when the original iPhone was introduced in 2007. Today, developers need to be able to target an increasingly wide range of display sizes when designing user interface layouts for iOS apps. With size classes and trait variations, it is possible to target all screen sizes, resolutions, and orientations from within a single storyboard. This chapter has outlined the basics of size classes and trait variations and worked through a simple example user interface layout designed for both the iPad and iPhone device families.

25. Using Storyboards in Xcode 15

Storyboarding is a feature built into Xcode that allows the various screens that comprise an iOS app and the navigation path through those screens to be visually assembled. Using the Interface Builder component of Xcode, the developer drags and drops view and navigation controllers onto a canvas and designs the user interface of each view in the usual manner. The developer then drags lines to link individual trigger controls (such as a button) to the corresponding view controllers that are to be displayed when the user selects the control. Having designed both the screens (referred to in the context of storyboarding as *scenes*) and specified the transitions between scenes (referred to as *segues*), Xcode generates all the code necessary to implement the defined behavior in the completed app. The transition style for each segue (page fold, cross dissolve, etc.) may also be defined within Interface Builder. Further, segues may be triggered programmatically when behavior cannot be graphically defined using Interface Builder.

Xcode saves the finished design to a *storyboard file*. Typically, an app will have a single storyboard file, though there is no restriction preventing using multiple storyboard files within a single app.

The remainder of this chapter will work through creating a simple app using storyboarding to implement multiple scenes with segues defined to allow user navigation.

25.1 Creating the Storyboard Example Project

Begin by launching Xcode and creating a new project named *Storyboard* using the iOS *App* template with the language menu set to *Swift* and the *Storyboard* Interface option selected. Then, save the project to a suitable location by clicking the *Create* button.

25.2 Accessing the Storyboard

Upon creating the new project, Xcode will have created what appears to be the usual collection of files for a single-view app, including a storyboard named file *Main.storyboard*. Select this file in the project navigator panel to view the storyboard canvas as illustrated in Figure 25-1.

The view displayed on the canvas is the view for the *ViewController* class created for us by Xcode when we selected the *App* template. The arrow pointing inwards to the left side of the view indicates that this is the initial view controller and will be the first view displayed when the app launches. To change the initial view controller, drag this arrow to any other scene in the storyboard and drop it in place.

Figure 25-1

Objects may be added to the view in the usual manner by displaying the Library panel and dragging and dropping objects onto the view canvas. For this example, drag a label and a button onto the view canvas. Using the properties panel, change the label text to *Scene 1* and the button text to *Go to Scene 2*.

Figure 25-2

Using the *Resolve Auto Layout Issues* menu, select the *Reset to Suggested Constraints* option listed under *All Views in View Controller*.

It will be necessary first to establish an outlet to manipulate text displayed on the label object from within the app code. Select the label in the storyboard canvas and display the Assistant Editor (*Editor -> Assistant*). Check that the Assistant Editor is showing the content of the *ViewController.swift* file. Then, right-click on the label and drag the resulting line to just below the class declaration line in the Assistant Editor panel. In the resulting connection dialog, enter *scene1Label* as the outlet name and click on the *Connect* button. Upon completion of the connection, the top of the *ViewController.swift* file should read as follows:

```
import UIKit

class ViewController: UIViewController {

    @IBOutlet weak var scene1Label: UILabel!
.
.
```

25.3 Adding Scenes to the Storyboard

To add a second scene to the storyboard, drag a View Controller object from the Library panel onto the canvas. Figure 25-3 shows a second scene added to a storyboard:

Figure 25-3

Drag and drop a label and a button into the second scene and configure the objects so that the view appears as shown in Figure 25-4. Then, repeat the steps performed for the first scene to configure Auto Layout constraints on the two views.

Figure 25-4

As many scenes as necessary may be added to the storyboard, but we will use just two scenes for this exercise.

Having implemented the scenes, the next step is to configure segues between the scenes.

25.4 Configuring Storyboard Segues

As previously discussed, a segue is a transition from one scene to another within a storyboard. Within the example app, touching the *Go To Scene 2* button will segue to scene 2. Conversely, the button on scene 2 is intended to return the user to scene 1. To establish a segue, hold down the Ctrl key on the keyboard, click over a control (in this case, the button on scene 1), and drag the resulting line to the scene 2 view. Upon releasing the mouse button, a menu will appear. Select the *Present Modally* menu option to establish the segue. Once the segue has been added, a connector will appear between the two scenes, as highlighted in Figure 25-5:

Figure 25-5

As more scenes are added to a storyboard, it becomes increasingly difficult to see more than a few scenes at one time on the canvas. To zoom out, double-click on the canvas. To zoom back in again, double-click once again on the canvas. The zoom level may also be changed using the plus and minus control buttons located in the status bar along the bottom edge of the storyboard canvas or by right-clicking on the storyboard canvas background to access a menu containing several zoom level options.

25.5 Configuring Storyboard Transitions

Xcode allows changing the visual appearance of the transition that occurs during a segue. To change the transition, select the corresponding segue connector, display the Attributes Inspector, and modify the *Transition* setting. For example, in Figure 25-6, the transition has been changed to *Cross Dissolve:*

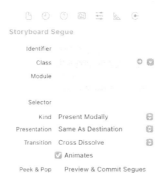

Figure 25-6

If animation is not required during the transition, turn off the *Animates* option. Run the app on a device or simulator and test that touching the "Go to Scene 2" button causes Scene 2 to appear.

25.6 Associating a View Controller with a Scene

At this point in the example, we have two scenes but only one view controller (the one created by Xcode when we selected the iOS *App* template). To add any functionality behind scene 2, it will also need a view controller. The first step is to add the class source file for a view controller to the project. Right-click on the *Storyboard* target at the top of the project navigator panel and select *New File...* from the resulting menu. In the new file panel, select *iOS* in the top bar, followed by *Cocoa Touch Class* in the main panel, and click *Next* to proceed. On the options screen, ensure that the *Subclass of* menu is set to *UIViewController* and that the *Also create XIB file* option is deselected (since the view already exists in the storyboard there is no need for a XIB user interface file), name the class *Scene2ViewController* and proceed through the screens to create the new class file.

Select the *Main.storyboard* file in the project navigator panel and click the View Controller button located in the panel above the Scene 2 view, as shown in Figure 25-7:

Figure 25-7

With the view controller for scene 2 selected within the storyboard canvas, display the Identity Inspector (*View -> Inspectors -> Identity*) and change the *Class* from *UIViewController* to *Scene2ViewController:*

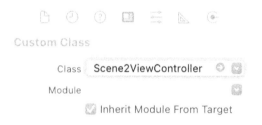

Figure 25-8

Scene 2 now has a view controller and corresponding Swift source file where code may be written to implement any required functionality.

Select the label object in scene 2 and display the Assistant Editor. Next, ensure that the *Scene2ViewController. swift* file is displayed in the editor, and then establish an outlet for the label named *scene2Label*.

25.7 Passing Data Between Scenes

One of the most common requirements when working with storyboards involves transferring data from one scene to another during a segue transition. Before the storyboard runtime environment performs a segue, a call is made to the *prepare(for segue:)* method of the current view controller. If any tasks need to be performed before the segue, implement this method in the current view controller and add code to perform any necessary tasks. Passed as an argument to this method is a segue object from which a reference to the destination view controller may be obtained and subsequently used to transfer data.

To see this in action, begin by selecting *Scene2ViewController.swift* and adding a new property variable:

```
import UIKit

class Scene2ViewController: UIViewController {

    @IBOutlet weak var scene2Label: UILabel!

    var labelText: String?
    .
    .
    .
```

This property will hold the text to be displayed on the label when the storyboard transitions to this scene. As such, some code needs to be added to the *viewDidLoad* method located in the *Scene2ViewController.swift* file:

```
override func viewDidLoad() {
    super.viewDidLoad()
    scene2Label.text = labelText
}
```

Finally, select the *ViewController.swift* file and implement the *prepare(for segue:)* method as follows:

```
override func prepare(for segue: UIStoryboardSegue, sender: Any?) {
    let destination = segue.destination
                            as! Scene2ViewController
    destination.labelText = "Arrived from Scene 1"
}
```

This method obtains a reference to the destination view controller and then assigns a string to the *labelText* property of the object so that it appears on the label.

Rerun the app and note that the new label text appears when scene 2 is displayed. This is because we have, albeit using an elementary example, transferred data from one scene to the next.

25.8 Unwinding Storyboard Segues

The next step is configuring the button on scene 2 to return to scene 1. It might seem that the obvious choice is to implement a segue from the button in scene 2 to scene 1. Instead of returning to the original instance of scene 1, however, this would create an entirely new instance of the ViewController class. If a user were to perform this transition repeatedly, the app would continue using more memory and eventually be terminated by the operating system.

The app should instead make use of the Storyboard *unwind* feature. This involves implementing a method in the view controller of the scene to which the user is to be returned and then connecting a segue to that method from the source view controller. This enables an unwind action to be performed across multiple scene levels.

To implement this in our example app, begin by selecting the *ViewController.swift* file and implementing a method to be called by the unwind segue named *returned*:

```
@IBAction func returned(segue: UIStoryboardSegue) {
    scene1Label.text = "Returned from Scene 2"
}
```

All this method requires for this example is that it sets some new text on the label object of scene 1. Once the method has been added, it is important to save the *ViewController.swift* file before continuing.

The next step is to establish the unwind segue. To achieve this, locate scene 2 within the storyboard canvas and right-click and drag from the button view to the Exit entry in the document outline panel, as shown in Figure 25-9. Release the line and select the *returnedWithSegue* method from the resulting menu:

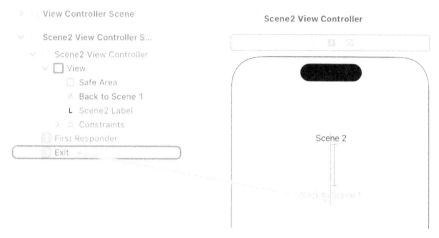

Figure 25-9

Once again, run the app and note that the button on scene 2 now returns to scene 1 and, in the process, calls the *returned* method resulting in the label on scene 1 changing.

25.9 Triggering a Storyboard Segue Programmatically

In addition to wiring up controls in scenes to trigger a segue, it is possible to initiate a preconfigured segue from within the app code. This can be achieved by assigning an identifier to the segue and then making a call to the *performSegue(withIdentifier:)* method of the view controller from which the segue is to be triggered.

To set the identifier of a segue, select it in the storyboard canvas, display the Attributes Inspector, and set the value in the *Identifier* field.

Assuming a segue with the identifier of *SegueToScene1*, this could be triggered from within code as follows:

```
self.performSegue(withIdentifier: "SegueToScene1", sender: self)
```

25.10 Summary

The Storyboard feature of Xcode allows for the navigational flow between the various views in an iOS app to be visually constructed without the need to write code. In this chapter, we have covered the basic concepts behind storyboarding, worked through creating an example iOS app using storyboards, and explored the storyboard unwind feature.

26. Organizing Scenes over Multiple Storyboard Files

The storyboard created in the preceding chapter is a small example consisting of only two scenes. When developing complex apps, however, it is not unusual for a user interface to consist of many more scenes. Once a storyboard grows in terms of the number of scenes, it can become challenging to navigate and locate specific scenes. This problem can be alleviated by organizing the scenes over multiple storyboards and then using *storyboard references* to reference a scene in one storyboard from within another storyboard.

Continuing to use the project created in the preceding chapter, this chapter will cover how to organize scenes in separate storyboard files and use storyboard references to establish segues between scenes in different storyboard files.

26.1 Organizing Scenes into Multiple Storyboards

The storyboard created in the previous chapter is a small example consisting of only two scenes. When developing complex apps, however, it is not unusual for a user interface to consist of many more scenes. Therefore, existing scenes in a storyboard file can be exported to a second storyboard file using a simple menu selection. To see this in action, select the *Main.storyboard* file and drag an additional view controller onto the storyboard canvas. Next, add button and label views so that the scene appears as illustrated in Figure 26-1 using the same steps as those followed for the previous scenes:

Figure 26-1

Before moving the new scene to a different storyboard file, add a second button to Scene 2 labeled "Go to Scene 3" and establish a modal presentation segue to the newly added scene. As before, set the Auto Layout settings to suggested constraints.

To move this new scene to a second storyboard, select it in the storyboard and choose the *Editor -> Refactor to Storyboard...* menu option (note that although only a single scene is being exported in this case, multiple scenes can also be selected and moved in a single operation). Once the menu option is selected, a panel (Figure 26-2) will appear seeking the name to be given to the new storyboard. In the *Save As:* field, name the file *Second.storyboard*:

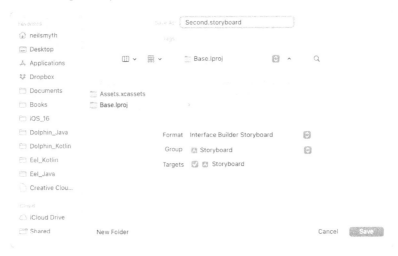

Figure 26-2

Click on the Save button to save the scene to the new storyboard. Once saved, two changes will have taken place. First, a review of the Project Navigator panel will reveal the presence of a new storyboard file named *Second. storyboard,* which, when selected, will reveal that it contains the third scene that was initially located in the *Main.storyboard* file.

Second, a review of the *Main.storyboard* file will show that the third scene has now been replaced by a storyboard reference, as shown in Figure 26-3, and that the segue is still in place:

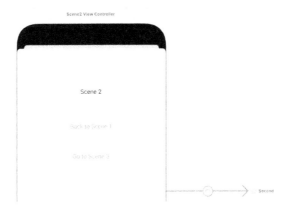

Figure 26-3

Select the *Second* storyboard reference and display the Attributes Inspector panel. Note that the Storyboard property is set to the Second storyboard file and that, by default, it is configured to display the *Initial View Controller* within that storyboard, which in this case is the only scene within the second storyboard:

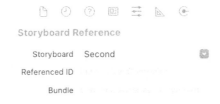

Figure 26-4

Compile and run the app and verify that the *Go to Scene 3* button does indeed segue to the third scene.

26.2 Establishing a Connection between Different Storyboards

The previous section explored separating existing scenes within a storyboard into separate storyboard files. Consider a segue that needs to be established between two scenes in two different storyboards where no reference has yet been established. To see this in action, select the *File -> New File...* menu option and, in the resulting panel, locate the *User Interface* section and select the *Storyboard* option. Click *Next* and name the file *Third.storyboard* before clicking on *Create*.

Select the *Third.storyboard* file from the Project Navigator panel, add a label to the view, and change the text to read *Scene 4* before setting appropriate Auto Layout constraints.

The objective is now to establish a segue from the "Go to Scene 4" button in the scene in the *Second.storyboard* file to the new scene in the *Third.storyboard* file.

The first step is to assign a storyboard ID to scene 4. Within the *Third.storyboard* file, select the View Controller, so it is highlighted in blue, display the Identity Inspector (*View -> Inspectors -> Identity*) and change the Storyboard ID setting to *Scene4Controller*.

The next step is to add a reference to this scene from within the *Second.storyboard* file. Select this file and drag a Storyboard Reference object from the Library onto the canvas. Select the reference object, display the Attributes Inspector, change the Storyboard menu to *Third* and enter *Scene4Controller* into the *Referenced ID* field as shown in Figure 26-5:

Figure 26-5

The storyboard reference is now configured to reference the scene 4 view controller in the Third storyboard file and can be used as the target for a segue. Remaining in the *Second.storyboard* file, right-click on the Go to Scene 4 button and drag the resulting line to the storyboard reference object. Release the line and select *Present Modally* from the popup menu.

Compile and run the app a final time and verify that the button initiates the segue to the fourth scene as configured.

26.3 Summary

This chapter has covered the steps involved in organizing scenes over multiple storyboard files. In addition, it has covered the exporting of scenes from an existing storyboard file to a new storyboard file and outlined the steps required to manually establish storyboard references between scenes residing in different storyboard files.

27. Using Xcode 15 Storyboards to Create an iOS 17 Tab Bar App

Having worked through a simple Storyboard-based app in the previous chapter, the goal of this chapter will be to create a slightly more complex storyboard example.

So far in this book, we have worked primarily with apps that present a single view to the user. In practice, however, it is more likely that an app will need to display various content depending on the user's actions. This is typically achieved by creating multiple views (often referred to as content views) and then providing a mechanism for the user to navigate from one view to another. One of several mechanisms for achieving this involves using either the UINavigationBar or UITabBar components. In this chapter, we will begin by using the storyboard feature of Xcode to implement a multiview app using a Tab Bar.

27.1 An Overview of the Tab Bar

The UITabBar component is typically located at the bottom of the screen. It presents an array of tabs containing text and an optional icon that the user may select to display a different content view. Typical examples of the tab bar in action include the iPhone's built-in Music and Phone apps. The Music app, for example, presents a tab bar with options to display different music options. Depending on the selection made from the tab bar, a different content view is displayed to the user.

27.2 Understanding View Controllers in a Multiview App

In the preceding chapters, we have discussed the model-view-controller concept in relation to each view having its own view controller (for additional information on this, read the chapter entitled *"The iOS 17 App and Development Architecture"*). In a multiview app, on the other hand, each content view will still have a view controller associated with it to handle user interaction and display updates. Multiview apps, however, also require an additional controller.

Multiview apps need a visual control that the user will use to switch from one content view to another, and this often takes the form of a tab or navigation bar. Both of these components are also *views* and as such, also need to have a *view controller*. In a multiview app, this is known as the *root controller* and is responsible for controlling which content view is currently displayed to the user. As an app developer, you are free to create your own root controller by subclassing from the UIViewController class, but in practice, it usually makes more sense to use an instance of either the UIKit UITabBarController or UINavigationController classes.

Regardless of the origins of your chosen root controller, it is the first controller that is loaded by the app when it launches. Once loaded, it is responsible for displaying the first content view to the user and switching the various content views in and out as required based on the user's subsequent interaction with the app.

Since this chapter is dedicated to creating a tab bar-based app, we will be using an instance of the UITabBarController as our root controller.

27.3 Setting up the Tab Bar Example App

The first step in creating our example app is to create a new Xcode project. To do so, launch Xcode and select the option to *Create a new Xcode project*.

On the template selection screen, select the iOS App option and click Next to proceed. On the next screen, enter TabBar as the product name. Then, proceed to the final screen and browse to a suitable location for the project files before clicking on the Create button.

27.4 Reviewing the Project Files

Based on our selections during the project creation process, Xcode has pre-populated the project with several files. In addition to the standard app delegate files, it has, for example, provided the file necessary for a single view controller-based app named *ViewController.swift*. In addition, a Main.storyboard file has also been created.

To start with an entirely clean project, select the *ViewController.swift* file in the project navigator panel and press the keyboard Delete key to remove the file from the project, choosing the option to move the file to the trash when prompted to do so.

27.5 Adding the View Controllers for the Content Views

The ultimate goal of this chapter is to create a tab bar-based app consisting of two tabs with corresponding views; each of these will require a view controller. The first step, therefore, is to add the view controller for the first view. To achieve this, select the *File -> New -> File...* menu option and, on the resulting panel, select the iOS option from the toolbar and Cocoa Touch Class from the list of templates. Click Next and on the next screen, name the new class Tab1ViewController and change the Subclass of menu to UIViewController. Ensure that the Also create XIB file option is switched off before clicking Next. Finally, select the desired location for creating the class files before clicking on Create.

Repeat the above steps to add a second view controller class named *Tab2ViewController*.

The scene within the storyboard file must now be associated with one of these view controller classes. Open the Main.storyboard file and select the scene added by Xcode so that it is highlighted with a blue border before displaying the Identity Inspector panel (*View -> Inspectors -> Identity*). Within the inspector panel, change the Class setting from UIViewController to Tab1ViewController.

The second view controller may be added to the storyboard simply by dragging and dropping one from the Library panel onto the storyboard canvas. Once it has been added, follow the same steps to change the view controller class within the Identity Inspector panel, this time selecting Tab2ViewController in the Class field.

27.6 Adding the Tab Bar Controller to the Storyboard

As previously explained, a Tab Bar Controller handles navigation between view controllers in a Tab Bar-based interface. It will be necessary, therefore, to add one of these to our storyboard. Begin by selecting the *Main.storyboard* file in the Xcode project navigator panel.

To add a Tab Bar Controller to the storyboard, select the Tab1ViewController in the storyboard design area, followed by the *Editor -> Embed In -> Tab Bar Controller* menu option. The Tab Bar Controller will subsequently appear in the storyboard already connected to the Tab 1 View Controller, as shown in Figure 27-1:

Figure 27-1

A relationship must now be established between the *Tab2ViewController* class and the Tab Bar Controller. To achieve this, right-click on the Tab Bar Controller object in the storyboard canvas and drag the line to the *Tab2ViewController* scene. Upon releasing the line select the *view controllers* menu option listed under *Relationship Segue,* as illustrated in Figure 27-2. This will add the *Tab2ViewController* to the *viewControllers* property of the Tab Bar Controller object so that it will be included in the tab navigation.

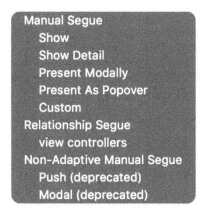

Figure 27-2

At this point in the design process, the storyboard should now consist of one Tab Bar Controller with relationships established with *Tab1ViewController* and *Tab2ViewController*. Allowing for differences in positioning of the storyboard elements, the canvas should now appear as shown in the following figure:

Figure 27-3

All that remains to complete the app is to configure the tab bar items and design rudimentary user interfaces for the two view controllers.

27.7 Designing the View Controller User interfaces

We will add labels to the views and change the background colors to visually differentiate the two view controllers. Begin by selecting the view of the Tab1ViewController scene. Then, within the Attributes Inspector panel, click on the white rectangle next to the *Background* label, select the *Custom…* menu option, and choose a shade of red from the resulting Colors dialog. Next, drag and drop a Label object from the Library panel and position it in the center of the red view. Double-click the label so it becomes editable, and change the text to *Screen One*. With the label still selected, use the Auto Layout Align menu to enable horizontal and vertical "in Container" constraint options.

Once completed, the Tab1ViewController storyboard scene should appear as shown in Figure 27-4. Repeat the above steps to change the background of the Tab2ViewController view to green and add a label displaying text that reads *Screen Two*.

Figure 27-4

27.8 Configuring the Tab Bar Items

As is evident from the tab bars across the bottom of the two view controller elements, the tab items are currently configured to display text that reads "Item". Therefore, the final task before compiling and running the app is rectifying this issue. First, begin by double-clicking on the word "Item" in the tab bar of Tab1ViewController so that the text highlights and enter *Screen One*. Next, repeat this step to change the text of the tab bar item for Tab2ViewController to *Screen Two*.

If you already have some icons suitable to be displayed on the tab bar items, feel free to use them for this project. Alternatively, example icons can be found in the *tabicons* folder of the sample code archive, which can be downloaded from the following URL:

https://www.payloadbooks.com/product/ios17xcode/

The icon archive contains two PNG format icon images named *first.png* and *second.png*.

Select the *Assets* entry in the Project Navigator panel, right-click in the left-hand panel of the asset catalog screen, and select the *Import…* menu option. Then, in the file selection dialog, navigate to and select the tabicons folder and click on the *Open* button to import the images into a new image set.

With the icons added to the project, click on the placeholder icon in the tab bar of the Tab1ViewController, and in the Attributes Inspector panel, use the *Image* drop-down menu to select *first* as the image file:

Figure 27-5

Note that it is also possible to select one of several built-in images using the *System Item* attribute menu and to display a different image when a tab is selected by providing an image for the *Selected Image* setting.

Perform the same steps to specify *second* as the image file for Tab2ViewController.

27.9 Building and Running the App

The design and implementation of the example app are complete, and all that remains is to build and run it. Click on the run button in the Xcode toolbar and wait for the code to compile and the app to launch within the iOS Simulator environment. The app should appear with the Tab1ViewController active and the two tab items in the tab bar visible across the bottom of the screen. Clicking on the Screen Two tab will navigate to the Tab2ViewController view:

Figure 27-6

27.10 Summary

The Storyboard feature of Xcode allows Tab Bar-based navigation to be quickly and easily built into apps. Perhaps the most significant point is that the example project created in this chapter was implemented without writing a single line of Swift code.

28. An Overview of iOS 17 Table Views and Xcode 15 Storyboards

If you have spent an appreciable amount of time using iOS, the chances are good that you have interacted with a UIKit Table View object. This is because table Views are the cornerstone of the navigation system for many iOS apps. For example, both the iPhone *Mail* and *Settings* apps extensively use Table Views to present information to users in a list format and to enable users to drill down to more detailed information by selecting a particular list item.

Historically, table views have been one of the more complex areas of iOS user interface implementation. In recognition of this, Apple introduced ways to implement table views using the Xcode Storyboard feature.

This chapter aims to provide an overview of the concept of the UITableView class and an introduction to how storyboards can be used to ease the table view implementation process. Once these basics have been covered, a series of chapters, starting with *"Using Xcode 15 Storyboards to Build Dynamic TableViews"*, will work through the creation of example projects intended to demonstrate the use of storyboards in the context of table views.

28.1 An Overview of the Table View

Table Views present the user with data in a list format and are represented by the UITableView class of the UIKit framework. The data is presented in rows, whereby the content of each row is implemented in the form of a UITableViewCell object. By default, each table cell can display a text label (textLabel), a subtitle (detailedTextLabel), and an image (imageView). More complex cells can be created by either adding subviews to the cell or subclassing UITableViewCell and adding your own custom functionality and appearance.

28.2 Static vs. Dynamic Table Views

When implementing table views using an Xcode storyboard, it is important to understand the distinction between *static* and *dynamic* tables. Static tables are helpful in situations when a fixed number of rows need to be displayed in a table. For example, the settings page for an app would typically have a predetermined number of configuration options and would be an ideal candidate for a static table.

On the other hand, dynamic tables (also known as prototype-based tables) are intended for use when a variable number of rows need to be displayed from a data source. Within the storyboard editor, Xcode allows you to visually design a prototype table cell which will then be replicated in the dynamic table view at runtime to display data to the user.

28.3 The Table View Delegate and dataSource

Each table view in an app must have a *delegate* and a *dataSource* associated with it (except for static tables, which do not have a data source). The dataSource implements the UITableViewDataSource protocol, which consists of several methods that define title information, how many rows of data are to be displayed, how the data is divided into different sections, and, most importantly, supplies the table view with the cell objects to be displayed. The delegate implements the UITableViewDelegate protocol and provides additional control over the table view's appearance and functionality, including detecting when a user touches a specific row, defining custom row heights and indentations, and implementing row deletion and editing functions.

28.4 Table View Styles

Table views may be configured to use either *plain* or *grouped* style. In the grouped style, the rows are grouped in sections separated by optional headers and footers. For example, Figure 28-1 shows a table view configured to use the grouped style:

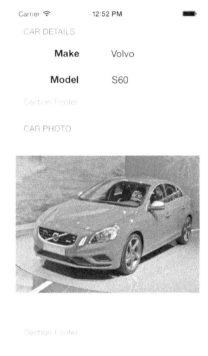

Figure 28-1

In the case of the plain style, the items are listed without separation and using the entire width of the display:

Figure 28-2

Table Views using plain style can also be *indexed*, whereby rows are organized into groups according to specified criteria, such as alphabetical or numerical sorting.

28.5 Self-Sizing Table Cells

With self-sizing cells, each row of a table is sized according to the content of the corresponding cell based on the Auto Layout constraints applied to the cell contents. Self-sizing will be demonstrated in the next chapter entitled *"Using Xcode 15 Storyboards to Build Dynamic TableViews"* but it is particularly important when the labels in a cell are configured to use dynamic type.

28.6 Dynamic Type

iOS allows users to select a preferred text size that apps must adopt when displaying text. The current text size can be configured on a device via the *Settings -> Display & Brightness -> Text Size* screen, which provides a slider to adjust the font size, as shown in Figure 28-3:

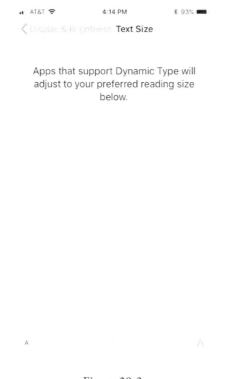

Figure 28-3

Almost without exception, the built-in iOS apps adopt the font size setting selected by the user when displaying text. Apple recommends that third-party apps also conform to the user's text size selection, and since iOS 8, support for dynamic type has been extended to table views. This is achieved by specifying a preferred text style setting for the font of any custom labels in a cell. iOS specifies various preferred text styles for this purpose, including headings, sub-headings, body, captions, and footnotes. The text style used by a label can be configured using Interface Builder or in code. To configure the text style in Interface Builder, select the label, display the Attributes Inspector, and click on the "T" button in the font setting field, as demonstrated in Figure 28-4. Next, from the drop-down menu, click on the Font menu button and select an item from the options listed under the *Text Styles* heading:

Figure 28-4

The preferred font is configured in code by setting the *preferredFont* property to one of the following pre-configured text style values:

- UIFontTextStyle.headline

- UIFontTextStyle.subheadline

- UIFontTextStyle.body

- UIFontTextStyle.callout

- UIFontTextStyle.footnote

- UIFontTextStyle.caption1

- UIFontTextStyle.caption2

The following code, for example, sets a dynamic type font on a label using the headline font style:

```
cell.myLabel.font =
        UIFont.preferredFont(forTextStyle: .headline)
```

The text size selected by a user will dictate the size of any cells containing labels that use dynamic type, hence the importance of using self-sizing to ensure the table rows are displayed using an appropriate height.

28.7 Table View Cell Styles

In addition to the style of the Table View itself, different styles may also be specified for the individual table cells (unless custom table cells are being used). The iOS SDK currently supports four different cell styles:

- **UITableViewCellStyle.default** – only the labelText in black and left aligned.

- **UITableViewCellStyle.subtitle** – labelText in black and left aligned with the detailLabelText positioned beneath it in a smaller font using a gray foreground.

- **UITableViewCellStyle.value1** – labelText in black, left aligned, and the smaller detailLabelText in blue, on the same line and right-aligned.

- **UITableViewCellStyle.value2** – labelText in blue on the left side of the cell, right aligned and detailedLabelText on the right of the cell, left aligned and black.

28.8 Table View Cell Reuse

At the basic level, a table view comprises a UITableView object and a UITableViewCell for each row to be displayed. The code for a typical iOS app using a table view will not directly create instances of a cell. The reasoning behind this becomes evident when performance and memory requirements are considered. Consider, for example, a table view that is required to display 1000 photo images. It can be assumed with a reasonable degree of certainty that only a small percentage of cells will be visible to the user at any one time. If the app were permitted to create each 1000 cells in advance, the device would quickly run into memory and performance limitations.

Instead, the app begins by registering with the table view object the class to be used for cell objects and the *reuse identifier* previously assigned to that class. If the cell class was written in code, the registration is performed using the *register* method of the UITableView object. For example:

```
self.tableView.register(AttractionTableViewCell.self,
                forCellReuseIdentifier: "MyTableCell")
```

If the cell is contained within an Interface Builder NIB file, the *registerNib* method is used instead.

Perhaps the most critical point to remember from this chapter is that if the cell is created using prototypes within a storyboard, it is unnecessary to register the class. Doing so will prevent the cell or view from appearing when the app runs.

As the table view initializes, it calls the *tableView(_:cellForRowAt:)* method of the datasource class passing through the index path for which a cell object is required. This method will then call the *dequeueReusableCell* method of the table view object, passing through both the index path and the reuse ID assigned to the cell class when it was registered to find out if there is a reusable cell object in the queue that can be used for this new cell. Since this is the initialization phase and no cells have been deemed eligible for reuse, the method will create a new cell and return it. Once all the visible cells have been created, the table view will stop asking for more cells. The code for the *tableView(_:cellForRowAt:)* method will typically read as follows (the code to customize the cell before returning it will be implementation specific):

```
override func tableView(_ tableView: UITableView, cellForRowAt indexPath:
    IndexPath) -> UITableViewCell {

    let cell =
        self.tableView.dequeueReusableCell(withIdentifier:
            "MyTableCell", for: indexPath)
                as! MyTableViewCell

    // Configure the cell here
    return cell
}
```

As the user scrolls through the table view, some cells will move out of the visible frame. When this happens, the table view places them on the reuse queue. As cells are moving out of view, new ones will likely come into view. For each cell moving into the view area, the table view will call *tableView(_:cellForRowAt:)*. This time, however, when a call to the *dequeueReusableCell* method is made, it is most likely that an existing cell object will be returned from the reuse queue, thereby avoiding the necessity to create a new object.

28.9 Table View Swipe Actions

The TableView delegate protocol provides delegate methods that allow the app to respond to left and right swipes over table rows by displaying an action button. Figure 28-5, for example, shows a leading swipe action configured with an action titled "Share":

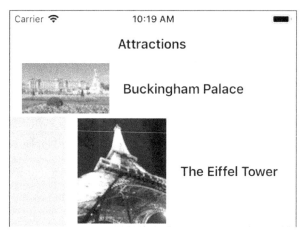

Figure 28-5

The two delegate methods are declared as follows:

```
override func tableView(_ tableView: UITableView,
  leadingSwipeActionsConfigurationForRowAt indexPath: IndexPath) ->
   UISwipeActionsConfiguration? {


}


override func tableView(_ tableView: UITableView,
 trailingSwipeActionsConfigurationForRowAt indexPath: IndexPath) ->
  UISwipeActionsConfiguration? {
}
```

The methods return a UISwipeActionsConfiguration object configured with the action to be performed. This consists of a UIContextualAction object configured with a style (either *destructive* or *normal*), the title to appear in the action, and a completion handler to be called when the user taps the action button, for example:

```
override func tableView(_ tableView: UITableView,
 leadingSwipeActionsConfigurationForRowAt indexPath: IndexPath) ->
  UISwipeActionsConfiguration? {

   let configuration = UISwipeActionsConfiguration(actions: [
       UIContextualAction(style: .normal, title: "Share",
         handler: { (action, view, completionHandler) in

           // Code here will be executed when the user selects the action

           completionHandler(true)
```

```
        })
    ])
    return configuration
}
```

Destructive actions appear in red when displayed and remove the corresponding row from the table view when selected, while normal actions appear in gray and do not remove the row.

28.10 Summary

While table views provide a popular mechanism for displaying data and implementing view navigation within apps, implementation has historically been a complex process. That changed with the introduction of storyboard support in Xcode. Xcode provides a mechanism for visually implementing a considerable amount of Table View functionality with minimal coding. Such table views can be either *static* or *dynamic* depending on the requirements of the table and the nature of the data being displayed.

The text within a table cell should be configured using text styles rather than specific font settings. This allows the text to appear in accordance with the user's device-wide text preferences as defined in the Settings app.

iOS also supports swipe actions within TableViews, allowing options to be presented when the user swipes left or right on a table cell.

29. Using Xcode 15 Storyboards to Build Dynamic TableViews

One of the most powerful features of Xcode storyboards is the implementation of table views through prototype table cells. Prototype cells allow the developer to visually design the user interface elements that will appear in a table cell (such as labels, images, etc.) and then replicate that prototype cell on demand within the table view of the running app. Before the introduction of Storyboards, this would have involved a considerable amount of coding work combined with trial and error.

This chapter aims to work through a detailed example to demonstrate dynamic table view creation within a storyboard using table view prototype cells. Once this topic has been covered, the next chapter (entitled *"Implementing iOS 17 TableView Navigation using Storyboards"*) will explore the implementation of table view navigation and data passing between scenes using storyboards.

29.1 Creating the Example Project

Start Xcode and create an iOS App project named TableViewStory with the Swift programming language option selected.

A review of the files in the project navigator panel will reveal that, as requested, Xcode has created a view controller subclass for us named ViewController. In addition, this view controller is represented within the Storyboard file, the content of which may be viewed by selecting the *Main.storyboard* file.

To fully understand how to create a Storyboard-based TableView app, we will start with a clean slate by removing the view controller added for us by Xcode. Within the storyboard canvas, select the View Controller scene to highlight it in blue, and press the Delete key on the keyboard. Next, select and delete the corresponding *ViewController.swift* file from the project navigator panel. Finally, select the option to move the file to the trash in the resulting panel.

At this point, we have a template project consisting solely of a storyboard file and the standard app delegate code file. We are ready to build a storyboard-based app using the UITableView and UITableViewCell classes.

29.2 Adding the TableView Controller to the Storyboard

From the user's perspective, the entry point into this app will be a table view containing a list of tourist attractions, with each table view cell containing the attraction's name and corresponding image. As such, we will need to add a Table View Controller instance to the storyboard file. Select the *Main.storyboard* file so that the canvas appears in the center of the Xcode window. Display the Library panel, drag a Table View Controller object, and drop it onto the storyboard canvas as illustrated in Figure 29-1:

Figure 29-1

With the new view controller selected in the storyboard, display the Attributes Inspector and enable the *Is initial View Controller* attribute, as shown in Figure 29-2. Without this setting, the system will not know which view controller to display when the app launches.

Figure 29-2

Within the storyboard, we now have a table view controller instance. Within this instance is a prototype table view cell that we can configure to design the cells for our table. At the moment, these are generic UITableViewCell and UITableViewController classes that do not give us much in the way of control within our app code. So that we can extend the functionality of these instances, we need to declare them as subclasses of UITableViewController and UITableViewCell, respectively. Before doing so, however, we need to create those subclasses.

29.3 Creating the UITableViewController and UITableViewCell Subclasses

We will declare the Table View Controller instance within our storyboard as being a subclass of UITableViewController named AttractionTableViewController. Currently, this subclass does not exist within our project, so we need to create it before proceeding. To achieve this, select the *File -> New -> File...* menu option, and in the resulting panel, select the option to create a new iOS Source Cocoa Touch class. Click *Next* and on the subsequent screen, name the class AttractionTableViewController and change the *Subclass of* menu to *UITableViewController*. Ensure that the *Also create XIB file* option is turned off and click *Next*. Select a location into which to generate the new class files before clicking the *Create* button.

Within the Table View Controller added to the storyboard in the previous section, Xcode also added a prototype table cell. Later in this chapter, we will add a label and an image view object to this cell. To extend this class, it is necessary to, once again, create a subclass. Perform this step by selecting the *File -> New -> File...* menu option. Within the new file dialog, select *Cocoa Touch Class* and click *Next*. On the following screen, name the new class *AttractionTableViewCell*, change the *Subclass of* menu to *UITableViewCell* and proceed with the class creation. Select a location into which to generate the new class files and click on *Create*.

Next, the items in the storyboard need to be configured to be instances of these subclasses. Begin by selecting the *Main.storyboard* file and the Table View Controller scene, highlighting it in blue. Within the Identity Inspector panel, use the *Class* drop-down menu to change the class from *UITableViewController* to *AttractionTableViewController,* as illustrated in Figure 29-3:

Figure 29-3

Similarly, select the prototype table cell within the table view controller storyboard scene and change the class from *UITableViewCell* to the new *AttractionTableViewCell* subclass.

With the appropriate subclasses created and associated with the objects in the storyboard, the next step is to design the prototype cell.

29.4 Declaring the Cell Reuse Identifier

Later in the chapter, some code will be added to the project to replicate instances of the prototype table cell. This will require that the cell be assigned a reuse identifier. With the storyboard still visible in Xcode, select the prototype table cell and display the Attributes Inspector. Within the inspector, change the *Identifier* field to *AttractionTableCell*:

Figure 29-4

29.5 Designing a Storyboard UITableView Prototype Cell

Table Views are made up of multiple cells, each of which is either an instance of the UITableViewCell class or a subclass thereof. A helpful feature of storyboarding allows the developer to visually construct the user interface elements that are to appear in the table cells and then replicate that cell at runtime. For this example, each table cell needs to display an image view and a label which, in turn, will be connected to outlets that we will later declare in the AttractionTableViewCell subclass. Much like any other Interface Builder layout, components may be dragged from the Library panel and dropped onto a scene within the storyboard. With this in mind, drag a Label and an Image View object onto the prototype table cell. Resize and position the items so that the cell layout resembles that illustrated in Figure 29-5, making sure to stretch the label object to extend toward the right-hand edge of the cell.

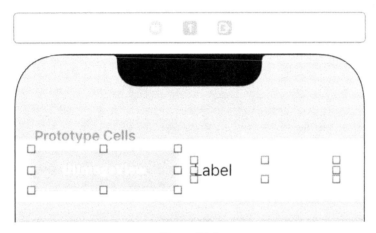

Figure 29-5

Select the Image View and, using the Auto Layout *Add New Constraints* menu, set *Spacing to nearest neighbor* constraints on the view's top, left, and bottom edges with the Constrain to margins option switched off. Before adding the constraints, also enable the Width constraint.

Select the Label view, display the Auto Layout Align menu and add a *Vertically in Container* constraint to the view. With the Label still selected, display the *Add New Constraints* menu and add a *Spacing to nearest neighbor* constraint on the left and right-hand edges of the view with the Constrain to margins option off.

Having configured the storyboard elements for the table view portion of the app, it is time to begin modifying the table view and cell subclasses.

29.6 Modifying the AttractionTableViewCell Class

Within the storyboard file, a label and an image view were added to the prototype cell, which, in turn, has been declared as an instance of our new AttractionTableViewCell class. We must establish two outlets connected to the objects in the storyboard scene to manipulate these user interface objects from within our code. Begin, therefore, by selecting the image view object, displaying the Assistant Editor, and making sure that it is displaying the content of the *AttractionTableViewCell.swift* file. If it is not, use the bar across the top of the Assistant Editor panel to select this file:

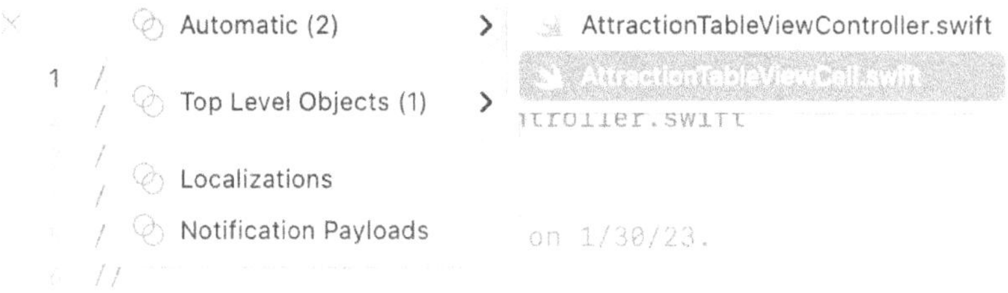

Figure 29-6

Right-click on the image view object in the prototype table cell and drag the resulting line to a point just below the class declaration line in the Assistant Editor window. Release the line and use the connection panel to establish an outlet named *attractionImage*.

Repeat these steps to establish an outlet for the label named *attractionLabel*.

29.7 Creating the Table View Datasource

Dynamic Table Views require a datasource to display the user's data within the cells. By default, Xcode has designated the AttractionTableViewController class as the *datasource* for the table view controller in the storyboard. Consequently, within this class, we can build a simple data model for our app consisting of several arrays. The first step is to declare these as properties in the *AttractionTableViewController.swift* file:

```
import UIKit

class AttractionTableViewController: UITableViewController {

    var attractionImages = [String]()
    var attractionNames = [String]()
    var webAddresses = [String]()
.
.
.
```

In addition, the arrays need to be initialized with some data when the app has loaded, making the *viewDidLoad* method an ideal location. Remaining within the *AttractionTableViewController.swift* file, add a method named initialize and call it from the *viewDidLoad* method as outlined in the following code fragment:

```
override func viewDidLoad() {
    super.viewDidLoad()
    initialize()
}

func initialize() {
    attractionNames = ["Buckingham Palace",
                       "The Eiffel Tower",
                       "The Grand Canyon",
                       "Windsor Castle",
                       "Empire State Building"]
```

```
webAddresses = ["https://en.wikipedia.org/wiki/Buckingham_Palace",
                "https://en.wikipedia.org/wiki/Eiffel_Tower",
                "https://en.wikipedia.org/wiki/Grand_Canyon",
                "https://en.wikipedia.org/wiki/Windsor_Castle",
                "https://en.wikipedia.org/wiki/Empire_State_Building"]

attractionImages = ["buckingham_palace.jpg",
                    "eiffel_tower.jpg",
                    "grand_canyon.jpg",
                    "windsor_castle.jpg",
                    "empire_state_building.jpg"]

tableView.estimatedRowHeight = 50
}
```

In addition to initializing the arrays, the code also sets an estimated row height for the table view. This will prevent the row heights from collapsing when table view navigation is added later in the tutorial and also improves the performance of the table rendering.

Several methods must be implemented for a class to act as the datasource for a table view controller. The table view object will call these methods to obtain information about the table and the table cell objects to display. When we created the AttractionTableViewController class, we specified that it was to be a subclass of UITableViewController. As a result, Xcode created templates of these data source methods for us within the *AttractionTableViewController.swift* file. To locate these template datasource methods, scroll down the file until the *// MARK: – Table view data source* marker comes into view. The first template method, named *numberOfSections*, must return the number of sections in the table. For this example, we only need one section, so we will return a value of 1 (also note that the #warning line needs to be removed):

```
override func numberOfSections(in tableView: UITableView) -> Int {
    return 1
}
```

The next method is required to return the number of rows to be displayed in the table. This is equivalent to the number of items in our *attractionNames* array, so it can be modified as follows:

```
override func tableView(tableView: UITableView,
            numberOfRowsInSection section: Int) -> Int {
    return attractionNames.count
}
```

The above code returns the *count* property of the *attractionNames* array object to obtain the number of items in the array and returns that value to the table view.

The final datasource method that needs to be modified is *tableView(_:cellForRowAt:)*. Each time the table view controller needs a new cell to display, it will call this method and pass through an index value indicating the row for which a cell object is required. This method's responsibility is to return an instance of our *AttractionTableViewCell* class and extract the correct attraction name and image file name from the data arrays based on the index value passed through to the method. The code will then set those values on the appropriate outlets on the AttractionTableViewCell object. Begin by removing the comment markers (/* and */) from around the template of this method and then re-write the method so that it reads as follows:

```
override func tableView(_ tableView: UITableView,
```

```
                cellForRowAt indexPath: IndexPath) -> UITableViewCell {

    let cell =
        self.tableView.dequeueReusableCell(withIdentifier:
        "AttractionTableCell", for: indexPath)
            as! AttractionTableViewCell

    let row = indexPath.row
    cell.attractionLabel.font =
        UIFont.preferredFont(forTextStyle: UIFont.TextStyle.headline)
    cell.attractionLabel.text = attractionNames[row]
    cell.attractionImage.image = UIImage(named: attractionImages[row])
    return cell
}
```

Before proceeding with this tutorial, we need to take some time to deconstruct this code to explain what is happening.

The code begins by calling the *dequeueReusableCell(withIdentifier:)* method of the table view object passing through the cell identifier assigned to the cell (AttractionTableCell) and index path as arguments. The system will find out if an AttractionTableViewCell cell object is available for reuse or create a new one and return it to the method:

```
let cell =
    self.tableView.dequeueReusableCell(withIdentifier:
        "AttractionTableCell", for: indexPath)
            as! AttractionTableViewCell
```

Having either created a new cell or obtained an existing reusable cell, the code simply uses the outlets previously added to the AttractionTableViewCell class to set the label with the attraction name, using the row from the index path as an index into the data array. Because we want the text displayed on the label to reflect the preferred font size selected by the user within the Settings app, the font on the label is set to use the preferred font for headline text.

The code then creates a new UIImage object configured with the image of the current attraction and assigns it to the image view outlet. Finally, the method returns the modified cell object to the table view:

```
let row = indexPath.row
cell.attractionLabel.font =
        UIFont.preferredFont(forTextStyle: UIFont.TextStyle.headline)
cell.attractionLabel.text = attractionNames[row]
cell.attractionImage.image = UIImage(named: attractionImages[row])
return cell
```

29.8 Downloading and Adding the Image Files

Before a test run of the app can be performed, the image files referenced in the code need to be added to the project. An archive containing the images may be found in the *attractionImages* folder of the code sample archive, which can be downloaded from the following URL:

https://www.payloadbooks.com/product/ios17xcode/

Select the *Assets* entry in the Project Navigator panel, right-click in the left-hand panel of the asset catalog screen, and select the *Import...* menu option. Then, navigate to and select the attractionImages folder in the file selection dialog and click on the *Open* button to import the images into a new image set.

29.9 Compiling and Running the App

Now that the storyboard work and code modifications are complete, the next step in this chapter is to run the app by clicking on the run button in the Xcode toolbar. Once the code has been compiled, the app will launch and execute within an iOS Simulator session, as illustrated in Figure 29-7.

Clearly, the table view has been populated with multiple instances of our prototype table view cell, each of which has been customized through outlets to display different text and images. Note that the self-sizing rows feature has automatically caused the rows to size to accommodate the attraction images.

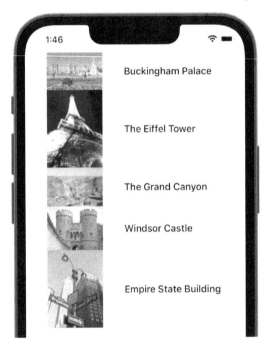

Figure 29-7

Verify that the preferred font size code works by running the app on a physical iOS device, displaying *Settings -> Display & Brightness -> Text Size,* and dragging the slider to change the font size. If using the Simulator, use the slider on the *Settings -> Accessibility -> Larger Text Size* screen. Stop and restart the app and note that the attraction names are now displayed using the newly selected font size.

29.10 Handling TableView Swipe Gestures

The final task in this chapter is to enhance the app so that the user can swipe left on a table row to reveal a delete button that will remove that row from the table when tapped. This will involve the addition of a table view trailing swipe delegate method to the AttractionTableViewController class as follows:

```
override func tableView(_ tableView: UITableView,
  trailingSwipeActionsConfigurationForRowAt indexPath: IndexPath) ->
    UISwipeActionsConfiguration? {

  let configuration = UISwipeActionsConfiguration(actions: [
        UIContextualAction(style: .destructive, title: "Delete",
```

```
            handler: { (action, view, completionHandler) in

                let row = indexPath.row
                self.attractionNames.remove(at: row)
                self.attractionImages.remove(at: row)
                self.webAddresses.remove(at: row)
                completionHandler(true)
                tableView.reloadData()
            })
        ])
    return configuration
}
```

The code within the method creates a new UISwipeActionsConfiguration instance configured with a destructive contextual action with the title set to "Delete". Declaring the action as destructive ensures that the table view will remove the entry from the table when the user taps the Delete button. Although this will have removed the visual representation of the row in the table view, the entry will still exist in the data model, causing the row to reappear the next time the table reloads. To address this, the method implements a completion handler to be called when the deletion occurs. This handler identifies the swiped row and removes the matching data model array entries.

Build and run the app one final time and swipe left on one of the rows to reveal the delete option (Figure 29-8). Tap the delete button to remove the item from the list.

Figure 29-8

The next step, which will be outlined in the following chapter entitled "*Implementing iOS 17 TableView Navigation using Storyboards*", will be to use the storyboard to add navigation capabilities to the app so that selecting a row from the table results in a detail scene appearing to the user.

29.11 Summary

The storyboard feature of Xcode significantly eases the process of creating complex table view-based interfaces within iOS apps. Arguably the most significant feature is the ability to visually design the appearance of a table view cell and then have that cell automatically replicated at run time to display information to the user in table form. iOS also includes support for automatic table cell sizing and the adoption of the user's preferred font setting within table views. Finally, iOS also includes support for swipe interactions within table views. This chapter demonstrated the implementation of a destructive trailing swipe handler designed to allow the user to delete rows from a table view.

30. Implementing iOS 17 TableView Navigation using Storyboards

The objective of this chapter is to extend the app created in the previous chapter (entitled *"Using Xcode 15 Storyboards to Build Dynamic TableViews"*) and, in so doing, demonstrate the steps involved in implementing table view navigation within a storyboard. In other words, we will modify the attractions example from the previous chapter such that selecting a row from the table view displays a second scene in which a web page providing information about the chosen location will be displayed to the user. As part of this exercise, we will also explore data transfer between different scenes in a storyboard.

30.1 Understanding the Navigation Controller

Navigation-based apps present a hierarchical approach to displaying information to the user. Such apps typically take the form of a navigation bar (UINavigationBar) and a series of Table based views (UITableView). Selecting an item from the table list causes the view associated with that selection to be displayed. The navigation bar will display a title corresponding to the currently displayed view and a button that returns the user to the previous view when selected. For an example of this concept in action, spend some time using the iPhone *Mail* or *Music* apps.

When developing a navigation-based app, the central component of the architecture is the *navigation controller*. In addition, each scene has a view and a corresponding view controller. The navigation controller maintains a stack of these view controllers. When a new view is displayed, it is *pushed* onto the navigation controller's stack and becomes the currently active controller. The navigation controller automatically displays the navigation bar and the "back" button. When the user selects the button in the navigation bar to move back to the previous level, that view controller is *popped* off the stack, and the view controller beneath it moves to the top, becoming the currently active controller.

The view controller for the first table view that appears when the app is started is called the *root view controller*. The root view controller cannot be popped off the navigation controller stack.

30.2 Adding the New Scene to the Storyboard

For this example, we will add a new View Controller to our storyboard to act as the second scene. With this in mind, begin by loading the *TableViewStory* project created in the previous chapter into Xcode.

Once the project has loaded, we will need to add a new UIViewController subclass to our project files, so select the *File -> New -> File...* menu item and choose the *Cocoa Touch Class* option from the *iOS* category. On the options screen, ensure that the *Subclass of* menu is set to UIViewController, name the new class *AttractionDetailViewController*, and make sure that the *Also create XIB file* option is switched off. Click *Next* before clicking on *Create*.

Next, select the *Main.storyboard* file from the project navigator to make the storyboard canvas visible. Then, from the Library, select a View Controller and drag and drop it to the right of the existing table view controller as outlined in Figure 30-1. With the new view controller added, select it, display the Identity inspector, and change the class setting from UIViewController to AttractionDetailViewController.

Figure 30-1

The detail scene has now been added and assigned to the newly created subclass, where code can be added to bring the scene to life.

30.3 Adding a Navigation Controller

Once the app is completed, selecting a row from the Table View will trigger a segue to display the detail view controller. The detail view will contain a button that, when selected by the user, will navigate back to the table view. This functionality will be made possible by adding a Navigation Controller to the storyboard. This can be added by selecting the Attraction Table View Controller scene in the storyboard so that it highlights in blue and then selecting the Xcode *Editor -> Embed In -> Navigation Controller* menu option. Once performed, the storyboard will appear as outlined in Figure 30-2:

Figure 30-2

30.4 Establishing the Storyboard Segue

When the user selects a row within the table view, a segue must be triggered to display the attraction detail view controller. To establish this segue, right-click on the *prototype cell* in the Attraction Table View Controller scene and drag the resulting line to the Attraction Detail View Controller scene. Upon releasing the line, select the *Show* option from the *Selection Segue* section of the resulting menu. The storyboard will update to display a segue connection between the table view cell and the view controller. We will need to reference this segue in code implemented later in this chapter. To do so, it must, therefore, be given an identifier. Click on the segue connection between Attraction Table View Controller and Attraction Detail View Controller, display the Attributes Inspector (*View -> Utilities -> Show Attributes Inspector*), and change the Identifier value to *ShowAttractionDetails*.

In addition, a toolbar should have appeared in both scenes. Click in the Attraction Table View Controller toolbar area to select the Navigation Item component, display the Attributes inspector panel and change the title property to "Attractions". Next, drag a Navigation Item view from the Library and drop it onto the toolbar of the Attraction Detail View Controller. Select the new item and change the title property in the Attributes inspector to "Attraction Details":

Figure 30-3

Build and run the app and note that selecting a row in the table view now displays the second view controller, which, in turn, contains a button in the toolbar to return to the "Attractions" table view. Clearly, we need to work on the AttractionDetailViewController class to display information about the selected tourist location in the view.

30.5 Modifying the AttractionDetailViewController Class

For this example app, the attraction detail view will display a WebKit View loaded with a web page relating to the selected tourist attraction. To achieve this, the class will need a WKWebView object which will later be added to the view.

In addition to the WebKit View, the class will also need an internal data model that contains the URL of the web page to be displayed. It will be the job of the table view controller to update this variable before the segue occurs to reflect the selected attraction. For the sake of simplicity, the data model will take the form of a String object. Select the *AttractionDetailViewController.swift* file and modify it as follows to declare this variable and also to import the WebKit framework, which will be used in the next step:

```
import UIKit
import WebKit


class AttractionDetailViewController: UIViewController {


    var webSite: String?
.
.
```

The next step is to add the WebKit View to the view controller. Select the storyboard file in the Project Navigator, and drag and drop a WebKit View from the Library panel onto the Attraction Detail scene. Resize the view so that it fills the entire scene area, as illustrated in Figure 30-4:

Figure 30-4

With the WebKit View selected in the storyboard canvas, display the Auto Layout *Add New Constraints* menu and add *Spacing to nearest neighbor* constraints on all four sides of the view with the *Constrain to margins* option disabled.

Display the Assistant Editor panel and verify that the editor is displaying the contents of the *AttractionDetailViewController.swift* file. Right-click on the WebKit View and drag to a position just below the class declaration line in the Assistant Editor. Release the line, and in the resulting connection dialog, establish an outlet connection named *webView*.

When the detail view appears, the WebKit View will need to load the web page referenced by the *webSite* string variable. This can be achieved by adding code to the *viewDidLoad* method of the *AttractionDetailViewController. swift* file as follows:

```
override func viewDidLoad() {
    super.viewDidLoad()

    if let address = webSite,
        let webURL = URL(string: address) {
        let urlRequest = URLRequest(url: webURL)
        webView.load(urlRequest)
    }
}
```

30.6 Using prepare(for segue:) to Pass Data between Storyboard Scenes

The last step in the implementation of this project is to add code so that the data model contained within the AttractionDetailViewController class is updated with the URL of the selected attraction when the user touches a table view row. As previously outlined in *"Using Xcode 15 Storyboards to Build Dynamic TableViews"*, the *prepare(for segue:)* method on an originating scene is called before a segue is performed. This is the ideal place to add code to pass data between source and destination scenes. The *prepare(for segue:)* method needs to be added to the *AttractionTableViewController.swift* file as outlined in the following code fragment:

```
override func prepare(for segue: UIStoryboardSegue, sender: Any?) {
    if segue.identifier == "ShowAttractionDetails" {
        let detailViewController = segue.destination
            as! AttractionDetailViewController
        let myIndexPath = self.tableView.indexPathForSelectedRow!
        let row = myIndexPath.row
        detailViewController.webSite = webAddresses[row]
    }
}
```

The first task performed by this method is to check that the triggering segue is the *ShowAttractionDetails* segue we added to the storyboard. Having verified that to be the case, the code then obtains a reference to the view controller of the destination scene (in this case, an instance of our AttractionDetailViewController class). The table view object is then interrogated to find out the index of the selected row, which, in turn, is used to prime the URL string variable in the AttractionDetailViewController instance.

30.7 Testing the App

Compile and run the app, click on the run button in the Xcode toolbar, and wait for the app to launch. Select an entry from the table and watch as the second view controller appears and loads the appropriate web page:

Figure 30-5

30.8 Customizing the Navigation Title Size

Including a navigation controller in this example caused a navigation bar to appear on each scene within the app. By default, this includes a title navigation item and, when necessary, a "back" button to return to the previous view controller. Many of the built-in apps provided with iOS now use a larger text size for these titles. The title text size within the navigation bar can be increased to conform with the general look and feel of the standard iOS apps by setting the *prefersLargeTitles* property on the navigation bar to *true*. To see this in action, modify the *initialize* method within the *AttractionTableViewController.swift* file to set this property:

```
func initialize() {
.

.

    navigationController?.navigationBar.prefersLargeTitles = true
}
```

Rerun the app and note that the title now appears in the larger text:

Attractions

Buckingham Palace

Figure 30-6

By default, this change will propagate down to any other view controllers displayed by the navigation controller. Selecting an entry from the table, for example, will show that the AttractionDetailViewController navigation bar has inherited the larger title property:

‹ Attractions

Attraction Details

☰ WIKIPEDIA   Q

Buckingham Palace

Figure 30-7

To prevent the setting from applying to this view controller, a property is available on the navigation bar's navigation item, which specifies the display mode for the title. Modify the *viewDidLoad* method of the *AttractionDetailViewController.swift* file to set this property so that the larger title is not used on this screen:

```
override func viewDidLoad() {
    super.viewDidLoad()

    navigationItem.largeTitleDisplayMode = .never
    if let address = webSite {
        let webURL = URL(string: address)
        let urlRequest = URLRequest(url: webURL!)
```

```
            webView.load(urlRequest)
        }
}
```

The full range of settings for this property are as follows:

- **automatic** – The default behavior. This causes the navigation item to inherit the size setting from the previous navigation bar item.

- **always** – The navigation item title always uses large text.

- **never** – The title always uses smaller text.

30.9 Summary

A key component of implementing table view navigation using storyboards involves using segues and transferring data between scenes. In this chapter, we used a segue to display a second scene based on table view row selections. The use of the *prepare(for segue:)* method as a mechanism for passing data during a segue has also been explored and demonstrated.

When a navigation controller is embedded into a storyboard, a navigation bar appears at the top of each view controller scene. The title size displayed in this navigation bar can be increased by setting a property on the navigation bar. To prevent this larger title from being inherited by other scenes in the navigation stack, change the display mode on the corresponding navigation item.

31. Integrating Search using the iOS UISearchController

The previous chapters have covered creating a table view using prototype cells and introduced table view navigation using a navigation controller. In this final chapter dedicated to table views and table view navigation, we will cover the integration of a search bar into the navigation bar of the TableViewStory app created in the earlier chapters.

31.1 Introducing the UISearchController Class

The UISearchController class is designed to be used alongside existing view controllers to provide a way to integrate search features into apps. The UISearchController class includes a search bar (UISearchBar) into which the user enters the search text.

The search controller is assigned a *results updater* delegate which must conform to the UISearchResultsUpdating protocol. The *updateSearchResults(for searchController:)* method of this delegate is called repeatedly as the user enters text into the search bar and is responsible for filtering the results. The results updater object is assigned to the search controller via the controller's *searchResultsUpdater* property.

In addition to the results updater, the search controller also needs a view controller to display the search results. The results updater object can also serve as the results view controller, or a separate view controller can be designated for the task via the search controller's *searchViewController* property.

The app can intercept a wide range of notifications relating to the user's interaction with the search bar by assigning classes that conform to the UISearchControllerDelegate and UISearchBarDelegate protocols.

Integrating the search controller into a navigation bar is achieved by assigning the search controller instance to the *searchController* property of the navigation bar's navigation item.

Once all of the configuration criteria have been met, the search bar will appear within the navigation bar, as shown in Figure 31-1:

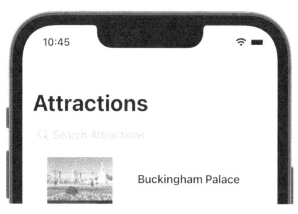

Figure 31-1

31.2 Adding a Search Controller to the TableViewStory Project

To add search to the TableViewStory app, begin by editing the *AttractionTableViewController.swift* file and adding search-related delegate declarations, a UISearchController instance, and a new array into which any matching search results will be stored. Also, add a Boolean variable that will be used to track whether or not the user is currently performing a search:

```
class AttractionTableViewController: UITableViewController,
        UISearchResultsUpdating, UISearchBarDelegate {

    var attractionImages = [String]()
    var attractionNames = [String]()
    var webAddresses = [String]()

    var searching = false
    var matches = [Int]()
    let searchController = UISearchController(searchResultsController: nil)
.
.
```

Next, modify the *initialize* method to designate the table view controller instance as both the search bar and results updater delegates for the search controller. The code also sets properties to display some placeholder text in the search text field and to prevent the search from obscuring the search results view controller:

```
func initialize() {
.
.

    navigationController?.navigationBar.prefersLargeTitles = true

    searchController.searchBar.delegate = self
    searchController.searchResultsUpdater = self
    searchController.obscuresBackgroundDuringPresentation = false
    searchController.searchBar.placeholder = "Search Attractions"
}
```

With the search controller configured, it can now be added to the navigation item, the code for which can be added at the end of the *initialize* method as follows:

```
func initialize() {
.
.

    navigationItem.searchController = searchController
    definesPresentationContext = true
}
```

The *definesPresentationContext* setting is a property of the view controller and ensures that any view controllers displayed from the current controller can navigate back to the current view controller.

31.3 Implementing the updateSearchResults Method

With AttractionTableViewController designated as the results updater delegate, the next step is to implement the *updateSearchResults(for searchController:)* method within this class file as follows:

```
func updateSearchResults(for searchController: UISearchController) {
    if let searchText = searchController.searchBar.text,
                    !searchText.isEmpty {
        matches.removeAll()

        for index in 0..<attractionNames.count {
            if attractionNames[index].lowercased().contains(
                            searchText.lowercased()) {
                matches.append(index)
            }
        }
        searching = true
    } else {
        searching = false
    }
    tableView.reloadData()
}
```

The method is passed a reference to the search controller object, which contains the text entered into the search bar. The code accesses this text property and verifies that it contains text. If no text has been entered, the method sets the *searching* variable to false before returning. This variable will be used later to identify if the table view is currently displaying search results or the full list of attractions.

If search text has been entered, any existing entries in the *matches* array are removed, and a *for* loop is used to iterate through each entry within the *attractionNames* array, checking to see if each name contains the search text. If a match is found, the index value of the matching array item is stored in the *matches* array.

Finally, the *searching* variable is set to true, and the table view data is reloaded.

31.4 Reporting the Number of Table Rows

Since the AttractionTableViewController is being used to display the full list of attractions and the search results, the number of rows displayed will depend on whether or not the controller is in search mode. In search mode, for example, the number of rows will be dictated by the number of items in the *matches* array. Locate the *tableView(_:numberOfRowsInSection:)* table view data source delegate method and modify it as follows:

```
override func tableView(_ tableView: UITableView,
            numberOfRowsInSection section: Int) -> Int {
    return searching ? matches.count : attractionNames.count
}
```

The method now uses a ternary statement to return either the total number of attractions or the number of matches based on the current value of the *searching* variable.

31.5 Modifying the cellForRowAt Method

The next step is ensuring that the tableView(_:cellForRowAt:) method returns the appropriate cells when the view controller displays search results. Specifically, if the user is currently performing a search, the index into the attraction arrays must be taken from the array of index values in the *matches* array. Modify the method so that it reads as follows:

```
override func tableView(_ tableView: UITableView, cellForRowAt indexPath:
            IndexPath) -> UITableViewCell {
```

```
let cell =
    self.tableView.dequeueReusableCell(withIdentifier:
        "AttractionTableCell", for: indexPath)
        as! AttractionTableViewCell

let row = indexPath.row
cell.attractionLabel.font =
    UIFont.preferredFont(forTextStyle: UIFont.TextStyle.headline)

cell.attractionLabel.text =
    searching ? attractionNames[matches[row]] : attractionNames[row]
let imageName =
    searching ? attractionImages[matches[row]] : attractionImages[row]

cell.attractionImage.image = UIImage(named: imageName)

return cell
}
```

Once again, ternary statements are being used to control which row index is used based on the prevailing setting of the *searching* variable.

31.6 Modifying the Trailing Swipe Delegate Method

The previous chapter added a trailing swipe delegate method to the table view class to allow users to delete rows from the table. This method also needs to be updated to allow items to be removed during a search operation. Locate this method in the *AttractionTableViewController.swift* file and modify it as follows:

```
override func tableView(_ tableView: UITableView,
    trailingSwipeActionsConfigurationForRowAt indexPath: IndexPath) ->
        UISwipeActionsConfiguration? {

    let configuration = UISwipeActionsConfiguration(actions: [
            UIContextualAction(style: .destructive,
             title: "Delete", handler: { (action, view, completionHandler) in

                let row = indexPath.row

                if self.searching {
                    self.attractionNames.remove(at: self.matches[row])
                    self.attractionImages.remove(at: self.matches[row])
                    self.webAddresses.remove(at: self.matches[row])
                    self.matches.remove(at: indexPath.row)
                    self.updateSearchResults(for: self.searchController)
                } else {
                    self.attractionNames.remove(at: row)
                    self.attractionImages.remove(at: row)
```

```
                  self.webAddresses.remove(at: row)
             }
             completionHandler(true)
             tableView.reloadData()
         })
    ])
    return configuration
}
```

31.7 Modifying the Detail Segue

When search results are displayed in the table view, the user can still select an attraction and segue to the details view. When the segue is performed, the URL of the selected attraction is assigned to the *webSite* property of the AttractionDetailViewController class so that the correct page is loaded into the WebKit View. The *prepare(forSegue:)* method now needs to be modified to handle the possibility that the user triggered the segue from a list of search results. Locate this method in the AttractionTableViewController class and modify it as follows:

```
override func prepare(for segue: UIStoryboardSegue, sender: Any?) {
    if segue.identifier == "ShowAttractionDetails" {

        let detailViewController = segue.destination
            as! AttractionDetailViewController

        let myIndexPath = self.tableView.indexPathForSelectedRow!
        let row = myIndexPath.row
        detailViewController.webSite =
            searching ? webAddresses[matches[row]] : webAddresses[row]
    }
}
```

31.8 Handling the Search Cancel Button

The final task is to ensure the view controller switches out of search mode when the user clicks the Cancel button in the search bar and displays the complete list of attractions. Since the AttractionTableViewController class has already been declared as implementing the UISearchBarDelegate protocol, all that remains is to add the *searchBarCancelButtonClicked* delegate method in the *AttractionTableViewController.swift* file. All this method needs to do is set the *searching* variable to false and instruct the table view to reload data:

```
func searchBarCancelButtonClicked(_ searchBar: UISearchBar) {
    searching = false
    tableView.reloadData()
}
```

31.9 Testing the Search Controller

Build and run the app, begin entering text into the search bar, and confirm that the list of results narrows with each keystroke to display only matching attractions:

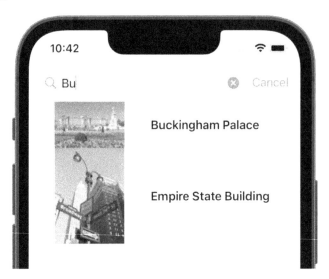

Figure 31-2

Verify that the correct images are displayed for the attraction results and that selecting an attraction from the list presents the correct web page in the detail view controller. Then, return to the search results screen and tap the Cancel button to return to the full list of attractions. Also, confirm that deleting a row from the search results removes the item from the full attraction list.

31.10 Summary

The UISearchController class provides an easy way to integrate a search bar into iOS apps. When assigned to a navigation item, the search bar appears within the navigation bar of view controllers with an embedded navigation controller. At a minimum, a search controller needs delegates to filter the search and display those results. This chapter has worked through an example search controller implementation in the context of a table view and navigation controller configuration.

![Chapter 32](black banner)

32. Working with the iOS 17 Stack View Class

With hindsight, it seems hard to believe, but until the introduction of iOS 9, there was no easy way to build stack-based user interface layouts that would adapt automatically to different screen sizes and changes in device orientation. While such results could eventually be achieved with careful use of size classes and Auto Layout, this was far from simple. That changed with the introduction of the UIStackView class in the iOS 9 SDK.

32.1 Introducing the UIStackView Class

The UIStackView class is a user interface element that allows subviews to be arranged linearly in a column or row orientation. The class extensively uses Auto Layout and automatically sets up many of the Auto Layout constraints needed to provide the required layout behavior. In addition, the class goes beyond simply stacking views, allowing additional Auto Layout constraints to be added to subviews, and providing a range of properties that enable the layout behavior of those subviews to be modified to meet different requirements.

The UIStackView object is available for inclusion within Storyboard scenes simply by dragging and dropping either the *Horizontal Stack View* or *Vertical Stack View* from the Library panel onto the scene canvas. Once added to a scene, subviews are added simply by dragging and dropping the required views onto the stack view.

Existing views in a storyboard scene may be wrapped in a stack view simply by Shift-clicking on the views so that they are all selected before clicking on the Embed In button located at the bottom of the Interface Builder panel, as highlighted in Figure 32-1 and selecting the Stack View option. Interface Builder will decide whether to encapsulate the selected views into a horizontal or vertical stack depending on the layout positions of the views:

Figure 32-1

By default, the stack view will resize to accommodate the subviews as they are added. However, as with any other view type, Auto Layout constraints may be used to constrain and influence the resize behavior of the stack view in relation to the containing view and any other views in the scene layout.

Once added to a storyboard scene, a range of properties is available within the Attributes Inspector to customize the layout behavior of the object.

Stack views may be used to create simple column or row-based layouts or nested within each other to create more complex layouts. Figure 32-2, for example, shows an example layout consisting of a vertical stack view containing three horizontal stack views, each containing a variety of subviews:

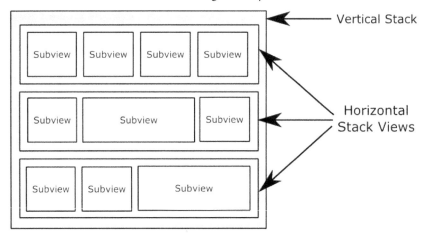

Figure 32-2

UIStackView class instances may also be created and managed from within the code of an iOS app. Stack view instances can be created in code and initialized with an array of subviews. Views may also be inserted and removed dynamically from within code, and the attributes of the stack view changed via a range of properties. The subviews of a stack view object are held in an array that can be accessed via the *arrangedSubviews* property of the stack view instance.

32.2 Understanding Subviews and Arranged Subviews

The UIStackView class contains a property named *subviews*. This is an array containing each of the child views of the stack view object. Figure 32-3, for example, shows the view hierarchy for a stack view with four subviews:

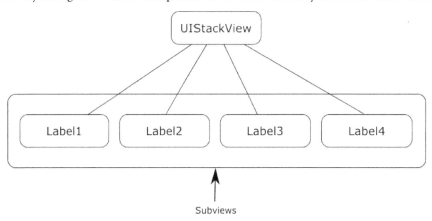

Figure 32-3

At any particular time, however, the stack view will not necessarily be responsible for arranging the layout and positions of all the subviews it contains. The stack view might, for example, only be configured to arrange the Label3 and Label4 views in the above hierarchy. This means that Label1 and Label2 may still be visible within the user interface but will not be positioned within the stack view. Subviews being arranged by the stack view are contained within a second array accessible via the *arrangedSubviews* property. Figure 32-4 shows both the subviews and the subset of the subviews which are currently being arranged by the stack view.

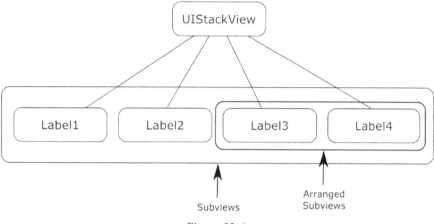

Figure 32-4

As will be outlined later in this chapter, the distinction between subview and arranged subviews is particularly important when removing arranged subviews from a stack view.

32.3 StackView Configuration Options

A range of options is available to customize how the stack view arranges its subviews. These properties are available both from within the Interface Builder Attributes Inspector panel at design time and also to be set dynamically from within the code of the app:

32.3.1 axis

The axis property controls the orientation of the stack in terms of whether the subviews are arranged in a vertical column layout or a horizontal row. When setting this property in code, the axis should be set to UILayoutConstraintAxis.vertical or UILayoutConstraintAxis.horizontal.

32.3.2 distribution

The distribution property dictates how the subviews of the stack view are sized. Options available are as follows:

- **Fill** – The subviews are resized to fill the entire space available along the stack view's axis. In other words, the height of the subviews will be modified to fill the full height of the stack view in a vertical orientation, while the widths will be changed for a stack view in a horizontal orientation. The amount by which each subview is resized relative to the other views can be controlled via the compression resistance and hugging priorities of the views (details of which were covered in the chapter entitled *"An Introduction to Auto Layout in iOS 17"*) and the position of the views in the stack view's arrangedSubviews array.

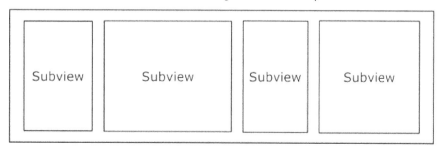

Figure 32-5

- **FillEqually** – The subviews are resized equally to fill the stack view along the view's axis. Therefore, all the subviews in a vertical stack will be equal in height, while the subviews in a horizontal axis orientation will be equal in width.

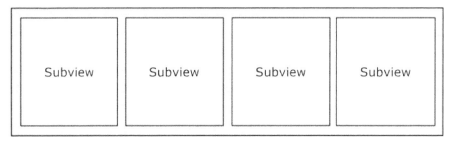

Figure 32-6

- **FillProportionally** – In this mode, the subviews are resized proportionally to their intrinsic content size along the axis of the stack view to fill the width or height of the view.

- **EqualSpacing** – Padding is used to space the subviews equally to fill the stack view along the axis. The size of the subviews will be reduced if necessary to fit within the available space based on the compression resistance priority setting and the position within the arrangedSubviews array.

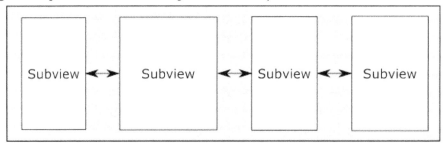

Figure 32-7

- **EqualCentering** – This mode positions the subviews along the stack view's axis with equal center-to-center spacing. The spacing in this mode is influenced by the spacing property (outlined below). Where possible, the stack view will honor the prevailing spacing property value but will reduce this value if necessary. If the views still do not fit, the size of the subviews will be reduced if necessary to fit within the available space based on the compression resistance priority setting and the position within the arrangedSubviews array.

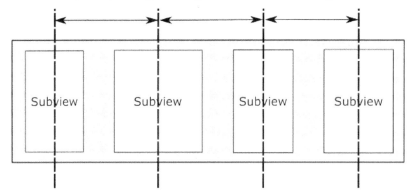

Figure 32-8

32.3.3 spacing

The spacing property specifies the distance (in points) between the edges of adjacent subviews within a stack view. When the stack view distribution property is set to *FillProportionally*, the spacing value dictates the spacing between the subviews. In *EqualSpacing* and *EqualCentering* modes, the spacing value indicates the minimum allowed spacing between the adjacent edges of the subviews. A negative spacing value causes subviews to overlap.

32.3.4 alignment

The alignment property controls the positioning of the subviews perpendicularly to the stack view's axis. Available alignment options are as follows:

- **Fill** – In fill mode, the subviews are resized to fill the space perpendicularly to the stack view's axis. In other words, the widths of the subviews in a vertical stack view are resized to fill the entire width of the stack view.

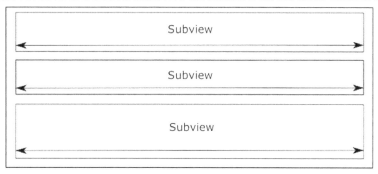

Figure 32-9

- **Leading** – In a vertically oriented stack view, the leading edges of the subviews are aligned with the leading edge of the stack view.

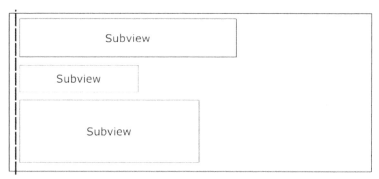

Figure 32-10

- **Trailing** - In a vertically oriented stack view, the trailing edges of the subviews are aligned with the trailing edge of the stack view.

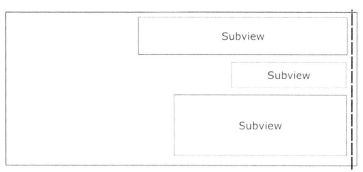

Figure 32-11

- **Top** – In a horizontally oriented stack view, the top edges of the subviews are aligned with the top edge of the stack view.

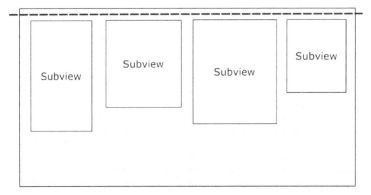

Figure 32-12

- **Bottom** - In a horizontally oriented stack view, the bottom edges of the subviews are aligned with the bottom edge of the stack view.

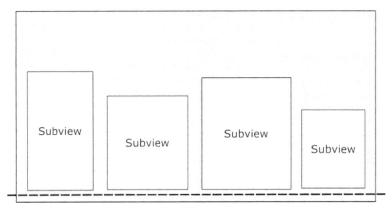

Figure 32-13

- **Center** – The centers of the subviews are aligned with the center axis of the stack view.

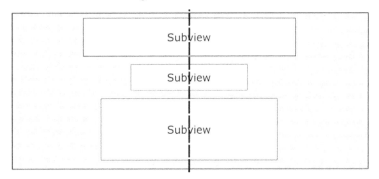

Figure 32-14

- **FirstBaseline** – Used only with horizontal stack views, this mode aligns all subviews with their first baseline. For example, an array of subviews displaying text content would all be aligned based on the vertical position of the first line of text.

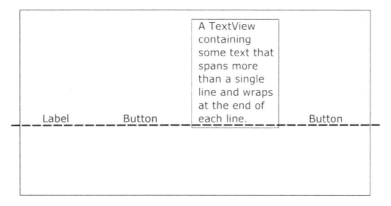

Figure 32-15

- **LastBaseline** – Similar to FirstBaseline, this mode aligns all subviews with their last baseline. For example, an array of subviews displaying text content would all be aligned based on the vertical position of the last line of text.

Figure 32-16

32.3.5 baseLineRelativeArrangement

Used only for vertical stack views, this property is a Boolean value that controls whether or not the vertical spacing between subviews is arranged relative to the baseline of the text contained within the views.

32.3.6 layoutMarginsRelativeArrangement

A Boolean value which, if set to true, causes subviews to be arranged relative to the layout margins of the containing stack view. If set to false, the subviews are arranged relative to the edges of the stack view.

32.4 Creating a Stack View in Code

UIStackView instances can be created in code by passing through an array object containing the subviews to be arranged by the stack. Once created, all the previously outlined properties may also be set dynamically from within the code. The following Swift code, for example, creates a new stack view object, configures it for horizontal axis orientation with *FillEqually* distribution, and assigns two Label objects as subviews:

```
let labelOne = UILabel(frame: CGRect(x: 0, y: 0, width: 200, height: 21))
labelOne.text = "Hello"
labelOne.backgroundColor = UIColor.red

let labelTwo = UILabel(frame: CGRect(x: 0, y: 0, width: 200, height: 21))
```

```
labelTwo.text = "There"
labelTwo.backgroundColor = UIColor.blue

let myStack = UIStackView(arrangedSubviews: [labelOne, labelTwo])

myStack.distribution = .fillEqually
myStack.axis = .horizontal
```

32.5 Adding Subviews to an Existing Stack View

Additional subviews may be appended to the end of a stack view's arrangedSubviews array using the *addArrangedSubview* method as follows:

```
myStack.addArrangedSubview(labelThree)
```

Alternatively, a subview may be inserted into a specific index position within the array of arranged subviews via a call to the *insertArrangedSubview:atIndex* method. The following line of code, for example, inserts an additional label at index position 0 within the arrangedSubviews array of a stack view:

```
myStack.insertArrangedSubview(labelZero, atIndex: 0)
```

32.6 Hiding and Removing Subviews

To remove an arranged subview from a stack view, call the *removeArrangedSubview* method of the stack view object, passing through the view object to be removed:

```
myStack.removeArrangedSubview(labelOne)
```

It is essential to be aware that the *removeArrangedSubview* method only removes the specified view from the *arrangedSubviews* array of the stack view. The view still exists in the subviews array and will probably still be visible within the user interface layout after removal (typically in the top left-hand corner of the stack view).

An alternative to removing the subview is to simply hide it. This has the advantage of making it easy to display the subview later within the app code. A helpful way to hide a subview is to obtain a reference to the subview to be hidden from within the arrangedSubviews array. For example, the following code identifies and then hides the subview located at index position 1 in the array of arranged subviews:

```
let subview = myStack.arrangedSubviews[1]
subview.hidden = true
```

If the subview is not needed again, however, it can be removed entirely by calling the *removeFromSuperview* method of the subview after it has been removed from the *arrangedSubviews* array as follows:

```
myStack.removeArrangedSubview(labelOne)
labelOne.removeFromSuperview()
```

This approach will remove the view entirely from the view hierarchy.

32.7 Summary

The UIStackView class allows user interface views to be arranged in rows or columns. A wide range of configuration options combined with the ability to dynamically create and manage stack views from within code make this a powerful and flexible user interface layout solution.

With the basics of the UIStackView class covered in this chapter, the next chapter will create an example iOS app that uses this class.

33. An iOS 17 Stack View Tutorial

The previous chapter covered a lot of detail relating to the UIStackView class. This chapter will create an iOS app project that uses a wide range of features of the UIStackView class and the Interface Builder tool. At the end of this tutorial, topics such as stack view nesting, adding and removing subviews both within Interface Builder and in code, and the use of Auto Layout constraints to influence stack view layout behavior will have been covered.

33.1 About the Stack View Example App

The app created in this chapter is intended as an example of many ways the UIStackView class can be used to design a user interface. The example will consist of a single scene (Figure 33-1) containing multiple stack view instances that combine to create the screen for a coffee ordering app.

Figure 33-1

33.2 Creating the First Stack View

Create a new Xcode iOS project based on the App template named *StackViewDemo*.

The first stack view to create within the user interface layout is a vertical stack view containing two labels. Select the *Main.storyboard* file from the Project Navigator panel and click on the current device setting in the bottom toolbar to display the device configuration bar. Select an iPad configuration from the bar (the layout will still work on iPhone-size screens, but the iPad setting provides more room in the scene when designing the layout). Drag two Labels from the Library panel onto the storyboard canvas and edit the text on each label so that the layout resembles that shown in Figure 33-2:

Figure 33-2

Select the uppermost label, display the Attributes Inspector panel and click on the T icon in the Font field to display the font selection menu. From within this menu, set the font for this label to Headline:

Figure 33-3

Finally, Shift-click on both labels and add them to a vertical stack view using the Embed In button in the lower right-hand corner of the storyboard canvas, as highlighted in Figure 33-4. From the resulting menu, select the *Stack View* option.

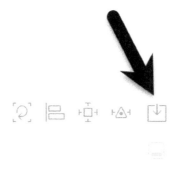

Figure 33-4

Once the button has been clicked, the two labels will be contained within a vertical stack view. Next, display the Document Outline panel, locate the newly inserted stack view from the hierarchy, select it, click on it a second time to enter editing mode, and change the name to "Title Stack View". Naming stack views in this way makes it easier to understand the layout of the user interface as additional stack views are added to the design:

Figure 33-5

33.3 Creating the Banner Stack View

The top section of the storyboard scene will consist of a banner containing an image of a coffee cup and the Title Stack View created above. Begin by dragging an Image View object onto the scene and positioning and resizing it so that it resembles the layout in Figure 33-6:

Figure 33-6

With the Image View object selected, display the Attributes Inspector panel and change the *Content Mode* setting to *Aspect Fit* so that the image's aspect ratio is retained when it is added to the view. Download the source code archive for the book and, using a Finder window, locate both the *BlueCoffeeCup.png* and *RedCoffeeCup.png* files in the *stackview_images* folder. Select the *Assets* entry in the Project Navigator panel and drag and drop the two image files beneath the AppIcon entry:

Figure 33-7

Display the *Main.storyboard* file again, select the image view and use the *Image* property menu to select the *BlueCoffeeCup* image. Once selected, the image should appear within the storyboard scene.

Shift-click on both the Image View object and the Title Stack View objects in the scene so both are selected, and click the Embed In button once again to add both to a new horizontal stack view instance. Next, locate the new stack view in the Document Outline panel, select it, and click on it a second time. Once in editing mode, change the name to Banner Stack View.

With the Banner Stack View entry still selected in the Document Outline panel, display the Attributes Inspector panel and change the Alignment property to *Center* and the Distribution property to *Fill Equally*. This will ensure that the content is centered vertically within the stack view.

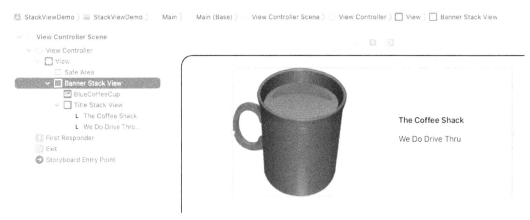

Figure 33-8

33.4 Adding the Switch Stack Views

The next stack views to create contain the two rows of Switch and Label objects. From the Library panel, drag four Label and four Switch objects onto the scene canvas so they are positioned beneath the Banner Stack View. Edit the text on the labels so that the views match those contained in Figure 33-9:

Figure 33-9

Use click and drag to select the first row of labels and switches so that all four views are selected. Add these views to a new horizontal stack view using the Embed In button at the bottom of the storyboard. Referring to the Document Outline panel, change the name of this stack view to "Switches 1 Stack View". Repeat these steps to add the second row to a stack view named "Switches 2 Stack View".

Select the Switches 1 Stack View in the Document Outline panel and change Alignment to Fill and Distribution to Equal Spacing using the Attributes Inspector panel. Repeat this step for the Switches 2 Stack View entry.

33.5 Creating the Top-Level Stack View

The next step is to add the existing stack views to a new vertical stack view. To achieve this, select the Banner Stack View and the two Switch stack views in the storyboard scene and use the Embed In button to add them to a vertical stack. Then, locate this new parent stack view within the Document Outline panel and change the name to "Top Level Stack View." At this point, verify that the view outline matches that of Figure 33-10:

Figure 33-10

With the Top Level Stack View object selected, change the Alignment and Distribution settings to *Fill.*

With these changes made, the storyboard scene should appear as shown in Figure 33-11:

Figure 33-11

33.6 Adding the Button Stack View

Two Button objects now need to be added to the Top Level Stack View, but instead of using the Embed In button, this time, the stack view and buttons will be added directly to the top-level stack. With the *Main.storyboard* file selected, locate the Horizontal Stack View in the Library panel and drag it to the bottom edge of the Top Level

Stack View in the storyboard scene so that a bold blue line appears together with a tag that reads "Top Level Stack View":

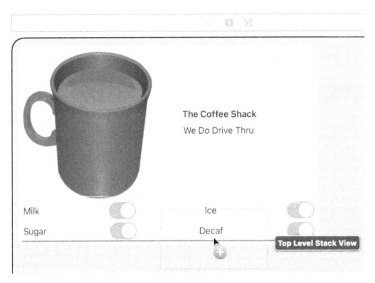

Figure 33-12

Release the stack view to add it as a subview of the top-level stack, then use the Document Outline panel to name the stack "Button Stack View". Next, drag two Button views from the Library onto the new stack view. Select the Button Stack View entry in the Document Outline and change the Distribution property to *Fill Equally*. The buttons should now be spread equally over the width of the top-level stack view.

Double-click on the left button and change the text to read "Add a Cup". Next, change the Background property in the View section of the Attributes Inspector panel to Custom, then change the Fill property to green. Next, repeat these steps for the right-hand button, setting the text to "Remove a Cup" and the background fill color cyan.

Display the Assistant Editor panel and establish action connections from the left and right buttons to methods named *addCup* and *removeCup,* respectively.

33.7 Adding the Final Subviews to the Top Level Stack View

Two final subviews need to be added to the top-level stack view to complete the layout. First, drag a Date Picker object from the Library panel and drop it immediately above the Switches 1 Stack View in the Document Outline panel. Be sure to move the object toward the left so that the blue insertion line extends to the left-hand edge of the Switches 1 Stack View entry (highlighted in Figure 33-13) before dropping the view to ensure that it is added as a subview of the Top Level Stack View and not the banner or title stack views. Once the Date view has been added, select it and use the Attributes Inspector to change the Preferred Style property to Wheels:

Figure 33-13

Repeat the above step to insert a Horizontal Stack View immediately above the Button Stack View, pulling the dragged view to the left before dropping to add the view to the Top Level Stack View. Once added, name the stack view "Cup Stack View".

With the Cup Stack View entry selected in the Outline Panel, display the Attributes Inspector panel and set the Alignment and Distribution properties to *Center* and *Fill Equally,* respectively.

Select the Top Level Stack View entry in the Document Outline panel and use the Auto Layout *Add New Constraints* menu to set *Spacing to nearest neighbor* constraints of 20 on all four edges of the view before clicking the *Add 4 Constraints* button:

Figure 33-14

At this point in the project, the layout of the storyboard scene should appear as illustrated in Figure 33-15:

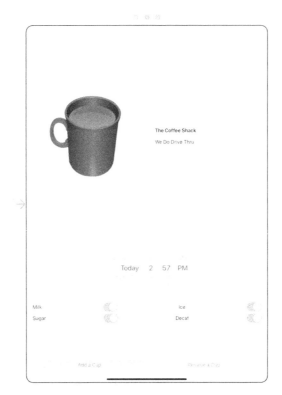

Figure 33-15

Compile and run the app on a physical device or Simulator session and verify that the layout appears correctly.

33.8 Dynamically Adding and Removing Subviews

The final step is to add the code to the two action methods to add and remove the subviews within the Cups Stack View. Select this view in the storyboard scene, display the Assistant Editor, and establish an outlet connection named *cupStackView*.

Within the *ViewController.swift* file, implement the code within the *addCup* method as follows:

```
@IBAction func addCup(_ sender: Any) {

    let cupImage = UIImageView(image: UIImage(named: "RedCoffeeCup"))
    cupImage.contentMode = .scaleAspectFit

    UIView.animate(withDuration: 0.75, animations: {
        self.cupStackView.addArrangedSubview(cupImage)
        self.cupStackView.layoutIfNeeded()
    })
}
```

The code begins by creating a new UIImageView object initialized with the red coffee cup image previously added to the asset catalog. This image view is then set to aspect fit mode so that the image will retain the original aspect ratio when displayed. An animation block is then used to animate the addition of the subview to the Cup Stack View instance.

The final step in this example is to add the code to remove the last coffee cup subview added to the stack within the *removeCup* method:

```
@IBAction func removeCup(_ sender: Any) {

    let lastAddedCup = self.cupStackView.arrangedSubviews.last

    if let cup = lastAddedCup
    {
        UIView.animate(withDuration: 0.25, animations: {
            self.cupStackView.removeArrangedSubview(cup)
            cup.removeFromSuperview()
            self.cupStackView.layoutIfNeeded()
        })
    }
}
```

This method accesses the arrangedSubviews array of the stack view to obtain the last added subview. This subview is then removed both from the arrangedSubviews array and the subviews of the parent view, all from within an animation block.

Compile and run the app and test that the buttons now add and remove coffee cup subviews and that the changes are animated.

33.9 Summary

This chapter has worked through the creation of an example app that makes use of the UIStackView class. The tutorial demonstrated the use of horizontal and vertical stack views, stack view nesting, the addition of subviews to a stack in Interface Builder both manually and using the Stack button, and the dynamic addition and removal of subviews from within code. The example also demonstrated the use of compression priority settings to fine-tune the layout behavior of a stack view.

34. A Guide to iPad Multitasking

Since the introduction of iOS 9, users can display and interact with two apps side by side on the iPad screen, a concept referred to as *multitasking*. Although the inclusion of support for multitasking within an iPadOS app is optional, enabling support where appropriate is recommended to provide the user with the best possible experience when using the app.

This chapter will introduce multitasking in terms of what it means to the user and the steps that can be taken to effectively adopt and support multitasking within an iOS app running on an iPad device. Once these areas have been covered, the next chapter (*"An iPadOS Multitasking Example"*) will create an example project designed to support multitasking.

Before reading this chapter, it is important to understand that multitasking support makes extensive use of both the Size Classes and Auto Layout features of iOS, topics which were covered in the *"An Introduction to Auto Layout in iOS 17"* and *"Using Trait Variations to Design Adaptive iOS 17 User Interfaces"* chapters of this book.

34.1 Using iPad Multitasking

Before implementing multitasking support for an iPad app, it is first essential to understand multitasking from the user's perspective. Traditionally, when an app was launched from the iPad screen, it would fill the entire display and continue to do so until placed into the background by the user. However, since the introduction of iOS 9, two apps can now share the iPad display.

Multitasking mode is initiated by tapping the three gray dots at the top of the screen to display the menu shown in Figure 34-1:

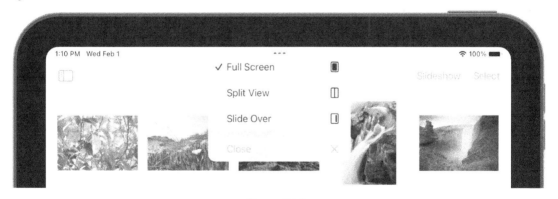

Figure 34-1

The Full Screen option, as the name suggests, will make the app currently in the foreground occupy the full device screen. On the other hand, the Split View option will split the screen between the current app and any other app of your choice. When selected, the current app will slide to the size allowing you to choose a second app from the launch screen:

Figure 34-2

Once a second app has been selected, both apps will appear in adjacent panels. Once the display is in Split View mode, touching and dragging the narrow white button located in the divider between the two panels (indicated in Figure 34-3) allows the position of the division between the primary and secondary apps to be adjusted:

Figure 34-3

In Slide Over Mode, the app will appear in a floating window, as is the case in Figure 34-4 below:

Figure 34-4

The three dots at the top of the secondary app can move the slide-over window to the left or right side of the screen by touching and dragging.

To hide a Slide Over view app, drag it sideways off the right side of the screen. Then, swipe left from the right-hand screen edge to restore the app.

34.2 Picture-In-Picture Multitasking

In addition to Split View and Slide Over modes, multitasking also supports the presentation of a movable and resizable video playback window over the top of the primary app window. This topic will be covered in the chapter entitled *"An iPadOS Multitasking Example"*.

34.3 Multitasking and Size Classes

A key part of supporting multitasking involves ensuring that the storyboard scenes within an app can adapt to various window sizes. Each of the different window sizes an app will likely encounter in a multitasking mode corresponds to one of the existing size classes outlined in the chapter entitled *"Using Trait Variations to Design Adaptive iOS 17 User Interfaces"*. As outlined in that chapter, the height and width available to an app are classified as *compact* or *regular*. So, for example, an app running in portrait mode on an iPhone 14 would use the compact width and regular height size class, while the same app running in portrait orientation would use the regular width and compact height size class.

When running in a multitasking environment, the primary and secondary apps will pass through a range of compact and regular widths depending on the prevailing multitasking configuration. The diagrams in Figure 34-4 illustrate how the different multitasking modes translate to equivalent regular and compact-size classes.

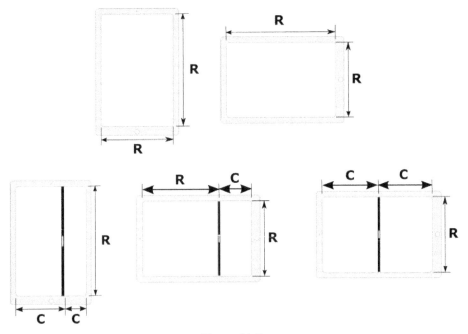

Figure 34-5

The above rules change slightly when the app runs in Split View mode on an iPad Pro. Due to the larger screen size of the iPad Pro, both apps are presented in Split View mode using the regular width, as illustrated in Figure 34-6:

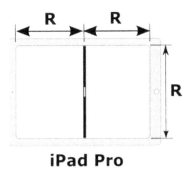

iPad Pro

Figure 34-6

Implementing multitasking support within an iOS app involves designing layouts that adapt appropriately to the different size classes outlined in the above diagram.

34.4 Handling Multitasking in Code

Much can be achieved using Auto Layout and Size Classes to adapt to the size changes associated with multitasking. There will, however, inevitably be instances where some code needs to be executed when a scene transitions from one size class to another (for example, when an app transitions from Slide Over to Split View). Fortunately, UIKit will call three delegate methods on the container instance (typically a view controller) of the current scene during the transition to notify it of the transition where code can be added to perform app-specific tasks at different points in the transition. These delegate methods are outlined below in the order in which they are called during the transition:

34.4.1 willTransition(to newcollection: with coordinator:)

This method is called immediately before the traits for the currently displayed view controller view are changed. For example, the UITraitCollection class represents a trait, which contains a collection of values consisting of size class settings, the display density of the screen, and the user interface idiom (which is simply a value indicating whether the device is on which the app is running is an iPhone or iPad).

When called, this method is passed a UITraitCollection object containing the new trait collection from which information can be accessed and used to decide how to respond to the transition. The following code, for example, checks that the app is running on an iPad before identifying whether the horizontal size class is transitioning to a regular or compact size class:

```
override func willTransition(to newCollection: UITraitCollection, with
        coordinator: UIViewControllerTransitionCoordinator) {

    super.willTransition(to: newCollection,
            with: coordinator)

    if newCollection.userInterfaceIdiom == .pad
        if newCollection.horizontalSizeClass == .regular {
            // Transitioning to Regular Width Size Class
        } else if newCollection.horizontalSizeClass == .compact {
            // Transitioning to Compact Width Size Class
        }
    }
}
```

The second argument passed through to the method is a UIViewControllerTransitionCoordinator object. This is the coordinator object that is handling the transition and can be used to add additional animations to those being performed by UIKit during the transition.

34.4.2 viewWillTransition(to size: with coordinator:)

This method is also called before the size change is implemented and is passed a CGSize value and a coordinator object. The size object can be used to obtain the new height and width to which the view is transitioning. The following sample code outputs the new height and width values to the console:

```
override func viewWillTransition(to size: CGSize,
                    with coordinator:
    UIViewControllerTransitionCoordinator) {

    super.viewWillTransition(to: size,
                    with: coordinator)

    print("Height = \(size.height), Width = \(size.width)")
}
```

34.4.3 traitCollectionDidChange(_:)

This method is called once the transition from one trait collection to another is complete and is passed the UITraitCollection object for the previous trait. In the following example implementation, the method checks to find out whether the previous horizontal size class was regular or compact:

```
override func traitCollectionDidChange(_ previousTraitCollection:
                UITraitCollection?) {

    super.traitCollectionDidChange(previousTraitCollection)

    if previousTraitCollection?.horizontalSizeClass == .regular {
        // The previous horizontal size class was regular
    }

    if previousTraitCollection?.horizontalSizeClass == .compact {
        // The previous horizontal size class was compact
    }
}
```

34.5 Lifecycle Method Calls

In addition to the transition delegate methods outlined above, several lifecycle methods are called on the app's application delegate during a multitasking transition. For example, when the user moves the divider, the *applicationWillResignActive* method is called at the point that the divider position changes. Likewise, when the user slides the divider to the edge of the screen so that the app is no longer visible, the *applicationDidEnterBackground* delegate method is called.

These method calls are particularly important when considering what happens behind the scenes when the user moves the divider. As the divider moves, the system repeatedly resizes the app off-screen and takes snapshots of various sizes as the slider moves. These snapshots make the sliding transition appear to take place smoothly. The *applicationWillResignActive* method may need to be used to preserve the state of the user interface so that when the user releases the divider, the same data and navigation position within the user interface is presented as before the slider change.

34.6 Opting Out of Multitasking

To disable multitasking support for an app, add the UIRequiresFullScreen key to the project's *Info.plist* file with the value set to true. This can be set manually within the *Info.plist* file itself or the *Deployment Info* section of the *General* settings panel for the project target:

Figure 34-7

34.7 Summary

Multitasking allows the user to display and interact with two apps concurrently when running on recent models of iPad devices. Multitasking apps are categorized as primary and secondary and can be displayed in either Slide Over or Split View configurations. Multitasking also supports a "Picture-in-Picture" option whereby video playback is displayed in a floating, resizable window over the top of the existing app.

Supporting multitasking within an iOS app primarily involves designing the user interface to support both regular and compact-size classes. A range of delegate methods also allows view controllers to receive size change notifications and respond accordingly.

Projects created in Xcode 15 are configured to support multitasking by default. However, it is also possible to opt out of multitasking with a change to the project *Info.plist* file.

35. An iPadOS Multitasking Example

With the basics of multitasking in iOS covered in the previous chapter, this chapter will involve the creation of a simple example app that uses multitasking within an app when running on an iPad device. In addition to using size classes, the example will also demonstrate how the UIStackView class can be of particular use when implementing multitasking user interface adaptability.

35.1 Creating the Multitasking Example Project

Begin by launching Xcode and creating a new project using the iOS App template with the Swift and Storyboard options selected, entering *MultitaskingDemo* as the product name.

35.2 Adding the Image Files

The completed app will include two images that need to be added to the project's asset catalog. Both image files are contained within the *multitasking_images* folder of the sample code download.

Within Xcode, locate and select the *Assets* entry within the Project Navigator panel to load the asset catalog into the main panel. Then, in the left-hand panel, right-click immediately beneath the existing *AppIcon* entry and select *New Image Set* from the resulting menu. Next, double-click on the new image set entry (which will default to the name *image*) and change the name to *Waterfalls*.

Open a Finder window, locate the *multitasking_images* folder from the code sample download, and drag and drop the *waterfall_landscape@2x.jpg* file onto the 2x placeholder within the image asset catalog. This portrait image will be displayed within the app when it is displayed using a regular width size class.

Remaining within the asset catalog and with the Waterfalls image set still selected, display the Attributes Inspector panel and change the *Width Class* property from *Any* to *Any & Compact*. The second row of image placeholders will now appear within the image set. Drag and drop the *waterfall_portrait@2x.jpg* image file from the Finder window onto the 2x Compact Width placeholder within the image set. On completion of these steps, the image set within the asset catalog should match that shown in Figure 35-1:

Figure 35-1

35.3 Designing the Regular Width Size Class Layout

The baseline user interface layout will be used for the regular width size class. In the next section, trait variations will be made to the layout for the compact width size class. Begin, therefore, by selecting the *Main.storyboard* file, displaying the device configuration bar (Figure 35-2), and selecting an iPad configuration:

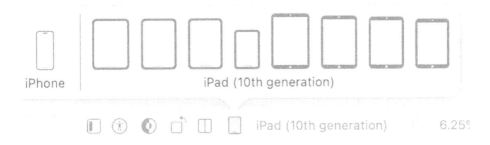

Figure 35-2

For this example, the layout will be controlled by a UIStackView instance, so drag and drop a Horizontal Stack View from the Library panel onto the scene canvas. With the Stack View selected, display the Auto Layout *Add New Constraints* menu and set *Spacing to nearest neighbor* constraints on all four sides of the view with the spacing set to 0 and the *Constrain to margins* option enabled as illustrated in Figure 35-3:

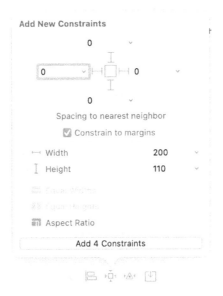

Figure 35-3

Display the Document Outline panel and select the Stack View entry. Then, using the Attributes Inspector panel, set the Alignment to *Center* and the Distribution property to *Fill Equally.*

Drag an Image object and drop it onto the stack view instance in the storyboard scene canvas. Locate the Text View object within the Library panel and drag it to the right-hand edge of the Image view within the scene canvas. When a bold blue vertical line appears (referenced by the arrow in Figure 35-4) indicating that the Text View will be placed to the right of the Image view in the stack, drop the Text View to add it to the scene:

Figure 35-4

With the Image View selected, use the Attributes Inspector panel to set the Content Mode attribute to *Aspect Fit* and the Image menu to *Waterfalls*. Next, select the Text View object and stretch it vertically so that all the Latin text is visible. Finally, with the Text View object still selected, display the Auto Layout *Add New Constraints* menu and enable the *Height* constraint option based on the current value before clicking on the *Add 1 Constraint* button. At this point, the user interface layout should resemble Figure 35-5:

Figure 35-5

The height constraint we have applied to the Text View is only required in regular width size class configurations. Therefore, we need to use a trait variation to prevent the height from being constrained in compact-width environments. Within the Document Outline panel, locate and select the height constraint as illustrated in Figure 35-6 below:

Figure 35-6

Next, refer to the Size inspector panel and add a wR hR variation as shown in Figure 35-7:

Figure 35-7

Finally, turn off the Installed checkbox for the default variation, and enable the new variation:

Figure 35-8

35.4 Designing the Compact Width Size Class

The compact size class will be used to arrange the scene layout when the app is displayed in Slide Over and specific Split View configurations. This size class must be designed within the project to ensure that the scene appears correctly. With the *Main.storyboard* file still loaded into Interface Builder, select the iPhone 14 device from the device configuration bar.

With Interface Builder now displaying the compact width, and regular height size class, the stack view needs to be configured to use vertical orientation to accommodate the narrower width available for the subviews.

Select the Stack View object within the Document Outline panel and display the Attributes Inspector panel. When the app is displayed in compact width, the axis orientation of the stack view object needs to change from horizontal to vertical. To configure this, click on the + button located to the left of the Axis setting in the Attributes Inspector and, from the resulting panel, set the Width option to *Compact* and Height option to *Regular*, leaving the Gamut set to *Any*. Once the options have been selected, click on the *Add Variation* button:

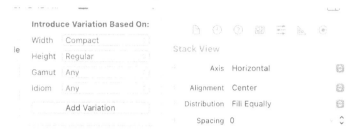

Figure 35-9

Once selected, a new Axis property setting will be added to the attributes list for the current size class labeled *wC hR*, as highlighted in Figure 35-10. Change the setting for this property to *Vertical*, and note that the scene's orientation has changed in the storyboard canvas.

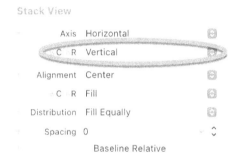

Figure 35-10

Repeat these steps to add an Alignment setting for the compact width and regular height size class set to *Fill*:

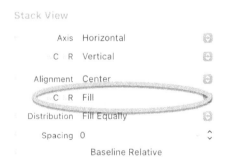

Figure 35-11

This setting will ensure that the Text View object expands to fill the width of the display in compact width mode.

35.5 Testing the Project in a Multitasking Environment

With the project completed, it is time to test that the layouts associated with the size classes work within the various multitasking modes. First, compile and run the app on an iPad model which supports multitasking or a suitable iOS simulator session.

Using the steps outlined in the previous chapter, display the app in a Slide Over window so that it appears, as shown in Figure 35-12. Note that the app is displayed using the compact width layout configuration:

Figure 35-12

Next, display the app in Split View mode and drag the divider to adjust the size of the example app. Note that the layout switches between the regular and compact width configurations depending on the size of the panel in which it is running:

Figure 35-13

35.6 Summary

In this chapter, we have created an example iPadOS project that uses size classes to display a user interface scene appropriately configured for both compact and regular width categories of size class. Once implemented, the app could adopt different layouts in various multitasking modes on an iPad.

36. An Overview of Swift Structured Concurrency

Concurrency can be defined as the ability of software to perform multiple tasks in parallel. Many app development projects will need to use concurrent processing at some point, and concurrency is essential for providing a good user experience. Concurrency, for example, allows an app's user interface to remain responsive while performing background tasks such as downloading images or processing data.

In this chapter, we will explore the *structured concurrency* features of the Swift programming language and explain how these can be used to add multi-tasking support to your app projects.

36.1 An Overview of Threads

Threads are a feature of modern CPUs and provide the foundation of concurrency in any multitasking operating system. Although modern CPUs can run large numbers of threads, the actual number of threads that can be run in parallel at any one time is limited by the number of CPU cores (depending on the CPU model, this will typically be between 4 and 16 cores). When more threads are required than there are CPU cores, the operating system performs thread scheduling to decide how the execution of these threads is to be shared between the available cores.

Threads can be thought of as mini-processes running within a main process, the purpose of which is to enable at least the appearance of parallel execution paths within application code. The good news is that although structured concurrency uses threads behind the scenes, it handles all of the complexity for you, and you should never need to interact with them directly.

36.2 The Application Main Thread

When an app is first started, the runtime system will typically create a single thread in which the app will run by default. This thread is generally referred to as the *main thread*. The primary role of the main thread is to handle the user interface in terms of UI layout rendering, event handling, and user interaction with views in the user interface.

Any additional code within an app that performs a time-consuming task using the main thread will cause the entire application to appear to lock up until the task is completed. This can be avoided by launching the tasks to be performed in separate threads, allowing the main thread to continue unhindered with other tasks.

36.3 Completion Handlers

As outlined in the chapter entitled *"Swift Functions, Methods and Closures"*, Swift previously used completion handlers to implement asynchronous code execution. In this scenario, an asynchronous task would be started, and a completion handler would be assigned to be called when the task finishes. In the meantime, the main app code would continue to run while the asynchronous task is performed in the background. On completion of the asynchronous task, the completion handler would be called and passed any results. The body of the completion handler would then execute and process those results.

Unfortunately, completion handlers tend to result in complex and error-prone code constructs that are difficult to write and understand. Completion handlers are also unsuited to handling errors thrown by asynchronous tasks and generally result in large and confusing nested code structures.

36.4 Structured Concurrency

Structured concurrency was introduced into the Swift language with Swift version 5.5 to make it easier for app developers to implement concurrent execution safely and in a logical and easy way to both write and understand. In other words, structured concurrency code can be read from top to bottom without jumping back to completion handler code to understand the logic flow. Structured concurrency also makes it easier to handle errors thrown by asynchronous functions.

Swift provides several options for implementing structured concurrency, each of which will be introduced in this chapter.

36.5 Preparing the Project

Launch Xcode and select the option to create a new iOS *App* project named ConcurrencyDemo. Once created, select the Main.storyboard file, display the Library, and drag a Button object onto the center of the scene layout. Next, double-click on the button and change the text to read "Async Test", then use the Align menu to add constraints to center the button horizontally and vertically in the container:

Figure 36-1

Display the Assistant Editor and establish an action connection from the button to a method named *buttonClick()*. Next, edit the *ViewController.swift* file and add two additional functions that will be used later in the chapter. Finally, modify the buttonCLick() method to call the doSomething function:

```
import UIKit
```

```
class ViewController: UIViewController {

    override func viewDidLoad() {
        super.viewDidLoad()
    }

    @IBAction func buttonClick(_ sender: Any) {
        doSomething()
    }

    func doSomething() {
    }

    func takesTooLong() {
    }
}
```

36.6 Non-Concurrent Code

Before exploring concurrency, we will first look at an example of non-concurrent code (also referred to as *synchronous code*) execution. Begin by adding the following code to the two stub functions. The changes to the *doSomething()* function print out the current date and time before calling the *takesTooLong()* function. Finally, the date and time are output once again before the *doSomething()* function exits.

The *takesTooLong()* function uses the system *sleep()* method to simulate the effect of performing a time-consuming task that blocks the main thread until it is complete before printing out another timestamp:

```
func doSomething() {
    print("Start \(Date())")
    takesTooLong()
    print("End \(Date())")
}

func takesTooLong() {
    sleep(5)
    print("Async task completed at \(Date())")
}
```

Run the app on a device or simulator and click on the "Async Test" button. Output similar to the following should appear in the Xcode console panel:

```
Start 2024-02-05 17:43:10 +0000
Async task completed at 2023-02-05 17:43:15 +0000
End 2024-02-05 17:43:15 +0000
```

The key point to note in the above timestamps is that the end time is 5 seconds after the start time. This tells us not only that the call to *takesTooLong()* lasted 5 seconds as expected but that any code after the call was made within the *doSomething()* function was not able to execute until after the call returned. During that 5 seconds, the app would appear to the user to be frozen.

The answer to this problem is implementing a Swift *async/await* concurrency structure. Before looking at *async/*

await, we will need a Swift concurrency-compatible alternative to the *sleep()* call used in the above example. To achieve this, add a new function to the *ViewController.swift* file that reads as follows:

```
func taskSleep(_: Int) async {
    do {
        try await Task.sleep(until: .now + .seconds(5), clock: .continuous)
    } catch { }
}
```

Ironically, the new function uses Swift concurrency before we covered the topic. Rest assured, the techniques used in the above code will be explained in the remainder of this chapter.

36.7 Introducing async/await Concurrency

The foundation of structured concurrency is the *async/await* pair. The *async* keyword is used when declaring a function to indicate that it will be executed asynchronously relative to the thread from which it was called. We need, therefore, to declare both of our example functions as follows (any errors that appear will be addressed later):

```
func doSomething() async {
    print("Start \(Date())")
    takesTooLong()
    print("End \(Date())")
}


func takesTooLong() async {
    await taskSleep(5)
    print("Async task completed at \(Date())")
}
```

Marking a function as async achieves several objectives. First, it indicates that the code in the function needs to be executed on a different thread to the one from which it was called. It also notifies the system that the function itself can be suspended during execution to allow the system to run other tasks. As we will see later, these *suspend points* within an async function are specified using the *await* keyword.

Another point to note about async functions is that they can generally only be called from within the scope of other async functions though, as we will see later in the chapter, the Task object can be used to provide a bridge between synchronous and asynchronous code. Finally, if an async function calls other async functions, the parent function cannot exit until all child tasks have also been completed.

Most importantly, once a function has been declared asynchronous, it can only be called using the await keyword. Before looking at the *await* keyword, we must understand how to call async functions from synchronous code.

36.8 Asynchronous Calls from Synchronous Functions

The rules of structured concurrency state that an async function can only be called from within an asynchronous context. If the entry point into your program is a synchronous function, this raises the question of how any async functions can ever get called. The answer is to use the Task object from within the synchronous function to launch the async function. Suppose we have a synchronous function named *main()* from which we need to call one of our async functions and attempt to do so as follows:

```
func main() {
    doSomething()
}
```

The above code will result in the following error notification in the code editor:

```
'async' call in a function that does not support concurrency
```

The only options we have are to make *main()* an async function or to launch the function in an unstructured task. Assuming that declaring *main()* as an async function is not a viable option, in this case, the code will need to be changed as follows:

```
func main() {
    Task {
        await doSomething()
    }
}
```

36.9 The await Keyword

As we previously discussed, the await keyword is required when making a call to an async function and can only usually be used within the scope of another async function. Attempting to call an async function without the await keyword will result in the following syntax error:

```
Expression is 'async' but is not marked with 'await'
```

To call the *takesTooLong()* function, therefore, we need to make the following change to the *doSomething()* function:

```
func doSomething() async {
    print("Start \(Date())")
    await takesTooLong()
    print("End \(Date())")
}
```

One more change is now required because we are attempting to call the async *doSomething()* function from a synchronous context (in this case, the buttonClick action method). To resolve this, we need to use the Task object to launch the *doSomething()* function:

```
@IBAction func buttonClick(_ sender: Any) {
    Task {
        await doSomething()
    }
}
```

When tested now, the console output should be similar to the following:

```
Start 2023-02-05 17:53:03 +0000
Async task completed at 2023-02-05 17:53:08 +0000
End 2023-02-05 17:53:08 +0000
```

This is where the await keyword can be a little confusing. As you have probably noticed, the *doSomething()* function still had to wait for the *takesTooLong()* function to return before continuing, giving the impression that the task was still blocking the thread from which it was called. In fact, the task was performed on a different thread, but the await keyword told the system to wait until it completed. The reason for this is that, as previously mentioned, a parent async function cannot complete until all of its sub-functions have also completed. This means that the call has no choice but to wait for the async *takesTooLong()* function to return before executing the next line of code. The next section will explain how to defer the wait until later in the parent function using the *async-let* binding expression. Before doing that, however, we need to look at another effect of using the await keyword in this context.

In addition to allowing us to make the async call, the await keyword has also defined a *suspend point* within the *doSomething()* function. When this point is reached during execution, it tells the system that the *doSomething()* function can be temporarily suspended and the thread on which it is running used for other purposes. This allows the system to allocate resources to any higher priority tasks and will eventually return control to the *doSomething()* function so that execution can continue. By marking suspend points, the *doSomething()* function is essentially being forced to be a good citizen by allowing the system to briefly allocate processing resources to other tasks. Given the speed of the system, it is unlikely that a suspension will last more than fractions of a second and will not be noticeable to the user while benefiting the overall performance of the app.

36.10 Using async-let Bindings

In our example code, we have identified that the default behavior of the await keyword is to wait for the called function to return before resuming execution. A more common requirement, however, is to continue executing code within the calling function while the async function is executing in the background. This can be achieved by deferring the wait until later in the code using an async-let binding. To demonstrate this, we first need to modify our *takesTooLong()* function to return a result (in this case, our task completion timestamp):

```
func takesTooLong() async -> Date {
    await taskSleep(5)
    return Date()
}
```

Next, we need to change the call within *doSomething()* to assign the returned result to a variable using a *let* expression but also marked with the *async* keyword:

```
func doSomething() async {
    print("Start \(Date())")
    async let result = takesTooLong()
    print("End \(Date())")
}
```

Now, we need to specify where within the doSomething() function we want to wait for the result value to be returned. We do this by accessing the result variable using the await keyword. For example:

```
func doSomething() async {
    print("Start \(Date())")
    async let result = takesTooLong()
    print("After async-let \(Date())")
    // Additional code to run concurrently with async function goes here
    print ("result = \(await result)")
    print("End \(Date())")
}
```

When printing the result value, we are using await to let the system know that execution cannot continue until the async *takesTooLong()* function returns with the result value. At this point, execution will stop until the result is available. Any code between the async-let and the await, however, will execute concurrently with the *takesTooLong()* function.

Execution of the above code will generate output similar to the following:

```
Start 2023-02-05 17:56:00 +0000
After async-let 2023-02-05 17:56:00 +0000
result = 2023-02-05 17:56:05 +0000
End 2023-02-05 17:56:05 +0000
```

Note that the "After async-let" message has a timestamp that is 5 seconds earlier than the "result =" call return stamp confirming that the code was executed while *takesTooLong()* was also running.

36.11 Handling Errors

Error handling in structured concurrency uses the throw/do/try/catch mechanism previously covered in the chapter entitled *"Understanding Error Handling in Swift 5"*. The following example modifies our original async *takesTooLong()* function to accept a sleep duration parameter and to throw an error if the delay is outside of a specific range:

```
enum DurationError: Error {
    case tooLong
    case tooShort
}
.
.
.
func takesTooLong(delay: Int) async throws {

    if delay < 5 {
        throw DurationError.tooShort
    } else if delay > 20 {
        throw DurationError.tooLong
    }

    await taskSleep(delay)
    print("Async task completed at \(Date())")
}
```

Now when the function is called, we can use a do/try/catch construct to handle any errors that get thrown:

```
func doSomething() async {
    print("Start \(Date())")
    do {
        try await takesTooLong(delay: 25)
    } catch DurationError.tooShort {
        print("Error: Duration too short")
    } catch DurationError.tooLong {
        print("Error: Duration too long")
    } catch {
        print("Unknown error")
    }
    print("End \(Date())")
}
```

When executed, the resulting output will resemble the following:

```
Start 2022-03-30 19:29:43 +0000
Error: Duration too long
End 2022-03-30 19:29:43 +0000
```

36.12 Understanding Tasks

Any work that executes asynchronously runs within an instance of the Swift *Task* class. An app can run multiple tasks simultaneously and structures these tasks hierarchically. When launched, the async version of our *doSomething()* function will run within a Task instance. When the *takesTooLong()* function is called, the system creates a *sub-task* within which the function code will execute. In terms of the task hierarchy tree, this sub-task is a child of the *doSomething()* parent task. Any calls to async functions from within the sub-task will become children of that task, and so on.

This task hierarchy forms the basis on which structured concurrency is built. For example, child tasks inherit attributes such as priority from their parents, and the hierarchy ensures that a parent task does not exit until all descendant tasks have been completed.

As we will see later in the chapter, tasks can be grouped to enable the dynamic launching of multiple asynchronous tasks.

36.13 Unstructured Concurrency

Individual tasks can be created manually using the Task object, a concept referred to as unstructured concurrency. As we have already seen, a common use for unstructured tasks is to call async functions from within synchronous functions.

Unstructured tasks also provide more flexibility because they can be externally canceled at any time during execution. This is particularly useful if you need to provide the user with a way to cancel a background activity, such as tapping on a button to stop a background download task. This flexibility comes with extra cost in terms of having to do a little more work to create and manage tasks.

Unstructured tasks are created and launched by calling the Task initializer and providing a closure containing the code to be performed. For example:

```
Task {
    await doSomething()
}
```

These tasks also inherit the configuration of the parent from which they are called, such as the actor context, priority, and task local variables. Tasks can also be assigned a new priority when they are created, for example:

```
Task(priority: .high) {
    await doSomething()
}
```

This provides a hint to the system about how the task should be scheduled relative to other tasks. Available priorities ranked from highest to lowest are as follows:

- .high / .userInitiated

- .medium

- .low / .utility

- .background

When a task is manually created, it returns a reference to the Task instance. This can be used to cancel the task or to check whether the task has already been canceled from outside the task scope:

```
let task = Task(priority: .high) {
    await doSomething()
```

```
}
.
.
if (!task.isCancelled) {
    task.cancel()
}
```

36.14 Detached Tasks

Detached tasks are another form of unstructured concurrency, but they differ in that they do not inherit any properties from the calling parent. Detached tasks are created by calling the *Task.detached()* method as follows:

```
Task.detached {
    await doSomething()
}
```

Detached tasks may also be passed a priority value, and checked for cancellation using the same techniques as outlined above:

```
let detachedTask = Task.detached(priority: .medium) {
    await doSomething()
}
.
.
if (!detachedTask.isCancelled) {
    detachedTask.cancel()
}
```

36.15 Task Management

Whether you are using structured or unstructured tasks, the Task class provides a set of static methods and properties that can be used to manage the task from within the scope.

A task may, for example, use the *currentPriority* property to identify the priority assigned when it was created:

```
Task {
    let priority = Task.currentPriority
    await doSomething()
}
```

Unfortunately, this is a read-only property so cannot be used to change the priority of the running task.

It is also possible for a task to check if it has been canceled by accessing the *isCancelled* property:

```
if Task.isCancelled {
    // perform task cleanup
}
```

Another option for detecting cancellation is to call the *checkCancellation()* method, which will throw a CancellationError error if the task has been canceled:

```
do {
    try Task.checkCancellation()
} catch {
    // Perform task cleanup
}
```

A task may cancel itself at any time by calling the *cancel()* Task method:

```
Task.cancel()
```

Finally, if there are locations within the task code where execution could safely be suspended, these can be declared to the system via the *yield()* method:

```
Task.yield()
```

36.16 Working with Task Groups

So far in this chapter, our examples have involved creating one or two tasks (a parent and a child). In each case, we knew how many tasks were required in advance of writing the code. Situations often arise, however, where several tasks need to be created and run concurrently based on dynamic criteria. We might, for example, need to launch a separate task for each item in an array or within the body of a *for* loop. Swift addresses this by providing *task groups*.

Task groups allow a dynamic number of tasks to be created and are implemented using either the *withThrowingTaskGroup()* or *withTaskGroup()* functions (depending on whether or not the async functions in the group throw errors). The looping construct to create the tasks is then defined within the corresponding closure, calling the group *addTask()* function to add each new task.

Modify the two functions as follows to create a task group consisting of five tasks, each running an instance of the *takesTooLong()* function:

```
func doSomething() async {
    await withTaskGroup(of: Void.self) { group in
        for i in 1...5 {
            group.addTask {
                let result = await self.takesTooLong()
                print("Completed Task \(i) = \(result)")
            }
        }
    }
}


func takesTooLong() async -> Date {
    await taskSleep(5)
    return Date()
}
```

When executed, there will be a 5-second delay while the tasks run before output similar to the following appears:

```
Completed Task 1 = 2022-03-31 17:36:32 +0000
Completed Task 2 = 2022-03-31 17:36:32 +0000
Completed Task 5 = 2022-03-31 17:36:32 +0000
Completed Task 3 = 2022-03-31 17:36:32 +0000
Completed Task 4 = 2022-03-31 17:36:32 +0000
```

Note that the tasks all show the same completion timestamp indicating that they were executed concurrently. It is also interesting to notice that the tasks did not complete in the order in which they were launched. When working with concurrency, it is important to remember that there is no guarantee that tasks will be completed in the order they were created.

In addition to the *addTask()* function, several other methods and properties are accessible from within the task group, including the following:

- **cancelAll()** - Method call to cancel all tasks in the group

- **isCancelled** - Boolean property indicating whether the task group has already been canceled.

- **isEmpty** - Boolean property indicating whether any tasks remain within the task group.

36.17 Avoiding Data Races

In the above task group example, the group did not store the results of the tasks. In other words, the results did not leave the scope of the task group and were not retained when the tasks ended. For example, let's assume we want to store the task number and result timestamp for each task within a Swift dictionary object (with the task number as the key and the timestamp as the value). When working with synchronous code, we might consider a solution that reads as follows:

```
func doSomething() async {

    var timeStamps: [Int: Date] = [:]

    await withTaskGroup(of: Void.self) { group in
        for i in 1...5 {
            group.addTask {
                timeStamps[i] = await self.takesTooLong()
            }
        }
    }
}
```

Unfortunately, the above code will report the following error on the line where the result from the *takesTooLong()* function is added to the dictionary:

```
Mutation of captured var 'timeStamps' in concurrently-executing code
```

The problem is that we have multiple tasks concurrently accessing the data and risk encountering a data race condition. A data race occurs when multiple tasks attempt to access the same data concurrently, and one or more of these tasks is performing a write operation. This generally results in data corruption problems that can be hard to diagnose.

One option is to create an *actor* in which to store the data. Another solution is to adapt our task group to return the task results sequentially and add them to the dictionary. We originally declared the task group as returning no results by passing Void.self as the return type to the *withTaskGroup()* function as follows:

```
await withTaskGroup(of: Void.self) { group in
.
.
```

The first step is to design the task group so that each task returns a tuple containing the task number (Int) and timestamp (Date) as follows. We also need a dictionary in which to store the results:

```
func doSomething() async {

    var timeStamps: [Int: Date] = [:]
```

```
await withTaskGroup(of: (Int, Date).self) { group in
    for i in 1...5 {
        group.addTask {
            return(i, await self.takesTooLong())
        }
    }
}
}
```

Next, we need to declare a second loop to handle the results as they are returned from the group. Because the results are being returned individually from async functions, we cannot simply write a loop to process them all at once. Instead, we need to wait until each result is returned. For this situation, Swift provides the *for-await* loop.

36.18 The for-await Loop

The *for-await* expression allows us to step through sequences of values that are being returned asynchronously and *await* the receipt of values as they are returned by concurrent tasks. The only requirement for using for-await is that the sequential data conforms to the AsyncSequence protocol (which should always be the case when working with task groups).

In our example, we need to add a for-await loop within the task group scope, but after the addTask loop as follows:

```
func doSomething() async {

    var timeStamps: [Int: Date] = [:]

    await withTaskGroup(of: (Int, Date).self) { group in

        for i in 1...5 {
            group.addTask {
                return(i, await self.takesTooLong())
            }
        }

        for await (task, date) in group {
            timeStamps[task] = date
        }
    }
}
```

As each task returns, the for-await loop will receive the resulting tuple and store it in the timeStamps dictionary. To verify this, we can add some code to print the dictionary entries after the task group exits:

```
func doSomething() async {
    .

    .

        for await (task, date) in group {
            timeStamps[task] = date
        }
    }
}
```

```
    for (task, date) in timeStamps {
        print("Task = \(task), Date = \(date)")
    }
}
```

When executed, the output from the completed example should be similar to the following:

```
Task = 2, Date = 2023-02-05 18:54:06 +0000
Task = 3, Date = 2023-02-05 18:54:06 +0000
Task = 4, Date = 2023-02-05 18:54:06 +0000
Task = 5, Date = 2023-02-05 18:54:06 +0000
Task = 1, Date = 2023-02-05 18:54:06 +0000
```

36.19 Asynchronous Properties

In addition to async functions, Swift also supports async properties within class and struct types. Asynchronous properties are created by explicitly declaring a getter and marking it as async as demonstrated in the following example. Currently, only read-only properties can be asynchronous.

```
struct MyStruct {
    var myResult: Date {
        get async {
            return await self.getTime()
        }
    }
    func getTime() async -> Date {
        sleep(5)
        return Date()
    }
}
.

.
func doSomething() async {

    let myStruct = MyStruct()

    Task {
        let date = await myStruct.myResult
        print(date)
    }
}
```

36.20 Summary

Modern CPUs and operating systems are designed to execute code concurrently, allowing multiple tasks to be performed simultaneously. This is achieved by running tasks on different *threads*, with the *main thread* primarily responsible for rendering the user interface and responding to user events. By default, most code in an app is also executed on the main thread unless specifically configured to run on a different thread. If that code performs tasks that occupy the main thread for too long, the app will appear to freeze until the task completes. To avoid this, Swift provides the structured concurrency API. When using structured concurrency, code that would block the main thread is instead placed in an asynchronous function (async properties are also supported) so that it is performed on a separate thread. The calling code can be configured to wait for the async code to complete before continuing using the *await* keyword or to continue executing until the result is needed using *async-let*.

Modern CPUs and operating systems are designed to execute code concurrently allowing multiple tasks to be performed at the same time. This is achieved by running tasks on different *threads* with the *main thread* being primarily responsible for rendering the user interface and responding to user events. By default, most code in an app is also executed on the main thread unless specifically configured to run on a different thread. If that code performs tasks that occupy the main thread for too long the app will appear to freeze until the task completes. To avoid this, Swift provides the structured concurrency API. When using structured concurrency, code that would block the main thread is instead placed in an asynchronous function (async properties are also supported) so that it is performed on a separate thread. The calling code can be configured to wait for the async code to complete before continuing using the *await* keyword, or to continue executing until the result is needed using *async-let*.

Tasks can be run individually or as groups of multiple tasks. The for-await loop provides a useful way to asynchronously process the results of asynchronous task groups.

37. Working with Directories in Swift on iOS 17

It is sometimes easy to forget that iOS is an operating system much like that running on many other computers today. Given this fact, it should come as no surprise that iOS has a file system much like any other operating system allowing apps to store persistent data on behalf of the user. Again, much like other platforms, the iOS file system provides a directory-based structure into which files can be created and organized.

Since the introduction of iOS 5, the iOS app developer has had two options in terms of storing data. Files and data may now be stored on the file system of the local device or remotely using Apple's iCloud service. In practice, however, it is most likely that an app will utilize iCloud storage to augment, rather than replace, the local file system, so familiarity with both concepts is still necessary.

The topic of iCloud-based storage will be covered in detail, beginning with the chapter entitled *"Preparing an iOS 17 App to use iCloud Storage"*. The goal of this chapter, however, is to provide an overview of how to work with local file system directories from within an iOS app. Topics covered include identifying the app's document and temporary directories, finding the current working directory, creating, removing, and renaming directories, and obtaining listings of a directory's content. Once the topic of directory management has been covered, we will move on to handling files in *"Working with Files in Swift on iOS 17"*.

37.1 The Application Documents Directory

An iPhone or iPad user can install multiple apps on a single device. However, the iOS platform ensures that these apps cannot interfere with each other regarding memory usage and data storage. Each app is restricted in where it can store data on the device's file system. iOS achieves this by allowing apps to read and write only to their own *Documents* and *tmp* directories. Within these two directories, the corresponding app can create files and subdirectories to any required level of depth. This area constitutes the app's *sandbox,* and the app cannot usually create or modify files or directories outside of these directories unless using the UIDocumentPickerViewController class.

37.2 The FileManager, FileHandle, and Data Classes

The Foundation Framework provides three classes that are indispensable when it comes to working with files and directories:

- **FileManager** - The FileManager class can perform basic file and directory operations such as creating, moving, reading, and writing files and reading and setting file attributes. In addition, this class provides methods for, amongst other tasks, identifying the current working directory, changing to a new directory, creating directories, and listing the contents of a directory.

- **FileHandle** - The FileHandle class is provided for performing lower-level operations on files, such as seeking to a specific position in a file and reading and writing a file's contents by a specified number of byte chunks, and appending data to an existing file. This class will be used extensively in the chapter entitled *"Working with Files in Swift on iOS 17"*.

- **Data** - The Data class provides a storage buffer into which the contents of a file may be read, or dynamically stored data may be written to a file.

37.3 Understanding Pathnames in Swift

As with macOS, iOS defines pathnames using the standard UNIX convention. Each path component is separated by a forward slash (/). When an app starts, the current working directory is the file system's *root directory* represented by a single /. From this location, the app must navigate to its own *Documents* and *tmp* directories to be able to write files to the file system. Path names that begin with a / are said to be *absolute path names* in that they specify a file system location relative to the root directory. For example, */var/mobile* is an absolute path name.

Paths that do not begin with a slash are interpreted to be *relative* to a current working directory. So, for example, if the current working directory is */User/demo* and the path name is *mapdata/local.xml,* then the file is considered to have an equivalent full, absolute pathname of */User/demo/mapdata/local.xml.*

37.4 Obtaining a Reference to the Default FileManager Object

The FileManager class contains a property named *default* that is used to obtain a reference to the app's default file manager instance:

```
let filemgr = FileManager.default
```

Having obtained the object reference, we can begin to use it to work with files and directories.

37.5 Identifying the Current Working Directory

As previously mentioned, when an app first loads, its current working directory is the app's root directory, represented by a / character. The current working directory may be identified at any time by accessing the *currentDirectoryPath* property of the file manager object. For example, the following code fragment identifies the current working directory:

```
let currentPath = filemgr.currentDirectoryPath
```

37.6 Identifying the Documents Directory

Each iOS app on a device has its own private *Documents* and *tmp* directories into which it can read and write data. Because the location of these directories is different for each app, the only way to find the correct path is to ask iOS. The exact location will also differ depending on whether the app is running on a physical iPhone or iPad device or in the iOS Simulator. The *Documents* directory for an app may be identified by making a call to a file manager method named *urls(for:),* passing through an argument (in this case *.documentDirectory*) indicating that we require the path to the Documents directory. The *.userDomainMask* argument indicates to the *urls(for:)* method that we are looking for the Documents directory located in the app's home directory. The method returns an object in the form of an array containing the results of the request. We can, therefore, obtain the path to the current app's Documents directory as follows:

```
let filemgr = FileManager.default

let dirPaths = filemgr.urls(for: .documentDirectory, in: .userDomainMask)

let docsDir = dirPaths[0].path
```

To access the path string contained within the URL, we access the *path* property of the URL at index position 0 in the array and assign it to the *docsDir* constant as outlined above.

When executed within the iOS Simulator environment, the path returned will take the form of the following:

```
/Users/<user name>/Library/Developer/CoreSimulator/Devices/<device id>/data/
Containers/Data/Application/<app id>/Documents
```

Where *<user name>* is the name of the user currently logged into the macOS system on which the simulator is running, *<device id>* is the unique ID of the device on which the app is running, and *<app id>* is the unique ID of the app, for example:

```
06A3AEBA-8C34-476E-937F-A27BDD2E450A
```

Clearly, this references a path on your macOS system, so feel free to open up a Finder window and explore the file system sandbox areas for your iOS apps.

When executed on a physical iOS device, however, the path returned by the function call will take the following form:

```
/var/mobile/Containers/Data/Application/<app id>/Documents
```

37.7 Identifying the Temporary Directory

In addition to the *Documents* directory, iOS apps are also provided with a *tmp* directory for storing temporary files. The path to the current app's temporary directory may be ascertained with a call to the *NSTemporaryDirectory* C function as follows:

```
let tmpDir = NSTemporaryDirectory()
```

Once executed, the string object referenced by tmpDir will contain the path to the temporary directory for the app.

37.8 Changing Directory

Having identified the path to the app's document or temporary directory, the chances are that you will need to make that directory the current working directory. The current working directory of a running iOS app can be changed with a call to the *changeCurrentDirectoryPath* method of a FileManager instance. The destination directory path is passed as an argument to the instance method in the form of a String object. Note that this method returns a Boolean *true* or *false* result to indicate whether the requested directory change was successful. A failure result typically indicates either that the specified directory does not exist or that the app lacks the appropriate access permissions:

```
let filemgr = FileManager.default

let dirPaths = filemgr.urls(for: .documentDirectory, in: .userDomainMask)

let docsDir = dirPaths[0].path

if filemgr.changeCurrentDirectoryPath(docsDir) {
    // Success
} else {
    // Failure

}
```

In the above example, the path to the *Documents* directory is identified and then used as an argument to the *changeCurrentDirectoryPath* method of the file manager object to change the current working directory to that location.

37.9 Creating a New Directory

A new directory on an iOS device is created using the *createDirectory(atPath:)* instance method of the FileManager class, once again passing through the pathname of the new directory as an argument and returning a Boolean success or failure result. The second argument to this method defines whether any intermediate directory levels should be created automatically. For example, if we wanted to create a directory with the path /

var/mobile/Containers/Data/Application/<app id>/Documents/mydata/maps and the *mydata* subdirectory does not yet exist, setting the *withIntermediateDirectories* argument to *true* will cause this directory to be created automatically before then creating the *maps* sub-directory within it. If this argument is set to *false,* then the attempt to create the directory will fail because *mydata* does not already exist, and we have not given permission for it to be created on our behalf.

This method also takes additional arguments in the form of a set of attributes for the new directory. Specifying *nil* will use the default attributes.

The following code fragment identifies the documents directory and creates a new sub-directory named *data* in that directory:

```
let filemgr = FileManager.default

let dirPaths = filemgr.urls(for: .documentDirectory, in: .userDomainMask)

let docsURL = dirPaths[0]

let newDir = docsURL.appendingPathComponent("data").path

do {
    try filemgr.createDirectory(atPath: newDir,
                withIntermediateDirectories: true, attributes: nil)
    } catch let error as NSError {
            print("Error: \(error.localizedDescription)")
}
```

37.10 Deleting a Directory

An existing directory may be removed from the file system using the *removeItem(atPath:)* method, passing through the directory's path to be removed as an argument. For example, to remove the data directory created in the preceding example, we might write the following code:

```
do {
    try filemgr.removeItem(atPath: newDir)
} catch let error {
    print("Error: \(error.localizedDescription)")
}
```

37.11 Listing the Contents of a Directory

A listing of the files contained within a specified directory can be obtained using the *contentsOfDirectory(atPath:)* method. This method takes the directory pathname as an argument and returns an array object containing the names of the files and sub-directories in that directory. The following example obtains a listing of the contents of the root directory (/) and displays each item in the Xcode console panel during execution:

```
do {
    let filelist = try filemgr.contentsOfDirectory(atPath: "/")

    for filename in filelist {
        print(filename)
    }
```

```
} catch let error {
    print("Error: \(error.localizedDescription)")
}
```

37.12 Getting the Attributes of a File or Directory

The attributes of a file or directory may be obtained using the *attributesOfItem(atPath:)* method. This takes as arguments the path of the directory and an optional Error object into which information about any errors will be placed (may be specified as *nil* if this information is not required). The results are returned in the form of an NSDictionary dictionary object. The keys for this dictionary are as follows:

```
NSFileType
NSFileTypeDirectory
NSFileTypeRegular
NSFileTypeSymbolicLink
NSFileTypeSocket
NSFileTypeCharacterSpecial
NSFileTypeBlockSpecial
NSFileTypeUnknown
NSFileSize
NSFileModificationDate
NSFileReferenceCount
NSFileDeviceIdentifier
NSFileOwnerAccountName
NSFileGroupOwnerAccountName
NSFilePosixPermissions
NSFileSystemNumber
NSFileSystemFileNumber
NSFileExtensionHidden
NSFileHFSCreatorCode
NSFileHFSTypeCode
NSFileImmutable
NSFileAppendOnly
NSFileCreationDate
NSFileOwnerAccountID
NSFileGroupOwnerAccountID
```

For example, we can extract the file type for the */Applications* directory using the following code excerpt:

```
let filemgr = FileManager.default

do {
    let attribs: NSDictionary =
            try filemgr.attributesOfItem(atPath: "/Applications") as NSDictionary
    let type = attribs["NSFileType"] as! String
    print("File type \(type)")
} catch let error {
    print("Error: \(error.localizedDescription)")
}
```

When executed, results similar to the following output will appear in the Xcode console:

```
File type NSFileTypeDirectory
```

37.13 Summary

iOS provides options for both local and cloud-based file storage. Like most other operating systems, iOS supports storing and managing files on local devices using a file and directory-based filesystem structure. Each iOS app installed on a device is provided with a filesystem area within which files and directories may be stored and retrieved. This chapter has explored how directories are created, deleted, and navigated from within Swift code. The next chapter will continue this theme by covering device-based file handling within iOS.

38. Working with Files in Swift on iOS 17

In the chapter entitled *"Working with Directories in Swift on iOS 17"*, we looked at the FileManager, FileHandle, and Data Foundation Framework classes. We discussed how the FileManager class enables us to work with directories when developing iOS-based apps. We also spent some time covering the file system structure used by iOS. In particular, we looked at the temporary and *Documents* directories assigned to each app and how the location of those directories can be identified from within the app code.

In this chapter, we move from working with directories to covering the details of working with files within the iOS SDK. Once we have covered file-handling topics in this chapter, the next chapter will work through an app example that puts theory into practice.

38.1 Obtaining a FileManager Instance Reference

Before proceeding, first, we need to recap the steps necessary to obtain a reference to the app's FileManager instance. As discussed in the previous chapter, the FileManager class contains a property named *default* that is used to obtain a reference. For example:

```
let filemgr = FileManager.default
```

Once a reference to the file manager object has been obtained, it can be used to perform some basic file-handling tasks.

38.2 Checking for the Existence of a File

The FileManager class contains an instance method named *fileExists(atPath:)*, which checks whether a specified file already exists. The method takes as an argument an NSString object containing the path to the file in question and returns a Boolean value indicating the presence or otherwise of the specified file:

```
let filemgr = FileManager.default

if filemgr.fileExists(atPath: "/Applications") {
    print("File exists")
} else {
    print("File not found")
}
```

38.3 Comparing the Contents of Two Files

The contents of two files may be compared for equality using the *contentsEqual(atPath:)* method. This method takes as arguments the paths to the two files to be compared and returns a Boolean result to indicate whether the file contents match:

```
let filePath1 = docsDir + "/myfile1.txt"
let filePath2 = docsDir + "/myfile2.txt"

if filemgr.contentsEqual(atPath: filePath1, andPath: filePath2) {
```

```
    print("File contents match")
} else {
    print("File contents do not match")
}
```

38.4 Checking if a File is Readable/Writable/Executable/Deletable

Most operating systems provide some level of file access control. These typically take the form of attributes designed to control the level of access to a file for each user or user group. As such, it is not certain that your program will have read or write access to a particular file or the appropriate permissions to delete or rename it. The quickest way to find out if your program has a particular access permission is to use the *isReadableFile(atPath:)*, *isWritableFile(atPath:)*, *isExecutableFile(atPath:)* and *isDeletableFile(atPath:)* methods. Each method takes a single argument in the form of the path to the file to be checked and returns a Boolean result. For example, the following code excerpt checks to find out if a file is writable:

```
if filemgr.isWritableFile(atPath: filePath1) {
    print("File is writable")
} else {
    print("File is read-only")
}
```

To check for other access permissions, substitute the corresponding method name in place of *isWritableFile(atPath:)* in the above example.

38.5 Moving/Renaming a File

A file may be renamed (assuming adequate permissions) using the *moveItem(atPath:)* method. This method takes as arguments the pathname for the file to be moved and the destination path. If the destination file path already exists, this operation will fail:

```
do {
    try filemgr.moveItem(atPath: filePath1, toPath: filePath2)
    print("Move successful")
} catch let error {
    print("Error: \(error.localizedDescription)")
}
```

38.6 Copying a File

File copying can be achieved using the *copyItem(atPath:)* method. As with the *move* method, this takes as arguments the source and destination pathnames:

```
do {
    try filemgr.copyItem(atPath: filePath1, toPath: filePath2)
    print("Copy successful")
} catch let error {
    print("Error: \(error.localizedDescription)")
}
```

38.7 Removing a File

The *removeItem(atPath:)* method removes the specified file from the file system. The method takes as an argument the pathname of the file to be removed:

```
do {
    try filemgr.removeItem(atPath: filePath2)
```

```
    print("Removal successful")
} catch let error {
    print("Error: \(error.localizedDescription)")
}
```

38.8 Creating a Symbolic Link

A symbolic link to a particular file may be created using the *createSymbolicLink(atPath:)* method. This takes as arguments the path of the symbolic link and the path to the file to which the link is to refer:

```
do {
    try filemgr.createSymbolicLink(atPath: filePath2,
            withDestinationPath: filePath1)
    print("Link successful")
} catch let error {
    print("Error: \(error.localizedDescription)")
}
```

38.9 Reading and Writing Files with FileManager

The FileManager class includes some basic file reading and writing capabilities. These capabilities are somewhat limited compared to the options provided by the FileHandle class but can be useful nonetheless.

First, the contents of a file may be read and stored in a Data object through the use of the *contents(atPath:)* method:

```
let databuffer = filemgr.contents(atPath: filePath1)
```

Having stored the contents of a file in a Data object, that data may subsequently be written out to a new file using the *createFile(atPath:)* method:

```
filemgr.createFile(atPath: filePath2, contents: databuffer,
                        attributes: nil)
```

In the above example, we have essentially copied the contents from an existing file to a new file. This, however, gives us no control over how much data is to be read or written and does not allow us to append data to the end of an existing file. Furthermore, if the file in the above example had already existed, any data it contained would have been overwritten by the source file's contents. Clearly, some more flexible mechanism is required. The Foundation Framework provides this in the form of the FileHandle class.

38.10 Working with Files using the FileHandle Class

The FileHandle class provides a range of methods designed to provide a more advanced mechanism for working with files. In addition to files, this class can also be used for working with devices and network sockets. In the following sections, we will look at some of the more common uses for this class.

38.11 Creating a FileHandle Object

A FileHandle object can be created when opening a file for reading, writing, or updating (in other words, both reading and writing). Having opened a file, it must subsequently be closed when we have finished working with it using the *closeFile* method. If an attempt to open a file fails, for example, because an attempt is made to open a non-existent file for reading, these methods return *nil*.

For example, the following code excerpt opens a file for reading and then closes it without actually doing anything to the file:

```
let file: FileHandle? = FileHandle(forReadingAtPath: filePath1)
```

```
    if file == nil {
        print("File open failed")
    } else {
        file?.closeFile()
    }
}
```

38.12 FileHandle File Offsets and Seeking

FileHandle objects maintain a pointer to the current position in a file. This is referred to as the *offset*. When a file is first opened, the offset is set to 0 (the beginning of the file). This means that any read or write operations performed using the FileHandle instance methods will take place at offset 0 in the file. Therefore, it is first necessary to seek the required offset to perform operations at different locations in a file (for example, append data to the end of the file). For example, to move the current offset to the end of the file, use the *seekToEndOfFile* method.

Alternatively, *seek(toFileOffset:)* allows you to specify the precise location in the file to which the offset is to be positioned. Finally, the current offset may be identified using the *offsetInFile* method. The offset is stored as an unsigned 64-bit integer to accommodate large files.

The following example opens a file for reading and then performs several method calls to move the offset to different positions, outputting the current offset after each move:

```
let file: FileHandle? = FileHandle(forReadingAtPath: filePath1)

if file == nil {
    print("File open failed")
} else {
    print("Offset = \(file?.offsetInFile ?? 0)")
    file?.seekToEndOfFile()
    print("Offset = \(file?.offsetInFile ?? 0)")
    file?.seek(toFileOffset: 30)
    print("Offset = \(file?.offsetInFile ?? 0)")
    file?.closeFile()
}
```

File offsets are a key aspect of working with files using the FileHandle class, so it is worth taking extra time to ensure you understand the concept. Without knowing where the current offset is in a file, it is impossible to know the location in the file where data will be read or written.

38.13 Reading Data from a File

Once a file has been opened and assigned a file handle, the contents of that file may be read from the current offset position. The *readData(ofLength:)* method reads a specified number of bytes of data from the file starting at the current offset. For example, the following code reads 5 bytes of data from offset 10 in a file. The data read is returned encapsulated in a Data object:

```
let file: FileHandle? = FileHandle(forReadingAtPath: filepath1)

if file == nil {
    print("File open failed")
} else {
    file?.seek(toFileOffset: 10)
    let databuffer = file?.readData(ofLength: 5)
```

```
file?.closeFile()
}
```

Alternatively, the *readDataToEndOfFile* method will read all the data in the file, starting at the current offset and ending at the end of the file.

38.14 Writing Data to a File

The *write* method writes the data contained in a Data object to the file starting at the location of the offset. Note that this does not insert data but overwrites any existing data in the file at the corresponding location.

To see this in action, let's assume the existence of a file named *quickfox.txt* containing the following text:

```
The quick brown fox jumped over the lazy dog
```

Next, we will write code that opens the file for updating, seeks to position 10, and then writes some data at that location:

```
let file: FileHandle? = FileHandle(forUpdatingAtPath: filePath1)

if file == nil {
    print("File open failed")
} else {
    if let data = ("black cat" as
        NSString).data(using: String.Encoding.utf8.rawValue) {
        file?.seek(toFileOffset: 10)
        file?.write(data)
        file?.closeFile()
    }
}
```

When the above program is compiled and executed, the contents of the *quickfox.txt* file will have changed to:

```
The quick black cat jumped over the lazy dog
```

38.15 Truncating a File

A file may be truncated at the specified offset using the *truncateFile(atOffset:)* method. To delete the entire contents of a file, specify an offset of 0 when calling this method:

```
let file: FileHandle? = FileHandle(forUpdatingAtPath: filePath1)

if file == nil {
    print("File open failed")
} else {
    file?.truncateFile(atOffset: 0)
    file?.closeFile()
}
```

38.16 Summary

Like other operating systems, iOS provides a file system to store user and app files and data locally. In this and the preceding chapter, file, and directory handling have been covered in some detail. The next chapter, entitled *"iOS 17 Directory Handling and File I/O in Swift – A Worked Example"*, will work through the creation of an example explicitly designed to demonstrate iOS file and directory handling.

39. iOS 17 Directory Handling and File I/O in Swift – A Worked Example

In the *"Working with Directories in Swift on iOS 17"* and *"Working with Files in Swift on iOS 17"* chapters of this book, we discussed in detail the steps involved in working with the iOS file system in terms of both file and directory handling from within iOS apps. The goal of this chapter is to put theory into practice by working through the creation of a simple app that demonstrates some of the key concepts outlined in the preceding chapters.

39.1 The Example App

The steps in this chapter involve creating an iOS app consisting of a text field and a button. When the user touches the button after entering text into the text field, that text is saved to a file. The next time the app has launched, the file's content is read by the app and pre-loaded into the text field.

39.2 Setting up the App Project

The first step in creating the app is to set up a new project. Begin by launching Xcode and creating a new project using the iOS App template with the Swift and Storyboard options selected, entering *FileExample* as the product name.

39.3 Designing the User Interface

The example app will consist of a button and a text field. To begin the user interface design process, select the *Main.storyboard* file to load it into the Interface Builder environment. Next, drag a Button and then a Text Field from the Library onto the view. Double-click on the button and change the text to *Save*. Position the components and resize the width of the text field so that the layout appears as illustrated in Figure 39-1:

Figure 39-1

Using the *Resolve Auto Layout Issues* menu, select the *Reset to Suggested Constraints* option listed under All Views in View Controller.

Select the Text Field object in the view canvas, display the Assistant Editor panel and verify that the editor is displaying the contents of the *ViewController.swift* file. Right-click on the text field object and drag it to a position just below the class declaration line in the Assistant Editor. Release the line, and in the resulting connection dialog, establish an outlet connection named *textBox*.

Right-click on the button object and drag the line to the area immediately beneath the *viewDidLoad* method in the Assistant Editor panel. Release the line and, within the resulting connection dialog, establish an Action method on the *Touch Up Inside* event configured to call a method named *saveText*.

39.4 Checking the Data File on App Startup

Each time the user launches the app, it will need to check to see if the data file exists (if the user has not previously saved any text, the file will not have been created). If the file exists, the contents need to be read by the app and displayed within the text field. An excellent place to put initialization code of this nature is in a method to be called from the *viewDidLoad* method of the view controller. With this in mind, select the *ViewController.swift* file, declare some variables that will be needed in the code and scroll down to the *viewDidLoad* method and edit the file as follows:

```swift
import UIKit


class ViewController: UIViewController {

    @IBOutlet weak var textBox: UITextField!

    var fileMgr: FileManager = FileManager.default
    var docsDir: String?
    var dataFile: String = ""

    override func viewDidLoad() {
        super.viewDidLoad()
        checkFile()
    }

    func checkFile() {

        let dirPaths = fileMgr.urls(for: .documentDirectory,
                                in: .userDomainMask)

        dataFile =
            dirPaths[0].appendingPathComponent("datafile.dat").path

        if fileMgr.fileExists(atPath: dataFile) {

            if let databuffer = fileMgr.contents(atPath: dataFile) {
                let datastring = NSString(data: databuffer,
                            encoding: String.Encoding.utf8.rawValue)
                textBox.text = datastring as String?
            }
        }
    }
}
```

.
.
.

Before proceeding, we need to take some time to talk about what the above code is doing. First, we declare some variables that will be used in the method and create an instance of the FileManager class. Because each iOS app on a device has its own *Documents* directory, we next make the appropriate calls to identify the path to that directory. Once we know where the documents directory is located, we construct the full path to our file (named datafile.dat) before checking whether the file exists. If it exists, we read the file's contents and assign it to the *text* property of our text field object so that it is visible to the user.

Now that we have the initialization code implemented, we need to write the code for our action method.

39.5 Implementing the Action Method

When the user enters text into our text field component and touches the save button, the text needs to be saved to the *datafile.dat* file in the app's *Documents* directory. We need to implement the code in our saveText action method to make this happen. Select the *ViewController.swift* file if it is not already open and modify the template *saveText* method we created previously so that it reads as follows:

```
@IBAction func saveText(_ sender: Any) {

    if let text = textBox?.text {

        let dataBuffer = text.data(using: String.Encoding.utf8)

        fileMgr.createFile(atPath: dataFile, contents: dataBuffer,
                         attributes: nil)
    }
}
```

This code converts the text in the text field object and assigns it to a Data object, the contents of which are written to the data file by calling the *createFile(atPath:)* method of the file manager object.

39.6 Building and Running the Example

Once the appropriate code changes have been made, test the app by clicking on the run button located in the toolbar of the main Xcode project window.

When the app has loaded, enter some text into the text field and click on the *Save* button. Next, stop the app by clicking on the stop button in the Xcode toolbar and then restart the app by clicking the run button again. On loading for a second time, the text field will be primed with the text saved during the previous session:

Figure 39-2

39.7 Summary

This chapter has demonstrated the use of the iOS FileManager class to read and write data to the file system of the local device. Now that the basics of working with local files have been covered, the following chapters will introduce cloud-based storage.

40. Preparing an iOS 17 App to use iCloud Storage

From the perspective of the average iPhone or iPad owner, iCloud represents a vast, remote storage service onto which device-based data may be backed up and music stored for subsequent streaming to multiple iCloud-supported platforms and devices.

From the iOS app developer's perspective, iCloud represents a set of programming interfaces and SDK classes that facilitate the storage of files and data on iCloud servers hosted at Apple's data centers from within an iOS app.

This chapter is intended to provide an overview of iCloud and to walk through the steps involved in preparing an iOS app to utilize the services of iCloud.

40.1 iCloud Data Storage Services

The current version of the iOS SDK provides support for four types of iCloud-based storage: *iCloud Document Storage, iCloud Key-Value Data Storage, iCloud Drive Storage,* and *CloudKit Data Storage.*

iCloud document storage allows an app to store data files and documents on iCloud in a special area reserved for that app. Once stored, these files may be retrieved from iCloud storage by the same app at any time as long as it runs on a device with the user's iCloud credentials configured.

The iCloud key-value storage service allows small amounts of data packaged in key/value format to be stored in the cloud. This service is intended to provide a way for the same app to synchronize user settings and status when installed on multiple devices. A user might, for example, have the same game app installed on an iPhone and an iPad. The game app would use iCloud key-value storage to synchronize the player's current position in the game and the prevailing score, thereby allowing the user to switch between devices and resume the game from the same state.

Every Apple user account has associated with it an iCloud Drive storage area into which files may be stored and accessed from different devices and apps. Unlike files stored using the iCloud Storage option (which is generally only accessible to the app that saved the file), however, files stored on iCloud Drive can also be accessed via the built-in *Files* app on iOS, other apps, the Finder on macOS, the iCloud Drive app on Windows and even via the iCloud.com web portal. Saving files to iCloud Drive will be outlined in the chapter entitled *"Using iCloud Drive Storage in an iOS 17 App"*.

CloudKit data storage provides apps with access to the iCloud servers hosted by Apple. It provides an easy-to-use way to store, manage and retrieve data and other asset types (such as large binary files, videos, and images) in a structured way. This allows users to store private data and access it from multiple devices and for the developer to provide publicly available data to all app users. CloudKit data storage is covered in detail, beginning with the chapter entitled *"An Introduction to CloudKit Data Storage on iOS 17"*.

40.2 Preparing an App to Use iCloud Storage

For an app to use iCloud services, it must be code signed with an App ID with iCloud support enabled. In addition to enabling iCloud support within the App ID, the app must also be configured with specific entitlements to enable one or more of the iCloud storage services outlined in the preceding section of this chapter.

Fortunately, both of these tasks can be performed within the *Capabilities* screen within Xcode 15.

Clearly, iOS developers who are not yet members of the iOS Developer Program will need to enroll before implementing any iCloud functionality. Details on enrolling in this program were outlined in the *Joining the Apple Developer Program* chapter of this book.

40.3 Enabling iCloud Support for an iOS 17 App

To enable iCloud support for an app, load the project into Xcode and select the app name target from the top of the project navigator panel (marked A in Figure 40-1). Then, from the resulting project settings panel, select the *Signing & Capabilities* tab (B) followed by the target entry (C):

Figure 40-1

Click on the "+ Capability" button (D) to display the dialog shown in Figure 40-2. Next, enter iCloud into the filter bar, select the result, and press the keyboard enter key to add the capability to the project:

Figure 40-2

Once you have enabled iCloud, the capabilities section provides options to enable key-value storage, iCloud Documents (which enables both the iCloud Storage and iCloud Drive capabilities), and CloudKit services. This is also where the iCloud containers used to store data are created and managed:

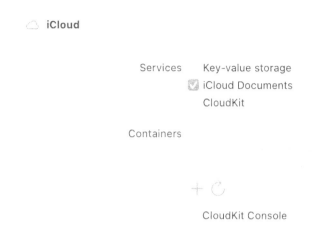

Figure 40-3

Enabling iCloud support will have automatically added the iCloud entitlement to the app's App ID and created an entitlements file to the project containing the app's iCloud container identifiers.

40.4 Reviewing the iCloud Entitlements File

Once iCloud capabilities have been enabled for an app within Xcode, a new file will appear in the project named *<product name>*.entitlements. Any apps that intend to use iCloud storage in any way must obtain entitlements appropriate to the iCloud features to be used. These entitlements are placed into this *entitlements file* and built into the app at compile time.

If the app is intended to use iCloud document storage, then the entitlements file must include a request for the *com.apple.developer.icloud-container-identifiers* entitlement. Similarly, if the key-value store is to be used, then the *com.apple.developer.ubiquity-kvstore-identifier* entitlement must be included. Apps that require both forms of iCloud storage must include both entitlements.

The entitlements file is an XML file in which the requests are stored in a key-value format. The keys are the entitlement identifiers outlined above, and the values are represented by one or more *container identifiers* comprised of the developer's ID and a custom string that uniquely identifies the app (the corresponding app's App ID is generally recommended, though not mandatory, for this value).

The entitlements file may be created either manually or, as outlined above, automatically from within the Xcode environment. The entitlements file will appear in the project navigator panel when using the Capabilities settings.

When using the Capabilities panel, a single iCloud container is added to the entitlements file. Additional containers may be added by selecting the *Specify custom containers* option and clicking on the '+' button located beneath the *Containers* list.

40.5 Accessing Multiple Ubiquity Containers

The *ubiquity-container-identifiers* value is an array that may reference multiple iCloud containers. If an app requires access to more than one ubiquity container, it will need to reference the identifier of the required container specifically. This is achieved by specifying the container identifier when constructing URL paths to documents within the iCloud storage. For example, the following code fragment defines a container identifier constant and then uses it to obtain the URL of the container in storage:

```
let UBIQUITY_CONTAINER_URL = "ABCDEF12345.com.yourdomain.icloudapp"
```

```
let ubiquityURL = FileManager.default.url(forUbiquityContainerIdentifier:
            UBIQUITY_CONTAINER_URL)?.appendingPathComponent("Documents")
```

Suppose nil is passed through as an argument in place of the container identifier. In that case, the method will simply return the URL of the first container in the *ubiquity-container-identifiers* array of the entitlements file:

```
let ubiquityURL = FileManager.default.url(
    forUbiquityContainerIdentifier: nil)?.appendingPathComponent("Documents")
```

40.6 Ubiquity Container URLs

When documents are saved to the cloud, they will be placed in subfolders of a folder on iCloud using the following path:

```
/private/var/mobile/Library/Mobile Documents/
<ubiquity container id>/Documents
```

40.7 Summary

iCloud brings cloud-based storage and app data synchronization to iOS 17-based apps. Before an app can take advantage of iCloud, it must first be provisioned with an iCloud-enabled profile and built against an appropriately configured entitlements file.

41. Managing Files using the iOS 17 UIDocument Class

Using iCloud to store files requires a basic understanding of the UIDocument class. Introduced as part of the iOS 5 SDK, the UIDocument class is the recommended mechanism for working with iCloud-based file and document storage.

The objective of this chapter is to provide a brief overview of the UIDocument class before working through a simple example demonstrating the use of UIDocument to create and perform read and write operations on a document on the local device file system. Once these basics have been covered, the next chapter will extend the example to store the document using the iCloud document storage service.

41.1 An Overview of the UIDocument Class

The iOS UIDocument class is designed to provide an easy-to-use interface for creating and managing documents and content. While primarily intended to ease the process of storing files using iCloud, UIDocument also provides additional benefits in terms of file handling on the local file system, such as reading and writing data asynchronously on a background queue, handling version conflicts on a file (a more likely possibility when using iCloud) and automatic document saving.

41.2 Subclassing the UIDocument Class

UIDocument is an *abstract class* that cannot be directly instantiated from within code. Instead, apps must create a subclass of UIDocument and, at a minimum, override two methods:

- **contents(forType:)** - This method is called by the UIDocument subclass instance when data is to be written to the file or document. The method is responsible for gathering the data to be written and returning it in the form of a Data or FileWrapper object.

- **load(fromContents:)** - Called by the subclass instance when data is being read from the file or document. The method is passed the content that has been read from the file by the UIDocument subclass and is responsible for loading that data into the app's internal data model.

41.3 Conflict Resolution and Document States

Storing documents using iCloud means that multiple instances of an app can potentially access the same stored document consecutively. This considerably increases the risk of a conflict occurring when app instances simultaneously make different changes to the same document. One option is to let the most recent save operation overwrite any changes made by the other app instances. A more user-friendly alternative, however, is to implement conflict detection code in the app and present the user with the option to resolve the conflict. Such resolution options will be app specific but might include presenting the file differences and letting the user choose which one to save or allowing the user to merge the conflicting file versions.

The current state of a UIDocument subclass object may be identified by accessing the object's *documentState* property. At any given time, this property will be set to one of the following constants:

- **UIDocumentState.normal** – The document is open and enabled for user editing.

- **UIDocumentState.closed** – The document is currently closed. This state can also indicate an error in reading a document.

- **UIDocumentState.inConflict** – Conflicts have been detected for the document.

- **UIDocumentState.savingError** – An error occurred when an attempt was made to save the document.

- **UIDocumentState.editingDisabled** – The document is busy and is not currently safe for editing.

- **UIDocumentState.progressAvailable** – The current progress of the document download is available via the *progress* property of the document object.

Clearly, one option for detecting conflicts is to periodically check the *documentState* property for a UIDocumentState. inConflict value. That said, it only really makes sense to check for this state when changes have been made to the document. This can be achieved by registering an observer on the *UIDocumentStateChangedNotification* notification. When the notification is received that the document state has changed, the code will need to check the *documentState* property for the presence of a conflict and act accordingly.

41.4 The UIDocument Example App

The remainder of this chapter will focus on creating an app designed to demonstrate the use of the UIDocument class to read and write a document locally on an iOS 17-based device or simulator.

To create the project, launch Xcode and create a new product named *iCloudStore* using the iOS *App* template and the Swift programming language.

41.5 Creating a UIDocument Subclass

As previously discussed, UIDocument is an abstract class that cannot be directly instantiated. Therefore, it is necessary to create a subclass and implement some methods in that subclass before using the features that UIDocument provides. The first step in this project is to create the source file for the subclass, so select the Xcode *File -> New -> File…* menu option, and in the resulting panel, select *iOS* in the tab bar and the *Cocoa Touch Class* template before clicking on *Next*. Next, on the options panel, set the *Subclass of* menu to *UIDocument,* name the class *MyDocument* and click *Next* to create the new class.

With the basic outline of the subclass created, the next step is implementing the user interface and the corresponding outlets and actions.

41.6 Designing the User Interface

The finished app will have a user interface comprising a UITextView and UIButton. The user will enter text into the text view and save it to a file by touching the button.

Select the *Main.storyboard* file and display the Library dialog. Drag and drop the Text View and Button objects into the view canvas, resizing the text view so that it occupies only the upper area of the view. Double-click on the button object and change the title text to "Save":

Figure 41-1

Click on the Text View so that it is selected, and use the Auto Layout *Add New Constraints* menu to add *Spacing to nearest neighbor* constraints on the top, left, and right-hand edges of the view with the *Constrain to margins* option switched on. Before adding the nearest neighbor constraints, also enable the *Height* constraint so that the view's height is preserved at runtime.

Having configured the constraints for the Text View, select the Button view and use the Auto Layout Align menu to configure a *Horizontal Center in Container* constraint. With the Button view still selected, display the *Add New Constraints* menu and add a *Spacing to nearest neighbor* constraint on the top edge of the view using the current value and with the *Constrain to margins* option switched off.

Remove the example Latin text from the text view object by selecting it in the view canvas and deleting the value from the *Text* property in the Attributes Inspector panel.

With the user interface designed, it is time to connect the action and outlet. Select the Text View object in the view canvas, display the Assistant Editor panel and verify that the editor is displaying the contents of the *ViewController.swift* file. Right-click on the Text View object and drag it to a position just below the "class ViewController" declaration line in the Assistant Editor. Release the line, and in the resulting connection dialog, establish an outlet connection named *textView*.

Finally, right-click on the button object and drag the line to the area immediately beneath the *viewDidLoad* method declaration in the Assistant Editor panel. Release the line and, within the resulting connection dialog, establish an Action method on the *Touch Up Inside* event configured to call a method named *saveDocument*.

41.7 Implementing the App Data Structure

So far, we have created and partially implemented a UIDocument subclass named *MyDocument* and designed the user interface of the app together with corresponding actions and outlets. As previously discussed, the *MyDocument* class will require two methods for interfacing between the *MyDocument* object instances and the app's data structures. Before implementing these methods, we first need to implement the app data structure. In this app, the data simply consists of the string entered by the user into the text view object. Given the simplicity of this example, we will declare the data structure, such as it is, within the *MyDocument* class, where it can be easily accessed by the *contents(forType:)* and *load(fromContents:)* methods. To implement the data structure, albeit a single data value, select the *MyDocument.swift* file and add a declaration for a String object:

```
import UIKit


class MyDocument: UIDocument {
```

```
    var userText: String? = "Some Sample Text"
}
```

Now that the data model is defined, it is time to complete the *MyDocument* class implementation.

41.8 Implementing the contents(forType:) Method

The *MyDocument* class is a subclass of UIDocument. When an instance of MyDocument is created, and the appropriate method is called on that instance to save the app's data to a file, the class makes a call to its *contents(forType:)* instance method. This method's job is to collect the data stored in the document and pass it back to the MyDocument object instance as a Data object. The content of the Data object will then be written into the document. While this may sound complicated, most of the work is done for us by the parent UIDocument class. All the method needs to do is get the current value of the *userText* String object, put it into a Data object, and return it.

Select the *MyDocument.swift* file and add the *contents(forType:)* method as follows:

```
override func contents(forType typeName: String) throws -> Any {
    if let content = userText {

        let length =
            content.lengthOfBytes(using: String.Encoding.utf8)
        return NSData(bytes:content, length: length)
    } else {
        return Data()
    }
}
```

41.9 Implementing the load(fromContents:) Method

The *load(fromContents:)* instance method is called by an instance of MyDocument when the object is instructed to read the contents of a file. This method is passed a Data object containing the document's content and is responsible for updating the app's internal data structure accordingly. All this method needs to do, therefore, is convert the Data object contents to a string and assign it to the *userText* object:

```
override func load(fromContents contents: Any, ofType typeName: String?)
  throws {
    if let userContent = contents as? Data {
        userText = NSString(bytes: (contents as AnyObject).bytes,
                length: userContent.count,
                encoding: String.Encoding.utf8.rawValue) as String?
    }
}
```

The implementation of the MyDocument class is now complete, and it is time to begin implementing the app functionality.

41.10 Loading the Document at App Launch

The app's ultimate goal is to save any text in the text view to a document on the device's local file system. When the app is launched, it needs to check if the document exists and, if so, load the contents into the text view object. If, on the other hand, the document does not yet exist, it will need to be created. As is usually the case, the best place to perform these tasks is the *viewDidLoad* method of the view controller.

Before implementing the code for the *viewDidLoad* method, we first need to perform some preparatory work. First, both the *viewDidLoad* and *saveDocument* methods will need access to a URL object containing a reference to the document and an instance of the *MyDocument* class, so these need to be declared in the view controller implementation file. Then, with the *ViewController.swift* file selected in the project navigator, modify the file as follows:

```
import UIKit

class ViewController: UIViewController {

    @IBOutlet weak var textView: UITextView!

    var document: MyDocument?
    var documentURL: URL?
    .
    .
    .
}
```

The first task for the *viewDidLoad* method is to identify the path to the app's *Documents* directory (a task outlined in *"Working with Directories in Swift on iOS 17"*) and construct a full path to the document named *savefile.txt*. The method will then need to use the document URL to create an instance of the *MyDocument* class. The code to perform these tasks can be implemented as outlined in the following code fragment:

```
let filemgr = FileManager.default

let dirPaths = filemgr.urls(for: .documentDirectory,
                            in: .userDomainMask)

documentURL = dirPaths[0].appendingPathComponent("savefile.txt")
if let url = documentURL {
    document = MyDocument(fileURL: url)
    document?.userText = ""
```

The next task for the method is identifying whether the saved file exists. If it does, the *open(completionHandler:)* method of the *MyDocument* instance object is called to open the document and load the contents (thereby automatically triggering a call to the *load(fromContents:)* method created earlier in the chapter).

The *open(completionHandler:)* method allows for a code block to be written to, which is passed a Boolean value indicating the success or otherwise of the file opening and reading process. On a successful read operation, this handler code simply needs to assign the value of the *userText* property of the *MyDocument* instance (which has been updated with the document contents by the *load(fromContents:)* method) to the text property of the *textView* object thereby making it visible to the user.

If the document does not yet exist, the *save(to:)* method of the *MyDocument* class will be called using the argument to create a new file:

```
if filemgr.fileExists(atPath: (url.path)!) {

    document?.open(completionHandler: {(success: Bool) -> Void in
        if success {
```

```
                print("File open OK")
                self.textView.text = self.document?.userText
        } else {
            print("Failed to open file")
        }
    })
} else {
    document?.save(to: url, for: .forCreating,
            completionHandler: {(success: Bool) -> Void in
        if success {
            print("File created OK")
        } else {
            print("Failed to create file ")
        }
    })
}
```

Note that print calls have been made at key points in the process for debugging purposes. These can be removed once the app is verified to be working correctly.

Bringing the above code fragments together results in the following fully implemented *loadFile* method, which will need to be called from the *viewDidLoad* method:

```
override func viewDidLoad() {
    super.viewDidLoad()
    loadFile()
}
.
.
func loadFile() {
    let filemgr = FileManager.default

    let dirPaths = filemgr.urls(for: .documentDirectory,
                            in: .userDomainMask)

    documentURL = dirPaths[0].appendingPathComponent("savefile.txt")

    if let url = documentURL {
        document = MyDocument(fileURL: url)
        document?.userText = ""

        if filemgr.fileExists(atPath: (url.path)) {

            document?.open(completionHandler: {(success: Bool) -> Void in
                if success {
                    print("File open OK")
                    self.textView.text = self.document?.userText
```

```
        } else {
            print("Failed to open file")
        }
    })
} else {
    document?.save(to: url, for: .forCreating,
        completionHandler: {(success: Bool) -> Void in
        if success {
            print("File created OK")
        } else {
            print("Failed to create file ")
        }
    })
}
    }
}
```

41.11 Saving Content to the Document

When the user touches the app's save button, the content of the text view object needs to be saved to the document. An action method has already been connected to the user interface object for this purpose, and it is now time to write the code for this method.

Since the *viewDidLoad* method has already identified the path to the document and initialized the *document* object, all that needs to be done is to call that object's *save(to:)* method using the *.saveForOverwriting* option. The *save(to:)* method will automatically call the *contents(forType:)* method implemented previously in this chapter. Before calling the method, therefore, the userText property of the document object must be set to the current text of the *textView* object.

Bringing this all together results in the following implementation of the *saveDocument* method:

```
@IBAction func saveDocument(_ sender: Any) {
    document?.userText = textView.text

    if let url = documentURL {
        document?.save(to: url,
                for: .forOverwriting,
                completionHandler: {(success: Bool) -> Void in
                if success {
                    print("File overwrite OK")
                } else {
                    print("File overwrite failed")
                }
        })
    }
}
```

41.12 Testing the App

All that remains is to test that the app works by clicking on the Xcode run button. Upon execution, any text entered into the text view object should be saved to the *savefile.txt* file when the Save button is touched. Once some text has been saved, click on the stop button located in the Xcode toolbar. After restarting the app, the text view should be populated with the previously saved text.

41.13 Summary

While the UIDocument class is the cornerstone of document storage using the iCloud service, it is also of considerable use and advantage in using the local file system storage of an iOS device. UIDocument must be subclassed as an abstract class, and two mandatory methods must be implemented within the subclass to operate. This chapter worked through an example of using UIDocument to save and load content using a locally stored document. The next chapter will look at using UIDocument to perform cloud-based document storage and retrieval.

42. Using iCloud Storage in an iOS 17 App

The two preceding chapters of this book were intended to convey the knowledge necessary to begin implementing iCloud-based document storage in iOS apps. Having outlined the steps necessary to enable iCloud access in the chapter entitled *"Preparing an iOS 17 App to use iCloud Storage"* and provided an overview of the UIDocument class in *"Managing Files using the iOS 17 UIDocument Class"*, the next step is to begin to store documents using the iCloud service.

Within this chapter, the *iCloudStore* app created in the previous chapter will be re-purposed to store a document using iCloud storage instead of the local device-based file system. The assumption is also made that the project has been enabled for iCloud document storage following the steps outlined in *"Preparing an iOS 17 App to use iCloud Storage"*.

Before starting on this project, it is important to note that membership to the Apple Developer Program will be required as outlined in *"Joining the Apple Developer Program"*.

42.1 iCloud Usage Guidelines

Before implementing iCloud storage in an app, a few rules must first be understood. Some of these are mandatory rules, and some are simply recommendations made by Apple:

- Apps must be associated with a provisioning profile enabled for iCloud storage.

- The app projects must include a suitably configured entitlements file for iCloud storage.

- Apps should not make unnecessary use of iCloud storage. Once a user's initial free iCloud storage space is consumed by stored data, the user will either need to delete files or purchase more space.

- Apps should, ideally, provide the user with the option to select which documents are to be stored in the cloud and which are to be stored locally.

- When opening a *previously created* iCloud-based document, the app should never use an absolute path to the document. The app should instead search for the document by name in the app's iCloud storage area and then access it using the result of the search.

- Documents stored using iCloud should be placed in the app's *Documents* directory. This gives the user the ability to delete individual documents from the storage. Documents saved outside the *Documents* folder can only be deleted in bulk.

42.2 Preparing the iCloudStore App for iCloud Access

Much of the work performed in creating the local storage version of the *iCloudStore* app in the previous chapter will be reused in this example. The user interface, for example, remains unchanged, and the implementation of the UIDocument subclass will not need to be modified. The only methods that need to be rewritten are the *saveDocument* and *viewDidLoad* methods of the view controller.

Load the *iCloudStore* project into Xcode and select the *ViewController.swift* file. Locate the *saveDocument* method and remove the current code from within the method so that it reads as follows:

```
@IBAction func saveDocument(_ sender: Any) {

}
```

Next, locate the *loadFile* method and modify it accordingly to match the following fragment:

```
func loadFile() {

}
```

42.3 Enabling iCloud Capabilities and Services

Before writing any code, we need to add the iCloud capability to our project, enable the iCloud Documents service, and create an iCloud container.

Begin by selecting the iCloudStore target located at the top of the Project Navigator panel (marked A in Figure 42-1) so that the main panel displays the project settings. From within this panel, select the *Signing & Capabilities* tab (B) followed by the CoreDataDemo target entry (C):

Figure 42-1

Click on the "+ Capability" button (D) to display the dialog shown in Figure 42-2. Enter iCloud into the filter bar, select the result and press the keyboard enter key to add the capability to the project:

Figure 42-2

If iCloud is not listed as an option, you will need to pay to join the Apple Developer program as outlined in the chapter entitled *"Joining the Apple Developer Program"*. If you are already a member, use the steps outlined in the chapter entitled *"Installing Xcode 15 and the iOS 17 SDK"* to ensure you have created a *Developer ID Application* certificate.

Within the iCloud entitlement settings, make sure that the iCloud Documents service is enabled before clicking on the "+" button indicated by the arrow in Figure 42-3 below to add an iCloud container for the project:

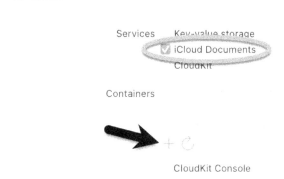

Figure 42-3

After clicking the "+" button, the dialog shown in Figure 42-4 will appear containing a text field into which you need to enter the container identifier. This entry should uniquely identify the container within the CloudKit ecosystem, generally includes your organization identifier (as defined when the project was created), and should be set to something similar to *iCloud.com.yourcompany.iCloudStore*.

Add a new container

Xcode will create a new container if the named container doesn't already
exist, add it to your App ID, and add the new container to your app's
entitlements.

Cancel   OK

Figure 42-4

Once you have entered the container name, click the OK button to add it to the app entitlements. Returning to the *Signing & Capabilities* screen, make sure that the new container is selected:

Figure 42-5

42.4 Configuring the View Controller

Before writing any code, several variables need to be defined within the view controller's *ViewController.swift* file in addition to those implemented in the previous chapter.

Creating a URL to the document location in the iCloud storage will also be necessary. When a document is stored on iCloud, it is said to be *ubiquitous* since the document is accessible to the app regardless of the device on which it is running. Therefore, the object used to store this URL will be named *ubiquityURL*.

As previously stated, when opening a stored document, an app should search for it rather than directly access it using a stored path. An iCloud document search is performed using an *NSMetaDataQuery* object which needs to be declared in the view controller class, in this instance, using the name *metaDataQuery*. Note that declaring the object locally to the method in which it is used will result in the object being released by the automatic reference counting system (ARC) before it has completed the search.

To implement these requirements, select the *ViewController.swift* file in the Xcode project navigator panel and modify the file as follows:

```
import UIKit

class ViewController: UIViewController {

    @IBOutlet weak var textView: UITextView!

    var document: MyDocument?
    var documentURL: URL?
    var ubiquityURL: URL?
    var metaDataQuery: NSMetadataQuery?

.
.
.
}
```

42.5 Implementing the loadFile Method

The purpose of the code in the view controller *loadFile* method is to identify the URL for the ubiquitous file version to be stored using iCloud (assigned to *ubiquityURL*). The ubiquitous URL is constructed by calling the *url(forUbiquityContainerIdentifier:)* method of the FileManager passing through *nil* as an argument to default to the first container listed in the entitlements file.

```
ubiquityURL = filemgr.url(forUbiquityContainerIdentifier: nil)
```

The app will only be able to obtain the ubiquityURL if the user has configured a valid Apple ID within the iCloud page of the iOS Settings app. Therefore, some defensive code must be added to notify the user and return from the method if a valid ubiquityURL cannot be obtained. For testing in this example, we will output a message to the console before returning:

```
guard ubiquityURL != nil else {
    print("Unable to access iCloud Account")
    print("Open the Settings app and enter your Apple ID into iCloud settings")
    return
}
```

Since it is recommended that documents be stored in the *Documents* sub-directory, this needs to be appended to the URL path along with the file name:

```
ubiquityURL =
        ubiquityURL?.appendingPathComponent("Documents/savefile.txt")
```

The final task for the *loadFile* method is to initiate a search in the app's iCloud storage area to find out if the *savefile.txt* file already exists and to act accordingly, subject to the result of the search. The search is performed by calling the methods on an instance of the *NSMetaDataQuery* object. This involves creating the object, setting a predicate to indicate the files to search for, and defining a ubiquitous search scope (in other words instructing the object to search within the Documents directory of the app's iCloud storage area). Once initiated, the search is performed on a separate thread and issues a notification when completed. For this reason, it is also necessary to configure an observer to be notified when the search is finished. The code to perform these tasks reads as follows:

```
metaDataQuery = NSMetadataQuery()

metaDataQuery?.predicate =
    NSPredicate(format: "%K like 'savefile.txt'",
        NSMetadataItemFSNameKey)
metaDataQuery?.searchScopes = [NSMetadataQueryUbiquitousDocumentsScope]

NotificationCenter.default.addObserver(self,
    selector: #selector(
            ViewController.metadataQueryDidFinishGathering),
    name: NSNotification.Name.NSMetadataQueryDidFinishGathering,
    object: metaDataQuery!)

metaDataQuery?.start()
```

Once the *start* method is called, the search will run and call the *metadataQueryDidFinishGathering* method when the search is complete. The next step, therefore, is to implement the *metadataQueryDidFinishGathering* method. Before doing so, however, note that the *loadFile* method is now complete, and the full implementation should read as follows:

```
func loadFile() {

    let filemgr = FileManager.default

    ubiquityURL = filemgr.url(forUbiquityContainerIdentifier: nil)

    guard ubiquityURL != nil else {
        print("Unable to access iCloud Account")
        print("Open the Settings app and enter your Apple ID into iCloud
settings")
        return
    }

    ubiquityURL = ubiquityURL?.appendingPathComponent(
                        "Documents/savefile.txt")
```

```
metaDataQuery = NSMetadataQuery()

metaDataQuery?.predicate =
    NSPredicate(format: "%K like 'savefile.txt'",
        NSMetadataItemFSNameKey)
metaDataQuery?.searchScopes =
            [NSMetadataQueryUbiquitousDocumentsScope]

NotificationCenter.default.addObserver(self,
    selector: #selector(
            ViewController.metadataQueryDidFinishGathering),
    name: NSNotification.Name.NSMetadataQueryDidFinishGathering,
    object: metaDataQuery!)

metaDataQuery?.start()
}
```

42.6 Implementing the metadataQueryDidFinishGathering Method

When the metadata query was triggered in the *loadFile* method to search for documents in the Documents directory of the app's iCloud storage area, an observer was configured to call a method named *metadataQueryDidFinishGathering* when the initial search was completed. The next logical step is to implement this method. The first task of the method is to identify the query object that caused this method to be called. This object must then disable any further query updates (at this stage, the document either exists or doesn't exist, so there is nothing to be gained by receiving additional updates) and stop the search. Finally, removing the observer that triggered the method call is also necessary. When combined, these requirements result in the following code:

```
let query: NSMetadataQuery = notification.object as! NSMetadataQuery

query.disableUpdates()

NotificationCenter.default.removeObserver(self,
        name: NSNotification.Name.NSMetadataQueryDidFinishGathering,
        object: query)

query.stop()
```

The next step is to make sure at least one match was found and to extract the URL of the first document located during the search:

```
if query.resultCount == 1 {
    let resultURL = query.value(ofAttribute: NSMetadataItemURLKey,
                forResultAt: 0) as! URL
```

In all likelihood, a more complex app would need to implement a *for* loop to iterate through more than one document in the array. Given that the iCloudStore app searched for only one specific file name, we can check the array element count and assume that if the count is one, then the document already exists. In this case, the ubiquitous URL of the document from the query object needs to be assigned to our *ubiquityURL* member property and used to create an instance of our MyDocument class called *document*. The *document object's open(completionHandler:) method* is then called to open the document in the cloud and read the contents. This will trigger a call to the *load(fromContents:)* method of the *document* object, which, in turn, will assign the contents of the document to the *userText* property. Assuming the document read is successful, the value of *userText* needs to be assigned to the *text* property of the text view object to make it visible to the user. Bringing this together results in the following code fragment:

```
document = MyDocument(fileURL: resultURL as URL)

document?.open(completionHandler: {(success: Bool) -> Void in
    if success {
        print("iCloud file open OK")
        self.textView.text = self.document?.userText
        self.ubiquityURL = resultURL as URL
    } else {
        print("iCloud file open failed")
    }
})
} else {
}
```

Suppose the document does not yet exist in iCloud storage. In that case, the code needs to create the document using the *save(to:)* method of the *document* object passing through the value of *ubiquityURL* as the destination path on iCloud:

```
.
.
.
} else {
    if let url = ubiquityURL {
        document = MyDocument(fileURL: url)

        document?.save(to: url,
                    for: .forCreating,
                    completionHandler: {(success: Bool) -> Void in
                     if success {
                         print("iCloud create OK")
                     } else {
                         print("iCloud create failed")
                     }
        })
    }
}
```

The individual code fragments outlined above combine to implement the following *metadataQueryDidFinishGathering* method, which should be added to the *ViewController.swift* file:

```
@objc func metadataQueryDidFinishGathering(notification: NSNotification)
    -> Void
{
    let query: NSMetadataQuery = notification.object as! NSMetadataQuery

    query.disableUpdates()
```

```
NotificationCenter.default.removeObserver(self,
        name: NSNotification.Name.NSMetadataQueryDidFinishGathering,
        object: query)


query.stop()

if query.resultCount == 1 {
    let resultURL = query.value(ofAttribute: NSMetadataItemURLKey,
                            forResultAt: 0) as! URL

    document = MyDocument(fileURL: resultURL as URL)

    document?.open(completionHandler: {(success: Bool) -> Void in
        if success {
            print("iCloud file open OK")
            self.textView.text = self.document?.userText
            self.ubiquityURL = resultURL as URL
        } else {
            print("iCloud file open failed")
        }
    })
} else {
    if let url = ubiquityURL {
        document = MyDocument(fileURL: url)

        document?.save(to: url,
                    for: .forCreating,
                    completionHandler: {(success: Bool) -> Void in
                     if success {
                         print("iCloud create OK")
                     } else {
                         print("iCloud create failed")
                     }
                })
    }
}
}
```

42.7 Implementing the saveDocument Method

The final task before building and running the app is implementing the *saveDocument* method. This method needs to update the *userText* property of the *document* object with the text entered into the text view and then call the *saveToURL* method of the *document* object, passing through the *ubiquityURL* as the destination URL using the *.forOverwriting* option:

```
@IBAction func saveDocument(_ sender: Any) {
    document?.userText = textView.text
```

```
if let url = ubiquityURL {
    document?.save(to: url,
            for: .forOverwriting,
            completionHandler: {(success: Bool) -> Void in
             if success {
                 print("Save overwrite OK")
             } else {
                 print("Save overwrite failed")
             }
        })
    }
}
```

All that remains now is to build and run the iCloudStore app on an iOS device, but first, some settings need to be checked.

42.8 Enabling iCloud Document and Data Storage

When testing iCloud on an iOS Simulator session, it is important to ensure that the simulator is configured with a valid Apple ID within the Settings app. Launch the simulator, load the Settings app, and click on the iCloud option to configure this. If no account information is configured on this page, enter a valid Apple ID and corresponding password before proceeding with the testing.

Whether or not apps are permitted to use iCloud storage on an iOS device or Simulator is controlled by the iCloud settings. To review these settings, open the Settings app on the device or simulator, select your account at the top of the settings list and, on the resulting screen, select the *iCloud* category. Scroll down the list of various iCloud-related options and verify that the *iCloud Drive* option is set to *On*:

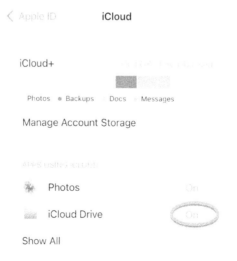

Figure 42-6

42.9 Running the iCloud App

Once you have logged in to an iCloud account on the device or simulator, test the iCloudStore app by clicking the run button. Once running, edit the text in the text view and touch the *Save* button. Next, in the Xcode toolbar, click on the stop button to exit the app, followed by the run button to re-launch the app. On the second launch, the previously entered text will be read from the document in the cloud and displayed in the text view object.

42.10 Making a Local File Ubiquitous

In addition to writing a file directly to iCloud storage, as illustrated in this example app, it is also possible to transfer a pre-existing local file to iCloud storage, making it ubiquitous. This can be achieved using the *setUbiquitous* method of the FileManager class. For example, assuming that *documentURL* references the path to the local copy of the file and *ubiquityURL* the iCloud destination, a local file can be made ubiquitous using the following code:

```
do {
    try filemgr.setUbiquitous(true, itemAt: documentUrl,
                destinationURL: ubiquityURL)
} catch let error {
    print("setUbiquitous failed: \(error.localizedDescription)")
}
```

42.11 Summary

The objective of this chapter was to work through the process of developing an app that stores a document using the iCloud service. Both techniques of directly creating a file in iCloud storage and making an existing locally created file ubiquitous were covered. In addition, some important guidelines that should be observed when using iCloud were outlined.

43. Using iCloud Drive Storage in an iOS 17 App

The previous chapter designed an app that used iCloud Storage to store a text file remotely. While the presence of the stored file could be confirmed by accessing the iCloud Storage section of the iOS Settings app, the file and its content were only accessible to the iCloudStore example app. This chapter will create a simple app that uses iCloud Drive to store a sample text file and show how the file can be accessed in various ways from outside the app.

43.1 Preparing an App to use iCloud Drive Storage

As with other forms of iCloud storage, several steps must be taken to add support for iCloud Drive to an Xcode app project. The first step is to enable the iCloud Documents capability as outlined in the chapter entitled *"Preparing an iOS 17 App to use iCloud Storage"*.

When an app stores files on iCloud Drive, it places them within the Documents folder of an iCloud ubiquitous container. Any files stored at this location will appear within iCloud Drive within a Folder with the name assigned to the container (by default, this is simply the app name).

The ubiquitous container is configured for the project via an NSUbiquitousContainers key entry which needs to be added to the project's *Info.plist* file, which takes the following form:

```
<key>NSUbiquitousContainers</key>
<dict>
    <key>iCloud.$(PRODUCT_BUNDLE_IDENTIFIER)</key>
    <dict>
        <key>NSUbiquitousContainerIsDocumentScopePublic</key>
        <true/>
        <key>NSUbiquitousContainerName</key>
        <string>MyAppName</string>
        <key>NSUbiquitousContainerSupportedFolderLevels</key>
        <string>None</string>
    </dict>
</dict>
```

The first entry in the dictionary consists of the app's bundle identifier pre-fixed with "iCloud." (for example, iCloud.com.ebookfrenzy.MyApp). This entry must match the app's bundle identifier. Otherwise, the stored files will not appear in iCloud Drive. Since Xcode has already declared the bundle ID in the *Info.plist* file via the PRODUCT_BUNDLE_IDENTIFIER key, the safest option is to reference this key as follows:

```
<key>iCloud.$(PRODUCT_BUNDLE_IDENTIFIER)</key>
```

Next, the *access scope* of the container is declared. If set to false, the contents of the container will be accessible to the app but will not otherwise be visible within iCloud Drive (in other words, it will not show up in the iOS Files app or macOS Finder).

The *container name* entry defines the container's name and represents the folder name under which the files will be listed in iCloud Drive.

Finally, the number of directory levels within the container to which the user will have access via iCloud Drive is declared. If this is set to *None*, iCloud Drive only has access to the container's Documents directory, and sub-directories cannot be created using apps such as Files or Finder. A setting of *One* allows iCloud Drive to access and create sub-folders up to one level beyond the Documents folder. Finally, a setting of *Any* allows sub-directories of any level to be accessed and created via iCloud Drive.

Once these preparations have been made, working with iCloud Drive from within an iOS app is simply a matter of obtaining the URL of the ubiquitous container and using it to perform the necessary file operations.

43.2 Making Changes to the NSUbiquitousContainers Key

When making modifications to the iCloud Drive container settings in the *Info.plist* file, it is important to be aware that once the app has been run once, subsequent changes to these settings may not be registered with iCloud unless the CFBundleVersion number value in the *Info.plist* file is incremented, for example:

```
.
.

    <key>CFBundleVersion</key>
            <string>2</string>

.
.
```

43.3 Creating the iCloud Drive Example Project

Begin by launching Xcode and creating a new project using the iOS App template with the Swift and Storyboard options selected, entering *TestDrive* as the product name. Next, follow the steps outlined in the *"Preparing an iOS 17 App to use iCloud Storage"* chapter to add the iCloud capability, enable the iCloud Documents Service, and create and enable a container for the app.

43.4 Modifying the Info.plist File

Locate the *Info.plist* file in the project navigator panel, right-click on it and select the *Open As -> Source Code* menu option. With the file open in the editor, add the NSUbiquitousContainers entry as follows:

```
<?xml version="1.0" encoding="UTF-8"?>
<!DOCTYPE plist PUBLIC "-//Apple//DTD PLIST 1.0//EN" "http://www.apple.com/DTDs/
PropertyList-1.0.dtd">
<plist version="1.0">
<dict>
      <key>UIApplicationSceneManifest</key>
      <dict>
.
.

                              <string>Main</string>
                      </dict>
              </array>
          </dict>
      </dict>
   <key>NSUbiquitousContainers</key>
   <dict>
```

```
    <key>iCloud.$(PRODUCT_BUNDLE_IDENTIFIER)</key>
    <dict>
        <key>NSUbiquitousContainerIsDocumentScopePublic</key>
        <true/>
        <key>NSUbiquitousContainerName</key>
        <string>TestDrive</string>
        <key>NSUbiquitousContainerSupportedFolderLevels</key>
        <string>None</string>
    </dict>
    </dict>
</dict>
</plist>
```

43.5 Designing the User Interface

The user interface will, once again, consist of a UITextView and a UIButton. The user will enter text into the text view and save that text to a file on iCloud Drive by clicking on the button.

Select the *Main.storyboard* file and display the Interface Builder Library panel. Drag and drop the Text View and Button objects into the view canvas, resizing the text view so that it occupies only the upper area of the view. Double-click on the button object and change the title text to "Save to iCloud Drive":

Figure 43-1

Display the *Resolve Auto Layout Issues* menu and select the *Reset to Suggested Constraints* option.

Remove the example Latin text from the text view object by selecting it in the view canvas and deleting the value from the *Text* property in the Attributes Inspector panel.

Select the Text View object in the view canvas, display the Assistant Editor panel and verify that the editor is displaying the contents of the *ViewController.swift* file. Right-click on the Text View object and drag it to a position just below the "class ViewController" declaration line in the Assistant Editor. Release the line, and in the resulting connection dialog, establish an outlet connection named *textView*.

Finally, right-click on the button object and drag the line to the area immediately beneath the *viewDidLoad* method declaration in the Assistant Editor panel. Release the line and, within the resulting connection dialog, establish an Action method on the *Touch Up Inside* event configured to call a method named *saveToDrive*.

43.6 Accessing the Ubiquitous Container

Each time the TestDrive app launches, it will need to obtain the URL of the container, check whether the text file already exists, and, if so, read the file content and display it within the Text View object. Edit the *ViewController. swift* file and modify it to read as follows:

```
import UIKit

class ViewController: UIViewController {

    @IBOutlet weak var textView: UITextView!

    let containerURL =
        FileManager.default.url(forUbiquityContainerIdentifier: nil)
    var documentURL: URL?

    override func viewDidLoad() {
        super.viewDidLoad()

        documentURL = containerURL?.appendingPathComponent(
                                "Documents/MyTextFile.txt")

        if let documentPath = documentURL?.path {
            if (FileManager.default.fileExists(atPath: documentPath,
                                    isDirectory: nil)) {

                if let databuffer = FileManager.default.contents(
                                        atPath: documentPath) {
                    let datastring = NSString(data: databuffer,
                            encoding: String.Encoding.utf8.rawValue)
                    textView.text = datastring as String?
                }
            }
        }
    }
.

.
```

The code changes begin by declaring a constant named *containerURL* and assigning to it the URL of the default ubiquity container and a variable into which the full URL of the text file will be stored:

```
let containerURL =
        FileManager.default.url(forUbiquityContainerIdentifier: nil)
var documentURL: URL?
```

The text file will be named *MyTextFile.txt* and must be stored in the container's Documents folder. This URL is constructed by appending it to the end of the containerURL as follows:

```
documentURL = containerURL?.appendingPathComponent(
                                    "Documents/MyTextFile.txt"
```

Finally, the FileManager class is used to check if the text file already exists. If it exists, the contents are read and displayed to the user:

```
if (FileManager.default.fileExists(atPath: documentPath, isDirectory: nil)) {
    if let databuffer = FileManager.default.contents(atPath: documentPath) {
        let datastring = NSString(data: databuffer,
                                    encoding: String.Encoding.utf8.rawValue)
        textView.text = datastring as String?
    }
}
```

43.7 Saving the File to iCloud Drive

The final task before testing the app is to implement the code in the *saveToDrive()* method to write the file to iCloud Drive. First, within the *ViewController.swift* file, locate the stub method and implement the code as follows:

```
@IBAction func saveToDrive(_ sender: Any) {

    if let url = documentURL {
        do {
            try textView.text.write(to: url, atomically:true,
              encoding:String.Encoding.utf8)
        } catch let error {
            print(error.localizedDescription)
        }
    }
}
```

Using the previously initialized *documentURL* constant, the method writes the Text View's contents to the text file stored on iCloud Drive, reporting an error in the event the write operation fails.

43.8 Testing the App

Build and run the app on a device or emulator on which the user's iCloud credentials have been configured, enter some text, and click the button to save the file to iCloud Drive. Then, stop the app, relaunch it, and make sure that the text entered previously is restored.

Place the app into the background, launch the iOS Files app, and select the Browse tab located at the bottom of the screen. From the Browse screen, select the iCloud Drive option from the Locations section. Among the folders already stored on iCloud Drive will be a folder named TestDrive, within which will reside the *MyTextFile. txt* file:

Figure 43-2

When selected, the file should open and display the text entered within the TestDrive app.

On a macOS system configured with the same iCloud user account, open the Finder window and navigate to *iCloud Drive -> TestDrive -> MyTextFile.txt,* where the preview panel should display the text saved to the file from within the TestDrive app:

Figure 43-3

43.9 Summary

The iCloud Drive support built into the iOS SDK allows apps to store and retrieve iCloud Drive-based files. This requires that the project's appropriate iCloud capabilities be enabled within Xcode and the addition of ubiquitous container settings within the *Info.plist* file. Once these steps have been taken, a reference to the URL of the container is obtained and used to read, write, delete, and copy files on iCloud Drive. This chapter outlined these steps before creating an example app that uses iCloud Drive to store and access a simple text file.

44. An Overview of the iOS 17 Document Browser View Controller

The previous chapters have introduced ways to integrate file handling into an iOS app in terms of local and cloud-based storage. In these chapters, the assumption has been made that all of the user interface aspects of the file handling and file system navigation will be provided in some way by the app itself. An alternative to integrating file handling in this way is to use the iOS document browser view controller.

This chapter provides a basic overview of this class in preparation for a tutorial in the next chapter.

44.1 An Overview of the Document Browser View Controller

The document browser view controller is implemented using the UIDocumentBrowserViewController class and provides a visual environment in which users can navigate file systems and select and manage files from within an iOS app. In addition, the document browser provides the user with access to the local device file system, iCloud storage, and third-party providers such as Google Drive.

To see the browser in action, take some time to explore the Files app included as standard with iOS 17. Figure 44-1, for example, shows the iOS Files app browsing a user's iCloud Drive files and folders:

Figure 44-1

When integrated into an app, the document browser provides the same functionality as the Files app in addition to the ability to create new files.

44.2 The Anatomy of a Document-Based App

The key elements that interact to provide the document browser functionality within an iOS app are a UIDocumentBrowserViewController instance, access to one or more file providers (for example, the local file system, iCloud Drive, Google Drive, etc.) and at least one additional view controller in which to present any selected file content to the user. When working with files in conjunction with the document browser, the use of the UIDocument class for the lower level file handling tasks is still recommended, so a subclass of UIDocument will also typically be included (the UIDocument class was covered in the chapter entitled *"Managing Files using the iOS 17 UIDocument Class"*).

Adding document browser support to an app is a multistep process that begins with creating a UIDocumentBrowserViewController instance. When doing this, the browser must be the app's root view controller. By far, the easiest way to start the development process is to use the Xcode iOS *Document App* template when creating a new project, as shown in Figure 44-2:

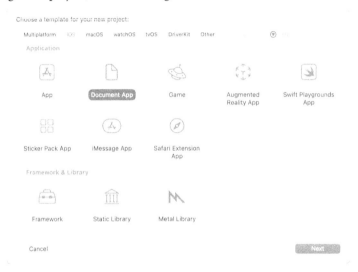

Figure 44-2

A project created using the Document Based App template will contain the following files by default:

- **DocumentBrowserViewController.swift** - The root view controller for the app derived from the UIDocumentBrowserViewController class. This file contains stub delegate methods ready to be completed to implement app-specific document browser behavior.

- **Document.swift** – A subclass of the UIDocument class containing stub methods.

- **DocumentViewController.swift** – A template view controller intended to present the selected files to the user. This template implementation simply displays the file name and a "Done" button to return to the document browser.

44.3 Document Browser Project Settings

Some *Info.plist* settings must be configured to enable document browser support within an app project. The first is the *Supports Document Browser* (UISupportsDocumentBrowser) key, which must be set to *YES*.

Next, the app must declare the *document types* it can handle and the action it can perform on those types (i.e., viewing only or viewing and editing). These settings dictate the types of files that will be selectable within the document browser.

Each supported type must, at a minimum, include the following key-value information:

- **CFBundleTypeName** - A string value that uniquely identifies the type within the app's context.

- **CFBundleTypeRole** – A string value indicating the action that the app will perform on the file (i.e., Editor or Viewer)

- **LSHandlerRank** – A string value that declares to the system how the app relates to the file type. If the app uses its own custom file type, this should be set to Owner. If the app is to be opened as the default app for files of this type, the value should be set to Default. If, on the other hand, the app can handle files of this type but is not intended to be the default handler, a value of Alternate should be used. Finally, None should be used if the app is not to be associated with the file type.

- **LSItemContentTypes** – An array of Universal Type Identifiers (UTI) indicating the file types supported by the app. These can be custom file types unique to the app or, more commonly, standard identifiers provided by Apple, such as public.image, public.text, public.plain-text, and public.rtf.

As outlined in the next chapter, the easiest way to configure these keys is within the *Info* panel of the Xcode project target screen.

44.4 The Document Browser Delegate Methods

When the user selects a file from within the document browser of an app, several delegate methods implemented within the document browser view controller will be called. These methods can be summarized as follows:

44.4.1 didRequestDocumentCreationWithHandler

This method is called when the user requests to create a new file within the document browser. This method is responsible for providing a template file and passing the URL for that file to the *importHandler* method. The template file can either be a file that is already bundled with the app or a file that is created on demand within the delegate method. This method also allows the app to display a selection screen to choose the template type if the app supports more than one file type or template option.

The *importHandler* method interacts with the appropriate file provider to create the file in the designated location. If, for example, the user was browsing an iCloud Drive location when making the file creation request, the *importHandler* method will work with the iCloud Drive file provider to create the new file in that location.

In addition to providing the URL of the template file, the *importHandler* method also needs to be passed a value indicating whether the template file should be moved (*.move*) or copied (*.copy*) to the location on the file provider. A move operation is more likely if the delegate method creates a temporary file to act as the template. However, for a template file bundled with the app, it will make more sense to copy the file since it will need to be available for future creation operations.

If the user cancels the creation process, the *importHandler* method must be called with a nil file URL and a none (*.none*) value. The following code shows an example method implementation that uses a bundled file named *template.txt* as the template:

```
func documentBrowser(_ controller: UIDocumentBrowserViewController,
  didRequestDocumentCreationWithHandler importHandler: @escaping (URL?,
   UIDocumentBrowserViewController.ImportMode) -> Void) {

    let newDocumentURL: URL? = Bundle.main.url(forResource: "template",
                              withExtension: "txt")

    if newDocumentURL != nil {
```

```
        importHandler(newDocumentURL, .copy)
    } else {
        importHandler(nil, .none)

    }

}
```

44.4.2 didImportDocumentAt

This method is called when a new document has been successfully created by the file provider (in other words, the *importHandler* method call was successful). When called, this method is passed both the local template file's source URL and the file's destination URL, now residing on the file provider. In addition, this method will typically display the view controller that is responsible for presenting the file content to the user:

```
func documentBrowser(_ controller: UIDocumentBrowserViewController,
  didImportDocumentAt sourceURL: URL, toDestinationURL destinationURL: URL) {

    presentDocument(at: destinationURL)

}
```

The *presentDocument* method called in the above example is a helpful utility method included as part of the Document Based App project template for the document browser view controller class.

44.4.3 didPickDocumentURLs

This method is called when the user requests to open one or more existing files within the document browser. The URLs for the selected files are passed to the method in the form of an array, and it is the responsibility of this method to pass these URLs to and present the document view controller. The default implementation for this method passes the first URL in the array to the *presentDocument* method:

```
func documentBrowser(_ controller: UIDocumentBrowserViewController,
  didPickDocumentURLs documentURLs: [URL]) {
        guard let sourceURL = documentURLs.first else { return }

    presentDocument(at: sourceURL)

}
```

44.4.4 failedToImportDocumentAt

Called when the document import request fails, this method should notify the user of the failure, details of which can be extracted from the error object:

```
func documentBrowser(_ controller: UIDocumentBrowserViewController,
  failedToImportDocumentAt documentURL: URL, error: Error?) {

    notifyUser(error?.localizedDescription

}
```

44.5 Customizing the Document Browser

Several properties are available for customizing the document browser. The *allowsPickingMultipleItems* property controls whether the user can select multiple files:

```
allowsPickingMultipleItems = false
```

The *allowsDocumentCreation* property defines whether the user can create new files (essentially defining whether or not the create file buttons appear in the browser):

```
allowsDocumentCreation = true
```

The visual appearance of the browser can be changed by setting the *browserUserInterfaceStyle* property to dark, light, or white:

```
browserUserInterfaceStyle = .dark
```

Finally, the tint color used by the browser (primarily the color used for text foreground and icons) can be changed via the *tintColor* property:

```
view.tintColor = .yellow
```

44.6 Adding Browser Actions

Performing a long press on a file within the document browser displays the edit menu (Figure 44-3) containing a range of built-in options, including copy, delete, rename, and share.

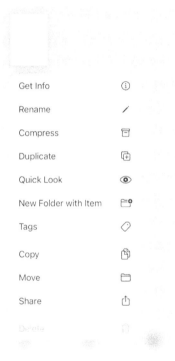

Figure 44-3

These options also appear in the navigation bar at the bottom of the screen when the user enters select mode by tapping the *Select* button in the top right-hand corner of the browser window.

Custom actions may be added to these menus by assigning an array of UIDocumentBrowserActions objects to the *customActions* property of the document browser view controller instance. A UIDocumentBrowserActions object consists of a unique identifier, a string to appear on the button, an array of locations where the action is to be available (options are menu and navigation bar), and a completion handler to be called when the action is selected. In addition, the completion handler is provided with an array of URLs representing the files selected when the action was triggered.

The action object also needs to be configured with the file types for which it is to appear and a property setting indicating whether the action can work with multiple file selections. The following example creates and assigns a browser action for text and plain text file types that works only with single file selections and displays "Convert" as the action title:

```
let action = UIDocumentBrowserAction(identifier:
    "com.ebookfrenzy.docdemo.convert", localizedTitle: "Convert",
        availability: [.menu, .navigationBar], handler: { urls in


    // Code to be executed when action is selected


})


action.supportedContentTypes = ["public.text", "public.plain-text"]
action.supportsMultipleItems = false
customActions = [action]
```

44.7 Summary

The UIDocumentBrowserViewController class provides an easy way to build document browsing into iOS apps. The document browser can be integrated with minimal programming effort and is designed to integrate with the local filesystem, iCloud Drive, and other third-party file providers such as Google Drive and DropBox. Integration primarily consists of adding a UIDocumentBrowserViewController as the root view controller, setting some *Info.plist* properties, and writing some delegate methods. Much preparatory work is performed automatically when a new Xcode project is created using the Document Based App template.

45. An iOS 17 Document Browser Tutorial

This chapter aims to work through creating an iOS app that uses the UIDocumentBrowserViewController class to integrate document browsing support. The app will demonstrate using the Document Based App template to create an app that can navigate all available file providers and create, open, and edit text-based documents.

45.1 Creating the DocumentBrowser Project

Launch Xcode and create a new iOS project named *DocumentBrowser* based on the iOS *Document App* template with Swift selected as the programming language.

Once the project has loaded, select the *File -> New -> File…* menu option, and scroll down the list of file types until the *Empty* option appears listed under *Other,* as shown in Figure 45-1:

Figure 45-1

Click *Next* and name the file *template.txt* before clicking on the *Create* button. This file will serve as the template when the user creates new documents. Select the file in the project navigator and add a line of text which reads as follows:

```
This is a template text file, add your own text.
```

45.2 Declaring the Supported File Types

The app will be configured to support text files (both plain text and text files containing markup such as HTML). Within Xcode, select the DocumentBrowser target at the top of the project navigator panel and, within the settings screen, select the *Info* tab highlighted in Figure 45-2:

Figure 45-2

Check that the *Supports Document Browser* key value is set to *YES*, then click on the disclosure arrow next to the *Document Types* heading to unfold the list of types currently supported, followed by the arrow next to the *Additional document type properties* section:

Figure 45-3

Note that Xcode has created a single document content type identifier set to *com.example.plain-text* with the handler rank set to *Default*:

Since this app is intended to edit text files, modify this entry as follows:

- **Name** – Plain Text

- **Types** – com.example.plain-text

- **CFBundleTypeRole** – Editor

- **Handler Rank** – Alternate

Next, add another document type by clicking on the + button beneath the Additional document type properties section. Fill in the information for this entry as follows:

- Name – Text

- Types – public.plain-text

- CFBundleTypeRole – Editor

- LSHandlerRank – Alternate

Build and run the app and make sure that the document browser appears and that it is possible to navigate around the local device or iCloud Drive for your account. Local files can be found by selecting the *On My iPad/ iPhone* location option. If this option is not listed, it usually means that no local files have been saved or that this option has not yet been enabled on the device. To check this, tap the menu button as indicated by the arrow in Figure 45-4 and select the Edit option:

Figure 45-4

After entering edit mode, enable the switches next to the locations to which you would like access from within the browser:

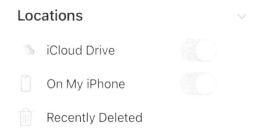

Figure 45-5

45.3 Completing the didRequestDocumentCreationWithHandler Method

Edit the *DocumentBrowserViewController.swift* file, add code to create a temporary template file, and pass the URL for that file to the *importHandler* method. Note that since the template file is bundled with the app, the file is copied to the file provider rather than moved. This ensures the template is still available for future creation requests:

```
func documentBrowser(_ controller: UIDocumentBrowserViewController,
    didRequestDocumentCreationWithHandler importHandler: @escaping (URL?,
        UIDocumentBrowserViewController.ImportMode) -> Void) {

    let newDocumentURL: URL? = Bundle.main.url(forResource:
                            "template", withExtension: "txt")

    if newDocumentURL != nil {
```

```
            importHandler(newDocumentURL, .copy)
        } else {
            importHandler(nil, .none)
        }
    }
}
```

Run the app, select the *Browse* item in the navigation bar at the bottom of the screen and verify that the browser has defaulted to the *DocumentBrowser* folder on iCloud Drive, as shown in Figure 45-6. If the browser displays a different location, navigate to the iCloud Drive *DocumentBrowser* folder before continuing.

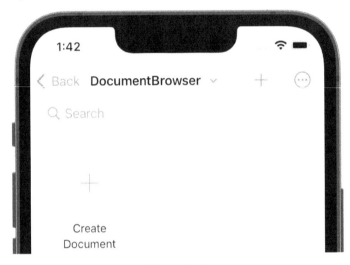

Figure 45-6

Click on the *Create Document* option, at which point the new document should be created, and the document view controller displayed containing the file's name and a Done button. Tap the Done button to return to the browser where the new file will be listed:

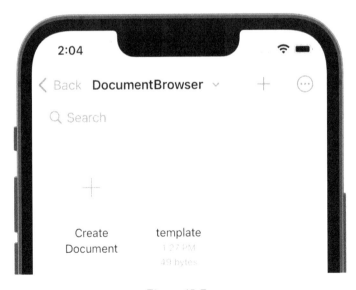

Figure 45-7

Before moving to the next step, scroll to the top of the *DocumentBrowserViewController.swift* class file and verify that the *allowsDocumentCreation* and *allowsPickingMultipleItems* properties are set to *true* and *false*, respectively, within the *viewDidLoad()* method:

```
allowsDocumentCreation = true
allowsPickingMultipleItems = false
```

45.4 Finishing the UIDocument Subclass

Xcode has provided a template UIDocument subclass in the *Document.swift* file. This class now needs to be completed so that it will read and write file content. This code is identical to that used in the chapter entitled *"Managing Files using the iOS 17 UIDocument Class"*. Edit the *Document.swift* file and modify it to reads as follows:

```
import UIKit


class Document: UIDocument {

    var userText: String? = ""

    override func contents(forType typeName: String) throws -> Any {

        if let content = userText {

            let length =
                content.lengthOfBytes(using: String.Encoding.utf8)
            return NSData(bytes:content, length: length)
        } else {
            return Data()
        }
    }


    override func load(fromContents contents: Any, ofType
            typeName: String?) throws {

        if let userContent = contents as? Data {
            userText = NSString(bytes: (contents as AnyObject).bytes,
                    length: userContent.count,
                    encoding: String.Encoding.utf8.rawValue) as String?
        }
    }
}
```

45.5 Modifying the Document View Controller

The final task is to modify the document view controller so that it displays the text file's content and allows it to be edited and saved. Begin by loading the *Main.storyboard* file into Interface Builder and locating the *Document View Controller* Scene. Drag and drop a TextView and a Button view onto the scene. Change the text on the Button to "Save" and, using the Attributes inspector panel, change the *Font* setting to *Title 2* to match the existing Done button. Position the new views so that the layout matches Figure 45-8 and set appropriate layout constraints:

Figure 45-8

Double-click on the Latin text in the TextView and press the keyboard Delete key to remove it. Display the Assistant Editor, confirm that it is displaying the *DocumentViewController.swift* file, and establish an outlet from the TextView to a variable named *documentText* and an action connection from the Save button to a method named *saveFile*.

Edit the *DocumentViewController.swift* file and modify the *updateViewsIfNecessary* method as follows:

```
.
.
func updateViewsIfNecessary() {
    // Check if the document is open and the view is loaded
    guard let document, !document.documentState.contains(.closed) else { return }
    guard isViewLoaded else { return }

    let mydoc = document as? Document

    // Display the content of the document, e.g.:
    self.documentNameLabel.text = document.localizedName
    self.documentText.text = mydoc?.userText
}
.
.
```

Finally, add code to the *saveFile* method to write the content of the TextView to the document:

```
@IBAction func saveFile(_ sender: Any) {
```

```
    let mydoc = document as? Document

    mydoc?.userText = documentText.text

    if let url = mydoc?.fileURL {
        mydoc?.save(to: url,
                       for: .forOverwriting,
                       completionHandler: {(success: Bool) -> Void in
                        if success {
                            print("File overwrite OK")
                        } else {
                            print("File overwrite failed")
                        }
        })
    }
}
```

45.6 Testing the Document Browser App

Run the app and select the *template.txt* file added earlier in the chapter. When the document view controller appears, enter new text into the TextView before clicking on Save, followed by Done to return to the document browser. The icon for the file should now reflect the extra text added to the file, and when selected, the document view controller should also load the new file content.

Place the app in the background and perform a long press on the app icon. When the pop-up appears, it should contain the recently created text file.

45.7 Summary

This chapter has provided a tutorial covering the steps involved in implementing a document browser using the Xcode Document Based App template. Topics covered included the declaration of supported document types, creation of a template document file, implementation of the *didRequestDocumentCreationWithHandler* method, use of the UIDocument class, and customization of the document view controller.

46. Synchronizing iOS 17 Key-Value Data using iCloud

When considering using iCloud in an app, it is important to note that the Apple ecosystem is not limited to the iOS platform. It also encompasses a range of macOS-based laptop and desktop computer systems, all of which have access to iCloud services. This increases the chance that a user will have the same app in one form or another on several different devices and platforms. Take, for the sake of an example, a hypothetical news magazine app. A user may have this app installed on an iPhone and an iPad. If the user begins reading an article on the iPhone instance of the app and then switches to the same app on the iPad later, the iPad app should take the user to the position reached in the article on the iPhone so that the user can resume reading.

This kind of synchronization between apps is provided by the Key-Value data storage feature of iCloud. This chapter aims to provide an overview of this service and work through a very simple example of the feature in action in an iOS app.

46.1 An Overview of iCloud Key-Value Data Storage

The primary purpose of iCloud Key-Value data storage is to allow small amounts of data to be shared between instances of apps running on different devices or even different apps on the same device. The data may be synchronized if encapsulated in an array, dictionary, String, Date, Data, Boolean, or Number object.

iCloud data synchronization is achieved using the NSUbiquitousKeyValueStore class introduced as part of the iOS 5 SDK. Values are saved with a corresponding key using the *set(forKey:)* method. For example, the following code fragment creates an instance of an NSUbiquitousKeyValueStore object and then saves a string value using the key "MyString":

```
var keyStore = NSUbiquitousKeyValueStore()
keyStore.set("Saved String", forKey: "MyString")
```

Once key-value pairs have been saved locally, they will not be synchronized with iCloud storage until a call is made to the *synchronize* method of the NSUbiquitousKeyValueStore instance:

```
keyStore.synchronize()
```

It is important to note that a call to the synchronize method does not immediately synchronize the locally saved data with the iCloud store. Instead, iOS will synchronize at what the Apple documentation refers to as "an appropriate later time."

A stored value may be retrieved by a call to the appropriate method corresponding to the data type to be retrieved (the format of which is *<datatype>*(forKey:)) and passing through the key as an argument. For example, the stored string in the above example may be retrieved as follows:

```
let storedString = keyStore.string(forKey: "MyString")
```

46.2 Sharing Data Between Apps

As with iCloud document storage, key-value data storage requires the implementation of appropriate iCloud entitlements. In this case, the app must have the *com.apple.developer.ubiquity-kvstore-identifier* entitlement key configured in the project's entitlements file. The value assigned to this key identifies which apps can share access to the same iCloud-stored key-value data.

If, for example, the *ubiquity-kvstore-identifier* entitlement key for an app named *MyApp* is assigned a value of *ABCDE12345.com.mycompany.MyApp* (where ABCDEF12345 is the developer's unique team or individual ID), then any other apps using the same entitlement value will also be able to access the same stored key-value data. This, by definition, will be any instance of the *MyApp* running on multiple devices but applies equally to entirely different apps (for example, *MyOtherApp*) if they also use the same entitlement value.

46.3 Data Storage Restrictions

iCloud key-value data storage is provided to meet the narrow requirement of performing essential synchronization between app instances, and the data storage limitations imposed by Apple reflect this.

The amount of data that can be stored per key-value pair is 1MB. The per-app key-value storage limit is 1024 individual keys which, combined, must also not exceed 1MB in total.

46.4 Conflict Resolution

If two app instances change the same key-value pair, the most recent change is given precedence.

46.5 Receiving Notification of Key-Value Changes

An app may register to be notified when another app instance changes stored values. This is achieved by setting up an observer on the *NSUbiquitousKeyValueStoreDidChangeExternallyNotification* notification. This notification is triggered when a change is made to any key-value pair in a specified key-value store and is passed an array of strings containing the keys that were changed together with an NSNumber indicating the reason for the change. If the available space for the key-value storage has been exceeded, this number will match the *NSUbiquitousKeyValueStoreQuotaViolationChange* constant value.

46.6 An iCloud Key-Value Data Storage Example

The remainder of this chapter is devoted to creating an app that uses iCloud key-value storage to store a key with a string value using iCloud. In addition to storing a key-value pair, the app will also configure an observer to receive a notification when another app instance changes the value.

Before starting on this project, it is important to note that membership to the Apple Developer Program will be required as outlined in *"Joining the Apple Developer Program"*.

Begin the app creation process by launching Xcode and creating a new iOS *App* project named *CloudKeys* with *Swift* selected as the programming language.

46.7 Enabling the App for iCloud Key-Value Data Storage

A mandatory step in the app development is configuring the appropriate iCloud entitlement. Following the steps outlined in the *"Preparing an iOS 17 App to use iCloud Storage"* chapter, add the iCloud capability and enable the Key-value storage service:

Figure 46-1

Once selected, Xcode will create an entitlements file for the project named *CloudKeys.entitlements* containing the appropriate iCloud entitlements key-value pairs. Select the entitlements file from the project navigator and note the value assigned to the *iCloud Key-Value Store* key. By default, this is typically comprised of your team or individual developer ID combined with the app's Bundle identifier. Any other apps that use the same value for the entitlement key will share access to the same iCloud-based key-value data stored by this app.

46.8 Designing the User Interface

The app will consist of a text field into which a string may be entered by the user and a button that, when selected, will save the string to the app's iCloud key-value data store. First, select the *Main.storyboard* file, display the Library panel, and drag and drop the two objects onto the view canvas. Next, double-click on the button object and change the text to *Store Key*. The completed view should resemble Figure 46-2:

Figure 46-2

Click on the background View component in the layout, display the *Resolve Auto Layout Issues* menu, and select the *Reset to Suggested Constraints* option listed under *All Views in the View Controller*.

Select the text field object in the view canvas, display the Assistant Editor panel and verify that the editor is displaying the contents of the *ViewController.swift* file. Right-click on the text field object and drag it to a position just below the class declaration line in the Assistant Editor. Release the line, and in the resulting connection dialog, establish an outlet connection named *textField*.

Finally, right-click on the button object and drag the line to the area immediately beneath the newly created outlet in the Assistant Editor panel. Release the line and, within the resulting connection dialog, establish an Action method on the *Touch Up Inside* event configured to call a method named *saveKey*.

46.9 Implementing the View Controller

In addition to the action and outlet references created above, an instance of the NSUbiquitousKeyStore class will be needed. Choose the *ViewController.swift* file, therefore, and modify it as follows:

```
class ViewController: UIViewController {

    var keyStore: NSUbiquitousKeyValueStore?

    @IBOutlet weak var textField: UITextField!
.
.
.
```

46.10 Modifying the viewDidLoad Method

The next step is to add a method to perform the initialization and call it from the *viewDidLoad* method of the view controller. Remaining within the *ViewController.swift* file, modify the code so that it reads as follows:

```
override func viewDidLoad() {
    super.viewDidLoad()

    initCloud()
}

func initCloud() {

    keyStore = NSUbiquitousKeyValueStore()

    let storedString = keyStore?.string(forKey: "MyString")

    if let stringValue = storedString {
        textField.text = stringValue
    }

    NotificationCenter.default.addObserver(self,
        selector: #selector(
        ViewController.ubiquitousKeyValueStoreDidChange),
        name: NSUbiquitousKeyValueStore.didChangeExternallyNotification,
        object: keyStore)
}
```

The method begins by allocating and initializing an instance of the NSUbiquitousKeyValueStore class and assigning it to the keyStore variable. Next, the *string(forKey:)* method of the keyStore object is called to check if the *MyString* key is already in the key-value store. If the key exists, the string value is assigned to the *text* field object's text property via the textField outlet.

Finally, the method sets up an observer to call the *ubiquitousKeyValueStoreDidChange* method when another app instance changes the stored key value.

Having implemented the code in the *initCloud* method, the next step is to write the *ubiquitousKeyValueStoreDidChange* method.

46.11 Implementing the Notification Method

Within the context of this example app, the *ubiquitousKeyValueStoreDidChange* method, triggered when another app instance modifies an iCloud-stored key-value pair, is provided to notify the user of the change via an alert message and to update the text in the text field with the new string value. The code for this method, which needs to be added to the *ViewController.swift* file, is as follows:

```
@objc func ubiquitousKeyValueStoreDidChange(notification: NSNotification) {

    let alert = UIAlertController(title: "Change detected",
            message: "iCloud key-value-store change detected",
        preferredStyle: UIAlertController.Style.alert)
```

```
let cancelAction = UIAlertAction(title: "OK",
        style: .cancel, handler: nil)


alert.addAction(cancelAction)
self.present(alert, animated: true,
            completion: nil)
textField.text = keyStore?.string(forKey: "MyString")
}
```

46.12 Implementing the saveData Method

The final coding task involves the implementation of the *saveData* action method. This method will be called when the user touches the button in the user interface and needs to be implemented in the *ViewController.swift* file:

```
@IBAction func saveKey(_ sender: Any) {
    keyStore?.set(textField.text, forKey: "MyString")
    keyStore?.synchronize()
}
```

The code for this method is quite simple. The *set(forKey:)* method of the keyStore object is called, assigning the current text property of the user interface textField object to the "MyString" key. The synchronize method of the keyStore object is then called to ensure that the key-value pair is synchronized with the iCloud store.

46.13 Testing the App

Click on the run button in the Xcode toolbar, and once the app is installed and running on the device or iOS Simulator, enter some text into the text field and tap the *Store Key* button. Next, stop the app from running by clicking on the stop button in the Xcode toolbar, then re-launch by clicking the run button. When the app reloads, the text field should be primed with the saved value string.

To test the change notification functionality, install the app on both a device and the iOS simulator. Then, with the app running on both, change the text on the iOS Simulator instance and save the key. After a short delay, the device-based instance of the app will detect the change, display the alert and update the text field to the new value.

46.14 Summary

iOS key-value data storage allows small amounts of data in the form of an array, dictionary, String, Date, Data, Boolean, or Number objects to be shared between instances of apps running on different devices running iOS and macOS. This chapter has outlined the steps in enabling and implementing this data sharing, including enabling key-value storage support and configuring a listener to detect changes.

47. iOS 17 Database Implementation using SQLite

While the preceding chapters of this book have looked at data storage within the context of iOS-based apps, this coverage has been limited to basic file and directory handling. However, in many instances, the most effective data storage and retrieval strategy require using some form of database management system.

To address this need, the iOS SDK includes everything necessary to integrate SQLite-based databases into iOS apps. Therefore, this chapter aims to provide an overview of how to use SQLite to perform basic database operations within your iOS app. Once the basics have been covered, the next chapter (*"An Example SQLite-based iOS 17 App using Swift and FMDB"*) will work through creating an actual app that uses an SQLite database to store and retrieve data.

47.1 What is SQLite?

SQLite is an embedded, relational database management system (RDBMS). Most relational databases (Oracle and MySQL being prime examples) are standalone server processes that run independently and cooperate with apps requiring database access. SQLite is referred to as *embedded* because it is provided as a library linked to apps. As such, there is no standalone database server running in the background. Instead, all database operations are handled internally within the app through calls to functions contained in the SQLite library.

The developers of SQLite have placed the technology into the public domain with the result that it is now a widely deployed database solution.

SQLite is written in the C programming language; therefore, using SQLite from within Swift code either requires some complex handling of C function calls, data types and pointers or the more straightforward approach of using an existing SQLite wrapper as a layer between SQLite and Swift. In this chapter, we will look at one such wrapper, FMDB.

For additional information about SQLite, refer to *https://www.sqlite.org*.

47.2 Structured Query Language (SQL)

Data is accessed in SQLite databases using a high-level language known as Structured Query Language. This is usually abbreviated to SQL and pronounced *sequel*. SQL is a standard language used by most relational database management systems. SQLite conforms mainly to the SQL-92 standard.

While some basic SQL statements will be used within this chapter, a detailed overview of SQL is beyond the scope of this book. However, many other resources provide a far better overview of SQL than we could ever hope to provide in a single chapter here.

47.3 Trying SQLite on macOS

For readers unfamiliar with databases and SQLite, diving right into creating an iOS app that uses SQLite may seem a little intimidating. Fortunately, macOS is shipped with SQLite pre-installed, including an interactive environment for issuing SQL commands from within a Terminal window. This is a helpful way to learn about SQLite and SQL and an invaluable tool for identifying problems with databases created by apps in the iOS simulator.

iOS 17 Database Implementation using SQLite

To launch an interactive SQLite session, open a Terminal window on your macOS system, change directory to a suitable location, and run the following command:

```
sqlite3 ./mydatabase.db
```

```
SQLite version 3.6.12
Enter ".help" for instructions
Enter SQL statements terminated with a ";"
sqlite>
```

At the *sqlite>* prompt, commands may be entered to perform tasks such as creating tables and inserting and retrieving data. For example, to create a new table in our database with fields to hold ID, name, address, and phone number fields, the following statement is required:

```
create table contacts (id integer primary key autoincrement, name text, address
text, phone text);
```

Note that each row in a table must have a *primary key* that is unique to that row. In the above example, we have designated the ID field as the primary key, declared it as being of type *integer*, and asked SQLite to increment the number each time a row is added automatically. This is a common way to ensure that each row has a unique primary key. The remaining fields are each declared as being of type *text*.

To list the tables in the currently selected database, use the *.tables* statement:

```
sqlite> .tables
contacts
```

To insert records into the table:

```
sqlite> insert into contacts (name, address, phone) values ("Bill Smith", "123
Main Street, California", "123-555-2323");
sqlite> insert into contacts (name, address, phone) values ("Mike Parks", "10
Upping Street, Idaho", "444-444-1212");
```

To retrieve all rows from a table:

```
sqlite> select * from contacts;
1|Bill Smith|123 Main Street, California|123-555-2323
2|Mike Parks|10 Upping Street, Idaho|444-444-1212
```

To extract a row that meets specific criteria:

```
sqlite> select * from contacts where name="Mike Parks";
2|Mike Parks|10 Upping Street, Idaho|444-444-1212
```

To exit from the sqlite3 interactive environment:

```
sqlite> .exit
```

When running an iOS app in the iOS Simulator environment, any database files will be created on the file system of the computer on which the simulator is running. This has the advantage that you can navigate to the location of the database file, load it into the sqlite3 interactive tool and perform tasks on the data to identify possible problems in the app code. If, for example, an app creates a database file named *contacts.db* in its documents directory, the file will be located on the host system in the following folder:

```
/Users/<user>/Library/Developer/CoreSimulator/Devices/<simulator id>/data/
Containers/Data/Application/<id>/Documents
```

Where *<user>* is the login name of the user logged into the macOS system, *<simulator id>* is the id of the simulator session, and *<id>* is the unique ID of the app.

47.4 Preparing an iOS App Project for SQLite Integration

By default, the Xcode environment does not assume that you will include SQLite in your app. When developing SQLite-based apps, a few additional steps are required to ensure the code will compile when the app is built. First, the project needs to be configured to include the *libsqlite3.tbd* dynamic library during the link phase of the build process. To achieve this, select the target entry in the Xcode project navigator (the top entry with the product name) to display the summary information. Next, select the *Build Phases* tab to display the build information.

The *Link Binary with Libraries* section lists the libraries and frameworks already included in the project. To add another library or framework, click the '+' button to display the complete list. From this list, select the required item (in this case, *libsqlite3.tbd*) and click *Add*.

47.5 SQLite, Swift, and Wrappers

As previously discussed, SQLite is written in the C programming language. While it was still possible to use the C-based SQLite API from within Objective-C code with relative ease, this is not the case when programming in Swift without dealing with complex issues when bridging the gap between C and Swift. A standard solution to this dilemma involves using an SQLite "wrapper." Several wrappers are now available for this purpose, many of which show considerable potential. For this book, however, we will work with the FMDB wrapper. Although this is essentially an Objective-C wrapper, it can be used efficiently within Swift code. FMDB has been chosen for the examples in this book because it has been available for some time, is considered stable and feature-rich, and will be familiar to the many developers who have previously used it with Objective-C. In addition, FMDB is an open-source project released under the terms of the MIT license.

Details on how to obtain FMDB and incorporate it into an iOS Xcode project are covered in detail in the next chapter (*"An Example SQLite-based iOS 17 App using Swift and FMDB"*).

47.6 Key FMDB Classes

When implementing a database using SQLite with FMDB, utilizing several FMDB classes contained within the wrapper will be necessary. A summary of the most commonly used classes is as follows:

- **FMDatabase** – Used to represent a single SQLite database. The object on which SQL statements are executed from within code.

- **FMResultSet** – Used to hold the results of a SQL query operation on an FMDatabase instance.

- **FMDatabaseQueue** – A version of FMDatabase designed to allow database queries to be performed from multiple threads.

For more detailed information, the FMDB Class Reference documentation is available online at:

http://ccgus.github.io/fmdb/html/Classes/FMDatabase.html

47.7 Creating and Opening a Database

Before work can commence on a database, it must first be created and opened. The following code opens the database file at the path specified by *<database file path>*. If the database file does not already exist, it will be created when the FMDatabase instance is initialized:

```
let myDatabase = FMDatabase(path: <database file path>)


if (myDatabase.open()) {
```

```
    // Database is ready
} else {
    print("Error: \(myDatabase.lastErrorMessage())")
}
```

47.8 Creating a Database Table

Database data is organized into *tables*. Before data can be stored in a database, therefore, a table must first be created. This is achieved using the SQL CREATE TABLE statement. The following code example illustrates the creation of a table named *contacts* using FMDB:

```
let sql_stmt = "CREATE TABLE IF NOT EXISTS CONTACTS (ID INTEGER PRIMARY KEY
AUTOINCREMENT, NAME TEXT, ADDRESS TEXT, PHONE TEXT)"


if !myDatabase.executeStatements(sql_stmt) {
    // Table creation failed
}
```

47.9 Extracting Data from a Database Table

Those familiar with SQL will know that data is retrieved from databases using the SELECT statement. Depending on the criteria defined in the statement, it is typical for more than one data row to be returned. It is essential, therefore, to learn how to retrieve data from a database using the SQLite FMDB wrapper.

In the following code excerpt, a SQL SELECT statement is used to extract the address and phone fields from all the rows of a database table named *contacts* via a call to the *executeQuery* method of the FMDatabase instance:

```
let querySQL = "SELECT address, phone FROM CONTACTS WHERE name =
            '\(name.text!)'"


do {
    let results:FMResultSet? = try myDatabase.executeQuery(querySQL,
                                            values: nil)
} catch {
    print("Error: \(error.localizedDescription)")
}
```

On completion of the query execution, the FMResults object returned from the method call contains the query results. Regardless of whether one or more results are expected, the *next* method of the returned FMResultSet object must be called. A *false* return value from the *next* method call indicates either that no results were returned or that the end of the result set has been reached.

If results were returned, the data can be accessed using the column name as a key. The following code, for example, outputs the "address" and "phone" values for all of the matching records returned as the result of the above query operation:

```
while results?.next() == true {
    print(results?.stringForColumn("address"))
    print(results?.stringForColumn("phone"))
}
```

47.10 Closing an SQLite Database

The database must be closed when an app has finished working on the database. This is achieved with a call to the *close* method of the FMDatabase instance:

```
myDatabase.close()
```

47.11 Summary

In this chapter, we have looked at the basics of implementing a database within an iOS app using the embedded SQLite relational database management system and the FMDB wrapper to make access to the database possible from within Swift code. In the next chapter, we will put this theory into practice and work through an example that creates a functional iOS app designed to store data in a database.

48. An Example SQLite-based iOS 17 App using Swift and FMDB

The chapter entitled *"iOS 17 Database Implementation using SQLite"* discussed the basic concepts of integrating an SQLite-based database into iOS apps. In this chapter, we will put this knowledge to use by creating a simple example app that demonstrates SQLite-based database implementation and management on iOS using Swift and the FMDB wrapper.

48.1 About the Example SQLite App

This chapter focuses on creating a somewhat rudimentary iOS app that stores contact information (names, addresses, and telephone numbers) in an SQLite database. In addition to data storage, a feature will also be implemented to allow the user to search the database for a specified contact name, address, and phone number. Some knowledge of SQL and SQLite is assumed throughout this tutorial. Those readers unfamiliar with these technologies in the context of iOS app development are encouraged to read the *previous chapter* before proceeding.

48.2 Creating and Preparing the SQLite App Project

Begin by launching the Xcode environment and creating a new iOS *App* project named *Database* configured for the Swift programming language.

Once the project has been created, the next step is to configure the project to include the SQLite dynamic library *(libsqlite3.tbd)* during the link phase of the build process. Failure to include this library will result in build errors.

To add this library, select the target entry in the Xcode project navigator (the top entry with the product name) to display the *General* information panel. Next, select the *Build Phases* tab to display the build information. Finally, the *Link Binary with Libraries* section lists the libraries and frameworks already included in the project. To add another library or framework, click the '+' button to display the full list. From this list, search for, and then select *libsqlite3.tbd* and click *Add.*

48.3 Checking Out the FMDB Source Code

To use FMDB, the source files for the wrapper will need to be added to the project. The source code for FMDB is stored on the GitHub source code repository and can be downloaded directly onto your development system from within Xcode. Begin by selecting the Xcode *Integrate -> Clone…* menu option to display the Clone dialog:

Figure 48-1

In the dialog, enter the following GitHub URL into the repository URL field and click on *Clone*:

https://github.com/ccgus/fmdb.git

Select the *master* branch, click the *Clone* button, and choose a location on your local file system into which the files are to be checked out before clicking the *Clone* button again. Xcode will check out the files and save them at the designated location. A new Xcode project window will also open containing the FMDB source files. Within the project navigator panel, unfold the *fmdb -> src -> fmdb* folder to list the source code files (highlighted in Figure 48-2) for the FMDB wrapper.

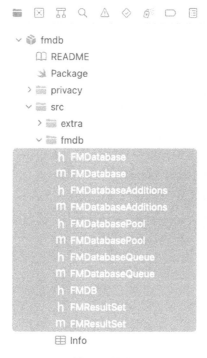

Figure 48-2

Shift-click on the first and last files in the *fmdb* folder to select all the .h and .m files in the navigator panel and drag and drop them onto the Database project folder in the Xcode window containing the Database project. On the options panel, click on the *Finish* button. Since these files are written in Objective-C rather than Swift, Xcode will offer to configure and add an *Objective-C bridging header* file, as shown in Figure 48-3:

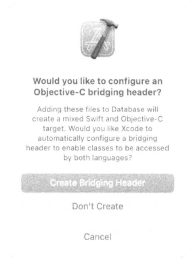

Figure 48-3

Click on the option to add the bridging file. Once added, it will appear in the project navigator panel with the name *Database-Bridging-Header.h*. Select this file and edit it to add a single line to import the FMDB.h file:

```
#import "FMDB.h"
```

With the project fully configured to support SQLite from within Swift app projects, the remainder of the project may now be completed.

48.4 Designing the User Interface

The next step in developing our example SQLite iOS app involves the design of the user interface. Begin by selecting the *Main.storyboard* file to edit the user interface and drag and drop components from the Library panel onto the view canvas and edit properties so that the layout appears as illustrated in Figure 48-4:

Figure 48-4

Before proceeding, stretch the status label (located above the two buttons) so that it is the same width as the combined labels and text field views, and change the text alignment in the Attributes Inspector so that it is centered. Finally, edit the label and remove the word "Label" so it is blank, display the *Resolve Auto Layout Issues* menu and select the *Reset to Suggested Constraints* option listed under *All Views in View Controller*.

Select the top-most text field object in the view canvas, display the Assistant Editor panel and verify that the editor is displaying the contents of the *ViewController.swift* file. Next, right-click on the text field object again and drag it to a position just below the class declaration line in the Assistant Editor. Release the line, and in the resulting connection dialog, establish an outlet connection named *name*.

Repeat the above steps to establish outlet connections for the remaining text fields and the label object to properties named *address*, *phone*, and *status*, respectively.

Right-click on the *Save* button object and drag the line to the area immediately beneath the existing *viewDidLoad* method in the Assistant Editor panel. Release the line and, within the resulting connection dialog, establish an Action method on the *Touch Up Inside* event configured to call a method named *saveContact*. Repeat this step to create an action connection from the *Find* button to a method named *findContact*.

Close the Assistant Editor panel, select the *ViewController.swift* file and add a variable to store a reference to the database path:

```
class ViewController: UIViewController {

    @IBOutlet weak var name: UITextField!
    @IBOutlet weak var address: UITextField!
    @IBOutlet weak var phone: UITextField!
    @IBOutlet weak var status: UILabel!

    var databasePath = String()

    override func viewDidLoad() {
        super.viewDidLoad()


    }

    @IBAction func saveContact(_ sender: Any) {
    }

    @IBAction func findContact(_ sender: Any) {
    }
.
.
.
}
```

48.5 Creating the Database and Table

When the app is launched, it will need to check whether the database file already exists and, if not, create both the database file and a table within the database to store the contact information entered by the user. The code to perform this task will be placed in a method named *initDB* which will be called from the *viewDidLoad* method of our view controller class. Select the *ViewController.swift* file and modify it as follows:

```
override func viewDidLoad() {
```

```
        super.viewDidLoad()
        initDB()
}


func initDB() {
    let filemgr = FileManager.default
    let dirPaths = filemgr.urls(for: .documentDirectory,
                                in: .userDomainMask)

    databasePath = dirPaths[0].appendingPathComponent("contacts.db").path

    if !filemgr.fileExists(atPath: databasePath) {

        let contactDB = FMDatabase(path: databasePath)

        if (contactDB.open()) {
            let sql_stmt = "CREATE TABLE IF NOT EXISTS CONTACTS (ID INTEGER
PRIMARY KEY AUTOINCREMENT, NAME TEXT, ADDRESS TEXT, PHONE TEXT)"
            if !(contactDB.executeStatements(sql_stmt)) {
                print("Error: \(contactDB.lastErrorMessage())")
            }
            contactDB.close()
        } else {
            print("Error: \(contactDB.lastErrorMessage())")
        }
    }
}
```

The code in the above method performs the following tasks:

- Identifies the app's Documents directory and constructs a path to the *contacts.db* database file.

- Checks if the database file already exists.

- If the file does not yet exist, the code creates the database by creating an FMDatabase instance initialized with the database file path. If the database creation is successful, it is then opened via a call to the *open* method of the new database instance.

- Prepares a SQL statement to create the *contacts* table in the database and executes it via a call to the FMDB *executeStatements* method of the database instance.

- Closes the database

48.6 Implementing the Code to Save Data to the SQLite Database

The saving of contact data to the database is the responsibility of the *saveContact* action method. This method will need to open the database file, extract the text from the three text fields and construct and execute a SQL INSERT statement to add this data as a record to the database. Having done this, the method will then need to close the database.

In addition, the code will need to clear the text fields ready for the next contact to be entered and update the status label to reflect the success or failure of the operation.

To implement this behavior, therefore, we need to modify the template method created previously as follows:

```
@IBAction func saveContact(_ sender: Any) {
    let contactDB = FMDatabase(path: databasePath)

    if (contactDB.open()) {

        let insertSQL = "INSERT INTO CONTACTS (name, address, phone) VALUES ('\
(name.text ?? "")', '\(address.text ?? "")', '\(phone.text ?? "")')"

        do {
            try contactDB.executeUpdate(insertSQL, values: nil)
        } catch {
            status.text = "Failed to add contact"
            print("Error: \(error.localizedDescription)")
        }

        status.text = "Contact Added"
        name.text = ""
        address.text = ""
        phone.text = ""

    } else {
        print("Error: \(contactDB.lastErrorMessage())")
    }
}
```

The next step in our app development process is to implement the action for the find button.

48.7 Implementing Code to Extract Data from the SQLite Database

As previously indicated, the user can extract a contact's address and phone number by entering the name and touching the find button. To this end, the *Touch Up Inside* event of the find button has been connected to the *findContact* method, the code for which is outlined below:

```
@IBAction func findContact(_ sender: Any) {
    let contactDB = FMDatabase(path: databasePath)

    if (contactDB.open()) {
        let querySQL =
            "SELECT address, phone FROM CONTACTS WHERE name = '\(name.text!)'"

        do {
            let results:FMResultSet? = try contactDB.executeQuery(querySQL,
                                       values: nil)

            if results?.next() == true {
                address.text = results?.string(forColumn: "address")
```

```
                phone.text = results?.string(forColumn: "phone")
                status.text = "Record Found"
            } else {
                status.text = "Record not found"
                address.text = ""
                phone.text = ""
            }
        } catch {
            print("Error: \(error.localizedDescription)")
        }
        contactDB.close()

    } else {
        print("Error: \(contactDB.lastErrorMessage())")
    }
}
```

This code opens the database and constructs a SQL SELECT statement to extract any records in the database that match the name entered by the user into the name text field. The SQL statement is then executed via a call to the *executeQuery* method of the FMDatabase instance. The search results are returned in the form of an FMResultSet object.

The *next* method of the FMResultSet object is called to find out if at least one match was found. If a match is found, the values corresponding to the address and phone columns are extracted and assigned to the text fields in the user interface.

48.8 Building and Running the App

The final step is to build and run the app. Click on the run button located in the toolbar of the main Xcode project window. Once running, enter details for a few contacts, pressing the *Save* button after each entry. Check the status label to ensure the data is saved successfully. Finally, enter the name of one of your contacts and click on the *Find* button. Assuming the name matches a previously entered record, the address and phone number for that contact should be displayed, and the status label should be updated with the message "Record Found":

Figure 48-5

48.9 Summary

In this chapter, we have looked at the basics of storing data on iOS using the SQLite database environment using the FMDB wrapper approach to using SQLite from within Swift code. However, for developers unfamiliar with SQL and reluctant to learn it, an alternative method for storing data in a database involves using the Core Data framework. This topic will be covered in detail in the next chapter entitled *"Working with iOS 17 Databases using Core Data"*.

49. Working with iOS 17 Databases using Core Data

The preceding chapters covered the concepts of database storage using the SQLite database. In these chapters, the assumption was made that the iOS app code would directly manipulate the database using SQLite API calls to construct and execute SQL statements. While this is a good approach for working with SQLite in many cases, it does require knowledge of SQL and can lead to some complexity in terms of writing code and maintaining the database structure. The non-object-oriented nature of the SQLite API functions further compounds this complexity. In recognition of these shortcomings, Apple introduced the Core Data Framework. Core Data is essentially a framework that places a wrapper around the SQLite database (and other storage environments), enabling the developer to work with data in terms of Swift objects without requiring any knowledge of the underlying database technology.

We will begin this chapter by defining some concepts that comprise the Core Data model before providing an overview of the steps involved in working with this framework. Once these topics have been covered, the next chapter will work through *"An iOS 17 Core Data Tutorial"*.

49.1 The Core Data Stack

Core Data consists of several framework objects that integrate to provide the data storage functionality. This stack can be visually represented as illustrated in Figure 49-1.

As shown in Figure 49-1, the iOS-based app sits on top of the stack and interacts with the managed data objects handled by the managed object context. Of particular significance in this diagram is that although the lower levels in the stack perform a considerable amount of the work involved in providing Core Data functionality, the app code does not interact with them directly.

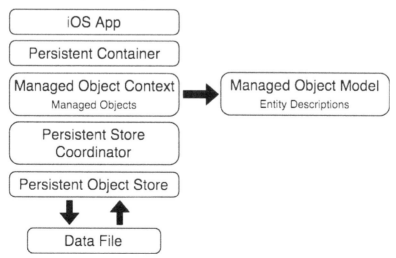

Figure 49-1

Before moving on to the more practical areas of working with Core Data, it is essential to explain the elements that comprise the Core Data stack in a little more detail.

49.2 Persistent Container

The *persistent container* handles the creation of the Core Data stack and is designed to be easily subclassed to add additional app-specific methods to the base Core Data functionality. Once initialized, the persistent container instance provides access to the *managed object context.*

49.3 Managed Objects

Managed objects are the objects that are created by your app code to store data. For example, a managed object may be considered a row or a record in a relational database table. For each new record to be added, a new managed object must be created to store the data. Similarly, retrieved data will be returned as managed objects, one for each record matching the defined retrieval criteria. Managed objects are actually instances of the NSManagedObject class or a subclass thereof. These objects are contained and maintained by the *managed object context.*

49.4 Managed Object Context

Core Data based apps never interact directly with the persistent store. Instead, the app code interacts with the managed objects contained in the managed object context layer of the Core Data stack. The context maintains the status of the objects in relation to the underlying data store and manages the relationships between managed objects defined by the *managed object model.* All interactions with the underlying database are held temporarily within the context until the context is instructed to save the changes. At this point, the changes are passed down through the Core Data stack and written to the persistent store.

49.5 Managed Object Model

So far, we have focused on managing data objects but have not yet looked at how the data models are defined. This is the task of the *Managed Object Model,* which defines a concept referred to as *entities.*

Much as a class description defines a blueprint for an object instance, entities define the data model for managed objects. Essentially, an entity is analogous to the schema that defines a table in a relational database. As such, each entity has a set of attributes associated with it that define the data to be stored in managed objects derived from that entity. For example, a *Contacts* entity might contain *name, address,* and *phone number* attributes.

In addition to attributes, entities can also contain *relationships, fetched properties,* and *fetch requests*:

- **Relationships** – In the context of Core Data, relationships are the same as those in other relational database systems in that they refer to how one data object relates to another. Core Data relationships can be one-to-one, one-to-many, or many-to-many.

- **Fetched property** – This provides an alternative to defining relationships. Fetched properties allow properties of one data object to be accessed from another as though a relationship had been defined between those entities. Fetched properties lack the flexibility of relationships and are referred to by Apple's Core Data documentation as "weak, one-way relationships" best suited to "loosely coupled relationships."

- **Fetch request** – A predefined query that can be referenced to retrieve data objects based on defined predicates. For example, a fetch request can be configured into an entity to retrieve all contact objects where the name field matches "John Smith."

49.6 Persistent Store Coordinator

The *persistent store coordinator* coordinates access to multiple *persistent object stores.* As an iOS developer, you will never directly interact with the persistence store coordinator. In fact, you will very rarely need to develop an app that requires more than one persistent object store. When multiple stores are required, the coordinator presents these stores to the upper layers of the Core Data stack as a single store.

49.7 Persistent Object Store

The term *persistent object store* refers to the underlying storage environment in which data are stored when using Core Data. Core Data supports three disk-based and one memory-based persistent store. Disk-based options consist of SQLite, XML, and binary. By default, the iOS SDK will use SQLite as the persistent store. In practice, the type of store used is transparent to you as the developer. Regardless of your choice of persistent store, your code will make the same calls to the same Core Data APIs to manage the data objects required by your app.

49.8 Defining an Entity Description

Entity descriptions may be defined from within the Xcode environment. For example, when a new project is created with the option to include Core Data, a template file will be created named *<projectname>*.xcdatamodeld. Selecting this file in the Xcode project navigator panel will load the model into the entity editing environment, as illustrated in Figure 49-2:

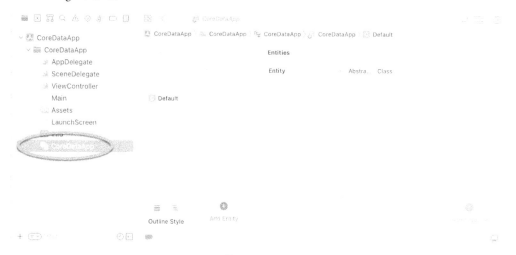

Figure 49-2

Create a new entity by clicking on the *Add Entity* button located in the bottom panel. The new entity will appear as a text box in the *Entities* list. By default, this will be named *Entity*. Double-click on this name to change it.

To add attributes to the entity, click the *Add Attribute* button in the bottom panel or use the + button beneath the *Attributes* section. Then, in the *Attributes* panel, name the attribute and specify the type and any other required options.

Repeat the above steps to add more attributes and additional entities.

The Xcode entity environment also allows relationships to be established between entities. Assume, for example, two entities named *Contacts* and *Sales*. First, select the Contacts entity and click on the + button beneath the Relationships panel to establish a relationship between the two tables. Then, in the detail panel, name the relationship, specify the destination as the *Sales* entity, and any options required for the relationship.

As demonstrated, Xcode makes the process of entity description creation reasonably straightforward. While a detailed overview of the process is beyond this book's scope, many other resources are dedicated to the subject.

49.9 Initializing the Persistent Container

The persistent container is initialized by creating a new NSPersistentContainer instance, passing through the name of the model to be used, and then making a call to the *loadPersistentStores* method of that object as follows:

```
let container = NSPersistentContainer(name: "CoreDataDemo")
         container.loadPersistentStores(completionHandler: {
                                 (description, error) in

             if let error = error {
                 fatalError("Unable to load persistent stores: \(error)")
             }
         })
```

49.10 Obtaining the Managed Object Context

Since many Core Data methods require the managed object context as an argument, the next step after defining entity descriptions often involves obtaining a reference to the context. This can be achieved by accessing the viewContext property of the persistent container instance:

```
let managedObjectContext = persistentContainer.viewContext
```

49.11 Getting an Entity Description

Before managed objects can be created and manipulated in code, the corresponding entity description must first be loaded. This is achieved by calling the *entity(forName:in:)* method of the NSEntityDescription class, passing through the name of the required entity and the context as arguments. For example, the following code fragment obtains the description for an entity with the name *Contacts:*

```
let entity = NSEntityDescription.entity(
            forName: "Contacts", in: context)
```

49.12 Setting the Attributes of a Managed Object

As previously discussed, entities and the managed objects from which they are instantiated contain data in the form of attributes. Once a managed object instance has been created, as outlined above, those attribute values can store the data before the object is saved. For example, assuming a managed object named *contact* with attributes named *name, address,* and *phone,* respectively, the values of these attributes may be set as follows before the object is saved to storage:

```
contact.name = "John Smith"
contact.address = "1 Infinite Loop"
contact.phone = "555-564-0980"
```

49.13 Saving a Managed Object

Once a managed object instance has been created and configured with the data to be stored, it can be saved to storage using the *save* method of the managed object context as follows:

```
do {
    try context.save()
} catch let error {
    // Handle error
}
```

49.14 Fetching Managed Objects

Once managed objects are saved into the persistent object store, those objects and the data they contain will likely need to be retrieved. Objects are retrieved by executing a fetch request and are returned in an array. The following code assumes that both the context and entity description have been obtained before making the fetch request:

```
let request: NSFetchRequest<Contacts> = Contacts.fetchRequest()
request.entity = entity
```

```
do {
    let results = try context.fetch(request as!
                    NSFetchRequest<NSFetchRequestResult>)
} catch let error {
    // Handle error
}
```

Upon execution, the *results* array will contain all the managed objects retrieved by the request.

49.15 Retrieving Managed Objects based on Criteria

The preceding example retrieved all managed objects from the persistent object store for a specified entity. More often than not, only managed objects that match specified criteria are required during a retrieval operation. This is performed by defining a *predicate* that dictates criteria a managed object must meet to be eligible for retrieval. For example, the following code implements a predicate to extract only those managed objects where the *name* attribute matches "John Smith":

```
let request: NSFetchRequest<Contacts> = Contacts.fetchRequest()
request.entity = entity

let pred = NSPredicate(format: "(name = %@)", "John Smith")
request.predicate = pred

do {
        let results = try context.fetch(request as!
                    NSFetchRequest<NSFetchRequestResult>)
} catch let error {
    // Handle error
}
```

49.16 Accessing the Data in a Retrieved Managed Object

Once results have been returned from a fetch request, the data within the returned objects may be accessed using *keys* to reference the stored values. The following code, for example, accesses the first result from a fetch operation results array and extracts the values for the *name*, *address,* and *phone* keys from that managed object:

```
let match = results[0] as! NSManagedObject

let nameString = match.value(forKey: "name") as! String
let addressString = match.value(forKey: "address") as! String
let phoneString = match.value(forKey: "phone") as! String
```

49.17 Summary

The Core Data Framework stack provides a flexible alternative to directly managing data using SQLite or other data storage mechanisms. Providing an object-oriented abstraction layer on top of the data makes managing data storage significantly easier for the iOS app developer. Now that the basics of Core Data have been covered, the next chapter, entitled *"An iOS 17 Core Data Tutorial"*, will work through creating an example app.

50. An iOS 17 Core Data Tutorial

In the previous chapter, entitled *"Working with iOS 17 Databases using Core Data"*, an overview of the Core Data stack was provided, together with details of how to write code to implement data persistence using this infrastructure. In this chapter, we will continue to look at Core Data in a step-by-step tutorial that implements data persistence using Core Data in an iOS 17 app.

50.1 The Core Data Example App

The app developed in this chapter will take the form of the same contact database app used in previous chapters, the objective being to allow the user to enter their name, address, and phone number information into a database and then search for specific contacts based on the contact's name.

50.2 Creating a Core Data-based App

As is often the case, we can rely on Xcode to do much of the preparatory work for us when developing an iOS app that will use Core Data. To create the example app project, launch Xcode and select the option to create a new project. In the new project window, select the iOS *App* project template. In the next screen, ensure the *Swift* and *Storyboard* options are selected. Next, enter *CoreDataDemo* into the *Product Name* field, select *Core Data* from the *Storage* menu, and click *Next* to select a location to store the project files.

Xcode will create the new project and display the main project window. In addition to the usual files that are present when creating a new project, an additional file named *CoreDataDemo.xcdatamodeld* is also created. This is the file where the entity descriptions for our data model will be stored.

50.3 Creating the Entity Description

The entity description defines the model for our data, much like a schema defines the model of a database table. To create the entity for the Core Data app, select the *CoreDataDemo.xcdatamodeld* file to load the entity editor:

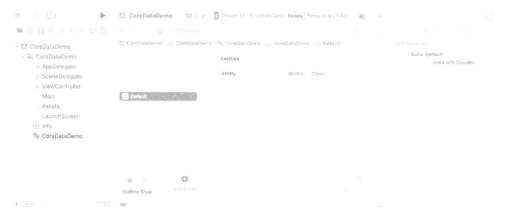

Figure 50-1

To create a new entity, click the Add Entity button in the bottom panel. Double-click on the new *Entity* item beneath the *Entities* heading and change the entity name to *Contacts*. With the entity created, the next step is to add some attributes that represent the data that is to be stored. To do so, click on the *Add Attribute* button. In the *Attribute* pane, name the attribute *name* and set the Type to *String*. Repeat these steps to add two other String attributes named *address* and *phone,* respectively:

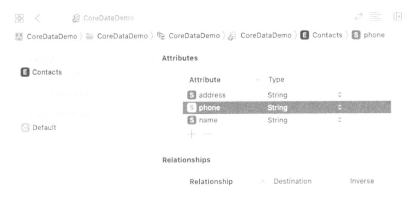

Figure 50-2

50.4 Designing the User Interface

With the entity defined, now is a good time to design the user interface and establish the outlet and action connections. Select the *Main.storyboard* file to begin the design work. The user interface and corresponding connections used in this tutorial are the same as those in previous data persistence chapters. The completed view should, once again, appear as outlined in Figure 50-3 (note that objects may be cut and pasted from the previous *Database* project to save time in designing the user interface layout):

Figure 50-3

Before proceeding, stretch the status label (located above the two buttons) so that it covers most of the width of the view and configure the alignment attribute so that the text is centered. Finally, edit the label and remove the word "Label" so it is blank.

Select the topmost text field object in the view canvas, display the Assistant Editor panel and verify that the editor displays the contents of the *ViewController.swift* file. Next, right-click on the text field object again and drag it to a position just below the class declaration line in the Assistant Editor. Release the line, and in the resulting connection dialog, establish an outlet connection named *name*.

Repeat the above steps to establish outlet connections for the remaining text fields and the label object to properties named *address, phone,* and *status,* respectively.

Right-click on the *Save* button object and drag the line to the area immediately beneath the *viewDidLoad* method in the Assistant Editor panel. Release the line and, within the resulting connection dialog, establish an Action method on the *Touch Up Inside* event configured to call a method named *saveContact*. Repeat this step to create an action connection from the *Find* button to a method named *findContact*.

50.5 Initializing the Persistent Container

The next step in this project is to initialize the Core Data stack and obtain a reference to the managed object context. Begin by editing the *ViewController.swift* file to import the Core Data framework and to declare a variable in which to store a reference to the managed object context object:

```
import UIKit
import CoreData

class ViewController: UIViewController {

    var managedObjectContext: NSManagedObjectContext?
.

.
```

Next, implement a method named *initCoreStack* to initialize the persistent container and access the managed object context. Also, modify the *viewDidLoad* method so that this new method is called when the View Controller starts:

```
override func viewDidLoad() {
    super.viewDidLoad()

    initCoreStack()
}


func initCoreStack() {
    let container = NSPersistentContainer(name: "CoreDataDemo")
    container.loadPersistentStores(completionHandler: {
                        (description, error) in
        if let error = error {
            fatalError("Unable to load persistent stores: \(error)")
        } else {
            self.managedObjectContext = container.viewContext
        }
    })
}
.

.
```

50.6 Saving Data to the Persistent Store using Core Data

When the user touches the Save button, the *saveContact* method is called. Therefore, within this method, we must implement the code to create and store managed objects containing the data entered by the user. Select the *ViewController.swift* file, scroll down to the template *saveContact* method, and implement the code as follows:

```
@IBAction func saveContact(_ sender: Any) {

    if let context = managedObjectContext, let entityDescription =
```

```
NSEntityDescription.entity(forEntityName: "Contacts",
                           in: context) {


    let contact = Contacts(entity: entityDescription,
                insertInto: managedObjectContext)


    contact.name = name.text
    contact.address = address.text
    contact.phone = phone.text

    do {
        try managedObjectContext?.save()
        name.text = ""
        address.text = ""
        phone.text = ""
        status.text = "Contact Saved"
    } catch let error {
        status.text = error.localizedDescription
    }

}

}
```

The above code uses the managed object context to obtain the Contacts entity description and then uses it to create a new instance of the Contacts managed object subclass. This managed object's name, address, and phone attribute values are then set to the current text field values. Finally, the context is instructed to save the changes to the persistent store with a call to the context's *save* method. The success or otherwise of the operation is reported on the status label, and in the case of a successful outcome, the text fields are cleared and ready for the next contact to be entered.

50.7 Retrieving Data from the Persistent Store using Core Data

To allow the user to search for a contact, implementing the findContact action method is now necessary. As with the save method, this method will need to identify the entity description for the Contacts entity and then create a predicate to ensure that only objects with the name specified by the user are retrieved from the store. Matching objects are placed in an array from which the attributes for the first match are retrieved using the *value(forKey:)* method and displayed to the user. A full count of the matches is displayed in the status field.

The code to perform these tasks is as follows:

```
@IBAction func findContact(_ sender: Any) {
    if let context = managedObjectContext {
        let entityDescription =
            NSEntityDescription.entity(forEntityName: "Contacts",
                                        in: context)

        let request: NSFetchRequest<Contacts> = Contacts.fetchRequest()
        request.entity = entityDescription

        if let name = name.text {
```

```
        let pred = NSPredicate(format: "(name = %@)", name)
        request.predicate = pred
    }

    do {
        let results =
            try context.fetch(request as!
                NSFetchRequest<NSFetchRequestResult>)

        if results.count > 0 {
            let match = results[0] as! NSManagedObject

            name.text = match.value(forKey: "name") as? String
            address.text = match.value(forKey: "address") as? String
            phone.text = match.value(forKey: "phone") as? String
            status.text = "Matches found: \(results.count)"
        } else {
            status.text = "No Match"
        }

    } catch let error {
        status.text = error.localizedDescription
    }
  }
}
```

50.8 Building and Running the Example App

The final step is to build and run the app. Click on the run button located in the toolbar of the main Xcode project window. If errors are reported, check the syntax of the code you have written using the error messages provided by Xcode as guidance. Once the app compiles, it will launch and load into the device or iOS Simulator. Next, enter some test contacts (some with the same name). Having entered some test data, enter the name of the contact for which you created duplicate records and tap the Find button. The address and phone number of the first matching record should appear together with an indication in the status field of the total number of matching objects retrieved.

50.9 Summary

The Core Data Framework provides an abstract, object-oriented interface to database storage within iOS apps. As demonstrated in the example app created in this chapter, Core Data does not require any knowledge of the underlying database system. Combined with Xcode's visual entity creation features, it allows database storage to be implemented relatively easily.

51. An Introduction to CloudKit Data Storage on iOS 17

The CloudKit Framework is one of the more remarkable developer features available in the iOS SDK solely because of the ease with which it allows for the structured storage and retrieval of data on Apple's iCloud database servers.

It is not an exaggeration to state that CloudKit allows developers to work with cloud-based data and media storage without any prior database experience and with minimal coding effort.

This chapter will provide a high-level introduction to the various elements that make up CloudKit, build a foundation for the CloudKit tutorials presented in the following two chapters and provide a basis from which to explore other capabilities of CloudKit.

51.1 An Overview of CloudKit

The CloudKit Framework provides apps with access to the iCloud servers hosted by Apple. It provides an easy-to-use way to store, manage and retrieve data and other asset types (such as large binary files, videos, and images) in a structured way. This provides a platform for users to store private data and access it from multiple devices and for the developer to provide publicly available data to all app users.

The first step in learning to use CloudKit is understanding the key components that constitute the CloudKit framework.

51.2 CloudKit Containers

Each CloudKit-enabled app has at least one container on iCloud. The container for an app is represented in the CloudKit Framework by the CKContainer class, and it is within these containers that the databases reside. Containers may also be shared between multiple apps.

A reference to an app's default cloud container can be obtained via the *default* property of the CKContainer class:

```
let container = CKContainer.default
```

51.3 CloudKit Public Database

Each cloud container contains a single public database. This is the database into which is stored data that all users of an app need. A map app, for example, might have a set of data about locations and routes that apply to all app users. This data would be stored within the public database of the app's cloud container.

CloudKit databases are represented within the CloudKit Framework by the CKDatabase class. A reference to the public cloud database for a container can be obtained via the *publicCloudDatabase* property of a container instance:

```
let publicDatabase = container.publicCloudDatabase
```

51.4 CloudKit Private Databases

Private cloud databases are used to store data that is private to each specific user. Each cloud container, therefore, will contain one private database for each app user. A reference to the private cloud database can be obtained via the *privateCloudDatabase* property of the container object:

```
let privateDatabase = container.privateCloudDatabase
```

51.5 Data Storage and Transfer Quotas

Data and assets stored in the public cloud database of an app count against the storage quota of the app. Anything stored in a private database, on the other hand, is counted against the iCloud quota of the corresponding user. Applications should, therefore, try to minimize the amount of data stored in private databases to avoid users having to unnecessarily purchase additional iCloud storage space.

At the time of writing, each application is provided with 1PB of free iCloud storage for public data for all of its users.

Apple also imposes limits on the volume of data transfers and the number of queries per second that are included in the free tier. While official documentation on these quotas and corresponding pricing is hard to find, it is unlikely that the average project will encounter these restrictions.

51.6 CloudKit Records

Data and assets stored in an app's public cloud database count against the app's storage quota. On the other hand, anything stored in a private database is counted against the iCloud quota of the corresponding user. Applications should, therefore, try to minimize the amount of data stored in private databases to avoid users having to unnecessarily purchase additional iCloud storage space.

Records in a database are categorized by a *record type* which must be declared when the record is created and takes the form of a string value. In practice, this should be set to a meaningful value that assists in identifying the purpose of the record type. Records in a cloud database can be added, updated, queried, and deleted using a range of methods provided by the CKDatabase class.

The following code demonstrates the creation of a CKRecord instance initialized with a record type of "Schools" together with three key-value pair fields:

```
let myRecord = CKRecord(recordType: "Schools")

myRecord.setObject("Silver Oak Elementary" as CKRecordValue?,
                          forKey: "schoolname")
myRecord.setObject("100 Oak Street" as CKRecordValue?,
                          forKey: "address")
myRecord.setObject(150 as CKRecordValue?, forKey: "studentcount")
```

Once created and initialized, the above record could be saved via a call to the *save* method of a database instance as follows:

```
publicDatabase.save(myRecord, completionHandler:
    ({returnRecord, error in

                if let err = error {
                    // save operation failed
                } else {
                    // save operation succeeded
                }

    }))
```

The method call passes through the record to be saved and specifies a completion handler as a closure expression to be called when the operation returns.

Alternatively, a group of record operations may be performed in a single transaction using the CKModifyRecordsOperation class. This class also allows timeout durations to be specified for the transaction and completion handlers to be called at various stages during the process. The following code, for example, uses the CKModifyRecordsOperation class to add three new records and delete two existing records in a single operation. The code also establishes timeout parameters and implements all three completion handlers. Once the modify operation object has been created and configured, it is added to the database for execution:

```
let modifyRecordsOperation = CKModifyRecordsOperation(
            recordsToSave: [myRecord1, myRecord2, myRecord3],
            recordIDsToDelete: [myRecord4, myRecord5])

let configuration = CKOperation.Configuration()

configuration.timeoutIntervalForRequest =  10
configuration.timeoutIntervalForResource = 10

modifyRecordsOperation.configuration = configuration

modifyRecordsOperation.perRecordCompletionBlock = { record, error in
    // Called after each individual record operation completes
}

modifyRecordsOperation.perRecordProgressBlock = { record, progress in
    // Called to update the status of an individual operation
    // progress is a Double value indicating progress so far
}

modifyRecordsOperation.modifyRecordsCompletionBlock = {
            records, recordIDs, error in
    // Called after all of the record operations are complete
}


privateDatabase?.add(modifyRecordsOperation)
```

It is important to understand that CloudKit operations are predominantly asynchronous, enabling the calling app to continue functioning. At the same time, the CloudKit Framework works in the background to handle the transfer of data to and from the iCloud servers. In most cases, therefore, a call to CloudKit API methods will require that a completion handler be provided. This handler code will then be executed when the corresponding operation completes and passed results data where appropriate or an error object in the event of a failure. Given the asynchronous nature of CloudKit operations, it is essential to implement robust error handling within the completion handler.

The steps involved in creating, updating, querying, and deleting records will be covered in greater detail in the next chapter entitled "An iOS 17 CloudKit Example".

The overall concept of an app cloud container, private and public databases, and records can be visualized as illustrated in Figure 51-1:

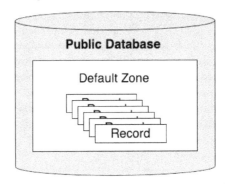

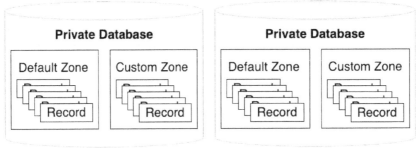

Figure 51-1

51.7 CloudKit Record IDs

Each CloudKit record has associated with it a unique record ID represented by the CKRecordID class. If a record ID is not specified when a record is first created, one is provided for it automatically by the CloudKit framework.

51.8 CloudKit References

CloudKit references are implemented using the CKReference class and provide a way to establish relationships between different records in a database. A reference is established by creating a CKReference instance for an originating record and assigning the record to which the relationship is to be targeted. The CKReference object is stored as a key-value pair field in the originating record. A single record can contain multiple references to other records.

Once a record is configured with a reference pointing to a target record, that record is said to be *owned* by the target record. When the owner record is deleted, all records that refer to it are also deleted, and so on down the chain of references (a concept referred to as *cascading deletes*).

51.9 CloudKit Assets

In addition to data, CloudKit may also be used to store larger assets such as audio or video files, large documents, binary data files, or images. These assets are stored within CKAsset instances. Assets can only be stored as part of a record, and it is not possible to directly store an asset in a cloud database. Once created, an asset is added to a record as another key-value field pair. The following code, for example, demonstrates the addition of an image asset to a record:

```
let imageAsset = CKAsset(fileURL: imageURL)


let myRecord = CKRecord(recordType: "Vacations")


myRecord.setObject("London" as CKRecordValue?, forKey: "city")
myRecord.setObject(imageAsset as CKRecordValue?, forKey: "photo")
```

51.10 Record Zones

CloudKit record zones (CKRecordZone) provide a mechanism for relating groups of records within a private database. Unless a record zone is specified when a record is saved to the cloud, it is placed in the *default zone* of the target database. Custom zones can be added to private databases and used to organize related records and perform tasks such as writing to multiple records simultaneously in a single transaction. Each record zone has a unique record zone ID (CKRecordZoneID) that must be referenced when adding new records to a zone.

Adding a record zone to a private database involves the creation of a CKRecordZone instance initialized with the name to be assigned to the zone:

```
let myRecordZone = CKRecordZone(zoneName: "MyRecordZone")
```

The zone is then saved to the database via a call to the *save* method of a CKDatabase instance, passing through the CKRecordZone instance together with a completion handler to be called upon completion of the operation:

```
privateDatabase.save(myRecordZone, completionHandler:
        ({returnRecord, error in
            if let err = error {
                // Zone creation failed
            } else {
                // Zone creation succeeded
            }
        }))
```

Once the record zone has been established on the cloud database, records may be added to that zone by including the record type and a record ID when creating CKRecord instances:

```
let myRecord = CKRecord(recordType: "Addresses",
                        recordID: CKRecord.ID(zoneID: zoneId))
```

In the above code, the zone ID is passed through to the CKRecord.ID initializer to obtain an ID containing a unique CloudKit-generated record name. The following is a typical example of a CloudKit-generated record name:

```
88F54808-2606-4176-A004-7E8AEC210B04
```

To manually specify the record name used within the record ID, modify the code to read as follows:

```
let myRecord = CKRecord(recordType: "Houses",
    recordID: CKRecord.ID(recordName: "MyRecordName", zoneID: zoneId))
```

However, when manually specifying a record name, care should be taken to ensure each has a unique name.

When the record is saved to the database, it will be associated with the designated record zone.

51.11 CloudKit Sharing

A CloudKit record contained within the public database of an app is accessible to all users of that app. Situations might arise, however, where a user wants to share specific records within a private database with others. This was made possible with the introduction of *CloudKit sharing* in iOS 10.

51.12 CloudKit Subscriptions

CloudKit subscriptions notify users when a change occurs within the cloud databases belonging to an installed app. Subscriptions use the standard iOS push notifications infrastructure and can be triggered based on various criteria, such as when records are added, updated, or deleted. Notifications can also be refined using predicates so that notifications are based on data in a record matching specific criteria. When a notification arrives, it is presented to the user in the same way as other notifications through an alert or a notification entry on the lock screen.

51.13 Obtaining iCloud User Information

Within the scope of an app's cloud container, each user has a unique, app-specific iCloud user ID and a user info record where the user ID is used as the record ID for the user's info record.

The record ID of the current user's info record can be obtained via a call to the *fetchUserRecordID(completionHandler:)* method of the container instance. Once the record ID has been obtained, this can be used to fetch the user's record from the cloud database:

```
container.fetchUserRecordID(completionHandler: { recordID,
        error in
            if let err = error {
                // Failed to get record ID
            } else {
                // Success - fetch the user's record here
            }
```

The record is of type CKRecordTypeUserRecord and is initially empty. However, once fetched, it can store data in the same way as any other CloudKit record.

CloudKit can also be used to perform user discovery. This allows the app to obtain an array of the users in the current user's address book who have also used the app. For the user's information to be provided, the user must have run the app and opted in to provide the information. User discovery is performed via a call to the *discoverAllIdentities(completionHandler:)* method of the container instance.

The discovered data is provided in the form of an array of CKApplicationUserInfo objects which contain the user's iCloud ID, first name, and last name. The following code fragment, for example, performs a user discovery operation and outputs to the console the first and last names of any users that meet the requirements for discoverability:

```
container.discoverAllIdentities(completionHandler: (
    {users, error in

        if let err = error {
            print("discovery failed %@",
                    err.localizedDescription)
        } else {

            for userInfo in user {
                let userRecordID = userInfo.userRecordID
                print("First Name = %@", userInfo.firstName)
                print("Last Name = %@", userInfo.lastName)
            }
        }
    })
```

51.14 CloudKit Console

The CloudKit Dashboard is a web-based portal that provides an interface for managing the CloudKit options and storage for apps. The dashboard can be accessed via the *https://icloud.developer.apple.com/dashboard/* URL or using the *CloudKit Dashboard* button located in the iCloud section of the Xcode Capabilities panel for a project, as shown in Figure 51-2:

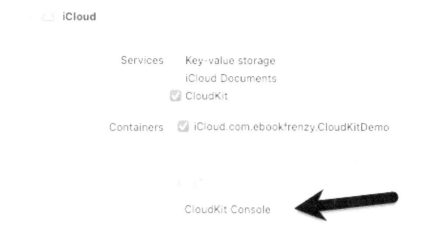

Figure 51-2

Access to the dashboard requires a valid Apple developer login and password and, once loaded into a browser window, will appear providing access to the CloudKit containers associated with your team account.

Once one or more containers have been created, the console provides the ability to view data, add, update, query, and delete records, modify the database schema, view subscriptions, and configure new security roles. It also provides an interface for migrating data from a development environment over to a production environment in preparation for an application to go live in the App Store

The Logs and Telemetry options provide an overview of CloudKit usage by the currently selected container, including operations performed per second, average data request size and error frequency, and log details of each transaction.

In the case of data access through the CloudKit Console, it is important to be aware that private user data cannot be accessed using the dashboard interface. Only data stored in the public and private databases belonging to the developer account used to log in to the console can be viewed and modified.

51.15 Summary

This chapter has covered a number of the key classes and elements that make up the data storage features of the CloudKit framework. Each app has its own cloud container, which, in turn, contains a single public cloud database in addition to one private database for each app user. Data is stored in databases in the form of records using key-value pair fields. Larger data, such as videos and photos, are stored as assets which, in turn, are stored as fields in records. Records stored in private databases can be grouped into record zones and may be associated with each other through the creation of relationships. Each app user has an iCloud user id and a corresponding user record, both of which can be obtained using the CloudKit framework. In addition, CloudKit user discovery can be used to obtain, subject to permission, a list of IDs for those users in the current user's address book who have also installed and run the app.

Finally, the CloudKit Dashboard is a web-based portal that provides an interface for managing the CloudKit options and storage for apps.

52. An Introduction to CloudKit Sharing

Before the release of iOS 10, the only way to share CloudKit records between users was to store those records in a public database. With the introduction of CloudKit sharing, individual app users can now share private database records with other users.

This chapter aims to provide an overview of CloudKit sharing and the classes used to implement sharing within an iOS app. The techniques outlined in this chapter will be put to practical use in the *"An iOS 17 CloudKit Sharing Example"* chapter.

52.1 Understanding CloudKit Sharing

CloudKit sharing provides a way for records within a private database to be shared with other app users, entirely at the discretion of the database owner. When a user decides to share CloudKit data, a *share link* in the form of a URL is sent to the person with whom the data is to be shared. This link can be sent in various ways, including text messages, email, Facebook, or Twitter. When the recipient taps on the share link, the app (if installed) will be launched and provided with the shared record information ready to be displayed.

The level of access to a shared record may also be defined to control whether a recipient can view and modify the record. It is important to be aware that when a share recipient accepts a share, they are receiving a reference to the original record in the owner's private database. Therefore, a modification performed on a share will be reflected in the original private database.

52.2 Preparing for CloudKit Sharing

Before an app can take advantage of CloudKit sharing, the CKSharingSupported key needs to be added to the project *Info.plist* file with a Boolean true value. Also, a CloudKit record may only be shared if it is stored in a private database and is a member of a record zone other than the default zone.

52.3 The CKShare Class

CloudKit sharing is made possible primarily by the CKShare class. This class is initialized with the root CKRecord instance that is to be shared with other users together with the permission setting. The CKShare object may also be configured with title and icon information to be included in the share link message. The CKShare and associated CKRecord objects are then saved to the private database. The following code, for example, creates a CKShare object containing the record to be shared and configured for read-only access:

```
let share = CKShare(rootRecord: myRecord)
share[CKShare.SystemFieldKey.title] = "My First Share" as CKRecordValue
share.publicPermission = .readOnly
```

Once the share has been created, it is saved to the private database using a CKModifyRecordsOperation object. Note the *recordsToSave:* argument is declared as an array containing both the share and record objects:

```
let modifyRecordsOperation = CKModifyRecordsOperation(
    recordsToSave: [myRecord, share], recordIDsToDelete: nil)
```

Next, a CKConfiguration instance needs to be created, configured with optional settings, and assigned to the operation:

```
let configuration = CKOperation.Configuration()

configuration.timeoutIntervalForResource = 10
configuration.timeoutIntervalForRequest = 10
```

Next, a lambda must be assigned to the modifyRecordsResultBlock property of the modifyRecordsOperation object. The code in this lambda is called when the operation completes to let your app know whether the share was successfully saved:

```
modifyRecordsOperation.modifyRecordsResultBlock = { result in
    switch result {
    case .success:
        // Handle completion
    case .failure(let error):
        print(error.localizedDescription)
    }
}
```

Finally, the operation is added to the database to begin execution:

```
self.privateDatabase?.add(modifyRecordsOperation)
```

52.4 The UICloudSharingController Class

To send a share link to another user, CloudKit needs to know both the identity of the recipient and the method by which the share link is to be transmitted. One option is to manually create CKShareParticipant objects for each participant and add them to the CKShare object. Alternatively, the CloudKit framework includes a view controller specifically for this purpose. When presented to the user (Figure 52-1), the UICloudSharingController class provides the user with a variety of options for sending the share link to another user:

Figure 52-1

The app is responsible for creating and presenting the controller to the user, the template code for which is outlined below:

```
let controller = UICloudSharingController {
      controller, prepareCompletionHandler in

      // Code here to create the CKShare and save it to the database
}

controller.availablePermissions =
        [.allowPublic, .allowReadOnly, .allowReadWrite, .allowPrivate]

controller.popoverPresentationController?.barButtonItem =
    sender as? UIBarButtonItem

present(controller, animated: true)
```

Note that the above code fragment also specifies the permissions to be provided as options within the controller user interface. These options are accessed and modified by tapping the link in the Collaboration section of the sharing controller (in Figure 52-1 above, the link reads "Only invited people can edit"). Figure 52-2 shows an example share options settings screen:

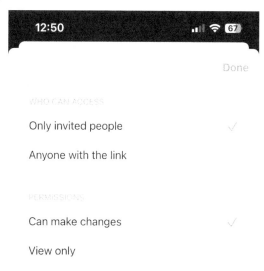

Figure 52-2

Once the user selects a method of communication from the cloud-sharing controller, the completion handler assigned to the controller will be called. As outlined in the previous section, the CKShare object must be created and saved within this handler. After the share has been saved to the database, the cloud-sharing controller must be notified that the share is ready to be sent. This is achieved by a call to the *prepareCompletionHandler* method that was passed to the completion handler in the above code. When *prepareCompletionHandler* is called, it must be passed the share object and a reference to the app's CloudKit container. Bringing these requirements together gives us the following code:

```
let controller = UICloudSharingController { controller,
    prepareCompletionHandler in

let share = CKShare(rootRecord: thisRecord)
```

```
share[CKShare.SystemFieldKey.title]
        = "An Amazing House" as CKRecordValue
share.publicPermission = .readOnly

// Create a CKModifyRecordsOperation object and configure it
// to save the CKShare instance and the record to be shared.
let modifyRecordsOperation = CKModifyRecordsOperation(
    recordsToSave: [myRecord, share],
    recordIDsToDelete: nil)

// Create a CKOperation instance
let configuration = CKOperation.Configuration()

// Set configuration properties to provide timeout limits
configuration.timeoutIntervalForResource = 10
configuration.timeoutIntervalForRequest = 10

// Apply the configuration options to the operation
modifyRecordsOperation.configuration = configuration

// Assign a completion block to the CKModifyRecordsOperation. This will
// be called the modify records operation completes or fails.

modifyRecordsOperation.modifyRecordsResultBlock = { result in
    switch result {
    case .success:
        // The share operation was successful. Call the completion
        // handler
        prepareCompletionHandler(share, CKContainer.default(), nil)
    case .failure(let error):
        print(error.localizedDescription)
    }
}

// Start the operation by adding it to the database
self.privateDatabase?.add(modifyRecordsOperation)
}
```

Once the *prepareCompletionHandler* method has been called, the app for the chosen form of communication (Messages, Mail, etc.) will launch preloaded with the share link. All the user needs to do at this point is enter the contact details for the intended share recipient and send the message. Figure 52-3, for example, shows a share link loaded into the Mail app ready to be sent:

Figure 52-3

52.5 Accepting a CloudKit Share

When the recipient user receives a share link and selects it, a dialog will appear, providing the option to accept the share and open it in the corresponding app. When the app opens, the *userDidAcceptCloudKitShareWith* method is called on the scene delegate class located in the project's *SceneDelegate.swift* file:

```
func windowScene(_ windowScene: UIWindowScene,
    userDidAcceptCloudKitShareWith cloudKitShareMetadata: CKShare.Metadata) {
}
```

When this method is called, it is passed a CKShare.Metadata object containing information about the share. Although the user has accepted the share, the app must also accept the share using a CKAcceptSharesOperation object. As the acceptance operation is performed, it will report the results of the process via two *result blocks* assigned to it. The following example shows how to create and configure a CKAcceptSharesOperation instance to accept a share:

```
let container = CKContainer(identifier: metadata.containerIdentifier)
let operation = CKAcceptSharesOperation(shareMetadatas: [metadata])
var rootRecordID: CKRecord.ID!

operation.acceptSharesResultBlock = { result in
    switch result {
    case .success:
        // The share was accepted successfully. Call the completion handler.
        completion(.success(rootRecordID))
    case .failure(let error):
        completion(.failure(error))
    }
}

operation.perShareResultBlock = { metadata, result in
```

```
    switch result {
    case .success:
        // The shared record ID was successfully obtained from the metadata.
        // Save a local copy for later.
        rootRecordID = metadata.hierarchicalRootRecordID

        // Display the appropriate view controller and use it to fetch, and
        // display the shared record.
        DispatchQueue.main.async {
            let viewController: ViewController =
                    self.window?.rootViewController as! ViewController
            viewController.fetchShare(metadata)
        }
    case .failure(let error):
        print(error.localizedDescription)
    }
}
```

The final step in accepting the share is to add the configured CKAcceptSharesOperation object to the CKContainer instance to accept share the share:

```
container.add(operation)
```

52.6 Fetching a Shared Record

Once a share has been accepted by both the user and the app, the shared record needs to be fetched and presented to the user. This involves the creation of a CKFetchRecordsOperation object using the root record ID contained within a CKShare.Metadata instance that has been configured with result blocks to be called with the results of the fetch operation. It is essential to be aware that this fetch operation must be executed on the *shared cloud database* instance of the app instead of the recipient's private database. The following code, for example, fetches the record associated with a CloudKit share:

```
let operation = CKFetchRecordsOperation(
                    recordIDs: [metadata.hierarchicalRootRecordID!])

operation.perRecordResultBlock = { recordId, result in
    switch result {
    case .success(let record):
        DispatchQueue.main.async() {
            // Shared record successfully fetched. Update user
            // interface here to present to the user.
        }
    case .failure(let error):
        print(error.localizedDescription)
    }
}

operation.fetchRecordsResultBlock = { result in
    switch result {
    case .success:
```

```
        break
    case .failure(let error):
        print(error.localizedDescription)
    }
}
```

```
CKContainer.default().sharedCloudDatabase.add(operation)
```

Once the record has been fetched, it can be presented to the user within the *perRecordResultBlock* code, taking the steps above to perform user interface updates asynchronously on the main thread.

52.7 Summary

CloudKit sharing allows records stored within a private CloudKit database to be shared with other app users at the discretion of the record owner. An app user could, for example, make one or more records accessible to other users so that they can view and, optionally, modify the record. When a record is shared, a share link is sent to the recipient user in the form of a URL. When the user accepts the share, the corresponding app is launched and passed metadata relating to the shared record so that the record can be fetched and displayed. CloudKit sharing involves the creation of CKShare objects initialized with the record to be shared. The UICloudSharingController class provides a pre-built view controller which handles much of the work involved in gathering the necessary information to send a share link to another user. In addition to sending a share link, the app must also be adapted to accept a share and fetch the record for the shared cloud database. This chapter has covered the basics of CloudKit sharing, a topic that will be covered further in a later chapter entitled *"An iOS 17 CloudKit Sharing Example"*.

53. An iOS 17 CloudKit Example

With the basics of the CloudKit Framework covered in the previous chapters, many of the concepts covered in those chapters will now be explored in greater detail by implementing an example iOS project. The app created in this chapter will demonstrate the use of the CloudKit Framework to create, update, query, and delete records in a private CloudKit database. In the next chapter, the project will be extended further to demonstrate the use of CloudKit subscriptions to notify users when new records are added to the app's database.

53.1 About the Example CloudKit Project

The steps outlined in this chapter are intended to use several key features of the CloudKit framework. The example will take the form of the prototype for an app designed to appeal to users while looking for a new home. The app allows the users to store addresses, take photos and enter notes about properties visited. This information will be stored on iCloud using the CloudKit Framework and include the ability to save, delete, update, and search for records.

Before starting this project, remember that membership to the Apple Developer Program will be required as outlined in *Joining the Apple Developer Program*.

53.2 Creating the CloudKit Example Project

Launch Xcode and create a new iOS *App* project named CloudKitDemo, with the programming language set to Swift.

Once the project has been created, the first step is to enable CloudKit entitlements for the app. Select the CloudKitDemo entry listed at the top of the project navigator panel and, in the main panel, click on the *Signing & Capabilities* tab. Next, click on the "+ Capability" button to display the dialog shown in Figure 53-1. Enter iCloud into the filter bar, select the result, and press the keyboard enter key to add the capability to the project:

Figure 53-1

If iCloud is not listed as an option, you will need to pay to join the Apple Developer program as outlined in the chapter entitled *"Joining the Apple Developer Program"*. If you are already a member, use the steps outlined in the chapter entitled *"Installing Xcode 15 and the iOS 17 SDK"* to ensure you have created a *Developer ID Application* certificate.

Within the iCloud entitlement settings, make sure that the CloudKit service is enabled before clicking on the "+" button indicated by the arrow in Figure 53-2 below to add an iCloud container for the project:

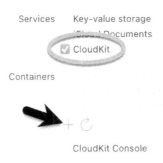

Figure 53-2

After clicking the "+" button, the dialog shown in Figure 53-3 will appear containing a text field into which you need to enter the container identifier. This entry should uniquely identify the container within the CloudKit ecosystem, generally includes your organization identifier (as defined when the project was created), and should be set to something similar to *iCloud.com.yourcompany.CloudkitDemo*.

Figure 53-3

Once you have entered the container name, click the OK button to add it to the app entitlements. Then, returning to the *Signing & Capabilities* screen, make sure that the new container is selected:

Figure 53-4

Note that if you are using the pre-created project version from the book sample download, you must assign your own Apple Developer ID to the project. To achieve this, use the *Team* menu in the Signing section of the *Signing & Capabilities* screen to select or add your Apple Developer ID to the project.

53.3 Designing the User Interface

The user interface layout for this project will consist of a Text Field, Text View, Image View, and a Toolbar containing five Bar Button Items. First, begin the design process by selecting the *Main.storyboard* file in the project navigator panel so that the storyboard loads into the Interface Builder environment.

Drag and drop views from the Library panel onto the storyboard canvas and resize, position, and configure the views so that the layout resembles that outlined in Figure 53-5, making sure to stretch the views horizontally so that they align with the margins of the containing view (represented by the dotted blue lines that appear when resizing a view). After adding the Text View and before adding the Image View, select the Text View object, display the Auto Layout *Add New Constraints* menu, and add a *Height* constraint:

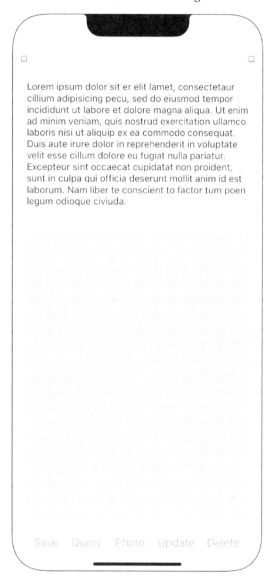

Figure 53-5

Select the Delete toolbar button, display the Attributes inspector and select the trash image:

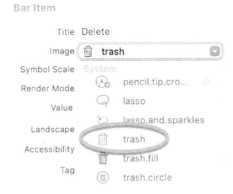

Figure 53-6

After selecting the image, the toolbar should match Figure 53-7:

Figure 53-7

Select the Text Field view, display the Attributes Inspector, and enter *Address* into the *Placeholder* attribute field. Next, select the Image View and change the Content Mode attribute to *Aspect Fit.*

Click on the white background of the view controller layout so that none of the views in the layout are currently selected. Then, using the *Resolve Auto Layout Issues* menu located in the lower right-hand corner of the Interface Builder panel, select the *Add Missing Constraints* menu option.

With the Text View selected in the storyboard, display the Attributes Inspector in the Utilities panel and delete the example Latin text.

53.4 Establishing Outlets and Actions

Display the Assistant Editor, select the Text Field view in the storyboard and right-click, drag from the view to a position beneath the "class ViewController" declaration, and release the line. In the resulting connection panel, establish an outlet connection named *addressField*. Repeat these steps for the Text View and Image View, establishing Outlets named *commentsField* and *imageView,* respectively.

Using the same technique, establish *Action* connections from the five Bar Button Items to action methods named *saveRecord, queryRecord, selectPhoto, updateRecord,* and *deleteRecord,* respectively (note that when selecting a Bar Button Item, you will need to click on it multiple times because initial clicks typically only select the Toolbar parent). Once the connections have been established, the *ViewController.swift* file should read as follows:

```
import UIKit


class ViewController: UIViewController {

    @IBOutlet weak var addressField: UITextField!
    @IBOutlet weak var commentsField: UITextView!
    @IBOutlet weak var imageView: UIImageView!
```

```
    override func viewDidLoad() {
        super.viewDidLoad()
    }


    @IBAction func saveRecord(_ sender: Any) {
    }


    @IBAction func queryRecord(_ sender: Any) {
    }


    @IBAction func selectPhoto(_ sender: Any) {
    }


    @IBAction func updateRecord(_ sender: Any) {
    }


    @IBAction func deleteRecord(_ sender: Any) {
    }
}
```

53.5 Implementing the notifyUser Method

The *notifyUser* method will display messages to the user and takes two string values representing a title and message as parameters. These strings are then used in the construction of an Alert View. Implement this method as follows:

```
func notifyUser(_ title: String, message: String) -> Void
{
    let alert = UIAlertController(title: title,
                                  message: message,
                                  preferredStyle: .alert)

    let cancelAction = UIAlertAction(title: "OK",
                                     style: .cancel, handler: nil)

    alert.addAction(cancelAction)
    DispatchQueue.main.async {
        self.present(alert, animated: true,
                     completion: nil)
    }
}
```

53.6 Accessing the Private Database

Since the information entered into the app is only relevant to the current user, the data entered into the app will be stored on iCloud using the app's private cloud database. Obtaining a reference to the private cloud database first involves gaining a reference to the app's container. Within the *ViewController.swift* file, make the following additions, noting the inclusion of import statements for frameworks that will be needed later in the tutorial, together with variables to store the current database record, record zone, and photo image URL:

An iOS 17 CloudKit Example

```swift
import UIKit
import CloudKit
import MobileCoreServices
import UniformTypeIdentifiers

class ViewController: UIViewController {

    @IBOutlet weak var addressField: UITextField!
    @IBOutlet weak var commentsField: UITextView!
    @IBOutlet weak var imageView: UIImageView!

    let container = CKContainer.default
    var privateDatabase: CKDatabase?
    var currentRecord: CKRecord?
    var photoURL: URL?
    var recordZone: CKRecordZone?

    override func viewDidLoad() {
        super.viewDidLoad()
        performSetup()
    }

    func performSetup() {
        privateDatabase = container().privateCloudDatabase

        recordZone = CKRecordZone(zoneName: "HouseZone")

        if let zone = recordZone {
            privateDatabase?.save(zone,
                completionHandler: {(recordzone, error) in

                if (error != nil) {
                    self.notifyUser("Record Zone Error",
                                    message: error!.localizedDescription)
                } else {
                    print("Saved record zone")
                }
            })
        }
    }
.
.
.
}
```

Note that the code added to the *performSetup* method also initializes the recordZone variable with a CKRecordZone object configured with the name "HouseZone" and saves it to the private database.

53.7 Hiding the Keyboard

It is important to include code to ensure the user can hide the keyboard after entering text into the two text areas in the user interface. Within the *ViewController.swift* file, override the *touchesBegan* method to hide the keyboard when the user taps the background view of the user interface:

```
override func touchesBegan(_ touches: Set<UITouch>,
                    with event: UIEvent?) {
    addressField.endEditing(true)
    commentsField.endEditing(true)
}
```

53.8 Implementing the selectPhoto method

The purpose of the Photo button in the toolbar is to allow the user to include a photo in the database record. Begin by declaring that the View Controller class implements the UIImagePickerControllerDelegate and UINavigationControllerDelegate protocols, then locate the template *selectPhoto* action method within the *ViewController.swift* file and implement the code as follows:

```
class ViewController: UIViewController, UIImagePickerControllerDelegate,
      UINavigationControllerDelegate {
.
.
@IBAction func selectPhoto(_ sender: Any) {

    let imagePicker = UIImagePickerController()

    imagePicker.delegate = self
    imagePicker.sourceType =
          UIImagePickerController.SourceType.photoLibrary
    imagePicker.mediaTypes = [UTType.image.identifier]

    self.present(imagePicker, animated: true,
                    completion:nil)
}
.
.
.
}
```

When executed, the code will cause the image picker view controller to be displayed, from which the user can select a photo from the photo library on the device to be stored along with the current record in the app's private cloud database. The final step in the photo selection process is to implement the delegate methods, which will be called when the user has either made a photo selection or canceled the selection process:

```
func imagePickerController(_ picker: UIImagePickerController,
didFinishPickingMediaWithInfo info: [UIImagePickerController.InfoKey : Any]) {
    self.dismiss(animated: true, completion: nil)
    let image =
        info[UIImagePickerController.InfoKey.originalImage] as! UIImage
    imageView.image = image
    photoURL = saveImageToFile(image)
```

```
}

func imagePickerControllerDidCancel(_ picker: UIImagePickerController) {
    self.dismiss(animated: true, completion: nil)
}
```

In both cases, the image picker view controller is dismissed from view. When a photo is selected, the image is displayed within the app via the Image View instance before being written to the device's file system. The corresponding URL is stored in the *photoURL* variable for later reference. The code expects the image file writing to be performed by a method named *saveImageToFile* which must now be implemented:

```
func saveImageToFile(_ image: UIImage) -> URL
{
    let filemgr = FileManager.default

    let dirPaths = filemgr.urls(for: .documentDirectory,
                                in: .userDomainMask)

    let fileURL = dirPaths[0].appendingPathComponent("currentImage.jpg")

    if let renderedJPEGData =
        image.jpegData(compressionQuality: 0.5) {
        try! renderedJPEGData.write(to: fileURL)
    }

    return fileURL
}
```

The method obtains a reference to the app's Documents directory and constructs a path to an image file named *currentImage.jpg*. The image is then written to the file in JPEG format using a compression rate of 0.5 to reduce the amount of storage used from the app's iCloud allowance. The resulting file URL is then returned to the calling method.

53.9 Saving a Record to the Cloud Database

When the user has entered an address and comments and selected a photo, the data is ready to be saved to the cloud database. This will require that code be added to the *saveRecord* method as follows:

```
@IBAction func saveRecord(_ sender: Any) {

    var asset: CKAsset?

    if (photoURL == nil) {
        notifyUser("No Photo",
            message: "Use the Photo option to choose a photo for the record")
        return
    } else {
        asset = CKAsset(fileURL: photoURL!)
    }
```

```
if let zoneId = recordZone?.zoneID {

    let myRecord = CKRecord(recordType: "Houses",
                            recordID: CKRecord.ID(zoneID: zoneId))

    myRecord.setObject(addressField.text as CKRecordValue?,
                       forKey: "address")

    myRecord.setObject(commentsField.text as CKRecordValue?,
                       forKey: "comment")

    myRecord.setObject(asset, forKey: "photo")

    let modifyRecordsOperation = CKModifyRecordsOperation(
        recordsToSave: [myRecord],
        recordIDsToDelete: nil)

    let configuration = CKOperation.Configuration()

    configuration.timeoutIntervalForRequest = 10
    configuration.timeoutIntervalForResource = 10

    modifyRecordsOperation.configuration = configuration

    modifyRecordsOperation.modifyRecordsResultBlock = { result in
        switch result {

        case .success():
            self.notifyUser("Success", message: "Record saved successfully")
            self.currentRecord = myRecord
        case .failure(_):
            self.notifyUser("Save Error", message: "Failed to save record")

        }
    }
    privateDatabase?.add(modifyRecordsOperation)
}
}
```

The method begins by verifying that the user has selected a photo to include in the database record. If one has not yet been selected, the user is notified that a photo is required (the *notifyUser* method will be implemented in the next section).

Next, a new CKAsset object is created and initialized with the URL to the photo image previously selected by the user. A new CKRecord instance is created and assigned a record type of "Houses." The record is then initialized with the Text Field and Text View content, the CKAsset object containing the photo image, and ID of the zone with which the record is to be associated.

Once the record is ready to be saved, a CKModifyRecordsOperation object is initialized with the record object and then executed against the user's private database. A completion handler is used to report the success or otherwise of the save operation. Since this involves working with the user interface, it is dispatched to the main thread to prevent the app from locking up. The new record is then saved to the *currentRecord* variable, where it can be referenced should the user decide to update or delete it.

53.10 Testing the Record Saving Method

Compile and run the app on a device or simulator on which you are signed into iCloud using the Apple ID associated with your Apple Developer account. Next, enter text into the address and comments fields and select an image from the photo library.

Tap the Save button to save the record and wait for the alert to appear, indicating that the record has been saved successfully. Note that CloudKit operations are performed asynchronously, so the amount of time for a successful save to be reported will vary depending on the size of the saved record, network speed, and responsiveness of the iCloud servers.

53.11 Reviewing the Saved Data in the CloudKit Console

Once some product entries have been added to the database, return to the *Signing & Capabilities* screen for the project (Figure 53-2) and click on the CloudKit Console button. This will launch the default web browser on your system and load the CloudKit Dashboard portal. Enter your Apple developer login and password, and once the dashboard has loaded, the home screen will provide the range of options illustrated in Figure 53-8:

Figure 53-8

Select the CloudKit Database option and, on the resulting web page, select the container for your app from the drop-down menu (marked A in Figure 53-9 below). Since the app is still in development and has not been published to the App Store, make sure that menu B is set to Development and not Production:

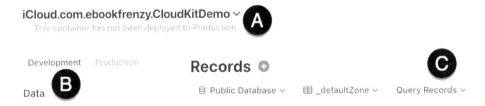

Figure 53-9

Next, we can query the records stored in the app container's private database. Set the row of menus (C) to *Private Database*, *HouseZone*, and *Query Records*, respectively. If HouseZone is not listed, make sure that the device or simulator on which the app is running is signed in using the same Apple ID used to log into the CloudKit Dashboard. Finally, set the Record Type menu to *Houses* and the *Fields* menu to All:

Records ⊕

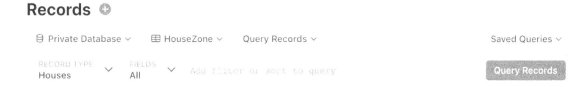

Figure 53-10

Clicking on the Query Records button should list any records saved in the database, as illustrated in Figure 53-11:

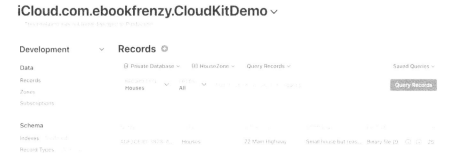

Figure 53-11

Within the records list, click on the record name to display the data and assets contained within that record. The information displayed in the *Record Details* panel (Figure 53-12) should match that entered within the CloudKitDemo app:

Figure 53-12

The next task is to implement the remaining action methods after verifying that the record was saved.

53.12 Searching for Cloud Database Records

The Query feature of the app allows a record matching a specified address to be retrieved and displayed to the user. Because a query operation can take some time to complete, it must be performed asynchronously from the main thread to prevent the app from freezing while awaiting a response from the CloudKit service. We will, therefore, perform query operations using Swift Concurrency, beginning with an async function that will perform the query. Within the *ViewController.swift* file, add a new method named *asyncQuery* as follows:

```swift
func asyncQuery(predicate: NSPredicate) async {

    let query = CKQuery(recordType: "Houses", predicate: predicate)

    do {
        let result = try await privateDatabase?.records(matching: query)

        if let records = result?.matchResults.compactMap({ try? $0.1.get() }) {

            if records.count > 0 {
                let record = records[0]
                self.currentRecord = record
                self.commentsField.text = record.object(forKey: "comment")
                                                            as? String
                let photo = record.object(forKey: "photo") as! CKAsset

                let image = UIImage(contentsOfFile:
                                    photo.fileURL?.path ?? "")

                if let img = image {
                    self.imageView.image = img
                    self.photoURL = self.saveImageToFile(img)
                }
            } else {
                self.notifyUser("No Match Found",
                        message: "No record matching the address was found")
            }
        }
    } catch {
        self.notifyUser("Error", message: "Unable to perform query")
    }
}
```

This method is passed an NSPredicate, which it uses to create a CKQuery object. This query object is then passed to the *records()* method of the private database, and the results are assigned to a constant using try await. The code then transforms the results into an array of records via a call to the Swift *compactMap()* method. Next, the first matching record is accessed, and the data and image contained therein are displayed to the user via the user interface outlet connections.

Next, edit the template *queryRecord* method in the *ViewController.swift* file and implement the body of the method to perform the query operation:

```
@IBAction func queryRecord(_ sender: Any) {


    if let text = addressField.text {
        let predicate = NSPredicate(format: "address = %@", text)
        Task.init {
            await asyncQuery(predicate: predicate)
        }
    }
}
```

This method extracts the address and uses it to create the predicate object, which is then passed to the asyncQuery() method. Since it is not possible to call async functions from within an IBAction function, we need to make this call using the Swift Concurrency Task.init construct.

Compile and run the app, enter the address used when the record was saved in the previous section, and tap the Query button. After a short delay, the display should update with the record's content.

53.13 Updating Cloud Database Records

When updating existing records in a cloud database, the ID of the record to be updated must be referenced since this is the only way to identify one record uniquely from another. In addition, in the case of the CloudKitDemo app, the record must already have been loaded into the app and assigned to the currentRecord variable, thereby allowing the recordID to be obtained and used for the update operation. With these requirements in mind, implement the code in the stub *updateRecord* method as follows:

```
@IBAction func updateRecord(_ sender: Any) {
    if let record = currentRecord, let url = photoURL {

        let asset = CKAsset(fileURL: url)

        record.setObject(addressField.text as CKRecordValue?,
                    forKey: "address")
        record.setObject(commentsField.text as CKRecordValue?,
                    forKey: "comment")
        record.setObject(asset, forKey: "photo")

        privateDatabase?.save(record, completionHandler:
            ({returnRecord, error in
                if let err = error {
                    self.notifyUser("Update Error",
                                    message: err.localizedDescription)
                } else {
                    self.notifyUser("Success", message:
                        "Record updated successfully")

                }
            }))
```

```
    } else {
        notifyUser("No Record Selected", message:
            "Use Query to select a record to update")
    }
}
```

This method performs similar tasks to the *saveRecord* method. This time, however, instead of creating a new CKRecord instance, the existing record assigned to the *currentRecord* variable is updated with the latest text and photo content entered by the user. When the save operation is performed, CloudKit will identify that the record has an ID that matches an existing record in the database and update that matching record with the latest data provided by the user.

53.14 Deleting a Cloud Record

CloudKit record deletions can be achieved by calling the *deleteRecordWithID* method of the CKDatabase instance, passing through as arguments the ID of the record to be deleted and a completion handler to be executed when the deletion operation returns. As with the *updateRecord* method, a deletion can only be performed when the record to be deleted has already been selected within the app and assigned to the *currentRecord* variable:

```
@IBAction func deleteRecord(_ sender: Any) {
    if let record = currentRecord {

        privateDatabase?.delete(withRecordID: record.recordID,
                completionHandler: ({returnRecord, error in
            if let err = error {
                self.notifyUser("Delete Error", message:
                                err.localizedDescription)
            } else {
                self.notifyUser("Success", message:
                    "Record deleted successfully")
            }
        }))
    } else {
        notifyUser("No Record Selected", message:
                    "Use Query to select a record to delete")
    }
}
```

53.15 Testing the App

With the app's basic functionality implemented, compile and run it on a device or simulator instance and add, query, update and delete records to verify that the app functions as intended.

53.16 Summary

CloudKit provides an easy way to implement the storage and retrieval of iCloud-based database records from within iOS apps. The objective of this chapter has been to demonstrate in practical terms the techniques available to save, search, update, and delete database records stored in an iCloud database using the CloudKit convenience API.

54. An iOS 17 CloudKit Sharing Example

The chapter entitled *"An Introduction to CloudKit Sharing"* provided an overview of how CloudKit sharing works and the steps involved in integrating sharing into an iOS app. The intervening chapters have focused on creating a project that demonstrates the integration of CloudKit data storage into iOS apps. This chapter will extend the project started in the previous chapter to add CloudKit sharing to the CloudKitDemo app.

54.1 Preparing the Project for CloudKit Sharing

Launch Xcode and open the CloudKitDemo project created in this book's chapter entitled *"An Introduction to CloudKit Sharing"*. If you have not completed the tasks in the previous chapter and are only interested in learning about CloudKit sharing, a snapshot of the project is included as part of the sample code archive for this book on the following web page:

https://www.payloadbooks.com/product/ios17xcode/

Once the project has been loaded into Xcode, the CKSharingSupported key needs to be added to the project *Info.plist* file with a Boolean value of true. Select the CloudKitDemo target at the top of the Project Navigator panel, followed by the *Info* tab in the main panel. Next, locate the bottom entry in the Custom iOS Target Properties list, and hover the mouse pointer over the item. When the plus button appears, click it to add a new entry to the list. Complete the new property with the key field set to *CKSharingSupported*, the type to Boolean, and the value to YES, as illustrated in Figure 54-1:

Figure 54-1

54.2 Adding the Share Button

The user interface for the app now needs to be modified to add a share button to the toolbar. First, select the *Main.storyboard* file, locate the Bar Button Item in the Library panel, and drag and drop an instance onto the toolbar to position it to the right of the existing delete button.

Once added, select the button item, display the Attributes inspector, and select the square and arrow image:

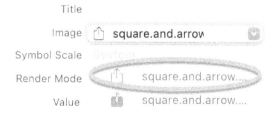

Figure 54-2

Once the new button has been added, the toolbar should match Figure 54-3:

Figure 54-3

With the new share button item still selected, display the Assistant Editor panel and establish an Action connection to a method named *shareRecord*.

54.3 Creating the CloudKit Share

The next step is to add some code to the *shareRecord* action method to initialize and display the UICloudSharingController and to create and save the CKShare object. Next, select the *ViewController.swift* file, locate the stub *shareRecord* method, and modify it so that it reads as follows:

```
@IBAction func shareRecord(_ sender: Any) {

    let controller = UICloudSharingController { controller,
        prepareCompletionHandler in

        if let thisRecord = self.currentRecord {
            let share = CKShare(rootRecord: thisRecord)

            share[CKShare.SystemFieldKey.title] =
                            "An Amazing House" as CKRecordValue
            share.publicPermission = .readOnly

            let modifyRecordsOperation = CKModifyRecordsOperation(
                recordsToSave: [thisRecord, share],
                recordIDsToDelete: nil)

            let configuration = CKOperation.Configuration()

            configuration.timeoutIntervalForResource = 10
            configuration.timeoutIntervalForRequest = 10

            modifyRecordsOperation.modifyRecordsResultBlock = {
                result in
                switch result {
                case .success:
                    prepareCompletionHandler(share, CKContainer.default(), nil)
                case .failure(let error):
                    print(error.localizedDescription)
                }
```

```
            }
            self.privateDatabase?.add(modifyRecordsOperation)
        } else {
            print("User error: No record selected")
        }
    }

    controller.availablePermissions = [.allowPublic, .allowReadOnly,
            .allowReadWrite, .allowPrivate]
    controller.popoverPresentationController?.barButtonItem =
        sender as? UIBarButtonItem

    present(controller, animated: true)
}
```

The code added to this method follows the steps outlined in the chapter entitled *"An Introduction to CloudKit Sharing"* to display the CloudKit sharing view controller, create a share object initialized with the currently selected record and save it to the user's private database.

54.4 Accepting a CloudKit Share

Now that the user can create a CloudKit share, the app needs to be modified to accept a share and display it to the user. The first step in this process is implementing the *userDidAcceptCloudKitShareWith* method within the project's scene delegate class. Edit the *SceneDelegate.swift* file and implement this method as follows:

```
.
.
import CloudKit
.
.
func windowScene(_ windowScene: UIWindowScene,
    userDidAcceptCloudKitShareWith cloudKitShareMetadata: CKShare.Metadata) {

    acceptCloudKitShare(metadata: cloudKitShareMetadata) { [weak self] result in
        switch result {
        case .success:
            DispatchQueue.main.async {
                let viewController: ViewController =
                    self?.window?.rootViewController as! ViewController
                viewController.fetchShare(cloudKitShareMetadata)
            }
        case .failure(let error):
            print(error.localizedDescription )
        }
    }
}
.
.
```

When the user clicks on a CloudKit share link, for example, in an email or text message, the operating system will call the above method to notify the app that shared CloudKit data is available. The above implementation of this method calls a method named acceptCloudKitShare and passes it the CloudKitShareMetadata object it received from the operating system. If the acceptCloudKitShare method returns a successful result, the delegate method obtains a reference to the app's root view controller and calls a method named fetchShare (which we will write in the next section) to extract the shared record from the CloudKit database and display it.

Next, we need to add the acceptCloudKitShare method as follows:

```
func acceptCloudKitShare(metadata: CKShare.Metadata,
    completion: @escaping (Result<CKRecord.ID, Error>) -> Void) {

    let container = CKContainer(identifier: metadata.containerIdentifier)
    let operation = CKAcceptSharesOperation(shareMetadatas: [metadata])
    var rootRecordID: CKRecord.ID!

    operation.perShareResultBlock = { metadata, result in
        switch result {
        case .success:
            rootRecordID = metadata.hierarchicalRootRecordID
        case .failure(let error):
            print(error.localizedDescription)
        }
    }

    operation.acceptSharesResultBlock = { result in
        switch result {
        case .success:
            completion(.success(rootRecordID))
        case .failure(let error):
            completion(.failure(error))
        }
    }
    container.add(operation)
}
```

54.5 Fetching the Shared Record

At this point, the share has been accepted and a CKShare.Metadata object provided, from which information about the shared record may be extracted. All that remains before the app can be tested is to implement the *fetchShare* method within the *ViewController.swift* file:

```
func fetchShare(_ metadata: CKShare.Metadata) {

    let operation = CKFetchRecordsOperation(recordIDs:
                            [metadata.hierarchicalRootRecordID!])

    operation.perRecordResultBlock = { recordId, result in
        switch result {
```

```
        case .success(let record):
            DispatchQueue.main.async() {
                self.currentRecord = record
                self.addressField.text =
                    record.object(forKey: "address") as? String
                self.commentsField.text =
                    record.object(forKey: "comment") as? String
                let photo =
                    record.object(forKey: "photo") as! CKAsset
                let image = UIImage(contentsOfFile:
                                        photo.fileURL!.path)
                self.imageView.image = image
                self.photoURL = self.saveImageToFile(image!)
            }
        case .failure(let error):
            print(error.localizedDescription)
        }
    }

    operation.fetchRecordsResultBlock = { result in
        switch result {
        case .success:
            break
        case .failure(let error):
            print(error.localizedDescription)
        }
    }
    CKContainer.default().sharedCloudDatabase.add(operation)
}
```

The method prepares a standard CloudKit fetch operation based on the record ID contained within the share metadata object and performs the fetch using the *sharedCloudDatabase* instance. On a successful fetch, the completion handler extracts the data from the shared record and displays it in the user interface.

54.6 Testing the CloudKit Share Example

To thoroughly test CloudKit sharing, two devices with different Apple IDs must be used. If you have access to two devices, create a second Apple ID for testing purposes and sign in using that ID on one of the devices. Once logged in, make sure that the devices can send and receive iMessage or email messages between each other and install and run the CloudKitDemo app on both devices. Once the testing environment is set up, launch the CloudKitDemo app on one of the devices and add a record to the private database. Once added, tap the Share button and use the share view controller interface to send a share link message to the Apple ID associated with the second device. When the message arrives on the second device, tap the share link and accept the share when prompted. Once the share has been accepted, the CloudKitDemo app should launch and display the shared record.

54.7 Summary

This chapter puts the theory of CloudKit sharing outlined in the chapter entitled *"An Introduction to CloudKit Sharing"* into practice by enhancing the CloudKitDemo project to include the ability to share CloudKit-based records with other app users. This involved creating and saving a CKShare object, using the UICloudSharingController class, and adding code to handle accepting and fetching a shared CloudKit database record.

55. An Overview of iOS 17 Multitouch, Taps, and Gestures

In terms of physical points of interaction between the device and the user, the iPhone and iPad provide four buttons (three in the case of the iPhone X), a switch, and a touch screen. Without question, the user will spend far more time using the touch screen than any other device aspect. Therefore, any app must be able to handle gestures (touches, multitouches, taps, swipes, pinches, etc.) performed by the user's fingers on the touch screen.

Before writing code to handle these gestures, this chapter will spend some time talking about the responder chain in relation to touch screen events before delving a little deeper into the types of gestures an iOS app is likely to encounter.

55.1 The Responder Chain

In the chapter entitled *"Understanding iOS 17 Views, Windows, and the View Hierarchy"*, we discussed the view hierarchy of an app's user interface and how that hierarchy also defined part of the app's *responder chain*. However, to fully understand the concepts behind handling touchscreen gestures, it is first necessary to spend a little more time learning about the responder chain.

When the user interacts with the touch screen of an iPhone or iPad, the hardware detects the physical contact and notifies the operating system. The operating system subsequently creates an *event* associated with the interaction and passes it into the currently active app's *event queue,* where it is then picked up by the *event loop* and passed to the current *first responder* object; the first responder being the object with which the user was interacting when this event was triggered (for example a UIButton or UIView object). If the first responder has been programmed to handle the type of event received, it does so (for example, a button may have an action defined to call a particular method when it receives a touch event). Having handled the event, the responder then has the option of discarding that event or passing it up to the *next responder* in the *response chain* (defined by the object's *next* property) for further processing, and so on up the chain. If the first responder is not able to handle the event, it will also pass it to the next responder in the chain and so on until it either reaches a responder that handles the event or it reaches the end of the chain (the UIApp object) where it will either be handled or discarded.

Take, for example, a UIView with a UIButton subview. If the user touches the screen over the button, then the button, as the first responder, will receive the event. If the button cannot handle the event, it will need to be passed up to the view object. If the view can also not handle the event, it would then be passed to the view controller.

When working with the responder chain, it is important to note that the passing of an event from one responder to the next in the chain does not happen automatically. If an event needs to be passed to the next responder, code must be written to make it happen.

55.2 Forwarding an Event to the Next Responder

To pass an event to the next responder in the chain, a reference to the next responder object must first be obtained. This can be achieved by accessing the *next* property of the current responder. Once the next responder has been identified, the method that triggered the event is called on that object and passed any relevant event data.

Take, for example, a situation where the current responder object cannot handle a *touchesBegan* event. To pass this to the next responder, the *touchesBegan* method of the current responder will need to make a call as follows:

```
override func touchesBegan(_ touches: Set<UITouch>, with event: UIEvent?) {
        self.next?.touchesBegan(touches, with: event)
}
```

In this case, the *touchesBegan* method is called on the next responder and passes the original touches and event parameters.

55.3 Gestures

Gesture is an umbrella term used to encapsulate any interaction between the touch screen and the user, starting at the point that the screen is touched (by one or more fingers) and the time that the last finger leaves the screen's surface. *Swipes, pinches, stretches,* and *flicks* are all forms of gesture.

55.4 Taps

As the name suggests, a tap occurs when the user touches the screen with a single finger and immediately lifts it from the screen. Taps can be single-taps or multiple-taps, and the event will contain information about the number of times a user tapped on the screen.

55.5 Touches

A *touch* occurs when a finger establishes contact with the screen. When more than one finger touches the screen, each finger registers as a touch, up to a maximum of five fingers.

55.6 Touch Notification Methods

Touch screen events cause one of four methods on the first responder object to be called. The method that gets called for a specific event will depend on the nature of the interaction. To handle events, therefore, it is important to ensure that the appropriate methods from those outlined below are implemented within your responder chain. These methods will be used in the worked example contained in the *"An Example iOS 17 Touch, Multitouch, and Tap App"* and *"Detecting iOS 17 Touch Screen Gesture Motions"* chapters of this book.

55.6.1 touchesBegan method

The *touchesBegan* method is called when the user first touches the screen. Passed to this method is an argument called *touches* of type NSSet and the corresponding UIEvent object. The touches object contains a UITouch event for each finger in contact with the screen. The *tapCount* method of any of the UITouch events within the *touches* set can be called to identify the number of taps, if any, performed by the user. Similarly, the coordinates of an individual touch can be identified from the UITouch event either relative to the entire screen or within the local view itself.

55.6.2 touchesMoved method

The *touchesMoved* method is called when one or more fingers move across the screen. As fingers move across the screen, this method gets called multiple times, allowing the app to track the new coordinates and touch count at regular intervals. As with the *touchesBegan* method, this method is provided with an event object and an NSSet object containing UITouch events for each finger on the screen.

55.6.3 touchesEnded method

This method is called when the user lifts one or more fingers from the screen. As with the previous methods, *touchesEnded* is provided with the event and NSSet objects.

55.6.4 touchesCancelled method

When a gesture is interrupted due to a high-level interrupt, such as the phone detecting an incoming call, the *touchesCancelled* method is called.

55.7 Touch Prediction

A feature introduced as part of the iOS 9 SDK is touch prediction. Each time the system updates the current coordinates of a touch on the screen, a set of algorithms attempt to predict the coordinates of the next location. For example, a finger sweeping across the screen will trigger multiple calls to the *touchesMoved* method passing through the current touch coordinates. Also passed through to the method is a UIEvent object on which a method named *predictedTouchesForTouch* may be called, passing through the touch object representing the current location. In return, the method will provide an array of UITouch objects that predict the next few locations of the touch motion. This information can then be used to improve the app's performance and responsiveness to the user's touch behavior.

55.8 Touch Coalescing

iOS devices are categorized by two metrics known as the *touch sample rate* and *touch delivery rate*. The touch sample rate is the frequency with which the screen scans for the current position of touches on the screen. The touch delivery rate, on the other hand, is the frequency with which that information is passed to the currently running app.

On most devices (including all recent iPhone models except the iPhone X), the sample and delivery rates run at 60 Hz (60 times a second). On other device models, however, the sample and delivery frequencies do not match. The iPhone X, for example, samples at 120 Hz but delivers at a slower 60 Hz, while an iPad Pro with an Apple Pencil samples at an impressive 240 Hz while delivering at only 120 Hz.

To avoid the loss of touch information caused by the gap in sampling and delivery frequencies, UIKit uses a system referred to as *touch coalescing* to deliver the additional touch data generated by the higher sampling frequencies.

With touch coalescing, the same touch notification methods are called and passed the same UITouch objects, which are referred to as the *main touches*. Also passed through to each method is a UIEvent object on which the *coalescedTouchesForTouch* method may be called, passing through as an argument the current main touch object. When called within an app running on a device where the sampling rate exceeds the delivery rate, the method will return an array of touch objects consisting of both a copy of the current main touch and the intermediate touch activity between the current main touch and the previous main touch. These intermediate touch objects are referred to as *coalesced touches*. On iOS devices with matching rates, no coalesced touch objects will be returned by this method call.

55.9 Summary

To fully appreciate the mechanisms for handling touchscreen events within an iOS app, it is first important to understand both the responder chain and the methods that are called on a responder depending on the type of interaction. We have covered these basics in this chapter. In the next chapter, entitled *"An Example iOS 17 Touch, Multitouch, and Tap App"*, we will use these concepts to create an example app demonstrating touch screen event handling.

56. An Example iOS 17 Touch, Multitouch, and Tap App

Now that we have covered the basic concepts behind the handling of iOS user interaction with an iPhone or iPad touchscreen in the previous chapter, this chapter will work through a tutorial designed to highlight the handling of taps and touches. Topics covered in this chapter include the detection of single and multiple taps and touches, identifying whether a user single or double-tapped the device display and extracting information about a touch or tap from the corresponding event object.

56.1 The Example iOS Tap and Touch App

The example app created in this tutorial will consist of a view and some labels. The view object's view controller will implement a number of the touch screen event methods outlined in *"An Overview of iOS 17 Multitouch, Taps, and Gestures"* and update the status labels to reflect the detected activity. The app will, for example, report the number of fingers touching the screen, the number of taps performed, and the most recent touch event that was triggered. In the next chapter, entitled *"Detecting iOS 17 Touch Screen Gesture Motions"*, we will look more closely at detecting the motion of touches.

56.2 Creating the Example iOS Touch Project

Begin by launching Xcode and creating a new project using the iOS App template with the Swift and Storyboard options selected, entering *Touch* as the product name. When the main Xcode project screen appears, we are ready to start writing the code and designing our app.

56.3 Designing the User Interface

Load the storyboard by selecting the *Main.storyboard* file. Then, using Interface Builder, modify the user interface by adding label components from the Library and modifying properties until the view appears as outlined in Figure 56-1.

When adding the rightmost labels, stretch them so that the right-hand edges reach approximately three-quarters across the overall layout width.

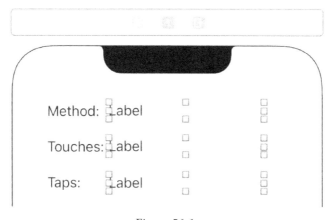

Figure 56-1

Display the *Resolve Auto Layout Issues* menu and select the *Reset to suggested constraints* option listed under *All Views in View Controller*.

Select the label to the right of the "Method" label, display the Assistant Editor panel, and verify that the editor displays the contents of the *ViewController.swift* file. Right-click on the same label object and drag it to a position just below the class declaration line in the Assistant Editor. Release the line, and in the resulting connection dialog, establish an outlet connection named *methodStatus*.

Repeat the above steps to establish outlet connections for the remaining label objects to properties named *touchStatus* and *tapStatus*. Finally, remove the text from the status labels, so they are blank.

56.4 Enabling Multitouch on the View

By default, views are configured to respond to only single touches (in other words, a single finger touching or tapping the screen at any one time). However, for this example, we plan to detect multiple touches. Therefore, to enable multitouch support, it is necessary to change an attribute of the view object. To achieve this, click on the background of the *View* window, display the Attributes Inspector (*View -> Utilities -> Show Attributes Inspector*), and make sure that the *Multiple Touch* option is selected in the *Interaction* section:

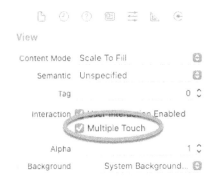

Figure 56-2

56.5 Implementing the touchesBegan Method

When the user touches the screen, the *touchesBegan* method of the first responder is called. We must implement this method in our view controller to capture these event types. In the Xcode project navigator, select the *ViewController.swift* file and add the *touchesBegan* method as follows:

```
override func touchesBegan(_ touches: Set<UITouch>, with event: UIEvent?) {
    let touchCount = touches.count
    if let touch = touches.first {
        let tapCount = touch.tapCount

        methodStatus.text = "touchesBegan"
        touchStatus.text = "\(touchCount) touches"
        tapStatus.text = "\(tapCount) taps"
    }
}
```

This method obtains a count of the number of touch objects contained in the *touches* set (essentially the number of fingers touching the screen) and assigns it to a variable. It then gets the tap count from one of the touch objects. The code then updates the *methodStatus* label to indicate that the *touchesBegan* method has been triggered, constructs a string indicating the number of touches and taps detected, and displays the information on the *touchStatus* and *tapStatus* labels accordingly.

56.6 Implementing the touchesMoved Method

When the user moves one or more fingers currently in contact with the surface of the touch screen, the *touchesMoved* method is called repeatedly until the movement ceases. To capture these events, it is necessary to implement the touchesMoved method in our view controller class:

```
override func touchesMoved(_ touches: Set<UITouch>, with event: UIEvent?) {
    let touchCount = touches.count
    if let touch = touches.first {
        let tapCount = touch.tapCount

        methodStatus.text = "touchesMoved";
        touchStatus.text = "\(touchCount) touches"
        tapStatus.text = "\(tapCount) taps"
    }
}
```

Once again, we report the number of touches and taps detected and indicate to the user that the touchesMoved method is being triggered this time.

56.7 Implementing the touchesEnded Method

When the user removes a finger from the screen, the *touchesEnded* method is called. We can, therefore, implement this method as follows:

```
override func touchesEnded(_ touches: Set<UITouch>, with event: UIEvent?) {
    let touchCount = touches.count
    if let touch = touches.first {
        let tapCount = touch.tapCount

        methodStatus.text = "touchesEnded";
        touchStatus.text = "\(touchCount) touches"
        tapStatus.text = "\(tapCount) taps"
    }
}
```

56.8 Getting the Coordinates of a Touch

Although not part of this particular example, it is worth knowing that the location coordinates on the screen where a touch has been detected may be obtained in the form of a CGPoint structure by calling the *location(in:)* method of the touch object. For example:

```
let touch = touches.first
let point = touch.location(in: self.view)
```

The X and Y coordinates may subsequently be extracted from the CGPoint structure by accessing the corresponding elements:

```
let pointX = point.x
let pointY = point.y
```

56.9 Building and Running the Touch Example App

Build and run the app on a physical iOS device by clicking on the run button located in the toolbar of the main Xcode project window. With each tap and touch on the device screen, the status labels should update to reflect the interaction:

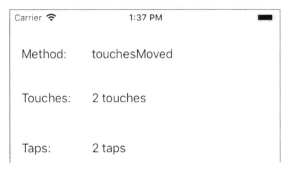

Figure 56-3

Note that when running within the iOS Simulator, multiple touches may be simulated by holding down the Option key while clicking in the simulator window.

56.10 Checking for Touch Predictions

Having implemented code to detect touches and touch motion on the screen, code will now be added to output to the console any touch predictions available within the UIEvent object passed to the *touchesMoved* method. Locate this method within the *ViewController.swift* file and modify it so that it now reads as follows:

```
override func touchesMoved(_ touches: Set<UITouch>, with event: UIEvent?) {
    let touchCount = touches.count
    if let touch = touches.first {
        let tapCount = touch.tapCount

        methodStatus.text = "touchesMoved";
        touchStatus.text = "\(touchCount) touches"
        tapStatus.text = "\(tapCount) taps"

        if let eventObj = event,
            let predictedTouches = eventObj.predictedTouches(for: touch) {
            for predictedTouch in predictedTouches {
                let point = predictedTouch.location(in: self.view)
                print("Predicted location X = \(point.x), Y = \(point.y)")
            }
            print("============")
        }
    }
}
```

The added code begins by checking that an event object was passed to the method before calling the *predictedTouches(for:)* method of that object. Then, for each touch object within the returned array, the X and Y coordinates of the predicted touch location are output to the console.

Compile and run the app again and monitor the console as a touch moves around the display. When it can do so, UIKit will provide predictions on future touch locations. Note that this feature would only work on a physical iOS device at the time of writing.

56.11 Accessing Coalesced Touches

The final task in this tutorial is to display any coalesced touch information that might be available. Once again, modify the *touchesMoved* method, this time implementing code to display the location information for any coalesced touches:

```
override func touchesMoved(_ touches: Set<UITouch>, with event: UIEvent?) {
    let touchCount = touches.count
    if let touch = touches.first {
        let tapCount = touch.tapCount

        methodStatus.text = "touchesMoved";
        touchStatus.text = "\(touchCount) touches"
        tapStatus.text = "\(tapCount) taps"

        if let eventObj = event,
           let coalescedTocuhes = eventObj.coalescedTouches(for: touch) {
            for coalescedTouch in coalescedTocuhes {
                let point = coalescedTouch.location(in: self.view)
                print("Coalesced location X = \(point.x), Y = \(point.y)")
            }
            print("============")
        }
    }
}
```

To test this functionality, running the app on a physical iPad Air 2 (or newer) device will be necessary. When run on such a device, moving a touch around the screen will cause the coordinates of the coalesced touches to be displayed to the Xcode console.

56.12 Summary

This chapter has created a simple example project designed to demonstrate the use of the *touchesBegan*, *touchesMoved,* and *touchesEnded* methods to obtain information about the touches occurring on the display of an iOS device. Using these methods, it is possible to detect when the screen is touched and released, the number of points of contact with the screen, and the number of taps being performed. Code was also added to detect and output information relating to touch predictions and coalesced touches.

57. Detecting iOS 17 Touch Screen Gesture Motions

The next area of iOS touchscreen event handling that we will look at in this book involves the detection of gestures involving movement. As covered in a previous chapter, a *gesture* refers to the activity that takes place between a finger touching the screen and the finger then being lifted from the screen. In the chapter entitled *"An Example iOS 17 Touch, Multitouch, and Tap App"*, we dealt with touches that did not involve movement across the screen surface. We will now create an example that tracks the coordinates of a finger as it moves across the screen.

Note that the assumption made throughout this chapter that the reader has already reviewed the *"An Overview of iOS 17 Multitouch, Taps, and Gestures"* chapter.

57.1 The Example iOS 17 Gesture App

This example app will detect when a single touch is made on the screen of the iPhone or iPad and then report the coordinates of that finger as it is moved across the screen surface.

57.2 Creating the Example Project

Begin by launching Xcode and creating a new project using the iOS App template with the Swift and Storyboard options selected, entering *TouchMotion* as the product name.

57.3 Designing the App User Interface

The app will display the X and Y coordinates of the touch and update these values in real-time as the finger moves across the screen. When the finger is lifted from the screen, the start and end coordinates of the gesture will then be displayed on two label objects in the user interface. Select the *Main.storyboard* file and, using Interface Builder, create a user interface that resembles the layout in Figure 57-1.

Be sure to stretch the labels so that they both extend to cover a little over half of the width of the view layout.

Select the top label object in the view canvas, display the Assistant Editor panel, and verify that the editor is displaying the contents of the *ViewController.swift* file. Right-click on the same label object and drag it to a position just below the class declaration line in the Assistant Editor. Release the line, and in the resulting connection dialog, establish an outlet connection named *xCoord*. Repeat this step to establish an outlet connection to the second label object named *yCoord*.

Figure 57-1

Next, review the *ViewController.swift* file to verify that the outlets are correct, then declare a property in which to store the coordinates of the start location on the screen:

```
import UIKit

class ViewController: UIViewController {

    @IBOutlet weak var xCoord: UILabel!
    @IBOutlet weak var yCoord: UILabel!

    var startPoint: CGPoint!
    .
    .
    .
}
```

57.4 Implementing the touchesBegan Method

When the user touches the screen, the location coordinates need to be saved in the *startPoint* instance variable, and those coordinates need to be reported to the user. This can be achieved by implementing the *touchesBegan* method in the *ViewController.swift* file as follows:

```
override func touchesBegan(_ touches: Set<UITouch>, with event: UIEvent?) {
    if let theTouch = touches.first {
        startPoint = theTouch.location(in: self.view)

        if let x = startPoint?.x, let y = startPoint?.y {

            xCoord.text = ("x = \(x)")
            yCoord.text = ("y = \(y)")
        }
    }
}
```

57.5 Implementing the touchesMoved Method

When the user's finger moves across the screen, the *touchesMoved* event will be called repeatedly until the motion stops. By implementing the *touchesMoved* method in our view controller, therefore, we can detect the motion and display the revised coordinates to the user:

```
override func touchesMoved(_ touches: Set<UITouch>, with event: UIEvent?) {
    if let theTouch = touches.first {

        let touchLocation = theTouch.location(in: self.view)
        let x = touchLocation.x
        let y = touchLocation.y

        xCoord.text = ("x = \(x)")
        yCoord.text = ("y = \(y)")
    }
}
```

57.6 Implementing the touchesEnded Method

When the user's finger lifts from the screen, the *touchesEnded* method of the first responder is called. The final task, therefore, is to implement this method in our view controller such that it displays the end point of the gesture:

```
override func touchesEnded(_ touches: Set<UITouch>, with event: UIEvent?) {
    if let theTouch = touches.first {

        let endPoint = theTouch.location(in: self.view)
        let x = endPoint.x
        let y = endPoint.y

        xCoord.text = ("x = \(x)")
        yCoord.text = ("y = \(y)")
    }
}
```

57.7 Building and Running the Gesture Example

Build and run the app using the run button in the toolbar of the main Xcode project window. When the app starts (either in the iOS Simulator or on a physical device), touch the screen and drag it to a new location before lifting your finger from the screen (or the mouse button in the case of the iOS Simulator). During the motion, the current coordinates will update in real-time. Once the gesture is complete, the end location of the movement will be displayed.

57.8 Summary

By implementing the standard touch event methods, the motion of a gesture can easily be tracked by an iOS app. However, much of a user's interaction with apps involves specific gesture types, such as swipes and pinches. Therefore, writing code correlating finger movement on the screen with a specific gesture type would be extremely complex. Fortunately, iOS makes this task easy through the use of *gesture recognizers*. In the next chapter, entitled *"Identifying Gestures using iOS 17 Gesture Recognizers"*, we will look at this concept in more detail.

58. Identifying Gestures using iOS 17 Gesture Recognizers

In the chapter entitled *"Detecting iOS 17 Touch Screen Gesture Motions"*, we looked at how to track the motion of contact with the touch screen of an iOS device. In practice, an app must respond to specific movements during a gesture. Swiping a finger across the screen might, for example, be required to slide a new view onto the display. Similarly, a pinching motion is typically used in iOS apps to enlarge or reduce an image or view.

Before iOS 4, identifying a gesture was the app developer's responsibility and typically involved the creation of complex mathematical algorithms. In recognition of this complexity, and given the importance of gestures to user interaction with the iOS device, Apple introduced the UIGestureRecognizer class in iOS 4, thereby making the task of identifying the types of gestures a much easier task for the app developer.

This chapter aims to provide an overview of gesture recognition within iOS 17. The next chapter will work through *"An iOS 17 Gesture Recognition Tutorial"*.

58.1 The UIGestureRecognizer Class

The UIGestureRecognizer class is used as the basis for a collection of subclasses, each designed to detect a specific type of gesture. These subclasses are as follows:

UITapGestureRecognizer – This class detects when a user taps on the device's screen. Both single and multiple taps may be detected based on the configuration of the class instance.

- **UIPinchGestureRecognizer** – Detects when the user makes a pinching motion on the screen. This motion is typically used to zoom in or out of a view or to change the size of a visual component.

- **UIPanGestureRecognizer** – Detects when the user makes a dragging or panning gesture.

- **UIScreenEdgePanGestureRecognizer** – Detects when a dragging or panning gesture starts near the edge of the display screen.

- **UISwipeGestureRecognizer** – Used to detect when the user makes a swiping gesture across the screen. Instances of this class may be configured to detect motion only in specific directions (left, right, up, or down).

- **UIRotationGestureRecognizer** – Identifies when the user makes a rotation gesture (essentially two fingers in contact with the screen opposite each other and moving in a circular motion).

- **UILongPressGestureRecognizer** – Used to identify when the user touches the screen with one or more fingers for a specified time (also referred to as "touch and hold").

These gesture recognizers must be attached to the view on which the gesture will be performed via a call to the view object's *addGestureRecognizer* method. Recognizers must also be assigned an action method to be called when the specified gesture is detected. Gesture recognizers may subsequently be removed from a view via a call to the view's *removeGestureRecognizer* method, passing through the recognizer to be removed as an argument.

58.2 Recognizer Action Messages

The iOS gesture recognizers use the target-action model to notify the app of the detection of a specific gesture. When an instance of a gesture recognizer is created, it is provided with the reference to the method to be called if the corresponding gesture is detected.

58.3 Discrete and Continuous Gestures

Gestures fall into two distinct categories – *discrete* and *continuous*. A discrete gesture only makes a single call to the corresponding action method. Tap gestures (including multiple taps) are considered to be discrete because they only trigger the action method once. On the other hand, gestures such as swipes, pans, rotations, and pinches are deemed to be continuous in that they trigger a constant stream of calls to the corresponding action methods until the gesture ends.

58.4 Obtaining Data from a Gesture

Each gesture action method is passed as an argument a UIGestureRecognizer sender object which may be used to extract information about the gesture. For example, the action method may obtain information about a pinch gesture's scale factor and speed. Similarly, the action method assigned to a rotation gesture recognizer may ascertain the amount of rotation performed by the user and the corresponding velocity.

58.5 Recognizing Tap Gestures

Tap gestures are detected using the UITapGestureRecognizer class. This must be allocated and initialized with an action selector referencing the method to be called when the gesture is detected. The number of taps that must be performed to constitute the full gesture may be defined by setting the *numberOfTapsRequired* property of the recognizer instance. The following code, for example, will result in a call to the *tapsDetected* method when two consecutive taps are detected on the corresponding view:

```
let doubleTap = UITapGestureRecognizer(target: self,
          action: #selector(tapDetected))
doubleTap.numberOfTapsRequired = 2

self.view.addGestureRecognizer(doubleTap)
```

A template method for the action method for this and other gesture recognizers is as follows:

```
@objc func tapDetected() {
     // Code to respond to gesture here
}
```

58.6 Recognizing Pinch Gestures

Pinch gestures are detected using the UIPinchGestureRecognizer class. For example:

```
let pinchRecognizer = UIPinchGestureRecognizer(target: self,
          action: #selector(pinchDetected))
self.view.addGestureRecognizer(pinchRecognizer)
```

58.7 Detecting Rotation Gestures

Rotation gestures are recognized by the UIRotationGestureRecognizer, the sample code for which is as follows:

```
let rotationRecognizer = UIRotationGestureRecognizer(target: self,
              action: #selector(rotationDetected))
self.view.addGestureRecognizer(rotationRecognizer)
```

58.8 Recognizing Pan and Dragging Gestures

Pan and dragging gestures are detected using the UIPanGestureRecognizer class. Pan gestures are essentially any *continuous* gesture. For example, the random meandering of a finger across the screen will generally be considered by the recognizer as a pan or drag operation:

```
let panRecognizer = UIPanGestureRecognizer(target: self,
                action: #selector(panDetected))
self.view.addGestureRecognizer(panRecognizer)
```

If both swipe and pan recognizers are attached to the same view, most swipes will likely be recognized as pans. Caution should be taken, therefore, when mixing these two gesture recognizers on the same view.

58.9 Recognizing Swipe Gestures

Swipe gestures are detected using the UISwipeGestureRecognizer class. All swipes, or just those in a specific direction, may be detected by assigning one of the following constants to the *direction* property of the class:

- UISwipeGestureRecognizerDirection.right

- UISwipeGestureRecognizerDirection.left

- UISwipeGestureRecognizerDirection.up

- UISwipeGestureRecognizerDirection.down

When programming in Swift, the above constants may be abbreviated to *.right*, *.left*, *.up*, and *.down*.

If no direction is specified, the default is to detect rightward swipes. The following code configures a UISwipeGestureRecognizer instance to detect upward swipes:

```
let swipeRecognizer = UISwipeGestureRecognizer(target: self,
            action: #selector(swipeDetected))
swipeRecognizer.direction = .up
self.view.addGestureRecognizer(swipeRecognizer)
```

58.10 Recognizing Long Touch (Touch and Hold) Gestures

Long touches are detected using the UILongPressGestureRecognizer class. The requirements for the gesture may be specified in terms of touch duration, number of touches, number of taps, and allowable movement during the touch. These requirements are specified by the *class's minimumPressDuration, numberOfTouchesRequired, numberOfTapsRequired, and allowableMovement properties*. For example, the following code fragment configures the recognizer to detect long presses of 3 seconds or more involving one finger. The default allowable movement is not set and therefore defaults to 10 pixels:

```
let longPressRecognizer = UILongPressGestureRecognizer(target: self,
        action: #selector(longPressDetected))
longPressRecognizer.minimumPressDuration = 3
longPressRecognizer.numberOfTouchesRequired = 1
self.view.addGestureRecognizer(longPressRecognizer)
```

58.11 Summary

In this chapter, we have provided an overview of gesture recognizers and outlined some examples of detecting the various types of gestures typically used by iOS device users. In the next chapter, we will work step-by-step through a tutorial designed to show these theories in practice.

59. An iOS 17 Gesture Recognition Tutorial

Having covered the theory of gesture recognition on iOS in the chapter entitled *"Identifying Gestures using iOS 17 Gesture Recognizers"*, this chapter will work through an example application intended to demonstrate the use of the various UIGestureRecognizer subclasses.

The application created in this chapter will configure recognizers to detect a number of different gestures on the iPhone or iPad display and update a status label with information about each recognized gesture.

59.1 Creating the Gesture Recognition Project

Begin by invoking Xcode and creating a new iOS *App* project named *Recognizer* using Swift as the programming language.

59.2 Designing the User Interface

The only visual component that will be present on our UIView object will be the label used to notify the user of the type of gesture detected. Since the text displayed on this label will need to be updated from within the application code it will need to be connected to an outlet. In addition, the view controller will also contain five gesture recognizer objects to detect pinches, taps, rotations, swipes and long presses. When triggered, these objects will need to call action methods in order to update the label with a notification to the user that the corresponding gesture has been detected.

Select the *Main.storyboard* file and drag a Label object from the Library panel to the center of the view. Once positioned, display the Auto Layout *Resolve Auto Layout Issues* menu and select the *Reset to Suggested Constraints* menu option listed in the *All Views in View Controller* section of the menu.

Select the label object in the view canvas, display the Assistant Editor panel, and verify that the editor is displaying the contents of the *ViewController.swift* file. Right-click on the same label object and drag to a position just below the class declaration line in the Assistant Editor. Release the line and, in the resulting connection dialog, establish an outlet connection named *statusLabel*.

Next, the non-visual gesture recognizer objects need to be added to the design. Scroll down the list of objects in the Library panel until the *Tap Gesture Recognizer* object comes into view. Drag and drop the object onto the View in the design area (if the object is dropped outside the view, the connection between the recognizer and the view on which the gestures are going to be performed will not be established). Repeat these steps to add Pinch, Rotation, Swipe, and Long Press Gesture Recognizer objects to the design. Note that the document outline panel (which can be displayed by clicking on the panel button in the lower left-hand corner of the storyboard panel) has updated to reflect the presence of the gesture recognizer objects, as illustrated in Figure 59-1. An icon for each recognizer added to the view also appears within the toolbar across the top of the storyboard scene.

Figure 59-1

Select the Tap Gesture Recognizer instance within the document outline panel and display the Attributes Inspector. Within the attributes panel, change the *Taps* value to 2 so that only double taps are detected.

Similarly, select the Long Press Recognizer object and change the *Min Duration* attribute to 3 seconds.

Having added and configured the gesture recognizers, the next step is to connect each recognizer to its corresponding action method.

Display the Assistant Editor and verify that it is displaying the content of *ViewController.swift*. Right-click on the *Tap Gesture Recognizer* object either in the document outline panel or in the scene toolbar and drag the line to the area immediately beneath the *viewDidLoad* method in the Assistant Editor panel. Release the line and, within the resulting connection dialog, establish an Action method configured to call a method named *tapDetected* with the *Type* value set to *UITapGestureRecognizer* as illustrated in Figure 59-2:

Figure 59-2

Repeat these steps to establish action connections for the pinch, rotation, swipe and long press gesture recognizers to methods named *pinchDetected*, *rotationDetected*, *swipeDetected* and *longPressDetected* respectively, taking care to select the corresponding type value for each action.

59.3 Implementing the Action Methods

Having configured the gesture recognizers, the next step is to add code to the action methods that will be called by each recognizer when the corresponding gesture is detected. The methods stubs created by Xcode reside in the *ViewController.swift* file and will update the status label with information about the detected gesture:

```
@IBAction func tapDetected(_ sender: UITapGestureRecognizer) {
```

```
        statusLabel.text = "Double Tap"
}


@IBAction func pinchDetected(_ sender: UIPinchGestureRecognizer) {
    let scale = sender.scale
    let velocity = sender.velocity
    let resultString =
        "Pinch - scale = \(scale), velocity = \(velocity)"

    statusLabel.text = resultString
}


@IBAction func rotationDetected(_ sender: UIRotationGestureRecognizer) {
    let radians = sender.rotation
    let velocity = sender.velocity
    let resultString =
        "Rotation - Radians = \(radians), velocity = \(velocity)"

    statusLabel.text = resultString
}


@IBAction func swipeDetected(_ sender: UISwipeGestureRecognizer) {
    statusLabel.text = "Right swipe"
}


@IBAction func longPressDetected(_ sender: UILongPressGestureRecognizer) {
    statusLabel.text = "Long Press"
}
```

59.4 Testing the Gesture Recognition Application

The final step is to build and run the application. Once the application loads on the device, perform the appropriate gestures on the display and watch the status label update accordingly. If using a simulator session, hold down the Option key while clicking with the mouse to simulate two touches for the pinch and rotation tests. Note that when testing on an iPhone, it may be necessary to rotate the device into landscape orientation to be able to see the full text displayed on the label.

59.5 Summary

The iOS SDK includes a set of gesture recognizer classes designed to detect swipe, tap, long press, pan, pinch, and rotation gestures. This chapter has worked through creating an example application that demonstrates how to implement gesture detection using these classes within the Interface Builder environment.

60. Implementing Touch ID and Face ID Authentication in iOS 17 Apps

In computer security, user authentication falls into three categories: something you know, something you have, and something you are. The "something you know" category typically involves a memorized password or PIN and is considered the least secure option. A more secure option is the "something you have" approach, which usually takes the form of a small authentication token or device which generates one-time access codes on request.

The final category, "something you are," refers to a physical attribute that is unique to the user. This involves biometrics in the form of a retina scan, facial or voice recognition, or fingerprint.

With the iPhone 5s, Apple introduced a built-in fingerprint scanner that enabled users to access the device and make purchases using fingerprint authentication in the iTunes, App, and iBooks stores. Since the introduction of iOS 8, this biometric authentication capability can now be built into your own apps. In addition, with the introduction of the iPhone X and iOS 11, biometric authentication using facial recognition can also be built into your iOS apps.

60.1 The Local Authentication Framework

Biometric authentication for iOS apps is implemented using the Local Authentication Framework. The key class within this framework is the LAContext class which, among other tasks, is used to evaluate the authentication abilities of the device on which the app is running and perform the authentication.

60.2 Checking for Biometric Authentication Availability

Not all iOS devices offer fingerprint scanners or facial recognition support, and even on devices with the necessary hardware support, not all users will have activated these authentication features. The first step in using biometric authentication, therefore, is to check that biometric authentication is a viable option on the device:

```
let context = LAContext()

var error: NSError?

if context.canEvaluatePolicy(
        LAPolicy.DeviceOwnerAuthenticationWithBiometrics,
            error: &error) {
        // Biometry is available on the device
} else {
        // Biometry is not available on the device
        // No hardware support, or the user has not set up biometric auth
}
```

If biometric authentication is not available, the reason can be identified by accessing the errorCode property of the error parameter and will fall into one of the following categories:

- **LAError.biometryNotEnrolled** – The user has not enrolled in biometric authentication on the device.

- **LAError.passcodeNotSet** – The user has not yet configured a passcode on the device.

- **LAError.biometryNotAvailable** – The device does not have the required biometric hardware support.

60.3 Identifying Authentication Options

If the device on which the app is running contains the necessary biometric hardware, it can be useful to identify the supported authentication type. This can be achieved by evaluating the *biometryType* property of the LAContext instance as follows:

```
let context = LAContext()

var error: NSError?

if context.canEvaluatePolicy(
    LAPolicy.deviceOwnerAuthenticationWithBiometrics,
        error: &error) {

    if (context.biometryType == LABiometryType.faceID) {
        // Device support Face ID
    } else if context.biometryType == LABiometryType.touchID {
        // Device supports Touch ID
    } else {
        // Device has no biometric support
    }
```

60.4 Evaluating Biometric Policy

If biometric authentication is available, the next step is to evaluate the policy. This task is performed by calling the *evaluatePolicy* method of the LAContext instance, passing through the authentication policy type, and a message to be displayed to the user. The task is performed asynchronously, and a *reply* closure expression is called once the user has provided input:

```
context.evaluatePolicy(
        LAPolicy.deviceOwnerAuthenticationWithBiometrics,
        localizedReason: "Authentication is required for access",
        reply: {(success, error) in
                // Code to handle reply here
    })
```

The reply closure expression is passed a Boolean value indicating the success or otherwise of the authentication and an NSError object from which the nature of any failure can be identified via the corresponding error code. Failure to authenticate will fall into one of the following three categories:

- **LAError.systemCancel** – The authentication process was canceled by the operating system. This error typically occurs when the app is placed in the background.

- **LAError.userCancel** - The authentication process was canceled by the user.

- **LAError.userFallback** – The user opted to authenticate using a password instead of Touch or Face ID.

In the event of the user fallback, it is the responsibility of the app to prompt for and verify a password before providing access.

If the authentication process is successful, the app should provide the user access to the protected screens, data, or functionality.

60.5 A Biometric Authentication Example Project

Launch Xcode and create a new project using the iOS *App* template with the Swift and Storyboard options selected, entering *BiometricID* as the product name.

Select the *Main.storyboard* file, display the Library, and drag and drop a Button view to position it in the center of the storyboard scene. Change the text on the button so that it reads *Authenticate*.

With the button selected, display the Auto Layout Align menu and configure both horizontal and vertical centers in container constraints.

Display the Assistant Editor, right-click on the button view, and drag the resulting line to a point beneath the ViewController class declaration line. On releasing the line, establish a connection to an outlet named *authButton*.

Finally, right-click and drag from the button view to a position just beneath the *viewDidLoad* method in the *ViewController.swift* file. Release the line and, in the connection dialog, establish an Action connection to a method named *authenticateUser*.

On completion of the user interface design, the layout should resemble Figure 60-1:

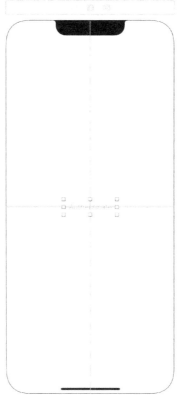

Figure 60-1

60.6 Checking for Biometric Availability

With the user interface design, the next step is to add some code to the *authenticateUser* method to verify that the device can handle biometric authentication. Select the *ViewController.swift* file, import the LocalAuthentication Framework, and add code to the *authenticateUser* method as follows:

```
import UIKit
import LocalAuthentication

class ViewController: UIViewController {

    override func viewDidLoad() {
        super.viewDidLoad()
        // Do any additional setup after loading the view, typically from a nib.
    }

    @IBAction func authenticateUser(_ sender: Any) {

        let context = LAContext()

        var error: NSError?

        if context.canEvaluatePolicy(
            LAPolicy.deviceOwnerAuthenticationWithBiometrics,
            error: &error) {

            // Device can use biometric authentication

        } else {
            // Device cannot use biometric authentication
            if let err = error {
                switch err.code{

                case LAError.Code.biometryNotEnrolled.rawValue:
                    notifyUser("User is not enrolled",
                        err: err.localizedDescription)

                case LAError.Code.passcodeNotSet.rawValue:
                    notifyUser("A passcode has not been set",
                        err: err.localizedDescription)


                case LAError.Code.biometryNotAvailable.rawValue:
                    notifyUser("Biometric authentication not available",
                        err: err.localizedDescription)
                default:
                    notifyUser("Unknown error",
```

```
                err: err.localizedDescription)
            }
        }
    }
}
```

In addition to evaluating the authentication policy, the above code identifies whether the device supports Face ID or Touch ID authentication and accordingly updates the text displayed on the authButton instance.

Before proceeding, implement the *notifyUser* method as follows:

```
func notifyUser(_ msg: String, err: String?) {
    let alert = UIAlertController(title: msg,
            message: err,
            preferredStyle: .alert)

    let cancelAction = UIAlertAction(title: "OK",
            style: .cancel, handler: nil)

    alert.addAction(cancelAction)

    self.present(alert, animated: true,
                    completion: nil)
}
```

60.7 Seeking Biometric Authentication

The next task is to attempt to obtain authentication from the user. This involves a call to the *evaluatePolicy* method of the local authentication context:

```
@IBAction func authenticateUser(_ sender: Any) {

    let context = LAContext()

    var error: NSError?

    if context.canEvaluatePolicy(
        LAPolicy.deviceOwnerAuthenticationWithBiometrics,
        error: &error) {

        // Device can use biometric authentication
        context.evaluatePolicy(
            LAPolicy.deviceOwnerAuthenticationWithBiometrics,
            localizedReason: "Access requires authentication",
            reply: {(success, error) in
                DispatchQueue.main.async {

                    if let err = error {

                        switch err._code {
```

```
                        case LAError.Code.systemCancel.rawValue:
                            self.notifyUser("Session canceled",
                                            err: err.localizedDescription)

                        case LAError.Code.userCancel.rawValue:
                            self.notifyUser("Please try again",
                                            err: err.localizedDescription)

                        case LAError.Code.userFallback.rawValue:
                            self.notifyUser("Authentication",
                                            err: "Password option selected")
                            // Custom code to obtain password here

                        default:
                            self.notifyUser("Authentication failed",
                                            err: err.localizedDescription)
                        }

                    } else {
                        self.notifyUser("Authentication Successful",
                                        err: "You now have full access")
                    }
                }
            })

    } else {
        // Device cannot use biometric authentication
        if let err = error {
            switch err.code {

            case LAError.Code.biometryNotEnrolled.rawValue:
                notifyUser("User is not enrolled",
                            err: err.localizedDescription)

            case LAError.Code.passcodeNotSet.rawValue:
                notifyUser("A passcode has not been set",
                            err: err.localizedDescription)


            case LAError.Code.biometryNotAvailable.rawValue:
                notifyUser("Biometric authentication not available",
                            err: err.localizedDescription)
            default:
                notifyUser("Unknown error",
```

```
                          err: err.localizedDescription)
                }
            }
        }
    }
```

The code added to the method initiates the authentication process and displays a message confirming a successful authentication. In the event of an authentication failure, a message is displayed to the user indicating the reason for the failure. The selection of the password option simply confirms that the option was selected. The action taken in this situation will be app specific but will likely involve prompting for a password and verifying it against a database of valid passwords.

60.8 Adding the Face ID Privacy Statement

Before testing, the final step is configuring the Face ID privacy statement within the project's *Info.plist* file. This is the statement displayed to the user when the app seeks permission to use Face ID authentication. To add this entry, select the BiometricID entry at the top of the Project navigator panel and, in the main panel, select the Info tab as shown in Figure 60-2:

Figure 60-2

Next, click on the + button contained with the last line of properties in the Custom iOS Target Properties section. Then, from the resulting menu, select the *Privacy – Face ID Usage Description* option and enter a description into the value field:

Figure 60-3

60.9 Testing the App

Biometric authentication can be tested on physical iOS devices, including biometric support, or using the simulator environment.

When testing Face ID support on a simulator, compile and run the app on an iPhone 14 or later simulator. Once the app has launched, select the simulator's *Features -> Face ID* menu and ensure the *Enrolled* option is enabled (as highlighted in Figure 60-4) before tapping the *Authenticate* button within the app.

Figure 60-4

At this point, the Face ID permission request dialog will appear, displaying the privacy statement that was previously entered into the *Info* screen, as shown in Figure 60-5:

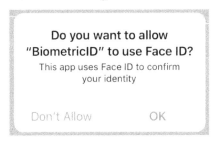

Figure 60-5

After granting permission by clicking on the OK button, the gray simulated Face ID panel (Figure 60-6) should appear:

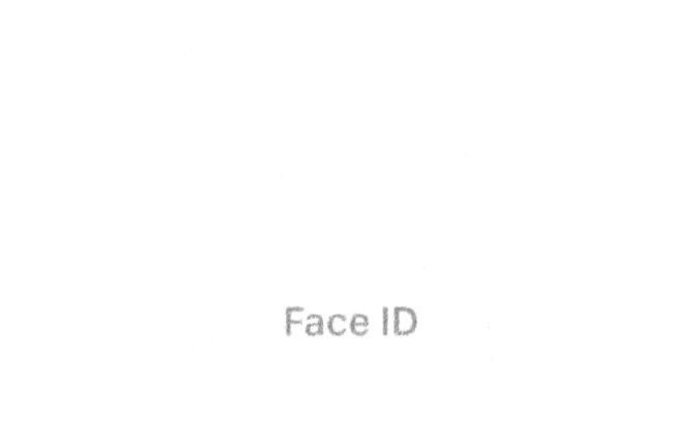

Face ID

Figure 60-6

To simulate a matching face, select the *Features -> Face ID -> Matching Face* menu option, after which the app should display the dialog shown in Figure 60-7 indicating that the authentication was successful:

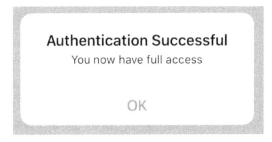

Figure 60-7

Repeat the authentication process, selecting the Non-matching menu option and verifying that the authentication fails.

Launch the app on a physical device with Touch ID support, or use a suitable simulator (for example, an iPhone 8) to test Touch ID authentication. If using a simulator, ensure that the *Features -> Touch ID -> Enrolled* option is enabled before clicking the *Authenticate* button. Then, when instructed to touch the home button, select the *Features -> Touch ID -> Matching Touch* menu option to test the authentication. After successful authentication, try again using the *Non-matching Touch* option.

60.10 Summary

Introduced with iOS 7 and the iPhone 5s device, Touch ID has been provided to iOS users to gain access to devices and make Apple-related purchases. Since the introduction of iOS 8, fingerprint authentication using the Touch ID system has been available to app developers. In addition, with the introduction of iOS 11 running on the iPhone X, authentication support has been extended to include facial recognition. This chapter has outlined the steps involved in using the Local Authentication Framework to implement biometric authentication using both the Touch ID and Face ID systems.

61. Drawing iOS 17 2D Graphics with Core Graphics

The ability to draw two-dimensional graphics on the iPhone and iPad is provided as part of the Core Graphics Framework in the form of the Quartz 2D API. The iOS implementation of Quartz on iOS is the same as that provided with macOS. It provides a graphics context object together with a set of methods designed to enable the drawing of 2D graphics in the form of images, lines, fill patterns, and gradients.

In this chapter, we will provide an overview of Quartz 2D. A later chapter, entitled *"An iOS 17 Graphics Tutorial using Core Graphics and Core Image"*, provides a step-by-step tutorial designed to teach the basics of two-dimensional drawing on iOS.

61.1 Introducing Core Graphics and Quartz 2D

Quartz 2D is a two-dimensional graphics drawing engine that makes up the bulk of the UIKit Core Graphics Framework. Quartz 2D drawing typically takes place on a UIView object (more precisely, a subclass thereof). Drawings are defined in terms of the paths a line must follow and rectangular areas into which shapes (rectangles, ellipses, etc.) must fit.

61.2 The draw Method

The first time a view is displayed, and each time part of that view needs to be redrawn due to another event, the *draw* method of the view is called. Therefore, drawing is achieved by subclassing the UIView class, implementing the draw method, and placing the Quartz 2D API calls within that method to draw the graphics.

When the *draw* method is not automatically called, a redraw may be forced via a call to the *setNeedsDisplay* or *setNeedsDisplayInRect* methods.

61.3 Points, Coordinates, and Pixels

The Quartz 2D API functions work based on *points*. These are essentially the x and y coordinates of a two-dimensional coordinate system on the device screen, with 0, 0 representing the top left-hand corner of the display. These coordinates are stored in the form of CGFloat variables.

An additional C structure named CGPoint contains both the x and y coordinates to specify a point on the display. Similarly, the CGSize structure stores two CGFloat values that designate an element's width and height on the screen.

Further, the position and dimension of a rectangle can be defined using the CGRect structure, which contains a CGPoint (the location) and CGSize (the dimension) of a rectangular area.

Of key importance when working with points and dimensions is that these values do not correspond directly to screen pixels. In other words, there is no one-to-one correlation between pixels and points. Instead, based on a scale factor, the underlying framework decides where a point should appear and what size relative to the display's resolution on which the drawing is taking place. This enables the same code to work on higher and lower resolution screens without the programmer having to worry about it.

For more precise drawing requirements, iOS version 4 and later allows the *scale factor* for the current screen to be obtained from UIScreen, UIView, UIImage, and CALayer classes allowing the correlation between pixels and points to be calculated for greater drawing precision.

61.4 The Graphics Context

Almost without exception, all Quartz API method calls are made on the *graphics context* object. Each view has its own context, which is responsible for performing the requested drawing tasks and subsequently rendering those drawings onto the corresponding view. The graphics context can be obtained with a call to the *UIGraphicsGetCurrentContext()* function, which returns a result of type *CGContextRef*:

```
let context = UIGraphicsGetCurrentContext()
```

61.5 Working with Colors in Quartz 2D

The Core Graphics CGColorRef data type stores colors when drawing with Quartz. This data type holds information about the *colorspace* of the color (RGBA, CMYK, or grayscale) together with a set of component values that specify the color and the transparency of that color. For example, red with no transparency would be defined with the RGBA components 1.0, 0.0, 0.0, 1.0.

A *colorspace* can be created via a Quartz API function call. For example, to create an RGB colorspace:

```
let colorSpace = CGColorSpaceCreateDeviceRGB()
```

If the function fails to create a colorspace, it will return a nil value.

Grayscale and CMYK color spaces may similarly be created using the *CGColorSpaceCreateDeviceGray()* and *CGColorSpaceCreateDeviceCMYK()* functions, respectively.

Once the colorspace has been created, the next task is to define the components. The following declaration defines a set of RGBA components for a semi-transparent blue color:

```
let components: [CGFloat] = [0.0, 0.0, 1.0, 0.5]
```

With both the colorspace and the components defined, the CGColorRef structure can be created:

```
let color = CGColor(colorSpace: colorSpace, components: components)
```

The color may then be used to draw using the graphics context drawing API methods.

Another useful method for creating colors involves the UIKit UIColor class. While this class cannot be used directly within Quartz API calls since it is a Swift class, it is possible to extract a color in CGColorRef format from the UIColor class by referencing the cgColor property.

The advantage offered by UIColor, in addition to being object-oriented, is that it includes a range of convenience methods that can be used to create colors. For example, the following code uses the UIColor class to create the color red and then accesses the cgColor property for use as an argument to the *setStrokeColor* context method:

```
context?.setStrokeColor(UIColor.red.cgColor)
```

The color selection and transparency can be further refined using this technique by specifying additional components. For example:

```
let color = UIColor(red:1.0 green:0.3 blue:0.8 alpha:0.5)
```

As we can see, the use of UIColor avoids the necessity to create colorspaces and components when working with colors. Refer to the Apple documentation for more details on the range of methods provided by the UIColor class.

61.6 Summary

This chapter has covered some basic principles behind drawing two-dimensional graphics on iOS using the Quartz 2D API. Topics covered included obtaining the graphics context, implementing the *draw* method, and handling colors and transparency. In *"An iOS 17 Graphics Tutorial using Core Graphics and Core Image"*, this theory will be implemented with examples of how to draw various shapes and images on an iOS device screen. Before moving on to the drawing tutorial, however, the next chapter will begin by exploring the Live Views feature of Interface Builder. Live Views are particularly useful when writing dynamic user interface code, such as drawing graphics.

62. Interface Builder Live Views and iOS 17 Embedded Frameworks

Two related areas of iOS development will be covered in this chapter in the form of Live Views in Interface Builder and Embedded Frameworks, both designed to make the tasks of sharing common code between projects and designing dynamic user interfaces easier.

62.1 Embedded Frameworks

Apple defines a framework as "a collection of code and resources to encapsulate functionality that is valuable across multiple projects." A typical iOS app project will use many Frameworks from the iOS SDK. For example, all apps use the Foundation Framework, while a game might also use the SpriteKit Framework.

Embedded Frameworks allow developers to create their own frameworks. Embedded frameworks are easy to create and provide several advantages, the most obvious of which is the ability to share common code between multiple app projects.

Embedded Frameworks are particularly useful when working with extensions. By nature, an extension will inevitably need to share code that already exists within the containing app. Rather than duplicate code between the app and the extension, a better solution is to place common code into an embedded framework.

Another benefit of embedded frameworks is the ability to publish code in the form of 3rd party frameworks that can be downloaded for use by other developers in their own projects.

However, one of the more intriguing features of embedded frameworks is that they facilitate a powerful feature of Interface Builder known as Live Views.

62.2 Interface Builder Live Views

Traditionally, designing a user interface layout using Interface Builder has involved placing static representations of view components onto a canvas. The app logic behind these views to implement dynamic behavior is then implemented within the view controller, and the app is compiled and run on a device or simulator to see the live user interface in action.

Live views allow the dynamic code behind the views to be executed from within the Interface Builder storyboard file as the user interface is being designed without compiling and running the app.

Live views also allow variables within the code behind a view to be exposed so that they can be accessed and modified in the Interface Builder Attributes Inspector panel, with the changes reflected in real-time within the live view.

The reason embedded frameworks and live views are covered in this chapter is that a prerequisite for live views is for the underlying code for a live view to be contained within an embedded framework.

The best way to better understand both embedded frameworks and live views is to see them in action in an example project.

62.3 Creating the Example Project

Launch Xcode and create a new project using the iOS *App* template with the Swift and Storyboard options selected, entering *LiveViewDemo* as the product name.

When the project has been created, select the *Main.storyboard* file and drag and drop a View object from the Library panel onto the view controller canvas. Resize the view, stretching it in each dimension until the blue dotted line indicates the recommended margin. Display the Auto Layout *Add New Constraints* menu and enable "spacing to nearest neighbor" constraints on all four sides of the view with the *Constrain to margins* option enabled as shown in Figure 62-1 before clicking on the *Add 4 Constraints* button:

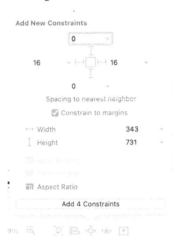

Figure 62-1

Once the above steps are complete, the layout should resemble that illustrated in Figure 62-2 below:

Figure 62-2

With the user interface designed, the next step is to add a framework to the project.

62.4 Adding an Embedded Framework

The framework to be added to the project will contain a UIView subclass containing some graphics drawing code.

Within Xcode, select the *File -> New -> Target…* menu option and, in the template selection panel, scroll to and select the *Framework* template (Figure 62-3):

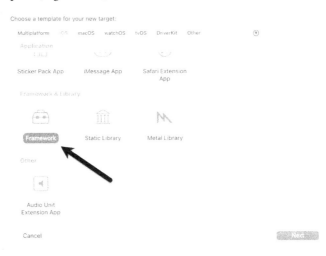

Figure 62-3

Click on the *Next* button and, on the subsequent screen, enter *MyDrawKit* into the product name field before clicking on the *Finish* button.

Within the project navigator panel, a new folder will have been added named *MyDrawKit,* into which will be stored the files that make up the new framework. Right-click on this entry and select the *New File…* menu option. In the template chooser panel, select *Cocoa Touch Class* before clicking on *Next*.

On the next screen, name the class *MyDrawView* and configure it as a subclass of UIView. Then, click the *Next* button and save the new class file into the *MyDrawKit* subfolder of the project directory.

Select the *Main.storyboard* file in the project navigator panel and click on the View object added in the previous section. Display the Identity Inspector in the Utilities panel and change the Class setting from *UIView* to *MyDrawView*:

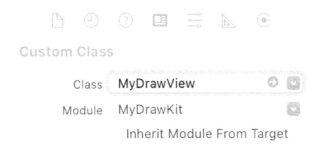

Figure 62-4

62.5 Implementing the Drawing Code in the Framework

The code to perform the graphics drawing on the View will reside in the *MyDrawView.swift* file in the *MyDrawKit* folder. Locate this file in the project navigator panel and double-click on it to load it into a separate editing window (thereby allowing the *Main.storyboard* file to remain visible in Interface Builder).

Remove the comment markers (/* and */) from around the template *draw* method and implement the code for this method so that it reads as follows:

```swift
import UIKit
import QuartzCore

class MyDrawView: UIView {

    var startColor: UIColor = UIColor.white
    var endColor: UIColor = UIColor.blue
    var endRadius: CGFloat = 100


    override func draw(_ rect: CGRect) {
        let context = UIGraphicsGetCurrentContext()

        let colorspace = CGColorSpaceCreateDeviceRGB()
        let locations: [CGFloat] = [ 0.0, 1.0]

        if let gradient = CGGradient(colorsSpace: colorspace,
                        colors: [startColor.cgColor, endColor.cgColor]
                                    as CFArray,
                        locations: locations) {

            var startPoint = CGPoint()
            var endPoint = CGPoint()

            let startRadius: CGFloat = 0

            startPoint.x = 130
            startPoint.y = 100
            endPoint.x = 130
            endPoint.y = 120

            context?.drawRadialGradient(gradient,
                    startCenter: startPoint, startRadius: startRadius,
                    endCenter: endPoint, endRadius: endRadius,
                    options: .drawsBeforeStartLocation)
        }
    }
}
```

62.6 Making the View Designable

At this point, the code has been added, and running the app on a device or simulator will show the view with the graphics drawn on it. The object of this chapter, however, is to avoid the need to compile and run the app to see the results of the code. To make the view "live" within Interface Builder, the class must be declared as being "Interface Builder designable." This is achieved by adding an *@IBDesignable* directive immediately before the class declaration in the *MyDrawView.swift* file:

```
import UIKit
import QuartzCore


@IBDesignable
class MyDrawView: UIView {

    var startColor: UIColor = UIColor.white
    var endColor: UIColor = UIColor.blue
    var endRadius: CGFloat = 100
.

.

.

}
```

As soon as the directive is added to the file, Xcode will compile the class and render it within the Interface Builder storyboard canvas (Figure 62-5):

Figure 62-5

Changes to the MyDrawView code will now be reflected in the Interface Builder live view. To see this in action, right-click on the *MyDrawView.swift* file and select the Open in New Window entry in the resulting menu. Then, with the Main storyboard scene visible, change the endColor variable declaration in the *MyDrawView.swift* file so that it is assigned a different color and observe the color change take effect in the Interface Builder live view:

```
var endColor: UIColor = UIColor.red
```

62.7 Making Variables Inspectable

Although it is possible to modify variables by editing the code in the framework class, it would be easier if they could be changed just like any other property using the Attributes Inspector panel. This can be achieved simply by prefixing the variable declarations with the *@IBInspectable* directive as follows:

```
@IBDesignable
class MyDrawView: UIView {

    @IBInspectable var startColor: UIColor = UIColor.white
    @IBInspectable var endColor: UIColor = UIColor.red
    @IBInspectable var endRadius: CGFloat = 100
.
.
.
}
```

With changes to the code, select the View in the storyboard file and display the Attributes Inspector panel. The properties should now be listed for the view (Figure 62-6) and can be modified. Any changes to these variables made through the Attributes Inspector will take effect in real time without requiring Xcode to recompile the framework code. When compiled and run on a device or simulator, these settings will also be generated into the app.

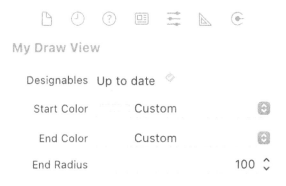

Figure 62-6

62.8 Summary

This chapter has introduced two concepts: embedded frameworks and Interface Builder live views. Embedded frameworks allow developers to place source code into frameworks that can be shared between multiple app projects. Embedded frameworks also provide the basis for the live views feature of Interface Builder. Before the introduction of live views, it was necessary to compile and run an app to see dynamic user interface behavior in action. With live views, the dynamic behavior of a view can now be seen within Interface Builder, with code changes reflected in real-time.

63. An iOS 17 Graphics Tutorial using Core Graphics and Core Image

As previously discussed in *"Drawing iOS 17 2D Graphics with Core Graphics"*, the Quartz 2D API is the primary mechanism by which 2D drawing operations are performed within iOS apps. Having provided an overview of Quartz 2D as it pertains to iOS development in that chapter, the focus of this chapter is to provide a tutorial that provides examples of how 2D drawing is performed. If you are new to Quartz 2D and have not yet read *"Drawing iOS 17 2D Graphics with Core Graphics"*, it is recommended to do so before embarking on this tutorial.

63.1 The iOS Drawing Example App

If you are reading this book sequentially and have created the *LiveViewDemo* project as outlined in the chapter entitled *"Interface Builder Live Views and iOS 17 Embedded Frameworks"*, then the code in this chapter may be placed in the *draw* method contained within the *MyDrawView.swift* file and the results viewed dynamically within the live view in the *Main.storyboard* file. On the other hand, if you have not yet completed the chapter titled *"Interface Builder Live Views and iOS 17 Embedded Frameworks"*, follow the steps in the next three sections to create a new project, add a UIView subclass and locate the *draw* method.

63.2 Creating the New Project

The app created in this tutorial will contain a subclassed UIView component within which the *draw* method will be overridden and used to perform various 2D drawing operations. Launch Xcode and create a new project using the iOS *App* template with the Swift and Storyboard options selected, entering *Draw2D* as the product name.

63.3 Creating the UIView Subclass

To draw graphics on the view, it is necessary to create a subclass of the UIView object and override the *draw* method. In the project navigator panel on the left-hand side of the main Xcode window, right-click on the *Draw2D* folder entry and select *New File…* from the resulting menu. In the *New File* window, select the iOS source *Cocoa Touch Class* icon and click *Next*. On the subsequent options screen, change the *Subclass of* menu to *UIView* and the class name to *Draw2D*. Click *Next*, and on the final screen, click on the *Create* button.

Select the *Main.storyboard* file followed by the UIView component in either the view controller canvas or the document outline panel. Display the Identity Inspector and change the *Class* setting from *UIView* to our new class named *Draw2D*:

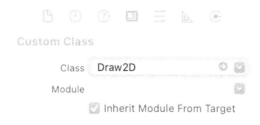

Figure 63-1

63.4 Locating the draw Method in the UIView Subclass

Now that we have subclassed our app's UIView, the next step is implementing the *draw* method in this subclass. Fortunately, Xcode has already created a template for this method for us. Select the *Draw2D.swift* file in the project navigator panel to locate this method. Having located the method in the file, remove the comment markers (/* and */) within which it is currently encapsulated:

```
import UIKit


class Draw2D: UIView {

    override func draw(_ rect: CGRect) {
        // Drawing code
    }
}
```

In the remainder of this tutorial, we will modify the code in the *draw* method to perform various drawing operations.

63.5 Drawing a Line

To draw a line on a device screen using Quartz 2D, we first need to obtain the graphics context for the view:

```
let context = UIGraphicsGetCurrentContext()
```

Once the context has been obtained, the width of the line we plan to draw needs to be specified:

```
context?.setLineWidth(3.0)
```

Next, we need to create a color reference. We can do this by specifying the RGBA components of the required color (in this case, opaque blue):

```
let colorSpace = CGColorSpaceCreateDeviceRGB()
let components: [CGFloat] = [0.0, 0.0, 1.0, 1.0]
let color = CGColor(colorSpace: colorSpace, components: components)
```

Using the color reference and the context, we can now specify that the color is to be used when drawing the line:

```
context?.setStrokeColor(color!)
```

The next step is to move to the start point of the line that is going to be drawn:

```
context?.move(to: CGPoint(x: 50, y: 50))
```

The above line of code indicates that the start point for the line is the top left-hand corner of the device display. We now need to specify the endpoint of the line, in this case, 300, 400:

```
context?.addLine(to: CGPoint(x: 300, y: 400))
```

Having defined the line width, color, and path, we are ready to draw the line:

```
context?.strokePath()
```

Bringing this all together gives us a *draw* method that reads as follows:

```
override func draw(_ rect: CGRect)
{
    let context = UIGraphicsGetCurrentContext()
    context?.setLineWidth(3.0)
    let colorSpace = CGColorSpaceCreateDeviceRGB()
```

```
let components: [CGFloat] = [0.0, 0.0, 1.0, 1.0]
let color = CGColor(colorSpace: colorSpace, components: components)
context?.setStrokeColor(color!)
context?.move(to: CGPoint(x: 50, y: 50))
context?.addLine(to: CGPoint(x: 300, y: 400))
context?.strokePath()
}
```

When compiled and run, the app should display as illustrated in Figure 63-2:

Figure 63-2

Note that we manually created the colorspace and color reference in the above example. As described in *"Drawing iOS 17 2D Graphics with Core Graphics"*, colors can also be created using the UIColor class. For example, the same result as outlined above can be achieved with fewer lines of code as follows:

```
override func draw(_ rect: CGRect) {
    let context = UIGraphicsGetCurrentContext()
    context?.setLineWidth(3.0)
    context?.setStrokeColor(UIColor.blue.cgColor)
    context?.move(to: CGPoint(x: 50, y: 50))
    context?.addLine(to: CGPoint(x: 300, y: 400))
    context?.strokePath()
}
```

63.6 Drawing Paths

As you may have noticed, we draw a single line in the above example by defining the path between two points. Defining a path comprising multiple points allows us to draw using a sequence of straight lines connected using repeated calls to the addLine(to:) context method. Non-straight lines may also be added to a shape using calls to, for example, the *addArc* method.

The following code, for example, draws a diamond shape:

```
override func draw(_ rect: CGRect)
{
```

```
    let context = UIGraphicsGetCurrentContext()
    context?.setLineWidth(3.0)
    context?.setStrokeColor(UIColor.blue.cgColor)
    context?.move(to: CGPoint(x:100, y: 100))
    context?.addLine(to: CGPoint(x: 150, y: 150))
    context?.addLine(to: CGPoint(x: 100, y: 200))
    context?.addLine(to: CGPoint(x: 50, y: 150))
    context?.addLine(to: CGPoint(x: 100, y: 100))
    context?.strokePath()
}
```

When executed, the above code should produce output that appears as shown in Figure 63-3:

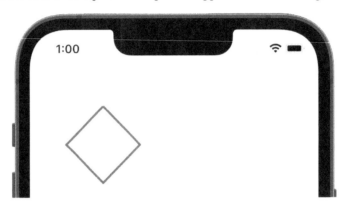

Figure 63-3

63.7 Drawing a Rectangle

Rectangles are drawn in much the same way as any other path is drawn, with the exception that the path is defined by specifying the x and y coordinates of the top left-hand corner of the rectangle together with the rectangle's height and width. These dimensions are stored in a CGRect structure and passed through as an argument to the *addRect* method:

```
override func draw(_ rect: CGRect)
{
    let context = UIGraphicsGetCurrentContext()
    context?.setLineWidth(4.0)
    context?.setStrokeColor(UIColor.blue.cgColor)
    let rectangle = CGRect(x: 90,y: 100,width: 200,height: 80)
    context?.addRect(rectangle)
    context?.strokePath()
}
```

The above code will result in the following display when compiled and executed:

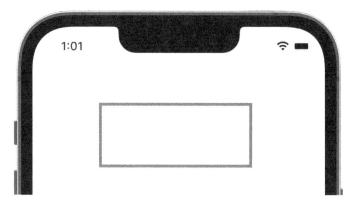

Figure 63-4

63.8 Drawing an Ellipse or Circle

Circles and ellipses are drawn by defining the rectangular area into which the shape must fit and then calling the *addEllipse(in:)* context method:

```
override func draw(_ rect: CGRect)
{
    let context = UIGraphicsGetCurrentContext()
    context?.setLineWidth(4.0)
    context?.setStrokeColor(UIColor.blue.cgColor)
    let rectangle = CGRect(x: 85,y: 100,width: 200,height: 80)
    context?.addEllipse(in: rectangle)
    context?.strokePath()
}
```

When compiled, the above code will produce the following graphics:

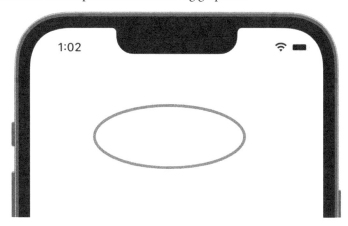

Figure 63-5

To draw a circle, simply define a rectangle with equal-length sides (a square, in other words).

63.9 Filling a Path with a Color

A path may be filled with color using a variety of Quartz 2D API functions. For example, rectangular and elliptical paths may be filled using the *fill(rect:)* and *fillEllipse(in:)* context methods, respectively. Similarly, a path may be filled using the *fillPath* method. Before executing a fill operation, the fill color must be specified using

449

An iOS 17 Graphics Tutorial using Core Graphics and Core Image

the *setFillColor* method.

The following example defines a path and then fills it with the color red:

```
override func draw(_ rect: CGRect)
{
    let context = UIGraphicsGetCurrentContext()
    context?.move(to: CGPoint(x: 100, y: 100))
    context?.addLine(to: CGPoint(x: 150, y: 150))
    context?.addLine(to: CGPoint(x: 100, y: 200))
    context?.addLine(to: CGPoint(x: 50, y: 150))
    context?.addLine(to: CGPoint(x: 100, y: 100))
    context?.setFillColor(UIColor.red.cgColor)
    context?.fillPath()
}
```

The above code produces the following graphics on the device or simulator display when executed:

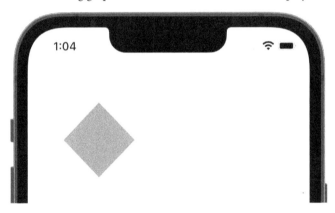

Figure 63-6

The following code draws a rectangle with a blue border and then once again fills the rectangular space with red:

```
override func draw(_ rect: CGRect)
{
    let context = UIGraphicsGetCurrentContext()
    context?.setLineWidth(4.0)
    context?.setStrokeColor(UIColor.blue.cgColor)
    let rectangle = CGRect(x: 85,y: 100,width: 200,height: 80)
    context?.addRect(rectangle)
    context?.strokePath()
    context?.setFillColor(UIColor.red.cgColor)
    context?.fill(rectangle)
}
```

When added to the example app, the resulting display should appear as follows:

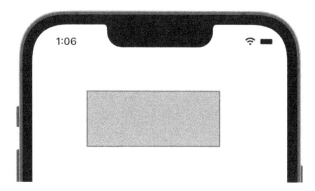

Figure 63-7

63.10 Drawing an Arc

An arc may be drawn by specifying two tangent points and a radius using the *addArc* context method, for example:

```
override func draw(_ rect: CGRect)
{
    let context = UIGraphicsGetCurrentContext()
    context?.setLineWidth(4.0)
    context?.setStrokeColor(UIColor.blue.cgColor)
    context?.move(to: CGPoint(x: 100, y: 100))
    context?.addArc(tangent1End: CGPoint(x: 100, y: 200),
            tangent2End: CGPoint(x: 300, y: 200), radius: 100)
    context?.strokePath()
}
```

The above code will result in the following graphics output:

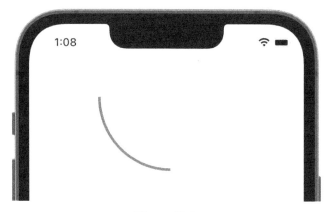

Figure 63-8

63.11 Drawing a Cubic Bézier Curve

A cubic Bézier curve may be drawn by moving to a start point and then passing two control points and an end point through to the *addCurve(to:)* method:

```
override func draw(_ rect: CGRect)
{
```

```
        let context = UIGraphicsGetCurrentContext()
        context?.setLineWidth(4.0)
        context?.setStrokeColor(UIColor.blue.cgColor)
        context?.move(to: CGPoint(x: 30, y: 30))
        context?.addCurve(to: CGPoint(x: 20, y: 50),
                        control1: CGPoint(x: 300, y: 250),
                        control2: CGPoint(x: 300, y: 70))
        context?.strokePath()
}
```

The above code will cause the curve illustrated in Figure 63-9 to be drawn when compiled and executed in our example app:

Figure 63-9

63.12 Drawing a Quadratic Bézier Curve

A quadratic Bézier curve is drawn using the *addQuadCurve(to:)* method, providing a control and end point as arguments having first moved to the start point:

```
override func draw(_ rect: CGRect)
{
    let context = UIGraphicsGetCurrentContext()
    context?.setLineWidth(4.0)
    context?.setStrokeColor(UIColor.blue.cgColor)
    context?.move(to: CGPoint(x: 10, y: 200))
    context?.addQuadCurve(to: CGPoint(x: 300, y: 200),
            control: CGPoint(x: 150, y: 10))
    context?.strokePath()
}
```

The above code, when executed, will display a curve that appears as illustrated in the following figure:

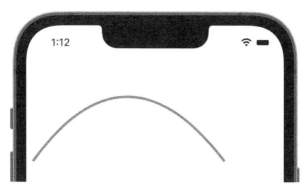

Figure 63-10

63.13 Dashed Line Drawing

So far in this chapter, we have performed all our drawing with a solid line. Quartz also provides support for drawing dashed lines. This is achieved via the Quartz *setLineDash* method, which takes as its arguments the following:

- **context** – The graphics context of the view on which the drawing is to take place

- **phase** - A floating point value that specifies how far into the dash pattern the line starts

- **lengths** – An array containing values for the lengths of the painted and unpainted sections of the line. For example, an array containing 5 and 6 would cycle through 5 painted unit spaces followed by 6 unpainted unit spaces.

- **count** – A count of the number of items in the lengths array

For example, a [2,6,4,2] lengths array applied to a curve drawing of line thickness 5.0 will appear as follows:

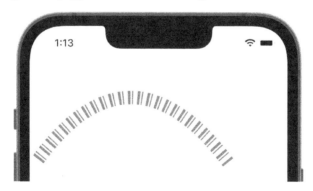

Figure 63-11

The corresponding *draw* method code that drew the above line reads as follows:

```
override func draw(_ rect: CGRect)
{
    let context = UIGraphicsGetCurrentContext()
    context?.setLineWidth(20.0)
    context?.setStrokeColor(UIColor.blue.cgColor)
    let dashArray:[CGFloat] = [2,6,4,2]
    context?.setLineDash(phase: 3, lengths: dashArray)
```

```
    context?.move(to: CGPoint(x: 10, y: 200))
    context?.addQuadCurve(to: CGPoint(x: 300, y: 200),
            control: CGPoint(x: 150, y: 10))
    context?.strokePath()
}
```

63.14 Drawing Shadows

In addition to drawing shapes, Core Graphics can also be used to create shadow effects. This is achieved using the *setShadow* method, passing through a graphics context, offset values for the position of the shadow relative to the shape for which the shadow is being drawn, and a value specifying the degree of blurring required for the shadow effect.

The following code, for example, draws an ellipse with a shadow:

```
override func draw(_ rect: CGRect)
{
    let context = UIGraphicsGetCurrentContext()
    let myShadowOffset = CGSize (width: -10,  height: 15)

    context?.saveGState()
    context?.setShadow(offset: myShadowOffset, blur: 5)
    context?.setLineWidth(4.0)
    context?.setStrokeColor(UIColor.blue.cgColor)
    let rectangle = CGRect(x: 60,y: 170,width: 200,height: 80)
    context?.addEllipse(in: rectangle)
    context?.strokePath()
    context?.restoreGState()
}
```

When executed, the above code will produce the effect illustrated in Figure 63-12:

Figure 63-12

63.15 Drawing Gradients

Gradients are implemented using the Core Graphics CGGradient class, which supports linear, radial, and axial gradients. The CGGradient class essentially involves the specification of two or more colors together with a set of location values. The location values indicate the points at which the gradient should switch from one color to another as the gradient is drawn along an axis line where 0.0 represents the start of the axis, and 1.0 is the endpoint. Assume, for example, that you wish to create a gradient that transitions through three different colors along the gradient axis, with each color being given an equal amount of space within the gradient. In this situation, three locations would be specified. The first would be 0.0 to represent the start of the gradient. Two more locations would then need to be specified for the transition points to the remaining colors. Finally, to equally divide the axis among the colors, these would need to be set to 0.3333 and 0.6666, respectively.

Having configured a CGGradient instance, a linear gradient is drawn via a call to the *drawLinearGradient* method of the context object, passing through the colors, locations, and start and end points as arguments.

The following code, for example, draws a linear gradient using four colors with four equally spaced locations:

```
override func draw(_ rect: CGRect)
{
    let context = UIGraphicsGetCurrentContext()

    let locations: [CGFloat] = [ 0.0, 0.25, 0.5, 0.75 ]

    let colors = [UIColor.red.cgColor,
                  UIColor.green.cgColor,
                  UIColor.blue.cgColor,
                  UIColor.yellow.cgColor]

    let colorspace = CGColorSpaceCreateDeviceRGB()

    let gradient = CGGradient(colorsSpace: colorspace,
                  colors: colors as CFArray, locations: locations)

    var startPoint = CGPoint()
    var endPoint =  CGPoint()

    startPoint.x = 0.0
    startPoint.y = 0.0
    endPoint.x = 600
    endPoint.y = 600

    if let gradient = gradient {
        context?.drawLinearGradient(gradient,
                                    start: startPoint, end: endPoint,
                                    options: .drawsBeforeStartLocation)
    }
}
```

When executed, the above code will generate the gradient shown in Figure 63-13:

Figure 63-13

Radial gradients involve drawing a gradient between two circles. When the circles are positioned apart from each other and given different sizes, a conical effect is achieved, as shown in Figure 63-14:

Figure 63-14

The code to draw the above radial gradient sets up the colors and locations for the gradient before declaring the center points and radius values for two circles. The gradient is then drawn via a call to the *drawRadialGradient* method:

```
override func draw(_ rect: CGRect)
{
    let context = UIGraphicsGetCurrentContext()

    let locations: [CGFloat] = [0.0, 0.5, 1.0]

    let colors = [UIColor.red.cgColor,
                  UIColor.green.cgColor,
                  UIColor.cyan.cgColor]

    let colorspace = CGColorSpaceCreateDeviceRGB()

    let gradient = CGGradient(colorsSpace: colorspace,
                     colors: colors as CFArray, locations: locations)

    var startPoint =  CGPoint()
    var endPoint  = CGPoint()

    startPoint.x = 100
    startPoint.y = 100
    endPoint.x = 200
    endPoint.y = 200
    let startRadius: CGFloat = 10
    let endRadius: CGFloat = 75

    if let gradient = gradient {
        context?.drawRadialGradient(gradient, startCenter: startPoint,
                              startRadius: startRadius,
                              endCenter: endPoint,
                              endRadius: endRadius, options: [])
    }
}
```

Interesting effects may also be created by assigning a radius of 0 to the starting point circle and positioning it within the circumference of the endpoint circle:

```
override func draw(_ rect: CGRect)
{
    let context = UIGraphicsGetCurrentContext()
    let locations: [CGFloat] = [0.0, 1.0]

    let colors = [UIColor.white.cgColor,
                    UIColor.blue.cgColor]

    let colorspace = CGColorSpaceCreateDeviceRGB()
```

```
    let gradient = CGGradient(colorsSpace: colorspace,
                    colors: colors as CFArray, locations: locations)

    var startPoint = CGPoint()
    var endPoint = CGPoint()
    startPoint.x = 180
    startPoint.y = 180
    endPoint.x = 200
    endPoint.y = 200
    let startRadius: CGFloat = 0
    let endRadius: CGFloat = 75

    if let gradient = gradient {
        context?.drawRadialGradient (gradient, startCenter: startPoint,
                            startRadius: startRadius,
                            endCenter: endPoint,
                            endRadius: endRadius,
                            options: .drawsBeforeStartLocation)
    }
}
```

When executed, the above code creates the appearance of light reflecting on the surface of a shiny blue sphere:

Figure 63-15

63.16 Drawing an Image into a Graphics Context

An image may be drawn into a graphics context either by specifying the coordinates of the top left-hand corner of the image (in which case the image will appear full size) or resized so that it fits into a specified rectangular area. Before we can display an image in our example app, that image must first be added to the project resources.

Begin by locating the desired image using the Finder and then drag and drop that image onto the project navigator panel of the Xcode main project window.

The following example *draw* method code displays the image in a file named *cat.png* full size located at 0, 0:

```
override func draw(_ rect: CGRect)
{
    let myImage = UIImage(named: "myImage.png")
    let imagePoint = CGPoint(x: 0, y: 0)
```

```
myImage?.draw(at: imagePoint)
}
```

As is evident when the app is run, the size of the image far exceeds the available screen size:

Figure 63-16

Using the *draw* method of the UIImage object, however, we can scale the image to fit better on the screen. In this instance, it is useful to identify the screen size since this changes depending on the device on which the app is running. This can be achieved using the *mainScreen* and *bounds* methods of the UIScreen class. The *mainScreen* method returns another UIScreen object representing the device display. Calling the *bounds* method of that object returns the dimensions of the display in the form of a CGRect object:

```
override func draw(_ rect: CGRect)
{
    let myImage = UIImage(named: "myImage.png")
    let imageRect = UIScreen.main.bounds
    myImage?.draw(in: imageRect)
}
```

This time, the entire image fits comfortably on the screen:

Figure 63-17

63.17 Image Filtering with the Core Image Framework

Having covered the concept of displaying images within an iOS app, now is a good time to provide a basic overview of the Core Image Framework.

Core Image was introduced with iOS 5 and provides a mechanism for filtering and manipulating still images and videos. Included with Core Image is a wide range of filters, together with the ability to build custom filters to meet specific requirements. Examples of filters that may be applied include cropping, color effects, blurring, warping, transformations, and gradients. A full list of filters is available in Apple's Core Image Filter Reference document, located in the Apple Developer portal.

A CIImage object is typically initialized with a reference to the image to be manipulated. A CIFilter object is then created and configured with the type of filtering to be performed, together with any input parameters required by that filter. The CIFilter object is then instructed to perform the operation, and the modified image is subsequently returned as a CIImage object. The app's CIContext reference may then be used to render the image for display to the user.

By way of an example of Core Image in action, we will modify the *draw* method of our Draw2D example app to render the previously displayed image in a sepia tone using the CISepiaTone filter. The first step, however, is to add the CoreImage Framework to the project. This is achieved by selecting the *Draw2D* target at the top of the project navigator and then selecting the *Build Phases* tab in the main panel. Next, unfold the *Link Binary with Libraries* section of the panel, click the + button and locate and add the *CoreImage.framework* library from the resulting list.

Having added the framework, select the *Draw2D.swift* file and modify the *draw* method as follows:

```
override func draw(_ rect: CGRect) {

    if let myimage = UIImage(named: "myImage.png"),
        let sepiaFilter = CIFilter(name: "CISepiaTone") {

        let cimage = CIImage(image: myimage)

        sepiaFilter.setDefaults()
        sepiaFilter.setValue(cimage, forKey: "inputImage")
        sepiaFilter.setValue(NSNumber(value: 0.8 as Float),
                             forKey: "inputIntensity")

        let image = sepiaFilter.outputImage

        let context = CIContext(options: nil)

        let cgImage = context.createCGImage(image!,
                                            from: image!.extent)

        let resultImage = UIImage(cgImage: cgImage!)
        let imageRect = UIScreen.main.bounds
        resultImage.draw(in: imageRect)
    }
}
```

The method begins by loading the image file used in the previous section of this chapter. Since Core Image works on CIImage objects, it is necessary to convert the UIImage to a CIImage. Next, a new CIFilter object is created and initialized with the CISepiaTone filter. The filter is then set to the default settings before being configured with the input image (in this case, our *cimage* object) and the filter's intensity value (0.8).

With the filter object configured, its *outputImage* method is called to perform the manipulation, and the resulting modified image is assigned to a new CImage object. The CIContext reference for the app is then obtained and used to convert the CImage object to a CGImageRef object. This, in turn, is converted to a UIImage object which is then displayed to the user using the object's *draw* method. When compiled and run, the image will appear in a sepia tone.

63.18 Summary

By subclassing the UIView class and overriding the *draw* method, various 2D graphics drawing operations may be performed on the view canvas. In this chapter, we have explored some of the graphics drawing capabilities of Quartz 2D to draw various line types and paths and present images on the iOS device screen.

Introduced in iOS 5, the Core Image Framework is designed to filter and manipulate images and video. In this chapter, we have provided a brief overview of Core Image and worked through a simple example that applied a sepia tone filter to an image.

64. iOS 17 Animation using UIViewPropertyAnimator

Most visual effects used throughout the iOS user interface are performed using *UIKit animation*. UIKit provides a simple mechanism for implementing basic animation within an iOS app. For example, if you need a user interface element to fade in or out of view gently, slide smoothly across the screen, or gracefully resize or rotate before the user's eyes, these effects can be achieved using UIKit animation in just a few lines of code.

This chapter will introduce the basics of UIKit animation and work through a simple example. While much can be achieved with UIKit animation, if you plan to develop a graphics-intensive 3D style app, it is more likely that Metal or SceneKit will need to be used, a subject area to which numerous books are dedicated.

64.1 The Basics of UIKit Animation

The cornerstone of animation in UIKit is the UIViewPropertyAnimator class. This class allows the changes made to the properties of a view object to be animated using a range of options.

For example, consider a UIView object containing a UIButton connected to an outlet named *theButton*. The app requires that the button gradually fades from view over 3 seconds. This can be achieved by making the button transparent through the use of the *alpha* property:

```
theButton.alpha = 0
```

However, setting the alpha property to 0 causes the button to become transparent immediately. To make it fade out of sight gradually, we need to create a UIViewPropertyAnimator instance configured with the duration of the animation. This class also needs to know the *animation curve* of the animation. This curve is used to control the speed of the animation as it is running. For example, an animation might start slow, speed up and then slow down again before completion. The timing curve of an animation is controlled by the UICubicTimingParameters and UISpringTimingParameters classes. For example, the following code configures a UIViewPropertyAnimator instance using the standard "ease in" animation curve dispersed over a 2-second duration:

```
let timing = UICubicTimingParameters(animationCurve: .easeIn)
let animator = UIViewPropertyAnimator(duration: 2.0,
                          timingParameters:timing)
```

Once the UIViewPropertyAnimator class has been initialized, the animation sequence to be performed needs to be added, followed by a call to the object's *startAnimation* method:

```
animator.addAnimations {
    self.theButton.alpha = 0
}
animator.startAnimation()
```

A range of other options is available when working with a UIViewPropertyAnimator instance. Animation may be paused or stopped anytime via calls to the *pauseAnimation* and *stopAnimation* methods. To configure the animator to call a completion handler when the animation finishes, assign the handler to the object's *completion* property. The animation may be reversed by assigning a true value to the *isReversed* property. The start of the animation may be delayed by passing through a delay duration when initializing the UIViewPropertyAnimator class as follows:

```
animator.startAnimation(afterDelay: 4.0)
```

64.2 Understanding Animation Curves

As previously mentioned, in addition to specifying the duration of an animation sequence, the linearity of the animation timeline may also be defined by specifying an *animation curve*. This setting controls whether the animation is performed at a constant speed, whether it starts out slow and speeds up, and provides options for adding spring-like behavior to an animation.

The UICubicTimingParameters class is used to configure time-based animation curves. As demonstrated in the previous section, one option when using this class is to use one of the following four standard animation curves provided by UIKit:

- **.curveLinear** – The animation is performed at a constant speed for the specified duration and is the option declared in the above code example.

- **.curveEaseOut** – The animation starts fast and slows as the end of the sequence approaches.

- **.curveEaseIn** – The animation sequence starts slow and speeds up as the end approaches.

- **.curveEaseInOut** – The animation starts slow, speeds up, and slows down again.

If the standard options do not meet your animation needs, a custom cubic curve may be created and used as the animation curve simply by specifying control points:

```
let timing = UICubicTimingParameters(
            controlPoint1: CGPoint(x:0.0, y:1.0),
             controlPoint2: CGPoint(x:1.0,y:0.0))
```

Alternatively, property changes to a view may be animated using a spring effect via the UISpringTimingParameters class. Instances of this class can be configured using mass, spring "stiffness," damping, and velocity values as follows:

```
let timing = UISpringTimingParameters(mass: 0.5, stiffness: 0.5,
        damping: 0.3, initialVelocity: CGVector(dx:1.0, dy: 0.0))
```

Alternatively, the spring effect may be configured using just the damping ratio and velocity:

```
let timing = UISpringTimingParameters(dampingRatio: 0.4,
                initialVelocity: CGVector(dx:1.0, dy: 0.0))
```

64.3 Performing Affine Transformations

Transformations allow changes to be made to the coordinate system of a screen area. This essentially allows the programmer to rotate, resize and translate a UIView object. A call is made to one of several transformation functions, and the result is assigned to the *transform* property of the UIView object.

For example, to change the scale of a UIView object named *myView* by a factor of 2 in both height and width:

```
myView.transform = CGAffineTransform(scaleX: 2, y: 2)
```

Similarly, the UIView object may be rotated using the *CGAffineTransform(rotationAngle:)* function, which takes as an argument the angle (in radians) by which the view is to be rotated. The following code, for example, rotates a view by 90 degrees:

```
let angle = CGFloat(90 * .pi / 180)
myView.transform = CGAffineTransform(rotationAngle: angle)
```

The key point to remember with transformations is that they become animated effects when performed within an animation sequence. The transformations evolve over the duration of the animation and follow the specified animation curve in terms of timing.

64.4 Combining Transformations

Two transformations may be combined to create a single transformation effect via a call to the *concatenating* method of the first transformation instance, passing through the second transformation object as an argument. This function takes as arguments the two transformation objects to be combined. The result may then be assigned to the transform property of the UIView object to be transformed. The following code fragment, for example, creates a transformation combining both scale and rotation:

```
let scaleTrans = CGAffineTransform(scaleX: 2, 2)

let angle = CGFloat(90 * .pi / 180)
let rotateTrans = CGAffineTransform(rotationAngle: angle)

scaleTrans.concatenating(rotateTrans)
```

Affine transformations offer an extremely powerful and flexible mechanism for creating animations, and it is impossible to do justice to these capabilities in a single chapter. However, a good starting place to learn about affine transformations is the *Transforms* chapter of Apple's *Quartz 2D Programming Guide*.

64.5 Creating the Animation Example App

The remainder of this chapter is dedicated to creating an iOS app that demonstrates the use of UIKit animation. The result is a simple app on which a blue square appears. When the user touches a location on the screen, the box moves to that location using a spring-based animation curve. Through the use of affine transformations, the box will rotate 180 degrees as it moves to the new location while also changing in size and color. Finally, a completion handler will change the color a second time once the animation has finished.

Launch Xcode and create a new project using the iOS *App* template with the Swift and Storyboard options selected, entering *Animate* as the product name.

64.6 Implementing the Variables

For this app, we will need a UIView to represent the blue square and variables to contain the rotation angle and scale factor by which the square will be transformed. These need to be declared in the *ViewController.swift* file as follows:

```
import UIKit

class ViewController: UIViewController {

    var scaleFactor: CGFloat = 2
    var angle: Double = 180
    var boxView: UIView?
.
.
.
```

64.7 Drawing in the UIView

Having declared the UIView reference, we need to initialize an instance object and draw a blue square at a specific location on the screen. We also need to add *boxView* as a subview of the app's main view object. These tasks only need to be performed once when the app first starts up, so a good option is within a new method to be called from the *viewDidLoad* method of the *ViewController.swift* file:

```
override func viewDidLoad() {
    super.viewDidLoad()

    initView()
}

func initView() {
    let frameRect = CGRect(x: 20, y: 20, width: 45, height: 45)
    boxView = UIView(frame: frameRect)

    if let view = boxView {
        view.backgroundColor = UIColor.blue
        self.view.addSubview(view)
    }
}
```

64.8 Detecting Screen Touches and Performing the Animation

When the user touches the screen, the blue box needs to move from its current location to the location of the touch. During this motion, the box will rotate 180 degrees and change in size. The detection of screen touches was covered in detail in *"An Overview of iOS 17 Multitouch, Taps, and Gestures"*. For this example, we want to initiate the animation at the point that the user's finger is lifted from the screen, so we need to implement the *touchesEnded* method in the *ViewController.swift* file:

```
override func touchesEnded(_ touches: Set<UITouch>, with event: UIEvent?) {

    if let touch = touches.first {
        let location = touch.location(in: self.view)
        let timing = UICubicTimingParameters(
                        animationCurve: .easeInOut)
        let animator = UIViewPropertyAnimator(duration: 2.0,
                        timingParameters:timing)

        animator.addAnimations {
            let scaleTrans =
                CGAffineTransform(scaleX: self.scaleFactor,
                                  y: self.scaleFactor)
            let rotateTrans = CGAffineTransform(
                rotationAngle: CGFloat(self.angle * .pi / 180))

            self.boxView!.transform =
                scaleTrans.concatenating(rotateTrans)
```

```
        self.angle = (self.angle == 180 ? 360 : 180)
        self.scaleFactor = (self.scaleFactor == 2 ? 1 : 2)
        self.boxView?.backgroundColor = UIColor.purple
        self.boxView?.center = location
    }

    animator.addCompletion {_ in
        self.boxView?.backgroundColor = UIColor.green
    }
    animator.startAnimation()
  }
}
```

Before compiling and running the app, we need to take some time to describe the actions performed in the above method. First, the method gets the UITouch object from the *touches* argument, and the *location(in:)* method of this object is called to identify the location on the screen where the touch took place:

```
if let touch = touches.first {
    let location = touch.location(in: self.view))
```

An instance of the UICubicTimingParameters class is then created and configured with the standard ease-in, ease-out animation curve:

```
let timing = UICubicTimingParameters(animationCurve: .easeInOut)
```

The animation object is then created and initialized with the timing object and a duration value of 2 seconds:

```
let animator = UIViewPropertyAnimator(duration: 2.0,
                        timingParameters:timing)
```

The animation closure is then added to the animation object. This begins the creation of two transformations for the view, one to scale the size of the view and one to rotate it 180 degrees. These transformations are then combined into a single transformation and applied to the UIView object:

```
let scaleTrans =
            CGAffineTransform(scaleX: self.scaleFactor,
                                    y: self.scaleFactor)
let rotateTrans = CGAffineTransform(
                    rotationAngle: CGFloat(self.angle * .pi / 180))

self.boxView?.transform = scaleTrans.concatenating(rotateTrans)
```

Ternary operators are then used to switch the scale and rotation angle variables ready for the next touch. In other words, after rotating 180 degrees on the first touch, the view will need to be rotated to 360 degrees on the next animation. Similarly, once the box has been scaled by a factor of 2, it needs to scale back to its original size on the next animation:

```
self.angle = (self.angle == 180 ? 360 : 180)
self.scaleFactor = (self.scaleFactor == 2 ? 1 : 2)
```

Finally, the location of the view is moved to the point on the screen where the touch occurred, and the color of the box changed to purple:

```
self.boxView?.backgroundColor = UIColor.purple
```

```
self.boxView?.center = location
```

Next, a completion handler is assigned to the animation and implemented such that it changes the color of the box view to green:

```
animator.addCompletion { _ in
    self.boxView?.backgroundColor = UIColor.green
}
```

After the animations have been added to the animation object, the animation sequence is started:

```
animator.startAnimation()
```

Once the *touchesEnded* method has been implemented, it is time to try out the app.

64.9 Building and Running the Animation App

Once all the code changes have been made and saved, click on the run button in the Xcode toolbar. Once the app has compiled, it will load into the iOS Simulator or connected iOS device.

When the app loads, the blue square should appear near the top left-hand corner of the screen. Tap the screen and watch the box glide and rotate to the new location, the size and color of the box changing as it moves:

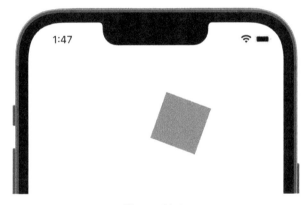

Figure 64-1

64.10 Implementing Spring Timing

The final task in this tutorial is to try out the UISpringTimingParameters class to implement a spring effect at the end of the animation. Edit the *ViewController.swift* file and change the timing constant so that it reads as follows:

```
.
.
let timing = UICubicTimingParameters(animationCurve: .easeInOut)

let timing = UISpringTimingParameters(mass: 0.5, stiffness: 0.5,
            damping: 0.3, initialVelocity: CGVector(dx:1.0, dy: 0.0))
.
.
```

Run the app once more, tap the screen, and note the spring effect on the box when it reaches the end location in the animation sequence.

64.11 Summary

UIKit animation provides an easy-to-implement interface to animation within iOS apps. From the simplest of tasks, such as gracefully fading out a user interface element, to basic animation and transformations, UIKit animation provides a variety of techniques for enhancing user interfaces. This chapter covered the basics of UIKit animation, including the UIViewPropertyAnimator, UISpringTimingParameters, and UICubicTimingParameters classes, before working step-by-step through an example to demonstrate the implementation of motion, rotation, and scaling animation.

65. iOS 17 UIKit Dynamics – An Overview

UIKit Dynamics provides a powerful and flexible mechanism for combining user interaction and animation into iOS user interfaces. What distinguishes UIKit Dynamics from other approaches to animation is the ability to declare animation behavior in terms of real-world physics.

Before moving on to a detailed tutorial in the next chapter, this chapter will provide an overview of the concepts and methodology behind UIKit Dynamics in iOS.

65.1 Understanding UIKit Dynamics

UIKit Dynamics allows for the animation of user interface elements (typically view items) to be implemented within a user interface, often in response to user interaction. To fully understand the concepts behind UIKit Dynamics, it helps to visualize how real-world objects behave.

Holding an object in the air and then releasing it, for example, will cause it to fall to the ground. This behavior is, of course, the result of gravity. However, whether or not, and by how much, an object bounces upon impact with a solid surface is dependent upon that object's elasticity and its velocity at the point of impact.

Similarly, pushing an object positioned on a flat surface will cause that object to travel a certain distance depending on the magnitude and angle of the pushing force combined with the level of friction at the point of contact between the two surfaces.

An object tethered to a moving point will react in various ways, such as following the anchor point, swinging in a pendulum motion, or even bouncing and spinning on the tether in response to more aggressive motions. However, an object similarly attached using a spring will behave entirely differently in response to the movement of the point of attachment.

Considering how objects behave in the real world, imagine the ability to selectively apply these same physics-related behaviors to view objects in a user interface, and you will begin understanding the basic concepts behind UIKit Dynamics. Not only does UIKit Dynamics allow user interface interaction and animation to be declared using concepts we are already familiar with, but in most cases, it allows this to be achieved with just a few simple lines of code.

65.2 The UIKit Dynamics Architecture

Before looking at how UIKit Dynamics are implemented in app code, it helps to understand the different elements that comprise the dynamics architecture.

The UIKit Dynamics implementation comprises four key elements: a *dynamic animator*, a set of one or more *dynamic behaviors*, one or more *dynamic items*, and a *reference view*.

65.2.1 Dynamic Items

The dynamic items are the view elements within the user interface to be animated in response to specified dynamic behaviors. A dynamic item is any view object that implements the *UIDynamicItem* protocol, which includes the UIView and UICollectionView classes and any subclasses thereof (such as UIButton and UILabel).

Any custom view item can work with UIKit Dynamics by conforming to the UIDynamicItem protocol.

65.2.2 Dynamic Behaviors

Dynamic behaviors are used to configure the behavior to be applied to one or more dynamic items. A range of predefined dynamic behavior classes is available, including *UIAttachmentBehavior, UICollisionBehavior, UIGravityBehavior, UIDynamicItemBehavior, UIPushBehavior,* and *UISnapBehavior.* Each is a subclass of the *UIDynamicBehavior* class, which will be covered in detail later in this chapter.

In general, an instance of the class corresponding to the desired behavior (UIGravityBehavior for gravity, for example) will be created, and the dynamic items for which the behavior is to be applied will be added to that instance. Dynamic items can be assigned to multiple dynamic behavior instances simultaneously and may be added to or removed from a dynamic behavior instance during runtime.

Once created and configured, behavior objects are added to the *dynamic animator* instance. Once added to a dynamic animator, the behavior may be removed at any time.

65.2.3 The Reference View

The reference view dictates the area of the screen within which the UIKit Dynamics animation and interaction are to take place. This is typically the parent superclass view or collection view, of which the dynamic item views are children.

65.2.4 The Dynamic Animator

The dynamic animator coordinates the dynamic behaviors and items and works with the underlying physics engine to perform the animation. The dynamic animator is represented by an instance of the *UIDynamicAnimator* class and is initialized with the corresponding reference view at creation time. Once created, suitably configured dynamic behavior instances can be added and removed as required to implement the desired user interface behavior.

The overall architecture for a UIKit Dynamics implementation can be represented visually using the diagram outlined in Figure 65-1:

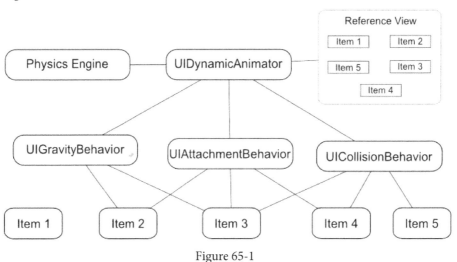

Figure 65-1

The above example has added three dynamic behaviors to the dynamic animator instance. The reference view contains five dynamic items, all but one of which have been added to at least one dynamic behavior instance.

65.3 Implementing UIKit Dynamics in an iOS App

The implementation of UIKit Dynamics in an app requires three very simple steps:

1. Create an instance of the *UIDynamicAnimator* class to act as the dynamic animator and initialize it with reference to the reference view.

2. Create and configure a dynamic behavior instance and assign to it the dynamic items on which the specified behavior is to be imposed.

3. Add the dynamic behavior instance to the dynamic animator.

4. Repeat from step 2 to create and add additional behaviors.

65.4 Dynamic Animator Initialization

The first step in implementing UIKit Dynamics is to create and initialize an instance of the UIDynamicAnimator class. The first step is to declare an instance variable for the reference:

```
var animator: UIDynamicAnimator?
```

Next, the dynamic animator instance can be created. The following code, for example, creates and initializes the animator instance within the *viewDidLoad* method of a view controller, using the view controller's parent view as the reference view:

```
override func viewDidLoad() {
    super.viewDidLoad()
    animator = UIDynamicAnimator(referenceView: self.view)
}
```

With the dynamic animator created and initialized, the next step is to configure behaviors, the details for which differ slightly depending on the nature of the behavior.

65.5 Configuring Gravity Behavior

Gravity behavior is implemented using the UIGravityBehavior class, the purpose of which is to cause view items to want to "fall" within the reference view as though influenced by gravity. UIKit Dynamics gravity is slightly different from real-world gravity in that it is possible to define a vector for the direction of the gravitational force using x and y components (x, y) contained within a CGVector instance. The default vector for this class is (0.0, 1.0), corresponding to downward acceleration at a speed of 1000 points per second^2. A negative x or y value will reverse the direction of gravity.

A UIGravityBehavior instance can be initialized as follows, passing through an array of dynamic items on which the behavior is to be imposed (in this case, two views named view1 and view2):

```
let gravity = UIGravityBehavior(items: [view1, view2])
```

Once created, the default vector can be changed if required at any time:

```
let vector = CGVectorMake(0.0, 0.5)
gravity.gravityDirection = vector
```

Finally, the behavior needs to be added to the dynamic animator instance:

```
animator?.addBehavior(gravity)
```

At any point during the app lifecycle, dynamic items may be added to, or removed from, the behavior:

```
gravity.addItem(view3)
gravity.removeItem(view)
```

Similarly, the entire behavior may be removed from the dynamic animator:

```
animator?.removeBehavior(gravity)
```

When gravity behavior is applied to a view, and in the absence of opposing behaviors, the view will immediately move in the direction of the specified gravity vector. In fact, as currently defined, the view will fall out of the bounds of the reference view and disappear. This can be prevented by setting up a collision behavior.

65.6 Configuring Collision Behavior

UIKit Dynamics is all about making items move on the device display. When an item moves, there is a high chance it will collide either with another item or the boundaries of the encapsulating reference view. As previously discussed, in the absence of any form of collision behavior, a moving item can move out of the visible area of the reference view. Such a configuration will also cause a moving item to simply pass over the top of any other items that happen to be in its path. Collision behavior (defined using the UICollisionBehavior class) allows such collisions to behave in ways more representative of the real world.

Collision behavior can be implemented between dynamic items (such that certain items can collide with others) or within boundaries (allowing collisions to occur when an item reaches a designated boundary). Boundaries can be defined such that they correspond to the boundaries of the reference view, or entirely new boundaries can be defined using lines and Bezier paths.

As with gravity behavior, a collision is generally created and initialized with an array object containing the items to which the behavior is to be applied. For example:

```
let collision = UICollisionBehavior(items: [view1, view2])
animator?.addBehavior(collision)
```

As configured, view1 and view2 will now collide when coming into contact. The physics engine will decide what happens depending on the items' elasticity and the collision's angle and speed. In other words, the engine will animate the items to behave as if they were physical objects subject to the laws of physics.

By default, an item under the influence of a collision behavior will collide with other items in the same collision behavior set and any boundaries set up. To declare the reference view as a boundary, set the *translatesReferenceBoundsIntoBoundary* property of the behavior instance to *true*:

```
collision.translatesReferenceBoundsIntoBoundary = true
```

A boundary inset from the edges of the reference view may be defined using the *setsTranslateReferenceBoundsIntoBoundaryWithInsets* method, passing through the required insets as an argument in the form of a *UIEdgeInsets* object.

The *collisionMode* property may be used to change default collision behavior by assigning one of the following constants:

- **UICollisionBehaviorMode.items** – Specifies that collisions only occur between items added to the collision behavior instance. Boundary collisions are ignored.

- **UICollisionBehaviorMode.boundaries** – Configures the behavior to ignore item collisions, recognizing only collisions with boundaries.

- **UICollisionBehaviorMode.everything** – Specifies that collisions occur between items added to the behavior and all boundaries. This is the default behavior.

The following code, for example, enables collisions only for items:

```
collision.collisionMode = UICollisionBehaviorMode.items
```

If an app needs to react to a collision, declare a class instance that conforms to the UICollisionBehaviorDelegate class by implementing the following methods and assign it as the delegate for the UICollisionBehavior object instance.

- collisionBehavior(_:beganContactForItem:withBoundaryIdentifier:atPoint:)

- collisionBehavior(_:beganContactForItem:withItem:atPoint:)

- collisionBehavior(_:endedContactForItem:withBoundaryIdentifier:)

- collisionBehavior(_:endedContactForItem:withItem:)

When implemented, the app will be notified when collisions begin and end. In most cases, the delegate methods will be passed information about the collision, such as the location and the items or boundaries involved.

In addition, aspects of the collision behavior, such as friction and the elasticity of the colliding items (such that they bounce on contact), may be configured using the UIDynamicBehavior class. This class will be covered in detail later in this chapter.

65.7 Configuring Attachment Behavior

As the name suggests, the UIAttachmentBehavior class allows dynamic items to be configured to behave as if attached. These attachments can take the form of two items attached or an item attached to an anchor point at specific coordinates within the reference view. In addition, the attachment can take the form of an imaginary piece of cord that does not stretch or a spring attachment with configurable damping and frequency properties that control how "bouncy" the attached item is in response to motion.

By default, the attachment point within the item itself is positioned at the center of the view. This can, however, be changed to a different position causing the real-world behavior outlined in Figure 65-2 to occur:

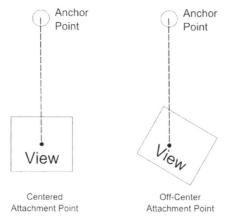

Figure 65-2

The physics engine will generally simulate animation to match what would typically happen in the real world. As illustrated above, the item will tilt when not attached in the center. If the anchor point moves, the attached view will also move. Depending on the motion, the item will swing in a pendulum motion and, assuming appropriate collision behavior configuration, bounce off any boundaries it collides with as it swings.

As with all UIKit Dynamics behavior, the physics engine performs all the work to achieve this. The only effort required by the developer is to write a few lines of code to set up the behavior before adding it to the dynamic animator instance. The following code, for example, sets up an attachment between two dynamic items:

```
let attachment = UIAttachmentBehavior(item: view1,
```

```
                                    attachedToItem: view2)
animator?.addBehavior(attachment)
```

The following code, on the other hand, specifies an attachment between view1 and an anchor point with the frequency and damping values set to configure a spring effect:

```
let anchorpoint = CGPoint(x: 100, y: 100)
let attachment = UIAttachmentBehavior(item: view1,
                    attachedToAnchor: anchorPoint)
attachment.frequency = 4.0
attachment.damping = 0.0
```

The above examples attach to the center point of the view. The following code fragment sets the same attachment as above, but with an attachment point offset 20, 20 points relative to the center of the view:

```
let anchorpoint = CGPoint(x: 100, y: 100)
let offset = UIOffset(horizontal: 20, vertical: 20)

let attachment = UIAttachmentBehavior(item: view1,
                        offsetFromCenter: offset,
                        attachedToAnchor: anchorPoint)
```

65.8 Configuring Snap Behavior

The UISnapBehavior class allows a dynamic item to be "snapped" to a specific location within the reference view. When implemented, the item will move toward the snap location as though pulled by a spring and, depending on the damping property specified, oscillate several times before finally snapping into place. Until the behavior is removed from the dynamic animator, the item will continue to snap to the location when subsequently moved to another position.

The damping property can be set to any value between 0.0 and 1.0, with 1.0 specifying maximum oscillation. The default value for damping is 0.5.

The following code configures snap behavior for dynamic item view1 with damping set to 1.0:

```
let point = CGPoint(x: 100, y: 100)
let snap = UISnapBehavior(item: view1, snapToPoint: point)
snap.damping = 1.0


animator?.addBehavior(snap)
```

65.9 Configuring Push Behavior

Push behavior, defined using the UIPushBehavior class, simulates the effect of pushing one or more dynamic items in a specific direction with a specified force. The force can be specified as continuous or instantaneous. In the case of a continuous push, the force is continually applied, causing the item to accelerate over time. The instantaneous push is more like a "shove" than a push in that the force is applied for a short pulse causing the item to gain velocity quickly but gradually lose momentum and eventually stop. Once an instantaneous push event has been completed, the behavior is disabled (though it can be re-enabled).

The direction of the push can be defined in radians or using x and y components. By default, the pushing force is applied to the center of the dynamic item, though, as with attachments, this can be changed to an offset relative to the center of the view.

A force of magnitude 1.0 is defined as being a force of one UIKit Newton, which equates to a view sized at 100 x 100 points with a density of value 1.0 accelerating at a rate of 100 points per second[2]. As explained in the next section, the density of a view can be configured using the UIDynamicItemBehavior class.

The following code pushes an item with instantaneous force at a magnitude of 0.2 applied on both the x and y axes, causing the view to move diagonally down and to the right:

```
let push = UIPushBehavior(items: [view1],
                          mode: UIPushBehaviorMode.instantaneous)
let vector = CGVector(dx: 0.2, dy: 0.2)
push.pushDirection = vector
```

Continuous push behavior can be achieved by changing the *mode* in the above code property to *UIPushBehaviorMode.continuous*.

To change the point where force is applied, configure the behavior using the *setTargetOffsetFromCenter(_:for:)* method of the behavior object, specifying an offset relative to the center of the view. For example:

```
let offset = UIOffset(horizontal: 20, vertical: 20)
push.setTargetOffsetFromCenter(offset, for:view1)
```

In most cases, an off-center target for the pushing force will cause the item to rotate as it moves, as indicated in Figure 65-3:

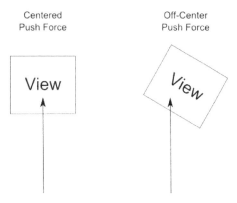

Figure 65-3

65.10 The UIDynamicItemBehavior Class

The UIDynamicItemBehavior class allows additional behavior characteristics to be defined that complement a number of the above primitive behaviors. This class can, for example, be used to define the density, resistance, and elasticity of dynamic items so that they do not move as far when subjected to an instantaneous push or bounce to a greater extent when involved in a collision. Dynamic items also can rotate by default. If rotation is not required for an item, this behavior can be turned off using a UIDynamicItemBehavior instance.

The behavioral properties of dynamic items that the UIDynamicItemBehavior class can govern are as follows:

- **allowsRotation** – Controls whether or not the item is permitted to rotate during animation.

- **angularResistence** – The amount by which the item resists rotation. The higher the value, the faster the item will stop rotating.

- **density** – The mass of the item.

- **elasticity** – The amount of elasticity an item will exhibit when involved in a collision. The greater the elasticity, the more the item will bounce.

- **friction** – The resistance exhibited by an item when it slides against another item.

- **resistance** – The overall resistance that the item exhibits in response to behavioral influences. The greater the value, the sooner the item will come to a complete stop during animation.

In addition, the class includes the following methods that may be used to increase or decrease the angular or linear velocity of a specified dynamic item:

- **angularVelocity(for:)** – Increases or decreases the angular velocity of the specified item. Velocity is specified in radians per second, where a negative value reduces the angular velocity.

- **linearVelocity(for:)** – Increases or decreases the linear velocity of the specified item. Velocity is specified in points per second, where a negative value reduces the velocity.

The following code example creates a new UIDynamicItemBehavior instance and uses it to set resistance and elasticity for two views before adding the behavior to the dynamic animator instance:

```
let behavior = UIDynamicItemBehavior(items: [view1, view2])
behavior.elasticity = 0.2
behavior.resistance = 0.5
animator?.addBehavior(behavior)
```

65.11 Combining Behaviors to Create a Custom Behavior

Multiple behaviors may be combined to create a single custom behavior using an instance of the UIDynamicBehavior class. The first step is to create and initialize each of the behavior objects. An instance of the UIDynamicBehavior class is then created, and each behavior is added to it via calls to the *addChildBehavior* method. Once created, only the UIDynamicBehavior instance needs to be added to the dynamic animator. For example:

```
// Create multiple behavior objects here

let customBehavior = UIDynamicBehavior()

customBehavior.addChildBehavior(behavior)
customBehavior.addChildBehavior(attachment)
customBehavior.addChildBehavior(gravity)
customBehavior.addChildBehavior(push)

animator?.addBehavior(customBehavior)
```

65.12 Summary

UIKit Dynamics provides a new way to bridge the gap between user interaction with an iOS device and corresponding animation within an app user interface. UIKit Dynamics takes a novel approach to animation by allowing view items to be configured such that they behave in much the same way as physical objects in the real world. This chapter has covered an overview of the basic concepts behind UIKit Dynamics and provided some details on how such behavior is implemented in terms of coding. The next chapter will work through a tutorial demonstrating many of these concepts.

66. An iOS 17 UIKit Dynamics Tutorial

With the basics of UIKit Dynamics covered in the previous chapter, this chapter will apply this knowledge to create an example app designed to show UIKit Dynamics in action. The example app created in this chapter will use the gravity, collision, elasticity, and attachment features in conjunction with touch handling to demonstrate how these key features are implemented.

66.1 Creating the UIKit Dynamics Example Project

Launch Xcode and create a new project using the iOS *App* template with the Swift and Storyboard options selected, entering *UIKitDynamics* as the product name.

66.2 Adding the Dynamic Items

The app's user interface will consist of two view objects drawn as squares colored blue and red, respectively. Therefore, the first step in the tutorial is to implement the code to create and draw these views. Within the project navigator panel, locate and select the *ViewController.swift* file and add variables for these two views so that the file reads as follows:

```
import UIKit

class ViewController: UIViewController {

    var blueBoxView: UIView?
    var redBoxView: UIView?
```

With the references declared, select the *ViewController.swift* file, add a new method (and call it from the *viewDidLoad* method) to draw the views, color them appropriately and then add them to the parent view so that they appear within the user interface:

```
override func viewDidLoad() {
    super.viewDidLoad()
    initViews()
}


func initViews() {

    var frameRect = CGRect(x: 10, y: 50, width: 80, height: 80)
    blueBoxView = UIView(frame: frameRect)
    blueBoxView?.backgroundColor = UIColor.blue

    frameRect = CGRect(x: 150, y: 50, width: 60, height: 60)
    redBoxView = UIView(frame: frameRect)
    redBoxView?.backgroundColor = UIColor.red
```

```
    if let blueBox = blueBoxView, let redBox = redBoxView {
        self.view.addSubview(blueBox)
        self.view.addSubview(redBox)
    }
}
```

Perform a test run of the app on either a simulator or physical iOS device and verify that the new views appear as expected within the user interface (Figure 66-1):

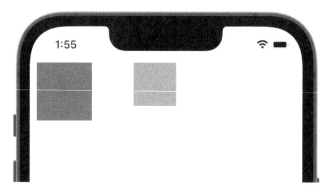

Figure 66-1

66.3 Creating the Dynamic Animator Instance

As outlined in the previous chapter, a key element in implementing UIKit Dynamics is an instance of the UIDynamicAnimator class. Select the *ViewController.swift* file and add an instance variable for a UIDynamicAnimator object within the app code:

```
import UIKit

class ViewController: UIViewController {

    var blueBoxView: UIView?
    var redBoxView: UIView?
    var animator: UIDynamicAnimator?
```

Next, modify the *initViews* method within the *ViewController.swift* file once again to add code to create and initialize the instance, noting that the top-level view of the view controller is passed through as the reference view:

```
func initViews() {

    var frameRect = CGRect(x: 10, y: 20, width: 80, height: 80)
    blueBoxView = UIView(frame: frameRect)
    blueBoxView?.backgroundColor = UIColor.blue

    frameRect = CGRect(x: 150, y: 20, width: 60, height: 60)
    redBoxView = UIView(frame: frameRect)
    redBoxView?.backgroundColor = UIColor.red
```

```
    if let blueBox = blueBoxView, let redBox = redBoxView {
        self.view.addSubview(blueBox)
        self.view.addSubview(redBox)

        animator = UIDynamicAnimator(referenceView: self.view)
    }
}
```

With the dynamic items added to the user interface and an instance of the dynamic animator created and initialized, it is time to begin creating dynamic behavior instances.

66.4 Adding Gravity to the Views

The first behavior to be added to the example app will be gravity. For this tutorial, gravity will be added to both views such that a force of gravity of 1.0 UIKit Newton is applied directly downwards along the y-axis of the parent view. To achieve this, the *initViews* method needs to be further modified to create a suitably configured instance of the UIGravityBehavior class and to add that instance to the dynamic animator:

```
func initViews() {

    var frameRect = CGRect(x: 10, y: 20, width: 80, height: 80)
    blueBoxView = UIView(frame: frameRect)
    blueBoxView?.backgroundColor = UIColor.blue

    frameRect = CGRect(x: 150, y: 20, width: 60, height: 60)
    redBoxView = UIView(frame: frameRect)
    redBoxView?.backgroundColor = UIColor.red

    if let blueBox = blueBoxView, let redBox = redBoxView {
        self.view.addSubview(blueBox)
        self.view.addSubview(redBox)

        animator = UIDynamicAnimator(referenceView: self.view)

        let gravity = UIGravityBehavior(items: [blueBox,
                                                redBox])
        let vector = CGVector(dx: 0.0, dy: 1.0)
        gravity.gravityDirection = vector

        animator?.addBehavior(gravity)
    }
}
```

Compile and run the app once again. Note that after launching, the gravity behavior causes the views to fall from the top of the reference view and out of view at the bottom of the device display. To keep the views within the bounds of the reference view, we need to set up a collision behavior.

66.5 Implementing Collision Behavior

In terms of collision behavior, the example requires that collisions occur both when the views impact each other and when making contact with the boundaries of the reference view. With these requirements in mind, the collision behavior needs to be implemented as follows:

```swift
func initViews() {

    var frameRect = CGRect(x: 10, y: 20, width: 80, height: 80)
    blueBoxView = UIView(frame: frameRect)
    blueBoxView?.backgroundColor = UIColor.blue

    frameRect = CGRect(x: 150, y: 20, width: 60, height: 60)
    redBoxView = UIView(frame: frameRect)
    redBoxView?.backgroundColor = UIColor.red

    if let blueBox = blueBoxView, let redBox = redBoxView {
        self.view.addSubview(blueBox)
        self.view.addSubview(redBox)

        animator = UIDynamicAnimator(referenceView: self.view)

        let gravity = UIGravityBehavior(items: [blueBox,
                                                redBox])
        let vector = CGVector(dx: 0.0, dy: 1.0)
        gravity.gravityDirection = vector

        let collision = UICollisionBehavior(items: [blueBox,
                                                    redBox])

        collision.translatesReferenceBoundsIntoBoundary = true

        animator?.addBehavior(collision)
        animator?.addBehavior(gravity)
    }
}
```

Running the app should now cause the views to stop at the bottom edge of the reference view and bounce slightly after impact. The amount by which the views bounce in the event of a collision can be changed by creating a UIDynamicBehavior class instance and changing the elasticity property. The following code, for example, changes the elasticity of the blue box view so that it bounces to a higher degree than the red box:

```swift
func initViews() {
.
.
.
        collision.translatesReferenceBoundsIntoBoundary = true

        let behavior = UIDynamicItemBehavior(items: [blueBox])
```

```
behavior.elasticity = 0.5

        animator?.addBehavior(behavior)
        animator?.addBehavior(collision)
        animator?.addBehavior(gravity)
    }
}
```

66.6 Attaching a View to an Anchor Point

So far in this tutorial, we have added some behavior to the app but have not yet implemented any functionality that connects UIKit Dynamics to user interaction. In this section, however, the example will be modified to create an attachment between the blue box view and the point of contact of a touch on the screen. This anchor point will be continually updated as the user's touch moves across the screen, thereby causing the blue box to follow the anchor point. The first step in this process is to declare within the *ViewController.swift* file some instance variables within which to store both the current location of the anchor point and a reference to a UIAttachmentBehavior instance:

```
import UIKit

class ViewController: UIViewController {

    var blueBoxView: UIView?
    var redBoxView: UIView?
    var animator: UIDynamicAnimator?
    var currentLocation: CGPoint?
    var attachment: UIAttachmentBehavior?
```

As outlined in the chapter entitled *"An Overview of iOS 17 Multitouch, Taps, and Gestures"*, touches can be detected by overriding the *touchesBegan*, *touchesMoved*, and *touchesEnded* methods. The *touchesBegan* method in the *ViewController.swift* file now needs to be implemented to obtain the coordinates of the touch and to add an attachment behavior between that location and the blue box view to the animator instance:

```
override func touchesBegan(_ touches: Set<UITouch>, with event: UIEvent?) {

    if let theTouch = touches.first, let blueBox = blueBoxView {

        currentLocation = theTouch.location(in: self.view) as CGPoint?

        if let location = currentLocation {
            attachment = UIAttachmentBehavior(item: blueBox,
                                    attachedToAnchor: location)
        }

        if let attach = attachment {
            animator?.addBehavior(attach)
        }
    }
}
```

As the touch moves around within the reference view, the anchorPoint property of the attachment behavior needs to be modified to track the motion. This involves overriding the *touchesMoved* method as follows:

```
override func touchesMoved(_ touches: Set<UITouch>, with event: UIEvent?) {
    if let theTouch = touches.first {

        currentLocation = theTouch.location(in: self.view)

        if let location = currentLocation {
            attachment?.anchorPoint = location
        }

    }
}
```

Finally, when the touch ends, the attachment needs to be removed so that the view will be pulled down to the bottom of the reference view by the previously defined gravity behavior. Remaining within the *ViewController. swift* file, implement the *touchesEnded* method as follows:

```
override func touchesEnded(_ touches: Set<UITouch>, with event: UIEvent?) {

    if let attach = attachment {
        animator?.removeBehavior(attach)
    }

}
```

Compile and run the app and touch the display. As the touch moves, note that the blue box view moves as though tethered to the touch point. Move the touch such that the blue and red boxes collide and observe that the red box will move in response to the collision while the blue box will rotate on the attachment point as illustrated in Figure 66-2:

Figure 66-2

Release the touch and note that gravity causes the blue box to fall once again and settle at the bottom edge of the reference view.

The code that creates the attachment currently attaches to the center point of the blue box view. Modify the *touchesBegan* method to adjust the attachment point so that it is off-center:

```
override func touchesBegan(_ touches: Set<UITouch>, with event: UIEvent?) {
```

```
    if let theTouch = touches.first, let blueBox = blueBoxView {

        currentLocation = theTouch.location(in: self.view) as CGPoint?

        if let location = currentLocation {
            let offset = UIOffset(horizontal: 20, vertical: 20)
            attachment = UIAttachmentBehavior(item: blueBox,
                                        offsetFromCenter: offset,
                                        attachedToAnchor: location)
        }

        if let attach = attachment {
            animator?.addBehavior(attach)
        }
    }
}
```

When the blue box view is now suspended by the anchor point attachment, it will tilt in accordance with the offset attachment point.

66.7 Implementing a Spring Attachment Between two Views

The final step in this tutorial is to attach the two views using a spring-style attachment. All that this involves is a few lines of code within the *viewDidLoad* method to create the attachment behavior, set the frequency and damping values to create the springing effect, and then add the behavior to the animator instance:

```
func initViews() {
.
.

    let behavior = UIDynamicItemBehavior(items: [blueBox])
    behavior.elasticity = 0.5

    let boxAttachment = UIAttachmentBehavior(item: blueBox,
                                        attachedTo: redBox)
    boxAttachment.frequency = 4.0
    boxAttachment.damping = 0.0

    animator?.addBehavior(boxAttachment)

    animator?.addBehavior(behavior)
    animator?.addBehavior(collision)
    animator?.addBehavior(gravity)
    }
}
```

When the app is now run, the red box will move in relation to the blue box as though connected by a spring (Figure 66-3). The views will even spring apart when pushed together before the touch is released.

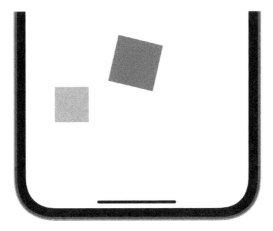

Figure 66-3

66.8 Summary

The example created in this chapter has demonstrated the steps involved in implementing UIKit Dynamics within an iOS app in the form of gravity, collision, and attachment behaviors. Perhaps the most remarkable fact about the animation functionality implemented in this tutorial is that it was achieved in approximately 40 lines of UIKit Dynamics code, a fraction of the amount of code that would have been required to implement such behavior in the absence of UIKit Dynamics.

67. Integrating Maps into iOS 17 Apps using MKMapItem

If there is one fact about Apple that we can state with any degree of certainty, it is that the company is passionate about retaining control of its destiny. Unfortunately, one glaring omission in this overriding corporate strategy has been the reliance on a competitor (in the form of Google) for mapping data in iOS. This dependency officially ended with iOS 6 through the introduction of Apple Maps.

In iOS 8, Apple Maps officially replaced the Google-based map data with data provided primarily by TomTom (but also technology from other companies, including some acquired by Apple for this purpose). Headquartered in the Netherlands, TomTom specializes in mapping and GPS systems. Of particular significance, however, is that TomTom (unlike Google) does not make smartphones, nor does it develop an operating system that competes with iOS, making it a more acceptable partner for Apple.

As part of the iOS 6 revamp of mapping, the SDK also introduced a class called MKMapItem, designed solely to ease the integration of maps and turn-by-turn directions into iOS apps. This was further enhanced in iOS 9 with the introduction of support for transit times, directions, and city flyover support.

For more advanced mapping requirements, the iOS SDK also includes the original classes of the MapKit framework, details of which will be covered in later chapters.

67.1 MKMapItem and MKPlacemark Classes

The MKMapItem class aims to make it easy for apps to launch maps without writing significant amounts of code. MKMapItem works in conjunction with the MKPlacemark class, instances of which are passed to MKMapItem to define the locations that are to be displayed in the resulting map. A range of options is also provided with MKMapItem to configure both the appearance of maps and the nature of directions to be displayed (i.e., whether directions are for driving, walking, or public transit).

67.2 An Introduction to Forward and Reverse Geocoding

It is difficult to talk about mapping, particularly when dealing with the MKPlacemark class, without first venturing into geocoding. Geocoding can best be described as converting a textual-based geographical location (such as a street address) into geographical coordinates expressed in longitude and latitude.

In iOS development, geocoding may be performed using the CLGeocoder class to convert a text-based address string into a CLLocation object containing the coordinates corresponding to the address. The following code, for example, converts the street address of the Empire State Building in New York to longitude and latitude coordinates:

```
let addressString = "350 5th Avenue New York, NY"

CLGeocoder().geocodeAddressString(addressString,
        completionHandler: {(placemarks, error) in

    if error != nil {
        print("Geocode failed with error: \(error!.localizedDescription)")
```

```
        } else if let marks = placemarks, marks.count > 0 {
            let placemark = marks[0]
            if let location = placemark.location {
                let coords = location.coordinate

                print(coords.latitude)
                print(coords.longitude)
            }
        }
    }
})
```

The code calls the *geocodeAddressString* method of a CLGeocoder instance, passing through a string object containing the street address and a completion handler to be called when the translation is complete. Passed as arguments to the handler are an array of CLPlacemark objects (one for each match for the address) together with an Error object which may be used to identify the reason for any failures.

For this example, the assumption is made that only one location matched the address string provided. The location information is then extracted from the CLPlacemark object at location 0 in the array, and the coordinates are displayed on the console.

The above code is an example of *forward geocoding* in that coordinates are calculated based on a text address description. *Reverse geocoding*, as the name suggests, involves the translation of geographical coordinates into a human-readable address string. Consider, for example, the following code:

```
let newLocation = CLLocation(latitude: 40.74835, longitude: -73.984911)


CLGeocoder().reverseGeocodeLocation(newLocation, completionHandler: {(placemarks,
error) in
    if error != nil {
        print("Geocode failed with error: \(error!.localizedDescription)")
    }

    if let marks = placemarks, marks.count > 0 {
        let placemark = marks[0]
        let postalAddress = placemark.postalAddress

        if let address = postalAddress?.street,
            let city = postalAddress?.city,
            let state = postalAddress?.state,
            let zip = postalAddress?.postalCode {

                print("\(address) \(city) \(state) \(zip)")
        }
    }
})
```

In this case, a CLLocation object is initialized with longitude and latitude coordinates and then passed through to the *reverseGeocodeLocation* method of a CLGeocoder object. Next, the method passes through an array of matching addresses to the completion handler in the form of CLPlacemark objects. Each placemark contains the address information for the matching location in the form of a CNPostalAddress object. Once again, the code assumes a single match is contained in the array and accesses and displays the address, city, state, and zip properties of the postal address object on the console.

When executed, the above code results in output that reads:

```
338 5th Ave New York New York 10001
```

It should be noted that the geocoding is not performed on the iOS device but rather on a server to which the device connects when a translation is required, and the results are subsequently returned when the translation is complete. As such, geocoding can only occur when the device has an active internet connection.

67.3 Creating MKPlacemark Instances

Each location to be represented when a map is displayed using the MKMapItem class must be represented by an MKPlacemark object. When MKPlacemark objects are created, they must be initialized with the geographical coordinates of the location together with an NSDictionary object containing the address property information. Continuing the example of the Empire State Building in New York, an MKPlacemark object would be created as follows:

```
import Contacts
import MapKit
.
.
let coords = CLLocationCoordinate2DMake(40.7483, -73.984911)

let address = [CNPostalAddressStreetKey: "350 5th Avenue",
               CNPostalAddressCityKey: "New York",
               CNPostalAddressStateKey: "NY",
               CNPostalAddressPostalCodeKey: "10118",
               CNPostalAddressISOCountryCodeKey: "US"]


let place = MKPlacemark(coordinate: coords, addressDictionary: address)
```

While it is possible to initialize an MKPlacemark object passing through a *nil* value for the address dictionary, this will result in the map appearing, albeit with the correct location marked, but it will be tagged as "Unknown" instead of listing the address. The coordinates are, however, mandatory when creating an MKPlacemark object. If the app knows the text address but not the location coordinates, geocoding will need to be used to obtain the coordinates before creating the MKPlacemark instance.

67.4 Working with MKMapItem

Given the tasks it can perform, the MKMapItem class is extremely simple to use. In its simplest form, it can be initialized by passing through a single MKPlacemark object as an argument, for example:

```
let mapItem = MKMapItem(placemark: place)
```

Once initialized, the *openInMaps(launchOptions:)* method will open the map positioned at the designated location with an appropriate marker, as illustrated in Figure 67-1:

```
mapItem.openInMaps(launchOptions: nil)
```

Figure 67-1

Similarly, the map may be initialized to display the current location of the user's device via a call to the MKMapItem *forCurrentLocation* method:

```
let mapItem = MKMapItem.forCurrentLocation()
```

Multiple locations may be tagged on the map by placing two or more MKMapItem objects in an array and then passing that array through to the *openMaps(with:)* class method of the MKMapItem class. For example:

```
let mapItems = [mapItem1, mapItem2, mapItem3]

MKMapItem.openMaps(with: mapItems, launchOptions: nil)
```

67.5 MKMapItem Options and Configuring Directions

In the example code fragments presented in the preceding sections, a *nil* value was passed through as the options argument to the MKMapItem methods. In fact, several configuration options are available for use when opening a map. These values need to be set up within an NSDictionary object using a set of pre-defined keys and values:

- **MKLaunchOptionsDirectionsModeKey** – Controls whether directions are to be provided with the map. If only one placemarker is present, directions from the current location to the placemarker will be provided. The mode for the directions should be either *MKLaunchOptionsDirectionsModeDriving*, *MKLaunchOptionsDirectionsModeWalking*, or *MKLaunchOptionsDirectionsModeTransit*.

- **MKLaunchOptionsMapTypeKey** – Indicates whether the map should display standard, satellite, hybrid, flyover, or hybrid flyover map images.

- **MKLaunchOptionsMapCenterKey** – Corresponds to a CLLocationCoordinate2D structure value containing the coordinates of the location on which the map is to be centered.

- **MKLaunchOptionsMapSpanKey** – An MKCoordinateSpan structure value designating the region the map should display when launched.

- **MKLaunchOptionsShowsTrafficKey** – A Boolean value indicating whether traffic information should be superimposed over the map when it is launched.

- **MKLaunchOptionsCameraKey** – When displaying a map in 3D flyover mode, the value assigned to this key takes the form of an MKMapCamera object configured to view the map from a specified perspective.

The following code, for example, opens a map with traffic data displayed and includes turn-by-turn driving directions between two map items:

```
let mapItems = [mapItem1, mapItem2]
let options = [MKLaunchOptionsDirectionsModeKey:
                    MKLaunchOptionsDirectionsModeDriving,
          MKLaunchOptionsShowsTrafficKey: true] as [String : Any]


MKMapItem.openMaps(with: mapItems, launchOptions: options)
```

67.6 Adding Item Details to an MKMapItem

When a location is marked on a map, the address is displayed together with a blue arrow, which displays an information card for that location when selected.

The MKMapItem class allows additional information to be added to a location through the *name*, *phoneNumber*, and *url* properties. The following code, for example, adds these properties to the map item for the Empire State Building:

```
mapItem.name = "Empire State Building"
mapItem.phoneNumber = "+12127363100"
mapItem.url = URL(string: "https://esbnyc.com")


mapItem.openInMaps(launchOptions: nil)
```

When the code is executed, the map place marker displays the location name instead of the address, together with the additional information:

Figure 67-2

A force touch performed on the marker displays a popover panel containing options to call the provided number or visit the website:

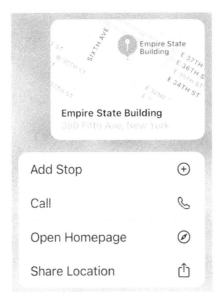

Figure 67-3

67.7 Summary

iOS 6 replaced Google Maps with maps provided by TomTom. Unlike Google Maps, which was assembled from static images, the new Apple Maps are dynamically rendered, resulting in clear and smooth zooming and more precise region selections. iOS 6 also introduced the MKMapItem class, which aims to make it easy for iOS app developers to launch maps and provide turn-by-turn directions with the minimum amount of code.

Within this chapter, the basics of geocoding and the MKPlacemark and MKMapItem classes have been covered. The next chapter, entitled "An Example iOS 17 MKMapItem App", will work through creating an example app that utilizes the knowledge covered in this chapter.

68. An Example iOS 17 MKMapItem App

This chapter aims to work through creating an example iOS app that uses reverse geocoding together with the MKPlacemark and MKMapItem classes. The app will consist of a screen into which the user will be required to enter destination address information. Then, when the user selects a button, a map will be launched containing turn-by-turn directions from the user's current location to the specified destination.

68.1 Creating the MapItem Project

Launch Xcode and create a new project using the iOS *App* template with the Swift and Storyboard options selected, entering *MapItem* as the product name.

68.2 Designing the User Interface

The user interface will consist of four Text Field objects into which the destination address will be entered, together with a Button to launch the map. Select the *Main.storyboard* file in the project navigator panel and, using the Library palette, design the user interface layout to resemble that of Figure 68-1. Take steps to widen the Text Fields and configure Placeholder text attributes on each one.

If you reside in a country not divided into States and Zip code regions, feel free to adjust the user interface accordingly.

Display the *Resolve Auto Layout Issues* menu and select the *Reset to Suggested Constraints* option under *All Views in View Controller*.

The next step is to connect the outlets for the text views and declare an action for the button. Next, select the *Street address* Text Field object, display the Assistant Editor, and ensure that the editor displays the *ViewController.swift* file.

Figure 68-1

Right-click on the *Street address* Text Field object and drag the resulting line to the area immediately beneath the class declaration directive in the Assistant Editor panel. Upon releasing the line, the configuration panel will appear. Configure the connection as an *Outlet* named *address* and click on the *Connect* button. Repeat these steps for the *City*, *State,* and *Zip* text fields, connecting them to outlets named *city, state,* and *zip*.

Right-click on the *Get Directions* button and drag the resulting line to a position beneath the new outlets declared in the Assistant Editor. In the resulting configuration panel, change the *Connection* type to *Action* and name the method *getDirections*. On completion, the beginning of the *ViewController.swift* file should read as follows:

```swift
import UIKit

class ViewController: UIViewController {

    @IBOutlet weak var address: UITextField!
    @IBOutlet weak var city: UITextField!
    @IBOutlet weak var state: UITextField!
    @IBOutlet weak var zip: UITextField!
.

.

    @IBAction func getDirections(_ sender: Any) {
    }
.

.

}
```

68.3 Converting the Destination using Forward Geocoding

When the user touches the button in the user interface, the *getDirections* method can extract the address information from the text fields. The objective will be to create an MKPlacemark object to contain this location. As outlined in *"Integrating Maps into iOS 17 Apps using MKMapItem"*, an MKPlacemark instance requires the longitude and latitude of an address before it can be instantiated. Therefore, the first step in the *getDirections* method is to perform a forward geocode translation of the address. Before doing so, however, it is necessary to declare a property in the *ViewController.swift* file in which to store these coordinates once they have been calculated. This will, in turn, requires that the *CoreLocation* framework be imported. Therefore, now is also an opportune time to import the *MapKit* and *Contacts* frameworks, both of which will be required later in the chapter:

```swift
import UIKit
import Contacts
import MapKit
import CoreLocation

class ViewController: UIViewController {

    @IBOutlet weak var address: UITextField!
    @IBOutlet weak var city: UITextField!
    @IBOutlet weak var state: UITextField!
    @IBOutlet weak var zip: UITextField!
    var coords: CLLocationCoordinate2D?
.

.
```

494

Next, select the *ViewController.swift* file, locate the *getDirections* method stub and modify it to convert the address string to geographical coordinates:

```
@IBAction func getDirections(_ sender: Any) {

    if let addressString = address.text,
        let cityString = city.text,
        let stateString = state.text,
        let zipString = zip.text {
        let addressString =
            "\(addressString) \(cityString) \(stateString) \(zipString)"

        CLGeocoder().geocodeAddressString(addressString,
                completionHandler: {(placemarks, error) in
            if error != nil {
                print("Geocode failed: \(error!.localizedDescription)")
            } else if let marks = placemarks, marks.count > 0 {
                    let placemark = marks[0]
                    if let location = placemark.location {
                    self.coords = location.coordinate
                    self.showMap()
                }
            }
        })
    }
}
```

The steps used to perform the geocoding translation mirror those outlined in *"Integrating Maps into iOS 17 Apps using MKMapItem"* with one difference: a method named *showMap* is called if a successful translation occurs. All that remains, therefore, is to implement this method.

68.4 Launching the Map

With the address string and coordinates obtained, the final task is implementing the *showMap* method. This method will create a new MKPlacemark instance for the destination address, configure options for the map to request driving directions, and launch the map. Since the map will be launched with a single map item, it will default to providing directions from the current location. With the *ViewController.swift* file still selected, add the code for the *showMap* method so that it reads as follows:

```
func showMap() {

    if let addressString = address.text,
        let cityString = city.text,
        let stateString = state.text,
        let zipString = zip.text,
        let coordinates = coords {
        let addressDict =
            [CNPostalAddressStreetKey: addressString,
```

```
                CNPostalAddressCityKey: cityString,
                CNPostalAddressStateKey: stateString,
                CNPostalAddressPostalCodeKey: zipString]


        let place = MKPlacemark(coordinate: coordinates,
                            addressDictionary: addressDict)
        let mapItem = MKMapItem(placemark: place)
        let options = [MKLaunchOptionsDirectionsModeKey:
            MKLaunchOptionsDirectionsModeDriving]
        mapItem.openInMaps(launchOptions: options)
    }
}
```

The method simply creates an NSDictionary containing the contact keys and values for the destination address. It then creates an MKPlacemark instance using the address dictionary and the coordinates from the forward-geocoding operation. Next, a new MKMapItem object is created using the placemarker object before another dictionary is created and configured to request driving directions. Finally, the map is launched.

68.5 Building and Running the App

Within the Xcode toolbar, click on the Run button to compile and run the app, either on a physical iOS device or the iOS Simulator. Once loaded, enter an address into the text fields before touching the *Get Directions* button. The map should subsequently appear with the route between your current location and the destination address. Note that if the app is running in the simulator, the current location will likely default to Apple's headquarters in California:

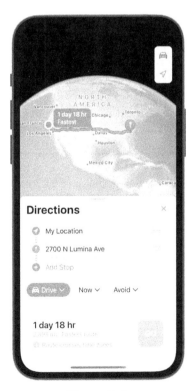

Figure 68-2

68.6 Summary

This chapter's goal has been to create a simple app that uses geocoding and the MKPlacemark and MKMapItem classes. The example app created in this chapter has demonstrated the ease with which maps and directions can be integrated into iOS apps.

69. Getting Location Information using the iOS 17 Core Location Framework

iOS devices can employ several techniques for obtaining information about the current geographical location of the device. These mechanisms include GPS, cell tower triangulation, and finally (and least accurately), using the IP address of available Wi-Fi connections. The mechanism used by iOS to detect location information is largely transparent to the app developer. The system will automatically use the most accurate solution available at any given time. All that is needed to integrate location-based information into an iOS app is understanding how to use the Core Location Framework, which is the subject of this chapter.

Once the basics of location tracking with Core Location have been covered in this chapter, the next chapter will provide detailed steps on how to create *"An Example iOS 17 Location App"*.

69.1 The Core Location Manager

The key classes contained within the Core Location Framework are CLLocationManager and CLLocation. An instance of the CLLocationManager class can be created using the following Swift code:

```
var locationManager: CLLocationManager = CLLocationManager()
```

Once a location manager instance has been created, it must seek permission from the user to collect location information before it can begin to track data.

69.2 Requesting Location Access Authorization

Before any app can begin tracking location data, it must first seek permission from the user. This can be achieved by calling one of two methods on the CLLocationManager instance, depending on the specific requirement. For example, suppose the app only needs to track location information when the app is in the foreground. In that case, a call should be made to the *requestWhenInUseAuthorization* method of the location manager instance. For example:

```
locationManager.requestWhenInUseAuthorization()
```

If tracking is also required when the app is running in the background, the *requestAlwaysAuthorization* method should be called:

```
locationManager.requestAlwaysAuthorization()
```

If an app requires *always* authorization, the recommended path to requesting this permission is first to seek *when in use* permission and then offer the user the opportunity to elevate this permission to *always* mode at the point that the app needs it. The reasoning behind this recommendation is that when seeking *always* permission, the request dialog displayed by iOS will provide the user the option of using either *when in use* or *always* location tracking. Given these choices, most users will typically select the *when in use* option. Therefore, a better approach is to begin by requesting *when in use* tracking and then explain the benefits of elevating to *always* mode in a later request.

Both location authorization request method calls require that specific key-value pairs be added to the Information

Property List dictionary contained within the app's *Info.plist* file. The values take the form of strings and must describe the reason why the app needs access to the user's current location. The keys associated with these values are as follows:

- **NSLocationWhenInUseUsageDescription** – A string value describing to the user why the app needs access to the current location when running in the foreground. This string is displayed when a call is made to the *requestWhenInUseAuthorization* method of the locationManager instance. The dialog displayed to the user containing this message will only provide the option to permit *when in use* location tracking. All apps built using the iOS 11 SDK or later must include this key regardless of the usage permission level being requested to access the device location.

- **NSLocationAlwaysAndWhenInUseUsageDesciption** – The string displayed when permission is requested for *always* authorization using the *requestAlwaysAuthorization* method. The request dialog containing this message will allow the user to select either *always* or *when in use* authorization. All apps built using the iOS 11 SDK or later must include this key when accessing device location information.

- **NSLocationAlwaysUsageDescription** – A string describing to the user why the app needs *always* access to the current location. This description is not used on devices running iOS 11 or later, though it should still be declared for compatibility with legacy devices.

69.3 Configuring the Desired Location Accuracy

The level of accuracy to which location information is to be tracked is specified via the *desiredAccuracy* property of the CLLocationManager object. It is important to keep in mind when configuring this property that the greater the level of accuracy selected, the greater the drain on the device battery. An app should, therefore, never request a greater accuracy than is needed.

Several predefined constant values are available for use when configuring this property:

- **kCLLocationAccuracyBestForNavigation** – Uses the highest possible level of accuracy augmented by additional sensor data. This accuracy level is intended solely for when the device is connected to an external power supply.

- **kCLLocationAccuracyBest** – The highest recommended level of accuracy for devices running on battery power.

- **kCLLocationAccuracyNearestTenMeters** - Accurate to within 10 meters.

- **kCLLocationAccuracyHundredMeters** – Accurate to within 100 meters.

- **kCLLocationAccuracyKilometer** – Accurate to within one kilometer.

- **kCLLocationAccuracyThreeKilometers** – Accurate to within three kilometers.

The following code, for example, sets the level of accuracy for a location manager instance to "best accuracy":

```
locationManager.desiredAccuracy = kCLLocationAccuracyBest
```

69.4 Configuring the Distance Filter

The default configuration for the location manager is to report updates whenever any changes are detected in the device's location. The *distanceFilter* property of the location manager allows apps to specify the amount of distance the device location must change before an update is triggered. If, for example, the distance filter is set to 1000 meters, the app will only receive a location update when the device travels 1000 meters or more from the location of the last update. For example, to specify a distance filter of 1500 meters:

```
locationManager.distanceFilter = 1500.0
```

The distance filter may be canceled, thereby returning to the default setting, using the *kCLDistanceFilterNone* constant:

```
locationManager.distanceFilter = kCLDistanceFilterNone
```

69.5 Continuous Background Location Updates

The location tracking options covered so far in this chapter only receive updates when the app is either in the foreground or background. The updates will stop as soon as the app enters the suspended state (in other words, the app is still resident in memory but is no longer executing code). However, if location updates are required even when the app is suspended (a key requirement for navigation-based apps), continuous background location updates must be enabled for the app. When enabled, the app will be woken from suspension each time a location update is triggered and provided the latest location data.

Enable continuous location updates is a two-step process beginning with the addition of an entry to the project *Info.plist* file. This is most easily achieved by enabling the location updates background mode in the Xcode *Signing & Capabilities* panel, as shown in Figure 69-1:

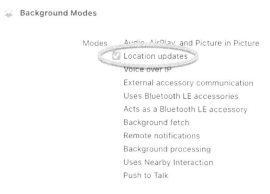

Figure 69-1

Within the app code, continuous updates are enabled by setting the *allowsBackgroundLocationUpdates* property of the location manager to *true*:

```
locationManager.allowsBackgroundLocationUpdates = true
```

To allow the location manager to suspend updates temporarily, set the *pausesLocationUpdatesAutomatically* property of the location manager to *true*.

```
locationManager.pausesLocationUpdatesAutomatically = true
```

This setting allows the location manager to extend battery life by pausing updates when it is appropriate to do so (for example, when the user's location remains unchanged for a significant amount of time). When the user starts moving again, the location manager will automatically resume updates.

Continuous location background updates are available for apps for both *always* and *when in use* authorization modes.

69.6 The Location Manager Delegate

Location manager updates and errors result in calls to two delegate methods defined within the CLLocationManagerDelegate protocol. Templates for the two delegate methods that must be implemented to comply with this protocol arc as follows:

```
func locationManager(_ manager: CLLocationManager,
              didUpdateLocations locations: [CLLocation])
```

```
{
    // Handle location updates here
}

func locationManager(_ manager: CLLocationManager,
        didFailWithError error: Error)
{
    // Handle errors here
}
```

Each time the location changes, the *didUpdateLocations* delegate method is called and passed as an argument an array of CLLocation objects with the last object in the array containing the most recent location data.

Changes to the location tracking authorization status of an app are reported via a call to the optional *didChangeAuthorization* delegate method:

```
func locationManager(_ manager: CLLocationManager,
        didChangeAuthorization status: CLAuthorizationStatus) {

    // App may no longer be authorized to obtain location
    //information. Check the status here and respond accordingly.
}
```

Once a class has been configured to act as the delegate for the location manager, that object must be assigned to the location manager instance. In most cases, the delegate will be the same view controller class in which the location manager resides, for example:

```
locationManager.delegate = self
```

69.7 Starting and Stopping Location Updates

Once suitably configured and authorized, the location manager can then be instructed to start tracking location information:

```
locationManager.startUpdatingLocation()
```

With each location update, the *didUpdateLocations* delegate method is called by the location manager and passed information about the current location.

To stop location updates, call the *stopUdatingLocation* method of the location manager as follows:

```
locationManager.stopUpdatingLocation()
```

69.8 Obtaining Location Information from CLLocation Objects

Location information is passed through to the *didUpdateLocation* delegate method in the form of CLLocation objects. A CLLocation object encapsulates the following data:

- Latitude

- Longitude

- Horizontal Accuracy

- Altitude

- Altitude Accuracy

69.8.1 Longitude and Latitude

Longitude and latitude values are stored as type CLLocationDegrees and may be obtained from a CLLocation object as follows:

```
let currentLatitude: CLLocationDistance =
        location.coordinate.latitude

let currentLongitude: CLLocationDistance =
        location.coordinate.longitude
```

69.8.2 Accuracy

Horizontal and vertical accuracy are stored in meters as CLLocationAccuracy values and may be accessed as follows:

```
let verticalAccuracy: CLLocationAccuracy =
        location.verticalAccuracy

let horizontalAccuracy: CLLocationAccuracy =
        location.horizontalAccuracy
```

69.8.3 Altitude

The altitude value is stored in meters as a type CLLocationDistance value and may be accessed from a CLLocation object as follows:

```
let altitude: CLLocationDistance = location.altitude
```

69.9 Getting the Current Location

If all that is required from the location manager is the user's current location without the need for continuous location updates, this can be achieved via a call to the *requestLocation* method of the location manager instance. This method will identify the current location and call the *didUpdateLocations* delegate once passing through the current location information. Location updates are then automatically turned off:

```
locationManager.requestLocation()
```

69.10 Calculating Distances

The distance between two CLLocation points may be calculated by calling the *distance(from:)* method of the end location and passing through the start location as an argument. For example, the following code calculates the distance between the points specified by *startLocation* and *endLocation*:

```
var distance: CLLocationDistance =
        endLocation.distance(from: startLocation)
```

69.11 Summary

This chapter has provided an overview of the use of the iOS Core Location Framework to obtain location information within an iOS app. This theory will be put into practice in the next chapter entitled *"An Example iOS 17 Location App"*.

70. An Example iOS 17 Location App

Having covered the basics of location management in iOS 17 apps in the previous chapter, we can put theory into practice and work step-by-step through an example app. This chapter aims to create a simple iOS app that tracks the latitude, longitude, and altitude of an iOS device. In addition, the level of location accuracy will be reported, together with the distance between a selected location and the device's current location.

70.1 Creating the Example iOS 17 Location Project

The first step, as always, is to launch the Xcode environment and start a new project to contain the location app. Once Xcode is running, create a new project using the iOS *App* template with the Swift and Storyboard options selected, entering *Location* as the product name.

70.2 Designing the User Interface

The user interface for this example location app will consist of some labels and a button connected to an action method. First, initiate the user interface design process by selecting the *Main.storyboard* file. Once the view has loaded into the Interface Builder editing environment, create a user interface that resembles as closely as possible the view illustrated in Figure 70-1:

Figure 70-1

In the case of the five labels in the right-hand column, which will display location and accuracy data, ensure that the labels are stretched to the right until the blue margin guideline appears. The data will be displayed to multiple levels of decimal points requiring space beyond the default size of the label.

Select the label object to the right of the "Current Latitude" label in the view canvas, display the Assistant Editor panel, and verify that the editor is displaying the contents of the *ViewController.swift* file. Right-click on the same Label object and drag it to a position just below the class declaration line in the Assistant Editor. Release the line and establish an outlet called *latitude* in the resulting connection dialog. Repeat these steps for the remaining labels, connecting them to properties named *longitude, hAccuracy, altitude, vAccuracy* and *distance,* respectively.

Stretch the distance label so that it is the same width until it is approximately half the overall width of the screen, then use the Attributes inspector to configure center alignment. Next, display the Resolve Auto Layout Issues menu and select the *Reset to Suggested Constraints* option under *All Views in View Controller.*

The final step of the user interface design process is to connect the button objects to action methods. Right-click on the *Reset Distance* button object and drag the line to the area immediately beneath the *viewDidLoad* method in the Assistant Editor panel. Release the line and, within the resulting connection dialog, establish an Action method on the *Touch Up Inside* event configured to call a method named *resetDistance*. Repeat this step for the remaining buttons, establishing action connections to methods named *startWhenInUse* and *startAlways,* respectively.

Close the Assistant Editor and add a variable to the ViewController class to store the start location coordinates and the location manager object. Now is also an opportune time to import the CoreLocation framework and to declare the class as implementing the CLLocationManagerDelegate protocol:

```
import UIKit
import CoreLocation

class ViewController: UIViewController, CLLocationManagerDelegate {

    @IBOutlet weak var latitude: UILabel!
    @IBOutlet weak var longitude: UILabel!
    @IBOutlet weak var hAccuracy: UILabel!
    @IBOutlet weak var altitude: UILabel!
    @IBOutlet weak var vAccuracy: UILabel!
    @IBOutlet weak var distance: UILabel!

    var locationManager: CLLocationManager = CLLocationManager()
    var startLocation: CLLocation!
.

.

}
```

70.3 Configuring the CLLocationManager Object

The next task is configuring the instance of the CLLocationManager class and ensuring that the app requests permission from the user to track the device's current location. Since this needs to occur when the view loads, an ideal location is in the view controller's *viewDidLoad* method in the *ViewController.swift* file:

```
override func viewDidLoad() {
    super.viewDidLoad()

    locationManager.desiredAccuracy = kCLLocationAccuracyBest
    locationManager.delegate = self
    startLocation = nil
```

}

The above code changes configure the CLLocationManager object instance to use the "best accuracy" setting. The code then declares the view controller instance as the app delegate for the location manager object.

70.4 Setting up the Usage Description Keys

As explained in the previous chapter, the two mandatory usage description key-value pairs now need to be added to the Information Property List dictionary. To add this entry, select the Location entry at the top of the Project navigator panel and select the Info tab in the main panel. Next, click on the + button contained with the last line of properties in the Custom iOS Target Properties section. Then, select the *Privacy – Location When in Use Usage Description* item from the resulting menu. Once the key has been added, double-click in the corresponding value column and enter the following text:

```
The application uses this information to show you your location
```

On completion of this step, the entry should match that of Figure 70-2:

Figure 70-2

Repeat this step, this time adding a *Privacy - Location Always and When In Use Usage Description* key set to the following string value:

```
Always mode is recommended for this app for improved location tracking
```

On completion of these steps, the usage description keys should appear in the property editor as follows:

> Supported interface orientations (iPad)	◇	(4 items)
Bundle version string (short)	◇	$(MARKETING_VERSION)
Privacy - Location When In Use Usage Description	◇	The application uses this information to show
Privacy - Location Always and When In Use Usage...	◇ ⊕ ⊖	Always mode is recommended for this app fo

Figure 70-3

70.5 Implementing the startWhenInUse Method

This action method will request when in use permission from the user before starting location updates. Locate the method stub in the *ViewController.swift* file and modify it as follows:

```
@IBAction func startWhenInUse(_ sender: Any) {
    locationManager.requestWhenInUseAuthorization()
    locationManager.startUpdatingLocation()
}
```

70.6 Implementing the startAlways Method

The *startAlways* method is intended to demonstrate the process of persuading the user to elevate location tracking to *always* mode after already granting *when in use* permission. In this method, the assumption is made that updates are already running, so the first step is to stop the updates. Once updates are stopped, the permission request is made before updates are restarted:

```
@IBAction func startAlways(_ sender: Any) {
    locationManager.stopUpdatingLocation()
    locationManager.requestAlwaysAuthorization()
    locationManager.startUpdatingLocation()
}
```

70.7 Implementing the resetDistance Method

The button object in the user interface is connected to the *resetDistance* action method, so the next task is to implement that action. All this method needs to do is set the *startLocation* variable to nil:

```
@IBAction func resetDistance(_ sender: Any) {
    startLocation = nil
}
```

70.8 Implementing the App Delegate Methods

When the location manager detects a location change, it calls the *didUpdateLocations* delegate method. Since the view controller was declared as the delegate for the location manager in the *viewDidLoad* method, it is necessary now to implement this method in the *ViewController.swift* file:

```
func locationManager(_ manager: CLLocationManager,
                    didUpdateLocations locations: [CLLocation]) {

    let latestLocation: CLLocation = locations[locations.count - 1]

    latitude.text = String(format: "%.4f",
                            latestLocation.coordinate.latitude)
    longitude.text = String(format: "%.4f",
                            latestLocation.coordinate.longitude)
    hAccuracy.text = String(format: "%.4f",
                                latestLocation.horizontalAccuracy)
    altitude.text = String(format: "%.4f",
                            latestLocation.altitude)
    vAccuracy.text = String(format: "%.4f",
                                latestLocation.verticalAccuracy)

    if startLocation == nil {
        startLocation = latestLocation
    }

    let distanceBetween: CLLocationDistance =
        latestLocation.distance(from: startLocation)

    distance.text = String(format: "%.2f", distanceBetween)
}
```

When the delegate method is called, an array of location objects containing the latest updates is passed, with the last item in the array representing the most recent location information. To begin with, the delegate method extracts the last location object from the array and works through the data contained in the object. In each case, it creates a string containing the extracted value and displays it on the corresponding user interface label.

If this is the first time the method has been called either since the app was launched or the user last pressed the *Reset Distance* button, the *startLocation* variable is set to the current location. The *distance(from:)* method of the location object is then called, passing through the *startLocation* object as an argument to calculate the distance between the two points. The result is then displayed on the distance label in the user interface.

The *didFailWithError* delegate method is called when the location manager instance encounters an error. This method should also, therefore, be implemented:

```
func locationManager(_ manager: CLLocationManager,
                    didFailWithError error: Error) {
    print(error.localizedDescription)
}
```

In this case, the error message is printed to the console. The action taken within this method is largely up to the app developer. The method, for example, might display an alert to notify the user of the error.

70.9 Building and Running the Location App

Select a suitable simulator and click on the run button located in the Xcode project window toolbar. Once the app has launched, click on the *When in Use* button, at which point the request dialog shown in Figure 70-4 will appear:

Figure 70-4

Note that this request uses the *when in use* description key and does not include the option to authorize *always* tracking. Click on the *Allow While Using App* button.

Once permission is granted, the app will begin tracking location information. By default, the iOS Simulator may be configured to have no current location causing the labels to remain unchanged. To simulate a location, select the iOS Simulator *Features -> Location* menu option and select either one of the pre-defined locations or journeys (such as City Bicycle Ride) or *Custom Location...* to enter a specific latitude and longitude. The following figure shows the app running in the iOS Simulator after the *City Run* location has been selected from the menu:

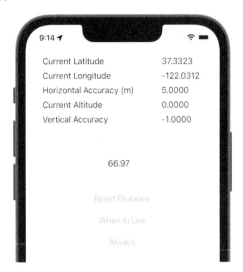

Figure 70-5

One point to note is that the distance data relates to the distance between two points, not the distance traveled. So, for example, if the device accompanies the user on a 10-mile trip that returns to the start location, the distance will be displayed as 0 (since the start and end points are the same).

Next, click on the *Always* button to display the permission request dialog. As shown in Figure 70-6, the request dialog will appear containing the second usage description key and options to retain the when in use setting or switch to *Always* mode.

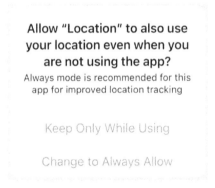

Figure 70-6

Click on the *Change to Always Allow* button and verify that the location data continues to update.

70.10 Adding Continuous Background Location Updates

The next step is to demonstrate continuous background location updates in action. Begin by modifying the *didUpdateLocations* delegate method to print the longitude and latitude value to the Xcode console. This will allow us to verify that updating continues after the app is suspended:

```
func locationManager(_ manager: CLLocationManager,
                    didUpdateLocations locations: [CLLocation]) {
.

.

    distance.text = String(format: "%.2f", distanceBetween)
```

```
    print("Latitude = \(latestLocation.coordinate.latitude)")
    print("Longitude = \(latestLocation.coordinate.longitude)")
}
```

After making this change, run the app and click the *When in Use* button. If necessary, select the *Freeway Drive* option from the *Features -> Location* menu and verify that the latitude and longitude updates appear in the Xcode console panel. Click on the home button (or select the *Device -> Home* menu option) and note that the location updates no longer appear in the console.

Within the *ViewController.swift* file, edit the *startWhenInUse* and *startAlways* methods to enable continuous background updates:

```
@IBAction func startWhenInUse(_ sender: Any) {
    locationManager.requestWhenInUseAuthorization()
    locationManager.startUpdatingLocation()
    locationManager.allowsBackgroundLocationUpdates = true
    locationManager.pausesLocationUpdatesAutomatically = true
}

@IBAction func startAlways(_ sender: Any) {
    locationManager.stopUpdatingLocation()
    locationManager.requestAlwaysAuthorization()
    locationManager.startUpdatingLocation()
    locationManager.allowsBackgroundLocationUpdates = true
    locationManager.pausesLocationUpdatesAutomatically = true
}
```

The project will also need to be configured to enable background location updates. First, select the Location target at the top of the project navigator panel, followed by the *Signing & Capabilities* tab in the main panel. Next, click the "+ Capability" button to display the dialog shown in Figure 70-7. Finally, enter "back" into the filter bar, select the result, and press the keyboard enter key to add the capability to the project:

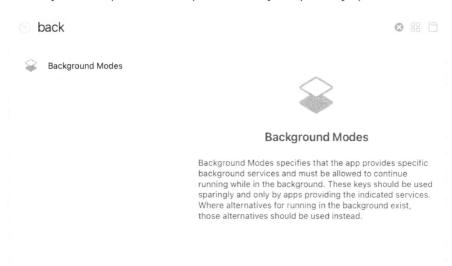

Figure 70-7

On returning to the capabilities screen, enable the checkbox for the *Location updates* in the Background modes section:

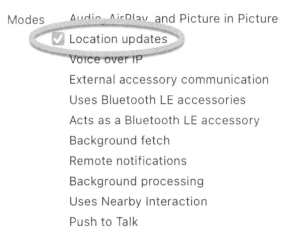

Figure 70-8

Re-run the app, and click on the *Always* button, followed by the Home button. Note that the location updates continue to appear in the Xcode console this time.

70.11 Summary

This chapter has made practical use of the features of the Core Location framework. Topics covered include the configuration of an app project to support core location updates, the differences between *always* and *when in use* location authorizations, and the code necessary to initiate and handle location update events. The chapter also included a demonstration of the use of continuous background location updates.

71. Working with Maps on iOS 17 with MapKit and the MKMapView Class

In the preceding chapters, we spent some time looking at handling raw geographical location information in the form of longitude, latitude, and altitude data. The next step is to learn about the presentation of location information to the user through maps and satellite images. Therefore, this chapter aims to provide an overview of the steps necessary to present the app user with location, map, and satellite imagery using the MapKit Framework and, in particular, the MKMapView class. This example app will be extended in the next chapters to use the Map Kit local search and directions features.

71.1 About the MapKit Framework

The MapKit Framework is based on the Apple Maps data and APIs and provides iOS developers with a simple mechanism for integrating detailed and interactive mapping capabilities into any app.

The core element of the MapKit Framework from the point of view of the app developer is the MKMapView class. This class is a subclass of UIView and provides a canvas onto which map and satellite information may be presented to the user. Information may be presented in map, satellite, or hybrid (whereby the map is superimposed onto the satellite image) form. The displayed geographical region may be changed manually by the user via a process of pinching, stretching, and panning gestures or programmatically from within the app code via method calls and property manipulation on the MkMapView instance. The device's current location may also be displayed and tracked on the map view.

The MapKit Framework also includes support for adding annotations to a map. This takes the form of a pin or custom image, title, and subview that may be used to mark specific locations on a map. Alternatively, the annotation can take the form of a custom view controller.

Implementation of the MKMapViewDelegate protocol allows an app to receive notifications of events relating to the map view, such as a change in either the user's location or region of the map displayed or the failure of the device to identify the user's current location or to download map data.

71.2 Understanding Map Regions

The area of the map that is currently displayed to the user is referred to as the *region*. This is defined in terms of a *center location* (declared by longitude and latitude) and the span of the surrounding area to be displayed. Adjusting the span has the effect of zooming in and out of the map relative to the specified center location. The region's span may be specified using either distance (in meters) or coordinate-based degrees. When using degrees, one degree of latitude is equivalent to 111 km. Latitude, however, varies depending on the longitudinal distance from the equator. Given this complexity, the map view tutorial in this chapter will declare the span in terms of distance.

71.3 Getting Transit ETA Information

A MapKit feature introduced in iOS 9 allows the departure and arrival times and estimated travel duration to a destination using public transit to be obtained from within an iOS app. This involves the use of MKDirections. Request object configured for travel by transit and initialized with start and end locations combined with a call to the *calculateETA(completionHandler:)* method of an appropriately configured MKDirections instance. The following method, for example, outputs the estimated arrival time for a journey by transit from the Empire State Building in New York to JFK Airport:

```
func getTransitETA() {
    let request = MKDirections.Request()
    let source = MKMapItem(placemark:
      MKPlacemark(coordinate:CLLocationCoordinate2D(latitude: 40.748384,
            longitude: -73.985479), addressDictionary: nil))
    source.name = "Empire State Building"
    request.source = source

    let destination = MKMapItem(placemark:
      MKPlacemark(coordinate:CLLocationCoordinate2D(latitude: 40.643351,
            longitude: -73.788969), addressDictionary: nil))
    destination.name = "JFK Airport"
    request.destination = destination

    request.transportType = MKDirectionsTransportType.transit

    let directions = MKDirections(request: request)
    directions.calculateETA {
        (response, error) -> Void in
        if error == nil {
            if let estimate = response {
                print("Travel time \(estimate.expectedTravelTime / 60)")
                print("Departing at \(estimate.expectedDepartureDate)")
                print("Arriving at \(estimate.expectedArrivalDate)")
            }
        }
    }
}
```

71.4 About the MKMapView Tutorial

This tutorial aims to develop an iOS app to display a map with a marker indicating the user's current location. In addition, buttons in a navigation bar are provided to allow the user to zoom in on the current location and toggle between map and satellite views. Through the implementation of the MKMapViewDelegate protocol, the map will update as the user's location changes so that the current location marker is always the center point of the displayed map region.

71.5 Creating the Map Project

Begin by launching Xcode and creating a new Xcode project using the iOS *App* template with the Swift and Storyboard options selected, entering *MapSample* as the product name.

71.6 Adding the Navigation Controller

The later stages of this tutorial will require the services of a navigation controller. Since the presence of the navigation bar will have implications for the layout of the user interface of the main view, it makes sense to add the controller now. Select the *Main.storyboard* file from the project navigator panel followed by the view controller view so that it highlights in blue and use the *Editor -> Embed In -> Navigation Controller* menu option to embed a controller into the storyboard as illustrated in Figure 71-1:

Figure 71-1

71.7 Creating the MKMapView Instance and Toolbar

The next step is to create an instance of the MKMapView class we will be using in our app and to add a toolbar instance to the user interface. Remaining in the *Main.storyboard* file, drag a *Toolbar* from the Library panel and place it at the bottom of the view canvas.

Next, drag and drop a Map Kit View object onto the canvas and resize and position it so that it takes up the remaining space in the view above the toolbar and below the navigation bar. By default, the Interface Builder tool will have added a single *Bar Button Item* to the new toolbar. However, two buttons will be required for this example, so drag and drop a second Bar Button Item from the Library panel onto the toolbar. Double-click on the toolbar button items and change the text to "Zoom" and "Type," respectively:

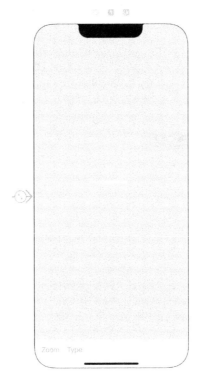

Figure 71-2

Select the MKMapView object in the scene and use the Auto Layout *Add New Constraints* menu in the lower right-hand corner of the Interface Builder panel to configure *Spacing to nearest neighbor* constraints of 0 on all four sides of the view with the *Constrain to margins* option switched off. Once the four constraints have been added to the MKMapView object, repeat these steps with the Toolbar view selected, this time with the bottom value set to 21.

Select the MKMapView object in the view canvas, display the Assistant Editor and verify that the editor is displaying the contents of the *ViewController.swift* file. Right-click on the MKMapView object and drag it to a position below the class declaration line in the Assistant Editor. Release the line, and in the resulting connection dialog, establish an outlet connection named *mapView*.

Click on the "Zoom" button to select it (note that to select a toolbar button item, it may be necessary to click on it twice since the first click selects the toolbar parent). With the button item selected, right-click on the button object and drag the line to the area immediately beneath the *viewDidLoad* method in the Assistant Editor panel. Release the line and, within the resulting connection dialog, establish an Action method on the *Touch Up Inside* event configured to call a method named *zoomIn*. Repeat this step to connect the "Type" button to a method named *changeMapType*.

Select the *ViewController.swift* file from the project navigator panel and verify that the outlets and actions have been set up correctly. Also, take this opportunity to import the MapKit framework and declare the class as implementing the MKMapViewDelegate protocol:

```
import UIKit
import MapKit

class ViewController: UIViewController, MKMapViewDelegate {
```

```
@IBOutlet weak var mapView: MKMapView!

override func viewDidLoad() {
    super.viewDidLoad()
}

@IBAction func zoomIn(_ sender: Any) {
}


@IBAction func changeMapType(_ sender: Any) {
}
.
.
.
}
```

Perform a test run of the app's progress by clicking on the run button in the Xcode toolbar. The app should run on the iOS simulator or device as illustrated in Figure 71-3:

Figure 71-3

71.8 Obtaining Location Information Permission

The next task is to request permission from the user to track the device's current location. Since this needs to occur when the app loads, an ideal location is in the app delegate *didFinishLaunchingWithOptions* method in the *AppDelegate.swift* file:

```
import UIKit
import CoreLocation

@main
class AppDelegate: UIResponder, UIApplicationDelegate {

    var locationManager: CLLocationManager?

    func application(_ application: UIApplication, didFinishLaunchingWithOptions
        launchOptions: [UIApplication.LaunchOptionsKey: Any]?) -> Bool {

        locationManager = CLLocationManager()
        locationManager?.requestWhenInUseAuthorization()

        return true
    }
    .
    .
}
```

71.9 Setting up the Usage Description Keys

The above code changes included a method call to request permission from the user to track location information when the app is running in the foreground. This method call must be accompanied by the usage description strings, which need to be added to the project's *Info.plist* file. To add this entry, select the *Location* entry at the top of the Project navigator panel and, in the main panel, select the Info tab. Next, click on the + button contained with the last line of properties in the Custom iOS Target Properties section. Then, from the resulting menu, select the *Privacy – Location When in Use Usage Description* item. Once the key has been added, double-click in the corresponding value column and enter the following text:

```
This information is required to show your current location
```

Repeat this step, this time adding a *Privacy - Location Always and When In Use Usage Description* key set to the following string value:

```
Always mode is recommended for this app for improved location tracking
```

71.10 Configuring the Map View

By default, the Map View does not indicate the user's current location. By setting the *showsUserLocation* property of the MKMapView class, the map is instructed to display a representation of the current location on the map in the form of a blue marker. Before user location information can be obtained, it is first necessary to seek permission from the user. To achieve these goals, select the *ViewController.swift* file and locate and modify the *viewDidLoad* method as follows:

```
override func viewDidLoad() {
    super.viewDidLoad()
    mapView.showsUserLocation = true
```

```
}
```

71.11 Changing the MapView Region

When the user taps the Zoom button, the map view region needs to be changed so that the user's current location is set as the central location and the region span needs to be changed to 2000 meters (analogous to zooming in to the map region). The code to implement this belongs in the *zoomIn* method, which now needs to be implemented in the *ViewController.swift* file:

```
@IBAction func zoomIn(_ sender: Any) {

    if let userLocation = mapView.userLocation.location?.coordinate {

        let region = MKCoordinateRegion(
                center: userLocation, latitudinalMeters: 2000,
                                longitudinalMeters: 2000)

        mapView.setRegion(region, animated: true)
    }
}
```

This method performs some very simple operations to achieve the desired effect in the mapView object. First, the user's current location coordinates are ascertained by accessing the *userLocation* property of the map view object, which, in turn, contains the user's coordinates. Next, the *MKCoordinateRegionMakeWithDistance* function is called to generate an MKCoordinateRegion object consisting of the user's location coordinates and a span that stretches 2000 meters to the North and South of the current location. Finally, this region object is passed through to the *setRegion* method of the mapView object.

Now that the Zoom functionality has been implemented, it is time to configure the map type switching feature of the app.

71.12 Changing the Map Type

The object's mapType property controls the map type of a map view. Supported values for this property are MKMapType.standard, MKMapType.mutedStandard, MKMapType.satellite MKMapType.hybrid, MKMapType.satelliteFlyover, and MKMapType.hybridFlyover. The map will switch between standard and satellite modes for this example app. Within the *ViewController.swift* file, modify the *changeMapType* action method connected to the Type button as follows:

```
@IBAction func changeMapType(_ sender: Any) {
    if mapView.mapType == MKMapType.standard {
        mapView.mapType = MKMapType.satellite
    } else {
        mapView.mapType = MKMapType.standard
    }
}
```

This simple method toggles between the two map types when the user taps the button.

71.13 Testing the MapView App

Now that more functionality has been implemented, it is a good time to build and run the app again, so click on the Xcode *Run* button to load it into the iOS Simulator. Once the app has loaded, a blue dot should appear over Northern California. Since the app is running in the simulator environment, the location information is simulated to match either the coordinates of Apple's headquarters in Cupertino, CA, or another simulated location depending on the current setting of the *Debug -> Location* menu.

Select the Type button to display the satellite view and then zoom in to get a better look at the region:

Figure 71-4

Load the app onto a physical iOS device to get real location information.

71.14 Updating the Map View based on User Movement

Assuming that you installed the app on a physical iOS device and went somewhere with the device in your possession (or used one of the debug location settings that simulated movement), you may have noticed that the map did not update as your location changed and that the blue dot marking your current location eventually went off the screen (also assuming, of course, that you had zoomed in to a significant degree).

To configure the app so the map automatically tracks the user's movements, the first step is to ensure the app is notified when the location changes. At the start of this tutorial, the view controller was declared as conforming to the MKMapViewDelegate delegate protocol. One method that comprises this protocol is the *mapView(didUpdate userLocation:)* method. When implemented, this method is called by the map view object whenever the location of the device changes. We must, therefore, first specify that the MapSampleViewController class is the delegate for the mapView object, which can be performed by adding the following line to the *viewDidLoad* method located in the *ViewController.swift* file:

```
mapView.delegate = self
```

The next task involves the implementation of the *mapView(didUpdate userLocation:)* method in the

ViewController.swift file:

```
func mapView(_ mapView: MKMapView, didUpdate
        userLocation: MKUserLocation) {
    mapView.centerCoordinate = userLocation.location!.coordinate
}
```

The delegate method is passed as an argument to an MKUserLocation object containing the current location coordinates of the user. This value is assigned to the center coordinate property of the mapView object such that the current location remains at the region's center. When the app is installed and run on a device, the current location will no longer move outside the displayed region as the device location changes. To experience this effect within the simulator, select the *Features -> Location -> Freeway Drive* menu option and then select the Zoom button in the user interface.

71.15 Summary

This chapter has demonstrated the basics of using the MKMapView class to display map-based information to the user within an iOS 17 app. The example created in the chapter also highlighted the steps involved in zooming into a map region, changing the map display type, and configuring a map to track the user's current location.

The next chapter will explore the use of the local search feature of the MapKit Framework before extending the example app to mark all the locations of a specified business type on the map.

72. Working with MapKit Local Search in iOS 17

This chapter will explore using the iOS MapKit MKLocalSearchRequest class to search for map locations within an iOS app. The example app created in the chapter entitled *"Working with Maps on iOS 17 with MapKit and the MKMapView Class"* will then be extended to demonstrate local search in action.

72.1 An Overview of iOS Local Search

Local search is implemented using the MKLocalSearch class. The purpose of this class is to allow users to search for map locations using natural language strings. Once the search has been completed, the class returns a list of locations within a specified region that match the search string. For example, a search for "Pizza" will return a list of locations for any pizza restaurants within a specified area. Search requests are encapsulated in instances of the MKLocalSearchRequest class, and results are returned within an MKLocalSearchResponse object which, in turn, contains an MKMapItem object for each matching location.

Local searches are performed asynchronously, and a completion handler is called when the search is complete. It is also important to note that the search is performed remotely on Apple's servers instead of locally on the device. Local search is, therefore, only available when the device has an active internet connection and can communicate with the search server.

The following code fragment, for example, searches for pizza locations within the currently displayed region of an MKMapView instance named *mapView*. Having performed the search, the code iterates through the results and outputs the name and phone number of each matching location to the console:

```
let request = MKLocalSearchRequest()
request.naturalLanguageQuery = "Pizza"
request.region = mapView.region

let search = MKLocalSearch(request: request)

    search.start(completionHandler: {(response, error) in

        if error != nil {
            print("Error occurred in search:
                    \(error!.localizedDescription)")
        } else if response!.mapItems.count == 0 {
            print("No matches found")
        } else {
            print("Matches found")

            for item in response!.mapItems {
                print("Name = \(item.name)")
                print("Phone = \(item.phoneNumber)")
```

```
            }
        }
    })
```

The above code begins by creating an MKLocalSearchRequest request instance initialized with the search string (in this case, "Pizza"). The region of the request is then set to the currently displayed region of the map view instance.

```
let request = MKLocalSearchRequest()
request.naturalLanguageQuery = "Pizza"
request.region = mapView.region
```

An MKLocalSearch instance is then created and initialized with a reference to the search request instance. The search is then initiated via a call to the object's *start(completionHandler:)* method.

```
search.start(completionHandler: {(response, error) in
```

The code in the completion handler checks the response to ensure that matches were found and then accesses the *mapItems* property of the response, which contains an array of mapItem instances for the matching locations. The *name* and *phoneNumber* properties of each mapItem instance are then displayed in the console:

```
if error != nil {
    print("Error occurred in search: \(error!.localizedDescription)")
} else if response!.mapItems.count == 0 {
    print("No matches found")
} else {
    print("Matches found")

    for item in response!.mapItems {
        print("Name = \(item.name)")
        print("Phone = \(item.phoneNumber)")
    }
  }
})
```

72.2 Adding Local Search to the MapSample App

The remainder of this chapter will extend the MapSample app so the user can perform a local search. The first step in this process involves adding a text field to the first storyboard scene. Begin by launching Xcode and opening the MapSample project created in the previous chapter.

72.3 Adding the Local Search Text Field

With the project loaded into Xcode, select the *Main.storyboard* file and modify the user interface to add a Text Field object to the user interface layout (reducing the height of the map view object accordingly to make room for the new field). With the new Text Field selected, display the Attributes Inspector and enter *Local Search* into the Placeholder property field. When completed, the layout should resemble that of Figure 72-1:

Figure 72-1

Select the Map Sample view controller by clicking on the toolbar at the top of the scene to highlight the scene in blue. Next, select the *Resolve Auto Layout Issues* menu from the toolbar in the lower right-hand corner of the storyboard canvas and select the *Reset to Suggested Constraints* menu option located beneath *All Views in View Controller*.

When the user touches the text field, the keyboard will appear. By default, this will display a "Return" key. However, a "Search" key would be more appropriate for this app. To make this modification, select the new Text Field object, display the Attributes Inspector, and change the *Return Key* setting from *Default* to *Search*.

Next, display the Assistant Editor and make sure that it displays the content of the *ViewController.swift* file. Right-click on the Text Field object, drag the resulting line to the Assistant Editor panel and establish an outlet named *searchText*.

Repeat the above step, setting up an Action for the Text Field to call a method named *textFieldReturn* for the *Did End on Exit* event. Be sure to set the Type menu to *UITextField,* as shown in Figure 72-2, before clicking on the *Connect* button:

Connection	Action
Object	View Controller
Name	textFieldReturn
Type	UITextField
Event	Did End On Exit
Arguments	Sender

Cancel   Connect

Figure 72-2

The *textFieldReturn* method will be required to perform three tasks when triggered. In the first instance, it will be required to hide the keyboard from view. When matches are found for the search results, an annotation for each location will be added to the map. The second task to be performed by this method is to remove any annotations created due to the previous search.

Finally, the *textFieldReturn* method will initiate the search using the user's string entered into the text field. Select the *ViewController.swift* file, locate the template *textFieldReturn* method, and implement it so that it reads as follows:

```
@IBAction func textFieldReturn(_ sender: UITextField) {
    _ = sender.resignFirstResponder()
    mapView.removeAnnotations(mapView.annotations)
    self.performSearch()
}
```

72.4 Performing the Local Search

The next task is to write the code to perform the search. When the user touches the keyboard *Search* key, the above *textFieldReturn* method is called, which, in turn, has been written to make a call to a method named *performSearch*. Remaining within the *ViewController.swift* file, this method may now be implemented as follows:

```
func performSearch() {

    matchingItems.removeAll()
    let request = MKLocalSearch.Request()
    request.naturalLanguageQuery = searchText.text
    request.region = mapView.region

    let search = MKLocalSearch(request: request)

    search.start(completionHandler: {(response, error) in

        if let results = response {

            if let err = error {
                print("Error occurred in search: \(err.localizedDescription)")
            } else if results.mapItems.count == 0 {
                print("No matches found")
            } else {
```

```
            print("Matches found")

            for item in results.mapItems {
                print("Name = \(item.name ?? "No match")")
                print("Phone = \(item.phoneNumber ?? "No Match")")

                self.matchingItems.append(item as MKMapItem)
                print("Matching items = \(self.matchingItems.count)")

                let annotation = MKPointAnnotation()
                annotation.coordinate = item.placemark.coordinate
                annotation.title = item.name
                self.mapView.addAnnotation(annotation)
            }
        }
    }
    })
}
```

Next, edit the *ViewController.swift* file to add the declaration for the *matchingItems* array referenced in the above method. This array is used to store the current search matches and will be used later in the tutorial:

```
import UIKit
import MapKit

class ViewController: UIViewController, MKMapViewDelegate {

    @IBOutlet weak var mapView: MKMapView!
    @IBOutlet weak var searchText: UITextField!
    var matchingItems: [MKMapItem] = [MKMapItem]()
.
.
```

The code in the *performSearch* method is largely the same as that outlined earlier in the chapter, the major difference being the addition of code to add an annotation to the map for each matching location:

```
let annotation = MKPointAnnotation()
annotation.coordinate = item.placemark.coordinate
annotation.title = item.name
self.mapView.addAnnotation(annotation)
```

Annotations are represented by instances of the MKPointAnnotation class and are, by default, represented by red pin markers on the map view (though custom icons may be specified). The coordinates of each match are obtained by accessing the placemark instance within each item. The annotation title is also set in the above code using the item's *name* property.

72.5 Testing the App

Compile and run the app on an iOS device and, once running, select the zoom button before entering the name of a type of business into the local search field, such as "pizza," "library," or "coffee." Next, touch the keyboard "Search" button and, assuming such businesses exist within the currently displayed map region, an annotation marker will appear for each matching location (Figure 72-3):

Figure 72-3

Local searches are not limited to business locations. For example, it can also be used as an alternative to geocoding for finding local addresses.

72.6 Customized Annotation Markers

By default, the annotation markers appear with a red background and a white push-pin icon (referred to as the *glyph*). To change the appearance of the annotations, the first step is to implement the *mapView(_:viewFor:)* delegate method within the *ViewController.swift* file. When implemented, this method will be called each time an annotation is added to the map. The method is passed the MKAnnotation object to be added and needs to return an MKMarkerAnnotationView object configured with appropriate settings ready to be displayed on the map. In the same way that the UITableView class reuses table cells, the MapView class also maintains a queue of MKMarkerAnnotationView objects ready to be used. This dramatically increases map performance when working with large volumes of annotations.

Within the *ViewController.swift* file, implement a basic form of this method as follows:

```
func mapView(_ mapView: MKMapView, viewFor annotation: MKAnnotation)
    -> MKAnnotationView? {

    let identifier = "marker"
    var view: MKMarkerAnnotationView
```

```
        if let dequeuedView = mapView.dequeueReusableAnnotationView(
                          withIdentifier: identifier)
                             as? MKMarkerAnnotationView {
        dequeuedView.annotation = annotation
        view = dequeuedView
    } else {
        view =
            MKMarkerAnnotationView(annotation: annotation,
              reuseIdentifier: identifier)
    }
    return view
}
```

The method begins by specifying an identifier for the annotation type. For example, if a map displays different annotation categories, each category will need a unique identifier. Next, the code checks to see if an existing annotation view with the specified identifier can be reused. If one is available, it is returned and displayed on the map. If no reusable annotation views are available, a new one consisting of the annotation object passed to the method and with the identifier string is created.

Run the app now, zoom in on the current location, and perform a search that will result in annotations appearing. Since no customizations have been made to the MKMarkerAnnotationView object, the location markers appear as before.

Modify the *mapView(_:viewFor:)* method as follows to change the color of the marker and to display text instead of the glyph icon:

```
func mapView(_ mapView: MKMapView, viewFor annotation: MKAnnotation)
  -> MKAnnotationView? {
.
.
    } else {
        view = MKMarkerAnnotationView(annotation: annotation,
            reuseIdentifier: identifier)
        view.markerTintColor = UIColor.blue
        view.glyphText = "Here"
    }
    return view
}
```

When the app is now tested, the markers appear with a blue background and display text which reads "Here" as shown in Figure 72-4:

Figure 72-4

A different image may also replace the default glyph icon. Ideally, two images should be assigned, one sized at 20x20px to be displayed on the standard marker and a larger one (40x40px) to be displayed when the marker is selected. To try this, open a Finder window and navigate to the *map_glyphs* folder of the sample code available from the following URL:

https://www.payloadbooks.com/product/ios17xcode/

This folder contains two image files named *small-business-20.png* and *small-business-40.png*. Within Xcode, select the *Assets* entry in the project navigator panel and drag and drop the two image files from the Finder window onto the asset panel as indicated in Figure 72-5:

Figure 72-5

With the glyphs added, modify the code in the *mapView(_:viewFor:)* method to use these images instead of the text:

.

.

```
} else {
    view = MKMarkerAnnotationView(annotation: annotation,
                        reuseIdentifier: identifier)
    view.markerTintColor = UIColor.blue
```

```
view.glyphText = "Here"
    view.glyphImage = UIImage(named: "small-business-20")
    view.selectedGlyphImage = UIImage(named: "small-business-40")
}
.
.
```

The markers will now display the smaller glyph when a search is performed within the app. Selecting a marker on the map will display the larger glyph image:

Figure 72-6

Another option for customizing annotation markers involves adding callout information, which appears when a marker is selected within the app. Modify the code once again, this time adding code to add a callout to each marker:

```
} else {
    view = MKMarkerAnnotationView(annotation: annotation,
            reuseIdentifier: identifier)
    view.markerTintColor = UIColor.blue
    view.glyphImage = UIImage(named: "small-business-20")
    view.selectedGlyphImage = UIImage(named: "small-business-40")
    view.canShowCallout = true
    view.calloutOffset = CGPoint(x: -5, y: 5)
    view.rightCalloutAccessoryView = UIButton(type: .detailDisclosure)
}
```

The new code begins by indicating that the marker can display a callout before specifying the position of the callout in relation to the corresponding marker. The final line of code declares a view to appear to the left of the callout text, in this case, a UIButton view configured to display the standard information icon. Since UIButton is derived from UIControl, the app can receive notifications of the button being tapped by implementing the *mapView(_: calloutAccessoryControlTapped:)* delegate method. The following example implementation of this method simply outputs a message to the console when the button is tapped:

```
func mapView(_: MKMapView, annotationView:
    MKAnnotationView, calloutAccessoryControlTapped: UIControl) {
        print("Control tapped")
```

}

Run the app again, zoom in, and perform a business search. When the result appears, select one of the annotations and note that the callout appears as is the case in Figure 72-7:

Figure 72-7

Click the information button to verify that the message appears in the console window.

72.7 Annotation Marker Clustering

When too many annotations appear close together on a map, it can be difficult to identify one marker from another without zooming into the area so that the markers move apart. MapKit resolves this issue by providing support for the clustering of annotation markers. Clustering is enabled by assigning cluster identifiers to the MKMarkerAnnotationView objects. When a group of annotations belonging to the same cluster is grouped too closely, a single marker appears, displaying the number of annotations in the cluster.

To see clusters in action, modify the *mapView(_:viewFor:)* delegate method one last time to assign a cluster identifier to each annotation marker as follows:

```
        .
        .
        .
} else {
    view = MKMarkerAnnotationView(annotation: annotation,
                                  reuseIdentifier: identifier)
    view.clusteringIdentifier = "myCluster"
    view.markerTintColor = UIColor.blue
        .
        .
        .
```

After building and relaunching the app, enter a search term without first zooming into the map. Because the map is zoomed out, the markers should be too close together to display, causing the cluster count (Figure 72-8) to appear instead:

Figure 72-8

72.8 Summary

The iOS MapKit Local Search feature allows map searches to be performed using free-form natural language strings. Once initiated, a local search will return a response containing map item objects for matching locations within a specified map region.

In this chapter, the MapSample app was extended to allow the user to perform local searches, use and customize annotations to mark matching locations on the map view, and marker clustering.

In the next chapter, the example will be further extended to cover the use of the Map Kit directions API to generate turn-by-turn directions and draw the corresponding route on a map view.

73. Using MKDirections to get iOS 17 Map Directions and Routes

This chapter will explore using the MapKit MKDirections class to obtain directions and route information from within an iOS app. Having covered the basics, the MapSample tutorial app will be extended to use these features to draw routes on a map view and display turn-by-turn driving directions.

73.1 An Overview of MKDirections

The MKDirections class was introduced into iOS as part of the iOS 7 SDK and generates directions from one geographical location to another. The start and destination points for the journey are passed to an instance of the MKDirections class in the form of MKMapItem objects contained within an MKDirections.Request instance. In addition to storing the start and end points, the MKDirections.Request class also provides several properties that may be used to configure the request, such as indicating whether alternate route suggestions are required and specifying whether the directions should be for driving or walking.

Once directions have been requested, the MKDirections class contacts Apple's servers and awaits a response. Upon receiving a response, a completion handler is called and passed the response as an MKDirections.Response object. Depending on whether or not alternate routes were requested (and assuming directions were found for the route), this object will contain one or more MKRoute objects. Each MKRoute object contains the distance, expected travel time, advisory notes, and an MKPolyline object that can be used to draw the route on a map view. In addition, each MKRoute object contains an array of MKRouteStep objects, each containing information such as the text description of a turn-by-turn step in the route and the coordinates at which the step is to be performed. In addition, each MKRouteStep object contains a polyline object for that step and the estimated distance and travel time.

The following code fragment demonstrates an example implementation of a directions request between the user's current location and a destination location represented by an MKMapItem object named *destination*:

```
let request = MKDirections.Request()
request.source = MKMapItem.forCurrentLocation()
request.destination = destination
request.requestsAlternateRoutes = false

let directions = MKDirections(request: request)

directions.calculate(completionHandler: {(response, error) in

    if error != nil {
        print("Error getting directions")
    } else {
        self.showRoute(response)
    }
})
```

The resulting response can subsequently be used to draw the routes on a map view using the following code:

```
func showRoute(_ response: MKDirections.Response) {

    for route in response.routes {

        routeMap.add(route.polyline,
                level: MKOverlayLevel.aboveRoads)
        for step in route.steps {
            print(step.instructions)
        }
    }
}
```

The above code iterates through the MKRoute objects in the response and adds the polyline for each route alternate as a layer on a map view. In this instance, the overlay is configured to appear above the road names on the map.

Although the layer is added to the map view in the above code, nothing will be drawn until the *rendererFor overlay* delegate method is implemented. This method creates an instance of the MKPolylineRenderer class and then sets properties such as the line color and width:

```
func mapView(_ mapView: MKMapView, rendererFor
        overlay: MKOverlay) -> MKOverlayRenderer {

    let renderer = MKPolylineRenderer(overlay: overlay)
    renderer.strokeColor = UIColor.blue
    renderer.lineWidth = 5.0
    return renderer
}
```

Note that this method will only be called if the class it resides in is declared as the delegate for the map view object. For example:

```
routeMap.delegate = self
```

Finally, the turn-by-turn directions for each step in the route can be accessed as follows:

```
for step in route.steps {
    print(step.instructions)
}
```

The above code outputs the text instructions for each step of the route. As previously discussed, additional information may be extracted from the MKRouteStep objects as required by the app.

With the basics of directions and routes in iOS covered, the MapSample app can be extended to implement some of this theory.

73.2 Adding Directions and Routes to the MapSample App

The MapSample app will now be modified to include a *Details* button in the toolbar of the first scene. When selected, this button will display a table view listing all locations' names and phone numbers matching the most recent local search operation. Selecting a location from the list will display another scene containing a map displaying the route from the user's current location to the selected destination.

73.3 Adding the New Classes to the Project

Load the MapSample app project into Xcode and add a new class to represent the view controller for the table view. To achieve this, select the *File -> New -> File...* menu option and create a new iOS Cocoa Touch Class file named *ResultsTableViewController* subclassed from *UITableViewController* with the *Also create XIB file* option disabled.

Since the table view will also need a class to represent the table cells, add another new class to the project named *ResultsTableCell*, subclassing from the UITableViewCell class.

Repeat the above steps to add a third class named *RouteViewController* subclassed from UIViewController with the *Also create XIB file* option disabled.

73.4 Configuring the Results Table View

Select the *Main.storyboard* file and drag and drop a Table View Controller object from the Library panel so that it is positioned to the right of the existing View Controller scene in the storyboard canvas (Figure 73-1):

Figure 73-1

With the new controller selected, display the Identity Inspector and change the class from *UITableViewController* to *ResultsTableViewController*.

Select the prototype cell at the top of the table view and change the class setting from *UITableViewCell* to *ResultsTableCell*. Then, switch to the Attributes Inspector with the table cell still selected and set the *Identifier* property to *resultCell*.

Drag two Label objects onto the prototype cell and position them as outlined in Figure 73-2, stretching them to extend to fill the cell's width.

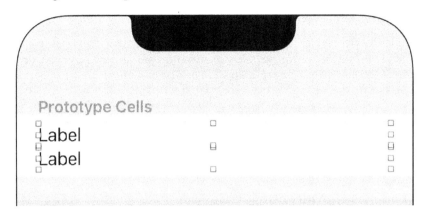

Figure 73-2

Shift-Click on the two Label views so that both are selected, display the Auto Layout *Resolve Auto Layout Issues* menu, and select the *Reset to Suggested Constraints* option listed under *Selected Views*.

Display the Assistant Editor, make sure that it displays the *ResultsTableCell.swift* file, and then establish outlets from the two labels named *nameLabel* and *phoneLabel,* respectively.

Next, edit the *ResultsTableViewController.swift* file and modify it to import the MapKit Framework and declare an array into which will be placed the MKMapItem objects representing the local search results:

```
import UIKit
import MapKit


class ResultsTableViewController: UITableViewController {

    var mapItems: [MKMapItem]?
.
.
.
}
```

Next, edit the file to modify the data source and delegate methods so that the table is populated with the location information when displayed (removing the #warning lines during the editing process). Note that the comment markers (/* and */) will need to be removed from around the *tableView(_:cellForRowAt:)* method:

```
override func numberOfSections(in tableView: UITableView) -> Int {
    return 1
}


override func tableView(_ tableView: UITableView, numberOfRowsInSection section:
Int) -> Int {
    return mapItems?.count ?? 0
}



override func tableView(_ tableView: UITableView, cellForRowAt indexPath:
IndexPath) -> UITableViewCell {
    let cell = tableView.dequeueReusableCell(
```

```
                withIdentifier: "resultCell", for: indexPath) as! ResultsTableCell

    // Configure the cell...
    let row = indexPath.row

    if let item = mapItems?[row] {
        cell.nameLabel.text = item.name
        cell.phoneLabel.text = item.phoneNumber
    }
    return cell
}
```

With the results table view configured, the next step is to add a segue from the first scene to this scene.

73.5 Implementing the Result Table View Segue

Select the *Main.storyboard* file and drag an additional Bar Button Item from the Library panel to the toolbar in the Map Sample View Controller scene. Double-click on this new button and change the text to *Details*:

Figure 73-3

Click on the Details button to select it (it may be necessary to click twice since the first click will select the Toolbar). Then, establish a segue by Clicking on the Details button, dragging to the Results Table View Controller, and selecting *Show* from the *Action Segue* menu.

When the segue is triggered, the *mapItems* property of the ResultsTableViewController instance needs to be updated with the array of locations created by the local search. This can be performed in the *prepare(for segue:)* method, which needs to be implemented in the *ViewController.swift* file as follows:

```
override func prepare(for segue: UIStoryboardSegue, sender: Any?) {

    let destination = segue.destination as!
                  ResultsTableViewController

    destination.mapItems = self.matchingItems
}
```

With the Results scene complete, compile and run the app on a device or simulator. Perform a search for a business type that returns valid results before selecting the Details toolbar button. The results table should subsequently appear (Figure 73-4), listing the names and phone numbers for the matching locations:

Figure 73-4

73.6 Adding the Route Scene

The last task is to display a second map view and draw the route from the user's current location to the location selected from the results table. The class for this scene (RouteViewController) was added earlier in the chapter, so the next step is to add a scene to the storyboard and associate it with this class.

Begin by selecting the *Main.storyboard* file and dragging a View Controller item from the Library panel to position it to the right of the Results Table View Controller scene (Figure 73-5). With the new view controller scene selected (so that it appears with a blue border), display the Identity Inspector and change the class from *UIViewController* to *RouteViewController*.

Figure 73-5

Drag and drop a MapKit View object into the new view controller scene and position it to occupy the entire view. Then, using the Auto Layout *Add New Constraints* menu, set *Spacing to nearest neighbor* constraints of 0 on all four sides of the view with the *Constrain to margins* option switched off.

Display the Assistant Editor, make sure it displays the content of the *RouteViewController.swift* file, and then establish an outlet from the map view instance named *routeMap*. Then, remaining in the *RouteViewController.swift* file, add an import directive to the MapKit framework, a property into which will be stored a reference to the destination map item, and a declaration that this class implements the MKMapViewDelegate protocol. With these changes implemented, the file should read as follows:

```
import UIKit
import MapKit


class RouteViewController: UIViewController {

    var destination: MKMapItem?
.
.
}
```

Now that the route scene has been added, it is time to add some code to it to establish the current location and generate and draw the route on the map.

73.7 Identifying the User's Current Location

Remaining within the *RouteViewController.swift* file, modify the *viewDidLoad* method to display the user's current location in the map view and set this class as the delegate for the map view:

```
override func viewDidLoad() {
    super.viewDidLoad()
    routeMap.delegate = self
    routeMap.showsUserLocation = true
}
```

The app will need to change the displayed map view region to be centered on the user's current location. One way to obtain this information would be to access the *userLocation* property of the MapView instance. The problem with this approach is that it is impossible to know when the map object calculates the current location. This exposes the app to the risk that an attempt to set the region will be made before the location information has been identified. To avoid this problem, the *requestLocation* method of a CLLocationManager instance will instead be used. Since this method triggers a delegate call when the current location has been obtained, we can safely put the code to use the location within that delegate method.

Begin by importing the CoreLocation framework into the *RouteViewController.swift* file and declaring the class as implementing both the MKMapViewDelegate and CLLocationManagerDelegate protocols. A constant referencing a CLLocationManager object and a variable in which to store the current location also needs to be declared:

```
import UIKit
import MapKit
import CoreLocation


class RouteViewController: UIViewController, MKMapViewDelegate,
CLLocationManagerDelegate {
```

```
    var destination: MKMapItem?
    @IBOutlet weak var routeMap: MKMapView!
    var locationManager: CLLocationManager = CLLocationManager()
    var userLocation: CLLocation?
.
.
.
```

Next, implement the two Core Location delegate methods:

```
func locationManager(_ manager: CLLocationManager,
        didUpdateLocations locations: [CLLocation]) {
    userLocation = locations[0]
    self.getDirections()

}

func locationManager(_ manager: CLLocationManager, didFailWithError error: Error)
{
    print(error.localizedDescription)
}
```

Next, add code to the *viewDidLoad* method to identify the current location, thereby triggering a call to the *didUpdateLocations* delegate method:

```
override func viewDidLoad() {
    super.viewDidLoad()
    routeMap.delegate = self
    routeMap.showsUserLocation = true
    locationManager.desiredAccuracy = kCLLocationAccuracyBest
    locationManager.delegate = self
    locationManager.requestLocation()
}
```

73.8 Getting the Route and Directions

Clearly, the last task performed by the Core *Location didUpdateLocations* method is to call another method named *getDirections* which now also needs to be implemented:

```
func getDirections() {

    let request = MKDirections.Request()
    request.source = MKMapItem.forCurrentLocation()

    if let destination = destination {
        request.destination = destination
    }

    request.requestsAlternateRoutes = false
```

```
    let directions = MKDirections(request: request)

    directions.calculate(completionHandler: {(response, error) in

        if let error = error {
            print(error.localizedDescription)
        } else {
            if let response = response {
                self.showRoute(response)
            }
        }
    })
}
```

This code largely matches that outlined at the start of the chapter, as is the case with the implementation of the *showRoute* method, which also now needs to be implemented in the *RouteViewController.swift* file along with the corresponding *mapView rendererFor overlay* method:

```
func showRoute(_ response: MKDirections.Response) {

    for route in response.routes {

        routeMap.addOverlay(route.polyline,
                        level: MKOverlayLevel.aboveRoads)

        for step in route.steps {
            print(step.instructions)
        }
    }

    if let coordinate = userLocation?.coordinate {
        let region =
            MKCoordinateRegion(center: coordinate,
                latitudinalMeters: 2000, longitudinalMeters: 2000)
        routeMap.setRegion(region, animated: true)
    }
}


func mapView(_ mapView: MKMapView, rendererFor
        overlay: MKOverlay) -> MKOverlayRenderer {
    let renderer = MKPolylineRenderer(overlay: overlay)

    renderer.strokeColor = UIColor.blue
    renderer.lineWidth = 5.0
    return renderer
}
```

The *showRoute* method adds the polygon for the route as an overlay to the map view, outputs the turn-by-turn steps to the console, and zooms in to the user's current location.

73.9 Establishing the Route Segue

All that remains to complete the app is to establish the segue between the results table cell and the route view. This will also require the implementation of the *prepare(for segue:)* method to pass the map item for the destination to the route scene.

Select the *Main.storyboard* file followed by the table cell in the Result Table View Controller scene (ensure the actual cell and not the view or one of the labels is selected). Right-click on the prototype cell and drag the line to the Route View Controller scene. Release the line and select *Show* from the resulting menu.

Finally, edit the *ResultsTableViewController.swift* file and implement the *prepare(for segue:)* method so that the destination property matches the location associated with the selected table row:

```
override func prepare(for segue: UIStoryboardSegue, sender: Any?) {
    let routeViewController = segue.destination
        as! RouteViewController

    if let indexPath = self.tableView.indexPathForSelectedRow,
        let destination = mapItems?[indexPath.row] {
            routeViewController.destination = destination
    }
}
```

73.10 Testing the App

Build and run the app on a suitable iOS device and perform a local search. Once search results have been returned, select the *Details* button to display the list of locations. Selecting a location from the list should now cause a second map view to appear containing the user's current location and the route from there to the selected location drawn in blue, as demonstrated in Figure 73-6:

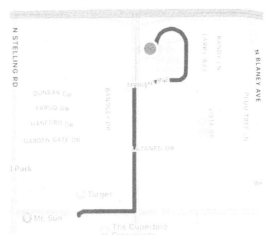

Figure 73-6

A review of the Xcode console should also reveal that the turn-by-turn directions have been output, for example:

```
Proceed to Infinite Loop
Turn right
Turn right onto Infinite Loop
```

```
Turn right onto Infinite Loop
Turn right onto N De Anza Blvd
Turn right to merge onto I-280 S
Take exit 10 onto Wolfe Road
Turn right onto N Wolfe Rd
Turn left onto Bollinger Rd
Turn right
The destination is on your left
```

73.11 Summary

The MKDirections class was added to the MapKit Framework for iOS 7, allowing directions from one location to another to be requested from Apple's mapping servers. Information returned from a request includes the text for turn-by-turn directions, the coordinates at which each journey step will take place, and the polygon data needed to draw the route as a map view overlay.

74. Accessing the iOS 17 Camera and Photo Library

The iOS SDK provides access to both the camera device and photo library through the UIImagePickerController class. It allows videos and photographs to be taken from within an app and for existing photos and videos to be presented to the user for selection.

This chapter will cover the basics and some of the theory behind using the UIImagePickerController class before working through the step-by-step creation of an example app in *"An Example iOS 17 Camera App"*.

74.1 The UIImagePickerController Class

The ultimate purpose of the UIImagePickerController class is to provide apps with either an image or video. It achieves this task by providing users access to the device's camera roll and photo libraries. In the case of the camera, the user can either take a photo or record a video depending on the device's capabilities and the app's configuration of the UIImagePickerController object. Regarding camera roll and library access, the object provides the app with the existing image or video the user selects. In addition, the controller also allows new photos and videos created within the app to be saved to the library.

74.2 Creating and Configuring a UIImagePickerController Instance

When using the UIImagePickerController, an instance of the class must first be created. In addition, properties of the instance need to be configured to control the source for the images or videos (camera, camera roll, or library). Further, the types of media acceptable to the app must also be defined (photos, videos, or both). Finally, another configuration option defines whether the user can edit a photo once it has been taken and before it is passed to the app.

The source of the media is defined by setting the *sourceType* property of the UIImagePickerController object to one of the three supported types:

- UIImagePickerController.SourceType.camera

- UIImagePickerController.SourceType.savedPhotosAlbum

- UIImagePickerController.SourceType.photoLibrary

The types of media acceptable to the app are defined by setting the *mediaTypes* property, an Array object that can be configured to support both video and images. The kUTTypeImage and kUTTypeMovie definitions in the MobileCoreServices Framework can be used as values when configuring this property.

Whether or not the user is permitted to perform editing before the image is passed on to the app is controlled via the *allowsEditing* Boolean property.

The following code creates a UIImagePickerController instance and configures it for camera use with image support and editing disabled before displaying the controller:

```
let imagePicker = UIImagePickerController()
```

```
imagePicker.delegate = self
imagePicker.sourceType = UIImagePickerController.SourceType.photoLibrary
imagePicker.mediaTypes = [kUTTypeImage as String]
imagePicker.allowsEditing = false

self.present(imagePicker, animated: true, completion: nil)
```

It should be noted that the above code also configured the current class as the delegate for the UIImagePickerController instance. This delegate is a key part of how the class works and is covered in the next section.

74.3 Configuring the UIImagePickerController Delegate

When the user is presented with the UIImagePickerController object user interface, the app essentially hands control to that object. That being the case, the controller needs some way to notify the app that the user has taken a photo, recorded a video, or made a library selection. It does this by calling delegate methods. The class that instantiates a UIImagePickerController instance should, therefore, declare itself as the object's delegate, conform to the UIImagePickerControllerDelegate and UINavigationControllerDelegate protocols and implement the *didFinishPickingMediaWithInfo* and *imagePickerControllerDidCancel* methods. For example, when the user has selected or created media, the *didFinishPickingMediaWithInfo* method is called and passed an NSDictionary object containing the media and associated data. If the user cancels the operation, the *imagePickerControllerDidCancel* method is called. In both cases, it is the responsibility of the delegate method to dismiss the view controller:

```
func imagePickerController(_ picker: UIImagePickerController,
didFinishPickingMediaWithInfo info: [UIImagePickerController.InfoKey : Any]) {
    let mediaType = info[UIImagePickerController.InfoKey.mediaType]
                                as! NSString

    self.dismiss(animated: true, completion: nil)
}

func imagePickerControllerDidCancel(_ picker: UIImagePickerController) {
    self.dismiss(animated: true, completion: nil)
}
```

The *info* argument passed to the *didFinishPickingMediaWithInfo* method is an NSDictionary object containing the data relating to the image or video created or selected by the user. The first step is typically to identify the type of media:

```
let mediaType = info[UIImagePickerController.InfoKey.mediaType] as! NSString

if mediaType.isEqual(to: kUTTypeImage as String) {

    // Media is an image

} else if mediaType.isEqual(to: kUTTypeMovie as String) {

    // Media is a video

}
```

The original, unedited image selected or photographed by the user may be obtained from the *info* dictionary as follows:

```
let image = info[UIImagePickerController.InfoKey.originalImage] as! UIImage
```

Assuming that editing was enabled on the image picker controller object, the edited version of the image may be accessed via the *UIImagePickerControllerEditedImage* dictionary key:

```
let image = info[UIImagePickerController.InfoKey.editedImage] as! UIImage
```

If the media is a video, the URL of the recorded media may be accessed as follows:

```
let url = info[UIImagePickerController.InfoKey.mediaURL]
```

Once the image or video URL has been obtained, the app can optionally save the media to the library and either display the image to the user or play the video using the AVPlayer and AVPlayerViewController classes as outlined later in the chapter entitled *"iOS 17 Video Playback using AVPlayer and AVPlayerViewController"*.

74.4 Detecting Device Capabilities

Not all iOS devices provide the same functionality. For example, iPhone models before the 3GS model do not support video recording. In addition, some iPod Touch models do not have a camera, so neither the camera nor camera roll are available via the image picker controller. These differences in functionality make it important to detect the capabilities of a device when using the UIImagePickerController class. Fortunately, this may easily be achieved by a call to the *isSourceTypeAvailable* class method of the UIImagePickerController. For example, to detect the presence of a camera:

```
if UIImagePickerController.isSourceTypeAvailable(
            UIImagePickerController.SourceType.camera) {
      // Code here
}
```

Similarly, to test for access to the camera roll:

```
if UIImagePickerController.isSourceTypeAvailable(
            UIImagePickerController.SourceType.savedPhotosAlbum) {
      // Code here
}
```

Finally, to check for support for photo libraries:

```
if UIImagePickerController.isSourceTypeAvailable(
            UIImagePickerController.SourceType.photoLibrary) {
      // Code here
}
```

74.5 Saving Movies and Images

Once a video or photo created by the user using the camera is handed off to the app, it is then the responsibility of the app code to save that media into the library. Photos and videos may be saved via calls to the *UIImageWriteToSavedPhotosAlbum* and *UISaveVideoAtPathToSavedPhotosAlbum* methods, respectively. These methods use a *target-action* mechanism whereby the save action is initiated, and the app continues to run. When the action is complete, a specified method is called to notify the app of the success or otherwise of the operation.

To save an image:

```
UIImageWriteToSavedPhotosAlbum(image, self,
                #selector(ViewController.image(image:didFinishSavingWithError:
                        contextInfo:)), nil)
```

To save a video:

```
if (UIVideoAtPathIsCompatibleWithSavedPhotosAlbum(videoPath))
{
    UISaveVideoAtPathToSavedPhotosAlbum(videoPath, self,
        #selector(ViewController.image(image:didFinishSavingWithError:
                    contextInfo:)), nil)
}
```

Last, but by no means least, is the *didFinishSavingWithError* method which will be called when the action is either complete or failed due to an error:

```
func image(image: UIImage, didFinishSavingWithError
      error: NSErrorPointer, contextInfo:UnsafeRawPointer) {
    if error != nil {
        // Report error to the user
    }
}
```

74.6 Summary

In this chapter, we have provided an overview of the UIImagePickerController and looked at how this class can allow a user to take a picture or record video from within an iOS app or select media from the device photo libraries. Now that the theory has been covered, the next chapter, entitled *"An Example iOS 17 Camera App"*, will work through the development of an example app designed to implement the theory covered in this chapter.

75. An Example iOS 17 Camera App

In the chapter entitled *"Accessing the iOS 17 Camera and Photo Library"*, we looked in some detail at the steps necessary to provide access to the iOS camera and photo libraries in an iOS app. This chapter aims to build on this knowledge by working through an example iOS app designed to access the device's camera and photo libraries.

75.1 An Overview of the App

The app user interface for this example will consist of an image view and a toolbar containing two buttons. When touched by the user, the first button will display the camera to the user and allow a photograph to be taken, which will subsequently be displayed in the image view. The second button will provide access to the camera roll, where the user may select an existing photo image. In the case of a new image taken with the camera, this will be saved to the camera roll.

Since we will cover the playback of video in the next chapter (*"iOS 17 Video Playback using AVPlayer and AVPlayerViewController"*), the camera roll and camera will be restricted to still images in this example. Adding video support to this app is left as an exercise for the reader.

75.2 Creating the Camera Project

Begin the project by launching Xcode and creating a new project using the iOS *App* template with the Swift and Storyboard options selected, entering *Camera* as the product name.

75.3 Designing the User Interface

The next step in this tutorial is to design the user interface. This simple user interface consists of an image view, a toolbar, and two bar button items. Select the *Main.storyboard* file and drag components from the Library onto the view. Position and size the components and set the text on the bar button items, so the user interface resembles Figure 75-1.

In terms of Auto Layout constraints, begin by selecting the toolbar view and clicking on the *Add New Constraints* menu in the toolbar located in the lower right-hand corner of the storyboard canvas and establish *Spacing to nearest neighbor* constraints on the bottom and two side edges of the view with the *Constrain to margins* option switched off. Also, enable the height constraint option to be set to the current value.

Next, select the Image View object and, once again using the *Add New Constraints* menu, establish *Spacing to nearest neighbor* constraints on all four sides of the view, with the *Constrain to margins* option enabled.

Finally, with the Image View still selected, display the Attributes Inspector panel and change the *Content Mode* attribute to *Aspect Fit*.

Select the image view object in the view canvas and display the Assistant Editor panel. Right-click on the image view object and drag it to a position just below the class declaration line in the Assistant Editor. Release the line and, in the resulting connection dialog, establish an outlet connection named *imageView*.

With the Assistant Editor still visible, establish action connections for the two buttons to methods named *useCamera* and *useCameraRoll,* respectively (keeping in mind that it may be necessary to click twice on each button to select it since the first click will typically select the toolbar parent object).

Figure 75-1

Close the Assistant Editor, select the *ViewController.swift* file and modify it further to add import and delegate protocol declarations together with a Boolean property declaration that will be required later in the chapter:

```
import UIKit
import MobileCoreServices
import UniformTypeIdentifiers


class ViewController: UIViewController, UIImagePickerControllerDelegate,
UINavigationControllerDelegate {

    @IBOutlet weak var imageView: UIImageView!
    var newMedia: Bool?
.
.
```

75.4 Implementing the Action Methods

The *useCamera* and *useCameraRoll* action methods now need to be implemented. The *useCamera* method first needs to check that the device on which the app is running has a camera. It then needs to create a UIImagePickerController instance, assign the cameraViewController as the delegate for the object and define the media source as the camera. Since we do not plan on handling videos, the supported media types property is set to images only. Finally, the camera interface will be displayed. The last task is to set the *newMedia* flag to true to indicate that the image is new and is not an existing image from the camera roll. Bringing all these requirements together gives us the following *useCamera* method:

```
@IBAction func useCamera(_ sender: Any) {

    if UIImagePickerController.isSourceTypeAvailable(
                UIImagePickerController.SourceType.camera) {

        let imagePicker = UIImagePickerController()
        imagePicker.delegate = self
        imagePicker.sourceType =
                UIImagePickerController.SourceType.camera
        imagePicker.mediaTypes = [UTType.image.identifier]
        imagePicker.allowsEditing = false

        self.present(imagePicker, animated: true,
                                completion: nil)
        newMedia = true
    }
}
```

The *useCameraRoll* method is remarkably similar to the previous method, with the exception that the source of the image is declared to be UIImagePickerController.SourceType.photoLibrary and the *newMedia* flag is set to *false* (since the photo is already in the library, we don't need to save it again):

```
@IBAction func useCameraRoll(_ sender: Any) {
    if UIImagePickerController.isSourceTypeAvailable(
                UIImagePickerController.SourceType.savedPhotosAlbum) {
        let imagePicker = UIImagePickerController()

        imagePicker.delegate = self
        imagePicker.sourceType =
                UIImagePickerController.SourceType.photoLibrary
        imagePicker.mediaTypes = [UTType.image.identifier]
        imagePicker.allowsEditing = false
        self.present(imagePicker, animated: true,
                completion: nil)
        newMedia = false
    }
}
```

75.5 Writing the Delegate Methods

As described in *"Accessing the iOS 17 Camera and Photo Library"*, some delegate methods must be implemented to fully implement an instance of the image picker controller delegate protocol. The most important method is *didFinishPickingMediaWithInfo* which is called when the user has finished taking or selecting an image. The code for this method in our example reads as follows:

```
func imagePickerController(_ picker: UIImagePickerController,
```

```
didFinishPickingMediaWithInfo info: [UIImagePickerController.InfoKey : Any]) {
    let mediaType = info[UIImagePickerController.InfoKey.mediaType]
                          as! NSString

    self.dismiss(animated: true, completion: nil)

    if mediaType.isEqual(to: UTType.image.identifier) {
        let image = info[UIImagePickerController.InfoKey.originalImage]
                          as! UIImage
        imageView.image = image

        if (newMedia == true) {
            UIImageWriteToSavedPhotosAlbum(image, self,
                #selector(ViewController.image(
                    image:didFinishSavingWithError:contextInfo:)), nil)
        } else if mediaType.isEqual(to: UTType.image.identifier) {
            // Code to support video here
        }

    }
}


@objc func image(image: UIImage, didFinishSavingWithError error: NSErrorPointer,
contextInfo:UnsafeRawPointer) {
    if error != nil {
        let alert = UIAlertController(title: "Save Failed",
            message: "Failed to save image",
            preferredStyle: UIAlertController.Style.alert)

        let cancelAction = UIAlertAction(title: "OK",
            style: .cancel, handler: nil)
        alert.addAction(cancelAction)
        self.present(alert, animated: true,
                    completion: nil)
    }
}
```

The code in this delegate method dismisses the image picker view and identifies the type of media passed from the image picker controller. If it is an image, it is displayed on the view image object of the user interface. If this is a new image, it is saved to the camera roll. When the save operation is complete, the didFinishedSavingWithError method is configured to be called. If an error occurs, it is reported to the user via an alert box.

It is also necessary to implement the *imagePickerControllerDidCancel* delegate method, which is called if the user cancels the image picker session without taking a picture or making an image selection. In most cases, all this method needs to do is dismiss the image picker:

```
func imagePickerControllerDidCancel(_ picker: UIImagePickerController) {
    self.dismiss(animated: true, completion: nil)
```

```
}
```

75.6 Seeking Camera and Photo Library Access

Access to both the camera and the photos stored on the device requires authorization from the user. This involves declaring three usage keys within the project *Info.plist* file.

To add these entries, select the *Camera* entry at the top of the Project navigator panel and select the Info tab in the main panel. Next, click on the + button contained with the last line of properties in the Custom iOS Target Properties section. Then, select the *Privacy – Camera Usage Description* item from the resulting menu. Once the key has been added, double-click in the corresponding value column and enter the following text:

```
This app allows you to take photos and store them in the photo library.
```

Repeat this step, this time adding a *Privacy – Photo Library Usage Description* key set to the following string value:

```
This app allows you to take photos and store them in the photo library.
```

Finally, add another key to the list, this time selecting the *Privacy - Photo Library Additions Usage Description* option from the drop-down menu. This permission is required to allow the app to add new photos to the user's photo library. Once the key has been selected, enter text similar to the following into the value field:

```
This app saves photos only to your photo library. This app saves photos only to
your photo library.
```

75.7 Building and Running the App

To experience the full functionality of this app, you will need to install it on a physical iOS device.

Click on the Xcode run button to launch the app. Once the app loads, select the *Camera* button to launch the camera interface and tap the Allow button when prompted to provide access to the camera and take a photo. Next, tap the *Use Photo* button, after which your photo should appear in the image view object of our app user interface:

Figure 75-2

Selecting the *Camera Roll* button will provide access to the camera roll and photo stream on the device where an image selection can be made:

Figure 75-3

75.8 Summary

This chapter has provided a practical example of how the UIImagePickerController class can access the camera and photo library within an iOS app. The example also demonstrated the need to configure appropriate privacy usage keys to seek permission from the user to access the device camera and search and add images to the photo library.

76. iOS 17 Video Playback using AVPlayer and AVPlayerViewController

Video playback support in iOS is provided by combining the AVFoundation AVPlayer and AVKit AVPlayerViewController classes.

This chapter presents an overview of video playback in iOS using these two classes, followed by a step-by-step example.

76.1 The AVPlayer and AVPlayerViewController Classes

The sole purpose of the AVPlayer class is to play media content. An AVPlayer instance is initialized with the URL of the media to be played (either a path to a local file on the device or the URL of network-based media). Playback can be directed to a device screen or, in the case of external playback mode, via AirPlay or an HDMI/VGA cable connection to an external screen.

The AVKit Player View Controller (AVPlayerViewController) class provides a view controller environment through which AVPlayer video is displayed to the user, together with several controls that enable the user to manage the playback experience. Playback may also be controlled from within the app code by calling the *play* and *pause* methods of the AVPlayer instance.

76.2 The iOS Movie Player Example App

The remainder of this chapter aims to create a simple app to play a video when a button is pressed. The video will be streamed over the internet from a movie file on a web server.

Launch Xcode and create a new project using the iOS *App* template with the Swift and Storyboard options selected, entering *AVPlayerDemo* as the product name.

76.3 Designing the User Interface

Select the *Main.storyboard* file and display the Library. Next, drag a single Button instance to the view window and change the text on the button to "Play Movie". With the button selected in the storyboard canvas, display the Auto Layout Align menu and add horizontal and vertical container constraints to the view with offset values set to 0.

From the Library panel, locate the AVKit Player View Controller object and drag it onto the storyboard to the right of the existing view controller. Right-click on the button in the first view controller and drag the resulting line to the AVKit Player View Controller. Release the line and select *Show* from the segue selection menu.

76.4 Initializing Video Playback

When the user taps the "Play Movie" button, the app will perform a segue to the AVPlayerViewController scene, but as yet, no AVPlayer has been configured to play video content. This can be achieved by implementing the *prepare(for segue:)* method within the *ViewController.swift* file as follows, the code for which relies on the AVKit iOS 17 Video Playback using AVPlayer and AVPlayerViewController

and AVFoundation frameworks having been imported:

```
import UIKit
import AVKit
import AVFoundation

class ViewController: UIViewController {
    .
    .
    .

    override func prepare(for segue: UIStoryboardSegue, sender: Any?) {

        let destination = segue.destination as!
                            AVPlayerViewController
        let url = URL(string:
                "https://www.payloadbooks.com/ios_book/movie/movie.mov")

            if let movieURL = url {
                destination.player = AVPlayer(url: movieURL)
            }
    }
    .
    .
```

The code in this above method begins by obtaining a reference to the destination view controller, in this case, the AVPlayerViewController instance. A URL object is then initialized with the URL of a web-based video file. Finally, a new AVPlayer instance is created, initialized with the video URL, and assigned to the *player* property of the AVPlayerViewController object.

Running the app once again should cause the video to be available for playback within the player view controller scene.

76.5 Build and Run the App

With the design and coding phases complete, all that remains is to build and run the app. First, click on the run button in the toolbar of the main Xcode project window. Assuming no errors occur, the app should launch within the iOS Simulator or device. Once loaded, touching the *Play Movie* button should launch the movie player in full-screen mode, and playback should automatically begin:

Figure 76-1

76.6 Creating an AVPlayerViewController Instance from Code

The example shown in this chapter used storyboard scenes and a transition to display an AVPlayerViewController instance. While this is a quick approach to working with the AVPlayerViewController and AVPlayer classes, the same result may be achieved directly by writing code within the app. The following code fragment, for example, initializes and plays a video within an app using these two classes without the use of a storyboard scene:

```
let player = AVPlayer(url: url)
let playerController = AVPlayerViewController()

playerController.player = player
self.addChildViewController(playerController)
self.view.addSubview(playerController.view)
playerController.view.frame = self.view.frame

player.play()
```

76.7 Summary

The basic classes needed to play back video from within an iOS app are provided by the AVFoundation and AVKit frameworks. The purpose of the AVPlayer class is to facilitate the playback of video media files. The AVPlayerViewController class provides a quick and easy way to embed an AVPlayer instance into a view controller environment with a set of standard on-screen playback controls.

77. An iOS 17 Multitasking Picture-in-Picture Tutorial

The topic of multitasking in iOS on iPad devices was covered in detail in the earlier chapter titled *"A Guide to iPad Multitasking"*. A multitasking area mentioned briefly in that chapter was Picture in Picture support. This chapter will provide a more detailed introduction to Picture in Picture multitasking before extending the *AVPlayerDemo* project created in the previous chapter to include Picture in Picture support.

77.1 An Overview of Picture-in-Picture Multitasking

Picture in Picture (PiP) multitasking allows the video playback within an app running on recent iPad models to appear within a floating, movable and resizable window. Figure 77-1, for example, shows an iPad screen's upper portion. In the figure, the PiP window is displayed in the top left-hand corner while the user interacts with a Safari browser session. Once displayed, the location of the PiP window can be moved by the user to any other corner of the display:

Figure 77-1

Video playback within a PiP window may only be initiated via user action. For example, when the user presses the Home button on the iPad device while full-screen video playback is in progress, the video will be transferred to a PiP window. Alternatively, the video playback can be moved to a PiP window using a button that appears in the top left corner of the video player window, as highlighted in Figure 77-2:

Figure 77-2

A set of controls is also available from within the PiP window to pause and resume playback, return to full-screen viewing or exit the playback entirely.

77.2 Adding Picture-in-Picture Support to the AVPlayerDemo App

The remainder of this chapter will work through the steps to integrate PiP support into the AVPlayerDemo app created in the previous chapter. The first step is to enable PiP support within the project capabilities.

If the project is not already loaded, start Xcode and open the AVPlayerDemo project. Then, in the Project Navigator panel, select the *AVPlayerDemo* project target at the top of the panel and click on the *Signing & Capabilities* tab in the main panel. Next, click the "+ Capability" button to display the dialog shown in Figure 77-3. Finally, enter "back" into the filter bar, select the result, and press the keyboard enter key to add the capability to the project:

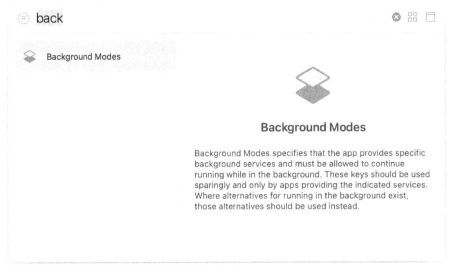

Figure 77-3

On returning to the capabilities screen, enable the checkbox for the *Audio, AirPlay, and Picture in Picture* in the Background modes section as highlighted in Figure 77-4:

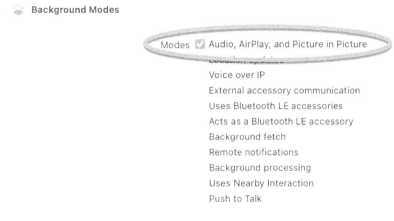

Figure 77-4

77.3 Adding the Navigation Controller

To better demonstrate the implementation of PiP support within an iOS app, the storyboard for the AVPlayerDemo will be adapted to include a navigation controller so that the user can navigate back to the main view controller scene from the AVKit Player scene. Within the Document outline panel, select the View Controller scene so that it highlights in blue, and choose the Xcode *Editor -> Embed In -> Navigation Controller* menu option.

77.4 Setting the Audio Session Category

The next step is configuring the app to use an appropriate audio session category. For this example, this will be set to *AVAudioSession.Category.playback*, the code for which should now be added to the *didFinishLaunchingWithOptions* method located in the *AppDelegate.swift* file as follows:

```
import UIKit
import AVFoundation
.
.
func application(_ application: UIApplication, didFinishLaunchingWithOptions
launchOptions: [UIApplication.LaunchOptionsKey: Any]?) -> Bool {

    let audioSession = AVAudioSession.sharedInstance()

    do {
        try audioSession.setCategory(AVAudioSession.Category.playback,
                    mode: .default)
    } catch {
        print("Unable to set audio session category")
    }

    return true
}
```

With these steps completed, launch the app on a physical iPad or iOS simulator session (keeping in mind that PiP support is unavailable on the first-generation iPad Mini or any full-size iPad models older than the first iPad Air). Once loaded, tap the Play Movie button and start video playback. Tap the PiP button in the video playback control bar, or use the device Home button and note that video playback is transferred to the PiP window:

Figure 77-5

With the PiP window visible and the three control buttons displayed, tap the button to toggle back to full-screen playback mode.

PiP support is now implemented except for one important step. To experience the need for this additional step, run the app again, begin movie playback, and switch playback to PiP mode. Then, remaining within the AVPlayerDemo app, tap the *Back* button in the navigation bar to return to the original view controller scene containing the Play Movie button. Next, tap the PiP button to return the movie playback to full screen, at which point the movie playback window will disappear, leaving just the initial view controller visible. This is because a delegate method must be implemented to present the full-size video playback view controller.

77.5 Implementing the Delegate

The AVPlayerViewController class can have assigned to it a delegate object on which methods will be called at various points during the playback of a video. This delegate object must implement the AVPlayerViewControllerDelegate protocol. For this example, the ViewController class will be designated as the delegate object for the class. Select the *ViewController.swift* file and modify it to declare that it now implements the AVPlayerViewControllerDelegate protocol:

```
import UIKit
import AVKit
import AVFoundation

class ViewController: UIViewController, AVPlayerViewControllerDelegate {

    override func viewDidLoad() {
        super.viewDidLoad()
        }
.
.
}
```

Having declared that the class implements the protocol, the *prepare(for segue:)* method now needs to be modified to assign the current instance of the class as the delegate for the player view controller instance:

```
override func prepare(for segue: UIStoryboardSegue, sender: Any?) {
```

```
    let destination = segue.destination as!
                            AVPlayerViewController
    let url = URL(string:
            "https://www.ebookfrenzy.com/ios_book/movie/movie.mov")

    destination.delegate = self

    if let movieURL = url {
        destination.player = AVPlayer(url: movieURL)
    }
}
```

When the user moves back from the PiP window to full-screen playback mode, the *restoreUserInterfaceForPictureInPictureStopWithCompletionHandler* method is called on the delegate object. This method is passed a reference to the player view controller and a completion handler. This method ensures that the player view controller is presented to the user before calling the completion handler with a Boolean value indicating the success or otherwise of the operation. Remaining within the *ViewController.swift* file, implement this method as follows:

```
func playerViewController(_ playerViewController: AVPlayerViewController,
    restoreUserInterfaceForPictureInPictureStopWithCompletionHandler
completionHandler: @escaping (Bool) -> Void) {

    let currentViewController =
            navigationController?.visibleViewController

    if currentViewController != playerViewController {
        if let topViewController =
            navigationController?.topViewController {

            topViewController.present(playerViewController,
                animated: true, completion: {()
                completionHandler(true)
            })
        }
    }
}
```

The delegate method is passed a reference to the player view controller instance and a completion handler. The code added to the method begins by identifying the currently visible view controller and checking if the current view controller matches the playerViewController instance. For example, suppose the current view controller is not the player view controller. In that case, the navigation controller obtains a reference to the top view controller, which, in turn, is used to display the player view controller. The completion handler is then called and passed a true value.

If, on the other hand, the current view controller is the playerViewController, no action needs to be taken since the system will automatically display the player controller to show the movie in full screen. In fact, attempting to present the player view controller when it is already the current view controller will cause the app to crash with an error that reads as follows:

```
Application tried to present modally an active view controller
<AVPlayerViewController>
```

Run the app again and verify that the full-screen playback view appears when the full-screen button is tapped in the PiP window after navigating back to the main view controller scene.

77.6 Opting Out of Picture-in-Picture Support

The default behavior for the AVPlayerViewController class is to support PiP. To disable PiP support for an AVPlayerViewController instance, set the allowsPictureInPicturePlayback property on the object to false. For example:

```
playerViewController.allowsPictureInPicturePlayback = false
```

With PiP support disabled, the PiP button will no longer appear in the full-screen view's playback control panel, and pressing the device Home button during video playback will no longer place the video into a PiP window.

77.7 Additional Delegate Methods

Several other methods are supported by the AVPlayerViewControllerDelegate protocol, which, if implemented in the designated delegate, will be called at various points in the life cycle of the video playback:

- **pictureInPictureControllerWillStartPictureInPicture** – Called before the transition to Picture in Picture mode starts.

- **pictureInPictureControllerDidStartPictureInPicture** - Called when the Picture in Picture playback has started. This method is passed a reference to the playback view controller object.

- **pictureInPictureControllerWillStopPictureInPicture** - Called when the Picture in Picture playback is about to stop. This method is passed a reference to the playback view controller object.

- **pictureInPictureControllerDidStopPictureInPicture** - Called when the Picture in Picture playback has stopped. This method is passed a reference to the playback view controller object.

77.8 Summary

Picture in Picture support leverages the multitasking capabilities of iOS to allow video playback to be placed within a floating, movable, and resizable window where it continues to play as the user performs other tasks on the device. This chapter has highlighted the steps in implementing PiP support within an iOS app, including enabling entitlements, configuring the audio session, and implementing delegate methods.

78. An Introduction to Extensions in iOS 17

Extensions are a feature originally introduced as part of the iOS 8 release designed to allow certain capabilities of an app to be made available for use within other apps. For example, the developer of a photo editing app might have devised some unique image filtering capabilities and decided that those features would be particularly useful to users of the iOS Photos app. To achieve this, the developer would implement these features in a Photo Editing extension which would then appear as an option to users when editing an image within the Photos app.

Extensions fall into various categories, and several rules and guidelines must be followed in the implementation process. While subsequent chapters will cover the creation of extensions of various types in detail, this chapter is intended to serve as a general overview and introduction to the subject of extensions in iOS.

78.1 iOS Extensions – An Overview

The sole purpose of an extension is to make a specific feature of an existing app available for access within other apps. Extensions are separate executable binaries that run independently of the corresponding app. Although extensions are individual binaries, they must be supplied and installed as part of an app bundle. The app with which an extension is bundled is called the *containing app*. Except for Message App extensions, the containing app must provide useful functionality. An empty app must not be provided solely to deliver an extension to the user.

Once an extension has been installed, it will be accessible from other apps through various techniques depending on the extension type. The app from which an extension is launched and used is referred to as a *host app*.

For example, an app that translates text to a foreign language might include an extension that can be used to translate the text displayed by a host app. In such a scenario, the user would access the extension via the Share button in the host app's user interface, and the extension would display a view controller displaying the translated text. On dismissing the extension, the user is returned to the host app.

78.2 Extension Types

iOS supports several different extension types dictated by *extension points*. An extension point is an area of the iOS operating system that has been opened up to allow extensions to be implemented. When developing an extension, it is important to select the extension point most appropriate to the extension's features. The extension types supported by iOS are constantly evolving, though the key types can be summarized as follows:

78.2.1 Share Extension

Share extensions provide a quick access mechanism for sharing content such as images, videos, text, and websites within a host app with social network sites or content-sharing services. It is important to understand that Apple does not expect developers to write Share extensions designed to post content to destinations such as Facebook or Twitter (such sharing options are already built into iOS) but rather as a mechanism to make sharing easier for developers hosting their own sharing and social sites. Share extensions appear within the activity view controller panel when the user taps the Share button from within a host app.

Share extensions can use the SLComposeServiceViewController class to implement the interface for posting content. This class displays a view containing a preview of the information to be posted and provides the ability to modify the content before posting it. In addition, a custom user interface can be designed using Interface Builder for more complex requirements.

The actual mechanics of posting the content will depend on how the target platform works.

78.2.2 Action Extension

The Action extension point enables extensions to be created that fall into the Action category. Action extensions allow the content within a host app to be transformed or viewed differently. As with Share extensions, Action extensions are accessed from the activity view controller via the Share button. Figure 78-1, for example, shows an example Action extension named "Change It Up" in the activity view controller of the iOS Notes app.

Figure 78-1

Action extensions are context-sensitive in that they only appear as an option when the type of content in the host app matches one of the content types for which the extension has declared support. For example, an Action extension that works with images will not appear in the activity view controller panel for a host app displaying text-based content.

Action extensions are covered in detail in the chapters entitled *"Creating an iOS 17 Action Extension"* and *"Receiving Data from an iOS 17 Action Extension"*.

78.2.3 Photo Editing Extension

The Photo Editing extension allows an app's photo editing capabilities to be accessed from within the built-in iOS Photos app. Photo Editing extensions are displayed when the user selects an image in the Photos app, chooses the edit option, and taps on the button in the top left-hand corner of the Photo editing screen. For example, Figure 78-2 shows the Photos app displaying two Photo Editing extension options:

Figure 78-2

Photo Editing Extensions are covered in detail in the chapter entitled *"Creating an iOS 17 Photo Editing*

Extension".

78.2.4 Document Provider Extension

The Document Provider extension allows a containing app to act as a document repository for other apps running on the device. Depending on the level of support implemented in the extension, host apps can import, export, open, and move documents to and from the storage repository the containing app provides. In most cases, the storage repository represented by the containing app will be a third-party cloud storage service providing an alternative to Apple's iCloud service.

A Document Provider extension consists of a Document Picker View Controller extension and an optional File Provider extension. The Document Picker View Controller extension provides a user interface, allowing users to browse and select the documents available for the Document Provider extension.

The optional File Provider extension provides the host app with access to the documents outside the app's sandbox and is necessary if the extension is to support move and open operations on the documents stored via the containing app.

78.2.5 Custom Keyboard Extension

As the name suggests, the Custom Keyboard Extension allows creating and installing custom keyboards onto iOS devices. Keyboards developed using the Custom Keyboard extension point are available to be used by all apps on the device and, once installed, are selected from within the keyboard settings section of the Settings app on the device.

78.2.6 Audio Unit Extension

Audio Unit Extensions allow sound effects, virtual instruments, and other sound-based capabilities to be available to other audio-oriented host apps such as GarageBand.

78.2.7 Shared Links Extension

The Shared Links Extension provides a mechanism for an iOS app to store URL links in the Safari browser shared links list.

78.2.8 Content Blocking Extension

Content Blocking allows extensions to be added to the Safari browser to block certain types of content from appearing when users browse the web. This feature is typically used to create ad-blocking solutions.

78.2.9 Sticker Pack Extension

An extension to the built-in iOS Messages App that allows packs of additional images to be provided for inclusion in the message content.

78.2.10 iMessage Extension

Allows interactive content to be integrated into the Messages app. This can range from custom user interfaces to interactive games. iMessage extensions are covered in the chapters entitled *"An Introduction to Building iOS 17 Message Apps"* and *"An iOS 17 Interactive Message App Tutorial"*.

78.2.11 Intents Extension

When integrating an app with the SiriKit framework, these extensions define the actions to be performed in response to voice commands using Siri.

78.3 Creating Extensions

By far, the easiest approach to developing extensions is to use the extension templates provided by Xcode. Once the project for a containing app is loaded into Xcode, extensions can be added as new targets by selecting the

File -> New -> Targets… menu option. This will display the panel shown in Figure 78-3, listing a template for each of the extension types:

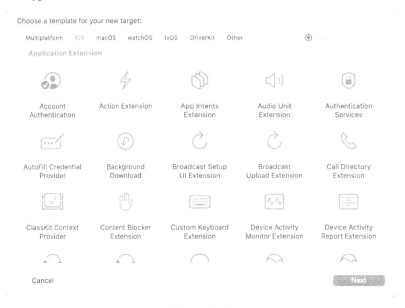

Figure 78-3

Once an extension template is selected, click on *Next* to name and create the template. Once the extension has been created from the template, the steps to implement the extension will differ depending on the type of extension selected. The next few chapters will detail the steps in implementing Photo Editing, Action, and Message app extensions.

78.4 Summary

Extensions in iOS provide a way for narrowly defined areas of functionality of one app to be made available from within other apps. iOS 17 currently supports a variety of extension types. When developing extensions, it is important to select the most appropriate extension point before beginning development work and to be aware that some app features may not be appropriate candidates for an extension.

Although extensions run as separate independent binaries, they can only be installed as part of an app bundle. The app with which an extension is bundled is called a *containing app*. An app from which an extension is launched is called a a *host app*.

Having covered the basics of extensions in this chapter, subsequent chapters will focus in detail on the more commonly used extension types.

79. Creating an iOS 17 Photo Editing Extension

The iOS Photo Editing extension's primary purpose is to allow an app's photo editing capabilities to be made available from within the standard iOS Photos app. Consider, for example, a scenario where a developer has published an app that allows users to apply custom changes and special effects to videos or photos. Before the introduction of extensions, the only way for a user to access these capabilities would have been to launch and work within that app. However, by placing some of the app's functionality into a Photo Editing extension, the user can now select videos or photos from within the Photos app and choose the extension from a range of editing options available on the device. Once selected, the user interface for the extension is displayed to the user so that changes can be made to the chosen image or video. Once the user has finished making the changes and exits the extension, the modified image or video is returned to the Photos app.

79.1 Creating a Photo Editing Extension

As with all extension types, using an Xcode template is the easiest starting point when creating a Photo Editing extension. For this chapter, create a new Xcode project using the iOS *App* template with the Swift and Storyboard options selected, entering *PhotoDemo* as the product name.

Once the app project has been created, a new target will be added for the Photo Editing extension. To achieve this, select the *File -> New -> Target...* menu option and choose the *Photo Editing Extension* template from the main panel as shown in Figure 79-1:

Figure 79-1

With the appropriate options selected, click the Next button and enter *MyPhotoExt* into the Product Name field. Leave the remaining fields to default values and click on Finish to complete the extension creation process. When prompted, click on the *Activate* button to activate the scheme created by Xcode to enable the extension to be built and run.

Once the extension has been added, it will appear in the project navigator panel under the *MyPhotoExt* folder. This folder will contain the Swift source code file for the extension's view controller named *PhotoEditingViewController*.

swift and the corresponding user interface storyboard file named *MainInterface.storyboard*. In addition, an *Info.plist* file will be present in the sub-folder.

79.2 Accessing the Photo Editing Extension

Before beginning work on implementing the extension's functionality, it is important to learn how to access such an extension from within the iOS Photos app. Begin by verifying that the *MyPhotoExt* build scheme is selected in the Xcode toolbar, as illustrated in Figure 79-2.

Figure 79-2

If the extension is not selected, click on the current scheme name and select *MyPhotoExt* from the drop-down menu. Having verified that the appropriate scheme is selected, click on the toolbar run button. Since this is an extension, it can only be run within the context of a host app. As a result, Xcode will display a panel listing the apps installed on the attached device. From this list of available apps (Figure 79-3), select the *Photos* app and click on the *Run* button.

Figure 79-3

After the extension and containing app have been compiled and installed, the Photos app will automatically launch. If it does not, launch it manually from the device screen. Once the Photos app appears, select a photo from those stored on the device and, once selected, tap on the *Edit* button located in the toolbar along the top edge of the screen, as illustrated in Figure 79-4, to enter the standard editing interface of the Photos app.

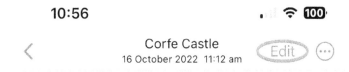

Figure 79-4

Within the tab bar along the bottom of the Photos editing tool is a small round button containing three dots (as highlighted in Figure 79-5):

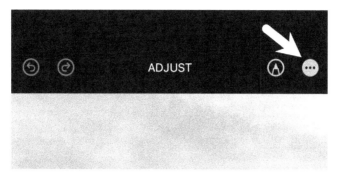

Figure 79-5

Tapping this button will display the action panel (as shown in Figure 79-6), where Photo Editing extensions may be chosen and used to edit videos and images.

Figure 79-6

Assuming that the extension for our *PhotoDemo* app is displayed, select it and wait for the extension to launch. Once the extension has loaded, it will appear in the form of the user interface as defined in the *MyPhotoExt -> MainInterface.storyboard* file.

79.3 Configuring the Info.plist File

A Photo Editing extension must declare the type of media it can edit. This is specified via the *PHSupportedMediaTypes* key within the *NSExtension* section of the extension's *Info.plist* file. By default, the Photo Editing template declares that the extension can only edit images. To confirm this, right-click on the *Info* entry within the MyPhotoExt folder in the Project Navigator and select the Open as Source code option and check that the NSExtension settings match the following:

```
<?xml version="1.0" encoding="UTF-8"?>
.

.

        <key>NSExtension</key>
        <dict>
                <key>NSExtensionAttributes</key>
                <dict>
                        <key>PHSupportedMediaTypes</key>
                        <array>
                                <string>Image</string>
```

Creating an iOS 17 Photo Editing Extension

```
                                </array>
                    </dict>
                    <key>NSExtensionMainStoryboard</key>
                    <string>MainInterface</string>
                    <key>NSExtensionPointIdentifier</key>
                    <string>com.apple.photo-editing</string>
            </dict>
</dict>
</plist>
```

If the extension is also able to edit video files, the *PHSupportedMediaTypes* entry within the file would be modified as follows:

```
<key>PHSupportedMediaTypes</key>
        <array>
            <string>Video</string>
            <string>Image</string>
        </array>
```

For this example, leave the *Info.plist* file unchanged with support for images only.

79.4 Designing the User Interface

The extension's user interface will consist of an Image View and a Toolbar containing three Bar Button Items. First, within the Xcode project navigator panel, locate and load the *MyPhotoExt -> MainInterface.storyboard* file into Interface Builder and select and delete the "Hello World" Label view. Then, with a clean canvas, design and configure the layout so that it consists of an Image View, a Toolbar, and three Toolbar Button Items, as shown in Figure 79-7:

Figure 79-7

Select the Image View, display the Attributes Inspector panel, and change the Content Mode setting to *Aspect Fit*.

With the Image View still selected, display the Auto Layout *Add New Constraints* menu and set *Spacing to nearest neighbor* constraints on all four sides of the view with the *Constrain to margins* option switched off.

Click to select the Toolbar view and use the Auto Layout *Add New Constraints* menu again to apply *Spacing to nearest neighbor* constraints on the left, right, and bottom edges of the view with the *Constrain to margins* option still switched off. Before adding the constraints, enable the *Height* constraint option using the currently displayed value.

Display the Assistant Editor and verify that it displays the source code for the *PhotoEditingViewController.swift* file. Next, select the Bar Button Item displaying the "Sepia" text (note that it may be necessary to click twice since the first click will select the parent Toolbar view). With the item selected, right-click on the item and drag the resulting line to a position immediately beneath the end of implementing the *viewDidLoad* method in the Assistant Editor panel. Next, release the line and, in the connection dialog, establish an Action named *sepiaSelected*. Repeat these steps for the "Mono" and "Invert" Bar Button Items, naming the Actions *monoSelected* and *invertSelected,* respectively.

Finally, right-click on the Image View and drag the resulting line to a position beneath the "class PhotoEditingViewController" declaration. Then, release the line and establish an Outlet for the Image View named *imageView*.

79.5 The PHContentEditingController Protocol

When Xcode created the template for the Photo Editing extension, it created a View Controller class named PhotoEditingViewController and declared it as implementing the PHContentEditingController protocol. It also generated stub methods for each method that must be implemented for the class to conform with the protocol. The remainder of implementing a Photo Editing extension primarily consists of writing the code for these methods to implement the required editing behavior. One of the first methods that will need to be implemented relates to the issue of adjustment data.

79.6 Photo Extensions and Adjustment Data

When the user selects a Photo Extension, a method named *canHandle(adjustmentData:)* is called on the view controller class of the extension. The method must return a true or false value depending on whether or not the extension supports adjustment data.

If an extension supports adjustment data, a copy of the original image or video is passed together with data outlining any earlier modifications made to the media during previous editing sessions. The extension then re-applies those changes to the file or video to get it back to the point where it was at the end of the last editing session. The advantage of this approach is that the extension can allow the user to undo any editing operations performed within previous sessions using the extension. Then, when editing is completed, the extension returns the modified image or video file and any new adjustment data reflecting edits performed during the current session.

If an image editing extension indicates that it does not support adjustment data, it is passed a copy of the modified image as it appeared at the end of the last editing session. This enables the user to perform additional editing tasks but does not allow previous edits to be undone. In the case of video editing extensions that do not support adjustment data, the extension will be passed the original video, and previous edits will be lost. Therefore, supporting adjustment data is an important requirement for video editing.

While the example contained within this tutorial will store and return adjustment data to the Photos app allowing for future improvements to the extension, it will not handle incoming adjustment data. Within the

PhotoEditingViewController.swift file, therefore, locate and review the *canHandle(adjustmentData:)* method and verify that it is configured to return a *false* value:

```
func canHandle(_ adjustmentData: PHAdjustmentData) -> Bool {
    return false
}
```

79.7 Receiving the Content

The next method called on the extension View Controller class is the *startContentEditing* method.

This method is passed as arguments a *PHContentEditingInput* object and a placeholder image. For images, this object contains a compressed version of the image suitable for displaying to the user, a URL referencing the location of the full-size image, information about the orientation of the image, and, in the case of extensions with adjustment data support, a set of adjustment data from previous edits.

As previously discussed, image extensions with adjustment data support implemented are passed the original image and a set of adjustments to be made to reach parity with the latest state of editing. Since it can take time to render these changes, the placeholder argument contains a snapshot of the image as it currently appears. This can be displayed to the user while the adjustment data is applied and the image is rendered in the background.

For this example, the *startContentEditing* method will be implemented as follows:

```
import UIKit
import Photos
import PhotosUI

class PhotoEditingViewController: UIViewController, PHContentEditingController {

    @IBOutlet weak var imageView: UIImageView!

    var input: PHContentEditingInput?
    var displayedImage: UIImage?
    var imageOrientation: Int32?
.

.

    func startContentEditing(with contentEditingInput:
        PHContentEditingInput, placeholderImage: UIImage) {

        input = contentEditingInput

        if let input = input {
            displayedImage = input.displaySizeImage
            imageOrientation = input.fullSizeImageOrientation
            imageView.image = displayedImage
        }
    }
.

.

.
```

}

The above changes declare two optional variables to reference the display-sized image and the image orientation. The code in the method then assigns the display-sized image from the *PHContentEditingInput* object passed to the method to the *displayedImage* variable and also stores the orientation setting in the *imageOrientation* variable. Finally, the display-sized image is displayed on the Image View in the user interface so that it is visible to the user.

Compile and run the extension, selecting the Photos app as the host app, and verify that the extension displays a copy of the image in the Image View of the extension View Controller.

79.8 Implementing the Filter Actions

The actions connected to the Bar Button Items will change the image by applying Core Image sepia, monochrome, and invert filters. Until the user commits the edits made in the extension, any filtering will be performed only on the display-sized image to avoid the rendering delays that are likely to be incurred working on the full-sized image. Having performed the filter, the modified image will be displayed on the image view instance.

Remaining within the *PhotoEditingViewController.swift* file, implement the three action methods as follows:

```
class PhotoEditingViewController: UIViewController,
 PHContentEditingController {

    @IBOutlet weak var imageView: UIImageView!

    var input: PHContentEditingInput?
    var displayedImage: UIImage?
    var imageOrientation: Int32?
    var currentFilter = "CIColorInvert"

    override func viewDidLoad() {
        super.viewDidLoad()
        // Do any additional setup after loading the view.
    }

    @IBAction func sepiaSelected(_ sender: Any) {
        currentFilter = "CISepiaTone"

        if let image = displayedImage {
            imageView.image = performFilter(image,
                                            orientation: nil)
        }
    }

    @IBAction func monoSelected(_ sender: Any) {
        currentFilter = "CIPhotoEffectMono"

        if let image = displayedImage {
            imageView.image = performFilter(image,
                                            orientation: nil)
```

```
            }
    }

    @IBAction func invertSelected(_ sender: Any) {
        currentFilter = "CIColorInvert"

        if let image = displayedImage {
            imageView.image = performFilter(image,
                                            orientation: nil)
        }
    }
    .
    .
    .
}
```

In each case, a method named *performFilter* is called to perform the image filtering task. The next step is to implement this method using the techniques outlined in the chapter entitled *"Drawing iOS 17 2D Graphics with Core Graphics"*:

```
func performFilter(_ inputImage: UIImage, orientation: Int32?)
    -> UIImage?
{
    var resultImage: UIImage?
    var cimage: CIImage

    cimage = CIImage(image: inputImage)!

    if let orientation = orientation {
        cimage = cimage.oriented(forExifOrientation: orientation)
    }

    if let filter = CIFilter(name: currentFilter) {
        filter.setDefaults()
        filter.setValue(cimage, forKey: "inputImage")

        switch currentFilter {

            case "CISepiaTone", "CIEdges":
                filter.setValue(0.8, forKey: "inputIntensity")

            case "CIMotionBlur":
                filter.setValue(25.00, forKey:"inputRadius")
                filter.setValue(0.00, forKey:"inputAngle")

            default:
                break
```

```
        }

        if let ciFilteredImage = filter.outputImage {
            let context = CIContext(options: nil)
            if let cgImage = context.createCGImage(ciFilteredImage,
                        from: ciFilteredImage.extent) {
                resultImage = UIImage(cgImage: cgImage)
            }
        }
    }
    return resultImage
}
```

The above method takes the image passed through as a parameter, takes steps to maintain the original orientation, and performs an appropriately configured filter operation on the image based on the value assigned to the *currentFilter* variable. The filtered image is then returned to the calling method.

Compile and run the extension again, this time using the filter buttons to change the appearance of the displayed image.

79.9 Returning the Image to the Photos App

When the user has finished making changes to the image and touches the *Done* button located in the extension toolbar, the *finishContentEditing(completionHandler:)* method of the View Controller is called. This is passed a reference to a completion handler which must be called once the image has been rendered and is ready to be returned to the Photos app.

Before calling the completion handler, however, this method performs the following tasks:

1. Obtains a copy of the full-size version of the image.

2. Ensures that the original orientation of the image is preserved through the rendering process.

3. Applies to the full-sized image all of the editing operations previously performed on the display-sized image.

4. Renders the new version of the full-sized image.

5. Packages up the adjustment data outlining the edits performed during the session.

Since the above tasks (particularly the rendering phase) are likely to take time, these must be performed within a separate asynchronous thread. The code to complete this example extension can now be implemented within the template stub of the method as follows:

```
func finishContentEditing(completionHandler: @escaping ((PHContentEditingOutput?)
-> Void)) {
    // Update UI to reflect that editing has finished, and output is being
rendered.

    // Render and provide output on a background queue.
    DispatchQueue.global().async {
        // Create editing output from the editing input.
        if let input = self.input {
            let output = PHContentEditingOutput(contentEditingInput: input)
```

```
            let url = self.input?.fullSizeImageURL

            if let imageUrl = url,
                let fullImage = UIImage(contentsOfFile: imageUrl.path),
                let resultImage = self.performFilter(fullImage,
                            orientation: self.imageOrientation) {

                if let renderedJPEGData =
                    resultImage.jpegData(compressionQuality: 0.9)  {
                    try! renderedJPEGData.write(to:
                        output.renderedContentURL)
                }

                do {
                    let archivedData =
                     try NSKeyedArchiver.archivedData(
                            withRootObject: self.currentFilter,
                      requiringSecureCoding: true)

                    let adjustmentData =
                        PHAdjustmentData(formatIdentifier:
                            "com.ebookfrenzy.photoext",
                                    formatVersion: "1.0",
                                    data: archivedData)

                    output.adjustmentData = adjustmentData
                } catch {
                    print("Unable to archive image data")
                }
            }
            completionHandler(output)
        }
    }
}
```

The code begins by creating a new instance of the *PHContentEditingOutput* class, initialized with the content of the input object originally passed into the extension:

```
if let input = self.input {
    let output = PHContentEditingOutput(contentEditingInput: input)
```

Next, the URL of the full-sized version of the image is extracted from the original input object, and the corresponding image is loaded into a UIImage instance. The full-sized image is then filtered via a call to the *performFilter* method:

```
if let imageUrl = url,
    let fullImage = UIImage(contentsOfFile: imageUrl.path),
    let resultImage = self.performFilter(fullImage,
```

```
                              orientation: self.imageOrientation) {
```

With the editing operations now applied to the full-sized image, it is rendered into JPEG format and written out to a location specified by the URL assigned to the *renderedContentURL* property of the previously created *PHContentEditingOutput* instance:

```
if let renderedJPEGData =
    resultImage.jpegData(compressionQuality: 0.9)  {
        try! renderedJPEGData.write(to: output.renderedContentURL)
}
```

Although the extension had previously indicated that it could not accept adjustment data, returning adjustment data reflecting the edits performed on the image to the Photos app is mandatory. For this tutorial, the name of the Core Image filter used to modify the image is archived into a Data instance with a revision number and a unique identifier. This object is then packaged into a *PHAdjustmentData* instance and assigned to the *adjustmentData* property of the output object:

```
let archivedData = try NSKeyedArchiver.archivedData(
                        withRootObject: self.currentFilter,
                        requiringSecureCoding: true)
let adjustmentData =
        PHAdjustmentData(formatIdentifier:
                        "com.ebookfrenzy.photoext",
                        formatVersion: "1.0",
                        data: archivedData)


output.adjustmentData = adjustmentData
```

If the extension were to be enhanced to handle adjustment data, code would need to be added to the *canHandle(adjustmentData:)* method to compare the *formatVersion* and *formatIdentifier* values from the incoming adjustment data with those specified in the outgoing data to verify that the data is compatible with the editing capabilities of the extension.

Finally, the completion handler is called and passed the fully configured output object. At this point, control will return to the Photos app, and the modified image will appear on the editing screen.

79.10 Testing the App

Build and run the extension using the Photos app as the host and take the familiar steps to select an image and invoke the newly created Photo Editing extension. Use a toolbar button to change the image's appearance before tapping the *Done* button. The modified image will subsequently appear within the Photos app editing screen (Figure 79-8 shows the results of the invert filter), where the changes can be committed or discarded:

Figure 79-8

79.11 Summary

The Photo Editing extension allows the image editing capabilities of a containing app to be accessed from within the standard iOS Photos app. A Photo Editing extension takes the form of a view controller, which implements the PHContentEditingController protocol and the protocol's associated delegate methods.

80. Creating an iOS 17 Action Extension

As with other extension types, the Action extension aims to extend elements of functionality from one app so that it is available for use within other apps. In the case of Action extensions, this functionality must generally fit the narrow definition of enabling the user to transform the content within a host app or view it differently. An app designed to translate text into different languages might, for example, provide an extension to allow the content of other apps to be similarly translated. An app designed to translate text into different languages might, for example, provide an extension to allow the content of other apps to be similarly translated.

This chapter will introduce the concept of Action extensions in greater detail and put theory into practice by creating an example app and Action extension.

80.1 An Overview of Action Extensions

Action extensions appear within the action view controller, which is the panel that appears when the user taps the Share button within a running app. Figure 80-1, for example, shows the action view controller panel as it appears from within the Safari web browser running on an iPhone. Action extensions appear within the action area of this panel alongside the built-in actions such as printing and copying of content.

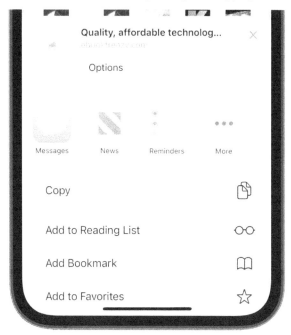

Figure 80-1

When an Action extension is created, it must declare the types of content with which it can work. The appearance or otherwise of the Action extension within the action view controller is entirely context-sensitive. In other words, an Action extension that can only work with text-based content will not appear as an option in the action view controller when the user is working with or viewing image or video content within a host app.

Unlike other extension types, there are two sides to an Action extension. In the first instance, there is the Action extension itself. An Action extension must be bundled with a containing app which must, in turn, provide some useful and meaningful functionality to the user. The other possibility is for host apps to be able to move beyond simply displaying the Action extension as an option within the action view controller. With the appropriate behavior implemented, a host app can receive modified content from an Action extension and make constructive use of it on the user's behalf. Both concepts will be implemented in the remainder of this chapter and the next chapter by creating an example Action extension and host app.

80.2 About the Action Extension Example

The tutorial in the remainder of this and the next chapter is divided into two distinct phases. The initial phase involves the creation of an Action extension named "Change it Up" designed to display the text content of host apps in upper case and using a larger font so that it is easier to read. For the sake of brevity, the containing app will not provide any additional functionality beyond containing the extension. However, it is important to remember that it will need to do so in the real world.

The second phase of the tutorial involves the creation of a host app that can receive modified content back from the Action extension and use it to replace the original content. This will be covered in the next chapter entitled "*Receiving Data from an iOS 17 Action Extension*".

80.3 Creating the Action Extension Project

An Action extension is created by adding an extension target to a containing app. Begin by launching Xcode and creating a new project using the iOS *App* template with the Swift and Storyboard options selected, entering *ActionDemo* as the product name.

80.4 Adding the Action Extension Target

With the newly created project loaded into Xcode, select the *File -> New -> Target...* menu option and, in the template panel (Figure 80-2), select the options to create an iOS Application Extension using the Action Extension template:

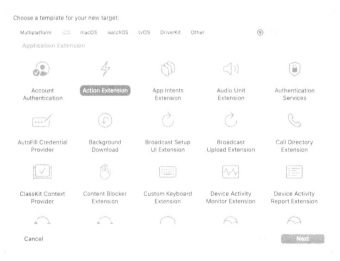

Figure 80-2

With the appropriate options selected, click the *Next* button and enter *MyActionExt* into the Product Name field. Leave the remaining fields to default values and click on *Finish* to complete the extension creation process.

When prompted, click on the *Activate* button to activate the scheme created by Xcode to enable the extension to be built and run.

Once the extension has been added, it will appear in the project navigator panel under the *MyActionExt* folder. This folder will contain the Swift source code file for the extension's view controller named *ActionViewController. swift*, a user interface storyboard file named *MainInterface.storyboard,* and an *Info.plist* file.

80.5 Changing the Extension Display Name

An important configuration change concerns the name that will appear beneath the extension icon in the action view controller. This is dictated by the value assigned to the *Bundle display name* key within the *Info.plist* file for the extension and currently reads "MyActionExt". To change this, select the ActionDemo entry at the top of the Project Navigator panel followed by MyActionExt listed under Targets. Finally, change the Display Name setting to "Change it Up" as illustrated below:

Figure 80-3

80.6 Designing the Action Extension User Interface

The user interface for the Action extension is contained in the *MyActionExt -> MainInterface.storyboard* file. Locate this file in the project navigator panel and load it into Interface Builder.

By default, Xcode has created a template user interface consisting of a toolbar, a "Done" button, and an image view. Therefore, the only change necessary for the purposes of this example is to replace the image view with a text view. First, select the image view in the storyboard canvas and remove it using the keyboard Delete key. Next, from the Library panel, drag and drop a Text View object onto the storyboard and position and resize it to fill the space previously occupied by the image view.

With the new Text View object still selected, display the *Resolve Auto Layout Issues* menu and select the *Reset to Suggested Constraints* menu option.

Display the Attributes Inspector for the Text View object, delete the default Latin text, and turn off the Editable option in the Behavior section of the panel. As previously outlined, one of the features of this extension is that the content is displayed in a larger font so take this opportunity to increase the font setting in the Attribute Inspector from System 14.0 to System 39.0.

Finally, display the Assistant Editor panel and establish an outlet connection for the Text View object named *myTextView*. Then, remaining within the Assistant Editor, delete the line of code declaring the imageView outlet.

With these changes made, the user interface for the Action extension view controller should resemble that of Figure 80-4:

Figure 80-4

80.7 Receiving the Content

The tutorial's next step is adding code to receive the content from a host app when the extension is launched. All extension view controllers have an associated *extension context* in the form of an instance of the NSExtensionContext class. A reference to the extension context can be accessed via the *extensionContext* property of the view controller.

The extension context includes a property named *inputItems* in the form of an array containing objects which provide access to the content from the host app. The input items are, in turn, contained within one or more NSExtensionItem objects.

Within the *ActionViewController.swift* file, locate the *viewDidLoad* method, remove the template code added by Xcode, and modify the method to obtain a reference to the first input item object:

```
override func viewDidLoad() {
    super.viewDidLoad()

    let textItem = self.extensionContext!.inputItems[0]
                    as! NSExtensionItem
}
```

Each NSExtensionItem object contains an array of *attachment* objects. These attachment objects are of type NSItemProvider and provide access to the data held by the host app. Once a reference to an attachment has been obtained, the *hasItemConformingToTypeIdentifier* method of the object can be called to verify that the host app has data of the type supported by the extension. In the case of this example, the extension supports text-based content, so the *UTType.text* uniform type identifier (UTI) is used to perform this test:

```
override func viewDidLoad() {
    super.viewDidLoad()

    let textItem = self.extensionContext!.inputItems[0]
            as! NSExtensionItem

    let textItemProvider = textItem.attachments![0]

    if textItemProvider.hasItemConformingToTypeIdentifier(UTType.text.identifier) {
    }
}
```

Assuming that the host app has data of the required type, it can be loaded into the extension via a call to the *loadItem(forTypeIdentifier:)* method of the attachment provider object, once again passing through as an argument the UTI content type supported by the extension. The loading of the data from the host app is performed asynchronously, so a completion handler must be specified, which will be called when the data loading process is complete:

```
override func viewDidLoad() {
    super.viewDidLoad()

    let textItem = self.extensionContext!.inputItems[0]
            as! NSExtensionItem

    let textItemProvider = textItem.attachments![0]

    if textItemProvider.hasItemConformingToTypeIdentifier(UTType.text.identifier) {
        textItemProvider.loadItem(
          forTypeIdentifier: UTType.text.identifier,
                  options: nil,
          completionHandler: { (result, error) in
        })
    }
}
```

When the above code is executed, the data associated with the attachment will be loaded from the host app, and the specified completion handler (in this case, a closure) will be called. The next step is to implement this completion handler. Remaining within the *ActionViewController.swift* file, declare a variable named *convertString* and implement the handler code in the closure so that it reads as follows:

```
import UIKit
import MobileCoreServices

class ActionViewController: UIViewController {

    @IBOutlet weak var myTextView: UITextView!
    var convertedString: String?
    .
    .
```

```
        if textItemProvider.hasItemConformingToTypeIdentifier(UTType.text.identifier) {
            textItemProvider.loadItem(forTypeIdentifier: UTType.text.identifier,
                            options: nil,
                completionHandler: { (result, error) in

                self.convertedString = result as? String

                if self.convertedString != nil {
                    self.convertedString = self.convertedString!.uppercased()

                    DispatchQueue.main.async {
                        self.myTextView.text = self.convertedString!
                    }
                }
            })
        }
```

.
.

The first parameter to the handler closure is an object that conforms to the NSSecureCoding protocol (in this case, a string object containing the text loaded from the host app). This string is assigned to a new variable within the method's body before being converted to upper case.

The converted text is then displayed on the Text View object in the user interface. It is important to be aware that because this is a completion handler, the code is being executed in a different thread from the main app thread. As such, any changes made to the user interface must be dispatched to the main thread, hence the *DispatchQueue* method wrapper.

80.8 Returning the Modified Data to the Host App

The final task of implementing the Action extension is to return the modified content to the host app when the user taps the Done button in the extension user interface. When the Action extension template was created, Xcode connected the Done button to an action method named *done*. Locate this method in the *ActionViewController. swift* file and modify it so that it reads as follows:

```
@IBAction func done() {
    let returnProvider =
        NSItemProvider(item: convertedString as NSSecureCoding?,
                    typeIdentifier: UTType.text.identifier)

    let returnItem = NSExtensionItem()

    returnItem.attachments = [returnProvider]
        self.extensionContext!.completeRequest(
            returningItems: [returnItem], completionHandler: nil)
}
```

This method essentially reverses the process of unpacking the input items. First, a new NSItemProvider instance is created and configured with the modified content (represented by the string value assigned to the *convertedString* variable) and the content type identifier. Next, a new NSExtensionItem instance is created, and the NSItemProvider object is assigned as an attachment.

Finally, the *completeRequest(returningItems:)* method of the extension context is called, passing through the NSExtensionItem instance as an argument.

As will be outlined later in this chapter, whether the host app does anything with the returned content items depends on whether the host app has been implemented to do so.

80.9 Testing the Extension

To test the extension, begin by making sure that the *MyExtAction* scheme (and not the *ActionDemo* containing app) is selected in the Xcode toolbar as highlighted in Figure 80-5:

Figure 80-5

Build and run the extension with a suitable device connected to the development system. As with other extension types, Xcode will prompt for a host app to work with the extension. An app that works with text content must be selected for the extension to be activated. Scroll down the list of apps installed on the device to locate and select the standard Notes app (Figure 80-6). Once selected, click on the *Run* button:

Figure 80-6

After the project has been compiled and uploaded to the device, the Notes app should automatically load (manually launch it if it does not). Select an existing note within the app, or add a new one if none exists, then tap the Share button in the top toolbar. If the Action extension does not appear in the action view controller panel, tap the *Edit Actions...* button and turn on the extension using the switch in the Activities list:

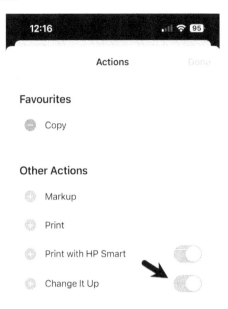

Figure 80-7

Once the extension has been enabled, it should appear in the action view controller panel:

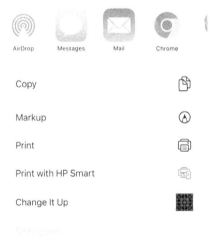

Figure 80-8

Once the extension is accessible, select it to launch the action. At this point, the extension user interface should appear, displaying the text from the note in uppercase using a larger font:

THIS IS SOME TEXT TO TEST AN ACTION EXTENSION

Figure 80-9

Note that there may be a delay of several seconds between selecting the Change it Up extension and the extension appearing. Having verified that the Action extension works, tap the Done button to return to the Notes app. Note that the content of the note did not change to reflect the content change to uppercase that was returned from the extension. This is because the Notes app has not implemented the functionality to accept modified content from an Action extension. As time goes by and Action extensions become more prevalent, it will become more common for apps to accept modified content from Action extensions. This raises the question of how this is implemented, an area that will be covered in the next chapter entitled *"Receiving Data from an iOS 17 Action Extension"*.

80.10 Summary

An Action extension is narrowly defined as a mechanism to transform the content in a host app or display that content to the user differently. An Action extension is context-sensitive and must declare the type of data it can use. There are essentially three key elements to an Action extension. First, the extension must load the content data from the host app. Second, the extension displays or transforms that content in some app-specific way. Finally, the transformed data is packaged and returned to the host app. Not all host apps can handle data returned from an Action extension, and in the next chapter, we will explore the steps necessary to add such a capability.

Chapter 81

81. Receiving Data from an iOS 17 Action Extension

The previous chapter covered the steps involved in creating an Action extension in iOS designed to modify and display text content from a host app. In developing the extension, steps were taken to ensure the modified content was returned to the host app when the user exited the extension. This chapter will work through creating an example host app that demonstrates how to receive data from an Action extension.

81.1 Creating the Example Project

Start Xcode and create a new project using the iOS App template with the Swift and Storyboard options selected, entering *ActionHostApp* as the product name.

The finished app will consist of a Text View object and a toolbar containing a Share button that will provide access to the Change it Up Action extension created in the previous chapter. When the Action extension returns, the host app will receive the modified content from the extension and display it to the user.

81.2 Designing the User Interface

Locate and load the *Main.storyboard* file into the Interface Builder tool and drag and drop a Toolbar instance to position it along the bottom edge of the layout canvas. Next, drag and drop a Text View object onto the canvas and resize and position it so it occupies the remaining space above the toolbar, stretching the view horizontally until the blue margin guidelines appear. With the TextView object selected, display the Attributes Inspector and change the displayed text to "This is some sample text":

Figure 81-1

Display the *Resolve Auto Layout Issues* menu and select the *Reset to Suggested Constraints* option listed under *All Views in View Controller*. Before proceeding, display the Assistant Editor panel and establish an outlet for the Text View object named *myTextView*.

81.3 Importing the Mobile Core Services Framework

The code added to this project will use a definition declared within the Mobile Core Services framework. To avoid compilation errors, this framework must be imported into the *ViewController.swift* file as follows:

```
import UIKit
import MobileCoreServices


class ViewController: UIViewController {

.

.

.

}
```

81.4 Adding an Action Button to the App

To access the "Change it Up" Action extension from within this host app, it will be necessary to implement an Action button. As the user interface currently stands, the toolbar contains a single button item displaying text which reads "Item". To change this to an Action button, select it in the storyboard layout (remembering that it may be necessary to click on it twice since the first click typically selects the parent toolbar rather than the button item).

With the button selected, display the Attributes Inspector and change the *System Item* menu from *Custom* to *Action*:

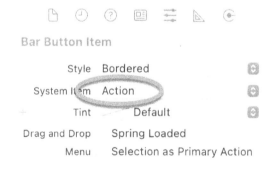

Figure 81-2

Once the change has been made, the button item should now have the standard appearance of an iOS Action button, as shown in Figure 81-3:

Figure 81-3

Now that the button looks like an Action button, some code needs to be added to display the activity view controller when the user taps it. First, with the Assistant Editor displayed, right-click on the button and drag the resulting line to a suitable location within the *ViewController.swift* file. Next, release the line and create an Action outlet named *showActionView*. Once created, implement the code in this method so that it reads as follows:

```
@IBAction func showActionView(_ sender: Any) {

    let activityViewController =
        UIActivityViewController(activityItems:
            [myTextView.text ?? ""], applicationActivities: nil)

    self.present(activityViewController,
                animated:true, completion: nil)

    activityViewController.completionWithItemsHandler =
        { (activityType, completed, returnedItems, error) in

        }
}
```

The code within the method creates a new UIActivityViewController instance initialized with the Text View content in the user interface. The activity view controller is then displayed to the user. Finally, a closure is assigned as the completion handler (the code for which will be implemented later) to be executed when the Action extension returns control to the app.

Compile and run the app and tap the Action button to test that the activity view controller appears. Next, select the "Change it Up" extension and verify that it displays the text extracted from the Text View. Finally, tap the Done button to return to the host app, noting that the original text content has not yet been converted to uppercase. This functionality now needs to be implemented within the completion handler method.

81.5 Receiving Data from an Extension

When the user exits from an Action extension, the completion handler assigned to the UIActivityViewController instance will be called and passed various parameters. One of those parameters will be an array of NSExtensionItem objects containing NSItemProvider objects that can be used to load any data the extension has returned.

Using the same techniques described in the previous chapter (*"Creating an iOS 17 Action Extension"*), this data can be extracted by making the following changes to the completion handler closure:

```
.
.
import UniformTypeIdentifiers
.
.
activityViewController.completionWithItemsHandler =
            { (activityType, completed, returnedItems, error) in

        if let items = returnedItems, items.count > 0 {

            let textItem: NSExtensionItem =
                items[0] as! NSExtensionItem

            let textItemProvider =
```

```
                textItem.attachments![0]

        if textItemProvider.hasItemConformingToTypeIdentifier(
            UTType.text.identifier) {

        textItemProvider.loadItem(
            forTypeIdentifier: UTType.text.identifier,
            options: nil,
            completionHandler: {(string, error) -> Void in
                let newtext = string as! String
                DispatchQueue.main.async(execute: {
                    self.myTextView.text = newtext
                })
            })
        }
    }
}
}
.
.
.
```

The method obtains a reference to the item provider and verifies that at least one item has been returned from the extension. A test is then performed to ensure that it is a text item. If the item is text-based, the item is loaded from the extension, and a completion handler is used to assign the new text to the Text View object. Note that the code to set the text on the TextView object is dispatched to the main thread for execution. This is because all user interface changes must be performed on the app's main thread, and completion handler code such as this is executed in a different thread.

81.6 Testing the App

Compile and run the app, select the Action button, and launch the "Change it Up" extension. On returning to the host app, the original text should now have been updated to be displayed in uppercase as modified within the extension.

81.7 Summary

In addition to providing an alternative view of the content in a host app, Action extensions can be used to somehow transform that content. This transformation can be performed and viewed within the extension, and a mechanism is also provided to return that modified content to the host app. By default, most host apps will not use the returned content. In reality, adding this support is a relatively simple task that involves implementing a completion handler method to handle the content returned from the extension into the host app and assigning that handler method to be called when the activity view controller is displayed to the user.

82. An Introduction to Building iOS 17 Message Apps

In much the same way that photo editing extensions allow custom photo editing capabilities to be added to the standard Photos app, message app extensions allow the functionality of the standard iOS Messages app to be extended and enhanced.

Message app extensions, introduced with iOS 10, allow app developers to provide users with creative ways to generate and send custom and interactive messages to their contacts. The possibilities offered by message apps range from simple sticker apps that allow images to be selected from sticker packs and inserted into messages through to more advanced possibilities such as fully interactive games.

Once created, Message app extensions are made available to customers through the Messages App Store, providing an additional source of potential revenue for app developers.

This chapter will provide a basic overview of message app extensions, along with an outline of how the key classes and methods of the Messages framework combine to enable the creation of message apps. The next chapter, entitled *"An iOS 17 Interactive Message App Tutorial"*, will work through creating an interactive message app project.

82.1 Introducing Message Apps

Message app extensions (often referred to simply as *message apps*) are built using the standard iOS extension mechanism. The one significant difference is that a message app extension does not require a containing app. Instead, users find and install message apps by browsing the Message App Store or when they receive a message created using a messaging app from another user. Once a messaging app has been installed, it appears within the *Messages App Drawer* of the Messages app on iOS devices. This app drawer is accessed by tapping the App Store icon located in the Messages app toolbar, as highlighted in Figure 82-1:

Figure 82-1

When a message app icon is tapped, the app extension is launched and displayed within the app drawer panel. When a message app is displayed, swiping left or right within the drawer scrolls through the different apps currently installed on the device. In Figure 82-2 below the app drawer displays a message app that allows animated images to be selected for inclusion in messages. When displayed in the app drawer, the message app is said to be using the *compact presentation style*.

Figure 82-2

The horizontal bar (highlighted in Figure 82-2 above) switches the app to *expanded presentation style* whereby the app user interface fills the entire screen area. Tapping the down arrow in the upper right-hand corner of the expanded presentation view will switch the app back to the compact style.

In addition to launching a message app from within the app drawer, selecting a message associated with a message app from the message transcript area will automatically launch the corresponding app in expanded presentation style.

If a user receives a message generated by a message app but does not currently have that particular app installed, tapping the app icon within the message will take the user to the Messages App Store, where the app may be purchased and installed. This is expected to have a viral effect in terms of selling message apps, with customers buying apps to interact with messages received from their contacts.

82.2 Types of Message Apps

iOS currently supports three different types of message app extensions. The first is simply a mechanism for providing collections of sticker images (referred to as *sticker packs*) to include in user messages. The second type of app allows various media content (such as text, images, web links, and videos) to be inserted into messages. The third, and most powerful option, allows fully interactive message apps to be created. When developing interactive message apps, the full range of iOS frameworks and user interface controls is available when implementing the app, essentially allowing a message app of any level of richness and complexity to be created using the same approach as that taken when developing regular iOS apps.

Since interactive message apps provide the greatest flexibility and opportunities for app developers, this will be the main focus of this chapter and the tutorial in the book's next chapter.

82.3 The Key Messages Framework Classes

Several classes provided by the Messages framework will need to be used in developing a message app. Therefore, understanding these classes and how they interact is essential. In this section, a brief overview of each class and the most commonly used properties and methods of those classes will be outlined.

82.3.1 MSMessagesAppViewController

The MSMessagesAppViewController class is responsible for displaying and managing the message app in both compact and expanded presentation styles. It allows for the presentation of a user interface to the user and provides a bridge between the user interface and the underlying app logic. The class also stores information about the app status via the following properties:

- **activeConversation** – Stores the MSConversation object for the currently active conversation.

- **presentationStyle** – Contains the current presentation style for the message app (compact or expanded).

Instances of this class also receive the following lifecycle method calls:

- **willBecomeActive** – The app is about to become active within the Messages app.

- **didBecomeActive** – Called immediately after the app becomes active.

- **willResignActive** – The app is about to become inactive.

- **didResignActive** – Called after the app has become inactive.

- **willSelect** – Called after the user selects a message from the transcript, but before the selectedMessage property of the conversation object is updated to reflect the current selection.

- **didSelect** – Called after the selectedMessage conversation property has been updated to reflect a message selection made by the user.

- **didReceive** – When an incoming message is received for the message app, and the message app is currently active, this method is called and passed corresponding MSMessage and MSConversation objects.

- **didStartSending** – Called when the user sends an outgoing message.

- **didCancelSending** – Called when the user cancels a message before sending it.

- **willTransition** – Called when the app is about to transition from one presentation style to another. Changes to the user interface of the message app to accommodate the presentation style change should be made here if necessary.

- **didTransition** – Called when the app has performed a transition between presentation styles.

Since MSMessagesAppViewController is a subclass of UIViewController, the class behaves in much the same way. Also, it receives the standard lifecycle method calls (such as *viewDidLoad*, *viewWillAppear*, *viewWillDisappear*, etc.) as the UIViewController class.

82.3.2 MSConversation

The MSConversation class represents the transcript area of the Messages app when a message app extension is active. This object stores the currently selected message (in the form of an MSMessage object via the *selectedMessage* property). In addition, it provides the following API methods that the message app may call to insert messages into the input field of the Messages app:

- **insert** – Inserts an MSMessage object or sticker into the input field of the Messages app.

- **insertText** – Inserts text into the input field of the Messages app.

- **insertAttachment** – Inserts an attachment, such as an image or video file, into the Messages app input field.

Once a message has been inserted into the Messages app input field, the user must send it via a tap on the send button. A message app can't send a message directly without the user taking this step.

In addition to the methods outlined above, the MSConversation class also contains the following properties:

- **localParticipantIdentifier** – Contains the UUID of the user of the local device. Accessing this item's uuidString property will provide the user's contact name in a format suitable for display within the message layout.

- **remoteParticipantIdentifiers** – Contains an array of UUID objects representing the identities of remote users currently participating in the message app conversation.

82.3.3 MSMessage

The MSMessage class represents individual messages within the Messages app transcript. The key elements of an MSMessage object are as follows:

- **layout** – The layout property takes the form of an MSMessageTemplateLayout object which defines how the message is to be displayed within the message bubble in the Messages app transcript area.

- **url** – The url property is used to encode the data that is to be sent along with the message. This can be a standard URL that points to a remote server where the data can be downloaded by the receiving app, or, for smaller data requirements, the URL itself can be used to encode the data to be transmitted with the message. The latter approach can be achieved using the URLComponents class, a process covered in detail in the next chapter entitled *"An iOS 17 Interactive Message App Tutorial"*.

- **session** – The use of sessions in message apps allows multiple messages to be designated as part of the same session. In addition, session messages are presented such that only the most recent message in the session is displayed in its entirety, thereby avoiding cluttering the Messages app transcript area with the full rendering of each message.

- **accessibilityLabel** – A localized string describing the message suitable for accessibility purposes.

- **senderParticipantIdentifier** – The UUID of the user that sent the message.

- **shouldExpire** – A Boolean value indicating whether the message should expire after the recipient has read it.

82.3.4 MSMessageTemplateLayout

The MSMessageTemplateLayout defines how an MSMessage instance is presented to the user within the transcript area of the Messages app.

When a message contained within an MSMessage object is presented to the user, it is displayed within a message bubble. Various aspects of how this message bubble appears can be defined and included within the MSMessage object.

The image, video, titles, and subtitles contained within the bubble are configured using an MSMessageTemplateLayout instance which is then assigned to the *layout* property of the MSMessage instance. For example, the diagram illustrated in Figure 82-3 provides a graphical rendering of an MSMessage-based message bubble with each of the configurable layout properties labeled accordingly:

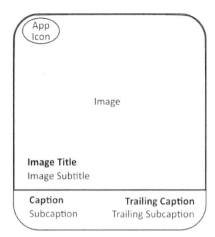

Figure 82-3

The settings in the above diagram correlate to the following properties of the MSMessageTemplateLayout class:

- **image** – The image to be displayed in the image area of the message. The recommended image size is 300pt x 300pt, and the Messages framework will automatically scale the image for different display sizes. To avoid rendering issues, it is recommended that text not be included in the image.

- **mediaFileURL** – The URL of a media file to be displayed in the image (such as a video or animated image file).

- **imageTitle** – The text to display in the Image Title location.

- **imageSubtitle** – The text to appear in the Image Subtitle location.

- **caption** – Text to appear in the Caption location.

- **subCaption** – Text to appear in the Subcaption location.

- **trailingCaption** - Text to appear in the Trailing Caption location.

- **trailingSubcaption** – Text to appear in the Trailing Subcaption location.

82.4 Sending Simple Messages

To send simple text, stickers, and image messages, it is not necessary to create an MSMessage object. The first step is to obtain a reference to the currently active conversation. From within an MSMessagesAppViewController instance, the currently active conversation can be obtained via the *activeConversation* property:

```
let conversation = self.activeConversation
```

The next step is to make a call to the appropriate method of the active conversation instance. To send a text message, for example, the code might read as follows:

```
let conversation = self.activeConversation
conversation?.insertText("Message Text Here") { error in
    // Handle errors
}
```

Once the above code is executed, the designated text will appear in the Messages app input field, ready to be sent by the user.

Similarly, an attachment may be sent using the *insertAttachment* method call, passing through a URL referencing the file to be attached to the message:

```
let conversation = self.activeConversation
conversation?.insertAttachment(myURL, withAlternateFilename: nil) { error in
      // Handle errors
}
```

82.5 Creating an MSMessage Message

To send an interactive message, it is necessary to use the MSMessage class. The first step, once again, is to obtain a reference to the currently active conversation:

```
let conversation = self.activeConversation
```

Next, a new MSMessage instance needs to be created within which to place the message content:

```
let message = MSMessage()
```

If the message is to be associated with a specific session, the message would be created as follows:

```
let session = MSSession()
let message = MSMessage(session: session)
```

The above example assigns a newly created session object to the message. If this message were being created in response to an incoming message that already had a session allocation, the session object from the incoming message would be used instead.

Once the message instance has been created, the layout needs to be configured using an MSMessageTemplateLayout instance. For example:

```
let layout = MSMessageTemplateLayout()
layout.imageTitle = "My Image Title"
layout.caption = "A Message Caption"
layout.subcaption = "A message subcaption"
layout.image = myImage
```

Once the layout has been defined, it needs to be assigned to the MSMessage object:

```
message.layout = layout
```

Next, a url needs to be assigned containing the data to be passed along with the message, for example:

```
message.url = myUrl
```

Once the message has been configured, it can be placed in the Messages app input field using the *insert* method of the active conversation:

```
conversation?.insert(message, completionHandler: {(error) in
            // Handle error
})
```

Once the message has been inserted, it is ready to be sent by the user.

82.6 Receiving a Message

When a message is received from another instance of a message app, and the message app is currently active, the *didReceive* method of the MSMessagesAppViewController instance will be called and passed both the MSMessage and MSConversation objects associated with the incoming message. When the user selects the message in the transcript, the app extension will launch, triggering a call to the *willBecomeActive* method, which will, in turn, be passed a copy of the MSConversation object from which a reference to the currently selected message may also be obtained.

Because the *didReceive* method is not called unless the message app is already active, the *willBecomeActive* method is typically the best place to access the incoming MSMessage object and update the app's status. The following sample implementation of the *willBecomeActive* method, for example, gets the selected message from the conversation object and then accesses the properties of the message to obtain the current session and the encoded URL:

```
override func willBecomeActive(with conversation: MSConversation) {
    if let message = conversation.selectedMessage? {
        let url = message.url
        let session = conversation.selectedMessage?.session
      // Decode the URL and update the app
    }
}
```

82.7 Supported Message App Platforms

The ability to create interactive messages using a message app extension is currently limited to devices running iOS 10 or later. Interactive messages will, however, be delivered to devices running macOS Sierra, watchOS 3, and iOS 10 in addition to older operating system versions.

When an interactive message is received on macOS Sierra, clicking on the message bubble will launch the URL contained within that message within the Safari browser. It is important to note that in this situation, the web server will need to be able to decode the URL and present content within the resulting web page that relates to the message. On watchOS 3, the interactive message can launch the full message app extension on a companion iOS 10 or later.

An incoming interactive message is delivered in two parts for older versions of macOS, watchOS, and iOS. The first contains the image assigned to the message layout, and the second is the URL contained within the message.

82.8 Summary

Message apps are custom apps installed as extensions to the built-in iOS Messages app. These apps create and send custom and interactive messages to other users. These extensions are made possible by the Messages framework. Message apps range in functionality from simple "sticker pack" apps to fully interactive experiences.

This chapter has outlined the basic concepts of message apps and the different classes typically required when developing a message app. The next chapter, entitled *"An iOS 17 Interactive Message App Tutorial"*, will use the information provided in this chapter to create an example interactive message app.

83. An iOS 17 Interactive Message App Tutorial

The previous chapter introduced message app extensions and described how the Messages framework allows custom, interactive messages to be sent and received from within the standard iOS Messages app.

In this chapter, many of the concepts described in the previous chapter will be put to practical use while working through the creation of an example interactive message app extension. Before following the tutorial, however, it is important to note that testing Message App extensions in a simulator environment has been unreliable for several years. Therefore, if you decide to complete this tutorial, you may only be able to test it if you have two iOS devices with separate Apple IDs or have a friend who will let you install the sample app on their device and play tic-tac-toe with you.

83.1 About the Example Message App Project

This tutorial will create an interactive message app extension project that implements a tic-tac-toe game designed to be played by two players via the Messages app. The first player begins the game by loading the app from the message app drawer and selecting from within the tic-tac-toe game grid. The current game status is then sent to a second player, appearing in the standard Messages app transcript area. Next, the second player selects the message to open the message app extension, where the next move can be made and sent back to the first player. This process repeats until the game is completed.

83.2 Creating the MessageApp Project

Launch Xcode and select the option to create a new Xcode project. Then, on the template selection screen, select the *iMessage App* option as illustrated in Figure 83-1 below and click on the *Next* button:

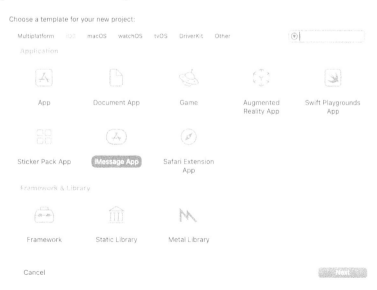

Figure 83-1

On the following screen, name the product *MessageApp* and select Swift as the language. Click the *Next* button, choose a location for the project files, and click the *Create* button.

A review of the project structure in the project navigator panel will reveal that both the main iOS app (named *MessageApp*) and an extension (*MessageExtension*) have been created:

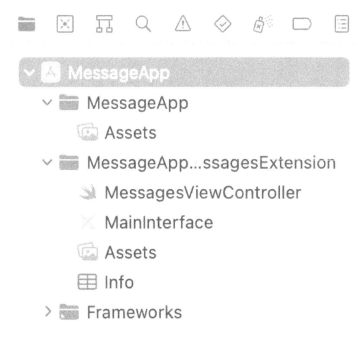

Figure 83-2

Within the MessagesExtension folder, the *MessagesViewController.swift* file contains the code for the MSMessagesAppViewController subclass, while the *MainInterface.storyboard* file contains the user interface for the message app extension. By default, the layout currently consists of a Label object configured to display "Hello World".

Before making any changes to the project, run the app on an iOS simulator and note that the Messages app launches and opens the message app extension. If the app does not load automatically, open the Messages app and click on the button indicated by the arrow in Figure 83-3:

Figure 83-3

From the resulting menu, select the More option followed by the MessageApp entry:

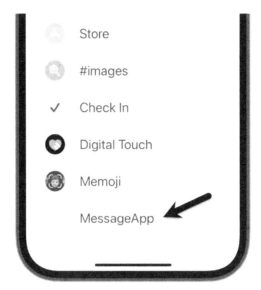

Figure 83-4

After the extension has loaded, the default "Hello World" user interface should appear (Figure 83-5):

Figure 83-5

Tapping the handle at the top of the extension panel (indicated by the arrow above) will switch the app from a compact to an expanded presentation style. Tap the handle at the top of the full-screen view to return to the compact presentation style.

83.3 Designing the MessageApp User Interface

The message app extension's user interface will consist of 9 Button objects arranged in a 3x3 grid using UIStackView layouts. Later in the tutorial, screenshots of the current game status will be taken and displayed in the interactive message bubbles. As a workaround for a problem with screenshots and the UIStackView class, the button collection will need to be contained within an additional UIView instance.

Begin the user interface design process by selecting the *MainInterface.storyboard* file and deleting the "Hello World" Label object. Next, drag and drop a View instance from the Library panel and position it so that it is centered horizontally and located along the bottom margin of the storyboard scene, as illustrated in Figure 83-6:

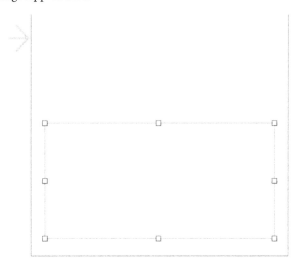

Figure 83-6

With the View selected, use the Add New Constraints button to add a constraint on the bottom edge of the view with the Constrain to Margins option enabled and both the Height and Width values set to 180. Next, use the Align men and enable the Horizontally in Container constraint. Once these constraints have been applied, the view should resemble Figure 83-7:

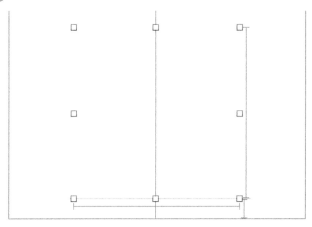

Figure 83-7

Drag a Button from the palette and place it within the newly added view. With the new button selected, display the Attributes Inspector panel and change the Background color to a light shade of gray. With the button still selected, change the Background property to Custom and the Fill color to a light shade of gray:

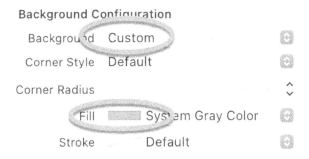

Figure 83-8

Double-click on the button and delete the current text, then use the Add New Constraints menu to set height and width values to 48 so that the parent view and button match the layout shown below (the button size constraints will take effect when it is embedded in a stack later):

Figure 83-9

Display the Assistant Editor panel and establish an action connection from the button to a method named *buttonPressed,* making sure to change the *Type* value from *Any* to *UIButton* before clicking on the *Connect* button.

Now that the first button has been added and configured, it must be duplicated eight times. Select the button in the layout, and use the Command-C keyboard shortcut to copy and Command-V to paste a duplicate. Position the new button to the right of the first button and continue pasting and moving button instances until there is a row of three buttons. Select the first button in the top row and then hold down the shift key while selecting the remaining two buttons in that row. With all three buttons selected, click on the Embed In button (highlighted in Figure 83-10) and select the *Embed In* menu option to add the buttons to a Stack View instance:

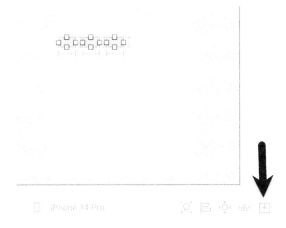

Figure 83-10

With the StackView instance selected, use the Attributes Inspector panel to change the Spacing attribute to 2.

Repeat these steps to add two more rows of buttons so that each row is contained within a horizontal Stack View.

Display the Document Outline panel, hold down the Command key and select each of the three Stack View instances:

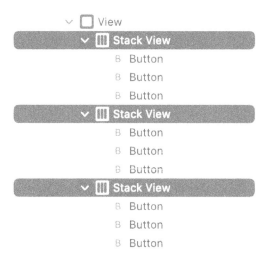

Figure 83-11

With the three Stack View entries selected, click on the Embed In button in the canvas toolbar once again to add the three horizontal stacks into a single vertical stack. Then, using the Attributes Inspector panel, increase the spacing property on the vertical stack view to 2.

With the vertical stack still selected, display the Auto Layout align menu and enable both the horizontal and vertical center in container options before clicking the *Add 2 Constraints* button. At this point, the view and grid layout should match Figure 83-12. Before proceeding, display the Assistant Editor and establish an outlet connection for the View object named *gridView*:

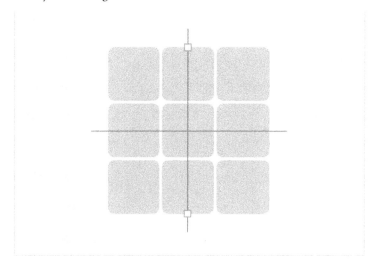

Figure 83-12

83.4 Creating the Outlet Collection

As is invariably the case, the code for the app will need to be able to access the buttons in the user interface via outlets. In this project, all buttons will be connected to the same outlet using an *outlet collection*.

Where a normal outlet contains a reference to a single user interface object, an outlet collection is an array of references to multiple user interface objects. First, display the Assistant Editor and select the first button on the top row of the grid (note that initial selection attempts may select the parent StackView objects, so continue clicking until only the button is selected). Next, create the outlet collection by right-clicking on the selected button and dragging it to a position beneath the class declaration line in the Assistant Editor panel. When the connection dialog appears, change the Connection menu setting from *Outlet* to *Outlet Collection* (Figure 83-13), name the connection *Buttons,* and click on the *Connect* button.

Figure 83-13

To add the second button in the first row, click on the outlet marker in the margin of the Assistant Editor panel and drag to the button as outlined in Figure 83-14:

Figure 83-14

Connect the outlet collection using this technique for the remaining buttons in the grid, taking care to work from left to right and row by row (the order in which the buttons are added to the collection is essential if the game is to function correctly).

Run the extension on the simulator and verify that the layout appears as designed in both compact and expanded presentation styles.

83.5 Creating the Game Model

The model for tracking the game's status is straightforward and consists of an array containing ten string elements. The first element in the array stores the current player ('X' or 'O'), while the remaining nine contain the corresponding buttons' current settings in the array ('X' or 'O'). In addition, the elements in this array are initialized with '-' characters to indicate unselected grid locations.

Open the *MessagesViewController.swift* file and add some variable declarations as follows:

```
class MessagesViewController: MSMessagesAppViewController {

    @IBOutlet weak var gridView: UIView!
    @IBOutlet var Buttons: [UIButton]!

    var gameStatus = [String](repeating: "-", count: 9)
    var currentPlayer: String = "X"
    var caption = "Want to play Tic-Tac-Toe?"
    var session: MSSession?

    .
    .
    .
```

In addition to the array declaration, the above changes include a variable to temporarily store the current player setting (which will be placed into the array when the user makes a selection), an initial setting of the message caption, and a variable to store the current MSSession instance.

83.6 Responding to Button Selections

Each game button was previously configured to call a method named *buttonPressed* when tapped. This method needs to identify which button was pressed, store the current player value into the matching element of the game status array, and then change the button's title to indicate that the current player has selected it. Within the *MessagesViewController.swift* file, locate the template *buttonPressed* method and implement the code as follows:

```
@IBAction func buttonPressed(_ sender: UIButton) {
    for (index, button) in Buttons.enumerated() {
        if button.isEqual(sender) {

            if gameStatus[index].isEqual("-") {
                gameStatus[index] = currentPlayer
                sender.setTitle(currentPlayer, for: .normal)
            }
        }
    }
}
```

When called, this method is passed a reference to the user interface object that triggered the event. The added code iterates through the *Buttons* outlet collection until it finds the matching button. Using the index value associated with this button, the code then ensures that the corresponding element in the gameStatus array contains a '-' character. This indicates that the button grid location has not already been selected. If the button is available, the current player's string value is stored at the corresponding location in the gameStatus array and set as the button title.

Compile and run the message app on a simulator session and verify that clicking on the buttons in the game grid causes an 'X' to appear on the clicked button. If the app crashes, then message app extensions probably still aren't working on the simulator, and you will need two physical iOS devices to continue testing.

83.7 Preparing the Message URL

Once the user has selected a game move, the message needs to be prepared and inserted into the message transcript, ready to be reviewed and sent by the user. Part of this message takes the form of a URL which will be used to encode the current game state so that it can be reconstructed when the second player receives the message.

For this example, the URLComponents class will build a URL containing a query item for the current player and nine other items representing each button position's status in the game grid. Below is an example of how the URL might appear partway through an ongoing game:

```
https://www.ebookfrenzy.com?currentPlayer=X&position0=X&position1=O&position2=-
&position3=-&position4=-&position5=-&position6=X&position7=-&position8=-
```

The first part of the URL contains the standard HTTP scheme and domain declaration, while the rest of the URL is comprised of query items. Each query item is represented by a URLQueryItem instance and contains a key-value pair. As seen in the example URL, the first query item contains the key "currentPlayer," which is currently assigned a value of "X". The remaining query items have keys ranging from position0 through to position8, with the value of each set to an 'X', 'O', or '-' to indicate the current status of the corresponding position in the button grid.

The code to create this URL is going to reside within a method named *prepareURL* which can now be added to the *MessagesViewController.swift* file so that it reads as follows:

```
func prepareURL() -> URL {
    var urlComponents = URLComponents()
    urlComponents.scheme = "https";
    urlComponents.host = "www.ebookfrenzy.com";
    let playerQuery = URLQueryItem(name: "currentPlayer",
                        value: currentPlayer)

    urlComponents.queryItems = [playerQuery]

    for (index, setting) in gameStatus.enumerated() {
        let queryItem = URLQueryItem(name: "position\(index)",
                                value: setting)
        urlComponents.queryItems?.append(queryItem)
    }
    return urlComponents.url!
}
```

The method begins by creating a URLComponents instance and configuring the scheme and host values. Next, a new query item comprising a key-value pair representing the current player information is created. The code then performs a looping operation through the elements of the gameStatus array. For each element, a new query item is created containing a key-value pair indicating the status of the corresponding grid position, which is then appended to the urlComponent object. Finally, the encoded array is returned.

This new method must be called from within the *buttonPressed* method when the user has selected a valid button. Now is also a good opportunity to add a call to a method named *prepareMessage* which will be created in the next section:

```
@IBAction func buttonPressed(_ sender: Any) {
    for (index, button) in Buttons.enumerated() {
        if button.isEqual(sender) {

            if gameStatus[index].isEqual("-") {
                gameStatus[index] = currentPlayer
                sender.setTitle(currentPlayer, for: .normal)
                let url = prepareURL()
                prepareMessage(url)
            }
        }
    }
}
```

83.8 Preparing and Inserting the Message

The steps to create the message will now be implemented within a method named *prepareMessage*. Add this method as follows to the *MessagesViewController.swift* file:

```
func prepareMessage(_ url: URL) {

    let message = MSMessage()

    let layout = MSMessageTemplateLayout()
    layout.caption = caption

    message.layout = layout
    message.url = url

    let conversation = self.activeConversation

    conversation?.insert(message, completionHandler: {(error) in
        if let error = error {
            print(error)
        }
    })
    self.dismiss()
}
```

The method creates a new MSMessage object and a template layout object with the caption set to the current value of the *caption* variable. The encoded url containing the current game status is then assigned to the url property of the message. Next, a reference to the currently active conversation is obtained before the message is inserted into the iMessage input field, ready to be sent by the player. Finally, the MessagesViewController instance is dismissed from view.

Rerun the message app and click the grid button. Note that the entry now appears in the Messages app input field, ready to be sent to the other player. Click on the send button (highlighted in Figure 83-15) to send the message.

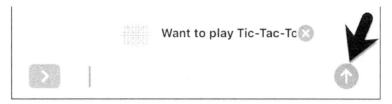

Figure 83-15

When testing messages in the simulator, the iMessage app simulates a conversation between two users named Kate Bell and John Appleseed. After the message has been sent, click the back arrow in the top left corner of the iMessage screen to move back to the conversation selection screen, select conversation entry and note that the message has arrived:

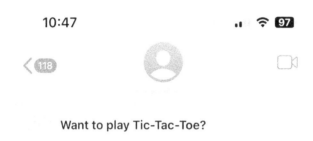

Want to play Tic-Tac-Toe?

Figure 83-16

Tap the message to load the message extension where the button grid will appear. A few areas of functionality, however, have yet to be implemented. First, the current state of play is not reflected on the buttons, all of which remain blank. Also, clicking on a button causes an 'X' character to appear. Since the first player is represented by 'X,' a current selection should display an 'O' on the button. Clearly, some code needs to be added to handle the receipt of a message and update the game model within the message app extension.

83.9 Message Receipt Handling

The first step in handling the incoming message is to write a method to decode the incoming url and update the gameStatus array with the current status. Within the *MessagesViewController.swift* file, implement a method for this purpose named *decodeURL*:

```
func decodeURL(_ url: URL) {

    let components = URLComponents(url: url,
                resolvingAgainstBaseURL: false)

    for (index, queryItem) in (components?.queryItems?.enumerated())! {

        if queryItem.name == "currentPlayer" {
            currentPlayer = queryItem.value == "X" ? "O" : "X"
        } else if queryItem.value != "-" {
            gameStatus[index-1] = queryItem.value!
            Buttons[index-1].setTitle(queryItem.value!, for: .normal)
        }
    }
}
```

This method performs the reverse of the *prepareURL* method in that it initiates a URLComponents object from a url and then extracts the value for the current player key, followed by the current setting for each button. If the status of a button is not a '-' character, then the current value (an X or O) is displayed on the corresponding button.

Next, the code to handle the incoming message needs to be implemented in the *willBecomeActive* method, a template for which has been placed within the *MessagesViewController.swift* file ready to be completed. When called by the Message framework, this method is passed an MSConversation object representing the currently active conversation. This object contains a property named *selectedMessage* referencing the MSMessage object selected by the user to launch the extension. From this object, the url containing the encoded game status data can be extracted, decoded, and used to update the game status within this instance of the message app.

Locate the *willBecomeActive* method template in the *MessagesViewController.swift* file and modify it as follows:

```
override func willBecomeActive(with conversation: MSConversation) {

    if let messageURL = conversation.selectedMessage?.url {
        decodeURL(messageURL)
        caption = "It's your move!"
    }

    for (index, item) in gameStatus.enumerated() {
        if item != "-" {
            Buttons[index].setTitle(item, for: .normal)
        }
    }
}
```

The method gets the url that was embedded into the message and passes it to the *decodeURL* method for decoding and updating the internal game status model. The caption variable is changed to indicate that this is an ongoing game before a *for* loop updates the titles displayed on the game buttons.

Test the game again and note that the current game status is preserved between players and that Os are displayed when the second player clicks on the grid buttons.

83.10 Setting the Message Image

Currently, the message bubbles in the message transcript area contain the default app icon and the text assigned to the message caption property. A better user experience would be provided if the message bubble's image property displayed the game's current status.

A quick way of achieving this result is to take a screenshot of the gameView View object in which the grid layout resides. This can be achieved by adding some code to the *prepareMessage* method as follows:

```
func prepareMessage(_ url: URL) {

    let message = MSMessage()
    let layout = MSMessageTemplateLayout()
    layout.caption = caption

    UIGraphicsBeginImageContextWithOptions(gridView.bounds.size,
            gridView.isOpaque, 0);
```

```
self.gridView.drawHierarchy(in: gridView.bounds,
        afterScreenUpdates: true)

layout.image = UIGraphicsGetImageFromCurrentImageContext()!
UIGraphicsEndImageContext()

message.layout = layout
message.url = url

let conversation = self.activeConversation
conversation?.insert(message, completionHandler: {(error) in
    if let error = error {
        print(error)
    }
})
self.dismiss()
}
```

This new code designates a graphic context covering the screen area containing the gridView object. A graphics rendering of the view hierarchy of which gridView is the parent is then drawn into the context. Finally, an image is generated and displayed as the image property of the message layout object.

When the app is tested, the message bubbles should now contain an image showing the current status of the tic-tac-toe grid:

Figure 83-17

83.11 Summary

The Message framework allows message app extensions to be integrated into the standard iOS Messages app. These extensions allow interactive messages to be sent between users. This process involves obtaining a reference to the currently active conversation and creating and configuring an MSMessage object, which is then inserted into the conversation. Data to be transferred with the message may be encoded into a URL using the URLComponents class and then assigned to the URL property of the MSMessage object. This data is then decoded when received by another instance of the app extension and used to restore the app's state.

This chapter has worked through creating an example app designed to demonstrate the key steps in developing an interactive message app.

84. An Introduction to Machine Learning on iOS

Machine learning is one of the key components of artificial intelligence. It involves using data analysis to teach software to perform tasks without specifically being programmed. Machine learning is used in many fields and industries to perform tasks such as identifying spam emails, detecting people and objects in images, fraud detection, and financial trading systems, for example.

Apple first introduced machine learning capabilities for iOS and macOS in 2017 with the introduction of the Core ML framework and has continued to add improvements in iOS 17 with the release of Create ML.

Machine learning is a large and complex technology area, so the goal of this and subsequent chapters is to provide an overview of the basics of this topic to get up to speed quickly and provide a knowledge basis on which to build more advanced machine learning skills.

84.1 Datasets and Machine Learning Models

Machine learning begins with the gathering of datasets to be used to train and create a learning model. To create a model that can detect happy or sad sentiments expressed in text messages, for example, the model would need to be trained with a dataset containing both types of messages, with each message labeled to indicate whether the message is happy or sad. Similarly, a model intended to identify a particular car model from photos would need to be trained with images of the model of the car in various colors taken from multiple angles and distances.

The model will be built by iterating through the training dataset and learning how to categorize similar data. Once the training is complete, the model is tested by applying it to a dataset containing data not previously included during training. The training results can then be analyzed to check for accuracy, and the model can be improved if necessary by providing additional training data and increasing the number of iterations performed during the training phase.

Once a model is complete, it is referred to as a *trained model* and is ready to be used in real-world situations.

84.2 Machine Learning in Xcode and iOS

The first step in implementing machine learning within an iOS app is to create the model. Once a complex and time-consuming task, this is now made easier through the introduction of Create ML. Create ML (in the form of the CreateMLUI class) can be used from within an Xcode playground to visually create a model by writing a few lines of code, dragging and dropping training and testing datasets into the Assistant Editor, and viewing the results. Alternatively, models may be created programmatically from within an app by using the CreateML class.

Training a model to identify whether an image contains a picture of a dog or cat, for example, can be as simple as creating a training folder containing one subfolder of cat images and another containing dog images. All that is necessary to train the model is to drag the training folder and drop it onto the model builder in the Xcode playground window.

Alternatively, the training dataset can consist of CSV or JSON data containing the training data. The following JSON excerpt, for example, is used to teach a model to distinguish between legitimate and spam email message titles:

```
[
    {
        "text": "Congratulations, you've won $1000!",
        "label": "spam"
    }, {
        "text": "Meeting reminder",
        "label": "not spam"
    }, {
        "text": "Lose 20lb in one month",
        "label": "spam"
    } ...
]
```

When dividing data into training and testing sets, the general recommendation is to use 80% of the data for training and 20% for testing.

Once the model has been sufficiently trained, it can be saved to a file and added to an Xcode app project simply by dragging and dropping the file onto the project navigator panel, where it is ready to be used in the app code.

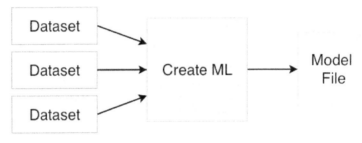

Figure 84-1

84.3 iOS Machine Learning Frameworks

When a trained model has been added to an app project, the classes of the Core ML framework are used to create and initiate requests to be performed using the model. In addition to Core ML, iOS also includes frameworks specifically for working with images (Vision framework), text and natural language (NaturalLangauge framework), and gameplaying (GameplayKit framework).

In a testament to the power in a device the size of an iPhone, machine learning operations run locally on the device using both the CPU and, for more intensive tasks, the GPU, maintaining user data privacy and avoiding reliance on a network connection.

84.4 Summary

This chapter has provided a basic introduction to machine learning in iOS, covered the creation of machine learning models using Create ML, and outlined the frameworks available for implementing machine learning within an iOS app. The next chapter will demonstrate the use of Create ML to build a machine learning model for image analysis, which will then be used in an iOS app in the *"An iOS Vision and Core ML Image Classification Tutorial"* chapter.

85. Using Create ML to Build an Image Classification Model

This chapter will demonstrate the use of Create ML to build an image classification model trained to classify images based on whether the image contains one of four specific items (an apple, banana, cat, or a mixture of fruits).

The tutorial will include the training and testing of an image recognition machine learning model using an Xcode playground. In the next chapter, this model will be integrated into an app to perform image classifications when a user takes a photo or selects an image from the photo library.

85.1 About the Dataset

As explained in the previous chapter, an image classification model is trained by providing it with a range of images that have already been categorized. Once the training process has been performed, the model is then tested using a set of images that were not previously used in the training process. Once the testing achieves a high enough level of validation, the model is ready to be integrated into an app project.

For this example, a dataset containing images of apples and bananas will be used for training. The dataset is contained within a folder named *CreateML_dataset,* which is included with the source code download available at the following URL:

https://www.payloadbooks.com/product/ios17xcode/

The dataset includes a *Training* folder containing images divided into two subfolders organized as shown in Figure 85-1:

Figure 85-1

The dataset also includes a *Testing* folder containing images for each classification, none of which were used during the training session. Once the dataset has been downloaded, take some time to browse the folders and images to understand the data's structure.

85.2 Creating the Machine Learning Model

With the dataset prepared, the next step is to create the model using the Create ML tool. Begin by launching Xcode, then select the *Xcode -> Open Developer Tool -> Create ML* menu option. When Create ML has loaded, it will display a Finder window where you can choose an existing model or create a new one. Within this window, click on the New Document button to display the template selection screen shown in Figure 85-2:

Using Create ML to Build an Image Classification Model

Figure 85-2

For this example, we will work with images, so select the *Image Classification* template followed by the Next button. Then, continue through the remaining screens, naming the project MyImageClassifier and selecting a suitable folder into which to create the model.

Once the model has been created, the screen shown in Figure 85-3 will appear ready for the training and tested data to be imported:

Figure 85-3

In the left-hand panel, click on the "MyImageClassifier 1" entry listed under Model Sources and change the name to MyImageClassifier.

85.3 Importing the Training and Testing Data

Click on the box labeled Training Data to display the finder dialog and navigate to and open the Training data set folder. Next, repeat these steps to import the test folder into the Testing Data box. Once the data has been imported, the Data section of the Create ML screen should resemble Figure 85-4:

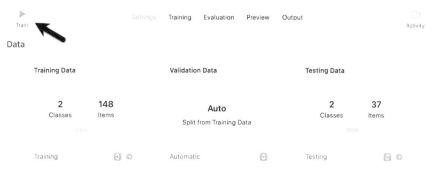

Figure 85-4

Next, increase the number of training iterations to 45 and set some augmentations to train the model to deal with image variations:

Figure 85-5

85.4 Training and Testing the Model

Now that we have loaded the data, we are ready to start training and testing the model by clicking on the Train button indicated by the arrow in Figure 85-4 above. Once the process is complete, select the Training tab to display a graph showing how accuracy improved with each training iteration:

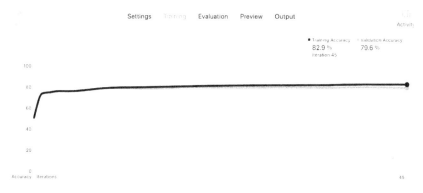

Figure 85-6

Next, switch to the Evaluation screen to review a more detailed breakdown of the training:

Figure 85-7

Finally, switch to the Preview screen and drag and drop images for each category that were not part of the training or testing data and see which are successfully classified by the model:

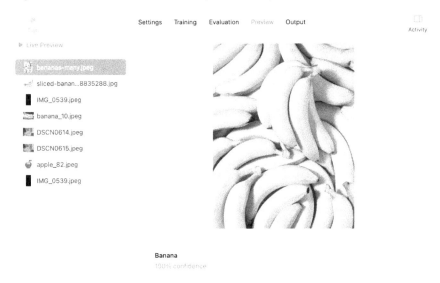

Figure 85-8

We now need to save the model in preparation for loading it into an Xcode project. To save the model, display the Output screen, click on the Get button highlighted in Figure 85-9, and select a name and location for the model file:

Figure 85-9

Before exiting from Create ML tool, save the project using the *File -> Save...* menu option.

85.5 Summary

A key component of any machine learning implementation is a well-trained model, and the accuracy of that model is dependent on the dataset used during the model training. Once comprehensive training data has been gathered, Create ML makes creating and testing machine learning models easy. This involves the use of the Create ML classifier builder. This chapter demonstrated the use of the Image classifier builder to create and save a model designed to identify several different object types within images. This model will be used in the next chapter to perform image identification within an existing iOS app.

86. An iOS Vision and Core ML Image Classification Tutorial

Now that we have created an image classification machine learning model in the previous chapter, this chapter will take that model and use it in conjunction with the iOS Core ML and Vision frameworks to build image classification features into an iOS app.

86.1 Preparing the Project

The project used as the basis for this tutorial is the Camera app created previously in the chapter entitled *"An Example iOS 17 Camera App"*. If you have not completed the Camera tutorial, a completed copy of the project can be found in the source code archive download.

Using a Finder window, duplicate the Camera project folder, name the copy Camera_ML and load it into Xcode.

86.2 Adding the Model

Using the Finder window once again, locate the *MyImageClassifier.mlmodel* file created in the previous chapter and drag it onto the Xcode Project navigator panel, accepting the defaults in the confirmation panel:

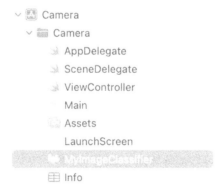

Figure 86-1

86.3 Modifying the User Interface

The existing user interface layout for the Camera app will need an additional Label view to be added so that the classification results can be presented to the user. Within Xcode, select the *Main.storyboard* file, display the Library panel, and drag and drop a Label onto the toolbar so that it is positioned as shown in Figure 86-2. Next, stretch the label so that the right-hand side reaches the right-hand margin of the parent view:

Figure 86-2

With the Label selected, use the *Add New Constraints* menu to add constraints to the left, right, and bottom edges of the Label with the *Constrain to Margins* option disabled.

Finally, display the Assistant Editor panel and establish an outlet connection from the Label to a variable named *identityLabel*.

86.4 Initializing the Core ML Request

When the user either takes or selects a photo, the app will need to pass a request to an instance of the VNImageRequestHandler class to perform the classification. This request takes the form of a VNCoreMLRequest instance initialized with the machine learning model to be used. This model is provided in the form of a VNCoreMLModel object which, in turn, must be initialized with the machine learning model (in this case, the model contained within the *MyImageClassifier.mlmodel* file).

The VNCoreMLRequest object also provides the option to specify a completion handler method to be called once the request has been processed. This method will be passed a VNRequest object from which the classification results can be checked and appropriate action taken.

Within the *ViewController.swift* file, add a method named *buildRequest()* to create a VNCoreMLRequest object, configure it with the MyImageClassifier model and assign a method named *checkResults()* as the completion handler to be called when the classification process finishes. This *buildRequest()* method will be called later in the tutorial when the VNImageRequestHandler instance is created:

```
.
.
import UIKit
import MobileCoreServices
import UniformTypeIdentifiers
import CoreML
import Vision

.
.
func buildRequest() -> VNCoreMLRequest {

    do {
        let defaultConfig = MLModelConfiguration()
        let model = try VNCoreMLModel(for: MyImageClassifier(
                              configuration: defaultConfig).model)
        let request = VNCoreMLRequest(model: model, completionHandler: {
            [weak self] request, error in
                self?.checkResults(for: request, error: error)
        })
        request.imageCropAndScaleOption = .centerCrop
        return request
    } catch {
        fatalError("Failed to load ML model: \(error)")
    }
}
.
.
```

86.5 Handling the Results of the Core ML Request

When the image analysis is completed, the completion handler for the above classification request is configured to call a method named checkResults(). This method now needs to be added to the *ViewController.swift* file as follows:

```
func checkResults(for request: VNRequest, error: Error?) {
    DispatchQueue.main.async {
        guard let results = request.results else {
            self.identityLabel.text =
                "Unable to classify image.\n\(error!.localizedDescription)"
            return
        }

        let classifications = results as! [VNClassificationObservation]

        if classifications.isEmpty {
            self.identityLabel.text = "Nothing recognized."
        } else {
            let bestClassifications = classifications.prefix(1)

            let bestMatch = bestClassifications[0]

            if bestMatch.confidence < 0.95 {
                self.identityLabel.text = "No Match"
            } else {
                self.identityLabel.text = bestMatch.identifier
            }
        }
    }
}
```

The code begins by dispatching the result-handling activities to a separate thread so that the code in the method is run asynchronously from the rest of the app:

```
func performClassification(for request: VNRequest, error: Error?) {
    DispatchQueue.main.async {
```

The method has been passed a VNRequest object which contains the results of the classification in the form of an array of VNClassificationObservation objects. The items in the array are positioned in order of best match to worst match. The method checks that the request object contains results and extracts the observations.

```
let classifications = results as! [VNClassificationObservation]
```

The code notifies the user if no matches are found; otherwise, the best match is taken from the results:

```
if classifications.isEmpty {
    self.identityLabel.text = "Nothing recognized."
} else {
    let bestClassifications = classifications.prefix(1)

    let bestMatch = bestClassifications[0]
```

Having identified the closest match, the match's confidence value is tested to ensure that the match was made with a greater than 95% degree of certainty. If the confidence level is high enough, the identifier for the match (in this case, "Apple," "Banana," "Cat," or "Mixed") is displayed on the Label view. Otherwise, "No match" is displayed:

```
if bestMatch.confidence < 0.95 {
    self.identityLabel.text = "No Match"
} else {
    self.identityLabel.text = bestMatch.identifier
}
```

86.6 Making the Classification Request

When the user either takes a picture or selects a photo library, the image picker delegate methods will need a way to make the Core ML classification request. Begin implementing this behavior by adding another method to the *ViewController.swift* file:

```
func startClassification(for image: UIImage) {

    if let orientation =
        CGImagePropertyOrientation(rawValue:
            UInt32(image.imageOrientation.rawValue)) {

        guard let ciImage = CIImage(image: image) else
        { fatalError("Unable to create \(CIImage.self) from \(image).") }

        DispatchQueue.global(qos: .userInitiated).async {
            let handler = VNImageRequestHandler(ciImage: ciImage,
            orientation: orientation)
            do {
                let request = self.buildRequest()
                try handler.perform([request])
            } catch {
                print("Classification failed: \(error.localizedDescription)")
            }
        }
    }
}
```

The method is passed a UIImage object from which the current orientation is obtained before being converted to a CIImage instance. Then, on a separate thread, a VNImageRequestHandler instance is created and initialized with the image object and orientation value. Next, the *buildRequest()* method created at the beginning of this chapter is called to obtain a VNCoreMLRequest object initialized with the trained model.

Finally, the request object is placed in an array (the VNImageRequestHandler class can handle multiple requests simultaneously) and passed to the *perform()* method of the handler. This will initiate a chain of events starting with the image classification analysis and ending with the resulting call to the *checkResults()* method, which, in turn, updates the Label view.

The last step before testing the app is to make sure the *startClassification()* method gets called from the *didFinishPickingMediaWithInfo* image picker delegate method:

```
func imagePickerController(_ picker: UIImagePickerController,
didFinishPickingMediaWithInfo info: [UIImagePickerController.InfoKey : Any]) {

    let mediaType =
            info[UIImagePickerController.InfoKey.mediaType] as! NSString

    self.dismiss(animated: true, completion: nil)

    if mediaType.isEqual(to: kUTTypeImage as String) {
        let image = info[UIImagePickerController.InfoKey.originalImage]
            as! UIImage

        imageView.image = image

        startClassification(for: image)
    .
    .
    .
}
```

86.7 Testing the App

Open the Photos app on your Mac, add some apple and banana images (including both dataset images and images downloaded from the internet) to your photo library, and wait for them to sync with your iOS device via iCloud. Next, compile and run the app on the physical device (at the time of writing, Core ML was not working on simulators) and tap the Camera Roll button. When the image picker appears, select one of the synced images to return to the Camera app and verify that the label updates with the correct identification:

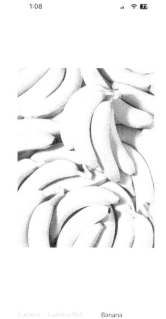

Figure 86-3

Finally, select a photo that is clearly neither a banana nor an apple, and verify that the status label indicates no match was found:

Figure 86-4

86.8 Summary

This chapter has demonstrated how a machine learning model can be used within an app to perform image classification tasks using classes from the Core ML and Vision frameworks together with minimal coding. The tutorial included creating and initiating a machine learning request object and handling results from a completed classification request.

87. An iOS 17 Local Notification Tutorial

Notifications provide a mechanism for an app to schedule an alert to notify the user about an event. These notifications take the form of a notification panel containing a message accompanied by a sound and the device's vibration.

Notifications are categorized as either local or remote. Notifications initiated by apps running on a device are referred to as local notifications. On the other hand, a remote notification is initiated by a remote server and *pushed* to the device, where it is displayed to the user.

Both local and remote notifications are managed using the classes of the UserNotifications framework in conjunction with the user notification center. In the course of covering the steps to create, send and manage local notifications, this chapter will also outline the various classes provided within the UserNotifications framework and the methods provided by the user notification center.

87.1 Creating the Local Notification App Project

The first step in demonstrating the use of local notifications is to create a new Xcode project. Begin by launching Xcode and creating a new project using the iOS App template with the Swift and Storyboard options selected, entering *NotifyDemo* as the product name.

87.2 Requesting Notification Authorization

Before an app can issue notifications, it must first seek permission from the user. This request involves making a call to the *user notification center*.

The user notification center handles, manages, and coordinates all notifications on a device. In this case, a reference to the current notification center instance needs to be obtained, and the *requestAuthorization* method is called on that object.

Edit the *ViewController.swift* file to import the UserNotifications framework, request authorization, and add a variable to store the subtitle of the message, which the user will be able to change from within the notification later in this tutorial:

```
import UIKit
import UserNotifications


class ViewController: UIViewController {


    var messageSubtitle = "Staff Meeting in 20 minutes"


    override func viewDidLoad() {
        super.viewDidLoad()
        UNUserNotificationCenter.current().requestAuthorization(options:
                [[.alert, .sound, .badge]],
```

```
                              completionHandler: { (granted, error) in
            // Handle Error
        })
    }
    .
    .
}
```

Run the app on an iOS device and tap the Allow button when the permission request dialog (Figure 87-1) appears:

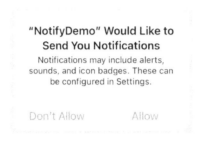

Figure 87-1

87.3 Designing the User Interface

Select the *Main.storyboard* file and drag and drop a Button object to position it in the center of the scene. Then, using the Auto Layout *Resolve Auto Layout Issues* menu, select the option to reset to suggested constraints for all views in the view controller.

Change the text on the button to read *Send Notification*, display the Assistant Editor panel and establish an action connection from the button to a method named *buttonPressed*.

Edit the *ViewController.swift* file and modify the *buttonPressed* action method to call a method named *sendNotification*:

```
@IBAction func buttonPressed(_ sender: Any) {
    sendNotification()
}
```

On completion of the layout work, the user interface should match that shown in Figure 87-2 below:

Figure 87-2

87.4 Creating the Message Content

The first part of the notification to be created is the message content. An instance of the UNMutableNotificationContent class represents the content of the message for a local notification. This class can contain various options, including the message title, subtitle, and body text. In addition, the message may contain media content such as images and videos. Within the *ViewController.swift* file, add the *sendNotification* method as follows:

```
func sendNotification() {
    let content = UNMutableNotificationContent()
    content.title = "Meeting Reminder"
    content.subtitle = messageSubtitle
    content.body = "Don't forget to bring coffee."
    content.badge = 1
}
```

Note also that the badge property of the content object is set to 1. This value configures the notification count that is to appear on the app launch icon on the device after a notification has been triggered, as illustrated in Figure 87-3:

Figure 87-3

87.5 Specifying a Notification Trigger

Once the content of the message has been created, a trigger needs to be defined that will cause the notification to be presented to the user. Local notifications can be triggered based on elapsed time intervals, a specific date and time, or a location change. For this example, the notification will be configured to trigger after 5 seconds have elapsed (without repeating):

```
func sendNotification() {
    let content = UNMutableNotificationContent()
    content.title = "Meeting Reminder"
    content.subtitle = messageSubtitle
    content.body = "Don't forget to bring coffee."
    content.badge = 1

    let trigger = UNTimeIntervalNotificationTrigger(timeInterval: 5,
                    repeats: false)
}
```

87.6 Creating the Notification Request

The next step is to create a notification request object containing the content and trigger objects together with an identifier that can be used to access the notification later if it needs to be modified or deleted. The notification request takes the form of a UNNotificationRequest object, the code for which will now need to be added to the *sendNotification* method:

```
func sendNotification() {
    let content = UNMutableNotificationContent()
    content.title = "Meeting Reminder"
    content.subtitle = messageSubtitle
    content.body = "Don't forget to bring coffee."
    content.badge = 1

    let trigger = UNTimeIntervalNotificationTrigger(timeInterval: 5,
                    repeats: false)

    let requestIdentifier = "demoNotification"
    let request = UNNotificationRequest(identifier: requestIdentifier,
                    content: content, trigger: trigger)
}
```

87.7 Adding the Request

The request object now needs to be added to the notification center, where it will be triggered when the specified time has elapsed:

```
func sendNotification() {
    let content = UNMutableNotificationContent()
    content.title = "Meeting Reminder"
    content.subtitle = messageSubtitle
    content.body = "Don't forget to bring coffee."
    content.badge = 1

    let trigger = UNTimeIntervalNotificationTrigger(timeInterval: 5,
                    repeats: false)

    let requestIdentifier = "demoNotification"
    let request = UNNotificationRequest(identifier: requestIdentifier,
            content: content, trigger: trigger)

    UNUserNotificationCenter.current().add(request,
            withCompletionHandler: { (error) in
            // Handle error
    })
}
```

87.8 Testing the Notification

Compile and run the NotifyDemo app on a device or simulator session. Once the app has loaded, tap the *Send Notification* button and press the Home button to place the app in the background. After 5 seconds have elapsed, the notification will appear as shown in Figure 87-4:

Figure 87-4

Open the app again and tap the button, but do not place the app in the background. This time the notification will not appear. This is the default behavior for user notifications. If the notifications issued by an app are to appear while that app is in the foreground, an additional step is necessary.

87.9 Receiving Notifications in the Foreground

As demonstrated in the previous section, when an app that issues a notification is currently in the foreground, the notification is not displayed. To change this default behavior, it will be necessary for the view controller to declare itself as conforming to the UNUserNotificationCenterDelegate protocol and implement the *userNotification:willPresent* method. In addition, the current class will also need to be declared as the notification delegate. Remaining within the *ViewController.swift* file, make these changes as follows:

```
import UIKit
import UserNotifications


class ViewController: UIViewController, UNUserNotificationCenterDelegate {
.
.

    override func viewDidLoad() {
        super.viewDidLoad()
        UNUserNotificationCenter.current().requestAuthorization(options: [[.alert,
                .sound, .badge]], completionHandler: { (granted, error) in
            // Handle Error
        })
        UNUserNotificationCenter.current().delegate = self
    }
.
.

    func userNotificationCenter(_ center: UNUserNotificationCenter, willPresent
notification: UNNotification, withCompletionHandler completionHandler: @escaping
(UNNotificationPresentationOptions) -> Void) {


    completionHandler([.banner, .sound])
}
```

The *userNotification:willPresent* method calls the provided completion handler, indicating that the notification should be presented to the user using both the banner message and sound. Rerun the app and test that the notification banner appears after the button is pressed with app remaining in the foreground.

87.10 Adding Notification Actions

The default action when the user taps a notification is to dismiss the notification and launch the corresponding app. However, the UserNotifications framework also allows action buttons to be added to notifications. These buttons are displayed when the user presses down with force on the notification message or swipes the message to the left. For this example, two action buttons will be added to the notification, one instructing the app to repeat the notification while the other will allow the user to input different text to appear in the message subtitle before repeating the notification.

This will require the creation of two notification action objects as follows:

```
let repeatAction = UNNotificationAction(identifier: "repeat",
                  title: "Repeat", options:[])


let changeAction = UNTextInputNotificationAction(identifier: "change",
                  title: "Change Message", options: [])
```

Next, these action objects need to be placed in a notification category object, and the category object added to the user notification center after being assigned an identifier:

```
let category = UNNotificationCategory(identifier: "actionCategory",
            actions: [repeatAction, changeAction],
            intentIdentifiers: [], options: [])


content.categoryIdentifier = "actionCategory"


UNUserNotificationCenter.current().setNotificationCategories([category])
```

Combining these steps with the existing *sendNotification* method results in code that reads as follows:

```
func sendNotification() {
    let content = UNMutableNotificationContent()
    content.title = "Meeting Reminder"
    content.subtitle = messageSubtitle
    content.body = "Don't forget to bring coffee."
    content.badge = 1

    let repeatAction = UNNotificationAction(identifier:"repeat",
            title: "Repeat", options: [])
    let changeAction = UNTextInputNotificationAction(identifier:
            "change", title: "Change Message", options: [])

    let category = UNNotificationCategory(identifier: "actionCategory",
            actions: [repeatAction, changeAction],
            intentIdentifiers: [], options: [])

    content.categoryIdentifier = "actionCategory"

    UNUserNotificationCenter.current().setNotificationCategories(
                                        [category])
```

.

.

}

Compile and run the app on a physical device, trigger the notification, and perform a long press on the message when it appears. The action buttons should appear beneath the message as illustrated in Figure 87-5 below:

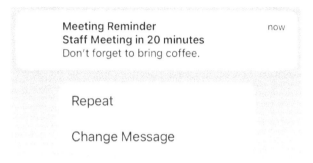

Figure 87-5

Tap the *Change Message* button and note that a text input field appears. Although the action buttons are now present, some work still needs to be performed to handle the actions within the view controller.

87.11 Handling Notification Actions

When an action is selected by the user, the *userNotification:didReceive* method of the designated notification delegate is called by the user notification center. Since the ViewController class has already been declared as implementing the UNUserNotificationCenterDelegate protocol and assigned as the delegate, all that needs to be added to the *ViewController.swift* file is the *userNotification:didReceive* method:

```
func userNotificationCenter(_ center: UNUserNotificationCenter, didReceive
 response: UNNotificationResponse, withCompletionHandler completionHandler:
  @escaping () -> Void) {

    switch response.actionIdentifier {
        case "repeat":
            self.sendNotification()
        case "change":
            let textResponse = response
                    as! UNTextInputNotificationResponse
            messageSubtitle = textResponse.userText
            self.sendNotification()
        default:
            break
    }
    completionHandler()
}
```

The method is passed a UNNotificationResponse object from which we can extract the identifier of the action that triggered the call. A switch statement is then used to identify the action and take appropriate steps. If the repeat action is detected, the notification is resent. In the case of the change action, the text entered by the user is obtained from the response object and assigned to the *messageSubtitle* variable before the notification is sent again.

Compile and run the app again and verify that the actions perform as expected.

87.12 Hidden Notification Content

iOS provides a range of options that allow the user to control the information displayed within a notification when it appears on the device lock screen. As we have seen in this example, the default setting is for all of the information contained within a notification (in this case, the title, subtitle, and body content) to be displayed when the notification appears on the lock screen.

These notification preview settings can be specified per app or globally for all installed apps. To view and change the current global settings, open the Settings app and select *Notifications -> Show Previews*. As shown in Figure 87-6, options are available to show notification previews always, only when the device is unlocked or never:

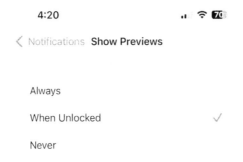

Figure 87-6

These global settings can be overridden for individual apps from within the Settings app by displaying the Notifications screen, selecting the app from the list, and scrolling down to the *Show Previews* option, as highlighted in Figure 87-7:

Figure 87-7

The current notification preview settings configured by the user may be identified by accessing the *showPreviewSettings* property of the current notification center settings. For example:

```
UNUserNotificationCenter.current().getNotificationSettings { (settings) in

    switch settings.showPreviewsSetting {
        case .always :
            print("Always")
        case .whenAuthenticated :
            print("When unlocked")
        case .never :
            print("Never")
    }
}
```

On the device on which the NotifyDemo app is installed, locate the notification preview settings for the app and change the current setting to *Never*. After making the change, run the app, trigger a notification, and immediately lock the device. When the notification appears, it will no longer contain any information except for the app name and the word *Notification* (Figure 87-8):

Figure 87-8

When creating a notification from within an app, it is possible to configure options that allow more information to be displayed in this situation. For example, when the notification code was implemented earlier in this chapter, a UNNotificationCategory object was created and initialized with information about the notification, including the identifier and the two actions. This category object was then assigned to the notification before it was sent:

```
.

.

let category = UNNotificationCategory(identifier: "actionCategory",
                         actions: [repeatAction, changeAction],
                 intentIdentifiers: [],
                         options: [])

content.categoryIdentifier = "actionCategory"

UNUserNotificationCenter.current().setNotificationCategories([category])

.

.
```

The category object also contains an array of options that were left empty in the above code. In this options array, properties can be declared that will allow the title, subtitle, or both to be displayed within the lock screen notification even when the preview mode is set to *When Unlocked*. The .hiddenPreviewsShowTitle and .hiddenPreviewsShowSubtitle option values represent the two settings. For example, modify the code for the NotifyDemo app so the category object is initialized as follows:

```
let category = UNNotificationCategory(identifier: "actionCategory",
```

```
actions: [repeatAction, changeAction],
intentIdentifiers: [],
options: [.hiddenPreviewsShowTitle])
```

Run the app, trigger a notification, and lock the device. This time when the notification appears, the title is included in the preview though the subtitle and body remain hidden:

Figure 87-9

Modify the options array once more, this time adding the subtitle option as follows:

```
let category = UNNotificationCategory(identifier: "actionCategory",
                actions: [repeatAction, changeAction],
                intentIdentifiers: [],
                options: [.hiddenPreviewsShowTitle,
                        .hiddenPreviewsShowSubtitle])
```

This time when a notification preview from the app appears on the lock screen, it will display both the title and subtitle while the body content remains hidden:

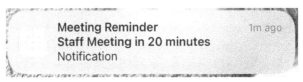

Figure 87-10

87.13 Managing Notifications

In addition to creating notifications, the UserNotifications framework also provides ways to manage notifications, both while they are still pending and after they have been delivered. One or more pending notifications may be removed by passing an array of request identifiers through to the removal method of the user notification center:

```
UNUserNotificationCenter.current()
 .removePendingNotificationRequests(withIdentifiers:
                [demoIdentifer, demoIdentifier2])
```

Similarly, the content of a pending intent may be updated by creating an updated request object with the same identifier containing the new content and adding it to the notifications center:

```
UNUserNotificationCenter.current().add(updatedRequest,
            withCompletionHandler: { (error) in
            // Handle error
})
```

Finally, previously delivered notifications can be deleted from the user's notification history by a call to the user notification center passing through one or more request identifiers matching the notifications to be deleted:

```
UNUserNotificationCenter.current()
 .removeDeliveredNotifications(withIdentifiers: [demoIdentifier])
```

87.14 Summary

An app can trigger notifications locally or remotely via a server. The UserNotifications framework manages both forms of notification. An app that needs to issue local notifications must first seek permission from the user.

A notification consists of a content object, a request object, and access to the notifications center. In addition, a notification may include actions that appear in the form of buttons when a force touch press is performed on the notification message. These actions include the ability for the user to input text to be sent to the app that initiated the intent.

iOS allows users to control content shown in the preview when the device is locked. The app can, however, configure options within the notification to display the title and subtitle content within the notification preview regardless of user settings.

88. Playing Audio on iOS 17 using AVAudioPlayer

The iOS SDK provides several mechanisms for implementing audio playback from within an iOS app. The easiest technique from the app developer's perspective is to use the AVAudioPlayer class, which is part of the AV Foundation Framework.

This chapter will provide an overview of audio playback using the AVAudioPlayer class. Once the basics have been covered, a tutorial is worked through step by step. The topic of recording audio from within an iOS app is covered in the next chapter entitled *"Recording Audio on iOS 17 with AVAudioRecorder"*.

88.1 Supported Audio Formats

The AV Foundation Framework supports the playback of various audio formats and codecs, including software and hardware-based decoding. Codecs and formats currently supported are as follows:

- AAC (MPEG-4 Advanced Audio Coding)

- ALAC (Apple Lossless)

- AMR (Adaptive Multi-rate)

- HE-AAC (MPEG-4 High-Efficiency AAC)

- iLBC (internet Low Bit Rate Codec)

- Linear PCM (uncompressed, linear pulse code modulation)

- MP3 (MPEG-1 audio layer 3)

- µ-law and a-law

If an audio file is to be included as part of the resource bundle for an app, it may be converted to a supported audio format before inclusion in the app project using the macOS *afconvert* command-line tool. For details on how to use this tool, run the following command in a Terminal window:

```
afconvert -h
```

88.2 Receiving Playback Notifications

An app receives notifications from an AVAudioPlayer instance by declaring itself as the object's delegate and implementing some or all of the following AVAudioPlayerDelegate protocol methods:

- **audioPlayerDidFinishPlaying** – Called when the audio playback finishes. An argument passed through to the method indicates whether the playback was completed successfully or failed due to an error.

- **audioPlayerDecodeErrorDidOccur** - Called when the AVAudioPlayer object encounters a decoding error during audio playback. An error object containing information about the nature of the problem is passed through to this method as an argument.

- **audioPlayerBeginInterruption** – Called when audio playback has been interrupted by a system event, such as an incoming phone call. Playback is automatically paused, and the current audio session is deactivated.

- **audioPlayerEndInterruption** - Called after an interruption ends. The current audio session is automatically activated, and playback may be resumed by calling the play method of the corresponding AVAudioPlayer instance.

88.3 Controlling and Monitoring Playback

Once an AVAudioPlayer instance has been created, audio playback may be controlled and monitored programmatically via the methods and properties of that instance. For example, the self-explanatory *play*, *pause* and *stop* methods may be used to control playback. Similarly, the *volume* property may be used to adjust the volume level of the audio playback. In contrast, the *playing* property may be accessed to identify whether or not the AVAudioPlayer object is currently playing audio.

In addition, playback may be delayed to begin later using the *playAtTime* instance method, which takes as an argument the number of seconds (as an NSTimeInterval value) to delay before beginning playback.

The length of the current audio playback may be obtained via the *duration* property while the current point in the playback is stored in the *currentTime* property.

Playback may also be programmed to loop back and repeatedly play a specified number of times using the *numberOfLoops* property.

88.4 Creating the Audio Example App

The remainder of this chapter will work through creating a simple iOS app that plays an audio file. The app's user interface will consist of play and stop buttons to control playback and a slider to adjust the playback volume level.

Begin by launching Xcode and creating a new project using the iOS App template with the Swift and Storyboard options selected, entering *AudioDemo* as the product name.

88.5 Adding an Audio File to the Project Resources

To experience audio playback, adding an audio file to the project resources will be necessary. For this purpose, any supported audio format file will be suitable. Having identified a suitable audio file, drag and drop it into the Project Navigator panel of the main Xcode window. For this tutorial, we will be using an MP3 file named *Moderato.mp3* which can be found in the *audiofiles* folder of the sample code archive, downloadable from the following URL:

https://www.payloadbooks.com/product/ios17xcode/

Locate and unzip the file in a Finder window and drag and drop it onto the Project Navigator panel.

88.6 Designing the User Interface

The app user interface will comprise two buttons labeled "Play" and "Stop" and a slider to adjust the playback volume. Next, select the *Main.storyboard* file, display the Library, drag and drop components from the Library onto the View window and modify properties so that the interface appears as illustrated in Figure 88-1:

Figure 88-1

With the scene view selected within the storyboard canvas, display the Auto Layout *Resolve Auto Layout Issues* menu and select the *Reset to Suggested Constraints* menu option listed in the *All Views in View Controller* section of the menu.

Select the slider object in the view canvas, display the Assistant Editor panel and verify that the editor is displaying the contents of the *ViewController.swift* file. Right-click on the slider object and drag it to a position just below the class declaration line in the Assistant Editor. Release the line, and in the resulting connection dialog, establish an outlet connection named *volumeControl*.

Right-click on the "Play" button object and drag the line to the area immediately beneath the *viewDidLoad* method in the Assistant Editor panel. Release the line and, within the resulting connection dialog, establish an Action method on the *Touch Up Inside* event configured to call a method named *playAudio*. Repeat these steps to establish an action connection on the "Stop" button to a method named *stopAudio*.

Right-click on the slider object and drag the line to the area immediately beneath the newly created actions in the Assistant Editor panel. Release the line and, within the resulting connection dialog, establish an Action method on the *Value Changed* event configured to call a method named *adjustVolume*.

Close the Assistant Editor panel, select the *ViewController.swift* file in the project navigator panel, and add an import directive and delegate declaration, together with a property to store a reference to the AVAudioPlayer instance as follows:

```
import UIKit
import AVFoundation

class ViewController: UIViewController, AVAudioPlayerDelegate {

    @IBOutlet weak var volumeControl: UISlider!
    var audioPlayer: AVAudioPlayer?
.
.
```

88.7 Implementing the Action Methods

The next step in our iOS audio player tutorial is implementing the action methods for the two buttons and the slider. Remaining in the *ViewController.swift* file, locate and implement these methods as outlined in the following code fragment:

```
@IBAction func playAudio(_ sender: Any) {
    audioPlayer?.play()
}


@IBAction func stopAudio(_ sender: Any) {
    audioPlayer?.stop()
}


@IBAction func adjustVolume(_ sender: Any) {
    audioPlayer?.volume = volumeControl.value
}
```

88.8 Creating and Initializing the AVAudioPlayer Object

Now that we have an audio file to play and appropriate action methods written, the next step is to create an AVAudioPlayer instance and initialize it with a reference to the audio file. Since we only need to initialize the object once when the app launches, a good place to write this code is in the *viewDidLoad* method of the *ViewController.swift* file:

```
override func viewDidLoad() {
    super.viewDidLoad()

    if let bundlePath = Bundle.main.path(forResource: "Moderato",
                                           ofType: "mp3") {

        let url = URL.init(fileURLWithPath: bundlePath)

        do {
            try audioPlayer = AVAudioPlayer(contentsOf: url)
            audioPlayer?.delegate = self
            audioPlayer?.prepareToPlay()
        } catch let error as NSError {
            print("audioPlayer error \(error.localizedDescription)")
        }
    }
}
```

In the above code, we create a URL reference using the filename and type of the audio file added to the project resources. Remember that this will need to be modified to reflect the audio file used in your projects.

Next, an AVAudioPlayer instance is created using the URL of the audio file. Assuming no errors were detected, the current class is designated as the delegate for the audio player object. Finally, a call is made to the audioPlayer object's *prepareToPlay* method. This performs initial buffering tasks, so there is no buffering delay when the user selects the play button.

88.9 Implementing the AVAudioPlayerDelegate Protocol Methods

As previously discussed, by declaring our view controller as the delegate for our AVAudioPlayer instance, our app will be able to receive notifications relating to the playback. Templates of these methods are as follows and may be placed in the *ViewController.swift* file:

```
func audioPlayerDidFinishPlaying(_ player: AVAudioPlayer, successfully
                flag: Bool) {

}

func audioPlayerDecodeErrorDidOccur(_ player: AVAudioPlayer,
                error: Error?) {

}

func audioPlayerBeginInterruption(_ player: AVAudioPlayer) {
}

func audioPlayerEndInterruption(player: AVAudioPlayer) {
}
```

For this tutorial, it is not necessary to implement any code for these methods, and they are provided solely for completeness.

88.10 Building and Running the App

Once all the requisite changes have been made and saved, test the app in the iOS simulator or a physical device by clicking on the run button in the Xcode toolbar. Once the app appears, click on the Play button to begin playback. Next, adjust the volume using the slider and stop playback using the Stop button. If the playback is not audible on the device, ensure that the switch on the side of the device is not set to silent mode.

88.11 Summary

The AVAudioPlayer class, part of the AVFoundation framework, provides a simple way to play audio from within iOS apps. In addition to playing back audio, the class also provides several methods that can be used to control the playback in terms of starting, stopping, and changing the playback volume. By implementing the methods defined by the AVAudioPlayerDelegate protocol, the app may also be configured to receive notifications of events related to the playback, such as playback ending or an error occurring during the audio decoding process.

89. Recording Audio on iOS 17 with AVAudioRecorder

In addition to audio playback, the iOS AV Foundation Framework provides the ability to record sound on iOS using the AVAudioRecorder class. This chapter will work step-by-step through a tutorial demonstrating using the AVAudioRecorder class to record audio.

89.1 An Overview of the AVAudioRecorder Tutorial

This chapter aims to create an iOS app to record and play audio. It will do so by creating an instance of the AVAudioRecorder class and configuring it with a file to contain the audio and a range of settings dictating the quality and format of the audio. Finally, playback of the recorded audio file will be performed using the AVAudioPlayer class, which was covered in detail in the chapter entitled *"Playing Audio on iOS 17 using AVAudioPlayer"*.

Audio recording and playback will be controlled by buttons in the user interface that are connected to action methods which, in turn, will make appropriate calls to the instance methods of the AVAudioRecorder and AVAudioPlayer objects, respectively.

The view controller of the example app will also implement the AVAudioRecorderDelegate and AVAudioPlayerDelegate protocols and several corresponding delegate methods to receive notification of events relating to playback and recording.

89.2 Creating the Recorder Project

Begin by launching Xcode and creating a new single view-based app named *Record* using the Swift programming language.

89.3 Configuring the Microphone Usage Description

Access to the microphone from within an iOS app is considered a potential risk to the user's privacy. Therefore, when an app attempts to access the microphone, the operating system will display a warning dialog to the user seeking authorization for the app to proceed. Included within the content of this dialog is a message from the app justifying using the microphone. This text message must be specified within the *Info.plist* file using the NSMicrophoneUsageDescription key. The absence of this key will result in the app crashing at runtime.

To add this setting:

1. Select the *Record* entry at the top of the Project navigator panel and select the *Info* tab in the main panel.

2. Click on the + button contained with the last line of properties in the Custom iOS Target Properties section.

3. Select the *Privacy - Microphone Usage Description* item from the resulting menu.

Once the key has been added, double-click in the corresponding value column and enter the following text:

```
The audio recorded by this app is stored securely and is not shared.
```

Once the rest of the code has been added and the app is launched for the first time, a dialog will appear, including the usage message. If the user taps the OK button, microphone access will be granted to the app.

89.4 Designing the User Interface

Select the *Main.storyboard* file and, once loaded, drag Button objects from the Library (*View -> Utilities -> Show Library*) and position them on the View window. Once placed in the view, modify the text on each button so that the user interface appears as illustrated in Figure 89-1:

Figure 89-1

With the scene view selected within the storyboard canvas, display the Auto Layout *Resolve Auto Layout Issues* menu and select the *Reset to Suggested Constraints* menu option listed in the *All Views in View Controller* section of the menu.

Select the "Record" button object in the view canvas, display the Assistant Editor panel and verify that the editor is displaying the contents of the *ViewController.swift* file. Next, right-click on the Record button object and drag to a position just below the class declaration line in the Assistant Editor. Release the line and establish an outlet connection named *recordButton*. Repeat these steps to establish outlet connections for the "Play" and "Stop" buttons named *playButton* and *stopButton,* respectively.

Continuing to use the Assistant Editor, establish Action connections from the three buttons to methods named *recordAudio*, *playAudio,* and *stopAudio*.

Close the Assistant Editor panel, select the *ViewController.swift* file and modify it to import the AVFoundation framework, declare adherence to some delegate protocols, and add properties to store references to AVAudioRecorder and AVAudioPlayer instances:

```
import UIKit
import AVFoundation


class ViewController: UIViewController, AVAudioPlayerDelegate,
AVAudioRecorderDelegate {

    var audioPlayer: AVAudioPlayer?
    var audioRecorder: AVAudioRecorder?
.
.
```

89.5 Creating the AVAudioRecorder Instance

When the app is first launched, an instance of the AVAudioRecorder class needs to be created. This will be initialized with the URL of a file into which the recorded audio will be saved. Also passed as an argument to the initialization method is a Dictionary object indicating the settings for the recording, such as bit rate, sample rate, and audio quality. A full description of the settings available may be found in the appropriate *Apple iOS reference materials*.

As is often the case, a good location to initialize the AVAudioRecorder instance is within a method to be called from the *viewDidLoad* method of the view controller located in the *ViewController.swift* file. Select the file in the project navigator and modify it so that it reads as follows:

```
.
.
override func viewDidLoad() {
    super.viewDidLoad()
    audioInit()
}


func audioInit() {
    playButton.isEnabled = false
    stopButton.isEnabled = false

    let fileMgr = FileManager.default

    let dirPaths = fileMgr.urls(for: .documentDirectory,
                                in: .userDomainMask)

    let soundFileURL = dirPaths[0].appendingPathComponent("sound.caf")

    let recordSettings =
       [AVEncoderAudioQualityKey: AVAudioQuality.min.rawValue,
                AVEncoderBitRateKey: 16,
                AVNumberOfChannelsKey: 2,
                AVSampleRateKey: 44100.0] as [String : Any]

    let audioSession = AVAudioSession.sharedInstance()

    do {
            try audioSession.setCategory(
              AVAudioSession.Category.playAndRecord, mode: .default)
    } catch let error as NSError {
       print("audioSession error: \(error.localizedDescription)")
    }

    do {
        try audioRecorder = AVAudioRecorder(url: soundFileURL,
            settings: recordSettings as [String : AnyObject])
```

```
        audioRecorder?.prepareToRecord()
    } catch let error as NSError {
        print("audioSession error: \(error.localizedDescription)")
    }
}
.
.
.
```

Since no audio has been recorded, the above method disables the play and stop buttons. It then identifies the app's documents directory and constructs a URL to a file in that location named *sound.caf*. A Dictionary object is then created containing the recording quality settings before an audio session, and an instance of the AVAudioRecorder class is created. Finally, assuming no errors are encountered, the audioRecorder instance is prepared to begin recording when requested to do so by the user.

89.6 Implementing the Action Methods

The next step is implementing the action methods connected to the three button objects. Select the *ViewController. swift* file and modify it as outlined in the following code excerpt:

```
@IBAction func recordAudio(_ sender: Any) {
    if audioRecorder?.isRecording == false {
        playButton.isEnabled = false
        stopButton.isEnabled = true
        audioRecorder?.record()
    }
}


@IBAction func stopAudio(_ sender: Any) {
    stopButton.isEnabled = false
    playButton.isEnabled = true
    recordButton.isEnabled = true

    if audioRecorder?.isRecording == true {
        audioRecorder?.stop()
    } else {
        audioPlayer?.stop()
    }
}


@IBAction func playAudio(_ sender: Any) {
    if audioRecorder?.isRecording == false {
        stopButton.isEnabled = true
        recordButton.isEnabled = false

        do {
            try audioPlayer = AVAudioPlayer(contentsOf:
                                (audioRecorder?.url)!)
            audioPlayer!.delegate = self
```

```
        audioPlayer!.prepareToPlay()
        audioPlayer!.play()
    } catch let error as NSError {
        print("audioPlayer error: \(error.localizedDescription)")
    }
  }
}
```

Each of the above methods performs the steps necessary to enable and disable appropriate buttons in the user interface and to interact with the AVAudioRecorder and AVAudioPlayer object instances to record or playback audio.

89.7 Implementing the Delegate Methods

To receive notification about the success or otherwise of recording or playback, it is necessary to implement some delegate methods. For this tutorial, we will need to implement the methods to indicate errors have occurred and also when playback is finished. Once again, edit the *ViewController.swift* file and add these methods as follows:

```
func audioPlayerDidFinishPlaying(_ player: AVAudioPlayer,
    successfully flag: Bool) {
    recordButton.isEnabled = true
    stopButton.isEnabled = false
}


func audioPlayerDecodeErrorDidOccur(_ player: AVAudioPlayer, error: Error?) {
    print("Audio Play Decode Error")
}


func audioRecorderDidFinishRecording(_ recorder: AVAudioRecorder, successfully
flag: Bool) {
}


func audioRecorderEncodeErrorDidOccur(_ recorder: AVAudioRecorder, error: Error?)
{
    print("Audio Record Encode Error")
}
```

89.8 Testing the App

Configure Xcode to install the app on a device or simulator session and build and run the app by clicking on the run button in the main toolbar. Once loaded onto the device, the operating system will seek permission to allow the app to access the microphone. Allow access and touch the Record button to record some sound. Touch the Stop button when the recording is completed and use the Play button to play back the audio.

89.9 Summary

This chapter has provided an overview and example of using the AVAudioRecorder and AVAudioPlayer classes of the AVFoundation framework to record and playback audio from within an iOS app. The chapter also outlined the necessity of configuring the microphone usage privacy key-value pair within the *Info.plist* file to obtain microphone access permission from the user.

90. An iOS 17 Speech Recognition Tutorial

When Apple introduced speech recognition for iOS devices, it was always assumed that this capability would one day be available to iOS app developers. That day finally arrived with the introduction of iOS 10.

The iOS SDK now includes the Speech framework, which can implement speech-to-text transcription within any iOS app. Speech recognition can be implemented with relative ease using the Speech framework and, as demonstrated in this chapter, may be used to transcribe both real-time and previously recorded audio.

90.1 An Overview of Speech Recognition in iOS

The speech recognition feature of iOS allows speech to be converted to text and supports a wide range of spoken languages. Most iOS users will no doubt be familiar with the microphone button that appears within the keyboard when entering text into an app. This dictation button is perhaps most commonly used to enter text into the Messages app.

Before the introduction of the Speech framework in iOS 10, app developers were still able to take advantage of the keyboard dictation button. Tapping a Text View object within any app displays the keyboard containing the button. Once tapped, any speech picked up by the microphone is transcribed into text and placed within the Text View. For basic requirements, this option is still available within iOS, though there are several advantages to performing a deeper integration using the Speech framework.

One of the key advantages of the Speech framework is the ability to trigger voice recognition without needing to display the keyboard and wait for the user to tap the dictation button. In addition, while the dictation button can only transcribe live speech, the Speech framework allows speech recognition to be performed on pre-recorded audio files.

Another advantage over the built-in dictation button is that the app can define the spoken language that is to be transcribed where the dictation button is locked into the prevailing device-wide language setting.

Behind the scenes, the service uses the same speech recognition technology as Siri. However, it is also important to know that the audio is typically transferred from the local device to Apple's remote servers, where the speech recognition process is performed. The service is, therefore, only likely to be available when the device on which the app is running has an active internet connection.

When working with speech recognition, it is important to note that the length of audio that can be transcribed in a single session is restricted to one minute at the time of writing. In addition, Apple also imposes undeclared limits on the total amount of time an app can freely use of the speech recognition service, the implication being that Apple will begin charging heavy users of the service at some point in the future.

90.2 Speech Recognition Authorization

As outlined in the previous chapter, an app must seek permission from the user before being authorized to record audio using the microphone. This is also the case when implementing speech recognition, though the app must also specifically request permission to perform speech recognition. This is particularly important given that the audio will be transmitted to Apple for processing. Therefore, in addition to an NSMicrophoneUsageDescription entry in the *Info.plist* file, the app must include the NSSpeechRecognitionUsageDescription entry if speech recognition is to be performed.

The app must also specifically request speech recognition authorization via a call to the *requestAuthorization* method of the SFSpeechRecognizer class. This results in a completion handler call which is, in turn, passed a status value indicating whether authorization has been granted. Note that this step also includes a test to verify that the device has an internet connection.

90.3 Transcribing Recorded Audio

Once the appropriate permissions and authorizations have been obtained, speech recognition can be performed on an existing audio file with just a few lines of code. All that is required is an instance of the SFSpeechRecognizer class together with a request object in the form of an SFSpeechURLRecognitionRequest instance initialized with the URL of the audio file. Next, a recognizer task is created using the request object, and a completion handler is called when the audio has been transcribed. For example, the following code fragment demonstrates these steps:

```
let recognizer = SFSpeechRecognizer()
let request = SFSpeechURLRecognitionRequest(url: fileUrl)
    recognizer?.recognitionTask(with: request, resultHandler: {
            (result, error) in
            print(result?.bestTranscription.formattedString)
})
```

90.4 Transcribing Live Audio

Live audio speech recognition makes use of the AVAudioEngine class. The AVAudioEngine class manages audio nodes that tap into different input and output buses on the device. In the case of speech recognition, the engine's input audio node is accessed and used to install a tap on the audio input bus. The audio input from the tap is then streamed to a buffer which is repeatedly appended to the speech recognizer object for conversion. These steps will be covered in greater detail in the next chapter entitled *"An iOS 17 Real-Time Speech Recognition Tutorial"*.

90.5 An Audio File Speech Recognition Tutorial

The remainder of this chapter will modify the Record app created in the previous chapter to provide the option to transcribe the speech recorded to the audio file. In the first instance, load Xcode, open the Record project, and select the *Main.storyboard* file so that it loads into the Interface Builder tool.

90.6 Modifying the User Interface

The modified Record app will require the addition of a Transcribe button and a Text View object into which the transcribed text will be placed as it is generated. Add these elements to the storyboard scene so that the layout matches that shown in Figure 90-1 below.

Select the Transcribe button view, display the Auto Layout Align menu, and apply a constraint to center the button in the horizontal center of the containing view. Next, display the *Add New Constraints* menu and establish a spacing to nearest neighbor constraint on the view's top edge using the current value and the *Constrain to margins* option disabled.

With the newly added Text View object selected, display the Attributes Inspector panel and delete the sample Latin text. Then, using the *Add New Constraints* menu, add spacing to nearest neighbor constraints on all four sides of the view with the *Constrain to margins* option enabled.

Figure 90-1

Display the Assistant Editor panel and establish outlet connections for the new Button and Text View named *transcribeButton* and *textView,* respectively.

Complete this tutorial section by establishing an action connection from the Transcribe button to a method named *transcribeAudio.*

90.7 Adding the Speech Recognition Permission

Select the *Record* entry at the top of the Project navigator panel and select the Info tab in the main panel. Next, click on the + button contained with the last line of properties in the Custom iOS Target Properties section. Then, select the *Privacy – Speech Recognition Usage Description* item from the resulting menu. Once the key has been added, double-click in the corresponding value column and enter the following text:

```
Speech recognition services are used by this app to convert speech to text.
```

90.8 Seeking Speech Recognition Authorization

In addition to adding the usage description key to the *Info.plist* file, the app must include code to seek authorization to perform speech recognition. This will also ensure that the device is suitably configured to perform the task and that the user has given permission for speech recognition to be performed. Before adding code to the project, the first step is to import the Speech framework within the *ViewController.swift* file:

```
import UIKit
import AVFoundation
import Speech

class ViewController: UIViewController, AVAudioPlayerDelegate,
AVAudioRecorderDelegate {
.
.
.
```

For this example, the code to perform this task will be added as a method named *authorizeSR* within the *ViewController.swift* file as follows:

```
func authorizeSR() {
    SFSpeechRecognizer.requestAuthorization { authStatus in

        OperationQueue.main.addOperation {
            switch authStatus {
            case .authorized:
                self.transcribeButton.isEnabled = true

            case .denied:
                self.transcribeButton.isEnabled = false
                self.recordButton.setTitle("Speech recognition access denied by
user", for: .disabled)

            case .restricted:
                self.transcribeButton.isEnabled = false
                self.transcribeButton.setTitle("Speech recognition restricted on
device", for: .disabled)

            case .notDetermined:
                self.transcribeButton.isEnabled = false
                self.transcribeButton.setTitle("Speech recognition not
authorized", for: .disabled)
            @unknown default:
                print("Unknown Status")
            }
        }
    }
}
```

The above code calls the *requestAuthorization* method of the SFSpeechRecognizer class with a closure specified as the completion handler. This handler is passed a status value which can be one of four values (authorized, denied, restricted, or not determined). A switch statement is then used to evaluate the status and enable the transcribe button or to display the reason for the failure on that button.

Note that the switch statement code is specifically performed on the main queue. This is because the completion handler can be called at any time and not necessarily within the main thread queue. Since the completion handler code in the statement changes the user interface, these changes must be made on the main queue to avoid unpredictable results.

With the authorizeSR method implemented, modify the end of the *viewDidLoad* method to call this method:

```
override func viewDidLoad() {
    super.viewDidLoad()
    audioInit()
    authorizeSR()
}
```

90.9 Performing the Transcription

All that remains before testing the app is to implement the code within the *transcribeAudio* action method. Locate the template method in the *ViewController.swift* file and modify it to read as follows:

```
@IBAction func transcribeAudio(_ sender: Any) {
    let recognizer = SFSpeechRecognizer()
    let request = SFSpeechURLRecognitionRequest(
                        url: (audioRecorder?.url)!)
    recognizer?.recognitionTask(with: request, resultHandler: {
        (result, error) in
            self.textView.text = result?.bestTranscription.formattedString
    })
}
```

The code creates an SFSpeechRecognizer instance, initializes it with a request containing the URL of the recorded audio, and then initiates a task to perform the recognition. Finally, the completion handler displays the transcribed text within the Text View object.

90.10 Testing the App

Compile and run the app on a physical device, accept the request for speech recognition access, tap the Record button, and record some speech. Next, tap the Stop button, followed by Transcribe, and watch as the recorded speech is transcribed into text within the Text View object.

90.11 Summary

The Speech framework provides apps with access to Siri's speech recognition technology. This access allows speech to be transcribed to text, either in real-time or by passing pre-recorded audio to the recognition system. This chapter has provided an overview of speech recognition within iOS and adapted the Record app created in the previous chapter to transcribe recorded speech to text. The next chapter, entitled *"An iOS 17 Real-Time Speech Recognition Tutorial"*, will provide a guide to performing speech recognition in real-time.

91. An iOS 17 Real-Time Speech Recognition Tutorial

The previous chapter, entitled *"An iOS 17 Speech Recognition Tutorial"*, introduced the Speech framework and the speech recognition capabilities available to app developers since the introduction of the iOS 10 SDK. The chapter also provided a tutorial demonstrating using the Speech framework to transcribe a pre-recorded audio file into text.

This chapter will build on this knowledge to create an example project that uses the speech recognition Speech framework to transcribe speech in near real-time.

91.1 Creating the Project

Begin by launching Xcode and creating a new single view-based app named *LiveSpeech* using the Swift programming language.

91.2 Designing the User Interface

Select the *Main.storyboard* file, add two Buttons and a Text View component to the scene, and configure and position these views so that the layout appears as illustrated in Figure 91-1 below:

Figure 91-1

Display the *Resolve Auto Layout Issues* menu, select the Reset to Suggested Constraints option listed under All Views in View Controller, select the Text View object, display the Attributes Inspector panel, and remove the sample Latin text.

Display the Assistant Editor panel and establish outlet connections for the Buttons named *transcribeButton* and *stopButton,* respectively. Next, repeat this process to connect an outlet for the Text View named *myTextView.* Then, with the Assistant Editor panel still visible, establish action connections from the Buttons to methods named *startTranscribing* and *stopTranscribing.*

91.3 Adding the Speech Recognition Permission

Select the *LiveSpeech* entry at the top of the Project navigator panel and select the Info tab in the main panel. Next, click on the + button contained with the last line of properties in the Custom iOS Target Properties section. Then, select the *Privacy – Speech Recognition Usage Description* item from the resulting menu. Once the key has been added, double-click in the corresponding value column and enter the following text:

```
Speech recognition services are used by this app to convert speech to text.
```

Repeat this step to add a *Privacy – Microphone Usage Description* entry.

91.4 Requesting Speech Recognition Authorization

The code to request speech recognition authorization is the same as that for the previous chapter. For this example, the code to perform this task will, once again, be added as a method named *authorizeSR* within the *ViewController.swift* file as follows, remembering to import the Speech framework:

```
.
.
import Speech
.
.
func authorizeSR() {
    SFSpeechRecognizer.requestAuthorization { authStatus in

        OperationQueue.main.addOperation {
            switch authStatus {
            case .authorized:
                self.transcribeButton.isEnabled = true

            case .denied:
                self.transcribeButton.isEnabled = false
                self.transcribeButton.setTitle("Speech recognition access denied
by user", for: .disabled)

            case .restricted:
                self.transcribeButton.isEnabled = false
                self.transcribeButton.setTitle(
                    "Speech recognition restricted on device", for: .disabled)

            case .notDetermined:
                self.transcribeButton.isEnabled = false
                self.transcribeButton.setTitle(
```

```
                   "Speech recognition not authorized", for: .disabled)
            @unknown default:
                print("Unknown state")
            }
        }
    }
}
```

Remaining in the *ViewController.swift* file, locate and modify the *viewDidLoad* method to call the *authorizeSR* method:

```
override func viewDidLoad() {
    super.viewDidLoad()
    authorizeSR()
}
```

91.5 Declaring and Initializing the Speech and Audio Objects

To transcribe speech in real-time, the app will require instances of the SFSpeechRecognizer, SFSpeechAudioBufferRecognitionRequest, and SFSpeechRecognitionTask classes. In addition to these speech recognition objects, the code will also need an AVAudioEngine instance to stream the audio into an audio buffer for transcription. Edit the *ViewController.swift* file and declare constants and variables to store these instances as follows:

```
import UIKit
import Speech

class ViewController: UIViewController {

    @IBOutlet weak var transcribeButton: UIButton!
    @IBOutlet weak var stopButton: UIButton!
    @IBOutlet weak var myTextView: UITextView!

    private let speechRecognizer = SFSpeechRecognizer(locale:
                    Locale(identifier: "en-US"))!

    private var speechRecognitionRequest:
            SFSpeechAudioBufferRecognitionRequest?
    private var speechRecognitionTask: SFSpeechRecognitionTask?
    private let audioEngine = AVAudioEngine()
.
.
.
```

91.6 Starting the Transcription

The first task in initiating speech recognition is to add some code to the *startTranscribing* action method. Since several method calls that will be made to perform speech recognition have the potential to throw exceptions, a second method with the *throws* keyword needs to be called by the action method to perform the actual work (adding the *throws* keyword to the *startTranscribing* method will cause a crash at runtime because action methods signatures are not recognized as throwing exceptions). Therefore, within the *ViewController.swift* file, modify the *startTranscribing* action method and add a new method named *startSession*:

.

.

.

```
@IBAction func startTranscribing(_ sender: Any) {
    transcribeButton.isEnabled = false
    stopButton.isEnabled = true

    do {
        try startSession()
    } catch {
        // Handle Error
    }
}


func startSession() throws {

    if let recognitionTask = speechRecognitionTask {
        recognitionTask.cancel()
        self.speechRecognitionTask = nil
    }

    let audioSession = AVAudioSession.sharedInstance()
    try audioSession.setCategory(AVAudioSession.Category.record,
                                    mode: .default)

    speechRecognitionRequest = SFSpeechAudioBufferRecognitionRequest()

    guard let recognitionRequest = speechRecognitionRequest else {
      fatalError(
      "SFSpeechAudioBufferRecognitionRequest object creation failed") }

    let inputNode = audioEngine.inputNode

    recognitionRequest.shouldReportPartialResults = true

    speechRecognitionTask = speechRecognizer.recognitionTask(
            with: recognitionRequest) { result, error in

        var finished = false

        if let result = result {
            self.myTextView.text =
                    result.bestTranscription.formattedString
            finished = result.isFinal
```

```
        }

        if error != nil || finished {
            self.audioEngine.stop()
            inputNode.removeTap(onBus: 0)

            self.speechRecognitionRequest = nil
            self.speechRecognitionTask = nil

            self.transcribeButton.isEnabled = true
        }
    }

    let recordingFormat = inputNode.outputFormat(forBus: 0)
    inputNode.installTap(onBus: 0, bufferSize: 1024, format: recordingFormat) {
      (buffer: AVAudioPCMBuffer, when: AVAudioTime) in

        self.speechRecognitionRequest?.append(buffer)
    }

    audioEngine.prepare()
    try audioEngine.start()
}
.
.
.
```

The startSession method performs various tasks, each of which needs to be broken down and explained for this to begin to make sense.

The first tasks to be performed within the *startSession* method are to check if a previous recognition task is running and, if so, cancel it. The method also needs to configure an audio recording session and assign an SFSpeechAudioBufferRecognitionRequest object to the *speechRecognitionRequest* variable declared previously. A test is then performed to ensure that an SFSpeechAudioBufferRecognitionRequest object was successfully created. If the creation fails, an exception is thrown:

```
if let recognitionTask = speechRecognitionTask {
    recognitionTask.cancel()
    self.speechRecognitionTask = nil
}

let audioSession = AVAudioSession.sharedInstance()
try audioSession.setCategory(AVAudioSession.Category.record, mode: .default)

speechRecognitionRequest = SFSpeechAudioBufferRecognitionRequest()

guard let recognitionRequest = speechRecognitionRequest else { fatalError("SFSpee
chAudioBufferRecognitionRequest object creation failed") }
```

Next, the code needs to obtain a reference to the inputNode of the audio engine and assign it to a constant. If an input node is not available, a fatal error is thrown. Finally, the recognitionRequest instance is configured to return partial results, enabling transcription to occur continuously as speech audio arrives in the buffer. If this property is not set, the app will wait until the end of the audio session before starting the transcription process.

```
let inputNode = audioEngine.inputNode

recognitionRequest.shouldReportPartialResults = true
```

Next, the recognition task is initialized:

```
speechRecognitionTask = speechRecognizer.recognitionTask(
    with: recognitionRequest) { result, error in

    var finished = false

    if let result = result {
        self.myTextView.text = result.bestTranscription.formattedString
        finished = result.isFinal
    }

    if error != nil || finished {
        self.audioEngine.stop()
        inputNode.removeTap(onBus: 0)

        self.speechRecognitionRequest = nil
        self.speechRecognitionTask = nil

        self.transcribeButton.isEnabled = true
    }
}
```

The above code creates the recognition task initialized with the recognition request object. A closure is then specified as the completion handler, which will be called repeatedly as each block of transcribed text is completed. Each time the handler is called, it is passed a result object containing the latest version of the transcribed text and an error object. As long as the *isFinal* property of the result object is false (indicating that live audio is still streaming into the buffer) and no errors occur, the text is displayed on the Text View. Otherwise, the audio engine is stopped, the tap is removed from the audio node, and the recognition request and recognition task objects are set to nil. The transcribe button is also enabled in preparation for the next session.

Having configured the recognition task, all that remains in this phase of the process is to install a tap on the input node of the audio engine, then start the engine running:

```
let recordingFormat = inputNode.outputFormat(forBus: 0)
inputNode.installTap(onBus: 0, bufferSize: 1024, format: recordingFormat) {
(buffer: AVAudioPCMBuffer, when: AVAudioTime) in

    self.speechRecognitionRequest?.append(buffer)
}

audioEngine.prepare()
```

```
try audioEngine.start()
```

Note that the *installTap* method of the inputNode object also uses a closure as a completion handler. Each time it is called, the code for this handler appends the latest audio buffer to the speechRecognitionRequest object, where it will be transcribed and passed to the completion handler for the speech recognition task, where it will be displayed on the Text View.

91.7 Implementing the stopTranscribing Method

Except for the *stopTranscribing* method, the app is almost ready to be tested. Within the *ViewController.swift* file, locate and modify this method to stop the audio engine and configure the status of the buttons ready for the next session:

```
@IBAction func stopTranscribing(_ sender: Any) {
    if audioEngine.isRunning {
        audioEngine.stop()
        speechRecognitionRequest?.endAudio()
        transcribeButton.isEnabled = true
        stopButton.isEnabled = false
    }
}
```

91.8 Testing the App

Compile and run the app on a physical iOS device, grant access to the microphone and permission to use speech recognition, and tap the Start Transcribing button. Next, speak into the device and watch as the audio is transcribed into the Text View. Finally, tap the Stop Transcribing button to end the session.

91.9 Summary

Live speech recognition is provided by the iOS Speech framework and allows speech to be transcribed into text as it is being recorded. This process taps into an AVAudioEngine input node to stream the audio into a buffer and appropriately configured SFSpeechRecognizer, SFSpeechAudioBufferRecognitionRequest, and SFSpeechRecognitionTask objects to perform the recognition. This chapter worked through creating an example app designed to demonstrate how these various components work together to implement near-real-time speech recognition.

92. An Introduction to iOS 17 Sprite Kit Programming

Suppose you have ever had an idea for a game but didn't create it because you lacked the skills or time to write complex game code and logic; look no further than Sprite Kit. Introduced as part of the iOS 7 SDK, Sprite Kit allows 2D games to be developed relatively easily.

Sprite Kit provides almost everything needed to create 2D games for iOS, watchOS, tvOS, and macOS with minimum coding. Sprite Kit's features include animation, physics simulation, collision detection, and special effects. These features can be harnessed within a game with just a few method calls.

In this and the next three chapters, the topic of games development with Sprite Kit will be covered to bring the reader up to a level of competence to begin creating games while also providing a knowledge base on which to develop further Sprite Kit development skills.

92.1 What is Sprite Kit?

Sprite Kit is a programming framework that makes it easy for developers to implement 2D-based games that run on iOS, macOS, tvOS, and watchOS. It provides a range of classes that support the rendering and animation of graphical objects (otherwise known as *sprites*) that can be configured to behave in specific programmer-defined ways within a game. Through *actions,* various activities can be run on sprites, such as animating a character so that it appears to be walking, making a sprite follow a specific path within a game scene, or changing the color and texture of a sprite in real-time.

Sprite Kit also includes a physics engine allowing physics-related behavior to be imposed on sprites. For example, a sprite can, amongst other things, be made to move by subjecting it to a pushing force, configured to behave as though affected by gravity, or to bounce back from another sprite as the result of a collision.

In addition, the Sprite Kit particle emitter class provides a useful mechanism for creating special effects within a game, such as smoke, rain, fire, and explosions. A range of templates for existing special effects is provided with Sprite Kit and an editor built into Xcode for creating custom particle emitter-based special effects.

92.2 The Key Components of a Sprite Kit Game

A Sprite Kit game will typically consist of several different elements.

92.2.1 Sprite Kit View

Every Sprite Kit game will have at least one SKView class. An SKView instance sits at the top of the component hierarchy of a game and is responsible for displaying the game content to the user. It is a subclass of the UIView class and, as such, has many of the traits of that class, including an associated view controller.

92.2.2 Scenes

A game will also contain one or more scenes. One scene might, for example, display a menu when the game starts, while additional scenes may represent multiple levels within the game. Scenes are represented in a game by the SKScene class, a subclass of the SKNode class.

92.2.3 Nodes

Each scene within a Sprite Kit game will have several Sprite Kit node children. These nodes fall into several different categories, each of which has a dedicated Sprite Kit node class associated with it. These node classes are all subclasses of the SKNode class and can be summarized as follows:

- **SKSpriteNode** – Draws a sprite with a texture. These textures will typically be used to create image-based characters or objects in a game, such as a spaceship, animal, or monster.

- **SKLabelNode** – Used to display text within a game, such as menu options, the prevailing score, or a "game over" message.

- **SKShapeNode** – Allows nodes to be created containing shapes defined using Core Graphics paths. If a sprite is required to display a circle, for example, the SKShapeNode class could be used to draw the circle as an alternative to texturing an SKSpriteNode with an image of a circle.

- **SKEmitterNode** – The node responsible for managing and displaying particle emitter-based special effects.

- **SKVideoNode** – Allows video playback to be performed within a game node.

- **SKEffectNode** – Allows Core Image filter effects to be applied to child nodes. A sepia filter effect, for example, could be applied to all child nodes of an SKEffectNode.

- **SKCropNode** – Allows the pixels in a node to be cropped subject to a specified mask.

- **SKLightNode** – The lighting node is provided to add light sources to a SpriteKit scene, including casting shadows when the light falls on other nodes in the same scene.

- **SK3DNode** – The SK3DNode allows 3D assets created using the Scene Kit Framework to be embedded into 2D Sprite Kit games.

- **SKFieldNode** – Applies physics effects to other nodes within a specified area of a scene.

- **SKAudioNode** – Allows an audio source using 3D spacial audio effects to be included in a Sprite Kit scene.

- **SKCameraNode** – Provides the ability to control the position from which the scene is viewed. The camera node may also be adjusted dynamically to create panning, rotation, and scaling effects.

92.2.4 Physics Bodies

Each node within a scene can have associated with it a physics body. Physics bodies are represented by the SKPhysicsBody class. Assignment of a physics body to a node brings a wide range of possibilities in terms of the behavior associated with a node. When a node is assigned a physics body, it will, by default, behave as though subject to the prevailing forces of gravity within the scene. In addition, the node can be configured to behave as though having a physical boundary. This boundary can be defined as a circle, a rectangle, or a polygon of any shape.

Once a node has a boundary, collisions between other nodes can be detected, and the physics engine is used to apply real-world physics to the node, such as causing it to bounce when hitting other nodes. The use of contact bit masks can be employed to specify the types of nodes for which contact notification is required.

The physics body also allows forces to be applied to nodes, such as propelling a node in a particular direction across a scene using either a constant or one-time impulse force. Physical bodies can also be combined using various join types (sliding, fixed, hinged, and spring-based attachments).

The properties of a physics body (and, therefore, the associated node) may also be changed. Mass, density, velocity, and friction are just a few of the properties of a physics body available for modification by the game developer.

92.2.5 Physics World

Each scene in a game has its own *physics world* object in the form of an instance of the SKPhysicsWorld class. A reference to this object, which is created automatically when the scene is initialized, may be obtained by accessing the *physicsWorld* property of the scene. The physics world object is responsible for managing and imposing the rules of physics on any nodes in the scene with which a physics body has been associated. Properties are available on the physics world instance to change the default gravity settings for the scene and also to adjust the speed at which the physics simulation runs.

92.2.6 Actions

An action is an activity performed by a node in a scene. Actions are the responsibility of SKAction class instances which are created and configured with the action to be performed. That action is then run on one or more nodes. An action might, for example, be configured to perform a rotation of 90 degrees. That action would then be run on a node to make it rotate within the scene. The SKAction class includes various action types, including fade in, fade out, rotation, movement, and scaling. Perhaps the most interesting action involves animating a sprite node through a series of texture frames.

Actions can be categorized as *sequence*, *group,* or *repeating* actions. An action sequence specifies a series of actions to be performed consecutively, while group actions specify a set of actions to be performed in parallel. Repeating actions are configured to restart after completion. An action may be configured to repeat several times or indefinitely.

92.2.7 Transitions

Transitions occur when a game changes from one scene to another. While it is possible to switch immediately from one scene to another, a more visually pleasing result might be achieved by animating the transition in some way. This can be implemented using the SKTransition class, which provides several different pre-defined transition animations, such as sliding the new scene down over the top of the old scene or presenting the effect of doors opening to reveal the new scene.

92.2.8 Texture Atlas

A large part of developing games involves handling images. Many of these images serve as textures for sprites. Although adding images to a project individually is possible, Sprite Kit also allows images to be grouped into a texture atlas. Not only does this make it easier to manage the images, but it also brings efficiencies in terms of image storage and handling. For example, the texture images for a particular sprite animation sequence would typically be stored in a single texture atlas. In contrast, another atlas might store the images for the background of a particular scene.

92.2.9 Constraints

Constraints allow restrictions to be imposed on nodes within a scene in terms of distance and orientation in relation to a point or another node. A constraint can, for example, be applied to a node such that its movement is restricted to within a certain distance of another node. Similarly, a node can be configured so that it is oriented to point toward either another node or a specified point within the scene. Constraints are represented by instances of the SKConstraint class and are grouped into an array and assigned to the *constraints* property of the node to which they are to be applied.

92.3 An Example Sprite Kit Game Hierarchy

To aid in visualizing how the various Sprite Kit components fit together, Figure 92-1 outlines the hierarchy for a simple game:

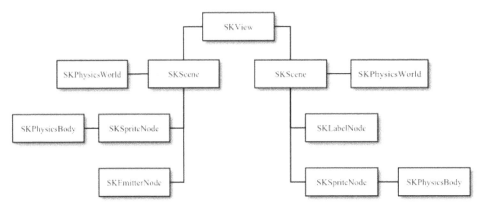

Figure 92-1

In this hypothetical game, a single SKView instance has two SKScene children, each with its own SKPhysicsWorld object. Each scene, in turn, has two node children. In the case of both scenes, the SKSpriteNode instances have been assigned SKPhysicsBody instances.

92.4 The Sprite Kit Game Rendering Loop

When working with Sprite Kit, it helps to understand how the animation and physics simulation process works. This process can best be described by looking at the Sprite Kit frame rendering loop.

Sprite Kit performs the work of rendering a game using a *game rendering loop*. Within this loop, Sprite Kit performs various tasks to render the visual and behavioral elements of the currently active scene, with an iteration of the loop performed for each successive frame displayed to the user.

Figure 92-2 provides a visual representation of the frame rendering sequence performed in the loop:

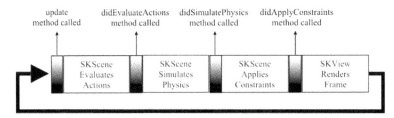

Figure 92-2

When a scene is displayed within a game, Sprite Kit enters the rendering loop and repeatedly performs the same sequence of steps as shown above. At several points in this sequence, the loop will make calls to your game, allowing the game logic to respond when necessary.

Before performing any other tasks, the loop begins by calling the *update* method of the corresponding SKScene instance. Within this method, the game should perform any tasks before the frame is updated, such as adding additional sprites or updating the current score.

The loop then evaluates and implements any pending actions on the scene, after which the game can perform more tasks via a call to the *didEvaluateActions* method.

Next, physics simulations are performed on the scene, followed by a call to the scene's *didSimulatePhysics* method, where the game logic may react where necessary to any changes resulting from the physics simulation.

The scene then applies any constraints configured on the nodes in the scene. Once this task has been completed, a call is made to the scene's *didApplyConstraints* method if it has been implemented.

Finally, the SKView instance renders the new scene frame before the loop sequence repeats.

92.5 The Sprite Kit Level Editor

Integrated into Xcode, the Sprite Kit Level Editor allows scenes to be designed by dragging and dropping nodes onto a scene canvas and setting properties on those nodes using the SKNode Inspector. Though code writing is still required for anything but the most basic scene requirements, the Level Editor provides a useful alternative to writing code for some of the less complex aspects of SpriteKit game development. The editor environment also includes both live and action editors, allowing for designing and testing animation and action sequences within a Sprite Kit game.

92.6 Summary

Sprite Kit provides a platform for creating 2D games on iOS, tvOS, watchOS, and macOS. Games comprise an SKView instance with an SKScene object for each game scene. Scenes contain nodes representing the game's characters, objects, and items. Various node types are available, all of which are subclassed from the SKNode class. In addition, each node can have associated with it a physics body in the form of an SKPhysicsBody instance. A node with a physics body will be subject to physical forces such as gravity, and when given a physical boundary, collisions with other nodes may also be detected. Finally, actions are configured using the SKAction class, instances of which are then run by the nodes on which the action is to be performed.

The orientation and movement of a node can be restricted by implementing constraints using the SKConstraint class.

The rendering of a Sprite Kit game takes place within the *game loop,* with one loop performed for each game frame. At various points in this loop, the app can perform tasks to implement and manage the underlying game logic.

Having provided a high-level overview in this chapter, the next three chapters will take a more practical approach to exploring the capabilities of Sprite Kit by creating a simple game.

93. An iOS 17 Sprite Kit Level Editor Game Tutorial

In this chapter, many of the Sprite Kit Framework features outlined in the previous chapter will be used to create a game-based app. In particular, this tutorial will demonstrate the practical use of scenes, textures, sprites, labels, and actions. In addition, the app created in this chapter will also use physics bodies to demonstrate the use of collisions and simulated gravity.

This tutorial will also demonstrate using the Xcode Sprite Kit Level, Live, and Action editors combined with Swift code to create a Sprite Kit-based game.

93.1 About the Sprite Kit Demo Game

The game created in this chapter consists of a single animated character that shoots arrows across the scene when the screen is tapped. For the game's duration, balls fall from the top of the screen, with the objective being to hit as many balls as possible with the arrows.

The completed game will comprise the following two scenes:

- **GameScene** – The scene which appears when the game is first launched. The scene will announce the game's name and invite the user to touch the screen to begin the game. The game will then transition to the second scene.

- **ArcheryScene** – The scene where the game-play takes place. Within this scene, the archer and ball sprites are animated, and the physics behavior and collision detection are implemented to make the game work.

In terms of sprite nodes, the game will include the following:

- **Welcome Node** – An SKLabelNode instance that displays a message to the user on the Welcome Scene.

- **Archer Node** – An SKSpriteNode instance to represent the archer game character. The animation frames that cause the archer to load and launch an arrow are provided via a sequence of image files contained within a texture atlas.

- **Arrow Node** – An SKSpriteNode instance used to represent the arrows as the archer character shoots them. This node has associated with it a physics body so that collisions can be detected and to make sure it responds to gravity.

- **Ball Node** – An SKSpriteNode represents the balls that fall from the sky. The ball has associated with it a physics body for gravity and collision detection purposes.

- **Game Over Node** – An SKLabelNode instance that displays the score to the user at the end of the game.

The overall architecture of the game can be represented hierarchically, as outlined in Figure 93-1:

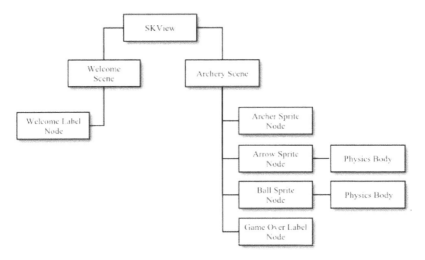

Figure 93-1

In addition to the nodes outlined above, the Xcode Live and Action editors will be used to implement animation and audio actions, which will be triggered from within the app's code.

93.2 Creating the SpriteKitDemo Project

To create the project, launch Xcode and select the *Create a new Xcode project* option from the welcome screen (or use the *File -> New -> Project…*) menu option. Next, on the template selection panel, choose the iOS *Game* template option. Click on the *Next* button to proceed and on the resulting options screen, name the product *SpriteKitDemo* and choose *Swift* as the language in which the app will be developed. Finally, set the Game Technology menu to *SpriteKit*. Click *Next* and choose a suitable location for the project files. Once selected, click *Create* to create the project.

93.3 Reviewing the SpriteKit Game Template Project

The selection of the SpriteKit Game template has caused Xcode to create a template project with a demonstration incorporating some pre-built Sprite Kit behavior. This template consists of a View Controller class (*GameViewController.swift*), an Xcode Sprite Kit scene file (*GameScene.sks*), and a corresponding GameScene class file (*GameScene.swift*). The code within the *GameViewController.swift* file loads the scene design contained within the *GameScene.sks* file and presents it on the view to be visible to the user. This, in turn, triggers a call to the *didMove(to view:)* method of the GameScene class as implemented in the *GameScene.swift* file. This method creates an SKLabelNode displaying text that reads "Hello, World!".

The GameScene class also includes a variety of touch method implementations that create SKShapeNode instances into which graphics are drawn when triggered. These nodes, in turn, are displayed in response to touches and movements on the device screen. To see the template project in action, run it on a physical device or the iOS simulator and perform tapping and swiping motions on the display.

As impressive as this may be, given how little code is involved, this bears no resemblance to the game that will be created in this chapter, so some of this functionality needs to be removed to provide a clean foundation on which to build. Begin the tidying process by selecting and editing the *GameScene.swift* file to remove the code to create and present nodes in the scene. Once modified, the file should read as follows:

```
import SpriteKit
import GameplayKit
```

```
class GameScene: SKScene {

    override func didMove(to view: SKView) {

    }

    override func touchesBegan(_ touches: Set<UITouch>, with event: UIEvent?) {

    }

    override func update(_ currentTime: TimeInterval) {
        // Called before each frame is rendered
    }
}
```

With these changes, it is time to start creating the SpriteKitDemo game.

93.4 Restricting Interface Orientation

The game created in this tutorial assumes that the device on which it is running will be in landscape orientation. Therefore, to prevent the user from attempting to play the game with a device in portrait orientation, the *Device Orientation* properties for the project need to be restricted. To achieve this, select the *SpriteKitDemo* entry located at the top of the Project Navigator and, in the resulting *General* settings panel, change the device orientation settings so that only the *Landscape* options are selected both for iPad and iPhone devices:

Figure 93-2

93.5 Modifying the GameScene SpriteKit Scene File

As previously outlined, Xcode has provided a SpriteKit scene file (*GameScene.sks*) for a scene named GameScene together with a corresponding class declaration contained within the *GameScene.swift* file. The next task is to repurpose this scene to act as the welcome screen for the game. Begin by selecting the *GameScene.sks* file so that it loads into the SpriteKit Level Editor, as shown in Figure 93-3:

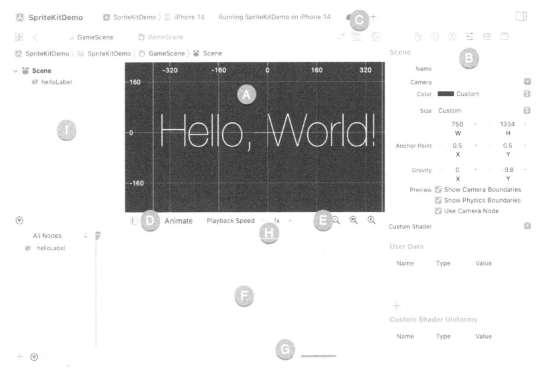

Figure 93-3

When working with the Level Editor to design SpriteKit scenes, there are several key areas of importance, each of which has been labeled in the above figure:

- **A – Scene Canvas** - This is the canvas onto which nodes may be placed, positioned, and configured.

- **B – Attribute Inspector Panel** - This panel provides a range of configuration options for the currently selected item in the editor panel. This allows SKNode and SKAction objects to be customized within the editor environment.

- **C – Library Button** – This button displays the Library panel containing a range of node and effect types that can be dragged and dropped onto the scene.

- **D – Animate/Layout Button** - Toggles between the editor's simulation and layout editing modes. Simulate mode provides a useful mechanism for previewing the scene behavior without compiling and running the app.

- **E – Zoom Buttons** – Buttons to zoom in and out of the scene canvas.

- **F – Live Editor** – The live editor allows actions and animations to be placed within a timeline and simulated within the editor environment. It is possible, for example, to add animation and movement actions within the live editor and play them back live within the scene canvas.

- **G – Timeline View Slider** – Pans back and forth through the view of the live editor timeline.

- **H – Playback Speed** – When in Animation mode, this control adjusts the playback speed of the animations and actions contained within the live editor panel.

- **I – Scene Graph View** – This panel provides an overview of the scene's hierarchy and can be used to select, delete, duplicate and reposition scene elements within the hierarchy.

Within the scene editor, click on the "Hello, World!" Label node and press the keyboard delete key to remove it from the scene. With the scene selected in the scene canvas, click on the *Color* swatch in the Attribute Inspector panel and use the color selection dialog to change the scene color to a shade of green. Remaining within the Attributes Inspector panel, change the Size setting from *Custom* to *iPad 9.7"* in *Landscape* mode:

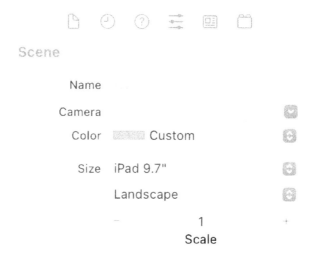

Figure 93-4

Click on the button (marked C in Figure 93-3 above) to display the Library panel, locate the Label node object, and drag and drop an instance onto the center of the scene canvas. With the label still selected, change the *Text* property in the inspector panel to read "SpriteKitDemo – Tap Screen to Play". Remaining within the inspector panel, click on the T next to the font name and use the font selector to assign a 56-point *Marker Felt Wide* font to the label from the *Fun* font category. Finally, set the *Name* property for the label node to "welcomeNode". Save the scene file before proceeding.

With these changes complete, the scene should resemble that of Figure 93-5:

Figure 93-5

93.6 Creating the Archery Scene

As previously outlined, the game's first scene is a welcome screen on which the user will tap to begin playing within a second scene. Add a new class to the project to represent this second scene by selecting the *File -> New -> File…* menu option. In the file template panel, make sure that the *Cocoa Touch Class* template is selected in the main panel. Click on the *Next* button and configure the new class to be a subclass of *SKScene* named *ArcheryScene*. Click on the *Next* button and create the new class file within the project folder.

The new scene class will also require a corresponding SpriteKit scene file. Select *File -> New -> File…* once again, this time selecting *SpriteKit Scene* from the Resource section of the main panel (Figure 93-6). Click *Next*, name the scene *ArcheryScene* and click the *Create* button to add the scene file to the project.

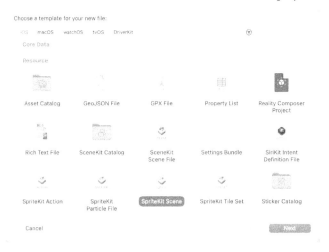

Figure 93-6

Edit the newly added *ArcheryScene.swift* file and modify it to import the SpriteKit Framework as follows:

```
import UIKit
import SpriteKit


class ArcheryScene: SKScene {


}
```

93.7 Transitioning to the Archery Scene

Clearly, having instructed the user to tap the screen to play the game, some code needs to be written to make this happen. This behavior will be added by implementing the *touchesBegan* method in the GameScene class. Rather than move directly to ArcheryScene, some effects will be added as an action and transition.

When implemented, the SKAction will cause the node to fade from view, while an SKTransition instance will be used to animate the transition from the current scene to the archery scene using a "doorway" style of animation. Implement these requirements by adding the following code to the *touchesBegan* method in the *GameScene.swift* file:

```
override func touchesBegan(_ touches: Set<UITouch>, with event: UIEvent?) {
    if let welcomeNode = childNode(withName: "welcomeNode") {
        let fadeAway = SKAction.fadeOut(withDuration: 1.0)
```

```
    welcomeNode.run(fadeAway, completion: {
        let doors = SKTransition.doorway(withDuration: 1.0)
        if let archeryScene = ArcheryScene(fileNamed: "ArcheryScene") {
            self.view?.presentScene(archeryScene, transition: doors)
        }
    })
}
}
```

Before moving on to the next steps, we will take some time to provide more detail on the above code.

From within the context of the *touchesBegan* method, we have no direct reference to the *welcomeNode* instance. However, we know that when it was added to the scene in the SpriteKit Level Editor, it was assigned the name "welcomeNode". Using the *childNode(withName:)* method of the scene instance, therefore, a reference to the node is being obtained within the *touchesBegan* method as follows:

```
if let welcomeNode = childNode(withName: "welcomeNode") {
```

The code then checks that the node was found before creating a new SKAction instance configured to cause the node to fade from view over a one-second duration:

```
let fadeAway = SKAction.fadeOut(withDuration: 1.0)
```

The action is then executed on the welcomeNode. A completion block is also specified to be executed when the action completes. This block creates an instance of the ArcheryScene class preloaded with the scene contained within the *ArcheryScene.sks* file and an appropriately configured SKTransition object. The transition to the new scene is then initiated:

```
let fadeAway = SKAction.fadeOut(withDuration: 1.0)

welcomeNode.run(fadeAway, completion: {
    let doors = SKTransition.doorway(withDuration: 1.0)
    if let archeryScene = ArcheryScene(fileNamed: "ArcheryScene") {
        self.view?.presentScene(archeryScene, transition: doors)
    }
})
```

Compile and run the app on an iPad device or simulator in landscape orientation. Once running, tap the screen and note that the label node fades away and that after the transition to the ArcheryScene takes effect, we are presented with a gray scene that now needs to be implemented.

93.8 Adding the Texture Atlas

Before textures can be used on a sprite node, the texture images must first be added to the project. Textures take the form of image files and may be added individually to the project's asset catalog. However, for larger numbers of texture files, it is more efficient (both for the developer and the app) to create a texture atlas. In the case of the archer sprite, this will require twelve image files to animate an arrow's loading and subsequent shooting. A texture atlas will be used to store these animation frame images. The images for this project can be found in the sample code download, which can be obtained from the following web page:

https://www.payloadbooks.com/product/ios17xcode/

Within the code sample archive, locate the folder named *sprite_images*. Located within this folder is the *archer.atlas* sub-folder, which contains the animation images for the archer sprite node.

To add the atlas to the project, select the *Assets* catalog file in the Project Navigator to display the image assets panel. Locate the *archer.atlas* folder in a Finder window and drag and drop it onto the asset catalog panel so that it appears beneath the existing AppIcon entry, as shown in the following figure:

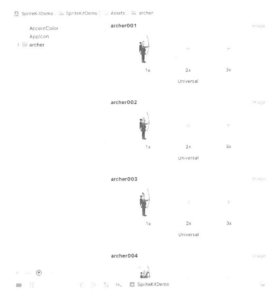

Figure 93-7

93.9 Designing the Archery Scene

The layout for the archery scene is contained within the *ArcheryScene.sks* file. Select this file so that it loads into the Level Editor environment. With the scene selected in the canvas, use the Attributes Inspector panel to change the color property to white and the Size property to landscape *iPad 9.7"*.

From within the SpriteKit Level Editor, the next task is to add the sprite node representing the archer to the scene. Display the Library panel, select the Media Library tab as highlighted in Figure 93-8 below, and locate the *archer001.png* texture image file:

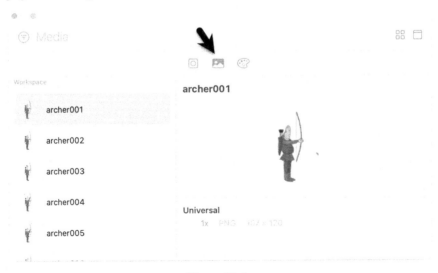

Figure 93-8

Once located, change the Size property in the Attributes Inspector to iPad 9.7", then drag and drop the texture onto the canvas and position it so that it is located in the vertical center of the scene at the left-hand edge, as shown in the following figure:

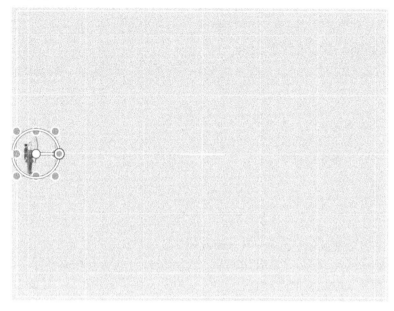

Figure 93-9

With the archer node selected, use the Attributes Inspector panel to assign the name "archerNode" to the sprite. The next task is to define the physical outline of the archer sprite. The SpriteKit system will use this outline when deciding whether the sprite has been involved in a collision with another node within the scene. By default, the physical shape is assumed to be a rectangle surrounding the sprite texture (represented by the blue boundary around the node in the scene editor). Another option is to define a circle around the sprite to represent the physical shape. A much more accurate approach is to have SpriteKit define the physical shape of the node based on the outline of the sprite texture image. With the archer node selected in the scene, scroll down within the Attribute Inspector panel until the *Physics Definition* section appears. Then, using the *Body Type* menu, change the setting to *Alpha mask*:

Figure 93-10

Before proceeding with the next phase of the development process, test that the scene behaves as required by clicking on the *Animate* button located along the bottom edge of the editor panel. Note that the archer slides down and disappears off the bottom edge of the scene. This is because the sprite is configured to be affected by gravity. For the game's purposes, the archer must be pinned to the same location and not subject to the laws of gravity. Click on the *Layout* button to leave simulation mode, select the archer sprite and, within the *Physical Definition* section, turn the *Pinned* option on and the *Dynamic, Allows Rotation,* and *Affected by Gravity* options off. Re-run the animation to verify that the archer sprite now remains in place.

93.10 Preparing the Archery Scene

Select the *ArcheryScene.swift* file and modify it as follows to add some private variables and implement the *didMove(to:)* method:

```
import UIKit
import SpriteKit

class ArcheryScene: SKScene {

    var score = 0
    var ballCount = 20

    override func didMove(to view: SKView) {
        let archerNode = self.childNode(withName: "archerNode")
        archerNode?.position.y = 0
        archerNode?.position.x = -self.size.width/2 + 40
        self.initArcheryScene()
    }
    .
    .
    .
}
```

When the archer node was added to the ArcheryScene, it was positioned using absolute X and Y coordinates. This means the node will be positioned correctly on an iPad with a 9.7" screen but not on any other screen sizes. Therefore, the first task performed by the didMove method is to position the archer node correctly relative to the screen size. Regarding the scene, position 0, 0 corresponds to the screen's center point. Therefore, to position the archer node in the vertical center of the screen, the y-coordinate is set to zero. The code then obtains the screen's width, performs a basic calculation to identify a position 40 points in from the screen's left-hand edge, and assigns it to the x-coordinate of the node.

The above code then calls another method named *initArcheryScene* which now needs to be implemented as follows within the *ArcheryScene.swift* file ready for code which will be added later in the chapter:

```
func initArcheryScene() {
}
```

93.11 Preparing the Animation Texture Atlas

When the user touches the screen, the archer sprite node will launch an arrow across the scene. For this example, we want the sprite character's loading and shooting of the arrow to be animated. The texture atlas already contains the animation frames needed to implement this (named sequentially from *archer001.png* through to *archer012.png*), so the next step is to create an action to animate this sequence of frames. One option would be to write some code to perform this task. A much easier option, however, is to create an animation action using the SpriteKit Live Editor.

Begin by selecting the *ArcheryScene.sks* file so that it loads into the editor. Once loaded, the first step is to add an

AnimateWithTextures action within the timeline of the live editor panel. Next, within the Library panel, scroll down the list of objects until the *AnimateWithTextures Action* object comes into view. Once located, drag and drop an instance of the object onto the live editor timeline for the archerNode as indicated in Figure 93-11:

Figure 93-11

With the animation action added to the timeline, the action needs to be configured with the texture sequence to be animated. With the newly added action selected in the timeline, display the Media Library panel so that the archer texture images are listed. Next, use the Command-A keyboard sequence to select all of the images in the library and then drag and drop those images onto the *Textures* box in the *Animate with Textures* attributes panel, as shown in Figure 93-12:

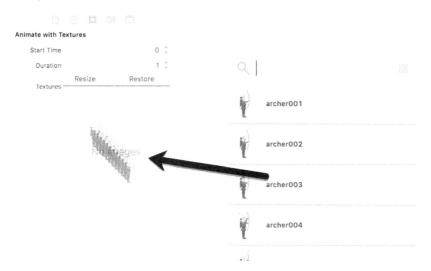

Figure 93-12

Test the animation by clicking on the *Animate* button. The archer sprite should animate through the sequence of texture images to load and shoot the arrow.

Compile and run the app and tap on the screen to enter the archery scene. On appearing, the animation sequence will execute once. The animation sequence should only run when the user taps the screen to launch an arrow. Having this action within the timeline, therefore, does not provide the required behavior for the game. Instead, the animation action needs to be converted to a *named action reference*, placed in an action file, and triggered from within the *touchesBegan* method of the archer scene class.

93.12 Creating the Named Action Reference

With the *ArcherScene.sks* file loaded into the level editor, right-click on the *Animate with Textures* action in the timeline and select the *Convert to Reference* option from the popup menu:

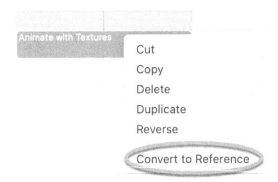

Figure 93-13

In the *Create Action* panel, name the action *animateArcher* and change the *File* menu to *Create New File*. Next, click on the *Create* button and, in the *Save As* panel, navigate to the *SpriteKitDemo* subfolder of the main project folder and enter *ArcherActions* into the *Save As:* field before clicking on *Create*.

Since the animation action is no longer required in the timeline of the archer scene, select the *ArcherScene.sks* file, right-click on the *Animate with Texture* action in the timeline, and select *Delete* from the menu.

93.13 Triggering the Named Action from the Code

With the previous steps completed, the project now has a named action (named *animateArcher*) which can be triggered each time the screen is tapped by adding some code to the *touchesBegan* method of the *ArcheryScene. swift* file. With this file selected in the Project Navigator panel, implement this method as follows:

```
override func touchesBegan(_ touches: Set<UITouch>, with event: UIEvent?) {

    if let archerNode = self.childNode(withName: "archerNode"),
        let animate = SKAction(named: "animateArcher") {
        archerNode.run(animate)
    }
}
```

Run the app and touch the screen within the Archery Scene. Each time a touch is detected, the archer sprite will run through the animation sequence of shooting an arrow.

93.14 Creating the Arrow Sprite Node

At this point in the tutorial, the archer sprite node goes through an animation sequence of loading and shooting an arrow, but no actual arrow is being launched across the scene. To implement this, a new sprite node must be added to the ArcheryScene. This node will be textured with an arrow image and placed to the right of the archer sprite at the end of the animation sequence. Then, a physics body will be associated with the arrow, and an impulse force will be applied to it to propel it across the scene as though shot by the archer's bow. This task will be performed entirely in code to demonstrate the alternative to using the action and live editors.

Begin by locating the *ArrowTexture.png* file in the *sprite_images* folder of the sample code archive and drag and drop it onto the left-hand panel of the *Assets* catalog screen beneath the *archer* texture atlas entry. Next, add a new method named *createArrowNode* within the *ArcheryScene.swift* file so that it reads as follows:

```
func createArrowNode() -> SKSpriteNode {

    let arrow = SKSpriteNode(imageNamed: "ArrowTexture.png")

    if let archerNode = self.childNode(withName: "archerNode"),
        let archerPosition = archerNode.position as CGPoint?,
         let archerWidth = archerNode.frame.size.width as CGFloat? {

        arrow.position = CGPoint(x: archerPosition.x + archerWidth,
                                 y: archerPosition.y)

        arrow.name = "arrowNode"
        arrow.physicsBody = SKPhysicsBody(rectangleOf:
                             arrow.frame.size)
        arrow.physicsBody?.usesPreciseCollisionDetection = true
    }
    return arrow
}
```

The code creates a new SKSpriteNode object, positions it to the right of the archer sprite node, and assigns the name *arrowNode*. A physics body is then assigned to the node, using the node's size as the boundary of the body and enabling precision collision detection. Finally, the node is returned.

93.15 Shooting the Arrow

A physical force needs to be applied to propel the arrow across the scene. The arrow sprite's creation and propulsion must be timed to occur at the end of the archer animation sequence. This timing can be achieved via some minor modifications to the *touchesBegan* method:

```
override func touchesBegan(_ touches: Set<UITouch>, with event: UIEvent?) {

    if let archerNode = self.childNode(withName: "archerNode"),
        let animate = SKAction(named: "animateArcher") {
        let shootArrow = SKAction.run({
            let arrowNode = self.createArrowNode()
            self.addChild(arrowNode)
            arrowNode.physicsBody?.applyImpulse(CGVector(dx: 60, dy: 0))
        })

        let sequence = SKAction.sequence([animate, shootArrow])

        archerNode.run(sequence)
    }
}
```

A new SKAction object is created, specifying a block of code to be executed. This run block calls the *createArrowNode* method, adds the new node to the scene, and then applies an impulse force of 60.0 on the X-axis of the scene. An SKAction sequence comprises the previously created animation action and the new run block action. This sequence is then run on the archer node.

When executed with these changes, touching the screen should now cause an arrow to be launched after the archer animation completes. Then, as the arrow flies across the scene, it gradually falls toward the bottom of the display. This behavior is due to gravity's effect on the physics body assigned to the node.

93.16 Adding the Ball Sprite Node

The game's objective is to score points by hitting balls with arrows. So, the next logical step is adding the ball sprite node to the scene. Begin by locating the *BallTexture.png* file in the *sprite_images* folder of the sample code package and drag and drop it onto the *Assets.xcassets* catalog.

Next, add the corresponding *createBallNode* method to the *ArcheryScene.swift* file as outlined in the following code fragment:

```
func createBallNode() {
    let ball = SKSpriteNode(imageNamed: "BallTexture.png")

    let screenWidth = self.size.width

    ball.position = CGPoint(x: CGFloat.random(
                    in: -screenWidth/2 ..< screenWidth/2-100),
                        y: self.size.height-50)

    ball.name = "ballNode"
    ball.physicsBody = SKPhysicsBody(circleOfRadius:
                    (ball.size.width/2))

    ball.physicsBody?.usesPreciseCollisionDetection = true
    self.addChild(ball)
}
```

This code creates a sprite node using the ball texture and then sets the initial position at the top of the scene but a random position on the X-axis. Since position 0 on the X-axis corresponds to the horizontal center of the screen (as opposed to the far left side), some calculations are performed to ensure that the balls can fall from most of the screen's width using random numbers for the X-axis values.

The node is assigned a name and a circular physics body slightly less than the radius of the ball texture image. Finally, precision collision detection is enabled, and the ball node is added to the scene.

Next, modify the *initArcheryScene* method to create an action to release a total of 20 balls at one-second intervals:

```
func initArcheryScene() {

    let releaseBalls = SKAction.sequence([SKAction.run({
    self.createBallNode() }),
    SKAction.wait(forDuration: 1)])

    self.run(SKAction.repeat(releaseBalls,
                        count: ballCount))
}
```

Run the app and verify that the balls now fall from the top of the scene. Then, attempt to hit the balls as they fall by tapping the background to launch arrows. Note, however, that when an arrow hits a ball, it simply bounces off:

Figure 93-14

The goal for the completed game is to have the balls burst with a sound effect when hit by the arrow and for a score to be presented at the end of the game. The steps to implement this behavior will be covered in the next chapters.

The balls fall from the top of the screen because they have been assigned a physics body and are subject to the simulated forces of gravity within the Sprite Kit physical world. To reduce the effects of gravity on both the arrows and balls, modify the *didMove(to view:)* method to change the current gravity setting on the scene's *physicsWorld* object:

```
override func didMove(to view: SKView) {
    let archerNode = self.childNode(withName: "archerNode")
    archerNode?.position.y = 0
    archerNode?.position.x = -self.size.width/2 + 40
    self.physicsWorld.gravity = CGVector(dx: 0, dy: -1.0)
    self.initArcheryScene()
}
```

93.17 Summary

The goal of this chapter has been to create a simple game for iOS using the Sprite Kit framework. In creating this game, topics such as using sprite nodes, actions, textures, sprite animations, and physical forces have been used to demonstrate the use of the Xcode Sprite Kit editors and Swift code.

In the next chapter, this game example will be further extended to demonstrate the detection of collisions.

94. An iOS 17 Sprite Kit Collision Handling Tutorial

In this chapter, the game created in the previous chapter, entitled *"An iOS 17 Sprite Kit Level Editor Game Tutorial"*, will be extended to implement collision detection. The objective is to detect when an arrow node collides with a ball node and increase a score count in the event of such a collision. In the next chapter, this collision detection behavior will be further extended to add audio and visual effects so that the balls appear to burst when an arrow hits.

94.1 Defining the Category Bit Masks

Start Xcode and open the SpriteKitDemo project created in the previous chapter if not already loaded.

When detecting collisions within a Sprite Kit scene, a delegate method is called each time a collision is detected. However, this method will only be called if the colliding nodes are configured appropriately using *category bit masks*.

Only collisions between the arrow and ball sprite nodes are of interest for this demonstration game. The first step, therefore, is to declare collision masks for these two node categories. Begin by editing the *ArcheryScene. swift* file and adding these declarations at the top of the class implementation:

```
import UIKit
import SpriteKit

class ArcheryScene: SKScene {

    let arrowCategory: UInt32 = 0x1 << 0
    let ballCategory: UInt32 = 0x1 << 1
.
.
```

94.2 Assigning the Category Masks to the Sprite Nodes

Having declared the masks, these need to be assigned to the respective node objects when they are created within the game. This is achieved by assigning the mask to the *categoryBitMask* property of the physics body assigned to the node. In the case of the ball node, this code can be added in the *createBallNode* method as follows:

```
func createBallNode() {
    let ball = SKSpriteNode(imageNamed: "BallTexture.png")
    let screenWidth = self.size.width

    ball.position = CGPoint(x: randomBetween(-screenWidth/2, max:
        screenWidth/2-200), y: self.size.height-50)

    ball.name = "ballNode"
    ball.physicsBody = SKPhysicsBody(circleOfRadius:
```

```
                                (ball.size.width/2))

        ball.physicsBody?.usesPreciseCollisionDetection = true
        ball.physicsBody?.categoryBitMask = ballCategory
        self.addChild(ball)
}
```

Repeat this step to assign the appropriate category mask to the arrow node in the *createArrowNode* method:

```
func createArrowNode() -> SKSpriteNode {

    let arrow = SKSpriteNode(imageNamed: "ArrowTexture.png")

    if let archerNode = self.childNode(withName: "archerNode"),
        let archerPosition = archerNode.position as CGPoint?,
        let archerWidth = archerNode.frame.size.width as CGFloat? {

        arrow.position = CGPoint(x: archerPosition.x + archerWidth,
                                 y: archerPosition.y)

        arrow.name = "arrowNode"
        arrow.physicsBody = SKPhysicsBody(rectangleOf:
                                arrow.frame.size)
        arrow.physicsBody?.usesPreciseCollisionDetection = true
        arrow.physicsBody?.categoryBitMask = arrowCategory
    }
    return arrow
}
```

94.3 Configuring the Collision and Contact Masks

Having assigned category masks to the arrow and ball nodes, these nodes are ready to be included in collision detection handling. However, before this can be implemented, code needs to be added to indicate whether the app needs to know about collisions, contacts, or both. When contact occurs, two nodes can touch or even occupy the same space in a scene. It might be valid, for example, for one sprite node to pass over another node, and the game logic needs to be notified when this happens. On the other hand, a collision involves contact between two nodes that cannot occupy the same space in the scene. The two nodes will typically bounce away from each other in such a situation (subject to prevailing physics body properties).

The type of contact for which notification is required is specified by assigning contact and collision bit masks to the physics body of one of the node categories involved in the contact. For this example, we will specify that notification is required for both contact and collision between the arrow and ball categories:

```
func createArrowNode() -> SKSpriteNode {

    let arrow = SKSpriteNode(imageNamed: "ArrowTexture.png")

    if let archerNode = self.childNode(withName: "archerNode"),
        let archerPosition = archerNode.position as CGPoint?,
        let archerWidth = archerNode.frame.size.width as CGFloat? {
```

```
        arrow.position = CGPoint(x: archerPosition.x + archerWidth,
                            y: archerPosition.y)


        arrow.name = "arrowNode"
        arrow.physicsBody = SKPhysicsBody(rectangleOf:
                            arrow.frame.size)
        arrow.physicsBody?.usesPreciseCollisionDetection = true
        arrow.physicsBody?.categoryBitMask = arrowCategory
        arrow.physicsBody?.collisionBitMask = arrowCategory | ballCategory
        arrow.physicsBody?.contactTestBitMask =
            arrowCategory | ballCategory
    }
    return arrow
}
```

94.4 Implementing the Contact Delegate

When the Sprite Kit physics system detects a collision or contact for which appropriate masks have been configured, it needs a way to notify the app code that such an event has occurred.

It does this by calling methods on the class instance registered as the *contact delegate* for the physics world object associated with the scene where the contact occurred. The system can notify the delegate at both the beginning and end of the contact if both the *didBegin(contact:)* and *didEnd(contact:)* methods are implemented. Passed as an argument to these methods is an SKPhysicsContact object containing information about the location of the contact and references to the physical bodies of the two nodes involved in the contact.

For this tutorial, we will use the ArcheryScene instance as the contact delegate and implement only the *didBegin(contact:)* method. Begin, therefore, by modifying the *didMove(to view:)* method in the *ArcheryScene. swift* file to declare the class as the contact delegate:

```
override func didMove(to view: SKView) {
    let archerNode = self.childNode(withName: "archerNode")
    archerNode?.position.y = 0
    archerNode?.position.x = -self.size.width/2 + 40
    self.physicsWorld.gravity = CGVector(dx: 0, dy: -1.0)
    self.physicsWorld.contactDelegate = self
    self.initArcheryScene()
}
```

Having made the ArcheryScene class the contact delegate, the *ArcheryScene.swift* file needs to be modified to indicate that the class now implements the SKPhysicsContactDelegate protocol:

```
import UIKit
import SpriteKit


class ArcheryScene: SKScene, SKPhysicsContactDelegate {
.
.
.
```

Remaining within the *ArcheryScene.swift* file, implement the *didBegin(contact:)* method as follows:

```swift
func didBegin(_ contact: SKPhysicsContact) {
    let secondNode = contact.bodyB.node as! SKSpriteNode

    if (contact.bodyA.categoryBitMask == arrowCategory) &&
        (contact.bodyB.categoryBitMask == ballCategory) {

        let contactPoint = contact.contactPoint
        let contact_y = contactPoint.y
        let target_y = secondNode.position.y
        let margin = secondNode.frame.size.height/2 - 25

        if (contact_y > (target_y - margin)) &&
            (contact_y < (target_y + margin)) {
            print("Hit")
            score += 1
        }
    }
}
```

The code starts by extracting references to the two nodes that have collided. It then checks that the first node is an arrow and the second a ball (no points are scored if a ball falls onto an arrow). Next, the point of contact is identified, and some rudimentary mathematics is used to check that the arrow struck the side of the ball (for a game of app store quality, more rigorous checking might be required to catch all cases). Finally, assuming the hit was within the defined parameters, a message is output to the console, and the game score variable is incremented.

Run the game and test the collision handling by ensuring that the "Hit" message appears in the Xcode console when an arrow hits the side of a ball.

94.5 Game Over

All that now remains is to display the score to the user when all the balls have been released. This will require a new label node and a small change to an action sequence followed by a transition to the welcome scene so the user can start a new game. Begin by adding the method to create the label node in the *ArcheryScene.swift* file:

```swift
func createScoreNode() -> SKLabelNode {
    let scoreNode = SKLabelNode(fontNamed: "Bradley Hand")
    scoreNode.name = "scoreNode"

    let newScore = "Score \(score)"

    scoreNode.text = newScore
    scoreNode.fontSize = 60
    scoreNode.fontColor = SKColor.red
    scoreNode.position = CGPoint(x: self.frame.midX,
                                 y: self.frame.midY)
    return scoreNode
}
```

Next, implement the *gameOver* method, which will display the score label node and then transition back to the welcome scene:

```
func gameOver() {
    let scoreNode = self.createScoreNode()
    self.addChild(scoreNode)
    let fadeOut = SKAction.sequence([SKAction.wait(forDuration: 3.0),
                                    SKAction.fadeOut(withDuration: 3.0)])
    let welcomeReturn =  SKAction.run({
        let transition = SKTransition.reveal(
            with: SKTransitionDirection.down, duration: 1.0)
        if let welcomeScene = GameScene(fileNamed: "GameScene") {
            self.scene?.view?.presentScene(welcomeScene,
                                    transition: transition)
        }
    })

    let sequence = SKAction.sequence([fadeOut, welcomeReturn])
    self.run(sequence)
}
```

Finally, add a completion handler that calls the *gameOver* method after the ball release action in the *initArcheryScene* method:

```
func initArcheryScene() {
    let releaseBalls = SKAction.sequence([SKAction.run({
    self.createBallNode() }),
    SKAction.wait(forDuration: 1)])

    self.run(SKAction.repeat(releaseBalls,
                    count: ballCount), completion: {
        let sequence =
                SKAction.sequence([SKAction.wait(forDuration: 5.0),
                    SKAction.run({ self.gameOver() })])
        self.run(sequence)
    })
}
```

Compile, run, and test. Also, feel free to experiment by adding other features to the game to gain familiarity with the capabilities of Sprite Kit. The next chapter, entitled *"An iOS 17 Sprite Kit Particle Emitter Tutorial"*, will cover using the Particle Emitter to add special effects to Sprite Kit games.

94.6 Summary

The Sprite Kit physics engine detects when two nodes within a scene come into contact with each other. Collision and contact detection is configured through the use of category masks together with contact and collision masks. When appropriately configured, the *didBegin(contact:)* and *didEnd(contact:)* methods of a designated delegate class are called at the start and end of contact between two nodes for which detection is configured. These methods are passed references to the nodes involved in the contact so that appropriate action can be taken within the game.

95. An iOS 17 Sprite Kit Particle Emitter Tutorial

In this, the last chapter dedicated to the Sprite Kit framework, the use of the Particle Emitter class and editor to add special effects to Sprite Kit-based games will be covered. Having provided an overview of the various elements that make up particle emitter special effects, the SpriteKitDemo app will be extended using particle emitter features to make the balls burst when an arrow hits. This will also involve the addition of an audio action.

95.1 What is the Particle Emitter?

The Sprite Kit particle emitter is designed to add special effects to games. It comprises the SKEmitterNode class and the Particle Emitter Editor bundled with Xcode. A particle emitter special effect begins with an image file representing the particle. The emitter generates multiple instances of the particle on the scene and animates each particle subject to a set of properties. These properties control aspects of the special effect, such as the rate of particle generation, the angle, and speed of motion of particles, whether or not particles rotate, and how the particles blend in with the background.

With some time and experimentation, a wide range of special effects, from smoke to explosions, can be created using particle emitters.

95.2 The Particle Emitter Editor

The Particle Emitter Editor is built into Xcode and provides a visual environment to design particle emitter effects. In addition to providing a platform for developing custom effects, the editor also offers a collection of pre-built particle-based effects, including rain, fire, magic, snow, and sparks. These template effects also provide an excellent starting point on which to base other special effects.

Within the editor environment, a canvas displays the current particle emitter configuration. A settings panel allows the various properties of the emitter node to be changed, with each modification reflected in the canvas in real time, thereby making creating and refining special effects much easier. Once the design of the special effect is complete, the effect is saved in a Sprite Kit particle file. This file actually contains an archived SKEmitterNode object configured to run the particle effects designed in the editor.

95.3 The SKEmitterNode Class

The SKEmitterNode displays and runs the particle emitter effect within a Sprite Kit game. As with other Sprite Node classes, the SKEmitterNode class has many properties and behaviors of other classes in the Sprite Kit family. Generally, an SKEmitterNode class is created and initialized with a Sprite Kit particle file created using the Particle Emitter editor. The following code fragment, for example, initializes an SKEmitterNode instance with a particle file, configures it to appear at a specific position within the current scene, and adds it to the scene so that it appears within the game:

```
if let burstNode = SKEmitterNode(fileNamed: "BurstParticle.sks") {
    burstNode.position = CGPoint(x: target_x, y: target_y)
    secondNode.removeFromParent()
    self.addChild(burstNode)
}
```

Once created, all of the emitter properties available within the Particle Emitter Editor are also controllable from within the code, allowing the effect's behavior to be changed in real time. The following code, for example, adjusts the number of particles the emitter is to emit before ending:

```
burstNode.numParticlesToEmit = 400
```

In addition, actions may be assigned to particles from within the app code to add additional behavior to a special effect. The particles can, for example, be made to display an animation sequence.

95.4 Using the Particle Emitter Editor

By far, the easiest and most productive approach to designing particle emitter-based special effects is to use the Particle Emitter Editor tool bundled with Xcode. To experience the editor in action, launch Xcode and create a new iOS Game-based project named *ParticleDemo* with the Language menu set to *Swift*.

Once the new project has been created, select the *File -> New -> File…* menu option. Then, in the resulting panel, choose the *SpriteKit Particle File* template option as outlined in Figure 95-1:

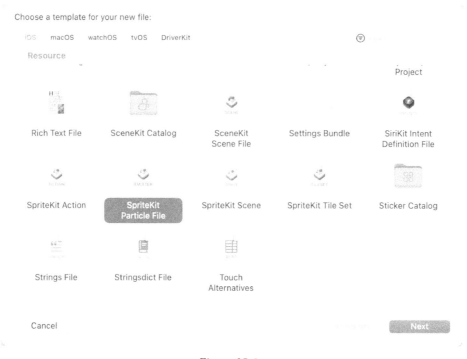

Figure 95-1

Click *Next* and choose a Particle template on which to base the special effect. For this example, we will use the *Fire* template. Click *Next* and name the file *RocketFlame* before clicking on *Create*.

At this point, Xcode will have added two files to the project. One is an image file named *spark.png* representing the particle, and the other is the *RocketFlame.sks* file containing the particle emitter configuration. In addition, Xcode should also have pre-loaded the Particle Emitter Editor panel with the fire effect playing in the canvas, as shown in Figure 95-2 (the editor can be accessed at any time by selecting the corresponding sks file in the project navigator panel).

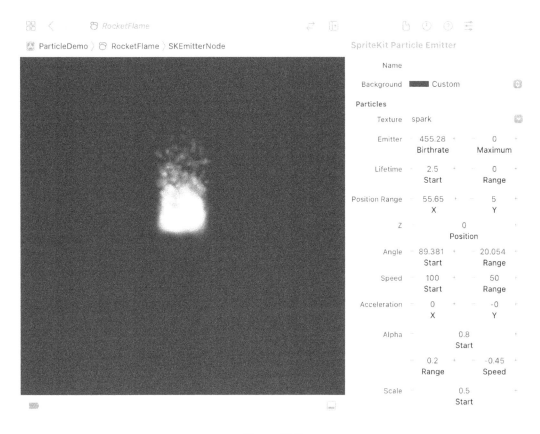

Figure 95-2

The right-hand panel of the editor provides access to and control of all of the properties associated with the emitter node. To access these property settings, click the right-hand toolbar button in the right-hand panel.

Much about particle emitter special effects can be learned through experimentation with the particle editor. However, before modifying the fire effects in this example, it will be helpful to provide an overview of what these properties do.

95.5 Particle Emitter Node Properties

A range of property settings controls the behavior of a particle emitter and associated particles. These properties can be summarized as follows:

95.5.1 Background

Though presented as an option within the editor, this is not actually a property of the emitter node. This option is provided so that the appearance of the effect can be tested against different backgrounds. This is particularly important when the particles are configured to blend with the background. Use this setting to test the particle effects against any background colors the effect is likely to appear with within the game.

95.5.2 Particle Texture

The image file containing the texture that will be used to represent the particles within the emitter.

95.5.3 Particle Birthrate

The birthrate defines the rate at which the node emits new particles. The greater the value, the faster new particles are generated. However, it is recommended that the minimum number of particles needed to achieve the desired effect be used to avoid performance degradation. Therefore, the total number of particles emitted may also be specified. A value of zero causes particles to be emitted indefinitely. If a limit is specified, the node will stop emitting particles when that value is reached.

95.5.4 Particle Life Cycle

The lifetime property controls the time in seconds a particle lives (and is therefore visible) before disappearing from view. The range property may be used to introduce variance in the lifetime from one particle to the next based on a random time value between 0 and the specified range value.

95.5.5 Particle Position Range

The position properties define the location from which particles are created. For example, the X and Y values can be used to declare an area around the center of the node location from which particles will be created randomly.

95.5.6 Angle

The angle at which a newly emitted particle will travel away from the creation point in counter-clockwise degrees, where a value of 0 degrees equates to rightward movement. Random variance in direction can be introduced via the range property.

95.5.7 Particle Speed

The speed property specifies the particles' initial speed at the creation time. The speed can be randomized by specifying a range value.

95.5.8 Particle Acceleration

The acceleration properties control the degree to which a particle accelerates or decelerates after emission in terms of both X and Y directions.

95.5.9 Particle Scale

The size of the particles can be configured to change using the scale properties. These settings cause the particles to grow or shrink throughout their lifetimes. Random resizing behavior can be implemented by specifying a range value. The speed setting controls the speed with which the size changes take place.

95.5.10 Particle Rotation

The rotation properties control the speed and amount of rotation applied to the particles after creation. Values are specified in degrees, with positive and negative values correlating to clockwise and counter-clockwise rotation. In addition, the speed of rotation may be specified in degrees per second.

95.5.11 Particle Color

The particles created by an emitter can be configured to transition through a range of colors during a lifetime. To add a new color in the lifecycle timeline, click on the color ramp at the location where the color is to change and select a new color. Change an existing color by double-clicking the marker to display the color selection dialog. Figure 95-3, for example, shows a color ramp with three color transitions specified:

Figure 95-3

To remove a color from the color ramp, click and drag it downward out of the editor panel.

The color blend settings control the amount by which the colors in the particle's texture blend with the prevailing color in the color ramp at any given time during the particle's life. The greater the Factor property, the greater the colors blend, with 0 indicating no blending. By adjusting the speed property, the blending factor can be randomized by specifying a range and the speed at which the blend is performed.

95.5.12 Particle Blend Mode

The Blend Mode property governs how particles blend with other images, colors, and graphics in Sprite Kit game scenes. Options available are as follows:

- **Alpha** – Blends transparent pixels in the particle with the background.

- **Add** – Adds the particle pixels to the corresponding background image pixels.

- **Subtract** – Subtracts the particle pixels from the corresponding background image pixels.

- **Multiply** - Multiplies the particle pixels by the corresponding background image pixels—resulting in a darker particle effect.

- **MultiplyX2** – This creates a darker particle effect than the standard Multiply mode.

- **Screen** – Inverts pixels, multiplies, and inverts a second time—resulting in lighter particle effects.

- **Replace** – No blending with the background. Only the particle's colors are used.

95.6 Experimenting with the Particle Emitter Editor

Creating compelling special effects with the particle emitter is largely a case of experimentation. As an example of adapting a template effect for another purpose, we will now modify the fire effect in the RocketFlame.sks file so that instead of resembling a campfire, it could be attached to the back of a sprite to represent the flame of a rocket launching into space.

Within Xcode, select the previously created *RocketFlame.sks* file so that it loads into the Particle Emitter Editor. The animation should appear and resemble a campfire, as illustrated in Figure 95-2.

1. The first step in modifying the effect is to change the angle of the flames so that they burn downwards. To achieve this, change the *Start* property of the *Angle* setting to 270 degrees. The fire should now be inverted.

2. Change the X value of the *Position Range* property to 5 so that the flames become narrower and more intense.

3. Increase the *Start* value of the *Speed* property to 450.

4. Change the *Lifetime* start property to 7.

The effect now resembles the flames a user might expect to see shooting out of the back of a rocket against a nighttime sky (Figure 95-4). Note also that the effects of the motion of the emitter node may be simulated by clicking and dragging the node around the canvas.

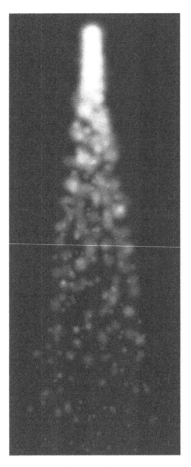

Figure 95-4

95.7 Bursting a Ball using Particle Emitter Effects

The final task is to update the SpriteKitDemo game so that the balls burst when they are hit by an arrow shot by the archer sprite.

The particles for the bursting ball will be represented by the *BallFragment.png* file located in the sample code download archive in the *sprite_images* folder. Open the SpriteKitDemo project within Xcode, locate the *BallFragment.png* file in a Finder window, and drag and drop it onto the list of image sets in the *Assets* file.

Select the *File -> New -> File…* menu option and, in the resulting panel, select the *SpriteKit Particle File* template option. Click *Next,* and on the template screen, select the *Spark* template. Click *Next*, name the file *BurstParticle,* and click *Create.*

The Particle Emitter Editor will appear with the spark effect running. Since the scene on which the effect will run has a white background, click on the black swatch next to *Background* in the Attributes Inspector panel and change the color to white.

Click on the Particles *Texture* drop-down menu, select the BallFragment image, and change the *Blend Mode* menu to *Alpha.*

Many ball fragments should now be visible, blended with the yellow color specified in the ramp. Set the Emitter *Birthrate* property to 15 to reduce the number of particles emitted. Click on the yellow marker at the start of the color ramp and change the color to *White* in the resulting color dialog. The particles should now look like fragments of the ball used in the game.

The fragments of a bursting ball would be expected to originate from any part of the ball. As such, the Position Range X and Y values need to match the dimensions of the ball. Set both of these values to 86 accordingly.

Finally, limit the number of particles by changing the Emitter *Maximum* property in the Particles section to 8.

The burst particle effect is now ready to be incorporated into the game logic.

95.8 Adding the Burst Particle Emitter Effect

When an arrow scores a hit on a ball node, the ball node will be removed from the scene and replaced with a *BurstParticle* SKEmitterNode instance. To implement this behavior, edit the *ArcheryScene.swift* file and modify the *didBegin(contact:)* method to add a new method call to extract the SKEmitterNode from the archive in the *BurstParticle* file, remove the ball node from the scene and replace it at the same position with the emitter:

```
func didBegin(_ contact: SKPhysicsContact) {
    let secondNode = contact.bodyB.node as! SKSpriteNode

    if (contact.bodyA.categoryBitMask == arrowCategory) &&
        (contact.bodyB.categoryBitMask == ballCategory) {

        let contactPoint = contact.contactPoint
        let contact_y = contactPoint.y
        let target_x = secondNode.position.x
        let target_y = secondNode.position.y
        let margin = secondNode.frame.size.height/2 - 25

        if (contact_y > (target_y - margin)) &&
            (contact_y < (target_y + margin)) {

            if let burstNode = SKEmitterNode(fileNamed: "BurstParticle.sks")
            {
                burstNode.position = CGPoint(x: target_x, y: target_y)
                secondNode.removeFromParent()
                self.addChild(burstNode)
            }
            score += 1
        }
    }
}
```

Compile and run the app. For example, when an arrow hits a ball, it should now be replaced by the particle emitter effect:

Figure 95-5

95.9 Adding an Audio Action

The final effect to add to the game is a bursting sound when an arrow hits the ball. We will again use the Xcode Action Editor to add this effect.

Begin by adding the sound file to the project. This file is named *burstsound.mp3* and is located in the *audiofiles* folder of the book code samples download. Locate this file in a Finder window and drag it onto the Project Navigator panel. In the resulting panel, enable the *Copy items if needed* option and click on *Finish*.

Within the Project Navigator panel, select the *ArcherScene.sks* file. Then, from the Library panel, locate the *Play-Sound-File-Named-Action* object and drag and drop it onto the timeline so that it is added to the archerNode object:

Figure 95-6

Select the new action object in the timeline and use the Attributes Inspector panel to set the *Filename* property to the *burstsound* file.

Right-click on the sound action and select the *Convert to Reference* menu option. Name the reference *audioAction* and click on the Create button. The action has now been saved to the *ArcherActions.sks* file. Next, select the object in the timeline, right-click, and select the Delete option to remove it from the scene file.

Finally, modify the *didBegin(contact:)* method to play the sound action when a ball bursts:

```
func didBegin(_ contact: SKPhysicsContact) {
    let secondNode = contact.bodyB.node as! SKSpriteNode
```

```
    if (contact.bodyA.categoryBitMask == arrowCategory) &&
        (contact.bodyB.categoryBitMask == ballCategory) {

        let contactPoint = contact.contactPoint
        let contact_y = contactPoint.y
        let target_x = secondNode.position.x
        let target_y = secondNode.position.y
        let margin = secondNode.frame.size.height/2 - 25

        if (contact_y > (target_y - margin)) &&
            (contact_y < (target_y + margin)) {
            print("Hit")

            if let burstNode = SKEmitterNode(fileNamed: "BurstParticle.sks")
            {
                burstNode.position = CGPoint(x: target_x, y: target_y)
                secondNode.removeFromParent()
                self.addChild(burstNode)
                if let audioAction = SKAction(named: "audioAction") {
                    burstNode.run(audioAction)
                }
            }
            score += 1
        }
    }
}
```

Run the app and verify that the sound file plays when a hit is registered on a ball.

95.10 Summary

The particle emitter allows special effects to be added to Sprite Kit games. All that is required is an image file to represent the particles and some configuration of the particle emitter properties. This work can be simplified using the Particle Emitter Editor included with Xcode. The editor is supplied with a set of pre-configured special effects, such as smoke, fire, and rain, which can be used as supplied or modified to meet many special effects needs.

96. Preparing and Submitting an iOS 17 Application to the App Store

After developing an iOS application, the final step is submitting it to Apple's App Store. Preparing and submitting an application is a multi-step process details of which will be covered in this chapter.

96.1 Verifying the iOS Distribution Certificate

The chapter entitled *"Joining the Apple Developer Program"* covered the steps involved in generating signing certificates. In that chapter, both a development and distribution certificate were generated. Up until this point in the book, applications have been signed using the development certificate so that testing could be performed on physical iOS devices. Before an application can be submitted to the App Store, however, it must be signed using the distribution certificate. The presence of the distribution certificate may be verified from within the Xcode settings.

With Xcode running, select the *Xcode -> Preferences...* menu option and select the *Accounts* category from the toolbar of the resulting window. Assuming that Apple IDs have been configured as outlined in *"Joining the Apple Developer Program"*, a list of one or more Apple IDs will be shown in the accounts panel, as illustrated in Figure 96-1:

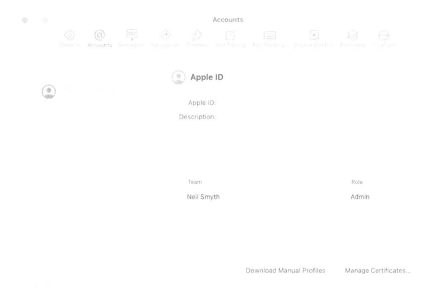

Figure 96-1

Select the Apple ID to be used to sign the application and click on the *Manage Certificates...* button to display the list of signing identities and provisioning profiles associated with that ID:

Signing certificates for "Neil Smyth":

Name	Creator	Date Created	Status
Apple Development Certificates			
☐ Neil's Mac mini	Neil Smyth	9/11/23	
☐ Neil's Mac mini	Neil Smyth	3/17/23	
Developer ID Application Certificates			
☐ Developer ID Application	Neil Smyth	9/11/23	
☐ Developer ID Application	Neil Smyth	3/13/22	

+ ⌄   Done

Figure 96-2

If no Apple Distribution certificate is listed, use the menu highlighted in Figure 96-3 to generate one:

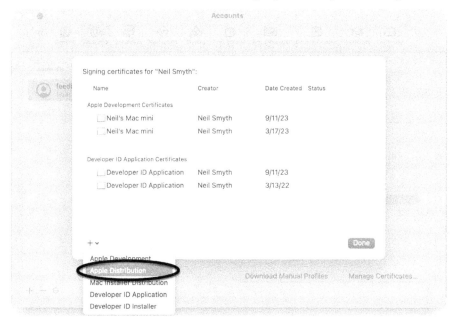

Figure 96-3

Xcode will then contact the developer portal and generate and download a new signing certificate suitable for use when signing applications for submission to the App Store. Once the signing identity has been generated, the certificate will appear in the list, as shown in Figure 96-4:

Signing certificates for "Neil Smyth":

Name	Creator	Date Created	Status
Apple Development Certificates			
Neil's Mac mini	Neil Smyth	9/11/23	
Neil's Mac mini	Neil Smyth	3/17/23	
Apple Distribution Certificates			
Apple Distribution	Neil Smyth	10/11/23	
Developer ID Application Certificates			
Developer ID Application	Neil Smyth	9/11/23	
Developer ID Application	Neil Smyth	3/13/22	

+ ∨   Done

Figure 96-4

96.2 Adding App Icons

Before rebuilding the application for distribution it is important to ensure that app icons have been added to the application. The app icons are used to represent your application on the home screen, settings panel and search results on the device. Each of these categories requires a suitable icon in PNG format and formatted for a number of different dimensions. Alternatively, you can add a single 1024 x 1024 icon to the project and Xcode will adapt it for each requirement.

App icons are added in the *Assets.xcassets* asset catalog within the AppIcon image set. When the AppIcon image set is selected, it will display a placeholder for an icon:

Figure 96-5

To add an images, simply drag and drop the PNG format image from a Finder window onto the placeholder in the asset catalog.

To add multiple image sizes, change the iOS Size menu in the Attributes inspector panel to *All Sizes*, as illustrated in Figure 96-6:

Figure 96-6

96.3 Assign the Project to a Team

As part of the submission process, the project must be associated with a development team to ensure that the correct signing credentials are used. In the project navigator panel, select the project name to display the project settings panel. Click the *Signing & Capabilities* tab and within the Identity section, select a team from the menu, as shown in Figure 96-7:

Figure 96-7

96.4 Archiving the Application for Distribution

The application must now be rebuilt using the previously installed distribution profile. To generate the archive, select the Xcode *Product -> Archive* menu option. Note that if the Archive menu is disabled this is most likely because a simulator option is currently selected as the run target in the Xcode toolbar. Changing this menu either to a connected device, or the generic *iOS Device* target option should enable the Archive option in the Product menu.

Xcode will proceed to archive the application ready for submission. Once the process is complete the archive will be displayed in the Archive screen of the Organizer dialog ready for upload and distribution:

Figure 96-8

Click the Validate App button and wait until the validation is complete. Correct any errors that are reported and archive and validate the product again until the validation is successful:

Figure 96-9

96.5 Configuring the Application in App Store Connect

Before an application can be submitted to the App Store for review it must first be configured in App Store Connect. Enrollment in the Apple Developer program automatically results in the creation of an App Store Connect account using the same login credentials. App Store Connect is a portal where developers enter tax and payment information, input details about applications and track the status of those applications in terms of sales and revenues.

Access App Store Connect by navigating to *https://appstoreconnect.apple.com* in a web browser and entering your Apple Developer program login and password details.

First time users should click on the *Agreements, Tax, and Banking* option and work through the various tasks to accept Apple's terms and conditions and to input appropriate tax and banking information for the receipt of sales revenue.

Once the administrative tasks are complete, select the *My Apps* option and click on the + button followed by *New App* to enter information about the application. Begin by selecting the *iOS* checkbox and entering a name for the application together with an SKU of your own creation. Also select or enter the bundle ID that matches the application that has been prepared for upload in Xcode:

Figure 96-10

Once the application has been added it will appear within the My Apps screen listed as *Prepare for submission*:

InAppDemo2018

iOS 1.0 Prepare for Submission

Figure 96-11

96.6 Validating and Submitting the Application

To validate the application, return to the Xcode archives window, make sure the application archive is selected and click on the *Distribute App* button. On the next screen, select the *TestFlight & App Store* option as highlighted in Figure 96-12 before clicking the Distribute button:

Figure 96-12

Xcode will connect to the App Store Connect service, locate the matching app entry added in the previous step and display the summary screen shown in Figure 96-13:

Figure 96-13

96.7 Configuring and Submitting the App for Review

On the My Apps screen of the App Store Connect portal, select the new app entry to display the configuration screen where options are available to set up pre-release test users, designate pricing, enter product descriptions and upload screenshots and preview videos. Once this information has been entered and saved and the app is ready for submission to the App Store, select the *Prepare for Submission* option (marked A in Figure 96-14) followed by the *Add for Review* button (marked B):

Figure 96-14

Once Apple has completed the review process an email will arrive stating whether the application has been accepted or not. In the event that the application has been rejected, reasons for the rejection will be stated and the application may be resubmitted once these issues have been addressed.

Index

Symbols

A

Index

Index

Index

N

O

P

Index

Index

Index

Index

www.ingramcontent.com/pod-product-compliance
Lightning Source LLC
LaVergne TN
LVHW080108070326
832902LV00015B/2476